MW00522656

BERKSHIRE ENCYCLOPEDIA OF

World Sport

BERKSHIRE ENCYCLOPEDIA OF

World Sport

VOLUME 1

David Levinson *and*
Karen Christensen

Editors

BERKSHIRE PUBLISHING GROUP

Great Barrington, Massachusetts U.S.A.

www.iWorldSport.com

For information:
  Berkshire Publishing Group LLC
  314 Main Street
  Great Barrington, Massachusetts 01230
  www.berkshirepublishing.com

Printed in the United States of America

Library of Congress Cataloging-in-Publication Data
Berkshire encyclopedia of world sport / David Levinson and Karen Christensen, general editors.
    p.   cm.
  Summary: "Covers the whole world of sport, from major professional sports and sporting events to community and youth sport, as well as the business of sports and key social issues"—Provided by publisher.
  Includes bibliographical references and index.
  ISBN 0-9743091-1-7
 1. Sports—Encyclopedias.   I. Levinson, David, 1947-   II. Christensen, Karen, 1957-

  GV567.B48 2005
  796.03–dc22

                                                        2005013050

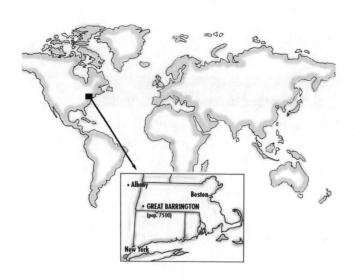

Editorial and Production Staff

Project Director
David Levinson

Editorial and Production Staff
Rachel Christensen, Tom Christensen, Elizabeth Eno,
Jess LaPointe, Courtney Linehan, Marcy Ross,
Gabby Templet

Photo Coordinator
Joseph DiStefano

Copy Editors
Eileen Clawson, Robin Gold, Mike Nichols,
Carol Parikh, Mark Siemens, Daniel Spinella

Information Management and Programming
Trevor Young

Designers
Joseph DiStefano and Linda Weidemann

Printers
Thomson-Shore

Composition Artists
Brad Walrod and Linda Weidemann

Production Coordinator
Marcy Ross

Proofreaders
Mary Bagg, Eileen Clawson, and Elizabeth Larson

Indexers
Peggy Holloway and Barbara Lutkins

Editorial Board

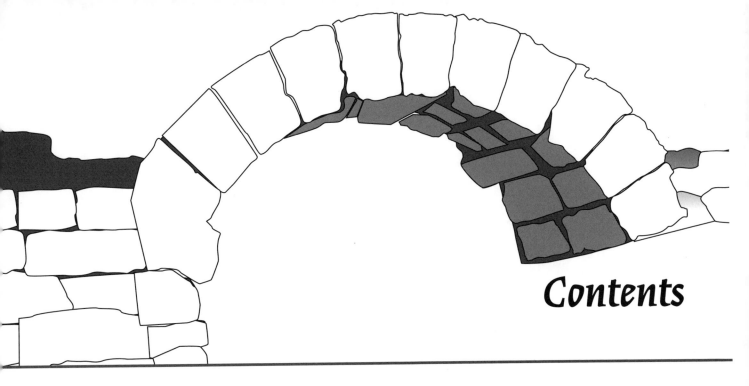

Contents

Entries

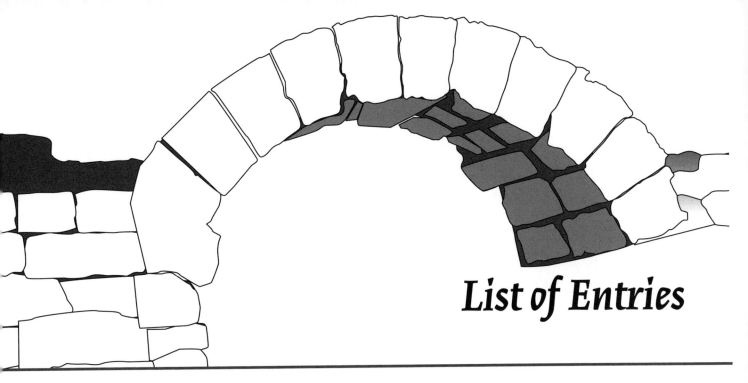

List of Entries

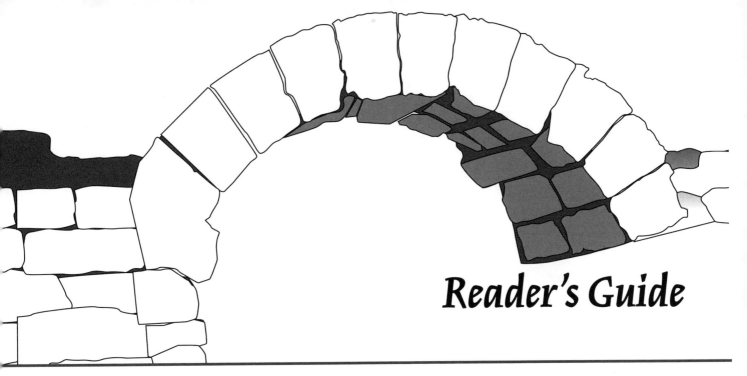

Reader's Guide

Management
Marketing
Memorabilia Industry
Ownership
Revenue Sharing
Salary Caps
Spectator Consumption Behavior
Sponsorship
Sport Tourism
Sporting Goods Industry
Unionism

Sport in Society

Aesthetics
American Sports Exceptionalism
Animal Rights
Art
Beauty
Body Image
Commercialization
Community
Competition
Cooperation
Country Club
Economics and Public Policy
Environment
Gender Equity
Globalization
International Politics
Law
Lesbianism
Literature
Masculinity
Movies
Prayer
Psychology
Psychology of Gender Differences
Religion
Scholar-Baller
Sexual Harassment
Sexuality
Social Class

Social Identity
Sport and National Identity
Technology
Values and Ethics
Violence

Sports—Air

Ballooning
Flying
Hang Gliding
Kite Sports
Parachuting
Soaring

Sports—Animal

Bullfighting
Buzkashi
Carriage Driving
Falconry
Foxhunting
Horse Racing
Horseback Riding
Hunting
Jousting
Polo
Rodeo

Sports—Ball

Basketball
Bowls and Bowling
Floorball
Footbag
Goalball
Handball, Team
Korfball
Mesoamerican Ball Court Games
Pelota
Netball
Volleyball
Volleyball, Beach
Sepak takraw
Speedball

Sports—Body Movement and Strength

Baton Twirling
Bodybuilding
Capoeira
Cheerleading
Dance
DanceSport
Gymnastics, Apparatus
Gymnastics, Rhythmic
Powerlifting
Rope Jumping
Tug of War
Weightlifting

Sports—Combative and Martial

Aikido
Archery
Arm Wrestling
Boxing
Bullfighting
Buzkashi
Fencing
Japanese Martial Arts, Traditional
Jousting
Judo
Jujutsu
Karate
Kendo
Mixed Martial Arts
Naginata
Shooting
Silat
Sumo
Taekwando
Wrestling
Wushu

Sports—Environmental

Fishing
Hunting

Youth Sports

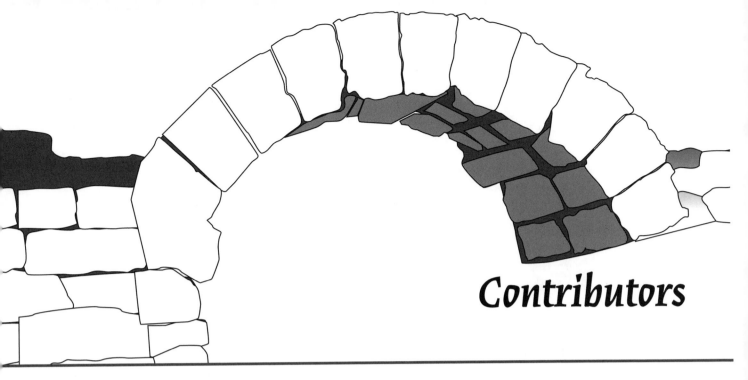

Contributors

Abbas, Andrea
University of Teeside, UK
Heptathlon

Abrams, Harvey
Harvey Abrams Books
Memorabilia Industry

Ackley, Brian
Freelance Sportswriter
Super Bowl

Adair, Daryl
University of Canberra
Flying

Adams, Mary Louise
Queen's University, Ontario
Skating, Ice Figure

Albers, Angela
University of North Dakota
*Track and Field—Jumping and
    Throwing*

Albers, Libby
Argosy University
Performance Enhancement

Albohm, Marjorie
Orthopaedic Research and
    Sports Medicine
Athletic Training

Allen, Dean
Independent Scholar
South Africa

Allen, E. John B.
Plymouth State College
Skiing, Alpine
Skiing, Cross-Country
St. Moritz

Althouse, Ronald C.
West Virginia University
College Athletes

Amdur, Ellis
Independent Scholar
Naginata

Anderson, Dean F.
Iowa State University
Spectator Consumption Behavior

Anderson, Julie
De Montfort University
Skating, Ice Speed

Anderson, Peter B.
University of New Orleans
Sex and Performance

Aplin, Nicholas G.
Nanyang Technological University
Singapore

Azoy, G. Whitney
Lawrenceville School
Buzkashi

Bailey, Ted
Independent Scholar
Boomerang Throwing

Baker, William
University of Maine
Religion

Bale, John
Keele University
Environment

Ballinger, Debra Ann
University of Rhode Island
British Open
Fishing
Golf

Barr, Carol A.
University of Massachusetts,
    Amherst
Title IX

Beal, Becky
University of the Pacific
Skateboarding

Beauchamp, Edward
University of Hawaii
Boxing

Bell, Daniel
International Games Archive
African Games
Arab Games
Asian Games
Central American and Caribbean Games
Commonwealth Games
Games of the New Emerging Forces (GANEFO)
South East Asian Games

Bell, Robert
University of Tennessee
Social Class

Belles, A. Gilbert
Western Illinois University
Handball, Team

Bennett, Alexander
Internation Research Centre for Japanese Studies
Kendo

Bensel-Meyers, Linda
University of Denver
Drake Group

Bernstein, Alina
Tel Aviv University
Womens Sports, Media Coverage of

Beunen, Gaston
Katholieke Universiteit Leuven
Growth and Development

Birkholz, Stefanie
Independent Scholar
Eurosport

Blanchard, Kendall
Fort Lewis College
Mascots

Blecking, Diethelm
Institut fur Sportgeschichte
Poland

Boggan, Tim
USA Table Tennis
Table Tennis

Bolin, Anne
Elon University
Bodybuilding

Bolz, Daphné
University of Strasbourg II and Free University Berlin
Foro Italico
Olympic Stadium (Berlin), 1936

Bonini, Gherardo
Historical Archives of European Union
India
Italy
Koreas
Luge
Motorcycle Racing
Romania
Senegal
Sledding—Skeleton

Booth, Douglas
University of Waikato
Bondi Beach
Extreme Surfing
Surf Lifesaving

Booth, Ross
Monash University
Revenue Sharing

Boucher, Stan
American Alpine Club
Mount Everest
Mountaineering

Bowman, John S.
Independent Scholar
Cooperation

Boyd, Jean A.
Arizona State University
Scholar-Baller

Bradley, Joseph M.
University of Stirling
Scotland

Brooks, Dana D.
West Virginia University
College Athletes

Brousse, Michel
Université de Bordeaux
Judo
Jujutsu

Brown, Matt
Ohio University
Collective Bargaining

Brownell, Susan
University of Missouri, St. Louis
Multiculturalism

Bruce, Toni
University of Waikato
Newspapers
Play-by-Play Announcing

Burdsey, Daniel
University of Brighton
Social Identity

Burnett, Cora
Rand Afrikaans University
Rituals

Bush, Anthony
Independent Scholar
Polo, Bicycle

Butler, Brian S.
University of Texas-Pan American
Astrodome

Cardoza, Monica
Independent Scholar
Karate

Cashman, Richard
University of Technology, Sydney
Australian Rules Football
Cricket
Cricket World Cup
Lord's Cricket Ground

Chandler, Timothy J.
Kent State University
Hurling

Chaplin, Patrick
Anglia Polytechnic University,
    Cambridge
Darts

Charlston, Jeffery A.
U.S. Army Center of Military
    History
Skating, In-line
Underwater Sports

Chase, Laura Frances
California State Polytechnic University, Pomona
Hockey, Ice
Stanley Cup

Chehabi, H. E.
Boston University
Iran

Chelladurai, Packianathan
Ohio State University
Management

Cherubini, Jeff
Manhattan College
Motivation

Chick, Garry
Pennsylvania State University
Auto Racing
Billiards
Indianapolis 500
Mesoamerican Ball Court Games

Christensen, Karen
Berkshire Publishing Group
Ashes, The

Clark, Becky
International Sports Sciences
    Association and
    Dr. Becky's Fitness
Deaflympics
Exercise and Health
Senior Sport
Special Olympics

Coakley, Jay
University of Colorado,
    Colorado Springs
Youth Sports

Cook, Philippa
Brunel University, UK
Postmodernism

Covil, Eric C.
Springfield College
Radio

Crawford, Russ
University of Nebraska, Lincoln
ESPN
Gymnastics, Apparatus
Movies
Spectators
World Series
Yankee Stadium

Crawford, Sally
Independent Scholar
Aerobics

Crawford, Scott A. G. M.
Eastern Illinois University
Auto Racing
Croquet
Netball
Shinty
Sled Dog Racing
Tug of War

Crawford, Simon J.
Illinois Wesleyan University
Parachuting

Crocker, Peter R. E.
University of British Columbia
Stress

Cronin, Mike
De Montfort University
Bobsledding
Camogie
Football, Gaelic
Ireland

Crum, Bart
Free University, Amsterdam
Korfball

Cumo, Christopher M.
Independent Scholar
Bulgaria
Cycling
Greece
Hunting
Strength
Sweden
Switzerland

Czech, Michaela
University of Goettingen
Biathlon and Triathlon

Daniels, Dayna B.
University of Lethbridge
Country Club
Lesbianism

Davis, Michael
Northern Missouri State
    University
Tai Chi

De Knop, Paul
Vrije Universiteit Brussel and
    Tilburg University
Sport Tourism

de Melo, Victor Andrade
Federal University of Rio de Janeiro
Brazil

DeMarco, Michael A.
Journal of the Asian Martial Arts
Wushu

DePauw, Karen P.
Virginia Polytechnic Institute and
    State University
Disability Sport

Depken, Craig A.
University of Texas, Arlington
Free Agency

DiBrezzo, Rosalie
University of Arkansas, Fayetteville
Biomechanics

Diketmüller, Rosa
University of Vienna
Austria

Doll-Tepper, Gudrun
Freie Universitat Berlin
Paralympics

Donnelly, Peter
University of Toronto
Interpretive Sociology

Drakich, Kristine
University of Toronto
Volleyball, Beach

Dyer-Bennet, Bonnie
Independent Scholar
Biathlon and Triathlon

Eichberg, Henning
University of Southern Denmark
Folk Sports

Eisen, George
Nazareth College of Rochester
Maccabiah Games

Elling, Agnes
Tilburg University
Gay Games

Emiola, Lasun
National Institute for Sports
Nigeria

Epstein, Adam
Central Michigan University
Law

Fair, John D.
Georgia College and
    State University
Powerlifting
Venice Beach
Weightlifting

Falcous, Mark
University of Otago, New Zealand
Media-Sports Complex

Fasting, Kari
Norwegian University of Sport
    and Physical Education
Gender Equity
Norway

Field, Russell
University of Toronto
Maple Leaf Gardens

Fort, Inza
University of Arkansas, Fayetteville
Biomechanics

Fragale, Mark
Independent Scholar
Surfing

Gaskin, Cadeyrn
Victoria University
Personality

Gelberg, J. Nadine
Rochester Institute of Technology
Technology

Gentner, Noah B.
Tennessee Wesleyan College
Mental Conditioning
Performance
Pilates

Georgiadis, Kostas
International Olympic Academy
International Olympic Academy

Ghent, Gretchen
University of Calgary Library
Magazines

Gildea, Dennis
Springfield College
Sportswriting and Reporting

Gill, Diane L.
University of North Carolina,
    Greensboro
Psychology of Gender Differences

Gladden, Jay
University of Massachusetts, Amherst
Brand Management

Gmelch, George
Union College
Baseball Nicknames
Baseball Stadium Life
Baseball Wives

Goksøyr, Matti
Norwegian University of Sport
    and Physical Education
Anthropology Days
Bislett Stadium
Holmenkollen Ski Jump
Holmenkollen Sunday
Ski Jumping

González Aja, Teresa
Universidad Politécnica de Madrid
Spain

Gragg, Derrick
University of Arkansas
Intercollegiate Athletics

Graham, Richard Neil
InlineHockeyCentral.com
Hockey, In-line

Green, B. Christine
University of Texas, Austin
Football, Flag

Gullion, Laurie
University of New Hampshire,
    Durham
Canoeing and Kayaking

Gundogan, Nese
National Olympic Committee of
    Turkey
Turkey

Guttmann, Allen
Amherst College
Art
Literature
Sexuality
Sumo
Sumo Grand Tournament Series

Hadd, Valerie
University of British Columbia
Stress

Handegard, Loretta A.
Florida State University
Officiating

Hanley, Elizabeth A.
Pennsylvania State University
DanceSport

Hargreaves, Jennifer
Brunel University, UK
Feminist Perspective
South Africa

Harris, John
University of Wales Institute,
    Cardiff
Diet and Weight Loss

Harris, Sally S.
Palo Alto Medical Clinic
Anemia

Harrison, C. Keith
Arizona State University
Scholar-Baller

Hartmann, Douglas
University of Minnesota
Community

Hasbrook, Cynthia A.
University of Wisconsin,
    Milwaukee
Family Involvement

Hasse, Manuela
Universidade Tecnica de Lisboa
Portugal

Hatfield, Disa
University of Connecticut
Sport Science

Hattery, Angela J.
Wake Forest University
Commercialization of College Sports
Violence

Heidemann, Berit
German Sport University Cologne
Adventure Education

Hennessey, Christina L.
Loyola Marymount University
Boat Race (Cambridge vs. Oxford)
Elfstedentocht
European Football Championship
Highland Games
Le Mans
Nextel (Winston) Cup

Henry, Amy
Bowling Green State University
*Track and Field—Running and
    Hurdling*

Hess, Robert
Victoria University
Australia

Heywood, Leslie
State University of New York,
    Binghamton
Cross-Country Running
Narrative Theory
Social Constructivism

Hofmann, Annette
University of Münster
Skiing, Freestyle
Snowboarding
Turner Festivals

Hong, Fan
De Montfort University
China

Horne, John D.
University of Edinburgh
Athletic Talent Migration
Sporting Goods Industry

Hudson, Ian
University of Manitoba
Economics and Public Policy

Huffman, Julie
University of California,
  Los Angeles
Maracana Stadium

Huggins, Mike
St. Martins College
Ascot

Hult, Joan
University of Maryland
Speedball

Humphreys, Brad R.
University of Illinois
Competitive Balance

Ikeda, Keiko M.
Yamaguchi University
Japan

Jackson, Steven J.
University of Otago, New Zealand
Athletes as Heroes

James, Jeffrey D.
Florida State University
Fan Loyalty

Jamison, Wesley V.
Dordt College
Animal Rights

Janning, Michelle Y.
Whitman College
Women's World Cup

Jarvie, Grant
University of Stirling
Racism

Jobling, Ian
Centre for Olympic Studies,
  University of Queensland
Olympics, 2004

Johnes, Martin
St. Martin's College
Soccer
United Kingdom

Jori, Alberto
University of Tübingen
Greece, Ancient
Rome, Ancient

Joseph, Janelle
University of Toronto
Alternative Sports
Gender Verification
Sport as Spectacle
Sportsmanship

Jutel, Annemarie
Otago Polytechnic
Body Image
Marathon and Distance Running

Kaufman, Haim
Wingate Institute
Israel

Kay, Joyce
University of Stirling
Horse Racing

Kidd, Bruce
University of Toronto
Canada

Kirby, Sandra
University of Winnipeg
Homophobia

Kleitman, Sabina
University of Sydney
School Performance

Klens-Bigman, Deborah
New York Budokai
Japanese Martial Arts, Traditional

Kozub, Francis M.
Indiana University
Adapted Physical Education

Kraemer, William J.
University of Connecticut
Sport Science

Ladda, Shawn
Manhattan College
Diving

Laine, Leena
Independent Scholar
Finland

LeCompte, Mary Lou
University of Texas, Austin
Rodeo

Lee, Jason
Troy State University
Prayer

Lennartz, Karl
German Sport University Cologne
Olympia
Olympics, Summer

Leonard, David J.
Washington State University
Internet

Levinson, David
Berkshire Publishing Group
Auto Racing
Boxing
Extreme Sports
Football, Canadian
Gymnastics, Rhythmic
Horseback Riding
Lake Placid
Madison Square Garden
Super Bowl
Wembley Stadium
Wrigley Field

Levy, Donald P.
University of Connecticut
Fantasy Sports

Lewis, Tina
International Footbag Players'
    Association
Footbag

Lidor, Ronnie
Zinman College of Physical
    Education and Sport Sciences
Psychology

Lincoln, Kate
Forbes Newspapers
Carriage Driving

Lockman Hall, Cara Joy
Positive Performance
Wakeboarding

Long, Kathy
Independent Scholar
Mixed Martial Arts

Lough, Nancy L.
University of New Mexico
*Commodification and
    Commercialization*
Sponsorship

Lowerson, John
University of Sussex
Bowls and Bowling
Foxhunting
Rounders and Stoolball

Lucas, Shelley
Boise State University
Mountain Biking

Ludwig, Ruth
BFA Publications
Ballooning

Maguire, Joseph A.
Loughborough University
Globalization

Marivoet, Salomé
Universidade de Coimbra
Euro 2004

Markovits, Andrei S.
University of Michigan, Ann Arbor
American Sports Exceptionalism

Marsh, David
University of Western Sydney
Television

Marsh, Herbert
Independent Scholar
School Performance

Mason, Daniel S.
University of Alberta
Agents
Franchise Relocation

Maughan, Ronald J.
Loughborough University
Nutrition

McConnell, Robin
University of Ulster
Academies and Camps, Sport
Clubsport Systems

McEvoy, Chad D.
Illinois State University
Collective Bargaining

McGehee, Richard V.
Concordia University, Austin
Argentina
Cuba
Gymnastics, apparatus
Honduras
Jamaica
Mexico
Pan American Games

McKernan, Tamara
Ringette Alberta
Ringette

McNeil, Teresa
Cuyamaca College
Pelota

Mellor, Gordon T.
De Montfort University
Falconry

Miller, Walter D.
Independent Scholar
Soaring

Mitchell, Timothy
Texas A & M University
Bullfighting

Mojer, Linda
American Amateur Racquetball
    Association
Racquetball

Mott, Morris
Brandon University, Manitoba
Curling

Mottola, Michelle F.
University of Western Ontario
Reproduction

Mulrooney, Aaron
Kent State University
Facility Management
Fenway Park

Myers, Helen
State University of New York,
    Geneseo
Dance

Nack, Annette
Independent Scholar
Fitness
Lacrosse
X Games

Nagel, Mark S.
Georgia State University
Collective Bargaining
Facility Naming Rights
Salary Caps

Nelson, Kelly
Arizona State University
Race Walking

Maria Newton
University of Utah
Tennis

Nicholson, Matthew
Victoria University
Australia

O'Sullivan, Robin K.
University of Texas, Austin
Sail Sports
Snowshoe Racing
Speedball
Tug of War
Ultimate

Ottesen, Laila
University of Copenhagen
Denmark

Page, Sarah E.
Independent Scholar
Yoga

Pagen, Claire
United States Hang Gliding
    Association
Hang Gliding

Paraschak, Vicky
University of Windsor
Iditarod
Native American Games and Sports

Park, Roberta J.
University of California, Berkeley
Human Movement Studies
Physical Education

Patel, Ashwin J.
University of Tennessee, Knoxville
All England Lawn Tennis and
    Croquet Club
Pilates

Pauka, Kirstin
University of Hawaii, Manoa
Silat

Pedersen, Inge Kryger
University of Copenhagen
Competition
Elite Sports Parents

Pfister, Gertrud
Institute of Exercise and Sports
    Sciences
Advertising
Beauty
Coeducational Sport
Eiger North Face
Fashion
Germany
Islamic Countries' Women's Sports
    Solidarity Games
Rope Jumping

Pike, Elizabeth C. J.
University College, Chichester
Injury
Injury Risk in Women's Sport

Pillsbury, Richard
Georgia State University
Auto Racing

Plummer III, Bill
Amateur Softball Association of
    America
Softball

Poliakoff, Michael B.
National Council on Teacher
    Quality
Wrestling

Polumbaum, Judy
University of Iowa
Boston Marathon
Ironman Triathlon
Jogging

Rahman, Nabilla Ahmed
Alexandria University
Egypt

Ransdell, Lynda B.
Boise State University
Mountain Biking
Tennis

Rascher, Daniel A.
University of San Francisco
Collective Bargaining

Reekie, Shirley
San José State University
Sailing

Reel, Justine
University of Utah
Cheerleading

Reilly, Erin
Auburn University, Montgomery
Taekwando

Renson, Roland
Katholieke Universiteit Leuven
Archery
Belgium
Olympics, Winter
World University Games

Riley, Dawn
America True and Women's Sports
    Foundation
America's Cup

Riordan, James
Committee on European Sports
    History
International Politics
Russia and USSR
Worker Sports

Roessler, Kirsten Kaya
University of Southern Denmark
Pain

Rosenthal, Joshua M.
State University of New York,
    Oneonta
Capoeira

Ruddle, Andrew
University of Manchester
Rowing

Rühl, Joachim K.
German Sport University Cologne
Jousting

Ryba, Tatiana V
University of Tennessee
Cultural Studies Theory
Yoga

Sachs, Michael
Temple University
Play vs. Organized Sport

Sack, Allen L.
University of New Haven
Amateur vs. Professional Debate

Sacks, David Neil
Florida State University
Officiating

Sagert, Kelly Boyer
Independent Scholar
Baseball
Basketball
Boomerang Throwing

Saint Sing, Susan
Independent Scholar
Henley Regatta

Sam, Michael
University of Otago, New Zealand
Sport and National Identity

San Antonio, Patricia
University of Maryland, Baltimore
    County
Baseball Stadium Life
Baseball Wives

Scherer, Jay
University of Otago, New Zealand
Sport and National Identity

Scott, Eugenia
Butler University
Goalball

Seeley, Andy
US ACRS
Skating, Roller

Seiler, Roland
Sport Science Institute
Orienteering

Sell, Katie
University of Utah
Cheerleader
Tennis
Wimbledon

Sheffer, Mary Lou
Louisiana State University
Sport as Religion

Shephard, Roy J.
University of Toronto
Osteoporosis

Shipley, Stan
Independent Scholar
Boxing

Shishida, Fumiaki
Waseda University, Tokyo
Aikido

Short, Martin
University of North Dakota
*Track and Field—Jumping and
    Throwing*

Simcock, Susie
World Squash Federation
Squash

Sisjord, Mari Kristin
Norwegian University of Sport
    and Physical Education
Wrestling

Skinner, Scott R.
Drachen Foundation
Kite Sports

Sloggett, Tony
Meadowbrook Farm
Masters
Pebble Beach
Ryder Cup
St. Andrews

Smith, D. Randall
Rutgers University
Home Field Advantage

Smith, Earl
Wake Forest University
*Commercialization of College
    Sports*
Violence

Smith, Ronald A.
Pennsylvania State University
Carnegie Report
Football

SooHoo, Sonya
University of Utah
Cheerleading

Spence, Kate
United States Badminton
    Association
Badminton

Spitzer, Giselher
University of Potsdam, Germany
East Germany

Stanley, Linda
University of British Columbia
Innebandy

Staurowsky, Ellen J.
Ithaca College
Hazing

Stotlar, David K.
University of Northern Colorado
Endorsements
Marketing

Strudler, Keith Andrew
Marist College
Duathlon

Styles, Alvy
Ashland University
Facility Management
Fenway Park

Su, Mila C.
Penn State Altoona College
Floorball
Hockey, Field

Sundgot-Borgen, Jorunn
Norwegian University of Sport
    and Physical Education
Disordered Eating

Szikora, Katalin
Hungarian University of Physical
    Education
Hungary

Teja, Angela
University of Cassino
Rome, Ancient

Terret, Thierry
University of Lyon
Cameroon
France
Interallied Games
Polo, Water
Swimming
Swimming, Synchronized
Tour de France

Thomas, Jonathan M.
St. Martin's College
Ownership
Polo
Professionalism
Rugby
Sport Politics

Thomson, Rex W.
Unitec New Zealand
New Zealand

Tikander, Vesa
Independent Scholar
Finland

Tishman, Jeffrey
United States Fencing Coaches
    Association
Fencing
Pentathlon, Modern

Toftegaard Nielson, Jan
Institute of Exercise and Sport
    Sciences, Copenhagen
Sexual Harassment

Toscano, Lisa
Manhattan College
Endurance

Townes, John
Berkshire Trade and Commerce
Arm Wrestling
Auto Racing
Boating, Ice
Karting
Motorboat Racing
Skiing, Water

Trail, Galen T.
University of Florida
Spectator Consumption Behavior

Trevithick, Alan
Independent Scholar
Sepak Takraw
Snowshoe Racing
Volleyball

Trumper, Ricardo
Okanagan University College
Athletes as Celebrities

Turner, Brian A.
Ohio State University
Management

Tymowski, Gabriela
University of New Brunswick
Child Sport Stars

Vamplew, Wray
University of Stirling
Horse Racing

van Bottenburg, Maarten
Utrect University
Netherlands

van Hilvoorde, Ivo
Universiteit Maastricht
Biotechnology
Fitness Industry

van Zwoll, Wayne C.
National Shooting Sports
    Foundation
Shooting

Vaverka, Frantisek
Palacky University
Czech Republic

Wachs, Faye Linda
California State Polytechnic
    University, Pomona
AIDS and HIV
Masculinity
Values and Ethics

Wade, Michael
University of Minnesota
Kinesiology

Waite, Barbara Teetor
Grinnell College
Coaching

Waldron, Jennifer J.
University of Northern Iowa
Burnout

Walk, Stephan
California State University,
    Fullerton
Injuries, Youth
Youth Culture and Sport

Wallbutton, Edward J.
World Squash Federation
Squash

Warner, Sally
University of Washington
Mountain Biking

Wassong, Stephan
German Sport University Cologne
Adventure Education
Olympia
Olympics, Summer

Wheaton, Belinda
University of Surrey Roehampton
Windsurfing

Wieting, Stephen
University of Iowa
Aesthetics
Kenya

Willman, Valerie Ludwick
Clinical Neuroscience Center
Baton Twirling

Wilson, Brian
University of British Columbia
Anti-Jock Movement

Wilson, Wayne
Amateur Athletic Foundation
American Youth Soccer
    Organization (AYSO)

Wise, Suzanne
Appalachian State University
Auto Racing

Woltmann, Bernard
Akademia Wychowania
    Fizycznego
Poland

Wong, Lloyd L.
University of Calgary
Athletes as Celebrities

Wrynn, Alison M.
California State University, Long
    Beach
Lifeguarding
Sports Medicine

Wushanley, Ying
Millersville University
Coliseum (Rome)
Davis Cup
World Cup

Zimbalist, Andrew
Smith College
Unionism

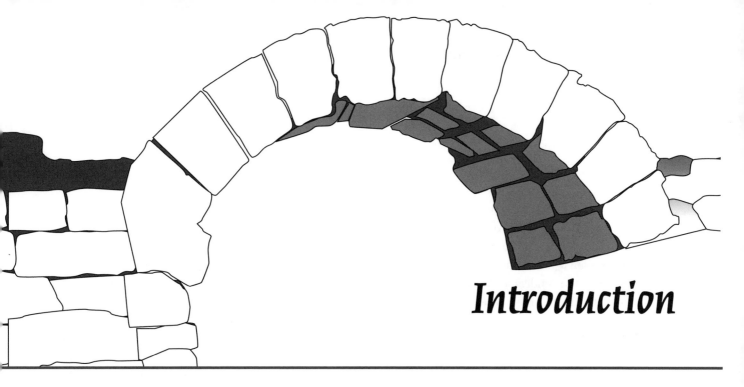

Introduction

The *Berkshire Encyclopedia of World Sport* is the first truly encyclopedic resource bringing together in one publication knowledge from all the disciplines involved in the study of sports. With sports studies now a diverse, global field, the integrated and interdisciplinary approach of the *Berkshire Encyclopedia of World Sport* is crucial because it fully meets the information needs of students, teachers, researchers, professionals, and sports enthusiasts of all interests.

The encyclopedia covers a range of topics in 430 articles. It covers individual sports themselves, with articles on the origins, history, and significance of major world sports such as basketball and cricket, as well as articles on regional and historic sports, including sumo and jousting. It covers issues both major and minor, from injuries and sponsorship to tailgate parties (see "Stadium Life") and mascots. Key social issues such as performance enhancement, racism, sexism, civic life, youth participation, and public policy are amply covered. Moreover, the encyclopedia reaches out to cover other sports topics, including the sports industry; famous arenas, stadiums, and events; media coverage; youth sports and college sports; health and fitness; and a survey of sports in nations around the world.

Berkshire developed the encyclopedia under the direction of eight leading scholars and educators, representing several sports disciplines and coming from three nations. Among them are the two first recipients of the International Olympic Committee's awards for sports history, Allen Guttmann and Roland Renson, and the past and present presidents of the International Society for the History of Physical Education and Sport, Gertrud Pfister and Thierry Terret. The board also well represents several other central interests in sports studies, including sport in society and youth sports (Jay Coakley), sports management and college sports (Allen L. Sack), education (Edward Beauchamp), women's studies and sports and the humanities (Leslie Heywood), and sports information and knowledge management (Wayne Wilson). Because several of the editors—and many of the contributors—are athletes themselves, their contributions are informed by both research and personal experience.

Audiences

The *Berkshire Encyclopedia of World Sport* creates a new arena in which to watch and explore the entire world of sports. It connects sports with academic learning, so kids and teachers who adore sports can use favorite sports topics—baseball or cricket or karate—as a way to learn about U.S. or world history, international relations, ethnicity and racism, or globalization. By making a resource such as this encyclopedia available, we hope to offer students (including reluctant readers, who often struggle with classroom materials but manage the sports page every day) a new and appealing tool for preparing class reports and presentations. When students are excited about learning, teachers' and parents' job educating them becomes easier; for more information on teaching uses of the encyclopedia see iworldsport.com.

For sports scholars in all disciplines, the encyclopedia provides an integrated state-of-the-art review of the sports that brings readers up to speed on what has been discovered in related fields. And for sports enthusiasts, it provides context for understanding new developments and issues that influence their chosen sports.

The Range of Sports Studies

Until not very long ago, sports studies was a limited enterprise, attracting mainly researchers and instructors in physical education departments and a few isolated scholars in history, sociology, and anthropology whose study of sports often dismayed their colleagues. Over the last fifteen or so years, sports studies has expanded and grown at an ever faster pace. It now includes a number of academic disciplines, each with its own interests, programs and departments, professional publications, and conferences. These include sports management, sport science, kinesiology, human movement studies, physical education, sports medicine, and sports law. In addition, sport remains an interest of scholars in recreation and leisure studies, history, sociology, economics, anthropology, and public policy. More and more sports research now looks at the role of sports in society, providing balance to the earlier emphasis on the historiography of individual sports. Sports studies is much more scientific now, and researchers use clinical and laboratory methods to study topics such as biomechanics, performance enhancement, and injury risk. In short, we now have a merging of the sports experience, social science, clinical and laboratory science, and policy analysis.

Because communication across disciplines is often limited, encyclopedias such as this are especially valuable. Our goal has been to integrate perspectives and knowledge from these different disciplines so that readers can have as full an understanding of what we know about sports in 2005 as possible.

The Global Nature of Sport

Sport is a part of globalization. When the British empire dominated the globe, British sports traveled to colonial outposts and took root around the world. With the rise of the United States in the twentieth century, it was the turn of sports such as basketball and volleyball to make a similar journey, along with new ideas about what sports means, what it takes or should take to win, and how sport fits into the overall human experience. The twentieth century was particularly notable for the political and nationalistic overtones that colored sports. Many nations invested heavily in the development of "world-class" sports programs, facilities, and athletes, intending to use international sports success to inspire national pride and patriotism. Sport has also inspired international cooperation, with athletes, coaches, sports delegations, international federations, and competitions more and more crossing national boundaries.

While there are many global sports, there are also vast numbers of regional and local sports. One might consider American football as an example: played as an exotic minority pastime in a few European nations, it does not seem poised to become a major global sport. Less well-known traditional sports and games include bicycle polo, pedestrianism, camogie (an Irish women's game), buzkashi (Afghan goat dragging), Finnish baseball, and Australian-rules football (which is quite similar to rugby).

Sports is also now a major global business, fed by a nearly insatiable demand among sports participants and fans for anything having to do with sports, and especially with their sport and their team. Leagues, teams, athletes, coaches, support personnel, equipment, fashion, memorabilia, scholarships, and fan loyalty are among the commodities to be bought and sold in this global marketplace. The media is so vital a component of the global sports industry that what is labeled the "media sports complex" is seen by some experts as the core of the entire enterprise. Round-the-clock coverage via satellite television and the Internet now makes it possible for sports fans to watch a staggering array of sports and for advertisers to sell their products nonstop.

An Overview of Our Coverage

The encyclopedia provides 430 articles, organized A through Z. For conceptual purposes, the articles can be

assigned to 12 general categories covering the world of sports, past and present:

- College Sports—7 articles (including Amateur vs. Professional Debate, Title IX)
- Culture of Sport—28 articles (including Officiating, Sex and Performance, Mascots)
- Events—51 articles (including Asian Games, Gay Games, The Olympics, Henley Regatta, Indianapolis 500)
- Health and Fitness—27 articles (including Diet and Weight Loss, Injury, Pilates)
- Media—10 articles (including ESPN, Internet)
- Nation and Region Profiles—49 articles
- Paradigms and Perspectives—10 articles (including Postmodernism, Sport Science
- Sports Industry—22 articles (including Brand Management, Fashion, Salary Caps)
- Sport in Society—39 articles (including Art, Prayer, Value and Ethics)
- Sports—149 articles on individual sports and groups of related sports
- Venues—26 articles (including Bondi Beach, Fenway Park, Mt. Everest)
- Youth Sports—12 articles (including Child Sport Superstars, School Performance)

It is important to define what we mean by sports. We have defined an activity as a sport if it meets three criteria: (1) there are clear rules agreed to by the participants; (2) there are clear criteria for determining the winner; (3) winning is based substantially on variability in the physical abilities of the competitors. This does not mean that strategy and luck cannot also be important, but physical ability must also matter. We do not cover sports in which animals are the only competitors, such as cock fighting, bear baiting, dog racing, or fish fighting, but we do cover animal sports with human competitors, such as horse racing. We also cover motor sports.

This encyclopedia is not meant to be a source of statistics, rules of play, or biographies, though we include some of this information. Statistical and biographical information changes rapidly and is easily available on the Web or in sport-specific statistical compendiums. The *Berkshire Encyclopedia of World Sport* is intended to provide context, the big picture, and a wealth of information and analysis that readers cannot get anywhere else. We want to know how well we have succeeded, and readers can be sure that we will be updating and adding to this collection of global knowledge on sports and the sporting world at iworldsport.com—visit us soon.

As with all Berkshire reference works, the encyclopedia offers more than just textual content. There are more than one thousand sidebars, quotes, photographs, and illustrations. Many of the sidebars are extracts from primary source material (participant accounts, journalism, literature, poetry, song) designed to give readers a first-hand sense of what the sports experience was or is like for participants. Each article is also followed by a rich annotation (Further Reading) of key sources, including both those used in writing the article and others of related interest.

How to Use the Encyclopedia

Given our emphasis on gathering information from different perspectives and on covering sports from a global perspective, it was important to us that the encyclopedia allow users to see connections across articles and to move around easily. We have provided four tools to facilitate such movement.

1. The Reader's Guide at the beginning of each volume classifies all articles into twenty-seven topical categories, with articles placed in as many categories as appropriate.
2. Several dozen blind entries throughout the volume direct readers who search for articles under one heading to their correct location under a different heading.
3. Extensive cross-references at the end of articles point readers to other related articles.
4. Volume 4 provides an extensive index of people, places, events, sports, concepts, and theories. The index indicates both volume and page numbers.

Acknowledgements

One reason we wanted to make sports part of our initial lineup as independent publishers was that we had so thoroughly enjoyed working with sports scholars on previous projects. Many of the contributors to this work have become friends. We have met them at conferences and visited them in their own countries. These relationships make the kind of publishing we do satisfying and fun—like sports themselves.

We are often asked how we became experts on world sport, and we have to give credit to the real experts, who have been coaching us for years. Allen Guttmann, who has written many well-known books on sports, including the recent, brilliantly titled *Sports: The First Five Millennia*, has our special thanks for providing a broad perspective on sports through history and a knowledge of historical scholarship that is unrivaled. He has provided us with many contacts, as well as with the illustration of a lovely Persian tapestry that adorns our cover.

Many of our experts are also athletes, coaches, and passionate fans. We have been inspired by their energy. Ed Beauchamp, who was the Japan editor for Berkshire's *Encyclopedia of Modern Asia*, is also a boxing enthusiast and actually got Karen to try it—and like it! He even sent a t-shirt that says, "A woman's place is in the ring." Wayne Wilson and his staff at the Amateur Athletic Foundation in Los Angeles graciously opened their world-class collection to us. Especially valuable was the historical collection, a source of many of our older sidebars and illustrations. Gertrud Pfister, Thierry Terret, and Roland Renson continually pulled us away from our U.S. experience and directed us to key people, ideas, and resources in the global sports study arena, while Jay Coakley, Allen Sack, and Leslie Heywood led us into the new worlds of sports management, youth and college sports, and paradigms and perspectives.

Contributors Becky Clark, Richard Graham, Rob Hess, Brad Humphreys, Bruce Kidd, Richard McGehee, and Michael Sachs merit special thanks for providing extra help by suggesting topics, recommending contributors, and reviewing articles. The national Shooting Sports Foundation secured the shooting-articles con-

tributor for us, and the International Council for Sport Science and Physical Education in Berlin provided assistance in identifying and locating sports experts outside the United States. A former editorial staffer, Robin O'Sullivan, also contributed several articles. In addition to copyediting many of the articles, Mike Nichols provided valuable help in researching and updating information in a number of the articles.

Several editors and contributors (and a couple of helpful noncontributors) were generous in supplying us with photos; these include Alex Bennett, Michel Brousse, Daniel Burdsey, Brian Butler, Patrick Chaplin, Becky Clark, Jo-Ann Enweazor, Allen Guttmann, Amy Henry, Annette Hofmann, Fan Hong, Keiko Ikeda, Sue Lane, Tina Lewis, Richard McGehee, Morris Mott, Kirstin Pauka, Gertud Pfister, Roland Renson, Philip St. Gelinas, Latazik Szikora, and Ying Wushanley.

The cover photo of the yacht was provided by Stephen Matthews, a London banker whom Karen worked for many years ago. The Sport Museum of Flanders also provided several photos.

We want to acknowledge the contributions of our staff to this project. Liz Eno was the initial project coordinator; Courtney Linehan ably continued her work after Liz left for graduate school. Jess LaPointe stepped in to move articles through at the end and to assist with copyediting and proofing. Gabby Templet took the lead in photo research, and Joe DiStefano prepared the photos and designed the letter openers and other elements. Marcy Ross edited articles, tracked down missing information, and managed the production process.

We would also like to share an important personal event that coincided with the completion of *Berkshire Encyclopedia of World Sport*. In April Karen was invited to Knoxville, Tennessee, to attend a charity event for the prevention of child abuse. Speaking at that event was one of our contributors, Becky Clark, a researcher and deaf athlete who wrote our article on "Deaflympics" and sent us the story of playing basketball as a Lady Vol under Pat Summitt, the famous Tennessee coach. At the time she was a Lady Vol, Becky was going deaf, and Coach Summitt taught her the importance of

anticipation—a story Becky recounted in the sidebar to our College Athletes article. Meeting contributors is always special, but this was something more—both because Becky is a person of unique courage and warmth, and because this event, which set sport within its social and personal context, showed what our encyclopedia is really about.

As it happened, Pat Summitt herself was also a speaker at the event. Listening to her, one was struck by the connection between sports and leadership. She is the "winningest" coach in NCAA history, having won more basketball games than any other college basketball coach, male or female. Her leadership style is not exactly what you would call empathetic. She is fierce. She yells. She demands.

But she also loves her players and clearly feels an immense sense of responsibility for, and to, them. Her toughness is not only about winning, but also courage, self-reliance, and determination—qualities that will help her players in every aspect of their lives. And coach is a role all of us have a chance to play—as teachers, parents, bosses, and even as friends. Sports can help us set our sights high. Summitt remarked that her Lady Vols sometimes ask her, "Coach, aren't you *ever* going to be satisfied?" She said, "I tell them I see more in them than they see in themselves." Working with the remarkable group of experts that has created this encyclopedia has helped us set our sights as publishers, and inspires us as a company to be the "winningest" team.

David Levinson and Karen Christensen

About the Editors

Editors

David Levinson and **Karen Christensen** have edited and written award-winning titles on an array of global topics. Among their personal favorites are the best-selling *Encyclopedia of World Sport* (ABC-CLIO 1996; one-volume edition, Oxford 1999) and the *International Encyclopedia of Women and Sport* (Macmillan 2001). Levinson is a cultural anthropologist and passionate sports spectator while Christensen is an environmental author and wannabe jock. They have been actively involved with NASSH (North American Society for Sport History) and ISHPES (International Society for the History of Physical Education and Sport) and decided in 2003 that it was time to create an expanded international team to develop a truly comprehensive reference work on the whole wide world of sports.

Levinson has been an editor of numerous multi-volume encyclopedias, most recently the *Berkshire Encyclopedia of World History* (2004), and he is author of *Ethnic Groups Worldwide*, *Toward Explaining Human*

Culture, and *Tribal Living Book*. Christensen has edited the *Encyclopedia of World Environmental History* (Routledge 2004), and she is author of *Eco Living, The Green Home*, and *The Armchair Environmentalist*.

Editorial Board

Edward Beauchamp (Professor Emeritus of Education and Japanese Studies, University of Hawaii) is author of a dozen books and editor of *Studies of Modern Japan* and *Perspectives on the Twentieth Century*.

Jay Coakley (Professor of Sociology, University of Colorado) is editor of the *Handbook of Sports Studies* and author of *Sport in Society: Issues and Controversies*.

Allen Guttmann (Emily C. Jordan Folger Professor of English and American Studies, Amherst College) won the first International Olympics Committee Award for sports history and is author of, among others, *From Ritual to Record* and in 2004 *Sports: The First Five Millennia*.

Leslie Heywood (Associate Professor of English, State University of New York, Binghamton) is author of

Bodymakers: A Cultural Anatomy of Women's Body-building and *Pretty Good for a Girl: A Sports Memoir.*

Gertrud Pfister (Professor at the Institute of Exercise and Sport Sciences, University of Copenhagen) is president of the International Sport Sociology Association, coauthor of *Sport and Women: Social Issues in International Perspective*, and coeditor of the *International Encyclopedia of Women and Sports.*

Roland Renson (Katholieke Universiteit Leuven, Belgium) is the author of *The Games Reborn: The VIIth Olympiad, Antwerp 1920,* coauthor of *The Olympic Games through the Ages: Greek Antiquity and Its Impact on Modern Sport,* and recipient of the second International Olympics Committee Award for sports history.

Allen L. Sack (Director of the Management of Sports Industries Program, University of New Haven) is the author of *College Athletes for Hire: The Evolution and Legacy of the NCAA's Amateur Myth* as well as numerous columns in the sports media.

Thierry Terret (Professor of Sports Science and History, University of Lyon, France) is president of the International Society for the History of Physical Education and Sport and author of *Les Jeux interalliés de 1919: Sport, guerre et relations internationals* and *Pratiques sportives et identités locales.*

Wayne Wilson (Vice-President for Research at the Amateur Athletic Foundation, Los Angeles) is executive producer of the CD-ROM *An Olympic Journey: The Story of Women in the Olympic Games* and coeditor of *Doping in Elite Sport: The Politics of Drugs in the Olympic Movement.*

BERKSHIRE ENCYCLOPEDIA OF

World Sport

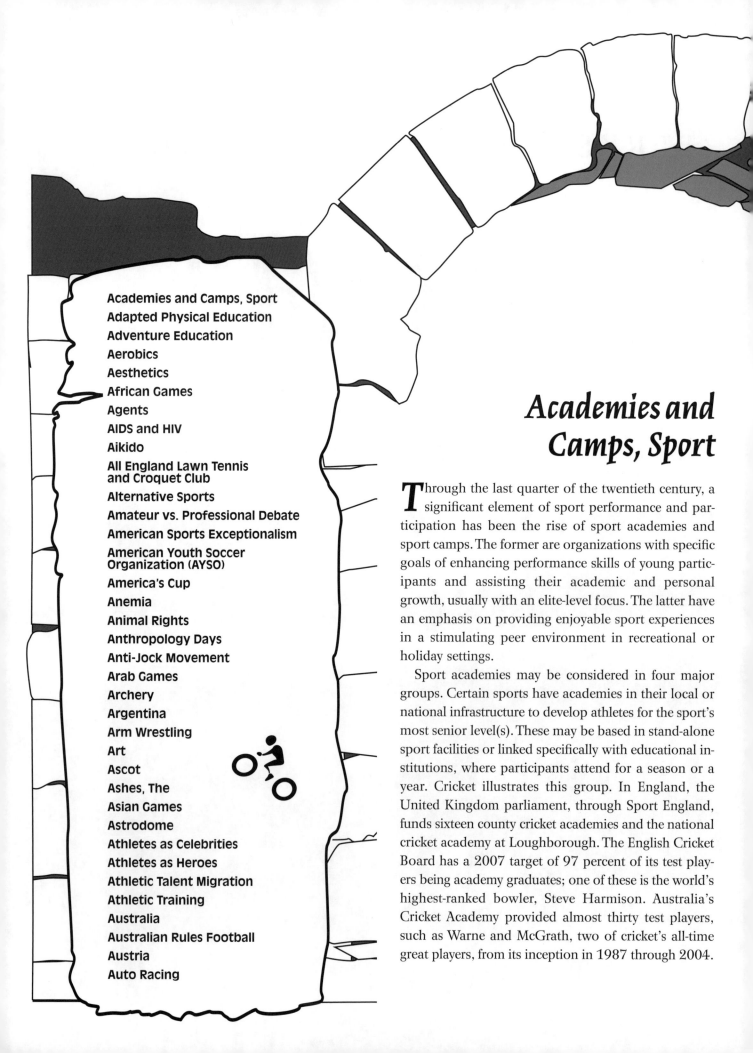

Academies and Camps, Sport

Through the last quarter of the twentieth century, a significant element of sport performance and participation has been the rise of sport academies and sport camps. The former are organizations with specific goals of enhancing performance skills of young participants and assisting their academic and personal growth, usually with an elite-level focus. The latter have an emphasis on providing enjoyable sport experiences in a stimulating peer environment in recreational or holiday settings.

Sport academies may be considered in four major groups. Certain sports have academies in their local or national infrastructure to develop athletes for the sport's most senior level(s). These may be based in stand-alone sport facilities or linked specifically with educational institutions, where participants attend for a season or a year. Cricket illustrates this group. In England, the United Kingdom parliament, through Sport England, funds sixteen county cricket academies and the national cricket academy at Loughborough. The English Cricket Board has a 2007 target of 97 percent of its test players being academy graduates; one of these is the world's highest-ranked bowler, Steve Harmison. Australia's Cricket Academy provided almost thirty test players, such as Warne and McGrath, two of cricket's all-time great players, from its inception in 1987 through 2004.

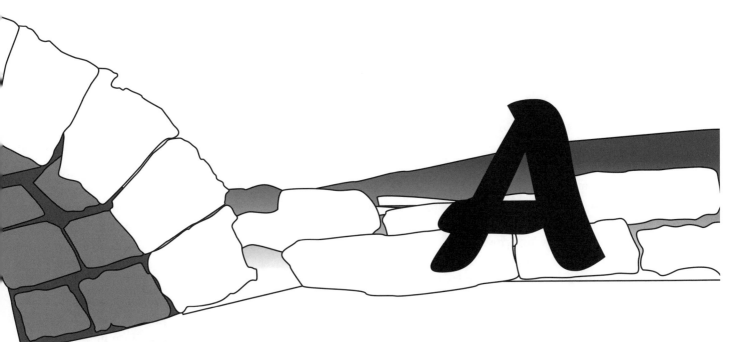

As with other academies in this group, athletes live on-site, develop their fitness, have access to medical support, continue academic or vocational studies, are monitored closely, receive dietary advice, and have assistance with personal development. Participants are in the broad 18–23-years age group. Virtually all sports have some type of academy or developmental group.

A second group has privately run academies with concomitant goals of skills development for potential elite-level sport achievers and generation of profit for academy owners. In tennis, the John Newcombe Academy in Texas illustrates this group. The Surfing Academy at Porthcawl, South Wales, and San Diego Surfing Academy in California are smaller examples of profit-making academies. A feature of sport academies and some sport camps is their association with famous names, such as the Evert and Newcombe tennis academies.

Tennis and other academies have generated criticism of perceived demands upon youngsters and the low proportion of their athletes who make a full-time living from professional sport. However, high-achieving youngsters annually come from the ranks of such academies. The International Tennis Federation (ITF) lists academies in eighteen countries. A camp in Russia, near the Black Sea, named for Yevgeny Kafilnikov, has been operative for forty years. Nick Bollettieri founded an academy in 1978 that has been associated with Agassi, Becker, Seles, Sharapova, and the Williams sisters. The seventy courts and two hundred acres are at the upper range of such establishments.

The third broad grouping encompasses small-scale academies, usually attached to educational institutions, businesses, or local or regional sports or nonsport bodies. A plethora of academies fits this group through the sport world. One of the few national networks planning to link with selected schools is that of the Hockey Canada Skills Academy programme. Year-long academies operate under the LA Kids program of Los Angeles, and the Combined Sports Academy provides for young people with learning difficulties at South East Derbyshire College in England. These particular athletes receive up to nine hours of sport tuition a week and engage in vocational and academic learning. At the highest educational level, the Queen's University in Belfast has sport academies, including one for Gaelic games. In India, the Tata Archery Academy and Tata Football Academy are run by the Tata Steel Company, which has its own sport complex.

In the final group of sport academies, "academy" terminology is used for what may be better described as a sport camp, conference, workshop, or short-term course. The Jai-Alai Academy in Miami fits the sport-camp model, and the two-day 2003 Yugoslav Handball Coaching Academy may be better described as a short course.

Internet analysis of sport structures reveals an increasing number and diversity in sport academies. In the 1990s in the small country of New Zealand, for example, the private International Rugby Academy of New Zealand (IRANZ) in Wellington was developed, as was a local soccer academy (Wynrs Academy) in Auckland. Each is typical of the second grouping noted above, in that they are privately operated for profit by prominent past international players. One of IRANZ's major goals is to encourage careers in playing or coaching rugby and "more importantly to achieve excellence in this area." The Wynrs Academy aims to "show these players a clear pathway to professional soccer." Additionally, the country has sport academies attached to a number of high schools and networks of regional rugby academies.

Sport camps may or may not have a goal of enhancing performance and are oriented to providing enjoyable sport experiences, usually in purpose-built vacation camps or in urban areas that have accommodation and access to sport facilities. They usually offer participation during school vacations. The placement of academies and camps near tourist destinations adds to their appeal, although the link between such centers and weather conducive to outdoor sport is also a significant factor. The financial demands on prospective participants can be daunting—the Evert "Fantasy Camps" in 2004 cost US$7,200 for three days. Camps may be run for profit (e.g., Tahoe Extreme Sports Camps) or for social or educational reasons. Camp networks have increased, as illustrated by the US Sports Camps network, which offers over five hundred camps. Certain camps, such as the Junior Tennis Camps at the John Newcombe Tennis Ranch, are linked with academies as opportunities for young athletes (eight to eighteen years old) to participate in recreational or competitive sport environments.

Children may be sent to such camps for social and sport reasons or for a sport-cum-leisure activity vacation. Certain camps may be seen as profit generating and oriented excessively to achievement, and the compulsory engagement of youngsters with sports in some settings may be counterproductive. But a well-run sport camp, with options and individual considerations, has the potential to positively engage children and young people.

The seeming proliferation of academies and camps, including sport and fantasy camps for adults, has rarely been examined in sport management. Academies, despite developing athletes for high performance, rarely provide any emphasis on systematic and in-depth leadership development (McConnell 2004). Academies for coaches and officials are few and, when offered, attempt to cover a range of topics in a brief period. Minority cultures and women are underrepresented in some sports (such as polo) that do not have wide-entry academies, although others espouse action to enhance wider participation and academy opportunities, such as with the Black Summit of skiers. Few academies or camps offer a focus on special populations. Longitudinal studies of academy members and their lives could provide valuable perspectives on the efficacy of such organizations.

Robin McConnell

See also Anti-Jock Movement; Child Sports Superstars; Youth Sports

Further Reading

Baschnagel, N.A. (1994, Summer). Specialty sports camps. *Pennsylvania Journal of Health, Physical Education, Recreation and Dance. 64(3)*, 31.

Finding your summer tennis getaway. (2002, July–August). *Tennis 38(6)*, 87–89.

Jeffreys, I. (2002). Soccer conditioning and academics, an alternative player development academy system in the UK. *Performance Conditioning Soccer, 8(6)*, 3–4; 11.

Labudova, J., & Markova, A. (2001). Sport-recreational camps for disabled children. In M. Bartoluci (Ed.), *Sport for all faculty of physical education* (pp. 139–142). Croatia: University of Zagreb.

McConnell, R. C. (2004). Developing leadership with young people: A critique and proposal for academies, camps and youth development programmes. Newtownabbey, Northern Ireland: University of Ulster.

Moreland, R. (1998). British Academy of Sport—a world class future. In *Taking sport to heart. Report of Institute of Sport & Recreation Management annual conference, at Kelvin Hall, Glasgow, October 1997* (pp. 55–68). UK: Melton Mowbray University.

Spanberg, E. (2003, September 8–14). Fantasy camps pitch opportunity of a lifetime. *Street & Smith's Sports Business Journal 6(20)*, 24.

Tristram, K. & Batty, R. (2000, Spring). Assessing the academy "boom." Sport academies in New Zealand secondary schools. *New Zealand Physical Educator 2(4)*, 16–17.

Wolverton, B. (1999, September). The dream factory. *Tennis 35(7)*, 106–111, 168.

Adapted Physical Education

*A*dapted *physical education, adapted physical activity,* and a host of other terms are sometimes used interchangeably to describe physical activity programming that is individualized to suit the unique motor needs of individuals with disabilities. More accurately, adapted physical activity is a broad term that includes adapted physical education. The latter is a subdiscipline specifically referring to specialized physical education services that help school-age children with disabilities learn. The purpose of this article is to clarify terms and discuss adapted physical education and adapted physical activity as they exist in today's society. Further, this article will discuss disability sport as a continuum of growing opportunities of competitive sport that has a past and a present consistent with other avenues of sport that permeate today's culture.

What Is Adapted Physical Education?

Adapted physical education is a program of study that targets the development of physical and motor fitness including basic movement patterns such as throwing, hopping, skipping, and a host of other age-appropriate skills that allow for participation in games and sports. Developmentally, children learn very simple locomotor patterns that later become more advanced and are used in conjunction with sport-specific skills required to engage in the games popular in our society. The focus in adapted physical education is on individualized instruction to help learners build on motor patterns that are necessary for later, more advanced sport and recreational participation. In physical education the goal is to instruct in this important curricular area rather than train to alleviate "cure" disability. The addition of "adapted" in front of "physical education" does not imply that the program has a therapy base, but rather it is a service that utilizes individualized educational services to reach goals similar to those outlined for general physical education. Although recreational play and even more basic functional movements can be part of a physical education program for individuals with disabilities, most advocate adapted physical education programs that are consistent with the intent of physical education for all children as stated in the National Association for Sport and Physical Education standards, including skills necessary to create lifelong learners and movers who choose physical activity over more sedentary pursuits.

Physical education (adapted or regular) is an important curricular area that has the potential to improve the quality of life for persons with disabilities. This is evident by the fact that physical education continues to be the only curricular area that is specifically mentioned in the Individuals with Disabilities Education Act of 1997. This is not to say that physical education is the most important area of development for school-age children with disabilities. However, two important foundational premises undoubtedly played a critical role in the minds of those who advocated that the current Individuals with Disabilities Education Act mention physical education. First, in the past many children with disabilities were denied appropriate physical education as a matter of practice, the idea being that some individuals were not "able" to benefit or perhaps had needs that were more important than those targeted in programs that focused on development of play and more general sport participation. Second, physical development is an avenue related to both personal enjoyment and lifetime health necessary in even the most basic functional skills. Even the most talented leaders would be of no use to society if they could not navigate curbs that line streets, lacked fitness abilities necessary for healthy living, or were unable to move from place to place. This is not to say that any person who needs physical assistance cannot be a leader, but rather to imply that all things in life are related to physical skills and even small improvements in physical areas are linked to independence. This was stated best by Paul Jansma, an early leader of

the adapted physical education movement, who believed that a "physical imperative" existed where independence and physical skills are closely linked.

In describing specifically how adapted physical education differs from physical education, it is important to understand the individualized nature of special education. School-age children with disabilities are eligible for individualized programs of instruction in physical education (adapted physical education) if unique motor needs exist. "Individualized" should in no way be confused with a different placement or setting for instruction from peers without disabilities but instead indicate services that are individualized to meet a child's needs. Many confuse adapted physical education to mean some segregated or highly specialized placement, but this is only true in a small number of cases, with students who have very serious disabilities. For most children with disabilities, successful physical education programming requires very basic modifications of the already existing program. These modifications occur in the same place where children without disabilities are also learning valuable lifetime physical activity skills. Adapted physical education is best characterized as a service rather than a placement, and this is consistent with descriptions of special education in general and the intent of the Individuals with Disabilities Education Act of 1997.

Debate about where services for most children with disabilities should occur began in the early 1980s. This spurred much discussion in the United States about appropriate education placements, related services, and legislative intent. Inclusion became a topic of considerable debate, debate that continues today as educators try to implement programs for children with disabilities in light of other educational issues, such as limited funding for schools. More recently, inclusion has become a focus for children with disabilities in physical education. Ethical and legal arguments that all children should receive physical education services in the same settings appeared in multiple publications by authors such as Martin E. Block and others who appeared to waiver over time on the extent that inclusion meant "all

children" in "all situations" belong in general physical education classes. However, inclusion is not the law in the United States, nor is this principle radically different from the legal concepts of least restrictive environment (LRE). Today, even the most steadfast "inclusionists" ponder earlier debates in light of what actually exists in public schools and what is best for some children with severe disabilities. In the end adapted physical education has little to do with inclusion movements and is based on the premise that some children require individualized attention that may or may not require segregated placements. Further, all children in general physical education classes can benefit from programs that take into account differences in abilities and learning styles.

In many school districts confusion exists over where medically oriented physical therapy programs are utilized over adapted physical education programs. It should be noted that all children with disabilities require physical education, whereas only a select few require additional physical therapy. This therapy is not synonymous with adapted physical education and is a separate service all together, by the terms of U.S. legislation. Physical education and physical therapy fall into two very different service categories; neither is substituted for the other. Physical education is considered a direct service (required for all who receive special education), while physical therapy is a related service (necessary only when a child needs therapy to benefit from his or her special education program). Both are equally important for some children. Further, these two different programs can work in tandem by targeting similar goals and having practitioners work collaboratively.

Adapted Physical Activity

As stated earlier, adapted physical activity includes many movement opportunities for individuals with disabilities, including adult recreational activities, family-based home programming, and even elite disability sport options. Given the pervasive nature of sport in the world, it is fitting that the concepts outlined earlier about physical education and adapted physical educa-

Strength does not come from winning. Your struggles develop your strengths. When you go through hardships and decide not to surrender, that is strength. ■ ARNOLD SCHWARZENEGGER

tion have their roots in sport. Since the early Olympic Games, sports and related physical activities as leisure pursuits have permeated society. The same is true for early movement opportunities for individuals with disabilities as more therapy-based programming led to competitive wheelchair games. This was initially the result of work done with many of the individuals around the world who returned from World War II with permanent physical disabilities. As these early movement opportunities developed, it was recognized that movement is enhanced by competitive play rather than training to alleviate disability.

The earliest sporting experiences for individuals with disabilities included the Stoke Mandeville Games in England. These and many postwar programs in the United States and abroad came in recognition of the value of sport and play as not only therapy for the body but also as vital to the human spirit. Since these earlier games, Special Olympics programs (outcomes of the 1965 task force on recreation for persons with mental retardation) and more recent Paralympic events have become mainstays in the broader sporting world, with the last growing in popularity and featuring outstanding athletic accomplishments as individuals with disabilities utilize advances in technology and training practices.

Adapted physical activity and specifically the sport participation of individuals with disabilities occur on a continuum. Joseph Winnick created one of the earlier and still relevant models outlining the potential sport-related options for persons with disabilities. His model includes regular sports with no modifications. As an example, Olympic athlete Oliver Halazy participated in an elite international athletic event alongside persons without disabilities and won an Olympic gold medal as part of the 1936 Hungarian water polo team. Next on the continuum, are regular sports with accommodations, such as judo, where a judoka with a visual impairment needs rule modifications that allow for integrated competition. For example, this would include rules requiring a grip must be maintained at all times during standing portions of the sport. The idea is to

equate play and not allow rule changes to alter the nature of the sport for participants. In the judo example, a visually impaired judoka would be at a disadvantage if a sighted opponent was not in physical contact, whereas maintaining a grip does not give one player an advantage over the other and still allows for a full range of throws to occur. This may alter strategy in play, but does not change the sport.

The issue of what changes the nature of participation or even creates an advantage for the person with a disability in integrated play between individuals with and without disabilities is covered by the Americans with Disabilities Act in the United States, and by other international sporting organizations. More recently, the court case of the golfer Casey Martin wanting to use a golf cart for Professional Golf Association (PGA) tour events in the United States illustrates this issue. In regular sports that make accommodations, not all changes to play are allowable, and each of these issues—such as a judoka requiring a basic rule change or a golfer requesting additional equipment (not available to all)—is handled on a case-by-case basis. The goal is to maintain the integrity of the sport involved while trying to afford equal opportunities to persons with disabilities.

Segregated sporting events are believed by many to not only be necessary for some individuals with disabilities, but their right. Winnick's classifications include a level of participation with events for the general population and persons with disabilities that occur at the same time, but do not involve direct competition between persons with and without disabilities. As in the Boston marathon, racers compete at the same time but within their locomotion category. This practice leads to an important debate in adapted physical activity related to who should participate in, for example, wheelchair races. Is it acceptable for a person with no or minimal disability to choose a wheelchair division over a bipedal competition? (This debate goes beyond the scope of the current paper and the reader is referred to Hans Lindstrom's 1992 work on the topic.)

Finally, there is the more traditional format of segregated sport in which based on predetermined criteria only individuals with disabilities compete in events and at times separate from individuals without disabilities. Take, for example, wheelchair basketball. Athletes who want to participate in Wheelchair USA basketball events are evaluated and, based on level and nature of limitations, are ranked and scored for equitable play. For example, a class I participant would be scored one point whereas a higher-functioning class III participant would be scored three points. A team can have a total of eleven points on the floor at a time. These scores equate play and ensure that participants of all levels are valued and that disability sport participation is maintained for individuals with disabilities. Other governing bodies may have similar grouping criteria aimed at creating fair play within a group of individuals who have similar disabilities.

What is important to note is that as society in general accepts athletes who participate in modified games or sports that can parallel more general events, such as judo or swimming, or even those who participate in more specialized events, such as goal ball or wheelchair races, disability sport has become a product worth selling. The same is true of all sport in society and this development marks a level of "arrival" or acceptance of persons with disabilities. Studies show that the marketing side of disability sport is on the rise and that products related to play are part of the endorsement deals, resulting in gains by companies in many areas that go beyond product sells and immediate profit. Today, the company that makes the fastest prosthetic limb is on par with golfing supply companies that make the drivers professionals use to hit the longest shots. This satisfies important corporate goals: Sport becomes an avenue of profits for companies producing superior products; in addition, "accepting" diversity enhances the corporate image. Finally, in society there is an overall understanding that sport excellence in any form has been and always will be valued. Media exposure and general acknowledgment by members of society that athletic abilities come in any type of body, even those that may on the surface appear different, is a sign of the times.

The significance of sports exposure as it relates to media coverage and product sales is an indicator of progress in the struggle for acceptance by individuals with disabilities. Claudine Sherrill, a leader in the adapted physical activity community, highlights the dichotomy of disability viewed as a form of diversity rather than less able. High-level competitive sport that accents the essence of human spirit helps others view the runner without sight, for example, as able rather than disabled. Today, it is clear that advances in training, technology, and general attitude make it likely that males and females, with and without disabilities, runners and those propelling themselves in a wheelchair, will reach the highest levels of athletic achievement. Programming that helps school-age children become more athletically proficient and interested in physical activity in general (as is the case for adapted programs for some children) feeds community programs whose participants vie for success similar to that of their counterparts without disabilities. In some cases elite athletes with disabilities emerge to compete for their countries at the highest Olympic and world levels.

The Future

So what does it all mean? From the perspective of an adapted physical educator, programs focus on the same types of learning experiences for children with disabilities as children without disabilities. In summary, adapted physical education is a part of the broader adapted physical activity and enjoyment of movement is an important theme. In today's society, marked by pervasive inactivity, where many diseases preventable through regular physical activity are on the rise, it is important to recognize the role that movement plays in preventing disease, improving the quality of life, and in some cases helping people become more able. Physical activity patterns by persons with disabilities are motivated by the same factors that encourage all humans to move. Adapted physical activity, and more specifically adapted physical education, should be presented in terms of how much fun they are, the educational goals they offer, and the opportunity for physical activity they present in a time when computers and other innovations make it likely that many humans will be less active today than they were yesterday.

Francis M. Kozub

See also Disability Sport

Further Reading

Block, M. E. (1999). Did we jump on the wrong bandwagon? Problems with inclusion in physical education (Part I). *PALAESTRA, 15*(3), 30–36.

Jansma, P. (1999). *Psychomotor domain training and serious disabilities* (5th ed.). New York: University Press of America.

Kozub, F. M. (2001). Adapted physical activity within the family for learners with disabilities: Application of family systems theory. *PALAESTRA, 17*(3), 30–38.

Legg, D., Emes, C., Stewart, D., & Steadward, R. (2004). Historical overview of the Paralympics, Special Olympics, and Deaflympics. *PALAESTRA, 20*(1), 30–35.

Lindstrom, H. (1992). Integration of sport for athletes with disabilities into sport programs for able-bodied athletes. *PALAESTRA, 8*(3), 28–58.

National Association for Sport and Physical Education. (1995). *Moving into the future: National standards for physical education.* New York: Mosby-Year Book.

National Wheelchair Basketball Association. (2004). *2003–2004 official rules and casebook.* Colorado Springs, CO: Author.

Ozturk, M. A., Kozub, F. M., & Kocak, S. (2004). Impact of sponsorship on companies that supported the 2002 Salt Lake City Winter Paralympics. *International Journal of Sport Marketing and Sponsorship. 5*(4), 45–56.

Sherrill, C. (2003). *Adapted physical activity, recreation, and sport: Crossdisciplinary and lifespan* (6th ed.). New York: McGraw-Hill.

Sherrill, C. (2004). A celebration of the history of adapted physical education. *PALAESTRA, 20*(1), 20–25.

Stein, J. U. (2004). Adapted physical activity: The golden years. *PALAESTRA, 20*(1), 26–29.

U.S. Department of Education Publications. (2002, September). *Individuals with Disabilities Education Act of 1997.* Retrieved March 29, 2004, from http://frewebgate.access.gpo.gov.

Winnick, J. P. (1987). An integration continuum for sport participation. *Adapted Physical Activity Quarterly, 4,* 157–161.

Adventure Education

The German educator and politician Kurt Hahn (1886–1974) is known as the "father" of adventure education, which teaches life skills through outdoor activities. As a progressive educator Hahn, who took British citizenship in 1940 after he was arrested by the National Socialists in 1933, regarded traditional education as too weak to counteract the political, social, and moral disease of modern society. By 1920 he began developing a progressive model of education. His emphasis did not lie in pure teaching, but more in character education. The central elements of his model were the physical fitness program, the expedition, the project, and service-oriented activities. According to Hahn, the educational value of the model was greatly diminished if only one element was missing.

He claimed that the physical fitness program helped prevent "underexercise," with its detrimental effect on the cardiovascular system. Hahn regarded physical activities as an educational means to develop self-discipline, fair play, team spirit, and goal-oriented behavior. Expeditions to the outdoors should inspire the spirit of adventure, he felt, and expeditions and their organizations should nourish character traits that each person should have, such as toughness, care for others, and decision making. The project was to offer people the chance to engage in a subject matter with full dedication and endurance to counteract the swift pace of industrialized life. According to Hahn, the restlessness of modern life decreases compassion. Service-oriented activities should help counteract this decrease and lead to the development of altruism and civic duty.

Hahn's model, with its four elements, came to fruition in Great Britain. Through various intermediate stages Hahn developed short-term schools. A month-long course was a mixture of athletic endeavors, cross-country route finding, expeditions into the outdoors, project-oriented activities, and service to local people. Participants were sent by schools, companies, the merchant navy, and police and fire departments. The British shipping magnate Lawrence Holt was particularly impressed by Hahn's educational model, which Holt regarded as an effective means to train his seamen. In 1941 Holt financed a professional training school named "Outward Bound Sea School Aberdovey." This name was well chosen because *outward bound* is the

A backpacker descends a switchbacked trail at Glacier National Park, Montana.

Source: istockphoto.com/Saturated.

nautical term for a ship's departure from the certainties of the harbor. During World War II many youngsters who were planning to join the armed forces attended this school.

Outward Bound

What became prominent as a wartime school for survival in Great Britain developed into a highly recognized educational program that used adventure experience to stimulate personal growth in the decades after World War II. Today Outward Bound has developed into a global movement. Each Outward Bound school has programs that are attended by participants from target groups, such as managers, pupils, students, drug addicts, and juvenile delinquents. Outward Bound has given rise to a whole industry of adventure education. Numerous organizations had been founded as spinoffs of Outward Bound, and each offers programs aimed at teaching personal growth by adventure.

The popularity of adventure education is a measure of personal needs, which are strongly influenced by current social structures and conditions. The pluralism and individualism of today's private and professional lives have led to a decrease in the validity of social rules and an increase in competing values. Stable social structures and bonds are replaced by the pressure of self-reliance and the compulsion to be responsible for one's own actions.

As social relationships begin to disintegrate, the acquisition of social competencies becomes more difficult. On the one hand, life offers more possibilities for experience, scope, and decision making in a heterogeneous and pluralistic society; on the other hand, life demands a higher degree of flexibility, decision-making ability, personal responsibility, and interpersonal patterns of behavior. Daily life is strongly influenced by mechanization and the modern media. The consumption of modern media and the interactive handling of information particularly lead to an estrangement from reality. The limits of reality and the virtual world become more blurred. The stimulus satiation by the modern media pushes people into a passive receptivity that leads to a loss of first-hand experience.

In professional life rationality, effectiveness, and achievement are often the only indicators of human quality. In education cognitive achievements are the most important goals. The result is a growing alienation from the body. Apart from this alienation, urbanization hinders first-hand natural experiences and an easy and healthy engagement in physical activities.

A consequence of this need for experience is an increase in leisure activities. People seek activities that promise to provide personal growth, well-being, and self-determination. In this context adventure education develops its effectiveness. Programs in adventure education have become popular not only in traditional educational settings such as schools, but also in training courses for managers or programs for the socialization of drug addicts, juvenile delinquents, or handicapped people. Rafting and canoeing trips, expeditions into the outdoors, and high rope courses have become popular because they teach social and moral values—traits that are difficult to realize in daily life.

Transferal

Although adventure education can nourish positive character traits, some people question whether the social and moral skills that participants are taught can be easily transferred to the participants' daily social and professional lives. The success of transferal is an element of uncertainty in adventure education. In adventure education people are confronted with nonspecific transferal, which means that the learning experiences in adventure education courses take place in an environment (mountains, rivers, lakes, etc.) that is different from the environment in which participants have to make use of such learning experiences.

Stephan Wassong and Berit Heidemann

Further Reading

Bacon, S. (1987). *The evolution of the Outward Bound process.* Greenwich, CT: Outward Bound.

Jenkins, J. M. (Ed.). (2003). *Encyclopedia of leisure and outdoor recreation.* London: Routledge.

Miles, J. C. (Ed.). (1990). *Adventure education.* State College, PA: Venture Publishing.

The word aerobics *comes from two Greek words:* aero, *meaning "ability to,"*
and bics, *meaning "withstand tremendous boredom."* ■ DAVE BARRY

Aerobics

The word *aerobic* means "with oxygen." Aerobics is a system of exercises designed to promote the supply and use of oxygen in the body. Aerobic exercises include biking, walking, running, dancing, rowing, and skating. Aerobic exercises increase cardiorespiratory fitness, which is the heart's ability to pump blood and deliver oxygen throughout the body. Benefits of cardiorespiratory fitness include increased endurance and energy, decreased heart disease, blood pressure, and cholesterol, and an increased ability to manage stress and control weight.

Development

The word *aerobics* is relatively new in the context of exercise and sport. Dr. Kenneth Cooper, a U.S. Air Force physician, in 1968 published a book entitled *Aerobics,* which was based on Cooper's research on coronary artery disease. Cardiovascular diseases, at their peak during the 1960s, accounted for 55 percent of all U.S. deaths annually. Cooper developed his aerobic exercise program in the spirit of preventive medicine, feeling that the contributions of aerobic exercise to cardiovascular health are significant. Cooper felt that if people lower their blood pressure and cholesterol, control their weight, and eat a proper diet they can lower the incidence of cardiovascular disease. One goal of Cooper's aerobic research was to develop a prescription for exercise, a specific program for people to follow. His book identified the quantity, kind, and frequency of such exercise. Cooper continued to spread his message with later books: *The New Aerobics* (1970), *Aerobics for Women* (1972), and *The Aerobics Way* (1977). Cooper traveled all over the world lecturing and explaining his beliefs and methods, contending that aerobics, exercise, and preventive medicine know no barriers of culture, language, or ethnicity. The Congress of International Military Sports in 1968 adopted Cooper's program for Sweden, the United States, Austria, Finland, Brazil, and Korea. His aerobic program spread from these military influences to civilian populations. For example, in Brazil runners ask, "Have you done your Cooper today?" meaning, "Have you done your running or jogging?"

Aerobic dancing developed as an alternative to running for women who wanted to improve their physical fitness. About the time Cooper was promoting his program in 1968, Judy Sheppard Missett was beginning an aerobic exercise program called "Jazzercise." It was a highly choreographed set of exercises set to music. It incorporated muscle group work with new dance trends. In 1969 Jackie Sorenson started "aerobic dance," which was also a choreographed set of dance patterns set to music with the goal of increased cardiovascular fitness. By the early 1970s people used the terms *aerobics, aerobic dance,* and *dance exercise* interchangeably to describe the combination of dance movements and exercise set to music. Most participants in the early aerobic dance classes were women.

To attract more men, by the late 1970s and early 1980s advocates shortened the term *aerobic dance* to *aerobics.* Co-educational classes were now offered, and the aerobics boom followed. Aerobic classes were offered in a variety of settings: churches, schools, community centers, and, of course, health clubs. The popularity of aerobics is attributable in part to the social support and reinforcement inherent in a group exercise situation. The U.S. movie actress Jane Fonda and the U.S. fitness expert Richard Simmons contributed to the growth of aerobics, and the boom spread all over the world. Fonda's early exercises primarily were resistance exercises for different parts of the body performed in one spot. Therefore, although she encouraged participants to work hard and to discipline themselves to obtain desired body changes, in the strict sense of the word, her programs did not contain aerobic exercises, and her early workouts were criticized as being unsuitable for ordinary exercisers. The emphasis of Simmons's exercise programs shifted from dance and fun to the weight-loss benefits of exercise. Aerobics consequently began to be connected closely with improved appearance.

Today many women celebrities (such as models Elle MacPherson and Cindy Crawford) promote their own exercise programs. Although these beautiful women might employ professional fitness experts to design and demonstrate their programs, they do further cement the notion that aerobics is a means to an improved body. When aerobics became a means to the perfect body, it also became increasingly commercialized, institutionalized, professionalized, and specialized.

Many of the early aerobic classes were what is called "high impact," that is, both of a participant's feet may be off the floor at any given time. High-impact aerobics was characterized by running or jogging in place or performing jumping jacks or small jumps or hops. This style was an exciting beginning; however, it created a tremendous amount of stress on the joints, and many participants developed impact-related injuries. Thus, "low-impact" aerobics was developed in response to the increase in injuries. "Low-impact" means that one foot is kept on the floor at all times; the routines are characterized by marching in place and traveling from one side of the room to the other. Next came variable-impact aerobics, which is a combination of high- and low-impact moves. This style combined the intensity of high impact with the safety of low impact. Many new types of aerobic classes have been developed. These include water aerobics, strength, sculpting, abdominal, sports conditioning, and circuit or interval classes. Step aerobics, which the U.S. gymnast Gin Miller developed while recovering from a knee injury, took the aerobic industry by storm. Step aerobics involves stepping up and down from a platform that is 15 to 30 centimeters high while performing step combinations.

As the boom spread, U.S. instructors began to travel to other countries to train new instructors. In the United States an estimated 6 million people participated in 1978, 19 million in 1982, and 22 million in 1987. By the late 1990s, some 25 million people participated. Forty-five percent of aerobic participants were women aged thirty to fifty, and aerobics was their only form of exercise. Another 45 percent of participants added aerobics to their regimen of sport and recreational activities. Ten percent of participants were instructors. Aerobics quickly evolved from its early

Aerobics

Kenneth Cooper on Aerobics

Countless people in every walk of life have found aerobics a workable way to achieve new levels of physical competence and personal well being. Professional athletic teams have found it to be an excellent way to maintain a high level of fitness during the off-season. Many colleges and universities throughout the country have adopted aerobics as part of their physical education program. All have shown interest in the program because it is the first scientific attempt to validate and quantify the effect of exercise—and to answer the questions of what kind, how often, and how much […] the widespread interest in exercise has caused physicians and public health authorities to take an appraising look at aerobic. If properly implemented and supervised, some of them see it as possible countermeasure to the Nations number one health problem: heart disease.

Source: Cooper, K. H. (1970). *The new aerobics* (pp. 9–10). New York: Bantam.

choreographed dance format to a varied form of dance, sport, and exercise movements set to music. Now virtually every community offers some sort of aerobic exercise class. Aerobics has even expanded into the home: One can see aerobic dance leaders on television at just about any hour or rent or buy aerobic videos.

Training and educational organizations have emerged to ensure safe and effective programs. In the United States the Aerobic and Fitness Association of America (AFAA) and the International Dance Exercise Association (IDEA) developed into two of the largest in the world, helping to promote aerobics in virtually every country. IDEA had more than nineteen thousand instructor-members in more than eighty countries in 2004. Such organizations helped to develop fundamental components of the aerobic exercise class. A well-designed aerobic exercise class consists of five segments: the warm-up or prestretch (10 minutes), the aerobic segment (20–45 minutes), cool-down (5–10 minutes),

A woman in southern Africa engaging in step aerobics using improvised apparatus.

aerobics presented in the United States. Its format and rules have become the international standard for aerobic competition around the world. In 1989 Howard Schwartz founded the International Competitive Aerobics Federation (ICAF), which became the governing body of the sport. The growth of the sport has been impressive: In 1990 the first World Aerobic Championship was held among sixteen countries. It was televised in thirty countries. In 1994 thirty-five countries took part. A year later the World Aerobic Championship was televised in 175 countries. More recently, the Federation of International Sports Aerobics and Fitness, which has some twenty-five member nations, has sponsored the Professional World Aerobic Championship in Adelaide, Australia (2004) and Ghent, Netherlands (2005).

Championship competitive aerobics is a rigorous display of both compulsory and freestyle moves choreographed into a two-minute routine set to music. People have called it the "toughest two minutes in sports." The performance showcases flexibility, strength, and endurance as well as creativity and dance. The competitors follow rules and regulations and are judged by an international panel.

Sally Crawford

See also Fitness

strength work (10–20 minutes), and the final stretch (5–10 minutes).

Aerobics helps participants to develop overall physical fitness. Aerobic dance, for example, can improve a participant's cardiovascular fitness, flexibility, strength, and body composition (percentage of body fat). The rhythmic movements performed to music also help to develop coordination and balance.

Competition

The sport of competitive aerobics has evolved naturally out of aerobic exercise classes. The National Aerobic Championship (NAC) was created in 1983 by Karen and Howard Schwartz, who founded competitive aerobics. The NAC was the first national competition for

Further Reading

Bishop, J. G. (1992). *Fitness through aerobic dance.* Scottsdale, AZ: Gorsuch Scarisbrick Publishing.

Casten, C., & Jordan, P. (1990). *Aerobics today.* St. Paul, MN: West Publishing.

Cole, C. L., & Hribar, A. (1995). Celebrity feminism: Nike style, sport-fordism, transcendence, and consumer power. *Sociology of Sport Journal, 12,* 347–269.

Cooper, K. (1968). *Aerobics.* New York: M. Evans and Co.

Cooper, K. (1970). *The new aerobics.* New York: M. Evans and Co.

Cooper, K. (1972). *Aerobics for women.* New York: M. Evans and Co.

Cooper, K. (1977). *The aerobics way.* New York: M. Evans and Co.

Fonda, J. (1981). *Jane Fonda's workout book.* New York: Simon & Schuster.

Francis, L. (1993). *Aerobic dance for health and fitness.* Madison, WI: Brown and Benchmark.

Kagan, E., & Morse, M. (1988). The body electronic: Aerobic exercise on video. *The Drama Review, 32,* 164–180.

What other people may find in poetry or art museums,
I find in the flight of a good drive. ■ ARNOLD PALMER

Markula, P. (1995). Firm but shapely, fit but sexy, strong but thin: The postmodern aerobicizing female bodies. *Sociology of Sport Journal, 12,* 424–453.

Mazzeo, K. S., & Mangili, L. M. (1993). *Fitness through aerobics and step training.* Englewood, CO: Morton Publishing.

Ryan, P. (1997, July–August). Beyond aerobics. *IDEA Today,* 60–71.

Sorensen, J. (1979). *Aerobic dancing.* New York: Rawson, Wade.

Tarantin, E. (1992, July–August). Aerobic competition yesterday, today and tomorrow. *IDEA Today,* 49–52.

Thomas, D. Q., & Rippe, N. E. (1992). *Is your aerobics class killing you?* Chicago: Chicago Review Press.

Aesthetics

Aesthetics captures a culture's ideas of beauty, proportion, and taste. It fulfills a purpose like politics, the economy, and religion, similarly addressing the social tasks a society must resolve. Vince Lombardi, the legendary coach of the U.S. professional football team, the Green Bay Packers, urged, "Winning is not everything; it is the only thing." Aesthetics appears in the injunction that, "It is not whether you win or lose, but how you play the game."

Eminent philosophers seriously contemplate aesthetic standards. Aristotle (384–322 BCE) is honored for his theories of knowledge and his political philosophy, but his *Poetics* develops his idea of beauty with consummate rigor. Immanuel Kant's (1724–1804) total philosophical system includes guidelines for evaluating knowledge (*Critique of Pure Reason*) and ethics (*Critique of Practical Reason*) but also his theory of aesthetics (*Critique of Judgment*). Standards of the good, proportion, and beauty infuse a culture with ultimate goals—aesthetics. Sport is physical, rule governed, usually an end in itself, and matters deeply to those who compete and watch. The activity is a serviceable medium of a culture's memories through stories, performances of athletes, and rituals surrounding sport.

Sport serves economic, political, and, possibly, religious ends. But in the forms of social memory, sport is most efficient when meeting expectations of a culture's aesthetics. Sport is especially serviceable as a vehicle of social memory, since it is a common vocabulary for citizens, it evokes attention from all our senses, and the characteristic clear winner rivets our interest within an ordinary world where performances are usually indistinguishable. Identifying the standards of quality in this type of social memory gives sport its potential for maximum importance in carrying its moral load; compromising of aesthetic standards portends loss of this vehicle of cultural memory. Two hundred countries participated in the 2004 Olympics; the outcome for each was heightened when the athletes faithfully embodied the cultures' aesthetic standards.

The Value of Stories

Stories appear exceedingly early in human civilization and are general; hence, they offer efficient entry into what is considered good in a culture. They do this by selection of topics, adequacy in evoking responses of accuracy by audiences, and their serviceability in showing the values of a society—what is prized and what is deplored. A very early sport story occurs in the *Iliad* (approximately eighth century BCE) when Achilles memorializes his fallen friend Patroclus with a round of athletic events, including a chariot race, boxing, wrestling, a footrace, javelin and discus throwing, archery, and sword fighting. Elaborate descriptions of the site, competitors, events, and prizes create an aura of authenticity (verisimilitude). Then, there is a narrative for each event that conveys not only the facts of performance but also the style and quality of conduct in each event.

SPORTS WRITING

For sixty years the best sports stories have been collected for North American sports, with the present series, *The Best American Sports Writing,* occurring since 1991. We know how the editors of the series evaluate sports performance by selection of type of sport, the degree of accuracy in evoking a sense of reality, how they sharply mark off prevailing values of society (intelligence, perseverance, motivation, self-sacrifice, for example) and how they negate bad values such as laziness, deceit, and personal aggrandizement. Cultures produce, select, and retain stories that encapsulate the values of their peoples. Often the achievements of a team or an individual are foregrounded as heroic, and the basis of the special achievement encapsulates the aesthetic of a culture.

CINEMA

Movies and critical evaluation of the cinema also convey aesthetic ideals of a society. While they may be driven by primarily commercial objectives, the themes occur and remain depending on the tastes of consuming publics. Several recent lists of the "best" suggest the operation of norms of goodness. The electronic version of *Sports Illustrated* listed these as the magazine's top ten: *Bull Durham* (baseball, 1988), *Rocky* (boxing, 1976), *Raging Bull* (boxing, 1980), *Hoop Dreams* (basketball, 1994), *Slap Shot* (hockey, 1977), *Hoosiers* (basketball, 1986), *Olympia* (Olympic Games, 1936), *Breaking Away* (cycling, 1979), *Chariots of Fire* (1924 Olympics, 1981), and *When We Were Kings* (boxing, 1996). Their listing in 2003 includes within-sport ordering of films in addition to the top-ten aggregate list, as well as a provision of aesthetic standards used in judgment.

The Body in Shape, Attire, and Performance

The rules of sport intend equal chances for competitors and some protection for participants, yet they must establish barriers for physical acumen so that the test creates a challenge that yields differences in success. Despite these factors, periods and sites display variations in the aesthetic features of performance. Artistic gymnastics and figure skating are examples where whole events include express and implied aesthetic criteria of performance. Derogatory comments on performances that technically accord with rules occur in all sports, such as displaying poor manners (one could not remove an article of clothing without penalty in the 1924 Tour de France), insufficient effort, clumsy execution, mean-spirited demeanor, or an inadequately flashy end ("the victory of a moribund," said Henri Degranges,

Statue of *The Archer* originally located in Dresden, Germany. *Source: istockphoto/heizfrosch.*

the race director, of Maurice de Waele's victory in the 1929 Tour de France).

Body proportions and comportment themselves may produce reasons for aesthetic valorization or criticism. The body of the gymnast was of a mature woman through the early 1970s, but with the performance of Nadia Comaneci in the 1976 Olympics, the women's-gymnastics body was required to conform to new standards. Dress conventions for athletes required to meet the same physical demands of contrived hazard show how standards of aesthetics override demands of the sport itself. While purity was expressed by nudity in the ancient Olympics, dress conventions of participants since that time reflect prevailing national standards. Participation in sports and interest itself may depend on a minimal preoccupation with the body as a medium of cultural identity and memory. Restrictions on clothing suitable for maximum athletic performance may exist in current cultures (Islamic, for example) that exclude women from performing since they may have to display, inappropriately, anatomical parts.

An athlete's nonathletic identity and orientation may enter into an aesthetic evaluation of the performer's sport proficiency and success. One's sexual orientation, for example, though entirely unrelated to eligibility to perform, quality of effort, and event success, may affect evaluations by other performers, journalists, and spectators.

In the mid-twentieth century, when public views of age- and sex-appropriate activities stereotyped older, married women as unfit for sport, aesthetic evaluations of momentous athletic accomplishments done by mothers could be muted or negative. Francina "Fanny" Blankers-Koen won four gold medals for Holland in the 1948 Games in London (100m and 200m runs, 80m hurdles, and the 4×100m relay). But her initial entry into the Games was strongly criticized by the public and press in her country, because she was married, had borne two children, and was thought too old to compete. (Aesthetic guidelines for tastes are often mutable, of course, as once this athlete had won, her country liberally welcomed her home as a heroine.)

Ritual in Sport

It is difficult to report a sporting contest where no rituals precede and conclude the events and punctuated revered activity. The ancient Olympics included several days of purification of athletes prior to the events, regularized procedures before and after the events, and closing ceremonies. The current Olympic Games set aside massive resources for rituals before and after the official schedule of competitions. Even impromptu sporting contests everywhere in the world include mechanisms of selection of sides, starting the action, and symbolizing venerated performances. Each day of the Tour de France ends with an elaborate ritual of the

Aesthetics
Bill Tilden on Tennis

Tennis is more than just a sport. It's an art, like the ballet. Or like a performance in the theater. When I step on the court I feel like Anna Pavlova. Or like Adelina Patti. Or even like Sarah Bernhardt. I see the footlights in front of me. I hear the whisperings of the audience. I feel an icy shudder. Win or die! Now or never! It's the crisis of my life.

stage winner and leader, wearing the yellow jersey. Softball players at the Olympics elaborately queue at the end of a game to shake hands respectfully with each of the opposing team's players.

Deviations from aesthetic standards yield strong censure among governing bodies and audiences. Tommie Smith and John Carlos won, respectively, gold and bronze medals in the 200m race in Mexico City in 1968. On the medal stand they displayed civil-rights badges (as did the silver medalist, Peter Norman of Australia). Smith and Carlos made the "black-power salute" with gloved fists during the playing of the U.S. national anthem. Their breach of ritual form infuriated the International Olympic Committee, which demanded the United States Olympic Committee send them home and banish them from further competition.

The Dark Side of Aesthetic Standards

Aesthetics defines the good in athletic memory, as found in stories, performances, and collective rituals. Defining the good marks off, in turn, the less valued aspects of sport for social valuation. These can be compromised by other forces such as economics and cheating, and the aesthetic ends of sport can vanish when a sport is expunged from a culture. Three instances show aesthetic standards warped, compromised, or lost altogether. They illustrate a certain dark side of these evaluations and prompt social vigilance in retaining aesthetic standards for sport in its role in storing venerated cultural memories.

A retro sign for a bowling alley, showing pins and a ball. The sign is illuminated with neon at night.

Source: istockphoto/Acerebel.

DEVALUATION BY EXCLUSION

First, aesthetic standards that valorize groups and performances in stories, bodily ideals, and ritual celebrations may intentionally or by inattention devalue other groups and performances. The culture's aesthetics, that is, may compromise other central social values such as equality and social justice—on the face not different from the "level playing field" component of sports at their core. The widely praised anthologies of sports writing examine each year thousands of potential stories. The inclusion, though, is of male sports endeavors. In the sample of fifty-nine entries in *The Best American Sports Writing of the Century,* there is no entry about a women's-sport performance. Among the twenty-five entries in *The Best American Sports Writing* of 2003, one focuses on a woman. The *Sports Illustrated* list of best films includes women participants only in *Olympia.* The sport television station, ESPN, extends its list to twenty films, and an investigator has to search through the continuation list to number 22 to find a film about women in sports (*A League of Their Own* records women's baseball played during World War II). There has been movement of female visibility in sport at secondary, collegiate, and international levels throughout the West and much of the East over the last decade. The virtual absence of valorized stories about women in sport shows a disturbing corner of omission of social valuation concerning women.

COMPROMISED STANDARDS

Second, have structural factors of increased volume and diversity of labor, advanced technology, and economic capital created an aura of compromised performance norms for elite athletes in international events? Rigid guidelines existed for competitors in the ancient Olympics for correct conduct before, during, and after the events. Rule violation in competition resulted in disqualification and public condemnation and could elicit flogging. While there were material rewards given at the early sport event at Patroclus's funeral and many of the early Greek minor-games sites, there was not at the main games—the "crown" games at Nemea, Isthmae, Delphi, and Olympia. The award to the winner denoted the supreme physical and aesthetic characteristics of *arete.* The victor embodied the credential, which "includes the concepts of excellence, goodness, valor, nobility, and virtue . . ." (Miller 2004, 242).

The valorization of *arete* in the early Olympic cycle when contrasted with the preoccupation of testing for drugs and exclusion of participation has to give warning that the very idea of an aesthetic standard within international sports is diminishing. By the end of the 2004 Olympic Games, twenty-four athletes, the most in any Games, had been cited for drug violations. The Tour de France is considered by event organizers and huge sectors of the French population as a cultural treasure. But since the notorious drug scandal in the 1998 race, which led to half of the competitors being forced out through some association with the drug arrests, the specter of drugs has continued to compromise the aesthetic integrity of the event through the last occurrence in the summer of 2004.

ROLE OF SPORT IN CULTURAL INTEGRITY

A third example comes from a district of Sudan where sport and a rigid cultural aesthetic carried by sport have been all but obliterated, with consequences for the integrity of the people. The Republic of the Sudan achieved independence from the United Kingdom in 1956. A military Islamist government has ruled since 1989, with continuous resistance from Christian groups and peoples with native religious beliefs. This conflict is being brokered in Kenya just now, with an apparent armistice between the government and the non-Islamist groups. But recently, Islamist rebels in the Southwest have violently attacked black groups and Christians, with the apparent acquiescence of the government in Khartoum.

The Nuba are a black population living in the Nuban Mountains, a remote area within the Kardofan district in central Sudan. Traditionally they had lived in an uneasy peace with the Arab groups to the north and west. But during the recent rebellion, comprising Nilotic groups to the south and east, both sides conscripted Nuba into their armies. One estimate is that as many as 40 percent of the military of the ruling Muslim/military government [National Congress Party (NCP), formerly the National Islamic Front] are Nuba. The opposition Christian group in the south, the Sudanese People's Liberation Party, have conscripted Nuba males and children as well.

S. F. Nadel, an anthropologist, was commissioned to study the Nuba in 1938. Following World War II, George Rodger, a Western photographer, began a journey across Africa seeking a certain humane purity, after his photographic work during the world conflict. He located the Nuba and in February and March 1949 captured vestiges of their disappearing life, including wrestling, in a series of photographs. Leni Reifenstahl, having encountered imprisonment and censure for her involvement with Nazi Germany, saw Rodger's work and sought to locate the Nuba in the 1960s. Between 1962 and 1969, she spent time among these tribes and produced her famous photographic volume, *The Last of the Nuba.*

In Nadel's commentary on wrestling in his study, and other forms of ritualized combat such as stick fighting, the sports assume an important role within the order and pace of the society. Wrestling in both Rodger's and Riefenstahl's recording occurs after the harvest season in the late fall and may continue through the spring. The sport of wrestling among the Nuba contains relatively noncomplicated rules for victory—simply throwing the other to the ground. But the ritual and meaning define age relations and relations among the sexes and mediate violence among subgroups of Nuba. The aesthetics of the sport, that is, are central to the integrity and social existence of this group. During the last ten years, wrestling has been prohibited. Nuba men have been conscripted into warring factions in the tragic conflict in the Sudan. The centrality of sport, as practiced within durable norms of form and proportion, is ending. Its loss for the Nuba signals diminution of the core of this people's civilization.

Stephen G. Wieting

See also Art; Beauty

Further Reading

Bale, J. (1998). Capturing the African body? Visual images and "imaginative sports." *Journal of Sport History,* 25 (Summer), 234–251.

Banner, L. (1983). *American beauty.* Chicago: University of Chicago Press.

Bissinger, B. (Ed.) (2003). *The best American sports writing.* Boston: Houghton Mifflin Company

Brownell, S. (1995). *Training the body for China.* Chicago: University of Chicago Press.

Daniels, B. C. (1995). *Puritans at play: Leisure and recreation in colonial New England.* New York: St. Martin's Griffin.

Fabos, B. (2001). Forcing the fairytale: Narrative strategies in figure skating competition coverage. In Wieting, S.J. (Ed.), *Sport and memory in North America* (pp. 184–212). London: Frank Cass.

Festle, M. J. (1996). *Playing nice: Politics and apologies in women's sport.* New York: Columbia University Press.

Golden, M. (2004). *Sport in the ancient world from A to Z.* London: Routledge.

Guttmann, A. (1996). *The erotic in sports.* New York: Columbia University Press.

Holt, R., & Mangan, J. (1996). *European heroes: Myth, identity, and sport.* London: Frank Cass.

MacAloon, J. J. (1981). *This great symbol: Pierre de Coubertin and the origins of the Olympic Games.* Chicago: University of Chicago Press.

Miller, S. G. (2004). *Ancient Greek Olympics.* New Haven, CT: Yale University Press.

Moore, O. K., & Anderson, A. R. (1969). Some principles for the design of clarifying environments. In D.A. Goslin (Ed.). *Handbook of socialization theory and research* (pp. 571–613). Chicago: Rand McNally.

Nadel, S. F. (1947). *The Nuba: An anthropological study of the Hill Tribes in Kordofan.* London: Oxford University Press.

Polumbaum, J., & Wieting, S. G. (1999). Stories of sport and the moral order: Unraveling the cultural construction of Tiger Woods. *Journalism & Communication Monographs. 1(2),* 69–118.

Riefenstahl, L. (1995) *The last of the Nuba.* London: Harvill Press. (Original work published 1976)

Rodger, G. (1999) *Village of the Nubas* (Liz Heron, Trans.). London: Phaedon. (Original work published 1955)

Ryan, J. (1996). *Little girls in pretty boxes: The making and breaking of elite gymnasts and figure skaters.* New York: Warner Books.

Wallechinsky, D. (2004). *The complete book of the summer Olympics.* Athens Edition. Wilmington, DE: Sport Media Publishing, Inc.

Walseth, K., & Fasting, K. (2003). Islam's view on physical activity and sport: Egyptian women interpreting Islam. *International Review for the Sociology of Sport, 38(1),* 45–60.

Wieting, S. G. (2000) Twilight of the hero in the Tour de France. *International Review for the Sociology of Sport, 35(2),* 348–363.

Wieting, S. G. (Ed.). (2001) *Sport and memory in North America.* London: Frank Cass.

African Games

A partheid, lack of economic resources, government instability, and war, issues affecting Africa in the postcolonial period, have all played a part in creating a difficult environment for continental games to take root in Africa.

The first attempts to organize games for the African continent occurred from 1925 to 1929. At the International Olympic Committee (IOC) session in Rome in 1923, a plan was unveiled to create regional games in Africa, to be held biennially. Algiers, Algeria, was to hold the first games in 1925, but this was too soon and the games were not held. The games were rescheduled for 1927 in Alexandria, Egypt, but facilities could not be prepared in time and once again the games were postponed, until 1929. Under the patronage of King Fouad I the games were set to open in April of 1929, when the British and French colonial rulers fearing that the games would prove dangerous to their power if African unity were to succeed, arranged for the games to be canceled at the very last minute.

The new stadium in Alexandria was reportedly built in the same spot as Alexandria's ancient Olympic stadium at the time of the Ptolemies. Though the stadium was not used for the canceled 1929 games, it made history when it hosted the first Mediterranean Games in 1951. Women were to be explicitly excluded from participation in the first games according to the published rules for the proposed 1927 games. However, women were to be included in lawn tennis in the 1929 edition.

Over three decades later, after regional games such as the West African Games and the French-backed Community-Friendship Games were held in Africa, the African games idea was revived. On 12 April 1963, the organizers of the West African Games and the Community-Friendship Games of the previous three years met in Dakar, Senegal, and awarded the first All-African Games to Brazzaville, Congo.

The original aim was to provide "a genuine means of fostering friendship, unity and brotherhood among African nations" (Mathias 1990, 16). South Africa and Rhodesia were specifically excluded from this gathering and would not be included in the games due to their apartheid policies. The International Association of Athletics Federations (IAAF) originally protested this exclusion, claiming that the organizers would need to choose a name other than African Games if South Africa were not allowed to compete.

The organizers replied that the IOC had excluded South Africa from the 1964 Olympic Games over the issue of apartheid, and also noted that all of the nations of Africa could easily join the new Games of the New Emerging Forces (GANEFO) movement and not become part of the Olympic movement. The IOC took the

threats seriously and began a closer working relationship with the organizing committee, in part so it could more closely control the preparations.

China had planned a political exhibition in Brazzaville during the 1965 games, specifically to take advantage of the large crowds that would be present. Games organizers made sure the exhibition did not take place as this would have been a violation of the rules set up by the IOC for regional games, which stated that regional games were not to be held in conjunction with other events or exhibitions, and "There must be no extraneous events connected with the Games, particularly those of a political nature" (Rules for Regional Games 1952, 12–13).

The 1965 African Games

The games opened under a tight ring of security. The Congo-Brazzaville army patrolled entrances to the city to guard against "counter-revolutionaries" that might want to disrupt the games. International Olympic Committee president Avery Brundage was present at the games and met with the organizers to discuss ways in which the IOC could help the African nations firmly establish the games. Jean-Claude Ganga of the Congo served as the head of the organizing committee for the 1965 games, and helped to found the Supreme Council for Sport in Africa (SCSA) in 1966, which became responsible for the organization of the African Games.

The 1973 African Games

Quadrennial plans for the games did not materialize. During the Brazzaville games, Bamako, Mali, was awarded the next games, to be held in 1969. A coup in 1968 canceled those games, which were then moved to Lagos, Nigeria, and rescheduled for 1971. The games were postponed once again and finally held in January of 1973.

Nigerian General Yakubu Gowon opened the 1973 games, with new IOC president Lord Killanin and former IOC president Avery Brundage in attendance. The games torch was relayed from Brazzaville to Lagos. According to a games report by IOC member Artur

Takacs, traffic and crowd control at the opening ceremonies was chaotic and eight IOC members could not get in the stadium to see the ceremony.

The 1978 African Games

Algiers, Algeria, hosted the 1978 games, but controversy began before the games when IOC members noted that an official poster for the games was overtly political in violation of the Olympic Charter. The poster featured an oversized continent of Africa, all in black, shaped into a large fist, poised to smash the continent of Europe, drawn in white. Several IOC members and international federation officials exchanged hasty letters, and IOC president Killanin contacted the organizers and was assured that all of the posters would be removed.

After beating Libya 1-0, the Egyptian soccer team was attacked by the Libyan football players and by spectators armed with clubs and metal bars. The violence was shown on live television and Egypt's Prime Minister Mamduh Salem ordered all Egyptian athletes home immediately. Kenya's Henry Rono, having already set four distance-running world records in 1978, would win the 3,000-meter steeplechase and 10,000-meter run in Algiers.

The issue of apartheid in South Africa and Rhodesia had not been solved and once again these nations were excluded from the games. Rhodesia never participated in the African Games. The nation became Zimbabwe

Table 1.

Locations of the African Games

Year	Location	Dates
1965	Brazzaville, Congo	July 18–25
1973	Lagos, Nigeria	January 7–18
1978	Algiers, Algeria	July 13–28
1987	Nairobi, Kenya	August 1–12
1991	Cairo, Egypt	September 20–October 1
1995	Harare, Zimbabwe	September 13–23
1999	Johannesburg, South Africa	September 10–19
2003	Abuja, Nigeria	October 4–18

and first competed in the 1987 African Games. South Africa had been reinstated by the IOC in time for the 1992 Barcelona Olympic Games and first competed in the 1995 African Games.

The 1987 African Games

After the 1978 games in Algiers, it was hoped the games could finally be organized on a quadrennial schedule and the 1982 games were awarded to Nairobi, Kenya. In December of 1980 Kenya informed the SCSA that they would not be able to hold the games on time. Pressure was put on the SCSA to move the games to Tunis, Tunisia, but the SCSA backed Nairobi. After several delays and near cancellation, and after China stepped in to help build the main stadium, the fourth African Games opened in August of 1987.

Kenyan distance runner Kip Keino and Kenyan Paralympian Japheth Musyoki started out the Fourth All-African Games month-long torch run with John Ngugi, Kenya's world champion cross-country star, lighting the cauldron during the opening ceremony. Morocco boycotted the games, pulling out of activities involving the Organization of African Unity over its dispute with Western Sahara.

The 1991 African Games

Cairo, Egypt, hosted the next games in 1991, the first time the games had been held in a four-year schedule. The Egyptians hoped to impress the IOC and convince them that an African city was ready to hold the Olympic Games. The games did not run as smoothly as expected. A stampede by spectators at the opening ceremonies prevented some dignitaries from getting inside the stadium. The Egyptians had spent some US$250 million for facilities for the games, and gave away most of the tickets to the games for free to fill the stands. Once the games began, the Egyptians were accused on numerous occasions of biased officiating, and computer systems did not work as well as expected. The medals for the diving events were struck from the records after the completion of the competition when it was ruled

that not enough nations had participated in order to make it an official competition.

The 1995 African Games

South Africa was finally welcomed to the games in 1995, when the games were held in Harare, Zimbabwe. The opening ceremony held in Harare's 60,000-seat National Sports Stadium had just 6,000 spectators in attendance. The games involved several protests, doping, poor sportsmanship, and a general lack of organization. Drug suspensions included Egyptian wrestler Mohy Abdel in the 100-kilogram class, Nigeria's 4 × 100-meter relay after team member Paul Egonye failed his drug test, and long jumpers Andrew Osuwu of Ghana, who lost the men's silver medal, and Karen Botha of South Africa, stripped of the women's long jump bronze medal.

Violence between the athletes and teams was especially disturbing at the games. The Zimbabwean security forces used police dogs to assist in escorting the football referee from the field after angry Nigerians confronted him after the match with Egypt. Boxers from Nigeria and fans from Egypt brawled in the boxing arena. Nigerians and Algerians fought during the volleyball competition. Women's handball teams from Zimbabwe and Egypt fought off court.

Controversies and arguments occurred over unfair judging in tae kwon do. The Egyptian team also protested that the South African women's gymnastics teams uniforms were too revealing. The Egyptian boxing contingent made claims that boxers from South Africa had AIDS, but later issued a retraction and an apology in an Egyptian newspaper. At the end of the games one Nigerian official stated that North Africans don't want to accept defeat and always think they are superior to black Africa.

Women's diving and netball were demoted to demonstration sports when not enough nations showed up to compete. South African hammer thrower Rumne Koprivchin won the gold medal but had only been given his South African citizenship in May, less than the

King Seezigeera, the last Tege King of Rwanda, with his bow.

Source: R. Bourgeois, Sport Museum Flanders.

had generally been the most successful nation in terms of medals won in previous games, but an instant rivalry was created when South Africa entered the games in 1995. The two nations both won 154 medals at the games, with South Africa claiming 64 gold medals and Egypt 61. The new rivalry was considered to be one of the reasons that the 1995 games were more contentious than most.

The games of Harare were the largest African Games up to that time with forty-six nations and 6,000 participants. International Olympic Committee president Juan Antonio Samaranch warned future African Games hosts not to copy the Olympic Games, that it would be harmful to try to organize games that were beyond the resources of most African nations.

The Seventh African Games

The seventh African Games were held in Johannesburg, South Africa, in September of 1999 with some 25,000 visitors, 6,000 athletes, and 3,000 officials from throughout the continent. Just prior to the 1999 African Games the SCSA met to discuss problems and issues in African sport and the sport movement worldwide, and passed a Code of Ethics for the African Sport Movement. The detailed code strongly emphasized that the members and associations of the African sport movement were to be ethical in all of their activities and stressed that there should be no discrimination or harassment of any kind, no doping, free and public elections, no forms of embezzlement, bribery, or conflict of interest, and no cheating or violence in sport.

Spectator interest in the Johannesburg games was low, however, with the opening ceremonies staged in a stadium with fewer than 15,000 spectators present. Johannesburg, which had lost to Athens for a bid for the 2004 Olympic Games, was hoping to impress the Fédération Internationale de Football Association (FIFA) in hopes of landing the 2006 World Cup, a bid Johannesburg did not win. Laborers protested outside games venues with a strike, pressing for higher wages. Police escorted the Egyptian basketball team from the

six months required for eligibility in the games, and was disqualified. Okkert Brits, a pole vaulter from South Africa, was the heavy favorite in the event. Traveling from Europe to compete in the games, his pole vaulting poles were lost. Organizers postponed the pole vault event for several days, until the equipment arrived allowing Brits to compete and win the gold medal.

One modern difficulty of the games is that many of the bigger athletics stars choose to skip the games, preferring to make money in other competitions, leading to a decline in spectator interest. In 1995 the main no-shows were Noureddine Morceli, Moses Kiptanui, Hassiba Boulmerka, Samuel Matete, Frankie Fredericks, and Haile Gebreselassie.

South Africa is a sporting power in Africa, and their participation changed the dynamics of the games. Egypt

African Games

The Importance of Sport for Young Africans

Charismatic athletes provide models for African youths. Filbert Bayi and Suleiman Nyambi Mujaya, for example, represented new possibilities for Tansanian hero-worshippers. "Our young people like to run, to compete. But all they have done in the past is run and they have been satisfied with beating whomever they happened to be racing against," observed Erasto Zambi, Tanzania's national coach, in 1976. "Now that there is talk of records and medals and trips abroad, they have something to aim for."

Source. Baker, W. J. (1987). The meaning of international sport for independent Africa. In J. A. Mangan, (Ed.), *Sport in Africa—Essays in social history* (p. 282). New York: American Publishing Company.

court after an on-court brawl between Angola and Egypt. Women's field hockey became a nonmedal event after the Nigerian team dropped out of the tournament and not enough teams were present to make it a medal sport.

Overall, though, the games impressed IOC president Juan Antonio Samaranch enough that he concluded that South Africa was ready to hold big events.

The Eighth African Games, Abuja, Nigeria

Labor unions once again called for strikes both before and during the eighth African Games in Abuja, Nigeria, in 2003, in protest over the government-mandated prices for fuel. The unions also asked spectators to boycott the games. At the closing ceremonies, spectators protesting the fuel prices and the cost of the games booed Nigerian president Olusegun Obasanjo, cutting his final speech short. Spectators also complained that ticket prices were out of reach for most Nigerians, and security was so tight and took so long that even those who had tickets had some difficulty getting into the venues.

Money and budget issues for the games were so severe that the Japanese television equipment company JVC (Japan Victor Company) refused to turn over the keys to the television equipment it had installed for the games because organizers had not paid for the work, and JVC was afraid they might never see the money. The issue was solved right at the beginning of the games and Nigerian television was allowed use of the equipment.

Nigeria's efforts to top the medals table brought protests from South Africa and Egypt and claims that Nigeria was counting several medals that were not official. Nigeria claimed that medals won by its disabled weightlifters counted in the medals table. The agreement was that disabled medals would count, but, in some of the events, South Africa and Egypt claimed that there were not enough competitors in the event to make the results official, that at least four nations had to participate in each weight class for official medals to be awarded. In one weight class, only one Nigerian competed and took home a medal. The games ended with the official count still in dispute. Sadly, several athletes and visitors contracted malaria while at the games and two Egyptians, one South African, and one Ethiopian died from the disease.

The Future

The next African Games are scheduled to be held in 2007 in Algiers, Algeria. Algiers should be well prepared to host the games after hosting the Arab Games in the fall of 2004. Algiers has already hosted the African Games, the Mediterranean Games, and the Arab Games, the only city on the world to have the distinction of hosting three of the major regional games. The continent of Africa is still hoping to host a future Olympic Games, with Egypt, South Africa, and Nigeria most often mentioned as possible hosts.

Daniel Bell

Further Reading

Bell, D. (2001). *African Games.* In K. Christensen, A. Guttmann, & G. Pfister (Eds.), *International encyclopedia of women and sports* (Vol. 1, pp. 15–17). New York: Macmillan Reference USA.

Bell, D. (2003). *Encyclopedia of international games.* Jefferson, NC: McFarland Publishing.

There are only two options regarding commitment, You're either in or you're out. There's no such thing as life in between. ■ ANONYMOUS

Brichford, M. (1996). *African Games*. In D. Levinson & K. Christensen (Eds.), *Encyclopedia of world sport* (Vol. 1, pp. 9–12). Santa Barbara, CA: ABC-CLIO.

Cairo hosts the 5th African Games. (1991). *Olympic Review*, 465–466. Retrieved December 21, 2004, from http://www.aafla.org/Olympic InformationCenter/OlympicReview/1991/ore287/ORE287q.pdf

The failure of the first African Games, in 1929. (1964). *Bulletin du Comité International Olympique, 86*, 83–84.

Kidane, F. (1995). The IOC and the African Games. *Olympic Review, 25*(4), 40–41.

Mathias, O. (1990, Winter). Socio-cultural forces in growth of all African Games. *Journal of the International Council for Health, Physical Education and Recreation, 26*(2), 16ff.

Meuwly, M. (1965, August). The first African Games in Brazzaville. *Bulletin du Comité International Olympique*, 39–40.

Reflection on sport in Africa. (1993). *Olympic Review, 16*(29), 24–27.

Rules for regional games. (1952, November). *Bulletin du Comité International Olympique*, 12–13.

The Second African Games. (1973). *Olympic Review*, (62–63), 58–59.

Zerguini, M. (1978). Algiers 1978: Festival of African Sports Youth. *Olympic Review*, (130–131), 516–518.

Agents

Although commercialized sports have been around since the nineteenth century, the widespread use of agents by athletes has been a relatively recent phenomenon. In using a skilled negotiator rather than negotiating on their own behalf, athletes have been able to compensate for an imbalance in bargaining position that has traditionally existed between themselves and management while freeing up the time to focus on developing their athletic skills.

Prior to the 1960s the bargaining position of professional athletes was weak; in professional team sports many people have described the historical relationship between players and teams as a dictatorship, with owners exercising considerable control over players. Owners were able to exercise such control through the use of the reserve clause, which bound a player to a specific team and was enforced by a lack of alternative employment opportunities available to professional athletes. This practice continued because athletes historically represented themselves and negotiated with a general manager or another representative of a club who likely had many years of negotiating experience. Players also understood that many other athletes were more than willing to replace them should they show any dislike for the terms offered by management. As a result many athletes felt exploited and underpaid. Thus, we can see the development of agents and players' associations in professional sports as an attempt by players to overcome their inferior bargaining position by acquiring the services of a skilled agent to negotiate the terms of their contracts and by collectively bargaining with owners as a single unit.

Agents have a close relationship with the players' associations in their clients' respective sports, and the agent's role is necessary because of the uniqueness of the representation provided by players' associations. In contrast to a decline in unionism in most industries, in sports players' associations have only recently emerged as powerful bargaining units, and their adversarial relationships with their respective leagues in North America have been the cause of frequent work stoppages in recent years. However, players' associations are different from other labor unions in that they do not focus on establishing individual salaries in the process of collective bargaining. For this reason agents have become an important part of the professional sports industry, while players' associations have focused on other means of increasing player salaries, by negotiating minimum salary levels and bargaining for mechanisms such as free agency and salary arbitration. The Major League Baseball (MLB) Players' Association leader, Donald Fehr, and other union leaders have acknowledged that agents are more effective at negotiating players' salaries than are unions because of the disparity of the various athletes' playing skills. Because playing skill is the prime determinant of an athlete's wages, the assistance of a capable agent can only increase potential earnings during an athlete's relatively short career span and assist the athlete in establishing a foundation for lifetime financial stability.

Agents began to emerge throughout professional sports during the mid-1960s, although agents had affiliated with prominent athletes for decades. The first widely known agent in professional sports was C. C. "Cash and Carry" Pyle, a promoter and movie theater manager who negotiated a playing salary and endorsement contracts for the U.S. college football great Red Grange in 1925. Pyle organized a series of playing tours that, combined with endorsement deals, resulted in earnings in excess of $325,000 for Grange. However, the true pioneers of the sports agent profession as it is known today are considered to be Bob Woolf and Marty Blackman and Mark McCormack of International Management Group (IMG).

Although many agents represented athletes independently, during the 1970s sports management organizations, such as IMG and Pro-Serv, emerged to look after the affairs of athletes. In 1975 IMG employed 250 people and had twelve offices throughout the world representing athletes in individual sports. By 1991 IMG had forty-three offices in twenty countries, employing one thousand people and representing more than four hundred athletes in a variety of sports. Today IMG is considered to be the largest sports management agency in the world, generating $1.4 billion in revenues in 2001 alone, employing more than thirty-five hundred people worldwide, and representing more than one thousand athletes.

Agent Services

An athlete delegates authority to an agent to negotiate contracts with the team that holds the athlete's rights and to provide other services, such as seeking endorsement opportunities. Today most agents charge a player a fee based on a percentage of the total salary or endorsements negotiated on behalf of the player, although the actual percentage has decreased as total transaction values have increased. The industry standard for contract negotiations in North America has decreased from 10 percent during the late 1960s and 1970s to between 2 percent and 5 percent, depending on the services provided to the player. With more agents vying to represent players, financial rewards for agents are likely to decrease as agents accept less favorable terms in order to contract with players. Thus, the agent business

is a highly competitive profession in which aspiring agents establish themselves only with difficulty.

Typically agents enter into a written contract with the players they represent. Similar to the standard player's contract that is negotiated with a team by the agent on behalf of a player, a standard representation contract (SRC) is negotiated between player and agent. The SRC establishes the rights and responsibilities between player and agent and clearly defines the period of service, exclusivity of representation, fee system, and if/how agent expenses are repaid. The terms of the SRC are created and enforced by the players' association. Although initiated to protect players, the SRC cannot fully police agent competence in the sense that the contract calls only for a good-faith effort on the part of the agent; in other words, the agent's efforts do not necessarily have to be successful. The player-agent relationship is also considered to be fiduciary: Agents are bound to act faithfully and honestly toward the players they represent. In this manner any breaches of contract are treated like breaches of service contracts that govern any other agency relationship, such as that between a vehicle owner and a mechanic. Thus, the agent is bound by two types of legal duty to the player: The agent must agree to perform the services contracted for and must act in the best interests of the player. Although this arrangement may seem straightforward, the ability of the agent to fulfill the terms of the contract can vary greatly.

In addition to negotiating a player's contract with a team, an agent may provide a number of other services. These may include (1) providing legal counseling, (2) obtaining endorsements and other income for the player, (3) providing financial planning and management, (4) providing career planning and counseling, (5) improving the player's public image, and (6) resolving disputes under the employment contract, such as arbitration. Agents are then compensated based on the services they provide, which is typically achieved in any of four ways: (1) on an hourly rate, (2) a flat rate, (3) a percentage of the athlete's salary, such as a commission, or (4) any combination of the preceding three ways. By far the most popular means of compensation is using a performance-contingent compensation (commission) system, although agents providing specific services may use a compensation scheme that is standard for their profession, such as attorneys who choose to bill at an hourly rate. Many agents do not represent players as a full-time occupation, and they perform services to other principals in the disciplines they have been trained in, such as financial planning or law. As salaries have escalated, the percentage that agents have charged players has decreased. Endorsements usually result in a substantially higher fee. The rationale for charging more is simple: An agent is more directly responsible for obtaining an endorsement and therefore expects to be paid more for the effort.

In order to perform the variety of services offered to players, agents must be cognizant of many issues in professional sports. Planning strategies, legal issues involved in creating personal service corporations, rights to publicity (an athlete's ability to retain the right to his or her name and likeness while agreeing to play for a team or in an event), tax planning, and state and local income taxation of professional athletes playing outside of their residences are important issues of which agents must be aware. In addition, agents must be aware of issues specific to the sport of their client, such as the application of revenue laws and codes to foreign-born athletes playing in other countries and the growing internationalization of sports, which today can involve complex transfer fees paid to foreign sports clubs or associations to release players to play elsewhere.

However, the relationship between player and agent cannot be defined solely on the basis of services that are provided in the SRC. Agents also provide a number of other benefits that are not so easily defined. Some contract negotiations can last for prolonged periods, which can be grueling for a player and strain relations between player and team and reduce team morale. In this instance an agent can act as a buffer between management and player. Because at contract time team management tries to minimize the player's contribution to the team in order to pay a lower salary, an agent can re-

duce any emotional trauma that the player might endure as result of having his or her abilities downplayed by team management. The agent also can act as a lightning rod for criticism; team management and local media members can more easily vilify an agent than a player for being greedy.

Agents are often expected to provide other services that are not necessarily addressed by a SRC. For example, the pioneer agent Bob Woolf recalled when his client, the former Boston Bruin Derek Sanderson, was on vacation in Hawaii and had left a number of urgent messages for Woolf at his office in Boston. Sanderson wanted Woolf to call the manager of the hotel that Sanderson was staying at in Hawaii to complain about the lack of hot water in his room.

Issues and Problems

Given the number of athletes in professional sports, the number of agents is relatively small compared with the number of agents in other industries, such as real estate. Despite this fact, sports agents have developed an unseemly reputation in the eyes of many people, a reputation that Bob Woolf claimed is a spillover from other fields such as the entertainment industry. Unfortunately for players, in many instances agents have not acted ethically and competently when performing services. The activities of several notorious agents have been well documented. However, estimating just how prevalent opportunistic behavior is in the agent profession would be difficult; media focus on the issue might lead one to assume that such behavior is commonplace. However, some commentators have claimed that agent opportunism is not as prevalent as media reports suggest.

One problem between players and agents in professional sports occurs when an agent misrepresents his or her ability in order to represent a player. Such misrepresentation can be largely attributed to a lack of standards of competency and explains why incidences of opportunism have occurred during the past three decades. Because no standard training is required for a person to become an agent—such as the law degree required for a person to become an attorney—players

have not always known or understood the types of training and experience that make a good agent. Thus, the likelihood of a player selecting an incompetent or unreliable agent is more likely to occur. The problem has been worsened by agents who have deliberately misrepresented their training and abilities in order to acquire a player as a client.

As player salaries have increased (increasing the potential financial benefits of representing professional athletes), competition between agents has grown; such competition may result in more abuses by agents who attempt to induce players to contract with them by any means possible. Some agents have resorted to soliciting players by providing prospective clients or their families with cars, money, or other perks. Problems of recruitment are compounded when an agent circumvents regulations set out by sports governing bodies such as the National Collegiate Athletic Association (NCAA) or when an agent is an attorney and violates solicitation rules set out in codes of conduct for the legal profession. Examples of agents lurking on college campuses have been well documented; players and their families have been forced to change their telephone numbers frequently and even forced out of their living accommodations to avoid persistent agents.

In other situations agents, although not guilty of putting forth inadequate effort, have been guilty of engaging in morally questionable behavior in order to contract with players. Given that an agent is willing to circumvent collegiate regulations and the law, that agent is capable of shirking his or her duties on behalf of the player in the future. In one instance a National Hockey League (NHL) team had an arrangement with an unscrupulous agent by which the team paid the agent money to negotiate on behalf of his players specifically with that team. Other agents have offered amateur coaches financial rewards to steer amateur athletes to those agents.

Another problem is conflicts of interest. The most common conflict of interest occurs when an agent represents multiple clients, such as players competing with each other for a position on the same team. Agents

should reveal such conflicts. Comprehensive sports management firms face another conflict. A large firm with multiple clients, such as IMG, may have conflicts in which the firm is also involved in event management. A player might be encouraged to attend or engage in a tournament that would further the interests of the firm but not necessarily those of the player.

Monitoring

Athletes have several means by which they can seek recourse for abuses by their agents. Just as teams and players may seek judicial and nonjudicial solutions to breaches of the standard player's contract, industry stakeholders have created methods by which players can obtain relief from breaches of the standard representation contract. Typically player-agent disputes are treated like disputes involving other principal-agent service contracts. In one high-profile case two football agents in the United States were convicted by invocation of the mail fraud statute.

In response to widespread claims of agent abuses in sports in the United States, individual states during the early 1980s began examining the possibilities of creating agent certification programs. In large part the motive for state involvement was the desire to address recruiting problems occurring on college campuses. Thus, a goal was to protect athletes and the collegiate athletic programs within a state's jurisdiction. Most state certification programs require agents to register and to post a bond. Registration fees vary widely from state to state, and several are contingent upon enforcement of the NCAA.

Because most athletes in North American professional sports receive their amateur training at U.S. colleges, the NCAA has also explored its own means of policing agents. In 1984 the NCAA created an annual registration for agents, often working in concert with state regulations. Obviously a motive for intervention by the NCAA was to prevent its member institutions from losing the eligibility of their high-profile athletes.

Other industry parties were concerned by agent abuses during the 1970s, and the agents themselves also expressed a desire to reduce agent abuses. As the agent profession developed a reputation as being unscrupulous, many competent, trustworthy agents recognized that the behavior of a few agents was hurting the image of the profession as a whole. Thus, the agents themselves sought to control and monitor behavior within their own ranks by creating a code of ethics for agents. The result was formation in 1978 of the Association of Representatives of Professional Athletes (ARPA), which grew to four hundred members by 1988. However, ARPA lacked the ability to sanction agents and folded.

Just as ARPA was created by agents to foster trustworthy behavior, lend credibility to their profession, and set standards of competency, other professions have developed similar codes of conduct. As a result some agents are influenced by codes of conduct of other professions in which they have been trained. When an agent has been trained and practices in another profession, such as law or accounting, that agent must also adhere to the standards of that profession. Other professions, such as financial advising, also have codes of conduct. Lawyers face additional constraints through their own professional standards; in the United States lawyers are bound by the code of the American Bar Association, which sets standards of professional ethics. If a lawyer engages in conduct that violates such a code, the lawyer risks being disbarred—a sanction that provides an additional means of deterring sports agent opportunism.

Finally, as a result of concern over agent opportunism, players' associations created their own agent certification programs. These programs remove the burden of regulation from other industry parties. In North America MLB, the NHL, National Football League (NFL), and National Basketball Association (NBA) have developed agent certification programs that establish the terms of the SRC, fees, and forms of dispute resolution.

The Future

Agents will continue to provide valuable services to athletes. During the past thirty years agents have become prominent stakeholders in professional sports as players have enjoyed significant salary increases and have been paid a higher percentage of total revenues generated in the industry. In addition, some players have substantially supplemented their playing salaries through endorsements obtained by agents. However, agents have at times acted opportunistically to the detriment of the athletes they represent. As a result industry stakeholders have regulated agent behavior. This trend will continue in the future.

Daniel S. Mason

See also Athletic Talent Migration; Free Agency

Further Reading

Brown, J. E. (1994). The battle fans never see: Conflicts of interest for sports lawyers. *Georgetown Journal of Legal Ethics, 7,* 813–838.

Cohen, G. (1993). Ethics and the representation of professional athletes. *Marquette Sports Law Journal, 4*(1), 149–197.

Cox, L. (1992). Targeting sports agents with the mail fraud statute: *United States v. Norby Walters and Lloyd Bloom. Duke Law Journal, 41,* 1157–1210.

Ehrhardt, C. W., & Rodgers, J. M. (1988). Tightening the defense against offensive sports agents. *Florida State University Law Review, 16,* 633–674.

Fraley, R. E., & Harwell, F. R. (1989). The sports lawyer's duty to avoid differing interests: A practical guide to responsible representation. *Hastings Commercial and Entertainment Law Journal, 11,* 165–217.

Gallner, S. (1974). *Pro sports: The contract game.* New York: Charles Scribner's Sons.

Levine, M. (1993). *Life in the trash lane: Cash, cars and corruption— A sports agent's true story.* Plantation, FL: Distinctive Publishing.

Mason, D. S., & Slack, T. (2001). Evaluating monitoring mechanisms as a solution to opportunism by professional hockey agents. *Journal of Sport Management, 15,* 107–134.

Narayanan, A. (1990). Criminal liability of sports agents: It is time to reline the playing field. *Loyola of Los Angeles Law Review, 24,* 273–336.

Powers, A. (1994). The need to regulate sports agents. *Seton Hall Journal of Sport Law, 4,* 253–276.

Ruxin, R. H. (1985). The regulation of sports agents. In J. Frey & A. Johnson (Eds.), *Government and sport: The public policy issues* (pp. 79–98). Totowa, NJ: Rowman and Allenheld.

Shropshire, K. L. (1989). Athlete agent regulation: Proposed legislative revisions and the need for reforms beyond legislation. *Cardozo Arts and Entertainment Law Journal, 8*(1), 85–112.

Shropshire, K. (1990). *Agents of opportunity: Sports agents and the corruption of collegiate sports.* Philadelphia: University of Pennsylvania Press.

Shropshire, K. L., & Davis, T. (2003). *The business of sports agents.* Philadelphia: University of Pennsylvania Press.

Sobel, L. S. (1987). The regulation of sports agents: An analytical primer. *Baylor Law Review, 39,* 702–786.

Steinberg, L. (1991). The role of sports agents. In P. D. Staudohar & J. A. Mangan (Eds.), *The business of professional sports* (pp. 247–263). Chicago: University of Illinois Press.

Stiglitz, J. (1997). A modest proposal: Agent deregulation. *Marquette Sports Law Journal*, 7(2), 361–372.

Trope, M., & Delsohn, S. (1987). *Necessary roughness: The other game of football exposed by its most controversial superagent.* Chicago: Contemporary Books.

AIDS and HIV

*I*n 1978 gay men in Sweden and the United States and heterosexuals in Tanzania and Haiti began developing unusual symptoms and ailments. In 1982, what at first seemed like a host of diseases was identified as a virus that attacked the immune system. Transmitted through sharing body fluids, the disease was named acquired immune deficiency syndrome or AIDS. Many individuals may be carriers prior to the onset of symptoms; these people have contracted the human immunodeficiency virus (HIV). Though HIV-positive individuals experience no symptoms, they may spread the virus to others. AIDS/HIV is generally contracted through unprotected sex, sharing contaminated needles, or prenatal contact (mother to fetus).

The AIDS epidemic has had tragic global consequences. Globally, AIDS is the leading cause of death due to infectious disease and the fourth leading cause of death overall. It is estimated that there are 33.6 million people worldwide living with HIV/AIDS. Though the majority of AIDS infections are found in poor nations (over 90 percent of cases reported), over a million people in the United States have contracted HIV since the emergence of the disease, and twenty thousand new cases are reported annually. The emergence of a deadly incurable contagious disease has had significant consequences in many areas of social life, including sports.

AIDS Enters the World of Sports

In the early stages of the epidemic, the emerging threat was largely ignored by the sports world in the United States. As it was incorrectly perceived as a disease contracted mainly by homosexuals, sporting institutions did not develop cohesive AIDS/HIV policies early on. The conflation of AIDS with gay men and the largely erroneous assumption that male athletes are heterosexual allowed sports leagues to avoid considering the risks posed by the disease. The role sports has played in defining masculinity in American culture, cultural conflations of effeminacy and male homosexuality, and the discrimination and loss of endorsement dollars that threaten out gay athletes led to a pervasive belief that there were and are no homosexual athletes in "manly sports" such as baseball, football, and basketball. Hence, the world of sports largely ignored HIV/AIDS during the early years of the epidemic.

The problem of the athlete with HIV and AIDS could no longer be ignored after 7 November 1991, when future Hall of Fame Laker point guard Earvin "Magic" Johnson announced that he had tested positive for HIV during a routine physical. Charismatic, popular, and respected, Johnson's announcement shook the world of sports. Johnson alleged that he had contracted HIV through heterosexual contact. This announcement revealed the risk of contagion among heterosexuals, something significantly underestimated in the United States. Because AIDS/HIV had long been associated with homosexuality, and specifically promiscuous homosexuality, the disease carried a significant social stigma, and Johnson's announcement was considered a courageous act. At the time Johnson choose to retire from the league, but he subsequently returned to play for the Lakers during the 1995–1996 season. He also continued to participate in basketball internationally after having been diagnosed. Though some expressed hesitation at competing with an athlete known to be infected, the public and league support Johnson received indicated a willingness to accept infected athletes, or at least extraordinarily talented ones.

Some debate has centered on the role of the media in "outing" those infected with the disease, and what obligations athletes have as public figures. Many point out that as public figures, athletes must raise awareness about the risks of the disease and the ability to live with contagion. By the same token, others are critical of a media that forces athletes to publicly discuss a painful diagnosis. This debate came to a head in 1992. When made aware that *USA Today* intended to reveal his previously undisclosed infection, Arthur Ashe announced he had AIDS. Ashe had previously contracted the virus during a blood transfusion in 1983. Though currently retired, former Wimbledon champion Ashe was still well known for his breaking down of racial barriers in the world of tennis and was a prominent philanthropist. Ashe died in 1993 of AIDS-related complications. Public response to Ashe was largely sympathetic, but the media's role in forcing Ashe to announce his status remains a point of contention.

Several other notable athletes have since announced HIV positive status or their status has been revealed posthumously. In 1995, diver Greg Louganis, arguably the best diver in the world for over a decade, revealed to Barbara Walters that he had AIDS and had been HIV positive in 1988 when he won two gold medals at the Olympic Games. Louganis had won his second medal only after recovering from an accident during competition, when he hit his head on the board and required stitches prior to continuing. In 1996 boxer Tommy Morrison, known for his portrayal of a young fighter in *Rocky V,* announced he had contracted HIV through heterosexual sex. Later he acknowledged it was most likely contracted through sharing needles while injecting steroids. Though banned from boxing in the United States, Morrison has participated in events since his retirement, including a much-publicized fund-raiser in which he knocked out his opponent in the first round. Other notables include former Olympic decathlete and founder of the Gay Games, Tom Waddell, who died of complications related to AIDS in 1987; Esteban de Jesus, the former World Boxing Council lightweight champion who died of AIDS while serving a life sentence for murder; Jon Curry, former Olympic and world champion figure skater who died from AIDS-related illness in 1994; and Glenn Burke, former Los Angeles Dodger and Oakland A's outfielder who died of AIDS-related complications in 1995. Further, Jerry Smith, for-

AIDS and HIV

The Magic Johnson Announcement

In a November 1991 press conference, the star basketball player Magic Johnson told the world he had tested positive for the HIV virus. In an instant, his announcement changed the face of AIDS/HIV from a "gay disease" to a disease that, in Johnson's words, "can happen to everybody." Below are excerpts from his announcement.

I plan on going on, living for a long time . . . and going on with my life. . . . I will now become a spokesman for the HIV virus. I want people, young people, to realize that they can practice safe sex. Sometimes you're a little naïve about it. . . . You only thought it could happen to other people. It *has* happened. But I'm going to deal with it. Life is going to go on for me, and I'm going to be a happy man. . . .

Source: Johnson, E. (1992). *My life* (pp. 266–267). New York: Random House.

mer member of the Washington Redskins, died of complications related to AIDS in 1986; stock car racer Tim Richmond died of complications caused by AIDS in 1989; Alan Wiggins, former member of the San Diego Padres and Baltimore Orioles, died of complications caused by AIDS in 1991; and Bill Goldsworthy, National Hockey League veteran and one of the original Minnesota North Stars, died of complications from AIDS in 1996. Certainly, the problems faced by many athletes after revealing their status may have led many others to remain silent.

Public Responses to Athletes with HIV/AIDS

The public response to athletes with AIDS has varied widely depending on the status and sexual orientation of the athlete. While heterosexual high profile Magic Johnson was labeled a hero for publicly acknowledging his HIV-positive status, Greg Louganis was faulted for failing to disclose his status to the doctor who treated

AIDS and HIV

HIV and Interscholastic Sports Policies

In the wake of Magic Johnson's announcement in 1991 that he tested positive for HIV, sports organizations scrambled to put policies in place concerning potential contact with HIV-positive athletes. Below is one such policy put forth by the state of Alaska in its Epidemiology Bulletin *(6 November 1992).*

Publicity surrounding Magic Johnson's infection with the human immunodeficiency virus (HIV), his participation in the Olympics, and his recent attempt to return to the National Basketball Association has focused attention on the possibility of HIV transmission through participation in sports. Concern among parents, coaches, and athletes is based on the fact that injuries and bleeding often occur during contact sports, and HIV can be transmitted through blood-to-blood contact with an infected individual. This widespread focus on athletic contact as a potential risk factor for HIV infection is misplaced, however, and diverts public attention from the activities repeatedly shown to be involved in HIV transmission: sexual intercourse and sharing contaminated needles and syringes for injection drug use.

As the HIV epidemic continues, we must use our knowledge and resources wisely to prevent transmission of HIV. The risk of HIV transmission through participation in interscholastic sports is infinitesimally small. It is important to remember that HIV is not transmitted through such things as saliva, sweat, tears, urine, respiratory droplets, handshaking, swimming pool water, communal bath water, showers, toilets, food, or drinking water. Numerous organizations . . . have carefully reviewed the available scientific evidence and developed recommendations for athletes, coaches, and others who participate in

sports. The following recommendations are consistent with the statements of these organizations:

1. Based on current scientific evidence, the risk of HIV transmission due to participation in contact sports is infinitesimally small. There have been no documented instances of HIV transmission between athletes during athletic training or competition.

2. There is no public health basis for excluding a player from participation in any sport because the player is infected with HIV. The decision for an HIV-infected person to continue participation in any sport is a medical decision involving the HIV-infected person and his or her personal physician.

3. There is no medical or public health justification for mandatory or routine HIV testing of participants in any sports activity.

4. Consistent with routine, sound medical practice, all sports teams should employ universal precautions when providing first-aid or cleaning-up blood or body fluids visibly contaminated with blood, as recommended by the National Centers for Disease Control and the Alaska Division of Public Health.

5. Athletes, coaches, and athletic trainers should receive training in prevention of HIV transmission. This training should concentrate on known high-risk behaviors associated with HIV transmission: sexual intercourse and blood-to-blood transmission associated with sharing contaminated drug injection equipment. Risks associated with sharing needles/syringes for anabolic steroid injection should be included in these discussions.

him during the 1988 Olympic Games. The doctor has publicly acknowledged his clear understanding of universal precautions and that he holds Louganis blameless. While Louganis was stigmatized as a carrier of the illness, sportscasters and writers lambasted athletes like

Karl Malone for having expressed concern at having to face Magic Johnson on the court, claiming their fears were groundless and citing ignorance about the disease. While heterosexual Arthur Ashe's illness was front page news, gay Glenn Burke's departure from baseball and subsequent death went largely unnoticed. Burke contended that he was blackballed from baseball because of his sexual orientation. Certainly the difference in the relative status of an athlete has some correlation with public exposure. However, athletes whose heterosexuality was unquestioned were treated very differently than openly gay or sexually ambiguous athletes. While Magic Johnson was appointed to presidential committees on HIV/AIDS, Greg Louganis was banned from speaking on a college campus and was unable to transition into a prominent diving commentator role in subsequent Olympic games. While the media was heavily criticized for forcing Ashe to reveal his illness, Greg Louganis was heavily criticized for failing to disclose his. It is clear that the social location of the athlete affects media and public response.

The Impact of AIDS on Sports

AIDS has impacted sporting bodies in a number of ways. In the first case, the world of sports has had to seriously consider risk of transmission. In addition to actual risk, the fear of risk of transmission also needs to be considered. Second, the ethical and legal consequences of policies and procedures must be considered. Special attention should be paid to the rights and protections afforded to infected and uninfected athletes. Third, the role of sports institutions in developing, adopting, and enforcing policies, procedures, and protections must be considered.

RISK OF TRANSMISSION

At the center of current debates is risk of transmission. The risk of transmission of HIV/AIDS through sports participation appears to be infinitesimally small. Most medical experts agree that there have been no cases of HIV being contracted during an athletic competition. Though a few anecdotal reports exist, these cases are questionable at best. Given the low level of risk, the question becomes, is the level of risk acceptable? Is the risk of contracting HIV/AIDS comparable with other risks assumed by athletes? Certainly, participating in sports carries with it the acceptance of an assortment of

varying degrees of risk of injury and infirmity that are far more likely and extremely debilitating. Studies on masculinity, gender, and sport by Brian Pronger, Michael Messner, Don Sabo, and others note the myriad of ways in which men's sports encourage risky behavior. For example, athletes routinely play with injuries, exacerbating the existing injury and risking further injury. Moreover, sports sometimes overlook medical evidence of risk in favor of preserving elements of a sport or competition. As Rodger Jackson (1999) notes, while U.S. boxing federations prohibit HIV-positive individuals from participating once diagnosed, other risky practices are ignored. Despite incontrovertible medical evidence that links blows to the head with the risk of death or long-term debilitation due to head injuries, headgear is not imposed at the professional level. In addition, many athletes engage in a variety of risky practices in an attempt to gain an athletic advantage. The triad of women's sports (eating disorders, exercise compulsion, amenorrhea) common among female athletes involved in sports such as track, cross country, figure skating, and gymnastics; rampant use and abuse of legal and illegal substances (recall that Tommy Morrison contracted HIV through sharing needles used to inject steroids); and excessive training regimes have lasting consequences on the health of individuals. Athletes are considered competent to accept these risks as part of participation in sports. While some of the risks assumed by athletes are questionable at best, the risk for contracting HIV/AIDS is extremely low, and therefore similar to or less than a host of other assumed risks. As a result, few sports organizations have chosen to ban HIV-positive individuals.

ETHICAL AND LEGAL CONSIDERATIONS

A host of ethical and legal considerations surround HIV-positive athletes' participation in sports. Foremost is the issue of confidentiality. Currently, most leagues and professional organizations do not require mandatory testing. However, U.S. boxers are tested when they apply for a license to fight and testing positive for HIV will lead to a revocation of the license. Boxers who compete against an opponent who he or she knows to be HIV positive also forfeits his or her license. The question of whether or not leagues can require testing and what the implications of that information should be is a thorny ethical dilemma. Given that the risk of contracting HIV is virtually nil, do leagues have the right to prohibit HIV-positive athletes from participation? Moreover, what responsibility do leagues and athletes have regarding informing other participants of potential risk? Does the perception of risk that the individual has matter? If mandatory testing is instituted, who would have access to information and what consequences are imposed on those who inappropriately disclose the status of others? What are the rules governing disclosure and what would be done to protect athletes from risk of disclosure? Indeed, an even more complex issue emerges when one considers how infected and noninfected athletes may use their status to intimidate or ostracize teammates or competitors. There are no clear-cut answers to such dilemmas. Ethicist Rodger Jackson (1999) suggests that any ethical inquiry into HIV/AIDS and sports should adhere to four rules: (1) specific details of any recommendations made must be given; (2) the goals of each recommendation must be stated clearly and honestly; (3) ethical and factual justification for the recommendation must be given; and (4) possible objections to the recommendation must be given.

In addition to ethical considerations are legal considerations. Leagues must deal with a host of issues pertaining to legal issues and HIV-positive athletes. In the first case, a person with HIV is viewed by the law as a person with a disability. Hence, leagues, personnel, and athletes must be familiar with the Rehabilitation Act of 1973 and the Americans with Disabilities Act (ADA) of 1990. The difficulty is that while the acts protect the rights of the disabled to restrict or limit physical activity, for athletes, sports participation is by its nature physical activity. The ADA further protects the rights of qualified athletes to reasonable accommodations from employers, unless undue hardship would result. Defining things like undue hardship and reasonable accommodations in the arena of professional and high-level amateur sports is difficult. Because physical ability is a necessity in sports, what types of accommodations are acceptable and what are not? What exactly constitutes an undue hardship and when is an athlete's performance problematic because of HIV as opposed to a host of other factors?

Currently, there are no clear legal precedents governing the participation of HIV-positive athletes, though access to health and fitness facilities for HIV-positive athletes is clearly protected. While most leagues permit the participation of HIV-positive athletes, and such practices have remained legal, leagues that have prohibited their participation, such as boxing, have received legal support as well. The problem becomes even more complex at the recreational level. The ADA requires that accommodations for recreational sports be made for disabled persons; however, for the HIV positive, it is generally unclear what these accommodations should be. At what point can leagues deem an athlete a danger to himself or herself or others? Past cases have suggested that leagues can ban an athlete to protect him or her from undue injury. At what point is an HIV-positive athlete a risk to himself or herself? Could beliefs about risk to the self or others be used to couch discrimination against HIV-positive athletes? Who is in a position to make such a decision and what are the legal repercussions for leagues who remove such athletes and leagues that do not?

Further, when considering athletes with HIV, one must consider ethical and legal issues pertaining to confidentiality. Who needs to know about an athlete's status? Recent legal cases have sent conflicting messages, sometimes ruling to protect the privacy of the individual, sometimes ruling that the HIV status of an individual should be revealed to colleagues. When considering such issues, two aspects are paramount: access to and control of the information. Recent rulings suggest that overall the confidentiality of the patient must be maintained. Given the complexity of the legal and ethical issues surrounding HIV-positive athletes, it is paramount that sports organizations develop clear legal guidelines in dealing with such athletes.

POLICIES AND PROCEDURES

Policies have now been adopted by most professional, amateur, and recreational sports leagues. Generally, most leagues advocate some variation of universal precautions. This means that leagues now operate on the assumption that any athlete may be infected and therefore have adopted safety policies and procedures to deal with bleeding athletes and blood spills. This requires that officials present be aware of policies and procedures for minimizing exposure to infectious agents. Policies and procedures vary by sport and league and generally focus on cleaning up blood, controlling bleeding, and exchanging or changing bloody uniforms. Teams or athletes requiring such accommodations are not penalized. Such issues become thornier in recreational settings, where there may be no qualified personnel to handle the situation.

The Future

While most sports have neither required testing nor banned HIV-positive athletes, the United States Boxing Commission denies licenses to HIV-positive boxers and bans them from further competition. Boxers are tested once a year, when they apply for a new license. By contrast, the National Collegiate Athletic Association institutes strict and extensive guidelines pertaining to blood-borne pathogens and communicable skin infections, but does not prohibit HIV-positive individuals from participating. Over time, leagues have developed what seem to be safe and reasonable policies for handling the threat of contagion.

Advances in treating HIV/AIDS mean that infected athletes can now enjoy prolonged involvement in sports. Further medical advances may eventually render fears about HIV/AIDS obsolete. In the meantime, it would seem that most leagues will adopt guidelines similar to the NCAA, adopting policies that regulate the

treatment of all bleeding athletes, rather than discriminating against specific individuals.

Faye Linda Wachs

See also Homophobia

Further Reading

Doughty, R. (1994). The confidentiality of AIDS related information: Responding to the resurgence of aggressive public health interventions in the AIDS epidemic. *California Law Review, 82*(1), 113–184.
Dworkin, S., & Wachs, F. L. (1998). "Disciplining the body": HIV positive male athletes, media surveillance, and the policing of sexuality. *Sociology of Sport Journal, 15*(1), 1–20.
Hums, M. A. (1999). Legal issues pertaining to HIV in sport. In G. Sankaran, K. A. E. Volkwein, & D. R. Bonsall (Eds.), *HIV/AIDS in sport: Impact, issues, and challenges* (chap. 9). Champaign, IL: Human Kinetics.
Jackson, R. (1999). HIV and sport: Constructing a framework for ethical deliberation. In G. Sankaran, K. A. E. Volkwein, & D. R. Bonsall (Eds.), *HIV/AIDS in sport: Impact, issues, and challenges* (chap. 7). Champaign, IL: Human Kinetics.
Odom, C. J., & Strobel, G. (1999). HIV, the game official, and control and prevention. In G. Sankaran, K. A. E. Volkwein, & D. R. Bonsall (Eds.), *HIV/AIDS in sport: Impact, issues, and challenges* (chap. 4). Champaign, IL: Human Kinetics.
Volkwein, K. A., & Bonsall, D. R. (1999). Transmission of HIV in sport. In G. Sankaran, K. A. E. Volkwein, and D. R. Bonsall (Eds.), *HIV/AIDS in sport: Impact, issues, and challenges* (chap. 1). Champaign, IL: Human Kinetics

Aikido

Aikido is a Japanese martial art that includes techniques for fighting empty handed, with weapons, or for subduing an armed opponent. The distinctive feature of aikido is characterized by a training method based on "kata" (a practice of aikido forms), while other Japanese martial arts, like judo, use two training methods, kata and randori (a free practice using the moves of kata in a more realistic and competitive setting). The kata method is well suited to younger and older people and to women because it is a safer and enjoyable way to practice a martial art. People are often impressed by aikido's graceful movements because, as many instructors point out, aikido movements maintain a person's stable center with an emphasis on spherical rotation characterized by flowing, circular, and dance-like motions.

Aikido is largely divided into two categories: joint (wrist, elbow, and shoulder, etc.) techniques (*kansetsu waza*) and striking techniques (*atemi waza*). Although aikido techniques have the power to kill and injure, their fundamental purpose is to seize and control an opponent. All of the principles of Japanese swordsmanship (eye contact, proper distance, timing, and cutting methods) are incorporated into the movements of aikido.

Morihei Ueshiba (1883–1969) founded aikido and promoted it throughout Japan with his son and heir Kisshomaru Ueshiba (1921–1999). He learned several forms of martial arts, but he derived the major techniques of aikido from the Daito-ryu jujitsu style, which he learned from Sokaku Takeda (1860–1943). Jujitsu is an art of weaponless fighting that employs holds, throws, and paralyzing blows to subdue an opponent. Ueshiba also established the Aiki-kai aikido association.

As to the meaning of aiki—the core concept of aikido—"ai" means to come together or harmonize, while "ki" means energy or spirit or mind. We can trace *aiki* back to martial arts literature of the Edo era (1600/1603–1868). *Toka Mondo* (Candlelight Discussion), written by a master of Kito-ryu jujitsu in 1764, says *aiki* means that two fighters come to a standstill in a bout when they have focused their attention on each other's breathing. Other interpretations exist. For example, the book *Budo-hiketsu Aiki no Jutsu* (Secret Keys to Martial Arts Techniques), published in 1892, says *aiki* is the ultimate goal in the study of martial arts and may be accomplished by "taking a step ahead of the enemy."

Organizations

There are three other major organizations that were established by Ueshiba's leading pupils in the world of aikido. The Ki-Society (established in 1974) is regarded in second position. Its founder is Koichi Tohei (b. 1920) who started aikido in 1939 and was at one time supposed to be Ueshiba's successor in Aiki-kai. He emphasizes the power of "*Ki*" in aikido, which he defines as the unification of mind and body, and became independent from Aiki-kai in 1974. Yoshinkan (established in 1955) is in third place. Its founder Gozo Shioda (1915–1994) practiced with Ueshiba beginning in 1932, and established a practical training method while teaching aikido at the police academy in Tokyo. The Japan Aikido Association (JAA, established in 1974) is in fourth place. Its founder Kenji Tomiki (1900–1979) originated the randori (free practice) training method of aikido in about 1961. It combines Ueshiba's techniques with judo, founder Jigoro Kano's theory on the modernization of Japanese schools of jujitsu. The JAA is the only school in the big four to promote the practice of both kata and competition. There are other smaller groups in Japan and other countries that are or were led by master instructors, among them Noriaki Inoue (Shineitaido school), Minoru Mochizuki (Youseikan), Minoru Hirai (Korindo), Kanshu Sunadomari (Manseikan), and Kenji Shimizu (Tendoryu).

Aikido Around the World

Aikido has the greatest number of schools in Japan, France, the United States, England, Germany, and Italy, in that order. Minoru Mochizuki was the first person to teach aikido in France, from 1951 to 1953. Then Tadashi Abe and Nobuyoshi Tamura of Aiki-kai followed. Aiki-kai aikido in France was promoted in affiliation with the French Judo Federation, which allowed aikido instructors to more easily receive government subsidies and to rent fully equipped gymnasiums at minimal cost. Consequently, tuition costs have been reasonable, a fact that has also helped to draw followers. France has approximately fourteen hundred clubs in two large organizations.

In North America Yoshimitsu Yamada and other younger instructors contributed to the rapid popularization of Aiki-kai aikido during the late 1960s. As of 2005 there were six hundred and forty clubs from various schools. The United States Aikido Federation (Aiki-kai, www.usaikifed.com) has the most with around two hundred and twenty clubs on the mainland. The United

An aikido dojo, with students being taught by their sensei.

Kingdom has around three hundred and thirty clubs under the British Aikido Board (BAB, www.bab.org.uk).

Three of the four main schools now have their own international organizations, the International Aikido Federation (Aiki-kai, www.aikido-international.org), the International Yoshinkan Aikido Federation (Yoshinkan, www.yoshinkan-aikido.org) and the Tomiki Aikido Network (JAA).

The Future

Aikido will likely develop on a large scale because there is significant demand from people who have tired of competitive sports and because many individuals have welcomed aikido as a unique form of physical activity that offers a combination of mental and physical stimulation not available elsewhere.

On the other hand, the increasing popularity and success of competitive martial arts such as judo and taekwondo in the Olympic Games bodes well for aikido, too. The Tomiki Aikido Network has held international competitions and contests since 1989, with widespread excitement evident among the participants, who enjoy the thrill of competition as in other athletic sports.

This enthusiasm for competition, however, is not generally shared by practitioners of other styles of aikido. Indeed, Aiki-kai strongly forbade competition after Kenji Tomiki created the free practice training method in 1961, which allows two aikido practitioners to compete. The reasoning behind the ban is that contests may produce a mind-set that is more interested in competition than cooperation.

More recently, however, a contest in the format of kata, with the winner being decided by a judging panel that scores each participant's performance, has become popular in many non-Tomiki aikido schools. Some clubs and some schools hold contests and give commendations to winning participants as an incentive, although strictly speaking this practice may result in producing a mind that wants to compete against other people. Going forward, the competitive mind-set—pro and con—is likely to remain a thorny issue in the aikido world.

Fumiaki Shishida

Further Reading

Pranin, S. (1991). *The Aiki News encyclopedia of aikido.* Tokyo: Aiki News.

Pranin, S. (1992). *Takeda Sokaku and Daito-ryu aiki jujutsu.* Tokyo: Aiki News.

Pranin, S. (1993). *Aikido masters: Prewar students of Morihei Ueshiba.* Tokyo: Aiki News.

Shioda, G. (1985). *Aikido jinsei* [My aikido life]. Tokyo: Takeuchi-shoten-shinsha.

Shishida, F. (1992). Martial arts diary by Admiral Isamu Takeshita and Morihei Ueshiba in about 1926 (in Japanese with English abstract). *Research Journal of Budo, 25*(2), 1–12.

Shishida, F., & Nariyama, T. (1985). *Aikido kyoshitsu* [Aikido class]. Tokyo: Taishukan.

Tomiki, K. (1991). *Budo-ron* [Budo theory]. Tokyo: Taishukan.

Ueshiba, K. (1977). *Aikido kaiso Ueshiba Morihei den* [A biography of Morihei Ueshiba: The founder of aikido]. Tokyo: Kodansha.

Ueshiba, K. (1981). *Aikido no kokoro* [The spirit of aikido]. Tokyo: Kodansha.

Westbrook, A., & Ratti, O. (1979). *Aikido and the dynamic sphere.* Rutland, VT: Charles E. Tuttle.

All England Lawn Tennis and Croquet Club

The All England Lawn Tennis and Croquet Club is the site of the most prestigious tournament in tennis: Wimbledon. Also known as "the Championships," Wimbledon challenges elite junior and professional players from around the world to compete on the club's famous grass courts. Of the four major tennis tournaments played every year that compose the Grand Slam of tennis—the Australian, the French, Wimbledon, and the U.S. Open—Wimbledon is the oldest and the only one played on grass. It is often referred to as the truest test of tennis because it requires players to adapt their playing style to the low bounces produced by the grass surface.

Traditions

Playing on the hallowed grounds of Wimbledon requires competitors to conform to some of the long-standing traditions of the club. While bowing on Center Court to the Royal Box (where members of the British Royal family sit on occasion) is no longer required, players must still wear all-white tennis apparel. Although over the years some players have protested Wimbledon's preeminent role in the sport, many players still view tradition-rich Wimbledon as the most important tournament to win.

History

The All England Croquet Club began in 1868 as a private club in the small town of Wimbledon just outside of London. In 1875 Major Walter C. Wingfield introduced a game called lawn tennis, which was immediately popular with club members. The game left such an impression on its members that two years later they decided to rename the club "The All England Croquet and Lawn Tennis Club." That same year the inaugural Lawn Tennis Championships were held using several of the same rules and regulations that govern the game today. The first Gentlemen's Singles champion was Spencer Gore, who bested a field of twenty-two participants.

In 1884 two significant events—the Ladies' Singles and the Gentlemen's Doubles—were added to the Championships. Maud Watson came out of a field of thirteen women to take the first Ladies' Singles Championship, while William and Earnest Renshaw took the Doubles title. At the turn of the century, the Championships began to display a more international flavor. In

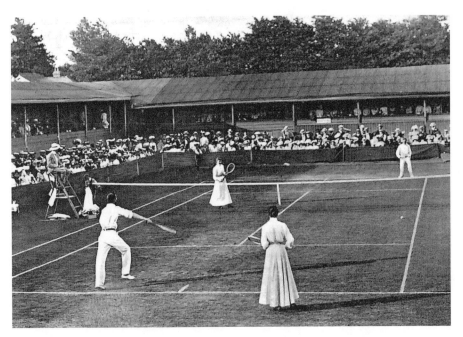

A mixed doubles match in the early years of the All England Lawn Tennis and Croquet Club.

Roy Emerson, and John Newcombe—who won sixteen of the next nineteen titles starting in 1956.

The Open Era

In the 1960s, those in charge of Wimbledon faced increased pressure from the ruling International Tennis Federation (ITF) to allow professional players to compete in its championships. For years, Wimbledon would permit only amateurs (that is, players who did not receive financial assistance from the ITF) to play in its tournament. However, with most of the world's top players now turning professional, the Lawn and Tennis Association decided to keep up with the times and permit professionals to compete with amateurs at Wimbledon. The inaugural winners in the 1968 Wimbledon Open Championships were Billie Jean King and Rod Laver. Since 1968 the Championships have continued uninterrupted.

Records Broken

Several records have been broken at the All England Lawn Tennis and Croquet Club over the past twenty-five years. In 1980, Sweden's Bjorn Borg won his fifth consecutive Wimbledon title, becoming the first male to do so in over a hundred years. His victory over John McEnroe, a five-set thriller that included a 34-point fourth-set tiebreaker, is arguably the most memorable match in tennis history. Other notable records include Boris Becker becoming the first unseeded and youngest male champion in the tournament's history; Martina Navratilova setting the all-time record of nine Singles titles in 1990; and Pete Sampras of the United States attaining his record seventh Gentlemen's Singles title in 2000.

Venue Today

While Wimbledon's present location has remained the same since 1922, many changes have been made to its grounds to accommodate the increasing number of

1905 May Sutton, an American, became the first non-British player to win the Championships. Two years later, Norman Brookes of Australia became the first foreigner to win the coveted Gentlemen's Singles title.

To help meet the growing popularity of the Championships, in 1922 the club was moved to its present location on Church Road. The current venue was opened by King George V and funded partly through the reserves of the club. After the move, Wimbledon's beautiful grounds were able to accommodate over fourteen thousand people. Initial concerns regarding ticket sales for the Championships were quickly dismissed—in fact, ticket demands became so great during the tournament's first year that tickets had to be allotted using ballots, a system still in use today.

Early Tournament Stars

In the early 1920s France's Suzanne Lenglen and the famous "Four Muskeeters" (Jean Borota, Jacques Brugnon, Henri Cochet, and Rene Lacoste) dominated Wimbledon. From 1927 through 1938, American Helen Willis continued the dominance started by Lenglen: She won eight championships, surpassing Lenglen's record six titles. British players reestablished themselves among the world's elite in the mid 1930s when Fred Perry and Dorothy Round won consecutive titles. Following the war, Americans dominated the tennis scene until the mid 1950s when they were supplanted by five Australian players—Lew Hoad, Neale Fraser, Rod Laver,

Tactics, fitness, stroke ability, adaptability, experience, and sportsmanship are all necessary for winning. ■ FRED PERRY

spectators who flock to London to watch the Championships each year. In 1997, a new Court 1, a media center, and two extra grass courts were built to help improve the quality of the tournament for fans, officials, and players. Including Centre Court and Court 1, the club now has nineteen grass courts in use for the Championships. Future plans for the club include erecting a retractable roof over Centre Court to help avoid the rain delays that have befallen these Championships over the years.

Ashwin J. Patel

Further Readings

Barrett, J. (1986). *One hundred Wimbledon Championships: A celebration.* London: Willow Books.
Barrett, J. (2001). *Wimbledon: The official story of the Championships.* London: Trafalgar Square.
Brady, M. (1957). *The centre court story.* London: Fireside Press.
Landon, C. (1981). *Classic moments of Wimbledon.* Derbyshire, UK: Moorland Publishing.
Little, A. (2004). *Wimbledon compendium.* Wimbledon: The All England Lawn Tennis and Croquet Club.
Medlycott, J. (1977). *One hundred years of the Wimbledon tennis championships.* London: Hamlyn Publishing.
Parsons, J. (2001). *Wimbledon: The Championships official annual 2000.* London: Hazelton Publishing.
Roberston, M. (1997). *Ballad of Worple Road: A poetic history of the early Wimbledon Championships.* London: Queen Anne Press.

Alternative Sports

Those activities known as "alternative sports" fall into various subheadings. Some are oriented toward play, self-challenge, risk-taking, or social affiliations. Others are associated with distinct nations or specific subcultures—groups of people whose identities and values contradict those of the mainstream society. Despite the various types of alternative sports, they are typically played by a small group of people, relative to the number of people who play and watch mainstream sports such as association and gridiron football, bas-

ketball, volleyball, baseball, and cricket worldwide. Alternative sports are played by athletes whose focus is on participation, not passive consumption. People interested in skateboarding, ultimate, power kiting, mountaineering, and capoeira are more likely to engage in the activity than to watch it. These five sports and physical activities differ in many ways from those team sports regularly seen on television and taught in schools.

Skateboarding

Skateboarders use their boards for transportation, kinetic expression, and rebellion. The board consists of a "deck," usually made of wood and covered with high-friction grip tape; two "trucks," for suspension and turning; and four wheels. The skateboard originated as a scooter in California in the 1930s, but by the 1950s the handlebars had been removed and the decks were shorter. Surfers took up the sport in hilly Californian coastal cities, which allowed them to recreate a sense of being on the sea.

HISTORY

In the 1960s skateboarding surfers took to riding the banks of empty backyard swimming pools, making tricks such as the kickturn (riding nearly vertically up a wall before lifting the front wheels and pivoting 180° to drop back down) possible. Skaters, as they became called, used all elements of the city and suburban landscape as their playground. Intentional "skate spaces" proliferated in the 1970s. Design and construction techniques were further refined and continually modified to keep up with improvements in skate techniques, which exploded in the 1980s. Renowned athletes such as Tony Hawk popularized aerial, ollie (jumping in the air while keeping the board on your feet) and flip variants of the 540° (1.5 full rotations); Danny Way began experimenting with 900° (2.5 full rotations) aerials in the 1990s. These extremely technical and dangerous moves were made possible with the help of bigger and better wooden-ramp skate parks often designed, owned, and managed by skaters themselves.

COMMUNICATIONS AMONG SKATEBOARDERS

Skateboarders' self-identities are tied to the number and difficulty of the moves they perform. Participants constantly try to invent even more spectacular (and dangerous) moves, working together at the skate park performing, practicing, and acting as mirrors for each other as well as relying on information in videos and magazines, the archives of skateboarding history. In the United States such magazines as *Skateboarder, Thrasher,* and *Big Brother* and in the United Kingdom *Skateboard!, R.A.D.,* and *Sidewalk Surfer* are the products of skateboarders who publish what the community has to say while recording the history-in-the-making of the subculture; the great proportion of still and high-speed sequence photographs reveal the performance emphasis of the skateboarding ethos.

ROLE OF WOMEN

The relative absence of women, or their sexualization, in skateboarding magazines and advertisements has been implicitly condoned by the skateboarding community, and heterosexist and misogynist attitudes have been promoted. This is slowly changing, however, partly due to the increasing popularity of skateboarding among girls. As these skateboarders age, they are redefining the values of this unique subculture.

One of the greatest paradoxes of skating is that although many recreational skaters idolize the professionals seen in television competitions and magazine advertisements, and some consume their products and emulate them, skateboarding has at its foundation an antimaterialistic, antiestablishment philosophy. As skateboarding gear (shoes, decks, hats, and apparel) becomes more popular, many skateboarders feel the need for a subcultural identity outside normative, mainstream lifestyles; these skaters resist the commodification of the sport by rejecting skateboarder-targeted products by companies such as Vans, Dcshoecousa, DirtBag Clothing, and Billabong. Skateboarding has been consistently repressed and legislated against, but participants continue to counter not through destruction but through boycotts, physical creativity, and appropriation of space. For many practitioners skateboarding is nothing less than a complete and alternative way of life.

Ultimate

Of the many stories surrounding the origins of the flying disc, the most popular legend is that of the Frisbie pie tin. In the mid-1940s, Yale students, as a game, tossed empty metal pie tins from a local bakery, embossed with the Frisbie Pie Company name. In the mid-1950s Warren Francioni and Fred Morrison had the idea of producing a plastic flying disc and, working in conjunction with the founders of the Wham-O company, produced the first plastic "Wham-O Pluto Platters." Two years later, after getting rights to the patent, "Frisbee" became a registered trademark. The discs have been used ever since to play a variety of games, the most formal of which is Ultimate.

DEVELOPMENT OF RULES

In the 1960s in Columbus, New Jersey, a high school's student council used the discs to create an after-school activity. The students called it "Frisbee Football," and today the game is known as "ultimate." In reaction to the mainstream sport paradigm of violent, ends oriented, gender segregated sports such as rugby, soccer, and gridiron football, ultimate developed with free-form ideals early on. Initially, the arbiters allowed as many as twenty to thirty players of all genders, shapes, and abilities, in any type of "uniform" in one game. They experimented with rules, concluding that the objective of the game is to get the disc across a rectangular pitch and into the other team's "end zone." If the disc is dropped or intercepted, the opposition takes possession. Running with the disc is not allowed. Instead, upon catching the disc players must stop for a maximum of ten seconds and throw it to a teammate. The student council decided to prohibit physical contact, picks, or screens between players, keeping the rules simple enough for inexperienced athletes to excel.

CODE OF CONDUCT

Before going off to college in 1970, the creators decided to print the rules and sent them to a number of other high schools in northern New Jersey, asking them to form Frisbee Football teams. The first interscholastic game was covered by the *Newark Evening News* in June 1969, and copies of the rules were subsequently requested by other schools eager to play this noncontact team sport. Today, it is estimated that ultimate is played by over ten thousand people in more than forty countries. Despite its high levels of organization in many communities and schools, rules are inclusive, and a code of conduct known as "the spirit of the game" forms its foundation. Games are refereed by the players themselves, even at World Championship level. If a player accused of committing a foul disagrees with the call, the play is redone. This places the responsibility for fair play on the participants themselves, who have proven that sport can be competitive without separating men and women, prioritizing individual skills or segregating respect among players, adherence to rules, or fun.

Power Kiting

Kites were first developed in China and were introduced to Europe in the thirteenth century by explorer Marco Polo. Initially, kites were used to provide entertainment, to celebrate religious events, to carry out scientific study, and as a platform for artistic expression. Today kites are used for aerial photography, advertising, hobby, and sport. Sport and stunt kites can be steered in any direction by means of two (dual) or four (quad) lines. They are mostly made with industrial materials such as carbon-fiber rods (spars) for the frame and a plastic coated rip-stop nylon for the sail, which is sometimes shaped like a parachute. They are easy to set up and handle on the ground and are stable in flight; traction kites propel participants on skis, on surfboards, or in buggies across land, water, sand, and snow.

KITE BUGGYING

Kite buggying is one of the most popular forms of power kiting. It is easy to learn, fun, and relatively safe —the buggy pilot sits in a small, light, easily maneuverable vehicle that sits close to the ground; the pilot flies a kite that pulls the buggy just as a sail pulls a sailboat. The pilot steers the buggy with pegs attached to the front forks and is able to accelerate, decelerate, stop the buggy at will, and safely navigate around people. Similarly, the kite is easily steered around trees or other kites. It is possible to buggy in wind as weak as 3 kph with a very large kite or as strong as 50 kph with a very small kite. Hardpacked beaches, dry lake beds, pavement, and grass are all viable kite-buggying venues. Of course, kite buggies can be raced, and competitions take place regularly in Europe and the United States.

KITE SKIING

Kite skiing can be accomplished on snow, land, or water. For snow skiing, conventional downhill skis and ski boots are used to travel over snowy hills, frozen lakes, or both. Kite waterskiing uses a variety of water skis to travel on rivers, lakes, or oceans, but this sport requires special apparel and a great deal of skill and planning to avoid getting marooned by a kite crash. Kite land skiing uses grass or sand skis to navigate across lawns, beaches, or deserts.

Kites can also be used to propel small boats, modified catamarans, participants on inline skates, or body surfers. Regardless of the medium participants travel through or the vehicle they travel on, the power of the kite gives them a sense of exhilaration and freedom not found in traditional sports. Every year technology furthers the power that kites can yield, and enthusiasts are ever more organized, with World Cup tournaments starting in the 1990s. Kiting is one of the fastest-growing sports, with a wide range of styles of competition and leisure available.

Mountaineering

Over the past century a small but distinct mountain-climbing subculture has developed. The hazards involved in climbing mountains are a major part of the sport's magnetism. Climbers may encounter fierce cold winds, animals, cliffs, or avalanches that can put their lives in jeopardy. In fact, most climbing journals have regular obituary sections, demonstrating that death is accepted without blame or fault in this subculture.

Climbing for sport began with some seriousness with the first ascent of Mont Blanc in 1786. Throughout the nineteenth century, men and women with sufficient money and leisure time used mountain climbing to escape city life. They were fascinated by the hazards, uncertainty, and jeopardy involved in the sport and took pleasure in defining themselves as different from nonclimbers and their sport as different from mainstream sports. Climbers have consistently rejected opportunities to establish an organizing body. The sport developed informally with an ethos of learning through experience and a rejection of social standards that prescribe bureaucracy.

The sport is paradoxical in that it has undergone a series of rapid transformations that have increased safety and climbing proficiency, such as guidebooks, training gyms, and improved equipment, but participants simultaneously focus on methods of maintaining or increasing risk. Guidebooks, which report the history, difficulty level, and special ecological conditions of the route, and indoor climbing gyms, which allow for year-round training and for less-affluent people to access rock climbing, both make judgment on the part of climbers redundant and competition (with external rewards) straightforward. Serious mountain climbers believe guidebooks and indoor gyms transform climbing from an interaction with nature to a commodified form of entertainment, to be consumed, objectified, controlled, and predicted. Climbers have generally accepted more advanced equipment, such as the Whillans harness created by Himalayan climber Don Whillans and friends, and the use of runners to limit fall potential because they increase control and safety and lead to better climbing experiences; however, use of bolts to create stairs in the rock, also a safety mechanism, is regarded with derision.

Climbers cherish peace and tranquility; they are possessive of the wilderness in general and are loath to popularize their activity lest it bring to the mountains the very conditions they seek to escape. The predictability, controllability, and safety of mainstream society are key elements of the dominant social value system that conflict with mountaineers' core values of adventure and risk. Anomie, the freedom from all constraints, is an essential element of mountaineering. Climbing's lack of external rewards and potential subversion of social and cultural values places it on the margins of the sport world.

Capoeira

Capoeira (kap-o-air-ah) has simultaneously been promoted as a game of slave resistance, a national martial art, and an Afro-Brazilian dance, depending on the context. The game-fight-dance was born among young enslaved Africans in Brazil, but in the early 1900s Brazilians of all ages, genders, classes, and ethnicities began to play, and in the mid- to late 1900s Brazilian migrants spread capoeira around the world. It is now played in small communities on every continent.

The artistry and athletics of capoeira combine in a physical activity in which two players confront each other inside a "roda" (ho-da) or circle of other participants who are playing musical instruments, singing songs in Portuguese, and clapping their hands. The lyrics of the songs comment on the action, praising or jeering the two players, who move to the rhythms, which dictate the pace and tone of the game.

A Game, a Fight, and a Dance

Capoeira is said to be a game because it is representative of the uninhibited, cooperative, and competitive activities seen among children. Capoeira is also a fight, but the martial aspects are often ritualized. Players can "show" a deadly move but stop at the last moment or move slowly enough for the opponent to escape. However, depending on the situation, games can change from friendly to violent, and serious injury can result. Capoeira also has its roots in African dance, the two most significant characteristics of which are the drums used to create rhythms of the music and the roda, with dancers in the center who are replaced after their exhibition.

Capoeira performances can be seen in music videos, at dance shows, in martial-arts tournaments, and on street corners as part of cultural exhibitions, group fundraisers, or players' idle lifestyles. Often performances are solos for a passive audience, in which players show their most spectacular moves in the style of a break-dancing show, as opposed to the traditional one-on-one fight. Yet players also get together without audiences and play with and for each other. In fact, one of the foremost contemporary teachers of capoeira in North America, Mestre Acordeon, hosted a twenty-four-hour roda in California in 2004. Players from around the world gathered to share their art and test their skills against one another.

Barefoot in white shirts and white pants, capoeira players spend much of their time upside down doing "aus" (cartwheels) and "macacos" (backwalkovers) when they aren't spinning, escaping, attacking, jumping, rolling, kicking, and dancing. African cultures tend to blur the limits between dance, fight, music, and religion, combining them in ways that might appear contradictory to Western eyes. At its most superficial level, capoeira can be used for fitness conditioning, cultural enrichment, recreation, and self-defense. For those embedded in the community, capoeira provides a family, a creed, a philosophy of life, and a complete lifestyle in its fusion of Afro-Brazilian music, dance, and street-fighting techniques.

The Future

These alternative-sport subcultures are in fact not separate or counter to hegemonic society. The participants choose to accept some aspects of the dominant social value system when it suits them and reject others when it does not fit with their beliefs. The structures, spaces, and communities surrounding alternative sport rely on mainstream sport for their definition. The proliferation of alternative sports can be accounted for by advancements in technology, individual creativity, international migration, and capitalist markets. People will constantly seek out novel ways to use their bodies, and once those

ways become mainstream, a new distraction will be discovered, invented, or appropriated.

Janelle Joseph

Further Reading

Borden, I. (2001). *Skateboarding, space and the city: Architecture and the body.* Oxford, U.K.; New York: Berg Publishers.

Brooke, M. (1999). *The concrete wave: The history of skateboarding.* Toronto, Canada: Warwick Publishing.

Capoeira, N. (2003). *Capoeira: Roots of the dance fight game.* Berkeley, CA: North Atlantic Books.

Chase, Philip. (1996). The Power Kiting Page, retrieved February 4, 2005, from http://dogwood.circa.ufl.edu/~pbc/kite/powerkite.html

Hardy, D. (2003). The rationalisation of the irrational: Conflicts between rock climbing culture and dominant value systems in society. In B. Humberstone, H. Brown, & K. Richards (Eds.), *Whose journeys? The outdoors and adventure as social and cultural phenomena: Critical explorations of relations between individuals, 'others' and the environment.* Penrith, Cumbria, U.K.: Institute for Outdoor Learning.

Studarus, J. (2003). *Fundamentals of ultimate: The complete guide to ultimate Frisbee.* California: Studarus Publishing.

Sydnor, S., & Rinehart, R. (Eds.) *To the extreme: Alternative sports inside and out.* Albany, NY: SUNY Press.

Williams, T., & Donnelly, P. (1985). Subcultural production, reproduction and transformation in climbing. *International Review for the Sociology of Sport. 10(1),* 3–17.

Amateur vs. Professional Debate

A characteristic of college sport in the United States has been its commercialization. In no other nation do colleges sell the broadcast rights to athletic events to television networks for millions of dollars and make millions more from the sale of corporate sponsorships, licensed apparel, luxury seating, parking, concessions, and other revenue streams. Although most people in the United States have come to accept commercialized college sport as a normal part of campus life, considerable debate continues regarding the status of college athletes.

Sports should always be fun. ■ CHARLES MANN

On one side of this debate people argue that regardless of the amount of money generated by college sport, college athletes are amateurs engaged in sport as an extracurricular activity during their free time. Thus, the primary rewards for athletic participation are, and ought to be, educational, social, and physical in nature. On the other side of this debate people argue that the unprecedented commercialization of college sport in recent years is transforming college athletes into professional entertainers for whom maintaining athletic eligibility often takes precedence over obtaining a meaningful education. Some people who take this position think that college athletes should be paid stipends in addition to their athletic scholarships and receive medical and other benefits not unlike those available to athletes in openly professional leagues.

How this debate is ultimately resolved is likely to have a profound effect on the future of college sport in the United States. Therefore, the major arguments on both sides of this debate deserve close scrutiny. Because controversies regarding amateurism and professionalism in college sport can be traced back to the late nineteenth century, and because the nature of these controversies has evolved through time, we should place this discussion in a historical context.

NCAA's Early Commitment to Amateurism

Since its inception in 1905 the National Collegiate Athletic Association (NCAA) has been a strong advocate of the concept of amateurism. At its first convention the NCAA took a firm stand against the practices that it thought violated amateur ideals. Included among those practices were "the offering of inducements to players to enter colleges because of their athletic abilities or supporting or maintaining players while students on account of their athletic abilities, either by athletic organizations, individual alumni, or otherwise directly or indirectly" (NCAA 1906, 33). Athletic scholarships, according to the NCAA, were a violation of amateurism. At this point in history the NCAA's views on

amateurism bore a close resemblance to those of British colleges.

The definition of an amateur athlete first appeared in NCAA bylaws in 1916. According to article VI(b), "an amateur is one who participates in competitive physical sports only for the pleasure, and the physical, mental, moral, and social benefits directly derived there from" (NCAA 1916, 118). This definition was amended in 1922 to include a phrase saying that college sport is an "avocation." The NCAA did not oppose financial aid for needy students. It opposed scholarships and other inducements awarded on the basis of athletic ability. Its concern was that paying the expenses of students because of their athletic ability might attract students for whom sport, not education, was the top priority. Such payments, the NCAA feared, would set athletes apart from other students as professionals.

Throughout the early twentieth century the NCAA continued to be philosophically opposed to athletic scholarships and other forms of professionalism. At that point in history, however, the NCAA had no enforcement power other than moral suasion. As a result, violations of amateurism were commonplace. According to a study carried out by the Carnegie Foundation in 1929, subsidization of athletes in violation of NCAA principles occurred in 81 of the 112 colleges studied, and other colleges likely were in violation but concealed such practices. During that period athletes were often paid for doing jobs that required little or no work. Alumni provided loans to athletes with no expectation of repayment. Some schools had slush funds totaling thousands of dollars from which they made under-the-table payments to talented athletes.

None of this was particularly surprising. During the early twentieth century sport at many colleges became far more than an extracurricular diversion for students. On the contrary, as spectator sport grew in popularity, winning teams not only attracted paying spectators and substantial media attention, but also provided a rallying point for alumni whose support was crucial to institutional growth. In many states winning athletic teams, especially football, provided tax-paying citizens with their only point of attachment with their state university. Schools made large investments in massive stadiums and athletic infrastructure to remain competitive. Given the high stakes involved, colleges could no longer trust the fortunes of their athletic teams to students engaging in sport as an extracurricular pastime. As a result, the pressure to recruit and subsidize talented athletes increased dramatically, and the NCAA's commitment to traditional amateur principles was increasingly put to the test.

NCAA Adopts Athletic Scholarships

The NCAA's early opposition to athletic scholarships was consistent with its vision that athletes be regular students rather than a separate class of athletic specialists, recruited and subsidized to provide entertainment for the general public. During the mid-1950s, however, rampant commercialism and the widespread practice of paying the educational and living expenses of athletes in defiance of the NCAA's amateur code forced the NCAA to reverse its position on athletic scholarships. In 1957 the NCAA decided to allow schools to pay the room, board, tuition, fees, and laundry expenses of athletes with no financial need or remarkable academic ability. This decision is a watershed in the history of college sport in the United States.

According to Walter Byers, executive director of the NCAA at the time, this decision was made in part because the NCAA believed it might help to eliminate some of the under-the-table payments to athletes from alumni that had become so common. Regardless of the NCAA's motives, by adopting athletic scholarships, the NCAA undeniably was sanctioning a practice that it had previously defined as a form of professionalism. Those people who believe that the scholarship system represented a significant break with amateurism have described it as a nationwide money-laundering scheme whereby money formally given to athletes under the table can now be funneled through a school's financial aid office.

Those people who do not see the NCAA's 1957 decision as a violation of amateur principles would argue, however, that because athletic scholarships were limited to educational and living expenses, they were not much different from academic scholarships that are awarded to help students with special talents complete their college degrees. From the NCAA's perspective, whether an athlete receives an athletic scholarship or not has no bearing on his or her amateur status. What matters is whether the amount of the award exceeds what the NCAA allows. According to the NCAA, "a professional athlete is one who receives any kind of payment, directly or indirectly, for athletics participation except as permitted by the governing legislation of the Association" (NCAA 1996, 69). Before the late 1950s athletic scholarships were considered to be pay; now they are not.

Scholarships: Gifts or Contracts for Hire?

When they were adopted, the NCAA's rules on athletic scholarships allowed them to be awarded for four years, and these scholarships could not be taken away for injury or failure to live up to a coach's expectations. The only condition for renewal was satisfactory academic progress. In other words, these early scholarships were gifts awarded to talented athletes to help them pay for their education. Even athletes who decided to voluntarily withdraw from sport could retain their scholarship. At this point in the evolution of athletic grants-in-aid, athletes were under no contractual obligation to play sport. Under these conditions one would have difficulty in arguing that scholarships constituted "pay for play."

During the 1960s coaches and athletic directors became concerned that athletes were accepting athletic grants and then refusing to participate. In 1967 the NCAA passed a rule to address this problem. This rule, referred to as the "fraudulent misrepresentation rule," allows a school to immediately cancel the financial aid of an athlete who has signed a letter of intent to play sport but voluntarily withdraws. The 1967 rule also allows the cancellation of aid to athletes who refuse to follow

Amateur vs. Professional Debate

The Amateur Spirit

Football is unquestionably the representative American college game. It has been wholly developed by college men, and they have naturally furnished its highest exponents. It is so widespread that practically every college and preparatory school in the country sends out a regularly organized team, and every institution which harbors an eleven takes pride in the men who compose it. The manly qualities which are necessary to the building up of a successful player call forth the best class of college men, and the wholesome attributes which the game itself promotes are shown in the splendid examples of mental and physical manhood to be found among football men. This is true only if the game is played in the proper spirit; how great, then, should be the solicitude lest the game lose aught, of its standing? It is doubtless, true that, college men as a whole seek to keep the game in its present high position, yet often-times effort is sadly misdirected. It is a serious and pertinent question, even with all that is being done, whether or not college men are really preserving to the utmost the true spirit of football, without which football must retrograde.

The greatest drawback to the wholesome conduct of the game is lack of the amateur spirit in players and managers. Good material and advantageous surroundings will not bring out the best results unless a true spirit of sport is the foundation. This spirit has been variously defined, and most teams pretend to accept its guidance, but too often it is mere pretense, and the quality of the playing and the character of the players deteriorates. The true spirit of football is absolute integrity and fairness in players and playing, and the dash and determination which can be built on that basis.

Source: Graves, H. S. (1900, January). Army and Navy football: The true spirit of play. *Outing, 4,* 453.

the directions of athletic staff members or who make only token appearances at practices. Because this rule makes athletic participation a contractual obligation and allows the cancellation of financial aid for insubordination, one can argue that it substantially increases the control that coaches have over their players.

The fraudulent misrepresentation rule allows coaches to withdraw financial aid from athletes who decide not to play or who do not make a serious effort to contribute to a team's success. However, the rule does not allow the withdrawal of aid from an athlete who is injured or who does not meet a coach's performance expectations. In 1973 the NCAA replaced four-year athletic scholarships with one-year renewable grants. Although these grants cannot be withdrawn during the one-year period of their award because of injury or poor athletic performance, renewal for a subsequent year can be conditioned on an athlete's performance or injury status. This rule, one can argue, creates a relationship between an athlete and a coach that is somewhat akin to employment.

Are College Athletes Amateurs or Paid Professionals?

The position of the NCAA and those who share its view of college sport is that college athletes are in fact amateurs and that athletic scholarships are educational gifts rather than contracts for hire. From their perspective, those people who argue that college athletes should be paid beyond what the NCAA currently allows are not only violating amateur principles but also are sending the message to young athletes that college sport is about money, not education. The NCAA argues that it is committed to maintaining college athletes as an integral part of the student body and maintaining athletics as an integral part of the educational program. Paying athletes more than their educational expenses would set athletes apart from the rest of the student body as paid professionals. Open professionalism, they argue, would also destroy the competitive balance so crucial to sport.

The NCAA and its supporters are aware that the NCAA has reversed its position on athletic scholarships since 1906, but they view this reversal as a necessary accommodation to the democratic values of modern U.S. life. The traditional—or British—approach to amateurism allows few but members of the elite leisure class to participate in sport as amateurs. By allowing athletic scholarships the NCAA has provided an opportunity to play college sport to students who would not have had time to do so if they had to work to pay college tuition. One can also argue that merit awards help colleges to attract students with special talents in a wide variety of areas, only one of which is athletics. Whether the area is music, art, or athletics, colleges ought to be committed to excellence.

Although the changes in NCAA rules regarding athletic scholarships are generally not mentioned in public debates over whether college athletes are, or should be, amateurs or professionals, these changes are crucial to this debate. Those people who are critical of the NCAA and accuse it of hypocrisy often argue that the NCAA abandoned amateurism in 1957 by adopting athletic scholarships. Then, by passing the fraudulent misrepresentation rule in 1967 and replacing four-year scholarships with one-year renewable ones in 1973, the NCAA completed the process of transforming amateur athletes into professional employees who can be "fired" for not performing to a coach's expectations.

In line with this argument, one could argue that the NCAA's insistence on defining college athletes as amateurs has more to do with maintaining a salary cap on how much money athletes can make from college sport than with protecting time-honored amateur and educational principles. In other words, amateurism has become an exploitative ideology that has little relationship to objective reality but rather defends the economic interests of those who control the college sport industry. According to this argument, the NCAA abandoned amateurism and transformed athletes into underpaid pro-

fessionals. Those people who insist that college athletes deserve a larger share of the revenue they generate are merely trying to ensure that athletes are treated fairly.

The Drake Group takes a slightly different position on the amateur versus professional debate. The Drake Group is an organization composed of faculty members and others committed to defending academic integrity in college sport. The Drake Group is totally opposed to paying college athletes for competing in what ought to be an extracurricular activity. However, it places the responsibility for professionalizing college sport directly on the NCAA and its member institutions. If the NCAA were truly committed to amateurism, argues the Drake Group, it would replace one-year renewable scholarships with grants that are based on financial need. This is the model of college sport that has been adopted in the Ivy League and in the NCAA's Division III. According to the Drake Group, athletes who receive athletically related financial aid are not amateurs and should have the same rights as other professional athletes. However, the Drake Group would prefer a return to what it views as true amateur sport.

The Future

As college sport becomes increasingly commercialized during the decades to come, demands by athletes for a greater share of the revenue they generate likely will increase, and athletes may well take their cases to the courts and to various legislative bodies. In 2003 the state of Nebraska passed legislation that would require college football players to be paid a stipend in addition to the scholarships they receive. Similar legislation is being considered in the state of California and elsewhere. The NCAA and the powerful academic institutions that it represents will undoubtedly oppose such legislation and take the position that amateur traditions must be preserved to protect academic integrity.

The argument that college sport is amateur and educational rather than an unrelated business of colleges has generally allowed the sport industry to hold off challenges that it has faced in court. For instance, injured players seeking workers' compensation benefits to this point have not been recognized by the courts as employees. The U.S. Internal Revenue Service has likewise been relatively unsuccessful in getting the courts to recognize revenue from college sport as taxable unrelated business income. Thus far the NCAA has functioned as an effective lobby to defend its claim that college athletes are amateurs and that college sport is not a business.

However, challenges to the claim that college sport is primarily educational and that athletes are merely amateurs are likely to increase during the years to come as college sport becomes increasingly commercialized. One significant court ruling that recognizes a college athlete as an employee with the same rights as other workers could radically alter the landscape of college sport. Until such a ruling is made, the amateur versus professional debate is likely to continue.

Allen L. Sack

See also College Athletes; Drake Group; Intercollegiate Athletics

Further Reading

Bowen, W. G., & Levin, S. A. (2003). *Reclaiming the game: College sports and educational values.* Princeton, NJ: Princeton University Press.

Byers, W. (1995). *Unsportsmanlike conduct: Exploiting college athletes.* Ann Arbor: University of Michigan Press.

Duderstadt, J. J. (2003). *Intercollegiate athletics and the American university: A university president's perspective.* Ann Arbor: University of Michigan Press.

Falla, J. (1981). *The voice of college sports: A diamond anniversary history, 1906–1981.* Mission, KS: National Collegiate Athletic Association.

Fleisher, R. A., III, Goff, B. L., & Tollison, R. D. (1992). *The National Collegiate Athletic Association: A study in cartel behavior.* Chicago: University of Chicago Press.

Gerdy, J. (1997). *The successful college athletic program: The new standard.* Westport, CT: Greenwood Publishing Group.

Knight Foundation Commission on Intercollegiate Athletics. (2001). *A call to action: Reconnecting college sports and higher education.* Miami, FL: John S. and James L. Knight Foundation.

National Collegiate Athletic Association. (1906). *Proceedings of the first annual convention.* Overland Park, KS: Author.

National Collegiate Athletic Association. (1916). *Proceedings of the eleventh annual convention.* Overland Park, KS: Author.

National Collegiate Athletic Association. (1996). *1995–96 NCAA manual.* Overland Park, KS: Author.

Sack, A. L., & Staurowsky, E. J. (1998). *College athletes for hire: The evolution and legacy of the NCAA's amateur myth.* Westport, CT: Praeger Publishers.

Savage, H. (1929). *American college athletics.* New York: Carnegie Foundation for the Advancement of Teaching.

Shulman, J. L., & Bowen, W. G. (2001). *The game of life: College sports and educational values.* Princeton, NJ: Princeton University Press.

Smith, R. (1988). *Sports and freedom: The rise of big-time college athletics.* New York: Oxford University Press.

Sperber, M. (1990). *College sports, inc.: The athletic department vs. the university.* New York: Henry Holt.

Sperber, M. (2000). *Beer and circus: How big-time sports is crippling undergraduate education.* New York: Henry Holt.

Thelin, J. R. (1996). *Games colleges play: Scandal and reform in intercollegiate athletics.* Baltimore: Johns Hopkins University Press.

Waterson, J. S. (2000). *College football: History, spectacle, controversy.* Baltimore: Johns Hopkins University Press.

Zimbalist, A. (1999). *Unpaid professionals: Commercialization and conflict in big-time college sports.* Princeton, NJ: Princeton University Press.

American Sports Exceptionalism

Contrary to the widely held opinion that *American exceptionalism* connotes a self-aggrandizing view by Americans of themselves, the term hails from a particular body of literature that is deeply anchored in how key European intellectuals of the nineteenth and early twentieth centuries characterized the main features of American politics and society in reference to those of their own. Thus, the very notion of "exceptionalism" bespeaks a profoundly Eurocentric epistemology because it was as an "exception" to the European norm that the United States fascinated these writers.

Origins of American Exceptionalism

The most prominent—and in my view still the most perceptive—European who compared the United States with Europe in every possible facet of public life was the French aristocrat Alexis de Tocqueville. But it was an essay by the German political economist Werner Sombart entitled, "Warum gibt es in den Vereinigten Staaten keinen Sozialismus?" (Why Is There No Socialism in the United States?) published in 1906 that really spawned

I'm a great believer in luck, and I find the harder I work, the more I have of it. ∎ THOMAS JEFFERSON

the huge body of literature in political science, sociology, and social history now found under the category, "American exceptionalism." To be sure, Sombart's formulation was seriously flawed since, of course, there was no socialism in the Europe of his day either. But Sombart's overly convenient and conceptually reductionist use of the term socialism did not alter the fact that he correctly observed a phenomenon in America that rendered the United States exceptional to all European societies of Sombart's time and would continue to do so to this very day. Rather than loosely using the term socialism in questioning America's exceptionalism, Sombart should have asked, albeit in a less elegant but more accurate way: What social forces, political arrangements, and historical structures have contributed to an outcome in which the United States is the only advanced industrial democracy in the world without a large and politically potent party anchored in the male, skilled, and industrial working class of the late nineteenth century? Or put differently, Why didn't the United States develop a politically potent mass movement of a social democratic and/or communist nature the way nearly all other industrial societies—including virtually all in Europe—most certainly did?

The answer to either question is quite simple: Because the United States constructed its own modernity that was orthogonal to Europe's—featuring many similarities but with sufficient differences to render them "exceptional."

The Other American Exceptionalism

Having been brought up completely biculturally in Europe and the United States, I have lived a constant comparison between the two every single day of my life. Furthermore, having been an avid sports fan on both continents, as well as a keen student of the many writings on the United States by European observers, I was well acquainted with Sombart's work and the huge debate that it spawned on both sides of the Atlantic. It was in this context that I embarked to investigate what in an analogy to the Sombartian debate I called "the other American exceptionalism," which addressed the following phenomenon: What were the social forces and historical reasons that rendered soccer a marginal also-ran in America's sports culture while elevating baseball, American football, basketball, and even ice hockey to importance in it, with the virtual opposite being the case in all of Europe and much of the rest of the world? The short answer is—like the answer to Sombart's question—equally simple: America constructed its own sports culture that features massive similarities with that of Europe by dint of a commonly held modernity, but that also exhibits sufficient differences to have constructed a sport culture in which millions follow and articulate a completely different discourse, namely, those of the Big Four of American sports and not of soccer, (which the rest of the world—tellingly—calls football). Please note that the concept of exceptionalism pertains solely to what millions of people *follow*, not what they *play*. Were it the latter, exceptionalism as a comparative axis would be meaningless because soccer has been played in America uninterruptedly since well before it was introduced to the European continent from its land of origin, England. Conversely, Europeans have played baseball, basketball, and even American football for nearly as long as these have existed as mainstays of American sports culture. Of course, only a few Europeans have done so and even those that did remained totally marginal to Europe's sports culture that—as of the 1920s at the latest—was dominated by what they called football and Americans have come to know as soccer. With the exception of basketball's rise after World War II and its meteoric ascent in the course of the Dream-Team era (the glory days of Larry Bird, Magic Johnson, and Michael Jordan), American sports continue to remain marginal in the sports cultures of European countries and much of the advanced industrial world's. Fascinatingly, whereas global popular culture has become completely American, this has had only one major exception: that of sports.

It is not the activity that matters here but rather the pervasive preoccupation with an activity of others that attains a meaning well beyond the event itself. That is the discourse of modern sport culture everywhere. The

A soccer coach instructing his team. *Source: istockphoto/Nick-Knacks.*

form and *structure*—as Allen Guttmann's path-breaking work has demonstrated—is ubiquitous. Secularism, equality of opportunity to compete, specialization of roles, rationalization, bureaucratic organization, quantification, and the quest for records pertains as much to baseball as it does to cricket, to basketball as it does to soccer, to ice hockey as it does to field hockey. What differs however substantially is the *content* of these entities that we call modern sports. Thus, even though Americans and Europeans partake in the comparable culture of modern sports that share large similarities, the actual sports languages are different. Americans understand signifiers such as "Hail Mary," the number "56" in baseball, a "double-double" in contrast to a "double play." Europeans have no idea what these mean but they in turn share a language with the rest of the world with concepts such as *"jogo bonito," "catenaccio,"* and "4-3-3" that baffle—and understandably bore—Americans.

This main "sports exceptionalism" has spawned many subordinate exceptionalisms that once again reflect America's own modernity. Among the most significant are the central role that college sports have played in

American sport culture, a phenomenon without parallel anywhere else in the world. Then, a fascinating new exceptionalism is the growth of participation in soccer among American women, who indeed have quickly advanced to be among the world's very best in a game that elsewhere—where soccer is the mainstay of sport culture—continues to remain an almost exclusively male bastion, just as football, baseball, basketball, and ice hockey still remain predominantly male domains in American sport culture. What renders these sport cultures so fascinating is their amazing resilience, their perseverance, their "stickiness," which have continued to make them relevant and beloved to millions of people throughout a century that has created the most profound changes that humanity has witnessed in its existence. The world of the late nineteenth century that created the social forces in Europe that Sombart conveniently (but wrongly) called socialism and that at the very same time spawned a reality in the United States that was devoid of this phenomenon—in other words American exceptionalism—also created the world of contemporary sport cultures in which American sports exceptionalism is still very much a reality. The continuing process of globalization and interdependence in the twentieth and early twenty-first centuries altered both at their respective margins but not in their cores.

Andrei S. Markovits

Further Reading

Guttmann, A.(1978). *From ritual to record: The nature of modern sports.* New York: Columbia University Press.

Guttmann, A. (1988). *A whole new ballgame: An interpretation of American sports.* Chapel Hill: The University of North Carolina Press.

Markovits, A. S. (1990). The other 'American Exceptionalism': Why IS there no soccer in the United States? *International Journal of the History of Sport, 7*(2).

Markovits, A. S., & Hellerman, S. L. (2001). *Offside: Soccer and American exceptionalism.* Princeton: Princeton University Press.

Sombart, W. (1976). *Why is there no socialism in the United States?* White Plains, NY: International Arts and Sciences Press.

Van Bottenburg, M. (2001). *Global games.* Urbana, IL: University of Illinois Press.

American Youth Soccer Organization (AYSO)

The American Youth Soccer Organization (AYSO) provides community-based soccer programs to young people. Nearly 680,000 boys and girls between the ages of four and nineteen play on more than fifty thousand AYSO teams, primarily in the United States. More than 80 percent of the participants are under the age of thirteen.

Five Philosophies

AYSO operates according to five philosophies: "everyone plays," "balanced teams," "open registration," "positive coaching," and "good sportsmanship." The goal of AYSO is to create a safe, enjoyable environment in which all children can learn the sport. Any child can play in AYSO. No team tryouts are held. Every team member is guaranteed the opportunity to play at least half of every game. League administrators create new teams at the beginning of each season and attempt to distribute player talent equally among the teams. AYSO stresses sportsmanship and nonabusive coaching styles.

Organization

Founded in 1964 in southern California with nine boys' teams, AYSO has expanded to all parts of the United States. Girls began playing in AYSO in 1971. Now approximately 40 percent of all players are girls.

The AYSO organization begins at the regional level. Regions combine to form areas. Areas, in turn, constitute fourteen sections across the United States. Volunteer administrators manage affairs at each organizational level. In 1995 AYSO expanded its operations, creating a program in Moscow, Russia. More recently, AYSO added programs in Puerto Rico, American Samoa, and Trinidad and Tobago.

A paid staff of about fifty people, based in Hawthorne, California, carries out the national administrative duties of the organization. Adult volunteers perform virtually all of the other tasks. Approximately 250,000 parents and other adults serve as volunteer coaches, referees, field maintenance personnel, and local administrators. The training of volunteer coaches, referees, and administrators is a central function of AYSO.

Funding comes from player registration fees, local sponsors, and national sponsors. AYSO regions establish player fees that cover local administrative costs. A charge of $11.75 is added to each registration fee and goes to the national office to cover the professional administrative expenses. Several national sponsorship and licensing options exist.

Innovative Programs

AYSO takes seriously its five philosophies. Since the 1990s AYSO has launched several initiatives designed to reinforce those philosophies and the organizational culture they represent. Among the most significant initiatives are the Very Important Players (VIP) Program, Safe Haven, and Kid Zone.

In sports . . . you play from the time you're eight years old,
and then you're done forever. ■ JOE MONTANA

The VIP Program expands AYSO services to reach children and some adults who have mental and physical disabilities. The program is a logical extension of AYSO's "everyone plays" philosophy. The VIP Program uses players from non-VIP teams to serve as "buddies" of players in VIP. About 160 VIP Programs exist in the United States.

Safe Haven developed in response to media reports about child abuse, including sexual abuse, in several youth sports settings. The purpose of Safe Haven is twofold. First, it attempts to identify and block from participation as AYSO volunteers those adults who have a history of sexual crimes and other specified criminal problems. Second, it trains and certifies adult volunteers. Such training and certification provide AYSO volunteers a measure of legal liability protection under the federal Volunteer Protection Act of 1997.

Kid Zone began in 1995 to counter what was perceived to be an increasing level of aggression and violence, particularly on the part of adults, in youth sports. Kid Zone is designed to promote nonviolent, positive behavior at AYSO games. It uses a kit that includes a video, signs, and badges to spread the message. In addition, AYSO parents must sign a pledge that states, in part, "I understand that the game is for the kids, and that I will encourage my child to have fun and keep sport in its proper perspective. I understand that athletes do their best when they are emotionally healthy, so I will be positive and supportive . . . I understand the importance of setting a good example of sportsmanship to my child . . . I will show respect for all involved in the game including coaches, players, opponents, opposing fans, and referees."

AYSO in the Context of U.S. Youth Soccer

In the context of U.S. youth soccer, AYSO represents the recreational end of the competitive spectrum. AYSO players and parents seeking a more competitive environment with professional coaches often gravitate toward private clubs after a few years in AYSO. Club teams typically are more expensive. They practice more often and play more games. Clubs are not obligated to select every player who wishes to join or to give every team member playing time.

Many AYSO regions attempt to meet the needs of more skillful and ambitious players by creating all-star or traveling teams who compete in tournaments after the regular season. AYSO has launched pilot efforts to create permanent AYSO teams of elite players and assess whether such teams fit the organization's values. Some parents and administrators believe that an inherent contradiction exists between AYSO's desire to abide by its fundamental principles and the organization's wish to satisfy the urge of some players and their parents to establish more competitive teams.

Despite its reputation for offering a relatively low-keyed form of soccer, AYSO has provided an introduction to the sport for many top U.S. players. AYSO alumni have played professionally in Europe and the United States and have played on men's and women's U.S. World Cup teams. Others have become professional coaches in the United States.

Issues

After four decades AYSO faces many of the problems that confront any youth sports organization in the United States. AYSO is concerned with how to retain children after the age of thirteen or fourteen, as well as how to generate sponsorship revenue, attract and train volunteers, increase membership, and maintain affordable player fees. In addition to these perennial youth sports issues, AYSO is evaluating the desirability of creating adult programs and expanding overseas programs. Finally, AYSO continues to investigate how to retain skilled players who seek a more competitive environment but remain true to its five philosophies.

Wayne Wilson

Further Reading

American Youth Soccer Association. (2005). Retrieved March 23, 2005, from http://soccer.org

America's Cup

The America's Cup is the oldest sporting trophy awarded in regular competition. The America's Cup race—held every three or four years—is the pinnacle of the sport of sailing and a major proving ground for new talent but even more so for new technology in the sailing industry. The America's Cup race has influenced history and has been influenced by history since 22 August 1851.

History

The schooner *America* sailed from the United States to England to participate in an 85-kilometer race around the Isle of Wright, held in conjunction with an industrial world's fair in 1851 that came to be known as "Prince Albert's Great Exhibition." The *America* finished first. England's Queen Victoria is reported to have asked who finished second. Her aide replied, "Your Majesty, there is no second," referring to how far ahead the *America* was.

Some controversy arose about the course that the *America* sailed during that race because the "outsiders" from the United States sailed inside of a shoal that by tradition—but not by rule—was observed as a mark of the course. The race committee upheld *America*'s win, but this race began a long history of competitors pushing the rules to the limit.

The trophy awarded for the race was brought back to the United States and on 24 October 1887 donated to the New York Yacht Club with a "deed of gift." In the deed George L. Schuyler, the sole survivor of the syndicate of people who owned *America* in 1851, stipulated that the trophy was to be held in trust for "friendly competition between foreign countries." The deed further stipulated that these countries would be represented by yacht clubs.

Thus began the 132-year winning streak of the United States, with thirteen America's Cup races being held off the harbor of New York (1870–1920). Eleven races were held off Newport, Rhode Island (1930–1983). In 1983 skipper Dennis Conner lost the trophy to Australian John Bertrand aboard *Australia II* with Ben Lexan's radical "winged keel," and the trophy went "down under" for the first time.

The 1987 America's Cup race, held in Fremantle, Australia, featured onboard cameras and award-winning coverage produced by then-fledgling cable television sports channel ESPN. Dennis Conner redeemed himself by winning the trophy and returning it to the United States. A delay in determining the rules for the next competition, now known as the "Protocol," allowed a rogue challenge by Sir Michael Fay of New Zealand with a 40-meter winged boat designed by Bruce Farr. However, Conner won with a smaller but faster dual-hulled catamaran. The New Zealand team appealed the race results to a New York superior court, which ruled that Conner's catamaran had held an unfair advantage. The ruling was overturned on appeal, and the final victor was Dennis Conner's *Stars & Stripes*.

In 1992 Bill Koch shared the helm of *America³* with Buddy Melges and defended the trophy against the Italian team. Koch said his team won with a combination of talent, teamwork, and technology. In 1995 the New Zealand team came into its own, defeating Dennis Conner five straight, and the trophy again went down under, but this time it was headed for Auckland, New Zealand. Sir Peter Blake (1948–2001) led the 1995 New Zealand team and its successful defense in 2000. Both times Russell Coutts was the helmsman. In 2003 Coutts and his core team left New Zealand to join the Swiss team, Alinghi, led by Ernesto Berterelli. Once again Coutts and team won, and Berterelli decided to hold the next race in Valencia, Spain, in 2007. That race will mark the first time the America's Cup race has been held in a non-Anglo Saxon country.

Rules

From 1851 until 1887 only general guidelines governed the type of boats that could enter the America's

 America's Cup

Beginning of the America's Cup

The letter below was sent to the secretaries of various yacht clubs in July 1857.

Sir: I am directed to inform the members of your association, that the One Hundred Guinea Cup, won by the yacht *America* at Cowes, England, Aug. 22, 1851, at the Regatta of the Royal Yacht Squadron, as a prize offered to yachts of all nations, has been presented to the New-York Yacht Club, subject to the following conditions, viz.:

"Any organized Yacht Club of any foreign country shall be always entitled, through any one or more of its members, to claim the right of sailing a match for this Cup, with any yacht or other vessel, of not less than thirty or more than three hundred tons, measured by the Custom House rule of the country to which the vessel belongs.

The parties desiring to sail for the Cup may make any match with the Yacht Club in possession of the same that may be determined upon by mutual consent; but in the case of disagreement as to terms, the match shall be sailed over the usual course for the Annual Regatta of the Yacht Club in possession of the Cup, and subject to its rules and sailing regulations; the challenging of the Cup, and subject to its rules and sailing regulations; the challenging party being bound to give six months notice in writing, fixing the day they wish to start—this notice to embrace the length, Custom House measurement, rig and name of the vessel.

It is to be distinctly understood that the Cup is to be the property of the Club, and not of the members thereof, or owners of the vessel winning the match, and that the condition of keeping it open to be sailed for by Yacht Clubs of all foreign countries, upon the terms above laid down, shall forever attach to it, thus making it perpetually a Challenge Cup for friendly competition between foreign countries."

The New-York Yacht Club, having accepted the gift, with the conditions above expressed, consider this a fitting occasion to present the subject to the Yacht Clubs of all nations, and invoke from them a spirited contest for the Championship, and trust that it may be the source of continued friendly strife between the institutions of this description throughout the world, and therefore request that this communication may be laid before your members at their earliest meeting, and earnestly invite a friendly competition for the possession of the prize, tendering to any gentlemen who may favor us with a visit, and who may enter into the contest, a liberal, hearty welcome, and the strictest fair play.

Respectfully, your obedient servant,
N. Bloodgood,
Secretary, New-York Yacht Club

Cup race. In 1893 the boats became very similar in that they were built to the maximum of 27-meter waterlines with overhangs of 6 to 7.6 meters at both ends—massive boats. In 1920 a universal rule was introduced with a formula creating the elegant "J-boats"—36-meter-long narrow boats with grand furnishings inside. In 1958 the 12-meter rule came into place with smaller (and less expensive) boats. During that time technology allowed for a transition to lighter materials, including aluminum. In 1987 the New Zealand team showed up with the *Plastic Fantastic,* built of fiberglass. That boat put the sailing world on notice: New Zealand was ready to compete. Sailor Dennis Conner of the United States responded by asking, "Why would you build a boat out of plastic unless you were trying to cheat?" The U.S. boat, *Stars & Stripes,* won.

Women in the America's Cup Race

Although sailing is a sport in which men and women can compete together, the history of women in the America's Cup race is relatively brief. Until the barrier-breaking 1995 *America*[3] all-women's team sponsored

America's Cup

Winning America's Cup Yachts

Year	Winner	Country
1851	America	USA
1870	Magic	USA
1871	Columbia/Sappho	USA
1876	Madeleine	USA
1881	Mischief	USA
1885	Puritan	USA
1886	Mayflower	USA
1887	Volunteer	USA
1893	Vigilant	USA
1895	Defender	USA
1899	Columbia	USA
1901	Columbia	USA
1903	Reliance	USA
1920	Resolute	USA
1930	Enterprise	USA
1934	Rainbow	USA
1937	Ranger	USA
1958	Columbia	USA
1962	Weatherly	USA
1964	Constellation	USA
1967	Intrepid	USA
1970	Intrepid	USA
1974	Courageous	USA
1977	Courageous	USA
1980	Freedom	USA
1983	Australia II	Australia
1987	Stars & Stripes	USA
1988	Stars & Stripes	USA
1992	America[3]	USA
1995	Black Magic	New Zealand
2000	Black Magic	New Zealand
2003	Alinghi	Switzerland

by Bill Koch, skippered by Leslie Egnot, and captained by Dawn Riley, only seven women had competed in the America's Cup Defender or Challenger trials or the finals. Hope Iselin, Phyllis Sopwith, and Gertrude "Gertie" Vanderbilt all served as timekeepers aboard their husbands' J-boats. Sis Morris Hovey, Christy Steinman Crawford, and Dory Vogel sailed on 12-meter boats. Dawn Riley was the only woman on the winning 1992 International America's Cup Class (IACC) team. Riley went on to become the first woman to head an America's Cup syndicate, America True. Twenty-five percent of the syndicate's team were women.

Significance

The America's Cup race has introduced many products and personalities to the world, including Sir Thomas Lipton's Lipton tea, Barron von Bic's Bic pens, and Ted Turner's ESPN cable TV channel. Modern captains of industry, such as Oracle software's Larry Ellison, ex-Microsoft executive Paul Allen, and Patricio Berterelli of apparel designer Prada, have been involved. The cost of competing is $45–100 million. The race is often controversial and contentious, but it has survived more than 153 years and may well survive as many more.

Dawn Riley

Further Reading

Herreshoff, H. (2004). History of America's Cup racing. Retrieved November 2, 2004, from http://www.herreshoff.org/frames/amchistory frame.htm

Jobson, G., Turner, T., & Levick, E. (2000). *An America's Cup treasury: The lost Levick photographs, 1893–1937.* Chicago: Independent Publishers Group.

Moritz, B. (2003). Maritime topics on stamps: The America's Cup. Retrieved November 2, 2004, from http://baegis.ag.uidaho.edu/~myron/html/amcup.htm

Rousmaniere, J. (1987). *Low black schooner.* Chicago: Independent Publishing Group.

Sparkman and Stephens, Inc. (2004). What are the 12-meter designs? Retrieved November 2, 2004, from http://www.sparkmanstephens.com/design/12_meter.html

Thompson, W. M., & Lawson, T. W. (1902). *The Lawson history of the America's Cup.* Boston: Rulon-Miller Books.

Wrightson, R. (2004). Women in the America's Cup. Retrieved November 2, 2004, from http://www.a3.org/95_Press_Releases/A3_95_History_Women_AC.html

Anemia

Anemia is the condition in which a person's body has fewer red blood cells than normal. It is one of the most common medical conditions affecting women athletes. Anemia, when untreated, can impair athletic performance and general well-being. It is easily diagnosed and treated and is usually preventable. Women athletes most often have iron deficiency anemia. However, two other types of exercise-related anemia—exercise-induced hemolysis and dilutional pseudoanemia—can afflict women athletes.

Diagnosis

Red blood cells carry oxygen from the lungs to the muscles. When the cells' carrying capacity is diminished, muscles fatigue more easily, and endurance is decreased. Athletes may feel tired, become easily fatigued, experience shortness of breath, muscle burning, and nausea, and become pale. Anemia is diagnosed by a simple blood test that measures hematocrit and hemoglobin, the components of red blood cells. Anemia is present when values for hemoglobin or hematocrit fall below the normal range. Normal ranges for adolescent and adult women are hemoglobin 12–16 g/dL (grams/deciliter) and hematocrit 36–46 percent. Values for hemoglobin are 0.5 g/dL lower in blacks. Values for hematocrit are 4 percent higher for each 1,999 meters increase in altitude. Significant overlap exists, on an individual basis, between normal and abnormal values; thus, the diagnosis of anemia must be made relative to a person's baseline normal range. For example, a hemoglobin value of 13 g/dL, although within the normal range, may represent anemia for a woman whose normal baseline hemoglobin level is 13.5 g/dL. Alternatively, a hemoglobin value of 11.5 g/dL, although below the normal range, may not represent anemia for a woman who has that normal baseline level.

Iron stores in the body are depleted before clinically recognized anemia occurs. Doctors therefore often look beyond hemoglobin and hematocrit when screening for the early stages of iron deficiency anemia and when differentiating iron deficiency anemia from other forms of anemia.

Sports Anemia

Low hemoglobin and hematocrit values in active women may not represent true anemia but may instead represent "sports anemia," also referred to as "dilutional pseudoanemia." In sports anemia hemoglobin is changed as a result of an increase in blood plasma volume, which is caused by endurance exercise training, resulting in artificially low values of hematocrit and hemoglobin. Endurance training increases blood plasma volume proportional to the intensity and amount of endurance exercise. A 5 percent increase in blood plasma volume, for example, can result from a moderate jogging program, whereas the training of an elite distance runner can cause a 20 percent increase. Although this dilutional effect decreases hemoglobin concentration, red blood cell mass remains normal or is often increased; therefore, oxygen-carrying capacity in the blood is not decreased (hence the terms *pseudoanemia* or *false anemia*).

Doctors most often see sports anemia in elite endurance athletes, athletes who are increasing their training intensity, and previously sedentary people who are initiating an exercise program. Sports anemia can be distinguished from iron deficiency anemia because the microscopic appearance of the red blood cells and measures of iron stores (such as the protein ferritin) are normal, it does not respond to iron supplementation, and it not likely to result in severe anemia—that is, levels will not become extremely low.

Not all women athletes are equally at risk for anemia. Risk factors include (1) recent childbirth, (2) excessive menstrual flow, (3) disadvantaged socioeconomic background, (4) dietary restrictions such as vegetarian diet, weight-loss diets, or fad diets, (5) intense or prolonged endurance training, (6) personal or family history of anemia, chronic disease, or bleeding disorders, (7) use of anti-inflammatory medications, and (8) recent blood donation.

Iron Deficiency Anemia

In studies of adolescent women athletes the prevalence of iron deficiency anemia ranges up to 20 percent and is particularly high in cross-country runners. Another 20–60 percent of women athletes are iron deficient but not yet anemic (low ferritin, normal hemoglobin). In studies development of iron deficiency during training was found to occur in 20 percent of women runners in the United States and was found to be preventable by iron supplementation. Adolescent girls may be especially susceptible because they need more iron to meet the demands of growth and to counter the loss of blood caused by the onset of menses as well as erratic dietary practices.

Although athletes may lose iron through urine, sweat, gastrointestinal sources, or hemolysis (destruction of red blood cells), these losses are usually negligible and not significant enough to cause appreciable iron deficiency. Excessive use of nonsteroidal anti-inflammatory medication (aspirin, ibuprofen) may increase gastrointestinal losses because of gastrointestinal bleeding. The most common cause of iron deficiency in women athletes and nonathletes alike is inadequate dietary intake of iron to compensate for menstrual losses. In the United States the recommended daily allowance (RDA) for iron to meet basic daily needs for women is 15 milligrams a day. The average diet in the United States contains 5–7 milligrams of iron per 1,000 calories. Therefore, women need about 3,000 calories per day to get at least the RDA of 15 milligrams of iron. However, many women athletes consume less than 2,000 calories a day, particularly women athletes who participate in sports (such as gymnastics) that emphasize lean body physique. In addition, in an attempt to eat healthfully and reduce fat intake, many women athletes eat little red meat, which is the primary food source of iron. Vegetarian diets pose an increased risk of anemia because of the lower quantities of iron in nonmeat foods and lower bioavailability (the degree and rate at which a substance is absorbed into a living system).

Exercise-Induced Hemolytic Anemia

Exercise-induced hemolytic anemia is caused by the hemolysis that can occur when exercise places physical stress on red blood cells. Hemolysis can occur in both high- and low-impact sports. In high-impact sports such as running, the physical trauma of repetitive, hard foot strikes leads to the destruction of red blood cells. For this reason the term *foot strike hemolysis* has been used to describe this condition. However, red blood cell destruction also occurs among competitive swimmers and other athletes who do not participate in running activities. Red blood cells may be damaged by lactic acid build-up (which occurs with intense or prolonged exercise), muscular contraction, or increased body temperature.

Exercise-induced hemolytic anemia is most commonly seen in middle-aged distance runners, particularly those runners who are overweight, wear poorly cushioned shoes, run on hard surfaces, and run with a heavy gait. Prevention and treatment center on encouraging runners to have lean body composition, wear well-cushioned shoes and insoles, run on soft surfaces, and run lightly on their feet. For most athletes exercise-induced hemolytic anemia is of little consequence because it seldom is severe enough to cause appreciable iron loss. However, small differences in red blood cell numbers may result in a competitive disadvantage for world-class athletes.

Effects on Performance

Anemia decreases physical performance and is linked to decreased maximum oxygen consumption, lower endurance, increased fatigue, decreased physical work capacity, and increased lactic acidosis (a byproduct of anaerobic metabolism). Experts are not certain that iron deficiency in the absence of anemia (nonanemic iron deficiency) decreases performance, although it probably represents a preanemic state.

Studies of the effects of iron supplementation on the performance of nonanemic iron deficient athletes have produced conflicting results. Some studies of women runners after iron supplementation have indicated im-

provements in measures of endurance, such as treadmill times, run times, and lower blood lactate levels during submaximal exercise (exercise that is intense but does not take the participant to the point of exhaustion and inability to continue). In many cases iron supplementation also led to improvements in hemoglobin levels, suggesting that the beneficial effects were because of correction of a mild anemia. Such studies demonstrate the important point that distinguishing mild anemia from nonanemic iron deficiency is clinically difficult and that although a hemoglobin value may technically fall within the normal range, it may nevertheless represent mild anemia that will respond to iron supplementation. Other studies, however, have failed to show that iron supplementation benefits the performance of nonanemic iron deficient athletes. Such studies suggest that when hemoglobin levels are not improved, iron supplementation does not improve performance, despite an increase in levels of ferritin.

Prevention

Prevention of anemia should emphasize adequate dietary intake of iron over supplements because iron has greater bioavailability in food sources—that is, the body better absorbs iron that comes from food. Ways to increase dietary intake of iron include (1) recognizing that meat sources of iron are absorbed better than non-meat sources of iron, (2) eating iron-rich foods such as lean red meat, dark meat of poultry, fish, cereals, pasta and bread enriched with iron, beans, dried fruits, tofu, and spinach, (3) enhancing iron absorption from foods by concurrently eating foods containing vitamin C, such as fruit juices, (4) cooking in iron skillets, (5) avoiding inhibitors of iron absorption such as tea, milk, wheat bran, and antacids, and (6) if unable to meet daily iron needs by diet, taking a supplement containing the RDA for iron (18 milligrams), such as a multivitamin with iron. Vegetarians have a number of nonmeat sources of dietary iron (dried fruit, eggs, kidney beans, cream of wheat, fortified cereal). However, if a person is unable to meet daily iron needs by diet alone, a daily multivit-

amin containing the RDA of iron is recommended. Iron supplementation is the mainstay of treatment of iron deficiency because people usually cannot increase dietary intake of iron enough to reverse iron deficiency.

Sally S. Harris

Further Reading

Clement, D. B., & Asmundson, R. C. (1984). Iron status and sports performance. *Sports Medicine, 1,* 65–74.

Fogelholm, M., Jaakkola, L., & Lampisjavi, T. (1992). Effects of iron supplementation in female athletes with low serum ferritin concentration. *International Journal of Sports Medicine, 13,* 158–162.

Harris, S. S. (1995). Helping active women avoid anemia. *Physician and Sportsmedicine, 23*(5), 35–48.

Haymes, E. M. (1993). Dietary iron needs in exercising women: A rational plan to follow in evaluating iron status. *Medicine, Exercise, Nutrition & Health, 2,* 203–212.

Haymes, E. M., & Spillman, D. M. (1989). Iron status of women distance runners, sprinters, and control women. *International Journal of Sports Medicine, 10,* 430–433.

Lamanca, J., & Haymes, E. (1989). Effects of dietary iron supplementation on endurance. *Medicine and Science in Sports & Exercise, 21*(2 Suppl), S1-117.

Newhouse, I. J., Clement, D. B., Taunton, J. E., & McKenzie, D. C. (1989). The effect of prelatent/latent iron deficiency on physical work capacity. *Medicine and Science in Sports & Exercise, 21,* 263–268.

Nickerson, H. J., Holubets, M., & Weiler, B. R. (1989). Causes of iron deficiency in adolescent athletes. *Journal of Pediatrics, 114,* 657–659.

Plowman, S. A., & McSwegin, P. C. (1981). The effects of iron supplementation on female cross country runners. *Journal of Sports Medicine and Physical Fitness, 21*(4), 407–416.

Risser, W. L., Lee, E. J., Poindexter, H. B., West, M. S., Pivarnik, J. M., Risser, J. M. H., & Hickson, J. F. (1988). Iron deficiency in female athletes: Its prevalence and impact on performance. *Medicine and Science in Sports & Exercise, 20,* 116–121.

Rowland, T. W., Black, S. A., & Kelleher, J. F. (1987). Iron deficiency in adolescent endurance athletes. *Journal of Adolescent Health Care, 8*(4), 322–326.

Rowland, T. W., Deisroth, M. B., Green, G. M., & Kelleher, J. F. (1988). The effect of iron therapy on the exercise capacity of nonanemic iron-deficient adolescent runners. *American Journal of Diseases of Children, 142,* 165–169.

Rowland, T. W., & Kelleher, J. F. (1989). Iron deficiency in athletes: Insights from high school swimmers. *American Journal of Diseases of Children, 143,* 197–200.

Selby, G. B., & Eichner, E. R. (1986). Endurance swimming, intravascular hemolysis, anemia, and iron depletion: New perspective on athlete's anemia. *American Journal of Medicine, 81,* 791–794.

Yoshida, T., Udo, M., & Chida, M. (1990). Dietary iron supplement during severe physical training in competitive female distance runners. *Sports Training and Medical Rehabilitation, 1,* 279–285.

Animal Rights

For the last several decades people have been questioning long accepted beliefs about the relationship between humans and the environment. Tension and conflict between those who seek to exploit the environment and those who seek to preserve it is now an established dynamic in our social order. From opposition to logging to protests over endangering species, concerns over the interrelationships between people and nature permeate modern society. Nowhere do these concerns appear more contentious than in the realm of human-animal relationships. Whether at a greyhound track or a pigeon shoot, on a deer hunt or at a horse show, a maturing mass movement questions the morality of people who interact with animals for sport.

Indeed, the animal rights movement attempts to protect animals from human exploitation. The movement is an intellectual and cultural phenomenon that has landed on modern Western culture's front porch. It is like a newborn child abandoned on the doorstep, and its seemingly sudden, unanticipated appearance and loud cries have left casual observers startled and perplexed, wondering, "Where did it come from?" "Why is it here?" "To whom does it belong?" and "What can we do now?" It did not spring full blown from the brow of contemporary philosophers and intellectuals. Rather, the movement has a historical antecedent, and like its predecessor, the contemporary animal rights movement represents a profound reaction to societal change. Unlike their predecessors, however, contemporary animal rights advocates carry the symbolic cause of animals out of the laboratory, beyond the barnyard gate, and into the realm of sport.

The animal rights movement is marked by utilitarianism (a belief that the useful is the good and that the usefulness of consequences should determine right conduct) and moral rights philosophy, is located within the middle and upper class, and is currently notable for the diversity of its criticism. The underlying causes of the movement's emergence and rapid growth include a unique convergence of four factors: rapid urbanization, scientific evidence linking animals and people, changes in the anthropomorphic (thought of as having human attributes) images of animals, and the ascendancy of egalitarianism (a belief in equality) as a universal political value. The animal rights movement poses many questions regarding relationships between animals and people. Indeed, animal rights activists ask, "If science tells us that we are related to other animals, that they are very similar to us, and that they have personalities and emotions like us, and if my experience supports these conclusions, then why shouldn't we extend protection to animals?" This question has already had a profound impact on sports involving animals, and the answer will continue to affect sporting enthusiasts and animal rights activists alike far into the future.

Origins

Historians and social scientists trace the origin of the contemporary animal rights movement to the nineteenth-century antivivisection movement, which opposed cutting into living animals, especially for scientific research. The antivivisection movement arose out of profound social reactions to increasing technological change and was concerned with the symbolic position of animals as liaisons between recently urbanized people and nature. Originally a puritanical reaction to both the Industrial Revolution and Victorian materialism, the antivivisection movement responded to perceptions of the increasing human exploitation of, and intrusion into, the natural world. Social scientists have discovered that, during periods of intense technological change and social displacement, people have often been receptive to criticism of forces in society that appear responsible for change. Hence, whether in the realm of agriculture or industry, technology came to be identified as a culprit, guilty of social disintegration and institutional impoverishment. When placed in this context, the antivivisection movement of the nineteenth and twentieth centuries as well as the current animal rights movement reflects widespread and deeply felt anxiety regarding social change.

*Animal liberationists do not separate out the human animal, so there is
no rational basis for saying that a human being has special rights.
A rat is a pig is a dog is a boy. They are all mammals.* ■ INGRID NEWKIRK

The Victorian antivivisection movement used sensationalized publicity along with popularized exposes of animal mistreatment and apocalyptic literature to mobilize public sentiment against animal experimentation, animal baiting, and the use of animals in sport. The movement depended heavily on aristocratic noblesse oblige (the obligation of honorable and responsible behavior associated with high birth) as a reservoir of support and played heavily upon public sensibilities concerning morality and brutality. The antivivisectionists opposed the relativistic (relating to a view that ethical truths depend on the people holding them) ideology of science, which to the Victorian was symbolic of the irreversible pollution and corruption of existing social order. Indeed, the relativistic ideology of science, with its technological Frankensteins, seemed responsible for the disintegration of society.

The Victorian movement had little impact upon the use of animals. Eventually the movement disintegrated; however, the symbolic reaction against the utilization of animals did not disappear all together. The movement's radical agenda for the transformation of society eventually dissolved into the social background, leaving the reformist animal welfare movement as its legacy. The antivivisectionists, although extreme in their abolitionist zeal, had sensitized society to the plight of animals. Less committed, and indeed less radical, people were motivated in part by antivivisectionist publicity to join animal welfare groups. Such groups, which sought reform of societal attitudes toward animals, perpetuated the cause.

Through the turn of the century animal welfare groups carried the torch, seeking to abate animal suffering, and antivivisection sentiments reemerged briefly during the 1950s in the form of a social reaction to various scientific phenomena. Nonetheless, animal welfare groups continued to predominate. However, beginning in the 1960s, the cause of animal protection was transformed from reformist calls for animal protection into the radical calls for societal redemption.

Whereas the nineteenth-century movement focused upon the experimental dissection of living animals and the mistreatment of companion animals, the contemporary animal rights movement has evolved to question virtually all forms of animal utilization and control. Like its Victorian predecessor, the animal rights movement has used publicity, exposés, and apocalyptic literature to frame the issues surrounding the status of animals in moralistic terms. However, unlike its progenitor, the radical animal rights movement extends rights-based claims for moral consideration and legal protection to animals.

Philosophies

The movement's claim of moral equivalency between human and nonhuman animals originates in two opposing philosophical schools: utilitarianism—a philosophy based on the maximization of pleasure and the reduction of pain—and moral rights. First, the utilitarian school posits that ethical decisions are dependent on their utility, stating that ethical decisions should maximize pleasure while minimizing pain. Its creed posits, "The greatest good, for the greatest number, for the longest time," as its justification. Animal liberationists—those who argue for the liberation of animals from a utilitarian perspective—argue that because animals and people both feel pain and pleasure, the utilitarian creed should be expanded to include nonhuman animals. In other words, they argue that the interests of nonhuman animals should be equivalent to those of humans in determining ethical decisions. The contemporary extension of utility outward from humans to nonhumans can be traced to a school of Oxford University utilitarian philosophers originating in the 1960s and 1970s. Finding its most popularized expression in Peter Singer's *Animal Liberation* (1975), the utilitarian justifications for moral consideration of animals are considered seminal to the movement's current growth.

Whereas utilitarian justifications rely on the utility of moral extensionism, the rights argument emphasizes similarities in the physiology, and therefore the inherent value, between higher mammals. Rights-based philosophers consider utilitarian moral considerations of nonhuman animals to be flawed in two aspects. First,

Animal Rights

Baiting the Opossum

From the 1832 Book of Sports:

Local boys need no introduction to the fighting attributed of the Vulpine Opossum, our *bushy-tail*, whose remarkably strong claws have left many a mark on incautious Europeans, both man and dog.

Mr. Ferguson's young terrier bitch was about sixteen months old, liver and white, weight about 25½ lbs. Mr. Jenkin's opossum from New South Wales was supposed to be about three years old and weighed 27 lbs.

The bitch and opossum fought on the 6th January, 1829, and the day being very rough, the fight was obliged to take place in a barn instead of Hempton Green, Norfolk, as had been contemplated, to the vexation of numbers, who could not get admission at any price; so much stir did the affair make in the neighborhood.

A great deal of betting took place previous to the match, at guineas to pounds, Possey the favourite. Some of our Norfolk knowing and learned country swells, who were acquainted with the *nature of the beast,* (after seeing the excellent trim he was got into by his trainer *Jemmy* Neal) even went as high as three to two, and it was said that even two to one was offered on the New South Wales favourite.

ROUND 1ST. Possey looked very fit, shook his bushy tail, and darted at the bitch as quick as lightening, caught her by the shoulder, and tore a piece out of it; he then drew back, made another spring at the fore leg, but missed it. Meantime, the bitch was not idle—she made several attempts at a hold, but the gentleman's furry coat deceived the poor bitch, who brought away a mouthful of his outer garment every time she sprung at him; at length, she caught

him *where the Irishmen put their lundy,* and punished him severely, while he returned by making use of his claws, with which he scratched dreadfully. At length he got away, and was taken to his house; and after two minutes rest, began.

ROUND 2ND. Both darted at one another, their heads met, and both were knocked over. Returning, Possey seized the bitch by the throat, and almost knocked all the wind out of the bitch (four to one on Possey freely offered—no takers). The bitch fought shy till she got a little wind, then made for him, seized his *proboscis,* and pulled him about in good style, in spite of his claws which made dreadful havoc with the bitch; Possey got away and was taken to his house. This lasted nine minutes and a half.

ROUND 3RD. The bitch made first play, and began by taking Mr. Possey by the nose, where she held him, and pulled him about for two minutes and a half he keeping his claws in exercise all the while when she lost her hold, and sprang at his neck (which in the previous round she had cleared of the fur) which she lacerated in a shocking manner, when he got away and was led to his house. Possey became rather weak from the loss of blood, but was restored by something being applied to his nostrils.

ROUND 4TH, AND LAST. The bitch again made for the foreigner's neck, where she left the marks of her toothy work; she then seized him by the shoulder, got an excellent hold, and for the first time Possey uttered a dismal yell, and, on getting away, made for his house, from whence he could no more be brought to the scratch. The bitch was consequently declared the winner.

The fight lasted thirty-seven minutes.

utilitarianism is based on the assumption that types of pains and pleasures are qualitatively different, and second, utilitarianism allows the exploitation of nonhuman animals if it is deemed necessary for the greater good. In response to utilitarianism's situational protection of animals, Tom Regan, an animal rights philosopher and university professor, advocates a rights-based approach. He believes that rights are dichotomous (having two parts) and absolute, thus extending protection under all circumstances. He argues that because nonhuman animals have consciousness, expectations, and desires, they likewise have personal autonomy. He attempts to protect their expectations and desires by granting personal autonomy through the extension of moral claims. Differentiating between moral and legal rights, he states that legal rights are provided to enfranchised citizens and consist of valid claims that have correlative duties. In his extension of moral rights to nonhuman animals, however, Regan argues that social justice calls for the respectful treatment of all beings that have inherent value.

The Animal Rights Movement

Each of the schools of thought has produced potent political and social critics of animal exploitation. The animal rights movement consists of various organizations, which can be subdivided into roughly three categories. According to James Jasper and Dorothy Nelkin in their book *The Animal Rights Crusade* (1992), these groups are the welfarists, the pragmatists, and the fundamentalists. Welfarists believe that animals are objects of compassion, deserving protection, and that some boundaries exist between species. Their goals include avoiding animal cruelty, limiting animal populations, and adopting animals. Welfarist strategies include advocating reformist legislation and humane education, funding animal shelters and animal birth control programs, and cooperating with existing agencies. The pragmatists believe that animals deserve moral and legal consideration, with a balance between human and nonhuman interests, and that some hierarchy of ani-

mals exists. Their explicit goals include the elimination of all unnecessary suffering by reducing and replacing existing uses of animals, and their strategy includes protests and debates, with pragmatic cooperation, negotiation, and acceptance of short-term compromises. The fundamentalists argue that animals have absolute moral and legal rights to personal autonomy and self-determination, with equal rights across species, especially among higher vertebrates. They seek total and immediate abolition of all animal exploitation and use moralistic rhetoric and public condemnation in conjunction with civil disobedience and direct actions to protest the use of animals. Interestingly, Jasper and Nelkin's somewhat dated analysis remains the template for understand the various factions involved in the animal rights movement.

Each of these groups is composed of dedicated activists who believe firmly in the morality of their cause. Yet, who are the activists? Although the animal rights movement is not monolithic, its activists tend to fit a uniform demographic profile. Social science data indicate that activists tend to be highly educated, middle-aged, middle-class Caucasian females from urban areas with the inclination and the political will to effect change. Although most animal protection activists are portrayed as ignorant, socially marginal people who are overly emotional about animals, what emerges from the data is a composite of a movement that is broad based and politically sophisticated and activists who are neither ignorant nor marginal. Indeed, animal rights activists are motivated by moralistic concerns rather than scientific, economic, or leisure-use justifications for animal exploitation.

Hence, during the 1960s the philosophical groundwork had been laid for a radical reinterpretation of the way people treat animals. Whereas people had traditionally viewed animals as objects to be used, albeit within some form of highly personal, existential (relating to or affirming existence) moral constraint, the animal rights movement argued that animals have personal autonomy and moral agencies and therefore should be protected from human exploitation through the provision of rights.

A few reasons exist for broader animal rights awareness. First, the rapid urbanization of U.S. culture since 1920 has facilitated a sentimental longing to return to an idealized rural life with its proximate relationships to nature and animals. Second, since the 1970s researchers who have studied primates and marine mammals have concluded that these animals have cognitive ability, complex social groups, and even forms of language. These conclusions, in turn, have further accentuated human empathy with animals. Third, evolutionary theory has indicated that humans and animals are biologically related and indeed that people are directly descended from other animals; in effect, scientists have argued that animals are much more similar to humans than previously thought and that people are biologically related to their fellow animals. These findings tantalized an urban population who experienced animals as highly anthropomorphized versions of themselves. Hence, the philosophical justifications of Singer and Regan for the moral consideration of animals were not widely rejected among the lay public. If indeed animals can think and feel and are intelligent, if indeed they are physically similar to people, if indeed they are evolutionary brothers and sisters of humans, and if indeed animals act almost "human," then why should they not be treated as the moral equivalent of people?

With these factors established within the public psyche, calls for moral and legal protection for animals were a given. In other words, animal rights philosophers and activists argue that the ethical distinction between animals and people has been dissolved by science and changing attitudes about animals; therefore, animals deserve rights. They believe that the exclusion of nonhuman animals from egalitarian protections based upon species constitutes "speciesism," a form of arbitrary discrimination no less repugnant than racism and sexism.

What has been the effect of this reinterpretation? In the case of the animal rights movement, activists are reacting to social unease. Confronting this unease, they seek a return to a simpler, less confusing and less complex time and to a bygone era when people lived in closer harmony with nature. Thus, animals assume highly symbolic roles as representations of an idealized natural world; they manifest iconographic status as bucolic exemplars of the purity and innocence of the prescientific, pre-industrial world. In effect, the animal rights movement attempts to protect its symbols of uncorrupted nature (animals) from desecration, and its mechanism has been through collective action. After egalitarianism is uncoupled from the traditional boundaries of universal human suffrage by evidence of evolutionary linkages between humans and nonhumans, the extension of rights to animals is not merely logical but inevitable. After egalitarian protections in the form of rights are extended outward to domesticated animals, their extension inexorably includes wild animals as well. Thus, whether it comes as critiques of animal-based biomedical or cosmetic research, feral and exotic animal control, the use of animals for sport or leisure, or the industrialized agricultural production of animals, animal rights philosophy extends egalitarianism to all animals in all contexts.

Feminism and Animal Rights

A large number of animal rights activists are women. Experts have offered various theories to explain why this is so. One theory, known as the "sociobiological hypothesis," holds that women are born as nurturers, are naturally emotive and intuitive, and thus are open to mothering instincts. Hence, women involved in the animal rights movement are supplementing their inherent mothering, nurturing, and protective instincts for human babies with the symbolic protection of animals. Studies have shown that most women activists are unmarried and childless. In this context, so the argument goes, women are responding to biological urges to behave in a nurturing fashion. This theory has an appeal that reflects fundamentalist and essentialist calls for a return to traditional family and social roles for women.

Another theory, known as the "philosophical-ideological hypothesis," argues that women are more re-

Joe W., the biggest trotter in Europe in the early twentieth century. Horse racing has long been criticized by animal rights supporters.

ceptive to the cause of animal rights because of their oppressed position in society. Women are themselves victims of systematic discrimination and oppression brought about by a women-hating patriarchal society and therefore consciously identify with the oppression of animals. As a result, women can experience, vicariously, the oppression of animals, as well as their liberation through animal rights activism. In this theory animal rights activism becomes a political outlet, and although women may be powerless to help themselves, they can nevertheless help animals to escape their oppression.

Neither theory sufficiently explains the participation of women in the movement. Both theories overlook the participation of men in the movement, and neither theory explains why most women in the United States are not animal rights activists. The philosophical-ideological hypothesis holds a circular charm in that evidence against it is used as proof of its validity. That most women are not animal rights activists proves only that society is oppressive. Interestingly, the French anthropologist Jacqueline Milliet (1998) argues that pet ownership—and animal activism in general—among women serves as a last remaining bulwark between women and an insipid anomie induced by rapidly changing and ill-defined social expectations and roles. In effect, she argues that pet ownership acts as a locus of control where women can legitimately regain control over the lives of an "intimate other" that symbolizes themselves: they control their pet's sexual reproduction (spaying and neutering), its eating habits, its sleeping habits, indeed most of their pet's experiences. This control, vicarious as it is, is a buttress against, and remedy for, the loss of meaning and control that they face. This provocative hypothesis remains speculative, and begs the issue of animals' moral status in society. Whether and why women (and men) advocate for the cause of animals is independent of animals' ability to feel pain and pleasure, their physiological similarities, their ethological resemblances, and the moral imperative of people to protect the weak.

Implications of the Movement

What are the implications for sports that involve riding, chasing, hunting, or just simply enjoying animals? The animal rights movement does not claim that animals have the right to vote; however, it does claim that animals have the right to life, liberty, and the pursuit of their own happiness. As philosopher Bernard Rollin has stated, "A deer has a right to its 'deerness,' a wolf to its 'wolfness,' and a pig to its 'pigness,'" independent of human-caused pain and suffering. The implications of this philosophy for sports cannot be overstated. Indeed, the impact of the animal rights movement upon sport is ubiquitous in nature and global in geography.

In England blood sports such as foxhunting have come under attack by the Hunt Saboteurs, an animal rights group whose protests and confrontational disruptions of fox hunts have been highly publicized. The Saboteurs, who believe that foxes have a right to their "foxness," oppose hunters who exploit the animals for mere pleasure. In response, some hunts now chase human marathon runners rather than foxes, ending

Animal Rights

Mission Statement of Kids for Animal Rights and Education (KARE)

Every year, millions of innocent lives are taken for fun, millions more to satisfy human appetites, and even more for the sake of unnecessary testing. The victims of these countless murders have unmarked graves in the stomachs, closets, and kitchens of human beings who are too heartless or too ignorant to see that all creatures, human or non-human, are deserving of a painless, peaceful life on the planet on which we were all once able to live in harmony. Kids for Animal Rights and Education was created in order to reach out to the people of the world—adults and children alike—and to inform them about the horrible, painful lives of the millions of creatures we share this planet with. KARE is an organization of kids from across the world who are willing to dedicate their time and love to making a difference in these innocent creatures' lives, and changing the hearts of millions of people in order to ensure that someday, we will all once again be able to live in a world free of blood sports, needless slaughter, and endless pain and suffering.

Source: KARE website. (n.d.) Retrieved February 22, 2005, from www.kare.homestead.com/

when the hounds catch the runners, and a good time is had by all. Indeed, in the face of such sustained intensity, in November of 2004 the House of Commons voted to ban foxhunting, thus ending a tradition rife with symbolic and class meaning. In continental Europe the movement is found in all sporting contexts. In Spain animal rights activists protest bullfighting, albeit unsuccessfully. In Germany catch-and-release anglers have been attacked by animal rights activists, and activists have accosted the Viennese for wearing fur on the promenades of Vienna. In Australia the animal rights movement opposes kangaroo hunts, while in Africa animal

rights groups protest big-game trophy safaris and claim to have been responsible for the shift toward noninjurious "photo safaris." In the Arctic animal rights groups protest subsistence trapping as well as trophy hunting, and they have affected both the fur industry and sporting enthusiasts. In the United States rodeos have been forced to justify their existence in the face of animal rights publicity. They have been picketed, and they now include contingency plans for disruptions caused by animal rights activists in their overall event planning. From greyhound racing to pig wrestling, from pigeon shoots to rattlesnake roundups, animal rights activists have periodically appeared at events to protest and disrupt, thus gaining publicity for their cause. Whether it be deer hunting to control overpopulation or to provide pleasure, whether it be falconry or competitive sheep herding, animal rights activists believe that the animals involved have the right to be left alone, regardless of human justifications.

Importantly, since the late 1990s an entire cable television channel—Animal Planet—has emerged to disseminate the science, mythology, and anthropomorphism of animals. From *The Pet Psychic* to *Growing up Bear* to *Animal Precinct*, Animal Planet's message is that animals are something other than mere animals. People often argue that animal rights activists, although highly visible at sporting events, have had little success in ending them. Nonetheless, the very presence of the activists—and vehicles like Animal Planet—indicates that the movement is growing, and the reports of the movement's impending demise have been greatly exaggerated.

Although the movement is fluid and decentralizing, perhaps the most striking example of the success of the animal rights movement came in California in 1990. California voters passed an initiative that banned mountain lion hunting despite the opposition of hunting, gun, and agricultural groups. This is a significant development to hunters for a variety of reasons. First, the California Department of Fish and Game (CDF&G) had conducted scientific studies that projected that mountain lions were sufficiently numerous to allow a

lotteried hunt. Although the lion had been both hunted and protected numerous times in state history, biologists for the CDF&G believed that the lions were multiplying and that a hunt was justified as a management tool. Animal rights activists, on the other hand, disputed the scientific justification, arguing instead that hunting the lions is morally wrong and evil. Second, the animal rights groups who passed the initiative contained a significant minority who wanted to ban hunting outright. The leadership of the animal rights groups agreed that an outright ban on hunting was premature and would have failed. Instead they identified a strategy of legislation that had a high likelihood of passing, banning the hunting of individual, charismatic megafauna. Third, the animal rights groups formed a coalition with environmentalists to redirect $900 million during thirty years from within other segments of the California budget toward habitat acquisition. This accomplishment is significant because the animal rights coalition redirected money away from the CDF&G and other hunter-friendly agencies as punishment for opposing them.

Thus, animal rights activists were able to ban one facet of sports (hunting) that they found to be offensive. They were likewise able to convince the electorate that the lions need protection. They were also able to punish state agencies that opposed them. Furthermore, a California ballot initiative to rescind the original legislation protecting the lions, and thus effectively to subject them to renewed hunting, was resoundingly defeated in the spring of 1996. Most important, activists have replicated this political model time and again throughout the United States. As a result, other states such as Oregon and Colorado have passed bans on specific types of hunting as well as hunting of certain species. Indeed, while the 2004 election found a ballot initiative in Maine to ban bear hunting that was ultimately defeated by a narrow margin, sporting enthusiasts should pause before pronouncing the movement dead; if the movement's past political savvy and adaptability is any lesson, activists will retool and continue their legislative agenda.

The lesson learned from the California initiative, regardless of whether it is ever repealed, is that the animal rights movement can affect its philosophy over the objections of sporting enthusiasts. And the lessons of those legislative actions that fail are that activists, fueled by redemptive zeal and supported by an urban culture, are adept at turning political setbacks into eventual public victories.

What are the implications of animal rights for people who interact with animals in general? The contemporary U.S. animal rights movement has attempted to realize nothing less than the radical extension of egalitarianism. Animal rights are a peculiar hybrid of liberal egalitarian ideals with a reaction to modernity. Having framed animal use issues in moral terms, having usurped the nomenclature of rights in the cause of animal protection, the animal rights movement has left its opponents unprepared to contest its philosophical underpinnings. Sporting enthusiasts are generally unprepared to discuss political theory, and their tacit reliance upon utilitarian justifications for animal uses is increasingly remote from the concerns of the culture within which they must exist.

Animal rights advocates attack all delineations between human and nonhuman animals as arbitrary and in their place posit new arbitrary distinctions based upon sentience (the ability to feel), species, or inherent value. How would hunters interact in a world devoid of hunting? How would sportspeople find solace in a world where their interactions with animals were strictly defined by the recognition of those animals' right to be left alone? Animal rights pose just such a dilemma.

Wesley V. Jamison

See also Foxhunting; Horse Racing

Further Reading

Adams, C., & Donovan, J. (1995). *Animals and women: Feminist theoretical explorations.* London: Duke University Press.

Dizard, J. (1994). *Going wild: Hunting, animal rights, and the contested meaning of nature.* Amherst: University of Massachusetts Press.

French, R. (1975). *Antivivisection and medical science in Victorian England.* Princeton, NJ: Princeton University Press.

[These events] will, of course, lose their appeal when black men, red men and yellow men learn to run, jump and throw, and leave the white men behind them. ∎ PIERRE DE COUBERTIN ON "ANTHROPOLOGY DAYS"

Herzog, H. (1993). "The movement is my life": The psychology of animal rights activism. *Journal of Social Issues, 49,* 103–119.

Jamison, W., & Lunch, W. (1992). Rights of animals, perceptions of science, and political activism: Profile of American animal rights activists. *Science, Technology & Human Values, 17*(4), 438–458.

Jasper, J., & Nelkin, D. (1992). *The animal rights crusade: The growth of a moral protest.* New York: Free Press.

Nash, R. (1989). *The rights of nature: A history of environmental ethics.* Madison: University of Wisconsin Press.

Regan, T. (1985). *The case for animal rights.* Berkeley and Los Angeles: University of California Press.

Singer, P. (1975). *Animal liberation: A new ethics for our treatment of animals.* New York: Avon Books.

Sperling, S. (1988). *Animal liberators: Research and morality.* Berkeley and Los Angeles: University of California Press.

Anthropology Days

Anthropology Days was an extraordinary event in modern Olympic history: It measured the performance of representatives of various non-Western peoples as they competed in mostly Western sports. Beneath the surface the event illuminated Western attitudes toward "others," that is, non-Western peoples.

Anthropology Days took place in St. Louis, Missouri, on 12–13 August 1904, approximately two weeks before the track and field competitions of the Olympic Games, which also took place in St. Louis. Organizers of Anthropology Days labeled the participants as more or less "savage" and divided them into eight groups: Africans, Asians (Turks and Syrians), Filipinos, Ainus (from Japan), Patagonian Indians (from South America), Cocopas (Native Americans from Mexico), Pueblos (Native Americans from North America), and Americanized Indians. With varying degrees of interest these participants competed in track events (100-yard, 440-yard, and 1-mile races), long jump, high jump, shot put, javelin, weight throw, and baseball throw for length and accuracy. Some participants threw bolos, and the "civilized" or "Americanized" Native Americans also ran a 120-yard hurdle race. Anthropology Days also included contests with which the participants were thought to be familiar, such as competing in archery and climbing a 15-meter pole.

Double Duty

The goal of Anthropology Days was to scientifically determine the physical abilities of the participants' respective cultural groups and to compare those abilities with the abilities of sport's dominant cultural group: white men. Thus, observers carefully measured the performances of participants. However, the participants in Anthropology Days had not come to St. Louis to compete in sports. They had come to St. Louis to be displayed by their colonial masters at the World's Fair. When placed on a starting line for a sports contest many of the participants did not understand what was expected of them. Still, observers to a surprisingly great degree took the participants' performances to be valid indications of the physical abilities of their respective cultural groups. Needless to say, the performances of the "savages" did not impress spectators or evaluators of the event. Indeed, the performances were ridiculed in the official report. Nevertheless, the report called the event a "brilliant success" because it taught "a great lesson." It laid bare the myth of "the natural all-round ability of the savage in athletic feats." High school championships probably displayed a higher level of athleticism than did Anthropology Days, observers said. These evaluations fit well with increasingly racist attitudes during the first decades of the twentieth century, and the event has earned a dubious reputation in Olympic and general history.

Why would people stage such an event? One has to consider the organizational, scientific, political, and cultural contexts and the close connection between the 1904 Olympics and the 1904 World's Fair. In 1904 the Olympics were part of the fair's Department of Physical Culture. Another department of the fair was the Anthropology Department, which provided living exhibits —human beings—for display at the fair. Anthropology Days was organized as a joint venture of the two departments.

The state of anthropology as a scientific discipline was also a factor in the staging of Anthropology Days. In 1904 anthropologists were inclined to study non-Western people in a more thorough way than had early

Anthropology Days

Wheel-Rolling in Africa

The so-called indigenous sports that were part of the Anthropology Days barely sampled the diversity of indigenous sports around the world. The following is a description of the wheel-rolling game played by the Baganda of Uganda.

Wheel-Rolling. This game was played by opposing teams and was played in the streets, as was the preceding one. The players stood opposite each other, each holding in his hand a "tangler" made of two pieces of corncob on a long string. One of the players stood in the middle of the road, rolled the wheel down, and the player on the other side tried to stop it with his tangler. If the end man failed the others tried. A player who stopped it sang out:

> It is all tangled! It is all tangled up!
> Spare it for me! Spare it for me!

Then the team which rolled the wheel came to examine the tangling. The player who had stopped it, when the tangles had been counted, stood where the wheel fell and held it in his outstretched hand. The three or four opponents (depending on the number of times the tanglers were found to be wrapped about the wheel) aimed at it with their tanglers. Those throws which succeeded made their throwers free, but the others were taken as servants by the opposing team and made to sweep the courts, where the wheels and tanglers were prepared.

The game continued with the different teams taking charge of the wheel alternately. Those who were taken captive might be redeemed by their successful team-mates. If one team lost more than three times it was captured. The winning team vaunted its accomplishment in the court of the other before the game proceeded.

There were several rules to this game:

1. The team which rolled the wheel the first time came only to see how the wheel was tangled and nothing was done. This was called "buying a village." This slogan has long been known to the Baganda. When a person goes to settle in a village he must first make a payment. This slogan has been adopted in many games.
2. The wheels must be tangled up only from the side where the player was supposed to stand and from nowhere else.
3. It was a forfeit if the wheel was tangled by two players of the same side. The other side did not send aimers.
4. A player might rush up and tangle the legs of one who had just tangled the wheel but had not yet moved from the court. This exempted him from having to aim at the wheel in his hand.
5. The team which rolled the wheel had the privilege of saying, "I tie my hand," to have it considered sufficient if their aimers tangled the arm holding the wheel instead of the wheel itself. If the other side shouted. "Tangle my arm," before they did, it meant that this would count as a miss and would mean a capture.
6. The side which tangled the wheel was not allowed to touch the wheel until the players of the other side had counted how many times the tangler encircled it. If they touched it the other side was exempt from the aiming.

Source: Kagwa, A. (1934). In E. B. Kalibala (Trans.), *The customs of the Baganda* (pp. 137–138). New York: Columbia University Press.

travelers and explorers. International politics had made such study easier. Western colonial powers often imported people and displayed them at world's fairs, especially during the heyday of colonialism from the 1880s to about 1960.

The Measure of a Myth

Another factor in the staging of Anthropology Days was the belief in evolution and anthropometry (the study of human body measurements, especially on a comparative basis). People did not require a giant step

I play the game for the game's own sake. ■ SHERLOCK HOLMES

to go from measuring skull dimensions and mental reactions to measuring strength, speed, and other physical abilities. The key problem that Anthropology Days illustrated was such measurements' lack of cultural validity.

Anthropology Days confirmed the colonial image of subordinate peoples: Such peoples were also subordinate in sports. The event gave a thin scientific legitimation to the racism that can be seen in sports literature of the first half of the twentieth century. The idea that a "noble savage" might exist in sports—portrayed as a "natural athlete" living a sound and healthy life far from Western civilization's alienation and sedentary life—was rejected. No athletic "threat" from the "savages" existed. The otherness of "others"—in this case non-Western peoples—was confirmed, as was the Western self-image of being the most developed.

Matti Goksøyr

Further Reading

Benedict, B. (1983). *The anthropology of world's fairs.* Berkeley, CA: Scholar Press.

Eichberg, H. (1988). Det olympiske og det barbariske. *Dansk Idrætshistorisk arbog.*

Goksøyr, M. (1990). One certainly expected a great deal more from the savages: The Anthropology Days in St. Louis, 1904, and their aftermath. *International Journal of the History of Sport,* 7(2).

Mallon, B. (1999). *The 1904 Olympic Games.* Jefferson, NC: McFarland.

Mandell, R. (1979). *The first modern Olympics.* Berkeley and Los Angeles: University of California Press.

Stanaland, P. (1979). Pre-Olympic "Anthropology Days," 1904: An aborted effort to bridge some cultural gaps. In A. T. Cheska (Ed.), *Play as context.* New York: Scribner.

The Anti-Jock Movement

The anti-jock movement refers to a loosely organized backlash against hypermasculine cultures often associated with high contact sports like gridiron football and hockey. Values usually associated with these hypermasculine cultures include "being tough," playing with pain, and extreme aggressiveness—values linked with notions of what it means to be a "real man" for many participants in and supporters of these cultures. Articles by researchers like Don Sabo and Joe Panepinto (1990) and Michael Messner and Don Sabo (1994) elaborate on this connection between participation in violent sports and the development of hyper-masculine "jock" identities and values.

What Is the Movement?

In an article entitled "The Anti-Jock Movement: Reconsidering Youth Resistance, Masculinity, and Sport Culture in the Age of the Internet" (2002) that appeared in the *Sociology of Sport Journal,* the anti-jock movement was described by the author of this entry as a series of websites put together by youth who critique negative aspects of these sport cultures. The anti-jock websites referred to included commentaries by young webpage writers and articles by journalists (that were linked from the webpages) that describe the excessive and unjust privileges that some athletes receive. Examples of these privileges included the "lack of punishment" for athletes who break school rules or laws and the overemphasis on athletic accomplishments in educational settings and elsewhere.

Also included on these sites were descriptions of incidents in which lower-status youth (often the authors of various webpages) have been bullied by members of "jock" high school cultures. Some anti-jock website authors used their concerns about "bullying by jocks" as departure points for discussions about the highly publicized school shootings carried out by two youth gunmen in 1999 in Littleton, Colorado, at Columbine High School. These shootings were viewed by many reporters as reactions by "outsider" youth who were seeking revenge against athletes and others who had bullied them. An article entitled "Dissecting Columbine's Cult of the Athlete" (1999) by Lorraine Adams and Dale Russakoff that appeared in the *Washington Post* is one of the more prominent essays about this conflict between marginalized/bullied youth and the dominant pro-football sport cultures. Some anti-jock webpage writers acknowledged that the Columbine shootings were intolerable and a tragedy, but they also explained the importance of the bullying-related issues that were highlighted because of the incident.

Some websites also included more encompassing critiques of the negative aspects of a North American sport culture that is believed by anti-jocks (and many other critics) to be excessive in its focus on and adulation of professional athletes and teams. On one website references were made to key academic and journalistic works that identify problems with many taken-for-granted assumptions about the benefits of sport. Included in this list of works were the books *Lessons of the Locker Room: The Myth of School Sports* (1994) by Andrew Miracle and Roger Rees, *Jock: Sports and Male Identity* (1980) edited by Don Sabo and Ross Runfola, and *Friday Night Lights: A Town, a Team, and a Dream* (1991) by H. G. Bissinger.

Why Is the Movement Important?

According to the argument put forth in this author's *Sociology of Sport* article, which was referred to earlier, the online incarnation of the anti-jock movement is relevant for sociologists who attempt to understand and explain forms of youth rebellion and resistance. He suggests that these young people are engaging in a form of online collective action that has possible political consequences. For example, concerns expressed by anti-jocks in school newspaper articles or through petitions against the funding of sport (both resistance strategies recommended on anti-jock sites) could potentially lead schools to rethink their emphasis on sports and athletic accomplishment or influence public opinion about issues such as the public funding of sports stadiums.

This form of resistance is different than less organized forms of resistance often associated with alternative sports like skateboarding, snowboarding, and surfing. In these youth sport cultures, participants rebel against mainstream sport conventions through their unique clothing, their aesthetically driven performance styles, and their engagement of a more communal (i.e., less competitive) sport lifestyle. In this way more typical

Anti-Jock Movement

Drop the Cap and Barley Bridge 1957

Games at which little boys might become rough were sham fights, running, leaping, wrestling, stone-casting, flinging bucklers, sliding, skating on bones, and whatever in these simple tests of skill developed or challenged the competitive spirit. Games that both boys and girls played, sometimes with much hilarity, were Drop the Cap (like Drop the Handkerchief) and Barley Bridge (like London Bridge). The singing and excitement of Drop the Cap culminated in the chase as the child behind whom the cap was dropped pursued the one who had dropped it. Sometimes when the caught person was kissed as penalty for being caught, there was a sharp contest that might become quite rough. Barley Bridge ended in a tug-of-war that strained muscles in the effort of the two sides to outtug each other and often was extremely rough. Drop the Cap was quite a different game when played by men and women on the village green, for they could engage in much pretty dalliance, but with children it was almost always an exciting game that might end in tears or squabbles.

Source: Pearson, L. E. (1957). *Elizabethans at home.* Stanford: Stanford University Press.

understandings of youth resistance as described by authors like Becky Beal in her *Sociology of Sport Journal* article, "Disqualifying the Official: An Exploration of Social Resistance through the Subculture of Skateboarding" (1995), were challenged by Wilson's interpretation of the anti-jock movement. That is to say, the anti-jock movement embodies the potential for political resistance and social change, while the subversion associated with skateboarding culture is largely symbolic and apolitical.

Interpreted more broadly, research and writing that is critical of hypermasculine sport cultures is pertinent to the term *anti-jock,* although researchers and authors writing in this vein would not be considered part of the "movement" per se. Included in this group of researchers and writers are those who examine issues such as homophobia in sport, sexual assault and athlete violence, hazing rituals in sport, and sport norms around pain tolerance. Work by authors like Jim McKay, Michael Messner, and Don Sabo (e.g., their 2000 edited collection *Masculinities, Gender Relations and Sport*); Phil White and Kevin Young (e.g., their 1999 edited book *Sport and Gender in Canada*); Brian Pronger (e.g., his 1992 book *The Arena of Masculinity*); and Laura Robinson (e.g., her 1998 book *Crossing the Line: Violence and Sexual Assault in Canada's National Sport*) is notable within the growing area of research on masculinity and sport.

In sum, these various reactions against and critiques of aspects of pro-sports culture are all associated with the term anti-jock, although the anti-jock movement is most directly associated with the series of youth-created websites. The extent to which the online anti-jock movement has actually led to any kind of political or public-opinion-related change remains unclear.

Brian Wilson

See also Youth Culture and Sports

Further Reading

Adams, L., & Russakoff, D. (1999, June 12). Dissecting Columbine's cult of the athlete, *Washington Post*, p. A1.

Beal, B. (1995). Disqualifying the official: An exploration of social resistance through the subculture of skateboarding. *Sociology of Sport Journal, 12*(3), 252–267.

Bissinger, H. G. (1991). *Friday night lights: A town, a team, and a dream.* New York: HarperCollins.

Connell, R. (1995). *Masculinities.* Berkeley: University of California Press.

McKay, J., Messner, M., & Sabo, D. (Eds.). (2000). *Masculinities, gender relations, and sport.* Thousand Oaks, CA: Sage.

Messner, M., & Sabo, D. (1994). *Sex, violence and power in sports: Rethinking masculinity.* Freedom, CA: The Crossing Press.

Miracle, A., & Rees, R. (1994). *Lessons of the locker room: The myth of school sports.* Amherst, NY: Prometheus Books.

Pronger, B. (1992). *The arena of masculinity: Sports, homosexuality, and the meaning of sex.* Toronto, Canada: University of Toronto Press.

Robinson, L. (1998). *Crossing the line: Violence and sexual assault in Canada's national sport.* Toronto, Canada: McClelland & Stewart.

Sabo, D., & Panepinto, J. (1990). Football ritual and the social reproduction of masculinity. In M. Messner and D. Sabo (Eds.), *Sport, men, and the gender order* (pp. 115–126). Champaign, IL: Human Kinetics Books.

Sabo, D., & Runfola, R. (Eds.). (1980). *Jock: Sports & male identity.* Englewood Cliffs, NJ: Prentice Hall.

White, P., & Young, K. (Eds.). (1999). *Sport and gender in Canada.* Toronto, Canada: Oxford University Press.

Wilson, B. (2002). The anti-jock movement: Reconsidering youth resistance, masculinity, and sport culture in the age of the Internet. *Sociology of Sport Journal, 19*(2), 206–233.

Arab Games

The Arab Games, created to promote unity among the Arab states, have a long history of strife, boycott, and violence. Established by the Arab League in 1951, the Arab Games were held for the first time in 1953 under the direction of Egypt's Ahmed Touny in Alexandria, Egypt. Women were not allowed to participate until the sixth games in 1985, in Casablanca.

Irregular Schedule

The goal is to hold the games every four years, like other regional games, and that goal was met for the first four occasions. These games were held in Alexandria, Egypt (1953), Beirut, Lebanon (1957), Casablanca, Morocco (1961), and Cairo, Egypt (1965).

Tripoli, Libya, was awarded the 1969 games, but a change in government stopped these plans. Sudan offered Khartoum as host in 1971, but instead Syria was asked to host games in 1974. The Israel-Arab war in October of 1973 interrupted those plans. Syria finally hosted the games in 1976. The next games were planned for 1980, but the ongoing Israeli-Palestinian conflict postponed plans to 1982, but the next games were not held until 1985 in Casablanca.

In January 1984, the Council of Arabian Ministers of Youth and Sports met in Algiers and attempted again to establish a quadrennial schedule. The council chose Iraq for the 1989 games, Jordan for 1993, and Tunisia for 1997. None of these games ever took place. The

*You have to do what others won't
to achieve what others don't.* ■ Unknown

proposed 1989 games were awarded to Iraq while they were actively at war with Iran.

Games were scheduled to be held in Beirut, Lebanon, in 1996, but construction delays and a slow recovery from the Israeli war slowed plans, and the games were set back one year to 1997. Unfortunately, this caused a schedule conflict with the Mediterranean Games, whose council had recently voted to switch those games to the year after, as opposed to the year before, the Olympic Games. The Arab Games Federation responded by moving their next games, planned for 2001 in Amman, to 1999 to avoid the overlapping schedules. The 2003 games, planned for Algiers, were postponed to 2004 after an earthquake in 2003 delayed the plans.

Political Difficulties

Political strife has followed the Arab Games throughout their history. Internal sports federation issues kept Egypt away from the second games in Beirut. Egypt had overwhelmed the other nations at the first games.

The 1961 games in Casablanca, Morocco, opened without teams from Iraq, Algeria, or Tunisia. The Iraqis boycotted, protesting the participation of Kuwait, which Iraq at the time was claiming as a part of its territory. Algeria's absence was due to a FIFA (Federation Internationale de Football Association) ban of some of its football (soccer) players, who had broken their contracts with teams in France in 1958 to return to Algeria and join the Algerian National Liberation Front. FIFA threatened to ban anyone who played against the Algerians. The Algerian government kept all its athletes from the games. Tunisia was involved in a small military action involving the French, the Bizerte crisis, and said that this prevented them from sending a team to the games. Both Algeria and Tunisia sent flagbearers as signs of goodwill.

In 1985, Egypt did not participate in the games after being sanctioned by the Arab League. In 1992, when Iraq was banned from the games for its invasion of Kuwait, Iraqi athletes traveled to the Syrian border to protest. In 1997, Iraq's participation was still an issue. Saudi Arabia, Kuwait, Oman, Bahrain, the United Arab Emirates, and Qatar threatened to boycott the games if Iraq took part. The Iraqis replied that even the United States had not prevented Iraqi participation in the 1996 Atlanta Olympic Games, and that they had invitations to the games from the Arab League. The Iraqi National Olympic Committee sent ninety-five Iraqi athletes to the Lebanese border, where the Lebanese authorities refused to let them cross. In 1999, Iraq was invited by Jordan to the games in Amman. Kuwait responded with a boycott of its own, claiming it would not participate with a nation that was still holding Kuwaiti prisoners of war. The president of the Kuwaiti Olympic Committee, Sheikh Ahmad al-Fahd al-Sabah, resigned from the Arab Sports Federation over the Iraq issue, citing interference from the Arab League.

The 1999 games were eventful, with soccer riots both on and off the field involving players and fans from Palestine, Libya, and Iraq, with destruction and minor injuries. This was the second games in a row in which soccer events had been interrupted by violence. The lack of goodwill carried over to basketball, and the Arab Games Organizing Committee called an emergency meeting to address the issue. Seven athletes failed drug tests at the games.

The 1999 games were also known as the Al Hussein tournament, in memoriam to Jordan's late King Hussein, who had died earlier in the year. During the

Table 1.

Locations of the Arab Games

Year	Location	Dates
953	Alexandria, Egypt	26 July–10 August
1957	Beirut, Lebanon	13–27 October
1961	Casablanca, Morocco	24 August–8 September
1965	Cairo, Egypt	2–14 September
1976	Damascus, Syria	6–21 October
1985	Casablanca, Morocco	2–16 August
1992	Damascus, Syria	4–18 September
1997	Beirut, Lebanon	13–27 July
1999	Amman, Jordan	12–31 August
2004	Algiers, Algeria	24 September–8 October

games, Saudi Arabia's Prince Faisal Fahd, an International Olympic Committee member and president of the Arab Sports Confederation, the governing body for the games, died of a heart attack. The Saudi Arabian delegation insisted that the games not be interrupted, though the prince was remembered in a moment of silence before each event began and flags were flown at half staff for three days. The closing ceremonies for the games were subdued, organizers canceling all festivities out of respect to Prince Fahd.

The 2004 Arab Games, held 24 September to 8 October in Algiers, Algeria, one month after the Athens

Olympic Games, were very orderly in comparison with past events, with no reported boycotts or violence.

The Future

The 2007 games are scheduled to be held in Libya. If held, these would be the first major international games held in the nation.

Daniel Bell

See also Islamic Countries' Women's Sports Solidarity Games

Further Reading

Bell, D. (2003). Arab Games. In D. Bell (Ed.), *Encyclopedia of international games* (pp. 39–47). Jefferson, NC: McFarland.
Henry, I., Amara, M., & Al-Tauqi, M. (2003). Sport, Arab nationalism, and the Pan-Arab Games. *International Review for the Sociology of Sport, 38*(3), 295–310.

A sports stadium under construction in Qatar in May 2004. *Source: istockphoto/PaulCowan.*

Archery

*S*ince ancient times, continuing through the legends of Robin Hood and William Tell, and on into the modern Olympics, people have taken up the bow and arrow for sport. Historians claim that all sports originated in the production process and that thus *Homo faber* (the tool-making human) preceded *Homo ludens* (the playful human). The bow and arrow was one tool that had a revolutionary impact on human culture. Prehistoric cave paintings in Spain and France depict bows and arrows as hunting equipment, and archaeologists have found stone arrowheads in excavations as evidence of the first human hunters. Moreover, researchers have found evidence of archery in almost every part of the world. Hence, we can assume that archery did not spread from one culture but rather that it originated independently in various areas. People also used bows and arrows as weapons in warfare. The teaching of archery for warfare led to competitions, which were prototypes of organized sports.

However, an opposing theory of the origin of sports is the so-called cultic historical school, which locates the origin of all sports in cultic rituals. People often linked archery with magic and symbolism. Among the ancient Hittites, for example, archery was part of a magic rite to cure impotence or homosexuality. A treatise on this subject describes how a patient dressed in a black cloak and how a priest intoned chants. The patient then had to undress and walk through a sacred gateway, carrying in his hand a spindle that symbolized womanhood. After he had passed through the gateway, he replaced the spindle with a war bow, which symbolized manhood. A magical formula then confirmed that the patient was cured and that all female elements had been removed.

From anthropological and historical perspectives we often have difficulty in differentiating how, where, and when archery was practiced purely for sport. The associations with warfare, hunting, and cultic rituals are never far away, but throughout history they have often been invoked as a rationalization for practicing archery purely for sport. Although archery as a sport is a contest between archers and not a practice of hunting or warfare, one can't trace the history of archery without alluding to the use of the bow and arrow in hunting and warfare.

Archery among the Ancients

When the English archaeologist Howard Carter (1873–1939) discovered the tomb of the Egyptian king Tutankhamen in 1922, the tomb revealed, among other artifacts for hunting, bows, arrows, quivers, arm guards, and a bow case that belonged to Tutankhamen's hunting chariot. The bows were of three kinds—composite, made of wood, horn, linen, and bark; self-bows of a single stave (staff); and bows of two staves—and ranged in length from 69 to 124 centimeters. One 36-centimeter self-bow was probably used by the king during his childhood. Carter also found 278 arrows ranging from 25 to 91 centimeters in length and one arrow of 15 centimeters, probably used by the king during his childhood. Pictures show that the king hunted with bow and arrow

not only from a sitting or standing position, but also from a moving chariot, in which he stood with the reins tied to his waist while shooting with his freed arms. The king, of course, hunted not for economic necessity but rather for enjoyment. Moreover, these royal hunting scenes were symbolic representations of Tutankhamen's military and physical fitness.

The Egyptian pharaohs also demonstrated their archery marksmanship before an admiring public. A granite relief from Karnak shows Amenophis II shooting at a target from a moving chariot. The inscription on the relief reads: "His Majesty performed these feats before the eyes of the whole land." A text found at Luxor states that the pharaoh not only challenged his soldiers to a shooting match, but also offered prizes to the winners. A stela (a usually carved or inscribed stone slab or pillar used for commemorative purposes) from Giza notes the sporting achievements of Amenophis II as he aimed at four targets of copper that had been set up at distances of twenty ells (an ell was the length of an arm and thus the perfect length for an arrow shaft).

However, sports Egyptologist Wolfgang Decker has argued that we should interpret such shooting records as mythological statements rather than as actual facts.

We also find the motif of the king hunting with bow and arrow in a two-wheeled chariot in ancient Mesopotamia, where ninth- and seventh-century BCE reliefs depict King Asshurnasirpal performing his hunting skills before spectators.

The ancient Greek Homer's epic poems, the *Iliad* and the *Odyssey,* also describe archery contests. A series of funeral games was organized to honor the Greek hero Patroclus, whom Hector had killed during the siege of Troy. For the archery contest Achilles had a ship's mast set up in the sandy soil, with a pigeon tied to it by a ribbon. Two entrants drew lots from a helmet, and Teucrus won first shot. His arrow hit the ribbon, and the pigeon flew away. The second entrant, Meriones, took the bow from Teucrus and aimed at the pigeon as it circled in the clouds. His arrow struck the pigeon, pierced its body, and came to earth with its tip buried in the ground at Meriones's feet. He won ten double axes, and Teucrus won ten ordinary axes. This scene from the *Iliad* presages popinjay shooting, which was an event of the Olympic Games in 1900 and 1920.

A story from the *Odyssey* tells of the archery skills of Odysseus. When he returned home after an absence of twenty years, he found his wife, Penelope, besieged by a hundred suitors, who were eating and drinking at his expense. His bow had been idle for twenty years. Penelope had declared that she would choose as her husband the man who was able to string the bow and shoot an arrow at a target through the eyes of twelve ax heads set up in a row, just as Odysseus used to do. One by one the suitors tried the feat but could not even string the great bow. Then the bow was handed to Odysseus, who was disguised as a beggar. He strung the bow and shot an arrow through the eyes of all the axes to the target. Then he revealed himself, took aim at Penelope's suitors, and struck them down one by one.

Roman soldiers were skilled with the bow and arrow, but they were more skilled with the sword. Roman legionnaires, until the fifth century CE, shot their bows by drawing the bow string to the chest, instead of to the face, which gives the arrow more accuracy. However, faithful to their slogan, "Castris uti, non palaestra" (barracks are important, not the sports field), historical evidence does not show that the Romans practiced archery for pleasure. Ironically, about 300 CE Saint Sebastian was martyred by being pierced with arrows because of his Christian faith. He was a Roman officer of the Imperial Guard. He became the patron saint of many medieval archery guilds in Europe.

Arrows Shot Around the World

Archery was among the first sports for which people kept records. A Turkish inscription from the thirteenth century praises Sultan Mahmud Khan for a shot of 1,215 arrow lengths. A seventeenth-century miniature portrays archers on Istanbul's Place of Arrows, where shots of great length were recorded. Latham and Paterson (1970), Faris and Elmer (1945), and Klopsteg (1934 and 1947) have documented archery among the Saracens, Arabs, and Turks.

Just as the Hun king Attila had terrorized the eastern borders of Europe with his horsemen-archers during the fifth century, the Mongol conqueror Genghis Khan rode westward with his cavalry in the thirteenth century. The Mongols used powerful composite bows, and their archery tradition survives today in Mongolia, where champion archers are esteemed.

The traditional Japanese art of archery, *kyudo,* is a branch of Zen Buddhism in which the bow and arrow are used to achieve a spiritual goal via physical and mental discipline. The samurai warriors were not only expert swordsmen but also expert archers. They shot from a galloping horse, a practice still known today as *yabusame.* They also shot on foot with a 2-meter laminated bamboo bow *(yumi).* Allen Guttmann (2004) has pointed out that "rationalization" of archery occurred in Japan as early as the tenth century through the transition from mimetic targets to abstract targets with concentric rings. A gallery in an ancient temple in Kyoto served as a shooting range in the so-called Oyakazu contest, which took place between 1606 and 1842. In this contest for twenty-four hours archers shot a maximum number of arrows through an aperture of 4.5 meters without touching the walls of the gallery. Interest in this contest declined drastically after 1686, when an archer scored 8,132 successes with 13,053 arrows and people thought his record impossible to break. This incident shows that the seventeenth-century Japanese understood the concept of the quantified sports record.

Archery is still used in Africa for hunting by isolated groups such as the Khoikhoi in the Kalahari Desert and the Pygmy in the rain forests, who use small bows and poisoned arrowheads. Arrow shooting for distance was practiced in the former kingdoms of Rwanda and Urundi, where participants determined the score by stepping the distance covered. Distances of up to 200 meters were mentioned. The young Intore warriors of Rwanda started their training by shooting at a vertical stick from 30 meters. Later they shot at a shell placed in the V-shaped branch of a tree from a distance of 30 to 40 meters. Archery contests for nonutilitarian pur-

Popinjay shooting in Flanders, Belgium, in 1981. *Source: Sport Museum Flanders.*

poses have not been recorded, except for children's play activities. Archery appears frequently as a children's game all over Africa.

Native Americans have long been associated with the bow and arrow. Types of bows and arrows varied widely among tribes. The Inuits of northern Alaska moved archery indoors during winter and used miniature bows and arrows to shoot at small wooden bird targets hung from the roof of the communal center. After the Spanish conquistadors introduced horses during the sixteenth century, Native American archers quickly adapted themselves to shooting from horseback. The artist George Catlin (1796–1872), who visited the Plains Native Americans during the mid-nineteenth century, painted a vivid scene of shooting for distance. Contests included shooting for accuracy at an arrow standing upright in the ground, at arrows arranged upright in a ring, at an arrow locked in a tree, at a suspended woven grass bundle, or at a roll of green cornhusks. Archers tried to have their first arrow remain in flight for as long as possible because the winner was the archer who could shoot the most arrows into the air before his first arrow hit the ground.

Archery is also widespread in South America, where competitions are usually contests of dexterity in which archers aim at a target (such as a doll, a ball, or fruits). Shooting for the longest distance is also common, especially in southern areas. A variation (for example, among the Yanomami of the Brazil-Venezuela border) is shooting blunt arrows at opponents who try to fend off the arrows.

Longbow Legacy of the English

The traditional English longbow holds a special position in the evolution of archery. The secret of the longbow lay in the properties of the yew tree *(Taxus baccata)*, which was cut in such a way that a layer of sapwood was left along the flattened back of the bow. The heartwood of yew withstands compression, whereas the sapwood of the yew is elastic; both woods return to their original straightness after the bow is loosed. People already had applied this combination in prehistoric times, as shown by Neolithic bows discovered in a peat bog in Somerset, England. Later the Saxons used bows only for hunting, not for warfare, because they considered only man-to-man combat with hand-held

A crossbow competition in Gubbio, Umbria, Italy, in May 1987.
Source: *Giuseppe Stuto, Sport Museum Flanders.*

tury to the sixteenth century all servants, laborers, yeomen, and other menfolk were required to have their own bows and to practice on Sundays and holy days. Target archery thus gradually lost its exclusive military nature and also became a social pastime.

Several acts to encourage archery were passed during the reign of King Henry VIII (1491–1547). One act ordered all physically fit men under the age of sixty, except for judges and clergymen, to practice shooting the longbow. During the Field of the Cloth of Gold Tournament in 1520, Henry VIII demonstrated his skill with the bow at the request of his great rival, King Francis I (1494–1547) of France. He also established and granted privileges to the Guild of St. George, an elite corps whose concern was "the science and feate of shootinge" with crossbow, longbow, and handgun.

Such firearms as the handgun made the bow obsolete, despite all the official encouragement and the publication of a treatise on archery, entitled *Toxophilus, the Schole of Shootinge*, in 1545. The author, Roger Ascham (1515–1568), an archer himself, pleaded for the retention of archery. Such a plea was, in itself, a sign of the decline of archery: "So shotinge is an exercyse of healthe, a pastyme of honest pleasure, and suche one also that stoppeth or auoydeth all noysome games gathered and increased by ill rull . . ." (Schroter 1983, 51).

Archery on the Continent

Many Frankish (relating to a Germanic tribal confederacy) knights had joined the First Crusade (1096–1099), motivated not only by religious zeal but also by adventure. During these expeditions to the Holy Land the knights became acquainted with a new weapon, the crossbow, a bow made by fastening a bow at right angles to a stock or tiller. The crossbow was so deadly that

weapons to be appropriate. This attitude would change, however, after the Norman invasion of England in 1066, when William the Conqueror used massed archery.

A better longbow, probably perfected by the Welsh, would make England a first-class military power. Folktales celebrated the lore of bow and arrow and featured such legendary archers as Robin Hood. Of particular importance in the spread of the English longbow was the victory in 1346 at the Battle of Crecy in France, where English archers routed the Genoese crossbowmen of the French army. The showers of arrows wounded the horses of the onrushing French knights, who were defeated. King Edward III's victorious army, which had been outnumbered by the enemy, consisted of thirteen thousand men, half of whom were archers. Even more notable was the English victory in the Battle of Agincourt in 1415, when King Henry V faced a French army five times as large as his five thousand archers and nine hundred men-at-arms. The yeoman archer became respected and feared and was imitated on the continent, where archers adopted the swift longbow side by side with the more precise but slower-to-load crossbow.

A government passed the first law concerning archery in the twelfth century; that law absolved an archer from charges of murder or manslaughter if he accidentally killed a man while practicing. From the thirteen cen-

A sportsman is a man who, every now and then, simply has to get out and kill something. ■ STEPHEN LEACOCK

it was forbidden to Christians by the second Lateran Council of 1139—another antiwar decree that has never been observed.

Elite troops had been established within the urban militias by the end of the thirteenth century; these were the guilds of the crossbowmen. The oldest records refer to the Saint George guilds of crossbowmen from the county of Flanders and the duchy of Brabant, such as those of Saint Omer, Ghent, Brussels, Ypres, Bruges, and Louvain, which were founded about 1300. During the Battle of the Golden Spurs in 1302, Flemish town militias killed six thousand members of French chivalry, who had stormed into battle as if to the joust. During the battle a French sally had been beaten off from Courtrai Castle by a company of crossbowmen from Ypres.

Inspired by the skill of the English longbowmen and their successes against the French in 1346 and 1415, on the continent several Saint Sebastian guilds of handbowmen arose, obtaining their charters and privileges during the fourteenth century. However, during the fifteenth century the invention of firearms diminished the military role of the crossbow and longbow guilds. Moreover, as a result of revolts by cities against centralized authority, many of the privileges of the cities were trimmed and their city walls and arms destroyed. The main pursuit of the archery guilds tended more and more toward representing the prestige of leading citizens. The guilds were unsurpassed in the organization of huge shooting festivities and banquets with plenty of food and drink. Although the guilds thus lost the character of training schools for the military, they maintained their traditional social status and political power.

Flanders, the Netherlands, and the Rhineland—in contrast to France and England—needed no legislative regulations to promote archery. On the contrary, rulers had difficulty in dealing with the many claims from villages, all requesting guild status for their archers. Peasants shot at butts (mounds of earth against which a shooting mark was placed) or at the popinjay (a wooden bird set on a high mast as a target).

Popinjay shooting remains popular in the northern (Flemish) part of France, in Belgium (mostly in Flanders but also in Wallonia), and in the Catholic southern provinces of the Netherlands. We can probably attribute this popularity to the fact that these regions were less affected by the drastic cultural changes of the Reformation and early industrialization.

A few cities in Italy keep alive their medieval crossbow traditions. During the yearly Palio della Balestra in Gubbio or San Marino, two rival societies of crossbowmen compete in medieval attire, accompanied by their drum corps and flag wavers.

Numerous *Schutzen* (rifle clubs) in Austria, Germany, and Switzerland originated as archery guilds. They have maintained a martial character, bringing together marksmen equipped with sophisticated firearms in local rifle associations.

Toxophilites and Revival

The Toxophilite Society of London, established in 1781 for the practice of archery as a sport, triggered the revival of archery at the end of the eighteenth century and influenced most of the later societies. At that time the form of archery varied from society to society, but rules for scoring, the number of arrows to be shot, and the distances to be shot would slowly evolve as people attempted to standardize the sport. Archers used targets with concentric rings in England as early as 1673. This practice can be seen as the beginning of "rationalization" of archery, one of the seven characteristics of modern sports, according to Guttmann.

Thomas Waring, who had inspired Sir Ashton Lever to form the Toxophilites, played a major role in this rationalization. Archery, which until then had been associated with the lower classes, was now rapidly adopted by the wealthy "leisure class." Archery tournaments were held on the grounds of fine country houses and drew large crowds. In 1787 the Royal British Bowmen was the first society to admit women as shooting members. Archery thus became an arena of fashion, elegance, and coquetry. *The Sporting Magazine* of November 1792 expressed the wish to "see the time when it can be said 'it is a reproach to be unskilful with the bow.'" The British prince regent's patronage of archery also contributed to its revival, which extended to Scotland. When King George IV visited Scotland in 1822, the Royal Company of Archers, founded in 1676 in Edinburgh, was given the honor of acting as royal bodyguard. Two members of this elite group fought a duel with bows and arrows in 1791. Although each man shot three arrows at the other "at point blank" range, neither man was injured.

In 1844 the first Grand National Meeting was held at York, England. Contestants shot a "York round," which consisted of shooting seventy-two arrows at 91 meters, forty-eight at 73 meters, and twenty-four at 55 meters. The championship of Great Britain is still based on these rules, decided upon by the Archers of the United Kingdom, assembled in 1844 on the Knavesmire race course near York. The circles on the targets were scored as follows: gold, nine; red, seven; blue, five; black, three; and white, one. Heath has attributed this innovation to the prince of Wales. In 1845 women competed for the first time in the second Grand National Meeting, although some women had already been members of various societies. Such meetings were still restricted to the Victorian upper classes, and the best newspapers reported the sport in their society columns. Victoria herself, before her accession to the throne, had not only been a patron of the Queen's Royal St. Leonard's Archers, but also had shot with them.

The archery tradition of England spread to the United States, where the first club was established in 1828 on the banks of the Schuylkill River in Pennsylvania. The United Bowmen of Philadelphia was a semi-secret society whose members adopted cryptic names. Members ordered a complete set of archery tackle from Thomas Waring Jr. in London, which they then copied.

The Civil War (1861–1865) was partly responsible for the renewed interest in archery in the United States. After the war men who had fought in the Confederate army were no longer allowed to use firearms. Two war veterans, the brothers William (1846–1918) and Maurice (1844–1901) Thompson, spent the time from 1866 to 1868 in the wilderness of Georgia's swamps and Florida's Everglades, living for the most part on the game they killed with bow and arrow. Maurice Thompson's book *The Witchery of Archery,* published in 1878, described their love of the sport. The book was widely read, and interest in archery spread. U.S. archery tackle had improved and was at least as good as that of the English. The National Archery Association was established and held its first championship meeting in Chicago in 1879. William Thompson won and repeated this victory in the next five tournaments. However, archery declined almost as quickly as it had spread. People in the United States sought their thrills in other fashionable outdoor sports such as tennis, baseball, rowing, and golf.

Archery also spread to the British colonies. In Australia, for example, archery was one of the few socially acceptable competitive sports for women and with tennis was organized in mixed clubs.

Precarious Olympic History

Archery originally was included in the Olympic Games only at the request of the national archery association of the host country. International rules did not exist; the rules of the host country were used. Archery first appeared during the 1900 games in Paris. Archery consisted of horizontal target shooting (*tir au berceau*), with the crossbow and with the handbow, and vertical popinjay shooting (*tir à la perche*) with the handbow. The crossbow contests were held at 35, 28, and 20 meters. The horizontal handbow contests, held at 50 and 33 meters, had two events: shooting at the large target (*au cordon doré*) and at the small target (*au chapelet*). Popinjay shooting was practiced at a 28-meter-tall mast. All medals were shared among French and Belgian entrants. Hubert Van Innis (1866–1961) from Belgium won two gold medals in the 33-meter target events and one silver medal in the 50-meter target *au cordon doré.*

During the 1904 Olympics women participated for the first time in archery. All competitors—men and women—were from the United States. The men shot the double York round (55, 46, and 37 meters) and the

**Ituri forest people from the Congo
with bows and bracers, c. 1990.**

Source: Pierre Cognie, Sport Museum Flanders.

double American round individually (55, 45, and 36 meters) and in teams (55 meters). The U.S. archery pioneer William Thompson won two bronze individual medals and one team gold medal as a member of the winning Potomac Archers from Washington, D.C. Among the women Mrs. M. C. Howell won three gold medals: in the double national round (55 and 45 meters), in the double Columbia round individually (45, 36, and 27 meters), and in teams (55, 45, and 44 meters) as member of the Cincinnati Archery Club. During the Olympics' so-called Anthropological Days, U.S. archers competed against a number of "savages" from different parts of the globe. Whereas the white U.S. contestants placed practically all their arrows at the 1.2-meter square target board at 36 meters, the "savages" hardly hit the target at all. This carnivalistic contest with racist undertones upset Olympics organizer Pierre de Coubertin of France, who had not been present and who called it a vulgar experiment not to be repeated.

For the 1908 Olympics in London, the Grand National Archery Society and the Royal Toxophilite Society joined to organize three days of shooting in the new stadium at Shepherd's Bush, England. They drew up clear rules of competition, including a regard for courtesy. For example, one rule stated: "Gentlemen will not be allowed to smoke at the ladies' targets." The competing teams consisted of twenty-five women and fifteen men from Britain, eleven men from France, and one man from the United States. British archers won gold and silver in the York round, but Henry B. Richardson, the U.S. champion, won the bronze medal. The only women competitors were British. French archers won all medals in the continental style (50 meters).

Archery next appeared in the Olympics in 1920 in Antwerp, Belgium. Archery was Belgium's national sport, but it was rather idiosyncratic. Hence, the Royal Toxophilite Society of England decided not to enter the competition because the rules restricted archery to popinjay shooting and to target shooting at "uncommon" distances. Only archers from Belgium, France, and the Netherlands took part. No women's events

were held. Popinjay shooting was practiced at a 31-meter-tall mast both in teams (six archers plus two reserves) and individually. Target archery contests were organized at 28 meters with a target of 60 centimeters, at 33 meters with a target of 72 centimeters, and at 50 meters with a target of 120 centimeters. Archers from Belgium won practically all the gold medals. After having already won three medals in Paris twenty years before, Hubert Van Innis of Belgium won three more gold and two more silver medals, making him the greatest archery *olympionike* ("Olympic champion" in Greek) in history. Archery then disappeared from the Olympics for more than fifty years, probably because of the lack of an international governing body. In 1931 the Federation Internationale de Tir a l'Arc (FITA) was founded at Lwow, Poland, with representatives from Poland, Belgium, France, and Sweden. This founding began a new era in international archery. FITA rules and regulations were internationally adopted. One year later the United Kingdom joined FITA. Under the leadership of

A typical archery lineup at a modern competition.

Oscar Kessels of Belgium (1957–1961) and Mrs. Inger K. Frith of Great Britain (1962–1977), archery was voted back into the Olympic Games in 1968.

FITA rules were recognized throughout the world. In the single FITA round, competitors shoot six sets of six arrows from distances of 90, 70, 50, and 30 meters. Women's rounds have distances of 70, 60, 50, and 30 meters. In Olympic competitions athletes shoot a double round, which comprises seventy-two arrows at the same distances. During the 1972 Olympics in Munich, Germany, two U.S. athletes—John Williams and Wilber Doreen—won gold medals in the men's double FITA and the women's double, respectively. Both established Olympic and world records.

The 1976 Olympics in Montreal, Canada, featured men and women archers from twenty-five countries. At the boycotted games of 1980 in Moscow and 1984 in Los Angeles, archery was represented but without splendor. At the 1988 games in Seoul, South Korea, the South Koreans dominated the team and the women's competitions. South Korean women dominated the individual and team competitions at the 1992 games in Barcelona, Spain, the 1996 games in Atlanta, Georgia, the 2000 games in Sydney, Australia, and the 2004 games in Athens, Greece. Among the men Simon Fairweather of Australia won gold in Sydney, and Marco Galiazzo of Italy won gold in Athens in the individual events; the Korean men won the team events in both Olympics.

Variations on a Theme

Archery lends itself to a variety of forms. For example, shooting from a wheelchair has become a standard sport practiced by many paraplegic persons, introduced in 1948 by Frank L. Bilson (1902–1980) at Stoke Mandeville in England. An alternative to formal target archery is field shooting, based on conditions that might be encountered in hunting. Oddly enough, this

*Desire is the most important factor in the success
of any athlete.* ■ WILLIE SHOEMAKER

more "natural" type of archery has also become standardized and is practiced either as the field round or as the hunters round. In both forms archers shoot fifty-six arrows from fourteen shooting positions, but in the first form at specified ranges and in the second form at unknown ranges.

Flight shooting, or shooting for maximum distance, is a reminder of the form that was developed by the Turks and was an honored pastime of the sultans. It has modern versions both in the United States and in Great Britain. Distances of more than 1,100 meters have been recorded.

In clout shooting archers shoot arrows with a high trajectory to fall into a target zone, marked by circles on the ground. A few traditionalist societies in England and Scotland still practice this form.

International crossbow shooting is regulated by the Union Internationale de Tir à l'Arbalète (UIA, www. arbalete.org). The UIA was founded in 1956 and has its headquarters in Switzerland, the land of the legendary William Tell. The first Crossbow World Championship was held in 1979 after eleven European championships had been held. Several variations exist both in terms of traditional crossbow types (for example, the bullet crossbow, still used in Belgium) and in terms of the targets (for example, popinjay shooting with the crossbow). Archers practice popinjay shooting not only at a tall mast, from which they must shoot down feathered "birds," but also horizontally in lanes, especially in Belgium.

Roland Renson

Further Reading

Acker, W. R. B. (1965). *Japanese archery.* Rutland, VT: Tuttle.

Brasch, R. (1972). *How did sports begin?* London: Longman.

Burke, E. H. (1957). *The history of archery.* New York: William Morrow.

Culin, S. (1907). *Games of the North American Indians.* Washington, DC: U.S. Government Printing Office.

Decker, W. (1990). The record of the ritual: The athletic records of ancient Egypt. In J. Carter & A. Kruger (Eds.), *Ritual and record* (pp. 21–30). New York: Greenwood Press.

De Vroede, E. (1996). Popinjay shooting in Flanders. In G. Pfister, T. Niewerth, & G. Steins (Eds.), *Spiele der Welt im Spannungsfeld von Tradition und Moderne* (Vol. 1, pp. 157–163.). Saint Augustin, Germany: Academia Verlag.

Dubay, P. (1978). *Arc et arbalète.* Paris: Albin Michel.

Faris, N., & Elmer, R. P. (1945). *Arab archery.* Princeton, NJ: Princeton University Press.

Frazer, J. G. (1890). *The golden bough: A study of magic and religion.* London: Macmillan.

Gasuku, J. (1989). L'Histoire de l'Education Physique et Sportive au Burundi d'avant la Colonisation jusqu'aujourd'hui. In H. Uberhorst (Ed.), *Geschichte der Leibesubungen: Band 6* (pp. 420–429). Berlin, Germany: Bartels & Wernitz.

Guttmann, A. (1978). *From ritual to record.* New York: Columbia University Press.

Guttmann, A. (2004). Targeting modernity: Archery and the modernization of Japan. *Sport History Review, 35,* 2031.

Habashi, Z. (1976). King Tutankhamun, sportsman in antiquity. In P. P. De Nayer, M. Ostyn, & R. Renson (Eds.), *The history, the evolution and diffusion of sports and games in different cultures* (pp. 71–83). Brussels, Belgium: BLOSO.

Hardy, R. (1976). *The longbow.* Cambridge, UK: Patrick Stephens.

Heath, E. G. (1973). *A history of target archery.* Newton Abbot, UK: David & Charles.

Herrigel, E. (1953). *Zen in the art of archery* (R. F. C. Hull, Trans.). New York: Pantheon.

Klopsteg, P. E. (1947). *Turkish archery and the composite bow* (2nd ed.). Evanston, IL: Author.

Lake, F., & Wright, H. (1974). *A bibliography of archery.* Manchester, UK: Manchester Museum.

Latham, J. D., & Paterson, W. F. (1970). *Saracen archery.* London: Holland Press.

Michaelis, H.-T. (1985). *Schutzengilden.* Munich, Germany: Keyser.

Ndejuru, A. (1989). Les Bases de l'Education et de l'Activite Physiques dans la Societe Traditionnelle Rwandaise. In H. Uberhorst (Ed.), *Geschichte der Leibesubungen: Band 6* (pp. 430–453). Berlin, Germany: Bartels & Wernitz.

Olivova, V. (1984). *Sports and games in the ancient world.* New York: St. Martin's Press.

Paterson, W. F. (1984). *Encyclopaedia of archery.* New York: St. Martin's Press.

Payne-Gallwey, R. (1903). *The cross-bow.* London: Longman.

Renson, R. (1976). The Flemish archery gilds: From defense mechanisms to sports institutions. In P. P. De Nayer, M. Ostyn, & R. Renson (Eds.), *The history, the evolution and diffusion of sports and games in different cultures* (pp. 135–159). Brussels, Belgium: BLOSO.

Renson, R. (1977). Play in exile: The continental pastimes of King Charles II (1630–1685). In *HISPA VIth International Congress* (pp. 508–522). Dartford, UK: Dartford College of Education.

Scheerder, J., & Renson, R. (1998). *Annotated bibliography of traditional play and games in Africa.* Berlin, Germany: International Council of Sport Science and Physical Education.

Schroter, H. (1983). *Roger Ascham, toxophilus: The schole of shootinge, London 1545.* Saint Augustin, Germany: Richarz.

Sollier, A., & Gyobiro, Z. (1969). *Japanese archery: Zen is action.* New York: Walker/Weatherhill.

Stamp, D. (1971). *The challenge of archery.* London: Adam & Charles Black.

Stein, H. (1925). *Archers d'autrefois; archers d'aujourd'hui.* Paris: Longuet.

Stein, H. J. (1985). *Die Kunst des Bogenschiessens: Kyuodo.* Bern, Switzerland: Scherz.

Van Mele, V., & Renson, R. (1992). *Traditional games in South America.* Schorndorf, Germany: Hofmann.

Weiler, I. (1981). *Der Sport bei den Volkern der alten Welt.* Darmstadt, Germany: Wissenschaftliche Buchgesellschaft.

Argentina

Argentina is the second largest country in South America, lying east of Chile in the "Southern Cone." Its other boundaries are with Brazil, Uruguay, Paraguay, Bolivia, and the Atlantic Ocean. The capital and largest city, Buenos Aires, is located in the northeast on an Atlantic estuary called Río de la Plata. Other major cities include Rosario and Córdoba (each with more than one million people). The national population in 2002 was 37,944,000.

History

By the early seventeenth century, a variety of sports existed in colonial Argentina. *El Pato* was played in extensive open spaces and involved one horsemen carrying the stuffed carcass of a duck and other riders who tried to grab the duck away and retain it. The modern version of the game employs an inflated ball outfitted with grabbing handles. Another traditional game from the same period is *las bochas*, a type of bowling game that today has its own national federation. Unlike some other Latin American countries where bullfighting survived to the present, Argentina prohibits it. Horse racing is a traditional Argentinean sport; over thirty tracks exist today.

British visitors and immigrants were largely responsible for the introduction of modern sports in Argentina. Much of the sport development in the late nineteenth and early twentieth centuries took place in private clubs, such as the Buenos Aires Lawn Tennis Club. The first club, the Buenos Aires Football Club, which later became the Buenos Aires Cricket & Rugby Club, was established in 1864. A second club, Rosario Athletic, was established in 1867.

Participant and Spectator Sports

Argentina is best known for its professional soccer league (which includes teams such as Independiente, River Plate, Estudiantes, Racing Club, and Boca Juniors) and the international successes of its national team. Soccer was introduced in Argentina in the second half of the nineteenth century by British residents, who formed the first league in 1891 and whose clubs dominated play until 1912. Early soccer success came with runner-up finishes in the Olympics of 1928 and the first World Cup in 1930. Argentina was the host nation and winner of the World Cup in 1978 (during the military dictatorship), winner in 1986 in Mexico City, and runner-up again in 1990. Argentina was the favorite in the 2002 World Cup but did not survive the first round. Through 2004 Argentinean soccer clubs had won the most (twenty) of the forty-four editions of the Copa Libertadores de América. Diego Maradona is perhaps the most famous player in recent Argentinean soccer.

Rugby teams composed of Britons played their first match in Argentina in 1873. In 1899 the River Plate Rugby Championship was founded (becoming the Unión Argentina de Rugby in 1951), and the first rugby club consisting of native Argentineans was formed in 1904. A visiting British team played in Argentina in 1910, the first of many international matches with visitors. The first Provincial Championship was held in 1945, and in 1951 the governing body organized a South American championship.

From 1965 onward, the national representative team, using the names Los Pumas, Jaguars, and Sudamérica, played and won many international matches (including the World Cup) at home and in South Africa, Europe, Australia, and New Zealand. The junior team, Los Pumitas, won the FIRA (Rugby Federation) championships in 1987, 1989, 1990, 1991, 1993, and 1997 (held in Buenos Aires). Argentina finished second in the

sional basketball player is Emanuel "Manu" Ginobili, star of the NBA's San Antonio Spurs.

Along with the many Argentinean Pan American and Olympic Games medalists in boxing, there was the powerful Argentinean professional heavyweight Luis Angel Firpo, who was known internationally in the 1920s. In a famous match with world champion Jack Dempsey in 1923, Firpo knocked Dempsey completely out of the ring. However, Dempsey was pushed back into the ring by fans and won the match. That same year Firpo defeated the American former world champion, Jess Willard.

World University Championships in 1988 and third in 1992. In 1995 Los Pumas won the first Pan American championship and were runners-up in the first Copa Latina, losing to France. When Argentina hosted the third Rugby World Cup sevens in Mar del Plata in 2001, Los Pumas ended in third place after losing to New Zealand in the semifinals. In 2002 Los Pumas won the South American Championship, undefeated.

Polo is one of the sports most closely associated with Argentina. Argentina has had outstanding performances in polo, including gold medals in the first Pan American Games and the 1924 and 1936 Olympics. The Argentinean Polo Association oversees the sport, and there are a large number of local clubs.

Juan Manuel Fangio began racing cars as a teenager in 1929. He competed in many long distance road races in South America, and, sponsored by the government, he began racing in the European circuit after World War II. Beginning in 1951, he won five major titles, including two World Championships and the German Grand Prix. He retired from racing in 1958.

Distinguished Argentineans in professional tennis have included Guillermo Vilas, Gabriela Sabatini, and Paola Suárez (U.S. Open women's doubles champion in 2003 and 2004). The best-known Argentinean profes-

SOUTH AMERICAN GAMES

In 1922 Argentina participated in athletic games in Rio de Janeiro, which were part of Brazil's celebration of independence. The movement for the establishment of a South American Sport Organization began in Argentina's Olympic Committee in 1976, but it lacked government support and eventually Bolivia assumed responsibility for holding the first Congress and the first Games. However, Argentina has participated in all editions of the series of South American Games that began in 1978 (first called Southern Cross Games), and, beginning with the third Games in Chile in 1986, Argentina has been the leader in the number of gold and total medals won. Rosario, Argentina, hosted the second Games in 1982.

Between 1978 and 2002, Argentina won South American Games gold medals in track and field, archery, boxing, bowling, canoeing, cycling, equestrian, fencing, gymnastics, judo, karate, racquetball, roller skating, rowing, shooting, soccer, swimming, taekwondo, team handball, tennis, triathlon, volleyball,

Argentina

Key Events in Argentina Sport History

1864	The Buenos Aires Football club is founded.
1867	Rosario Athletic club is founded.
1891	The first soccer league is formed.
1904	The first rugby club consisting of native Argentineans is formed.
1923	Boxer Luis Angel Firpo knocks world champion Jack Dempsey out of the ring but loses the fight.
1923	The Argentina Olympic Committee is formed.
1924	Argentina participates in Olympics for the first time and wins the gold medal in polo.
1928	Argentina participates in the Winter Olympics for the first time.
1930	Argentina wins its first World Cup in soccer.
1936	Argentina wins the gold medal in polo at the Olympics. Swimmer Jeannette Campbell is the first Argentinian woman to compete in the Olympics.
1945	The first Provincial Championship in rugby is held.
1951	Juan Manuel Fangio wins the first of five major international auto racing titles.
1951	Argentina hosts the first Pan American Games in Buenos Aires.
1978	Argentina hosts and wins the World Cup.
1978	Argentina participates in the first South American Games.
1979	Argentina wins the Youth World Cup.
1990	Argentina hosts the only Pan American Winter Games.
1995	Argentina hosts the Pan American Maccabiah Games.
2004	Argentina wins eight medals, four of them gold, at the Olympics.

weight lifting, wrestling, and yachting, as well as other medals in baseball, basketball, golf, minisoccer, mountain biking, softball, synchronized swimming, and table tennis. In six South American Games from 1978 through 2002 (data is not available for 1982), Argentina won 526 gold, 389 silver, and 353 bronze medals.

PAN AMERICAN GAMES

Preliminary planning for future Pan American Games began in meetings held during the 1932 and 1936 Olympics. Argentinean athletes took part in an Inter-American competition in Dallas, Texas, in 1937, and Argentina took a leading role in promoting a Western Hemisphere sport festival whose first host would be Buenos Aires. After delays due to World War II, Argentina held the first Pan American Games in 1951 (in Buenos Aires) and was host again in 1995 (in Mar del Plata), and has participated in all editions of this sport festival. In the initial games, the host nation won the most gold (64) and total (146) medals, including seven track and field events, all boxing categories, all-but-one cycling event, two equestrian events, several fencing and gymnastics events (men only in both), polo, all rowing events, eleven shooting events, soccer, four men's and women's swimming events, four tennis events, water polo, four wrestling categories, and one yachting event.

Argentina Olympics Results
2004 Summer Olympics: 2 Gold, 4 Bronze

In future games, Argentinean athletes participated in many Pan American sports, winning gold medals in men's and women's track and field (women's pole vault in 1999), men's basketball (1995), boxing, men's cycling, fencing (men), men's and women's field hockey, men's artistic gymnastics, rhythmic gymnastics, men's judo, men's karate, men's kayak, men's roller skating (including hockey on skates), women's roller skating (five of six gold in 1979 and six of seven in 1991), men's and women's rowing, men's and women's shooting, soccer (1955, 1959, 1971, 1995, and 2003), men's and women's swimming and tennis, men's and women's taekwondo, men's triathlon, men's volleyball (1995), water polo, weight lifting, wrestling, women's sambo wrestling (1983), and men's and women's yachting. Argentina was in fourth place overall for gold (232) and for total medals (796) won in Pan American Games from 1951 to 1999.

After its introduction as a men-only sport, Argentina won four consecutive Pan American Games titles in field hockey (1967–1979), winning again in 1991 and 1995, and taking silver in 1983, 1987, and 1999, and bronze in 2003. Argentina began winning Pan American Games women's field hockey with its introduction in 1987 and it won again in 1991, 1995, and 1999, and took silver in 2003. Argentina was South American Games men's field hockey champion in 2003. Men's teams participated in Olympic Games in 1972, 1976, 1988, 1992, 2000, and 2004, and women's teams participated in 1988, 2000 (silver), and 2004 (bronze).

Argentina has participated extensively in the Pan American Paralympics since the first Games were held in Mexico in 1999. Argentina hosted the only Pan American Winter Games, which were held in 1990 in the Mountain Sport Center at Las Leñas (in Mendoza Province), and the Pan American Maccabiah Games in 1995.

OLYMPIC GAMES

Argentina's first Olympic participation came with ninety-three men in Paris in 1924, who won polo, second place in triple jump (men only) and two boxing categories, and third place in two boxing categories. Other athletes competed in track and field, cycling, fencing, rowing, shooting, swimming, tennis, weight lifting, and yachting. Argentinean men won gold (in boxing, swimming, and marathon) and other medals (in boxing, fencing, and soccer) in all-male delegations in 1928 and 1932. The nation's first female Olympian was swimmer Jeannette Campbell, who won a silver medal in 1936. From 1936 through 2004, Argentinean athletes participated in and won medals in many Olympic sports, including gold medals in men's basketball (2004), boxing, marathon (Delfo Cabrera), polo, men's rowing, men's soccer (2004), and the men's exhibition sports of pelota and hockey on skates (1992). The nation did not send a delegation to the 1980 Olympics in Moscow.

Argentina's first participation in the Winter Olympic Games was in 1928 in St. Moritz, Switzerland (two bobsled teams). Since then, the nation has entered all Winter Games except for 1932, 1936, and 1956, competing in Alpine skiing all years, bobsled in 1928, 1948, 1952, and 1964, luge in 1964 and 1968, and Nordic skiing and biathlon in 1984 and 1988. Argentinean participation increased significantly in 1992, with competition in Alpine, Nordic, and freestyle skiing, biathlon, luge, and figure and speed skating.

From 1924 to 1952, Argentina was the Latin American country with most success in the Olympic Games, winning thirteen gold (seven of them in boxing) and thirty-six total medals. An Argentinean was a member of the first International Olympic Committee (IOC) and others have followed in this role. The nation currently has one member on the IOC, Antonio Rodríguez, who was elected in 1990.

Women and Sport

Argentinean women participated in Pan American Games from the beginning, and over time they increased their numbers and the number of sports they played. However, the nation was late adding women to its Olympic delegations—the first was Jeannette Campbell, who won a silver medal in swimming in 1936.

Trekking in North Patagonia, Batea Mahuida. *Source: istockphoto.com/laurag.*

Gabriela Sabatini, a professional and Olympic tennis player, is one of the most famous Argentinean women in sport. Currently, Paola Suárez is prominent in doubles tennis, having won the U.S. Open in 2003 and 2004. Roller skater Nora Alicia Vega won five world titles, eight Pan American Games medals, ten South American Championships, and fifty national tournaments. Argentinean women's field hockey teams won Pan American Games gold four times through 1999 and an Olympic bronze medal in 2004. Argentina's eighteen Olympic flag bearers between 1924 and 2004 have included five women (Isabel Avellán, swimmer, 1956; Cristina Hardekopf, diver and only female athlete, 1960; Jeannette Campbell, swimmer, 1964; Gabriela Sabatini, tennis, 1988; and Carolina Mariani, judo, 1996).

Argentina has a Commission for Women and Sport. A few young women are taking up the previously male-dominated sports of car racing, soccer, boxing, weight lifting, and polo.

Youth Sports

Young people are involved extensively in sport and there are age-group leagues and junior international competitions in sports such as soccer and rugby.

Organizations

The Argentinean National Olympic Committee, which was established 1923, maintains a comprehensive and useful website (http://www.coarg.org.ar/). Argentinean sport is organized into fifty-nine national associations, federations, and confederations under the Olympic committee. These organizations correspond to the mainstream international summer Olympic sports as well as to others, such as subaquatic activities, chess, billiards, bobsled and skeleton, *bochas,* bowling, boxing, bridge, netball, *colombófila* (pigeon racing), orienteering, military sport, sport law, water skiing, *faustball* (similar to volleyball but the ball may bounce between each of three hits per side), sport medicine, sport motorcycling, special Olympics, parachuting, *pelota vasca,* skiing and mountain climbing, and squash. The Secretaría de Deporte y Recreación is the principal government agency responsible for overseeing sport activities.

Sports in Society

Argentinean soccer is so popular that it inspires neighborhood, club, provincial, and national spirit, and, unfortunately, often produces violence among fans, especially since the restoration of democratic government in 1983. Soccer has had many connections with Argentinean politics at all levels. The directors of local clubs are elected by their memberships, and party politics commonly play a role in these elections. The president of the Argentinean Football Association (AFA) is usually linked to politics, and the federal government has a history of getting involved in soccer affairs.

National president Juan Perón (1946–1955) used sport to build national spirit and gain support for his government. His government strengthened sport, and the AFA in turn backed Perón in his presidential campaigns. Perón's popular wife, Eva, promoted participation in sport (including the Evita Youth Championships) as a means of improving young people's health. Some of the closest connections between soccer and politics occurred during the military dictatorship between 1976 and 1983. The generals wanted good publicity for the 1978 World Cup Finals in Argentina. In an effort to please their own people and impress the visitors, the government spent great amounts of money on infrastructure related to holding the Cup matches, and the (usually violent) neighborhood fan groups were convinced that they should show good manners. Argentina's World Cup victory in 1978 (as well as their Youth World Cup win in 1979) brought glory to the government and helped cover up the brutal repression it was carrying out during this period.

The Future

Argentina's long tradition in sport shows no sign of weakening in the future. The nation continues to maintain interest in centuries-old activities inherited from the colonial period and to participate in a wide spectrum of modern sports; it also seeks opportunities for hosting major international events. For over a half-century women have been increasing their participation in Argentinean sport. The nation experienced diminished Olympic success during the period from 1956 to 2000 (a total of seven silver and seven bronze medals in this period; no medals at all in 1976, 1984, and 2000), but the 2004 Games produced four gold and eight total medals, which perhaps indicates a positive future trend for Argentina in the Olympic Games. The nation's international prominence in soccer should continue, and it will probably increase its presence in rugby, men's basketball and volleyball, and other sports.

Richard V. McGehee

Further Reading

Arbena, J. L. (1990). Generals and *goles*: Assessing the connection between the military and soccer in Argentina. *The International Journal of the History of Sport, 7*(1), 120–130.

Arbena, J. L. (2002). In search of the Latin American female athlete. In J. L. Arbena and D. G. La France (Eds.), *Sport in Latin America and the Caribbean* (pp. 219–232). Wilmington, DE: Scholarly Resources.

Archetti, E. P. (1992). Argentinian football: A ritual of violence? *The International Journal of the History of Sport, 9*(2), 209–235.

Duke, V., & Crolley, L. (2002). *Fútbol*, politicians and the people: Populism and politics in Argentina. In J. A. Mangan and L. P. DaCosta (Eds.), *Sport in Latin American society: Past and present* (pp. 93–116). London: Frank Cass.

Galeano, E. (1998). *Soccer in sun and shadow*. New York: Verso.

Mason, T. (1995). *Passion of the people? Football in South America*. New York: Verso.

Morelli, L. (1990). *Mujeres deportistas* [Women Athletes]. Buenos Aires, Argentina: Editorial Planeta.

Moss, S., & Nye, D. (1991). *Fangio: A Pirelli album*. London: Pavilion Books.

Torres, C. R. (2002). Tribulations and achievements: The early history of Olympism in Argentina. In J. A. Mangan & L. P. DaCosta (Eds.), *Sport in Latin American society: Past and present* (pp. 59–92). London: Frank Cass.

Try and fail is the manner of losers; try and learn is the way of the strong. ■ ANONYMOUS

Arm Wrestling

Arm wrestling, a variation of the basic sport of wrestling, is a contest of willpower and strength between two contestants who face each other across a table or other flat surface. Each contestant places one elbow on the flat surface, holding his or her forearm upright at a V-shaped angle, and grips the opponent's hand with knuckles facing out. When the match begins, each contestant presses in an arc toward the flat surface, attempting to force the opponent's forearm, wrist, and hand to the surface beneath.

Wrist wrestling is a form of arm wrestling. Although people occasionally use the terms interchangeably, *wrist wrestling* refers to a technique in which opponents grip each other's unused arm across the flat surface. In contrast, *arm wrestling* refers to a technique in which opponents grip a peg or other object with their free hand or keep their free hand loose. Wrist wrestling is a less common sport.

Origins

Although no extensive documentation of arm wrestling in early history exists, scholars generally believe that people in ancient societies engaged in arm wrestling as a specialized form of wrestling. Scholars usually trace today's arm wrestling to indigenous people in North America, where it was adopted by later Anglo settlers. One traditional term for the sport, *Indian wrestling,* refers to these origins.

Arm-wrestling tournaments have long been conducted at fairs, taverns, and other social settings. Since the 1960s arm wrestling has become an international organized sport, with many tournaments and dedicated participants and fans. This modern arm-wrestling movement was originally most active in California, Connecticut, Virginia, and Pennsylvania. It spread to other regions of North America and other nations. Arm wrestling is popular in many regions of North America but also in India, where it is called *"punjah,"* and na-

tional championships attract thousands of spectators. Arm wrestling has also become increasingly popular in Brazil, England, Russia, and other states of the former Soviet Union.

Contemporary arm wrestling reflects its varied history. Some aspects are colorful and emphasize belligerence and machismo. Other aspects are serious and emphasize technique and discipline. Young boys often arm wrestle each other to test their strength. Arm wrestling has also traditionally been associated with bars, workplaces, and situations in which physical strength is considered an important attribute.

People usually compete in arm wrestling on a friendly basis, but they may also compete for serious purposes. For example, people have used arm wrestling to express animosity, settle disputes physically, or compare strength without engaging in actual combat. Like most other sports, arm wrestling has also been a basis for gambling: Two wrestlers bet each other on a match, or spectators bet on the outcome.

The 1987 movie *Over the Top,* starring Sylvester Stallone as a competitive arm wrestler, gave the sport wider publicity, although some enthusiasts believe the movie reinforces unwanted stereotypes. The major goals of many contemporary proponents of arm wrestling are to change the sport's rough-and-tumble image and to increase appreciation of it as a serious sport. In 1988 organized arm wrestling gained major corporate backing when Heublein, a liquor company, began to sponsor the Yukon Jack World Arm-Wrestling Championships.

More than 100,000 men and women compete in organized arm wrestling. The sport has produced many top athletes, including John Brezek, Moe Baker, David Patten, Cleve Dean, and Dot Jones. Arm wrestlers have diverse personalities and wrestling styles. Some are flamboyant, with extravagant tattoos and costumes and outrageous nicknames. They growl, pound the table, or engage in other antics before a match. This behavior reflects a sense of showmanship but is also intended to intimidate opponents. Other arm wrestlers have more subdued personalities.

Although the number of organized tournaments with cash prizes has increased since the 1980s, arm wrestling remains primarily an amateur sport, and most arm wrestlers hold other jobs. Many tournaments do not award cash prizes, and even top wrestlers usually win only enough to cover expenses. Traveling arm wrestlers have earned an income by challenging people to matches for money.

Women Get a Grip

Although most people see arm wrestling as a masculine contest of strength, women became increasingly active in arm sports during the 1970s as competitors, promoters, and officials. Many of the women who originally participated in arm sports had the encouragement of male relatives who arm wrestled. Prominent early women competitors included Karyn Jubinville (who entered the sport in 1971 at age twelve), Kari Tremblay, Cindy Baker, and Dot Jones. In 1985 Jeanette Davis won the first annual Female Armwrestler of the Year Award from the American Armwrestling Association. Grace Ann Swift earned four world titles between 1987 and 1994. Chris Baliko was the world champion four times between 1993 and 1997. Karen Brisson Curavoo gained recognition when she proved that the sport is also suited to older athletes. She began wrestling at age fifteen in 1978 and won three world titles during the late 1970s and early 1980s. She retired to raise a family but then, during the 1990s, returned to competition.

Practice

An arm-wrestling match is called a "pull." When a pull begins, each contestant presses his or her arm and hand in a downward arc toward the flat surface. In right-hand matches contestants press in a counterclockwise direction; in left-hand matches contestants press in a clockwise direction. Contestants press in the same direction, but because they are facing each other their arms and hands press in opposite directions. A pull ends in a pin when one opponent forces and keeps the other's forearm, wrist, and hand down. Pulls are not

The New York City Arm Wrestler of the Year and Super Heavyweight Champion Dan Sorrese (left) from Deer Park, New York wins the Empire State's Strongest Arm MVP award over Light Heavyweight Champion Ed Safarian from Bayside, New York. The fierce 1½-minute battle of arms took place at the Empire State Building's Observatory in Manhattan. *Source: Gene Camp.*

timed, so their duration depends on the time required for a pin to occur. Often a pull lasts less than a minute, although it may last several minutes. *Flashing* is a term used to describe a contest in which one opponent pins the other especially quickly.

Arm wrestlers use strategies to hold themselves and use their muscles and energy. In wrist wrestling the physical position of contestants tends to focus on the overall use of the upper body. In standard arm wrestling contestants have more mobility and emphasize techniques that use shoulders, arms, and hands. Basic movements include the shoulder roll, in which a contestant exerts pressure from the shoulder and triceps; the hook and drag, which emphasizes the use of wrist and triceps to press the opponent's arm down; and the top roll, which focuses on bending the opponent's wrist. These movements have many variations.

Although strong, well-developed upper arms and shoulders give a wrestler an obvious advantage, well-developed tendons and ligaments in the forearm and hand are also important, and many successful competitors are small and wiry or of average size. In addition to physical strength, technical strategies and psychological attributes are vital to success. Arm wrestlers develop techniques to focus their mental energy and to gain a psychological advantage over opponents. A contestant must be determined and sometimes endure intense physical pain during a pull.

Sanctioned events have rules that govern how a match is conducted and judged. These rules prohibit movements or positions that give a contestant an unfair advantage or that might harm the opponent. Matches are refereed, and illegal movements, such as letting go of the peg or removing one foot from the floor, result in a foul. Rules may vary among sponsors, although many rules are consistent throughout the sport. For example, in tournaments contestants are often required to keep their shoulders squared and to grip each other's hands at the thumb with the first knuckle visible. Tournaments are generally organized by weight classes and gender so contestants will be well matched physically. Typical weight classes include those for contestants less than 75 kilograms, between 75 and 90 kilograms, and more than 90 kilograms. Official matches often take place on special tables equipped with gripping pegs, elbow pads, and a pinning mat.

Governing Bodies

Arm wrestling's largest sanctioning body is the World Armsport Federation (www.waf.homestead.com), based in Scranton, Pennsylvania. The federation coordinates regional and national affiliated organizations in more than seventy nations, including the American Arm-wrestling Association (www.armsport.com) and United States Armsports (www.armwrestling.com). Affiliates of the World Armsport Federation hold local and national competitions, with winners representing their countries at an annual world championship. The Yukon Jack tournaments are a separate, corporate-sponsored, World Armsport Federation-sanctioned series for prize money, with remaining proceeds donated to charity. Smaller independent arm-wrestling associations also sponsor tournaments. Some private entrepreneurs organize tournaments as business ventures. During the 1980s and 1990s enthusiasts also initiated a drive to have arm wrestling included in the Olympics.

John Townes

Further Reading

Berkow, I. (1995, August 26). Wrist wars on the waterfront. *New York Times*.

Jordan, P. (1987, November 2). In Florida: "Lock up!" and the pulse pounds. *Time*.

Junod, T. (1993, June 14). Arms and the man. *Sports Illustrated*.

Art

The incidence of sports images in art is directly related to the cultural importance of sports. When sports are considered central to the everyday lives of ordinary men and women, which was true in ancient Greece and is true, once again, in the modern world, sports figure prominently in art.

Ancient Images

Among the earliest images of sports are carved reliefs depicting royal hunters such as the Assyrian king Ashurbanipal (seventh century BCE), who appears on horseback, spearing an attacking lion. In addition to hunting, Amenophis III and other ancient Egyptian rulers practiced a form of archery designed to demonstrate their physical fitness. This, too, was documented in stone reliefs. The prowess of the pharaoh's soldiers can be inferred from the gamut of wrestling holds and throws portrayed on Egyptian tomb walls. A bronze-age Minoan fresco, discovered by Sir Arthur Evans in the Palace of Minos in Crete, shows young men (colored red) and young women (colored white) boldly gripping the horns and vaulting over the body of a charging bull. The significance of this ritual was probably religious rather than political. An apparently secular image of two juvenile boxers survived on the island of Thera.

Images of athletes proliferated in the art of ancient Greece—as bronze and marbles statues, on black-

In this drawing by George Catlin in 1852, Native Americans of the prairie are shown competing in archery. *Source: Sport Museum Flanders.*

figured and red-figured vases, and as terra-cotta statuettes. *The Discus Thrower* (by Myron), the *Charioteer* (by Lysippos), and the *Spear Carrier* (by Polykleitos) are probably as famous as the anonymous *Venus de Milo.* Olympic victors were commemorated by statues erected near the stadium. Thousands of athletes appeared on the vases that were filled with olive oil and presented to the victors of the Panathenaic Games. Vases also carried images of Atalanta, the mythic runner who lost her race when she bent to retrieve a triad of golden apples. (Atalanta also inspired Renaissance artists such as Peter Paul Rubens and Guido Reni and modern artists like Paul Manship.) We know that Greek girls actually ran races from literary sources and from a pair of statues (an archaic bronze figure and a Hellenistic marble statue that has survived in several Roman copies). These girls were probably engaged in sports with religious significance, perhaps the games celebrated at Olympia in honor of the goddess Hera.

The aura of the sacred disappeared in the athletic art of Roman times. Mosaics depicting gladiators at their bloody sport decorated public and private sites throughout the Roman world. Chariots clatter silently across many marble reliefs. The most famous sport-centered work from this time is a bronze statue of a battered boxer. As for women's sports, the fourth-century (CE) Bikini Mosaic from the Piazza Armerina in Sicily presents ten athletic girls whose "sportswear" prompted the mosaic's name.

Modern Sports Images

Medieval peasants played folk-football and wrestled, but artistic attention was deflected by class bias. *A Wrestling Match* (c. 1650), by the greatly undervalued Flemish artist Michael Sweerts, is among the rare paintings devoted to vernacular sports. (Most genre painters seem to have been enchanted by drinkers and dancers rather than by wrestlers.) From the middle of the fifteenth century, when an anonymous Italian painted *The Tournament in the Piazza Santa Croce*, to the late sixteenth century, when Jost Amman produced *The Tournament of Emperor Maximilian at Vienna* (1565), wealthy patrons commissioned the combats and colorful pageantry of the knightly tournament. Woodcuts by Albrecht Dürer and Lucas Cranach suggest that there was also a market for inexpensive images of knightly combat. When tournaments declined in favor, elegant fencers began to appear in drawings such as Willem Swanenburg's *The Fencing Hall* (1608), which carefully placed the human figures in geometrically defined space.

In Renaissance art, aristocratic women occasionally appeared as hunters. Francesco Primaticcio portrayed

A late-sixteenth-century depiction of a Persian polo match by an unknown artist.

reproduced images of the archery contests that were a favorite amusement of Japanese noblemen. In the nineteenth century, inexpensive woodblock prints depicting hugely muscled (and hugely popular) sumo wrestlers were ubiquitous. Throughout Asia, polo was immensely popular. In Tang dynasty China (618–907 CE) craftsmen produced countless terra-cotta statuettes of male and female players. Sixteenth- and seventeenth-century Persian and Indian painters often adorned manuscripts with precise miniature depictions of the game. Even more common in Islamic art were hunting scenes.

During the seventeenth and eighteenth centuries, horse races were a major theme of English sporting art (just as they were, a century later, in the art of Edgar Degas and his fellow Impressionists). Among the masterpieces of the genre were *Race Horses Exercising on the Downs* and *Gimcrack on Newmarket Heath,* both by George Stubbs. Hunting offered a splendid opportunity for artists to paint men, women, and horses. John Wootton's *The Death of the Stagg* (1737) and *Lady Henrietta Harley Hunting with Harriers* (c. 1740) were typical of the genre. Wooten's French counterparts produced some mangnificant achievements: for example, Jean-Baptiste-Siméon Chardin's after-the-hunt still-life renditions of pheasants and hares and Jean-Baptiste Oudry's *Louis XV Hunting Stag in the Forest of St. Germain* (1730).

English artists found cricket, played on picturesque village greens, irresistible. Among the finest depictions was an anonymous painting entitled simply *The Game of Cricket* (c. 1790). As early as 1763, cricket entered the realm of American colonial art in Benjamin West's group portrait, *The Cricketers,* in which five young gentlemen from Virginia and South Carolina proudly pose with their sports equipment. John Singleton Copley, who followed West from America to England, added to the genre with his portrait of young Richard Heber (1782). Women also played the game, but they were more likely to be seen with bow and arrow. In an aquatint entitled *A Meeting of the Society of Royal British Archers* (1794), limned by Robert Smirke, the ladies

Diane de Poitiers, mistress of Henri II of France, in the guise of her namesake, the huntress-goddess Diana. (Diana has remained popular with artists. She appears in works by Jean Goujon, Titian, Peter Paul Rubens, Jean-Alexandre-Joseph Falguière, and Augustus Saint-Gaudens, who placed her statue on top of Madison Square Gardens).

In northern Europe, Hendrick Avercamp, Esaias van de Velde, Lucas Van Valckenborch, and Rembrandt van Rijn all produced lively scenes of skaters gliding gracefully across, or sprawling awkwardly upon, frozen ponds and canals. These wintry scenes seem magically to reappear centuries later in the paintings of William Glackens, Pierre Bonnard, Ernst Ludwig Kirchner, and Wassily Kandinsky.

Sports appear much less often in Asian than in European art, but they were by no means absent. As early as the thirteenth century, Japanese scrolls and screens

shoot while the gentlemen stand ready to assist and admire. One beautiful image of women's archery was William Powell Frith's *The Fair Toxophilites* (1872), a portrait of his daughters as a trio of archers.

Realism to Abstraction

In the late nineteenth and early twentieth centuries, sports attracted an array of talented American painters, including Thomas Eakins, Winslow Homer, and George Bellows:

- A rowing scene, *Max Schmitt in a Single Scull* (1871), represents Eakins at his artistic zenith. His fascination with anatomy inspired him to paint a number of boxers and wrestlers.
- Winslow Homer did a splendid series of oils devoted to male and female croquet enthusiasts. (Homer's Impressionist contemporary, Edouard Manet, was foremost among the Europeans interested in the game.)
- In oils and in lithographs, George Bellows portrayed tennis players, ice-skaters, polo players, and a great many boxers—some as famous as Jack Dempsey, others identified simply as "members of the club."

Baseball has captivated the imagination of American novelists and poets, but visual artists—with the exception of Eakins and William Morris Hunt—have seldom been interested in the "national game." There has been a curious neglect—everywhere in the world—of the world's most popular sport: association football. Billions of photographs document the history of soccer, but relatively few painters of stature have thought it worth their time to interpret the game. Umberto Boccioni's *Dynamism of a Soccer Player* and Nicolas de Stael's *Soccer Players* are among the rare canvases attempting to catch the complicated movements of a soccer match. (Both are abstract works.) Rugby players can boast that their sport inspired several of the world's most renowned painters:

- Henri Rousseau exhibited his charmingly primitive *The Football Players* in 1908.

- Robert Delaunay's *The Cardiff Rugby Team* (1912–1913) was emphatically modern, not only in its choice of sporting subject but also in its background: the Eiffel Tower, a Ferris wheel, an airplane.
- André Lhote's *Rugby* (1912) was even more abstract.
- The Expressionist Max Beckmann, in *Rugby Player* (1929), returned to a somewhat more representational (and comic) style.

American football has attracted very few major painters, but Frederic Remington, renowned for his paintings of cowboys, did a version of the Yale-Princeton football game of 27 November 1890. In the 1950s, Elaine de Kooning attempted to reproduce the action of a number of ball games, including American football.

In the fin de siècle period, tennis players appeared in the work of artists as different in their styles as the British academic John Lavery, the German Impressionist Max Liebermann, and the Belgian Symbolist Ferdinand Khnopff. In time, tennis appeared also in paintings by the French art déco specialist Marcel Gromaire, the Italian Surrealist Carlo Carrà, and the American pop-art painter Mike Francis. The mood of these pictures varies from the pastoralism of Lavery's *The Tennis Party* (1885) to the eroticism of Francis's *Advantage, Mrs. Cunningham* (1976), in which a male spectator's sunglasses reflect the naked buttocks of a female player.

Everywhere in the modern world, golf rivals tennis as the favorite participant sport of the affluent, but the bucolic pleasures of golf have seldom excited the artistic imagination. When Paul Cadmus painted *Aspects of Suburban Life: Golf* (1936), he indulged in Hogarthian satire. It may be that landscape artists are temperamentally opposed to sports events. There are, however, a few exceptions, including *The Dune Hazard* (1922), by the American Impressionist Childe Hassam.

Artists have never been as keen on Alpine skiing as on town-pond skating. (Too hard to sketch with frozen fingers?) We do have Tamara de Lempicka's *St. Moritz* (1929), in which the artist's self-portrait dwarfs the rather insignificant ski slopes, and Joan Miró's *The Skiing Course* (1966), which is so abstract that it was probably conceived and executed in his atelier.

Human Bodies

Just as artists fascinated by women's bodies have produced innumerable nudes (the adjective "female" is usually considered unnecessary), artists interested in the shape and motion of men's bodies have studied boxers and wrestlers. Among the painters and sculptors who have portrayed boxers, Eakins, Bellows, Mahonri Young, and Andy Warhol are among the most prominent. (Andy Warhol included Muhammad Ali in a 1978 series of ten pop-art acrylic portraits of athletes.) In addition to Eakins and Bellows, the list of modern artists who have painted wrestling scenes includes George Luks and the German Impressionist Max Slevogt. A surprisingly large number of renowned painters and sculptors took female wrestlers as their subject. Eugène Delacroix and Degas were both attracted by the erotic appeal of muscular female bodies. They—and their lesser contemporary Emmanuel Croisé—depicted Spartan girls as wrestlers. The great twentieth-century sculptor Aristide Maillol, best known for his larger-than-life bronze nudes, was true to form when he cast *Wrestling*

Women (1900). French artists were, however, hardly unanimous in their admiration for combative females. In 1868, the caricaturist Amadée-Charles-Henri Cham was clearly repelled by the sight of a pair of tubby women grappling before a crowd of leering men.

Focus on female wrestlers did not mean that conventionally feminine sports have been neglected. *Beach Scene, New London* (1919), a brightly Impressionistic canvas by Glackens, reminds the viewer that swimmers have, for centuries, attracted artists fascinated by the human body. The gentle game of shuttlecock caught the eye of Maurice Denis in 1900, as it had an even greater French artist, Chardin, in 1741. Chardin's indoor scene portrays a little girl holding her racquet and her shuttlecock. Denis preferred a game in progress; he set it in a peaceful forest glade and emphasized his arcadian motif with pastel shades of green and yellow.

Mechanized Motion

Several twentieth-century artists have expressed their fascination with "technological" sports. In the years just before World War I, Boccioni, Lyonel Feininger, Natalia Gontscharova, and Jean Metzinger all produced abstractions designed to give an impression of the cyclist's energy and speed. A generation later, Edward Hopper chose to paint—in haunting realism—an image of an exhausted cyclist between the laps of a six-day race. Automobiles at full throttle raced through the work of Italian Futurists such as Giacomo Balla and Luigi Russolo, careened across Gerardo Dottori's *Velocity Triptych,* and show no signs of

Shobu Aikido Dojo, showing the Kamiza altar and drawings, is an example of the importance of aesthetic elements in Asian martial arts.

Horse racing is animated roulette. ■ ROGER KAHN

stopping in contemporary pictures such as Jean Tinguely's collage, *Panorama Formula I-Circus.* Inevitably, the Futurists produced images of airplanes. Mario Sironi's *Yellow Airplane with View of the City* appeared in 1915, a year before the abstractionist Delaunay painted his *Hommage to Blériot* (the first pilot to fly the English Channel).

Obsession with mechanized motion did not mean that Delaunay and other early modernist artists lost interest in runners. Delaunay's *The Runners* appeared in 1926, six years after Paul Klee's composite abstraction, *Runner Hooker Boxer.* What Delaunay hoped to express by the faces of his five runners—a set of five reddish disks—is impossible to say. Willi Baumeister and Pablo Picasso were among the relatively few artists to portray female runners. Baumeister's boyishly slender runner, painted in 1927, is nude except for a blue headband. She seems to dance rather than to run. In contrast, the runners depicted in *The Race* (1922) have the massive bodies of Picasso's classical period. Their tunics and exposed left breasts are probably an allusion to the garb of ancient Spartan runners.

California is the symbolic, if not the actual, birthplace of skateboarding, rollerblading, and other postmodern sports, so it is hardly surprising that they appear in the work of California's artists. In Richard Cronk's *Venus on the Half Shell* and Peter Blake's *The Encounter or Bonjour Mr. Hockney,* both painted in 1981, young women glide by on roller skates. Both pictures were clever visual allusions—Blake's to Gustave Courbet's famous *Bonjour, Monsieur Courbet* (1854) and Cronk's to Sandro Botticelli's even more famous *Birth of Venus.* Both works remind the viewer that the images we use to document the history of sports are also an important facet of the history of art.

Allen Guttmann

See also Aesthetics; Beauty

Further Reading

Coombs, D. (1978). *Sport and the country side in English painting, watercolors, and prints.* Oxford:, UK Phaidon.
Deuchar, S. (1988). *Sporting art in eighteenth-century England.* New Haven, CT: Yale University Press.
Kühnst, P. (1996). *Sports: A cultural history in the mirror of art.* Dresden, Germany: Verlag der Kunst.
Musée des Beaux-Arts de Mons. (1984). *Art et sport.* Mons, Belgium: Musée des Beaux-Arts.

Ascot

The Ascot races are far more than mere horse races. For the British they have grown into a national institution. On the one hand, they are popular and democratic, attracting crowds from across London and the South, and showcasing horses from throughout the country. On the other, they still retain their associations with the British monarchy, enjoy long-standing traditions of elegance, extravagance, and glamour, and are attended by fashionable high society. Often known as "Royal Ascot," these races are still one of the supreme social functions of the British season. Queen Elizabeth II has attended regularly and often runs her better horses there. Even though the races are held during the week, which limits working-class attendance, as does their distance from London, they have always attracted large crowds, although well below those found at Epsom for the Derby.

History

The course is about ten kilometers from Windsor Castle, the main residence of Britain's royal family, and just over a kilometer from the gates of Windsor Great Park. Racing there had its beginnings in a series of match contests between hunting horses run for the private amusement of Queen Anne (the last of the Stuart monarchs) and her courtiers on Ascot Heath, a large clearing in Windsor Forest, in 1711. Although she weighed over 126 kilograms (278 pounds), she continued to follow racing and hunting until her death, and even provided a Queen's Plate as a prize. Following her death, the course had little patronage, though members of her former hunt, the Royal Buckhounds, who

Women in their best dresses and hats during a break in the racing at Ascot in the late nineteenth century.

hunted deer in the area, occasionally used it for hunters' races.

In the 1740s the patronage of William Duke of Cumberland once more created a high-status five- or four-day June meeting. Its first really valuable race, the Ascot Gold Cup, was instituted in 1807. It was watched by George III, Queen Charlotte, and Princesses Mary and Amelia, dressed in Spanish mantles and gypsy hats; the king's estranged son, the Prince of Wales, pointedly watched from his own pavilion opposite the judge's box.

The course's development was significantly influenced by royal patronage. This patronage is reflected in the titles of its famous races, which indicate the continuity of British racing life. Such races include the St.

James Palace Stakes (which began in 1834), the King Edward VII Stakes (1834), the Queen Anne Stakes (1840), the Royal Hunt Cup (1843), the Coronation Stakes (1840), and the Prince of Wales Stakes (1862). Queen Victoria attended Ascot regularly in the first half of the nineteenth century. By the early twentieth century Edward VII had made it probably the most fashionable event in the social calendar.

Beginning with the reign of George IV in the early nineteenth century, the royal procession to and along the course has been a key tradition. The public pageantry, pomp, and circumstance of this royal arrival have always been a major attraction for the crowd, helping to strengthen the hold of the monarchy on British society. In the 1920s, for example, there was a coach procession from Windsor that featured not just the royal family but postilions in quaint costumes with grey wigs and jockey caps, outriders in scarlet and gold uniforms and tops hats, and equerries in somber black. As the royal standard was raised above the Royal Box, voices would call out, "The King, the King!"

The ultimate privilege for the wealthy was admission to Ascot's royal enclosure, first created in front of the Royal Stand in the 1840s; acceptance was often a mark of arrival into elite society. Applications had to be made to the royal representative at St. James Palace and were carefully scrutinized. Court rules governing the nonadmission of divorced persons always applied. Correct clothing and appearance were expected, to signal the high status of visitors. Between the two World Wars, for example, men wore tailored dark suits, stiff-collared shirts, and high top hats, while women wore extravagant hats and elegant frocks. The royal family itself always watched the race from the Royal Box, and the ultimate accolade was to be invited to join them. The cream of British aristocracy would arrange house parties at country houses in the neighborhood of the races, and every crack military regiment quartered in England had a luncheon tent on the course.

Management of the races was usually carried out by the Master of the Buckhounds, who was invariably a member of the ultra-elite Jockey Club, the ruling body

*Wimbledon is getting a bit too like Royal Ascot. It's not what happens or
who wins so much, as what clothes do I have on.* ■ DAVID LLOYD

of British racing. Names of modern races such as the
Ribblesdale Stakes, the Cork and Orrery Stakes, and the
Hardwick Stakes all commemorate aristocrats who held
the office in the past. The racing cups were often made
by leading British silversmiths and usually incorporated
the Royal Arms. Between the wars these were often
chosen as the result of design competitions and exhibited in Goldsmith's Hall in London.

Contemporary Ascot

Even today, the racing is of a high standard. Royal
Ascot still takes place in June, and the vast majority of
Britain's leading June races are held there. Indeed, Ascot
has been described as "the finest festival of racing in Europe." Its races, because of their high status, have always
been attractive to sponsors, and prize money here has
always been greater that at most other racecourses. In
1878, for example, according to London's *Graphic*
newspaper, the total value of the stakes was "no less
than £28,890—sums beyond any which have ever been
run for at any race meeting in the world."

By the 1990s Ascot had expanded from a single
meeting to five fixtures and a total of thirteen days of
racing a year. In 1973 the one-and-a-half-mile King
George and Queen Elizabeth Stakes, run in July, became
the first £100,000 race in Britain. Originally founded in
1951 as part of the Festival of Britain to help stimulate
Britain's postwar revival, it has attracted winners of
many leading international races for three-year-olds and
upward. The course has always enjoyed better facilities
than most other British courses, with constant building
and upgrading.

Its prestige meant that the meeting attracted leading
horses, and all the leading British flat-race jockeys regularly appeared there. Between 1957 and 1982 former
champion jockey Lester Piggott won the Ascot Gold
Cup no fewer than eleven times. Frankie Dettori, the
British champion jockey in 2004, went through the
card there on 28 September 1996, the first time this
"magnificent seven" had been achieved in Britain.

Mike Huggins

Further Reading

Huggins, M. (2000). *Flat racing and British society 1790–1914.* Lon-
    don: Frank Cass.
Huggins, M. (2003). *Horseracing and the British 1919–1939.* Man-
    chester, UK: Manchester University Press.
Laird, D. (1976). *Royal Ascot.* London: Hodder and Stoughton.
Onslow, R. (1990). *Royal Ascot.* Ramsbury, UK: The Crowood Press.
Vamplew, W. (1976). *The turf.* London: Allen Lane.

Ashes, The

Symbol of global rivalry, and a colonial relationship
fraught with ambiguous feelings, the Ashes tour is a
major sporting event: the biennial cricket competition
between Australia and England. The Ashes themselves
truly are ashes—the cremated remains of a cricket bail
or stump, placed in a small brown urn and preserved
and cherished in the museum at Lord's Cricket Ground
in London.

History

The Ashes is cricket's oldest international contest and
has its origins in the third Australian tour to England.
The visitors horrified the host nation (and thrilled their
country's people) by beating England in its own green
and pleasant land on 29 August 1882.

The Australians had won four out of seven matches
before the Test Match at the Oval cricket ground in
south London. This in itself was considered humiliating
by the English, who commentators say were determined
to teach the Aussies a lesson, presumably about proper
filial behavior. (England was known as the "mother
country.")

The defeat at the Oval was made even worse because
the Australians came from behind to devastate a confident English team at the last moment. The following
mocking obituary was published the next day in the
Sporting Times:

In Affectionate Remembrance of English Cricket,
Which died at the Oval on 29th August, 1882,

Deeply lamented by a large circle of sorrowing
Friends and acquaintances.
R.I.P.
N.B. The body will be cremated and the ashes taken to
Australia.

When the English team next toured Australia, its captain, Ivo Bligh, stayed in a home in Sydney, where one of the young ladies of the family suggested she make a velvet bag in which he could store the imaginary ashes of English cricket. (This suggests that jokes about the situation could be made, at least in private.) This brown velvet bag, embroidered with the year 1883 in gold thread, still exists, but it was quickly deemed inappropriate for the storage of the Ashes. Supposedly the ladies of the household then burned a bail, one of the small wooden bars that rest on top of the three vertical stumps that stand behind a batsman. When the bails fall, the wicket is lost (a "wicket" is an "out").

Florence Morphy of Melbourne, Australia, is credited with having provided the brown urn in which the Ashes now rest. Bligh himself married Florence Morphy and settled in Australia, and after his death she presented the urn to the Marylebone Cricket Club. They have been on permanent display ever since, and a substitute is the Ashes trophy, which moves between England and Australia, depending on the results of the latest tour.

The original Ashes returned to Australia only once, for the country's bicentenary celebrations, flown by RAF aircraft and moved under police escort to and from Lord's.

The Ashes Tour

The England-Australia series was rechristened the Ashes tour and is played every two years, alternating between England and Australia. Because it is played in two hemispheres, some of the series are listed by two years, played in the Australian summer season.

THE "BODYLINE" ASSAULT

Americans associate cricket with the English and a privileged, leisured way of life. But cricket has been for well over a century an intensely global competition, a venue where the complex emotions of colonial relationships are played out. In the 1932–1933 series, a new edge was added to the legendary rivalry, when England's captain, Douglas Jardine, decided to implement a tactic that was not forbidden in the rules but which was aggressive and dangerous.

For the Australians, winning at cricket was about beating the English at their own game. For the English, the country's and the Empire's honor was at stake. But this was a new era, in which the British government was negotiating for a Commonwealth constitution with the Dominion governments (including Australia) that would assure loyalty to the Crown yet recognize Dominion autonomy. In this politically charged time, the British government wanted to avoid anything that would cause Australians to feel ill-will toward Britain.

One player said, when he heard that Jardine had been named captain, that England would "win the Ashes—but we may lose a Dominion." Jardine has been credited with the strategy known as the "bodyline," but

Illustration of British cricketers shows a wicket of the type burned for the Ashes.

it was only possible because he happened to have four star fast bowlers. The star of the Australian team was batsman Donald Bradman, known as the "Don," who took England's traditional spin bowling in stride but showed some uncertainty when faced with ace fast bowlers like Harold Larwood.

Jardine took advantage of this and ordered his bowlers to the attack, placing their balls in such a way that it would bounce right in front of the batsman and jump towards their heads. The bodyline itself was a line-up of fielders placed closely round the batsman, instead of spread over the pitch. The batsman was forced to respond defensively, and the ball would go straight into the hands of one of the close quarter fielders.

Like baseball, a catch is an out, and that batsman never comes back to bat. A technique that could knock out a player like the Don, who might get 200 or 300 runs, was of considerable value. But, as the crowds roared, it was not sportsmanlike. It was not cricket.

A diplomatic crisis ensued, with telegrams crossing the globe. An Australian player was quoted as saying that Jardine's tactics were unsportsmanlike, an insult so breathtakingly offensive that the British government demanded it be withdrawn. The crowds were wild, especially when several players were struck in the head and one Australian batsman sustained a fractured skull.

The 1984 Australian miniseries *Bodyline: It's Not Just Cricket* dramatized the legend. Jardine was portrayed as a sportsman not just obsessed with winning but as a sadistic Englishman who had to prove his superiority over the colonials. It was highly popular in both England and Australia.

CONTEMPORARY TOURS

In recent decades, fans have talked about England's cricket performance in a way akin to Americans talking about the Chicago Cubs or the Boston Red Sox (though there was no known curse on England). The 2004–2005 Ashes tour, however, revived English hopes of regaining the Ashes.

As it happened, Larwood, the star bowler of the bodyline series, settled in Australia and became some-thing of a hero. And in an ironic twist of modern commercialism and globalization, the Oval, where English cricket supposedly died in 1882, is now called the Foster's Oval, under the sponsorship of the Australian beer.

Karen Christensen

Further Reading

ABCs of cricket: The Ashes. (2004). Retrieved March 28, 2005, from http://www.abcofcricket.com/A_Legend_Is_Born/a_legend_is_born.htm

Cricket: The Ashes tour. (2003, January 25). Retrieved March 28, 2005, from news.bbc.co.uk/sport1/hi/cricket/the_ashes/history

Guttmann, A. (2004). *Sports, the first five millennia.* Amherst, MA: University of Massachusetts Press.

Holt, R. (1989). *Sport and the British.* Oxford, UK: Oxford University Press.

Lord's: The Ashes. (2002). Retrieved March 28, 2005, from http://www.lords.org.uk/history/ashes.asp

Asian Games

The original 1950 charter of the Asian Games begins, "The Asian Games shall be held every four years, exceptional circumstances apart, and assemble amateurs of Asian nations in fair and equal competition under conditions that are to be as perfect as possible. No discrimination is allowed against any country or person on grounds of color, religion or politics." Women were restricted to competition in athletics, fencing, gymnastics, swimming, canoeing, yachting, and art exhibitions. The charter allowed for Asian Winter Games to be held during the same year, but the first Asian Winter Games were not held until 1986, and thereafter in 1990, 1996, 1999, and 2003.

The games resumed competition between Asian nations that was interrupted during the 1930s. China, Japan, and the Philippines had hosted ten competitions of the Far East Championships from 1913 until 1934. Indian Prime Minister Jawaharlal Nehru proposed the idea to other Asian nations in 1947. The Indian Olympic Committee, led by G. D. Sohndi, continued the discussions with Asian neighbors at the 1948 Olympic Games and the first competitions were planned for 1950. Delays slowed the preparations and the first "Asiad" or Asian Games were held in New Delhi, India, in 1951. Since 1954 the Asian Games have been held regularly every four years on the even years between the Summer Olympic Games.

The 1951 Asian Games, New Delhi, India

New Delhi's National Stadium welcomed athletes from eleven nations in March of 1951 to the first Asian Games. A five-mile torch relay from New Delhi's Red Fort to National Stadium opened the games. The cauldron in the stadium was lit by India's Dalip Singh, a participant in the 1924 Olympic Games. China and Vietnam did not participate as India did not recognize their governments, and they were not invited to the games. Pakistan, newly independent from India, and still disputing the Kashmir regions with India, boycotted the games.

The 1954 Asian Games, Manila, Philippines

China declined to participate in the games of 1954, in Manila, Philippines, when the Taiwanese were invited to participate. The debate of athletic sovereignty between the "two Chinas" began in 1952 and continues to this day.

The 1958 Asian Games, Tokyo, Japan

In Tokyo, Japan built for the 1958 Asian Games what was said to be one of the most modern and beautiful stadiums of its time in the world. They also succeeded in impressing the International Olympic Committee to award them the 1964 Olympic Games. Gun laws in Japan were so severe that even starting pistols were restricted. The Japanese Diet (parliament) had to give special permission for the officials to use starting guns. Japanese commercial and government television stations broadcast the games. The torch for the games was lit in Manila's Rizal Stadium, host of the previous games, and carried by plane to southern Japan where it was relayed on foot to Tokyo. Japan's 1928 Olympic triple jump champion Mikio Oda lit the games cauldron. China again refused to compete when Taiwan was invited. North Korea wanted to field a separate team from South Korea but were not yet members of the Asian Games Federation and were expected to compete as part of a unified Korean team. The Japanese spent over $40 million on their new stadium, and lost money on the games, but were able to restore some of the international goodwill that had been lost in the region during the preceding decade of war. Mainland China, however, at the conclusion of the games broke off sporting relations with Japan over the issue of the participation of Taiwan.

The 1962 Asian Games, Jakarta, Indonesia

The games of 1962 were awarded to Jakarta, Indonesia, by a narrow 22–20 vote of the Asian Games Federation and with pessimism that Indonesia's complete lack of facilities and experience in organizing events of this kind would doom the games. The political tensions between mainland China and Taiwan resurfaced as a theme of these games in 1962, as did the issue of Israel's participation. Indonesia, having no diplomatic relations with either Taiwan or Israel, refused visas to both countries, excluding them from entering the country for the games. China, one month before the games were to begin, placed a great amount of diplomatic pressure on Indonesia to influence the decision concerning Taiwan. The Taiwanese protested and attempted to gain the support of other countries in a boycott if Taiwan was not invited to the games. During the week prior the games, with all of the nations except Taiwan and Israel in Jakarta, and the Indonesian government unwilling to budge, India's G. D. Sohndi, one of the original founders of the Asian Games, attempted to remove the official sanction from the games and have them called the Jakarta Games and not the Asian Games.

The main stadium of Thammasart University, Rangsit, Thailand, the locale for the Asian Games. *Source: istockphoto.com/palmbook.*

On 26 August, two days after the opening ceremony, a statement was issued to the press that the games would not be recognized as the Asian Games but would be called the Jakarta Games. The international federations for basketball and weightlifting immediately removed their sanction for those sports and the tournaments were canceled. Two days later the Asian Games Federation met again and reversed the decision, insisting the games had full sanction and setting up a committee to look into the issues with Taiwan and Israel.

In February of 1963, Sohndi, as part of the executive committee of the International Olympic Committee, moved to have sanctions placed against Indonesia and have them suspended from the Olympic movement. This led Indonesia to attempt to establish the Games of the New Emerging Forces (GANEFO) in protest, which were to be an ongoing alternative to the Olympic Games. The GANEFO games were held once, in Jakarta in 1963, and a smaller Asian GANEFO was held in 1966 in Cambodia, before the protest movement lost momentum. Israel and Taiwan were both invited back to the 1966 Asian Games held in Bangkok, Thailand, but the games were not considered to be well organized. One spectator died in a stampede of fans attempting to get in to the opening ceremony.

The 1970 Asian Games, Bangkok, Thailand

South Korea had been selected to host the 1970 games but ongoing domestic problems forced the Koreans to decline. Bangkok graciously offered to host the games for the second time in a row.

The 1974 Asian Games, Tehran, Iran

In 1974 in Tehran, Iran, the Asian Games were especially controversial when the political issues of Taiwan

Table 1.

Locations of the Summer Asian Games

Year	Location
1951	New Delhi, India
1954	Manila, Philippines
1958	Tokyo, Japan
1962	Jakarta, Indonesia
1966	Bangkok, Thailand
1970	Bangkok, Thailand
1974	Tehran, Iran
1978	Bangkok, Thailand
1982	New Delhi, India
1986	Seoul, South Korea
1990	Beijing, China
1994	Hiroshima, Japan
1998	Bangkok, Thailand
2002	Busan, South Korea

and Israel again became hot topics. The Asian Football Federation finally voted to eliminate Israel from all future football competitions at the games. Other nations boycotted Israel's participation in other sports, the Arab nations, North Korea, Pakistan, and China refusing to participate with Israel in tennis, fencing, basketball, and football. On the matter of Taiwan's participation, the international governing bodies of swimming (FINA, Federation Internationale de Natation) and athletics (IAAF, International Association of Athletics Federations) ruled opposite of one another on the issue. The IAAF said Taiwan could compete, while FINA voted against their inclusion, voting to include China instead, and in the end Taiwan did not participate.

The 1974 games saw accusations of professionalism against six boxers from Thailand and two drug suspensions handed out against weightlifters from North Korea and Japan.

The 1978 Asian Games, Bangkok, Thailand

Bangkok, Thailand, once again stepped in to rescue the games in 1978 after Islamabad, Pakistan, pulled out as

host. Israel was expelled entirely from the Asian Games Federation and Bangladesh, Lebanon, Saudi Arabia, United Arab Emirates, and Qatar were accepted as new members of the federation.

The 1982 Asian Games, New Delhi, India

In 1982 in New Delhi, police arrested more than seven hundred people three days before the games opened, fearful that Akali Sikh activists might try to disrupt the games. Ten thousand extra police were on hand for security during the games, which took place without incident. For the first time Japan was not atop the medals table; China had outscored the Japanese with sixty-one gold medals to Japan's fifty-seven gold medals.

The games organizing body was renamed in December of 1982 from the Asian Games Federation to the Olympic Council of Asia (OCA).

The 1986 Asian Games, Seoul, South Korea

Security was increased for the 1986 Asian Games in Seoul, South Korea. North Korea refused to participate in the games and gave indications that that they might attempt to disrupt the events. Five days before the games opening, a large bomb exploded inside Seoul's Kimpo Airport, killing five and injuring thirty-six. The South Korean government closed down five schools and universities during the games in an attempt to stop student demonstrations.

The 1990 Asian Games, Beijing, China

One month after Iraq invaded Kuwait in August of 1990, the Asian Games opened in Beijing, China. Iraq was expelled from the games and was not allowed to participate. During the Iraqi invasion on 2 August 1990 Sheikh Fahad al Sabah, president of the Olympic Council of Asia and a member of the International Olympic Committee from Kuwait, was murdered. International businesses shied away from sponsoring the games because of the June 1989 Tiananmen Square crackdown.

Being in politics is like being a football coach. You have to be smart enough to understand the game and dumb enough to think it's important. ■ EUGENE MCCARTHY

China dominated the medals table like no nation had before, winning 183 gold medals. The rest of the nations combined shared 127 gold medals.

The 1994 Asian Games, Hiroshima, Japan

The 1994 games in Hiroshima, Japan, were controversial again for the Chinese, with eleven Chinese athletes suspended for performance-enhancing drugs. South Korea had proposed that a unified North and South Korean team compete at these games, but North Korea rejected the offer for reasons connected to international inspections of its nuclear facilities.

The 1998 Asian Games, Bangkok, Thailand

Bangkok, Thailand, held the Asian Games in 1998, the fourth time since 1966 that the games were held in Thailand's capital. Worries about Bangkok's slow preparations began in 1995 and continued to 1997, with the OCA almost taking the games away from Bangkok. Bangkok eventually succeeded in pulling off a magnificent Asian Games. Monetary awards by various nations to their athletes were a visible part of the games. Singapore offered $154,000 for a gold medal, China $480. Despite the slogan "Friendship Beyond Frontiers," the games were not without the usual political disturbances. Saudi Arabia and Afghanistan withdrew before the games began, Afghanistan citing economic difficulties and protesting the amounts the Thai organizers were charging to stay in the village. The Saudi Arabians withdrew in part because the Muslim holy month of Ramadan began during the last week of the games. Iraq was not present for the third games in a row, still banned for its aggression against Kuwait in 1990.

The Chinese embassy protested when Taiwanese flags were found flying in various locations around Bangkok. Because of the political disputes between China and Taiwan it was agreed before the games that only the flag of the National Olympic Committee of Taiwan could be flown. North Korea insisted that it march before South Korea during the opening ceremonies but the Thai hosts said that the Thai alphabet would be used and the South Korean delegation would march in fourth or fifth while North Korea would be approximately the thirty-fifth team to walk into the stadium. The teams were also separated in the village as much as possible. The North Koreans were challenged to prove the ages of their female gymnasts, which some nations thought were under the required age of sixteen years. After inspecting their passports the OCA allowed them to compete.

China, South Korea, Taiwan, and the host Thailand all protested decisions of the judges in the tae kwon do competition with sit-ins and near riots in the stands. Police were called in to restore order several times. Pakistani and Indian billiards players hotly debated proper behavior during their match play and the Chinese reported that a few of their table tennis players had been approached and offered bribes to throw their matches; all of them refused.

When India's Jyotirmoy Sikhdar won India's very first gold medal of the games, the hosts mistakenly began to play the Chinese national anthem, the anthem heard most often at the games. After Indians in the crowd began to boo, the hosts realized their mistake and apologized. The Indian anthem was then played, and later in the day played again as a further apology. Drug suspensions caused other medals to come under dispute. Fakruddin Taher of the United Arab Emirates was disqualified for illegal drug use after winning the silver medal in the 60-kilogram class in karate. The OCA ruled that the two bronze medal winners (there is no bronze medal bout and two medals are awarded) would both be given silver medals and the fifth and sixth place winners moved up and both awarded bronze medals. Only four athletes failed drug tests at the games.

At the games, the Asian nations discussed the possibility of boycotting the 2002 World Cup in football, because FIFA (Federation Internationale de Football Association) had decided to reduce the number of qualifying positions for the Asian region from a possible four to two. If Korea and Japan were to go along with a proposed boycott this would put them in the most curious position of boycotting a tournament they would be hosting and organizing.

The 2002 Asian Games, Busan, South Korea

One legacy of the 2002 Asian Games in Busan, South Korea, was that for the first time a team from North Korea had participated in a games in South Korea. North Korea's national anthem and flag are normally banned by law in South Korea. These restrictions were set aside, in part, for the duration of the games. The flag could be waved, but only in official ceremonies, and by North Korean delegates in the stadium, not by spectators. South Korea even manufactured some North Korean flags for the first time. The anthem was played on official occasions, though South Korean military bands still refused to play the anthem. On the matter of China and Taiwan, Korean organizers, under pressure from China, arranged for Taiwan to march under a banner reading Chinese Taipei, using a phonetic Korean script, and not the usual Korean alphabetical order. This put them thirty-fifth in the parade, rather than second, and behind China. China also asked that the number of delegations be referred to as forty-four countries and territories, not forty-four countries, as China does not regard Taiwan, Hong Kong, or Macau as countries.

Badminton, boxing, bodybuilding, and tae kwon do were all hit with protests over officiating. Boxing judges were banned over questionable decisions. A large memorial wall, of athlete's hands and signatures, cast in bronze, was to be created after the games, symbolizing the friendship of the games.

The Future

The 2006 Asian Games are scheduled to be held in Doha, Qatar, in December of 2006. Organizers have said that there will be no restrictions or dress codes for women at the games. Guangdong, China, was named as host of the 2010 Asian Games at OCA meetings in June 2004.

Daniel Bell

See also South East Asian Games

Further Reading

Asian Games rules. (1950). Delhi, India: Asian Games Federation.

Bell, D. (2003). Asian Games. In *Encyclopedia of international games* (pp. 59–73). Jefferson, NC: McFarland.

Hanna, W. (1962). *The Politics of Sport: Indonesia as host to the Fourth Asian Games* (pp. 193–203). New York: American Universities Field Staff.

History of other Asian Games organisations. (1951). *Bulletin du Comité International Olympique, 25,* 24–25.

Official Report of the III Asian Games. (1958). Tokyo: Organizing Committee for the III Asian Games.

Report of the first Asian Games held at New Delhi. (1951, June). *Bulletin du Comité International Olympique, 27,* 43–44.

Astrodome

The Astrodome, or Harris County Domed Stadium, opened in Houston, Texas, in 1965 after more than five years' planning and three years' construction. When it opened, the stadium offered the first all-enclosed, multipurpose sports venue and was nicknamed the "Eighth Wonder of the World." The Astrodome was the home of the Houston Astros major league baseball team until 2000 and the Houston Oilers National Football League team until 1997. The stadium ushered in a new era in stadium design that saw the construction of many multipurpose domed stadiums.

History

The Harris County Board of Park Commissioners in Houston issued contracts to architects for the preliminary planning for a new stadium in 1958. The Astrodome, though, was the brainchild of former Houston mayor Judge Roy Hofheinz (1912–1982), who, from humble origins, had made a fortune and became a legendary figure in Houston politics and civic life as a state legislator, judge, and entrepreneur. Having consulted with Buckminster Fuller on the idea, Hofheinz brought a model of the domed stadium to the National League owners' meeting in Chicago in October 1960 and was awarded a National League franchise. In June 1961 Harris County officials turned to the architectural firms of Wilson, Morris, Crain & Anderson and

Lloyd & Morgan to design the stadium as the Associated Stadium Architects.

UNCONVENTIONAL DESIGN

Designers considered a number of dome styles, including Fuller's geodesic dome and an air-pressure-supported dome with a cloth or film covering. In the end, however, a lamella roof design was adopted with more than four thousand clear Lucite panels in a steel frame. When it was completed, it was the largest clear-span dome in the world. After two years' study, agronomists at Texas A&M University developed a Tifway Bermuda grass that would grow under the dome, but the roof design presented problems. During day games the glare off the roof panels was wreaking havoc on the fielders, who scrambled to find fly balls that were falling ten feet out of their reach. Hofheinz had the Lucite panels coated in an acrylic film, reducing the natural light by twenty-five to forty percent and thereby killing the grass. After finishing the season on a field of dead grass, Hofheinz installed an artificial turf, dubbed Astroturf, for the 1966 season.

CREATURE COMFORTS

While players had to adjust to climate-controlled baseball on an artificial field, the Astrodome offered fans comforts that no stadium had ever offered before. With a cooling capacity of 6,600 tons and seventy-two million BTUs, for example, the stadium air conditioner kept the venue at seventy-four degrees. When it opened, the stadium offered 46,000 seats for baseball and more than 50,000 seats for football. All seats were padded, and most were upholstered. For those who wanted the best, the Astrodome offered fifty-three skyboxes along the upper perimeter of the stadium. Each skybox included a bar, telephone, radio, closed-circuit television, Dow-Jones stock service, and toilet. With names like "Spanish Provano," "Roman Holiday," "Pagoda Den," "Egyptian Autumn," and "The Aztec," each box had a distinct theme. The "Las Vegas," for example, was furnished with coffee tables shaped like large dice.

What drew the attention of the majority of patrons, no doubt, was the massive $2 million dollar electronic

The Harris County Domed Stadium (Astrodome) in Houston, Texas, c. 1970.
Source: Brian S. Butler.

scoreboard in centerfield. More than four stories tall and stretching across 474 feet, it dwarfed every other scoreboard in the major leagues and truly revolutionized the fan experience. Aside from the perfunctory line score, lineup, and other stats, the scoreboard included a one-hundred-line television for animated or still pictures. For many fans the scoreboard was as much a spectacle and attraction as the dome itself.

SPACE-AGE THEME

The very nature of the Astrodome as an entertainment complex allowed for the incorporation of some notable images of the early space age. Hofheinz envisioned fans being transported to the stadium doors from the 30,000-space parking lot by way of "rocket trains." Once inside, they were ushered to their seats by "Spacettes" in gold-lamé miniskirts and blue boots. "Blast-off Girls" served customers in the "Countdown Cafeteria," while down on the field "Earthmen," attired in orange space suits and white helmets, worked as groundskeepers. Prior to the Astros' first official game against the Phillies, twenty-three of the twenty-six Gemini astronauts lined the field during pregame ceremonies, throwing out first pitches. Press reports and other accounts, moreover, noted the stadium resembled a spaceship.

NOTABLE EVENTS

By 1974 the Astrodome was America's third-most-popular manmade tourist attraction, drawing 7.5 million visitors a year, trailing only the Golden Gate Bridge and Mt. Rushmore. More than baseball and football, though, the venue was the site of a number of notable athletic and entertainment events. Aside from the 1968 and 1986 major-league baseball All-Star games, the Astrodome hosted the 1971 NCAA national basketball tournament, and the 1971 NBA-ABA All-Star game. In 1968 the Astrodome hosted the UCLA–University of Houston basketball game, which drew the largest crowd ever to see a basketball game to that time. Perhaps the most remarkable event in the dome's brief history was the 1973 "Battle of the Sexes" tennis match that saw Billie Jean King defeat Bobby Riggs before a national television audience. The dome also held auto races, boxing matches, rodeos, religious crusades, circuses, a record-breaking motorcycle jump by Evel Knievel, a tightrope walk by Karl "The Great" Wallenda, the production of Robert Altman's film *Brewster Mc-Cloud,* as well as concerts and shows by the likes of Bob Hope, Frank Sinatra, and Elvis Presley.

Venue Today

Today the aging stadium stands empty, and its future is in doubt. While Harris County rents the venue for the occasional high school football game or company softball game, maintenance on the aging stadium costs the county about $1 million annually. Among the proposals to save the stadium is one by the Astrodome Redevelopment Corporation to put a theme park in the venue. The Astrodome revolutionized the sport world and reshaped the fan experience. It remains a symbol of Houston and a remarkable achievement in stadium design.

Brian S. Butler

Further Reading

Gershman, M. (1993). *Diamonds: The evolution of the ballpark.* Boston: Houghton Mifflin.

Houston Sports Association. (1965). *Inside the Astrodome: Eighth wonder of the world.* Houston, TX: Houston Sports Association.

Ray, E. W. (1980). *The grand huckster: Houston's Judge Roy Hofheinz, genius of the Astrodome.* Memphis, TN: Memphis State University Press.

Smith, C. (2001). *Storied stadiums: Baseball's history through its ballparks.* New York: Carroll & Graf Publishers.

Smith, R. (2003). *The ballpark book: A journey through the fields of baseball magic.* St. Louis, MO: Sporting News Publishing Co.

Athletes as Celebrities

As a cultural phenomenon, sports resonates throughout societies, nations, and the world. As participants and workers in sports and sporting enterprises, athletes, particularly athletes who are celebrities, play a major role in this process.

Scholars have argued that *celebrity* is a very difficult concept to define, and its definition is slippery (Andrews & Jackson 2001; Turner, Bonner & Marshall 2000, 9). The word *celebrity* has Latin roots in "celebrem" and "celere," indicating a situation where the individual possesses both particularity and fame (Rojek 2001, 9), that is, a special ability and a fleeting renown. It is possible to "treat celebrity as the attribution of glamorous or notorious status to an individual within the public sphere" while recognizing that celebrities are cultural fabrications involving many actors and agents helping create personalities with enduring appeal for fans (Rojek 2001, 10–11). *Celebrity* is the result of a well-designed process developed in the mid-twentieth century that involves an industry that both gains from the manufacturing of celebrities and brings profits to the companies that use celebrities.

Celebrity is linked to a public that has volatile opinions. The process of "celebritydom" dynamically draws the attention of the media and constructs celebrities to represent other people's fantasies of lifestyle, luxury, consumption, and display (Whannel 2002, chapter 15). Determining when "celebrities" first emerged is difficult, but in 1959, an International Celebrity Register containing 2,200 names was published in the United States (Ponce de Leon 2002, 11).

Pre-1960s

At the beginning of the twentieth century, the print media helped create an industry of leisure out of "spectacles." Spectacles such as those involving extraordinary sporting events satisfied the newly created commodified needs of those with disposable time and income for leisure. Sports, along with visual artistic activities such

*I'm not a headline guy. I know that as long as I was following Ruth to the plate
I could have stood on my head and no one would have known the difference.* ■ LOU GEHRIG

as theater and opera, were thus transformed into profit-making functions with vast paying audiences. Ponce de Leon (2002, 7) points out that stars emerged at the beginning of the twentieth century when famous-personality journalism matured around 1900. The making of stars was contingent on the creation of media empires, mass-readership magazines, wire services, and feature syndicates. Show business and sports-renowned people emerged when newspapers and magazines began to cover these events in detail and to show the personalities who played in them. The renown of certain athletes increased when many major newspapers created a discrete sports pages and sections in the 1880s. Sports writers fashioned a way of thinking about sport that cut across social classes to reach wider audiences and sell more papers. As the sports columns were syndicated, they reached an even wider audience outside the big metropolitan centers, broadening the knowledge of sports stars who were a key element in these pages. Then, the use of photography in newspapers further aided in the creation of sport stars by individualizing athletes (Whannel 2002, 31). This coverage of sports stars helped to sell tickets to sports spectacles and to sell newspapers and magazines, which continues. The conventions of journalism established then remain the paradigm of celebrity creation today.

By the 1910s and 1920s, a new capitalism of mass production and mass consumption emerged, sometimes referred to as Fordist capitalism. Hollywood became important at this point. Dyer (1979) marks the year 1912 as the year of the first conscious attempt at manufacturing a movie star, the beginning of the deliberate marketing of stardom. The sports industry followed a similar path. By the 1920s, in addition to the print media, radio contributed to the promotion of sports and sport stars. The commercialization of sports climaxed in massive spectacles in the United States. Among these, baseball and boxing offered opportunities for entrepreneurs and media moguls to profit. These events depended on male stars. In baseball, Babe Ruth drew multitudes in the early 1900s, and in boxing Jack Dempsey and Gene Tunney attracted 120,000 people

to a Philadelphia stadium to watch the World Heavyweight Title fight in 1926. Driven by the search of profits, sport entrepreneurs and newspapers attempted to build images of celebrity athletes as both naturally talented and hardworking but also "sportsmanlike."

Sport stars and sports then grew in importance, to such an extent that they became symbols of nation, democracy, race, and politics. The 1936 Berlin Olympics proclaimed Jesse Owens, an African-American athlete, as a sport star, an icon of the American democratic supremacy over Nazi ideology of "Aryan" superiority. It is ironic and telling that, at the same time, the United States was steeped in racial segregation.

Post-1960s

Although sports celebrities in the first half of the 1900s reaped some benefits from stardom, they were secondary actors in sports spectacles. Television started to bring the spectacle of sports to broader mass audiences. In 1950, there were only five million television sets in the world, mostly in Great Britain, the United States, and the USSR. In 1956, the Melbourne Olympics were the first ever televised, and in 1962, the World Football Cup in Chile was televised for the first time. Thus began the era of what some scholars have now called the "televisualization of sport" and "sportification of television" (Miller et al. 2001, 93). In the 1950s and 1960s, however, the superstar status of athletes and their personal fortunes were still relatively limited; their personal lives were kept more apart from their sports identities, and their influence was limited to the particular sports they practiced. This started to change in the 1960s. The boxer Muhammad Ali best illustrates this period of transition. Ali was well known, in part, because of the marketing of his boxing abilities and in part because of the politically and ideologically controversial positions he took. Hence, he has also been described as a "trickster" who embodied both the "bad" in personal terms and the "good" as a sports person (Lemert 2003, p. 35).

In the 1970s and 1980s, there were economic, political, and technological changes. The current period, which is called post-Fordist capitalism, consists of the

Athletes as Celebrities

Lady Butterfield 1882

Near London these wakes, like Hampstead or Deptford wakes, were well kept up; and there was my Lady Butterfield in Epping Forest, of whose entertainment and calf-roasting we have already had a description through Ward's instrumentality. Here is one of her advertisements: "My Lady Butterfield gives a Challenge to all England, to Ride a Horse, Leap a Horse, Run on Foot or Hallow with any Woman in England Ten years younger, but not a Day older, because she would not under value herself. Gentlemen and Ladies, whilst in the Spring 'tis worth your while to come to hear the Nightingal Sing in Wanstead within a Mile of the Green Man, in Essex, at my Lady Butterfields at Nightingal Hall. This is to give notice to all Gentlemen and Ladies, and all the best of my Friends, that on the last Wednesday of April is my feast, where is very good Entertainment for that Day, and for all the Year after from my Lady Butterfield."

Or another:–

TO ALL GENTLEMEN AND LADIES.
If Rare Good young Beans and Pease can Tempt
   Ye,
Pray pass not by my Hall with Bellies Empty;
For Kind Good Usage every one can tell,
My Lady Butterfield does al excell;
At Wanstead Town, a Mile of the Green Man,
Come if you dare and stay away if you can.

Ashton, J. (1882). *Social life in the reign of Queen Anne taken from original sources.* London: Chatto and Windus.

---

dominance of transnational corporations, just-in-time production and the microchip, real-time communications and global media empires, globalized consumerism, and branding, all of which have transformed sports, athletes, and celebrity athletes. Cultural globalization has been one of the results of post-Fordism.

With cultural globalization, particularly of the media, there has been an extreme commercialization of sport and the creation of a global sport industry that is marketed across cultures (Westerbeek & Smith 2003). Some scholars have called this a "global media-sports-culture complex" (Miller et al. 2001, 68–71). In contrast with the pre-1960s, celebrity athletes now have a team of specialists who help make them into cultural products and become companies in themselves, with agents, managers, and other employees who deal with their multiple businesses and investments. What this means is that these athletes are "commodified" for a global corporate sports complex that operates in a media culture where the spectacle is dominant (Kellner 2003, chapter 1).

We have chosen two of these celebrities, Michael Jordan and David Beckham, to illustrate the new roles, because they have been the epicenter of the transformation of sports celebrity status in the post-Fordist era.

MICHAEL JORDAN

As a basketball player, Michael Jordan was nicknamed "Air Jordan," and off the court he soared by forging a new role for celebrity athletes in a globalizing world. As Klein (2002, p. 50) notes, "Any discussion of a branded celebrity leads to the same place: Michael Jordan . . . who has incorporated himself into the JORDAN brand." His presence has been almost universal. For example, Chinese children ranked him at par with founders of the Chinese Communist party as figures of the twentieth century. Jordan has been given a deity stature as people kneel before his statue in Chicago (LaFeber 1999, 27). A few other National Basketball Association (NBA) basketball players had similar characteristics, and other sports were more popular than basketball, but what made Jordan significant has been the convergence of several developments. First, in post-Fordist capitalism, sports has become one of the most important forms of entertainment and is centered around celebrities, much as in Hollywood. Second, before the 1980s, sports spec-

The day you take complete responsibility for yourself, the day you stop making any excuses, that's the day you start to the top. ■ O.J. SIMPSON

tacles generated profits primarily by capturing audiences to attend the actual event. This evolved to a situation where worldwide audiences, via satellite, could watch the spectacles in real time. Third, many large transnational corporations began to sell their products globally. In addition to Coca-Cola and a handful of already existing companies that aimed at global markets, many other companies began to draw a sizable part of profits from selling their products to consumers throughout the world.

Jordan's celebritydom was crucial in this process. He was directly associated with the large entrepreneurs who owned these companies such as Phil Knight (the former CEO of Nike), and Rupert Murdoch and Ted Turner (media moguls), and with corporate names such as McDonald's and NBC. Before the 1980s, basketball was not as popular as baseball and football in the United States. A concerted marketing effort around a few celebrity figures allowed the NBA to become a successful league and business. For example, one popular marketing strategy was one of a "race contest" between African-Americans, epitomized by Magic Johnson of the Los Angeles Lakers, and whites, symbolized by Larry Bird of the Boston Celtics. When Jordan was hired to play for the Chicago Bulls in the mid-1980s, the business of basketball was already beginning to flourish. At the same time, the post-Fordist system of production and sales was globalizing into a network of production facilities throughout the world and this included Nike, then primarily a maker of sneakers massively sold during the jogging boom of the early 1980s. At the end of this boom, Nike embarked on a project that used particularly talented athletes as its central feature. These talented athletes also include established superstar golfer Tiger Woods and emerging basketball player LeBron James to name a few, but Jordan was the company's main early promoter and superstar.

Klein (2002) offers a glimpse of the process that ensued and gave sports celebrities parity with movie and pop stars. Nike first re-packaged sports stars to make them celebrities in Hollywood fashion. Then, in a complicated process involving ideas of body, work, resistance against rules, and branding, Nike became one of the largest transnational corporations in the world, with a name brand and logo recognition similar to that of Coca-Cola or McDonald's. In this process, Nike boosted Michael Jordan to the same level of renown as stars in show business entertainment.

Jordan thus brought sports into the high levels of entertainment as technicians used close-ups and quick cuts to make him appear suspended in the air. Jordan's special quality was established both on and off the court. He was portrayed as the ideal sports performer who met the standards of a show business celebrity through radio, television, newspapers, and "specialized" sports magazines. His commercial presence was enhanced by commercials that were in turn sold by his guise and persona. He became Nike's main asset. Jordan became a special type of athlete, and he diversified into commercials endorsing Hanes underwear, McDonald's restaurants, Gatorade, and Wheaties cereal. McDonald and Andrews (2001) called Jordan "hyperreal."

As David Stern, the owner of the Chicago Bulls, put it, when Jordan commenced working for the Bulls, "the globalization of sports hadn't yet occurred" (LaFeber 1999, 153). When Jordan retired, basketball was a global phenomenon. He had become a semi-god, and Nike was a global phenomenon that dominated the sports product market. In turn, millions of spectators worldwide watched NBA basketball. Basketball, and sports in general, had become an integral part of an entertainment world that depended on images and commodities and that was made possible by the new global media sports complex. This complex includes magazines, newspapers, tabloids, television networks, cable and digital television, and film studios—all of which provide a global framework for entertainment and spectacles. Jordan not only sold products through his charisma and business acumen but had himself become a product, or a commodity, that sold other commodities. There has been a consumption of Michael Jordan's image as a celebrity as he became an American

> *I have come to accept that if I have a new haircut it is front page news.*
> *But having a picture of my foot on the front page of a national*
> *newspaper is a bit exceptional.* ■ DAVID BECKHAM

commodity sign (McDonald & Andrews 2001, 21, 33). The Jordan-Nike nexus reminds us that the media is one of the most important places where cultural icons are created as part of the sports/entertainment colossus (Kellner 2003, 89).

DAVID BECKHAM

As an iconic figure of the celebrity world, David Beckham was recently considered as becoming a Jordan (Cashmore 2002, 141). Beckham has fine skills as a footballer (soccer player), but he is much more than that. He is an icon that exists outside time and space in the imagination of people as "le beau ideal" (Cashmore 2002, 4). In some parts of the world, he has reached demi-god status—chocolate and gold leaf statues of him have been erected and worshipped (Beckham & Watt 2003, Statue, 31). A sculpture of Beckham was put in a spot of the Pariwas Temple in Bangkok that is normally reserved for minor deities. Like Michael Jordan, Beckham is a rich and famous global phenomenon who is, above all, a commodity. He is an image and a

person who has been packaged to be a product to be consumed globally. He also sells other brands and logos. Thus, also like Jordan, he is also a giant corporate enterprise in and of himself but also directly linked to the global media-sports-culture complex.

Beckham's celebrity status is partly because of Australian-born Murdoch, who has been instrumental in making sports a major part of show business through celebrity status. Murdoch's early ownership of British newspapers, such as the *Sun, Times,* and *Sunday Times,* used "full computerization and color printing . . . towards a collage style in which headlines and photo displays came to dominate" (Cashmore 2002, 67; Whannel 2001, 35). This permitted visual highlight stories of individuals that repackaged them into personalities and celebrities. Moreover, in the 1980s, the global visibility of sports became the fulcrum of spectacles such that the selling of "sponsorships" became the major source of revenue in the 1982 football World Cup and the 1984 Olympics. Television was central to this process, and Murdoch emerged as one of the major forces in television. Cashmore (2002, 64–66) argues that Murdoch created football anew, making it into an overblown spectacle and that since then, football is not just a sport anymore. Giant media companies have integrated vertically, buying sports clubs of different kinds; in many places, football clubs have become large capitalist enterprises. These include the Manchester United (Beckham's former team) and the Real Madrid (Beckham's team at the time of writing), both of which depend on their celebrity footballers to make profits. Football, like basketball, attracts huge audiences throughout many parts of the world that can be sold many commodities. Companies that manufacture these products pay for television spots and sign these footballers, such as Beckham, to endorse their products. Through these ads, Beckham has become one of the most watched, admired, and recognized figures of the planet: He is the main character of Barclay's Bank propaganda machine, of Brylcreem hair products, of Sondico shin pads, of Adidas' roster of sport celebrities, and of Pepsi Cola. Since his deal with Adidas, Beckham

Athletes as Celebrities

Joe DiMaggio and Mrs. Robinson

In 1969, Paul Simon and Art Garfunkel topped the charts with "Mrs. Robinson." Though the song's reference to Joe DiMaggio ("Where have you gone, Joe DiMaggio? A nation turns its lonely eyes to you . . .") was a metaphor for heroes of days gone by, DiMaggio took it personally. "What I don't understand is why you ask where I've gone," he once complained to Simon. "I just did a Mr. Coffee commercial!"

Source: *The Patterns on the Tenement Halls: A Tribute to the Late Joe DiMaggio* (1999). Retrieved February 24, 2005, from http://www.geocities.com/epanodist/gallery/dimaggio.html#article

has been represented by a publicist who specializes in show business public relations. Beckham's public image has been attentively created to show him as a family man and a common mortal too, one who is even "tempted" by extramarital affairs. Thus, he is marketed with the image of an extraordinary man, but one who could perhaps be imitated. All his career moves have enhanced his business interests, including his branding, his magazine, and his cookbooks. His 2003 transfer to the Real Madrid team adds another mammoth brand in the form of a football team. His marriage to Victoria Adams, a Spice Girl (a British band) and a brand in her own right, was an astute career move that has strengthened his image and his logo. Thus, as Cashmore (2002, 13) argues, Beckham can be depicted as the epitome of the late twentieth century to early twenty-first century post-Fordist capitalism.

Unlike most ordinary citizens, many sport celebrities are affluent transnational persons living and working in many countries and for multinational corporations. Jordan and Beckham are American and British citizens, respectively, but they are also transnational citizens. Jordan and Beckham have played for their national teams, and both the United States and Britain are intensely nationalistic societies; the media has represented both men as the norm of world citizenship. Thus, the creation of celebrity athletes has become part of the globalization process. Jordan and Beckham are associated and symbolized with the consumption of global brand mass products that are easily recognizable by their logos.

The Future

Inasmuch as an individual celebrity athlete is a cultural fabrication and invention, he or she will inevitably have a cultural death. This is currently happening to Michael Jordan and will eventually happen to David Beckham. The point remains, however, that celebritydom and celebrityhood will likely continue unabated, and new celebrity athletes will emerge. This process of the celebritydom of a few select athletes is intricately tied to the global media and corporate sports in post-Fordist

capitalism. Their celebritydom is a part of the resonance of sports in the social, cultural, and economic relationships of humanity.

Ricardo Trumper and Lloyd L. Wong

Further Reading

Andrews, D., & Jackson, S. (Eds.) (2001). Introduction: Sport celebrities, public culture, and private experience. In D. Andrews & S. Jackson (Eds.), *Sport stars: The cultural politics of sporting celebrity* (pp.1–19). New York: Routledge.

Beckham, D., & Watt, T. (2003). *Beckham—Both feet on the ground: An autobiography.* Toronto: HarperCollins Canada.

Cashmore, E. (2002). *Beckham.* London: Polity Press.

Dyer, R. (1979). *Stars.* London: Educational Advisory Service.

Kellner, D. (2003). *Media spectacle.* London: Routledge.

Klein, N. (2002). *No logo. Taking aim at the brand bullies.* Toronto: Vintage Canada.

LaFeber, W. (1999). *Michael Jordan and the new global capitalism.* New York: Norton.

Lemert, C. (2003). *Muhammad Ali: Trickster in the culture of irony.* Cambridge, MA: Polity Press.

McDonald, M. G., & Andrews, D. L. (2001). Michael Jordan: Corporate sport and postmodern celebrityhood. In D. Andrews & S. Jackson (Eds.), *Sport stars: The cultural politics of sporting celebrity* (pp. 20–35). New York: Routledge.

Miller, T., Lawrence, G., McKay, J., & Rowe, D. (2001). *Globalization and sport: Playing the world.* London: Sage.

Ponce de Leon, C. L. (2002). *Self exposure: Human-interest journalism and the emergence of celebrity in America, 1890–1940.* Chapel Hill: University of North Carolina Press.

Rojek, C. (2001). *Celebrity.* London: Reaktion Books.

Turner, G., Bonner, F., & Marshall, P. D. (2000). *Fame games. The production of celebrity in Australia.* Cambridge, UK: Cambridge University Press.

Westerbeek, H., & Smith, A. (2003). *Sport business in the global marketplace.* New York: Palgrave Macmillan.

Whannel, G. (2001). Punishment, redemption and celebration in the popular press: The case of David Beckham. In D. Andrews & S. Jackson (Eds.), *Sport stars: The cultural politics of sporting celebrity* (pp.138–151). New York: Routledge.

Whannel, G. (2002). *Media sport stars: Masculinities and moralities.* London: Routledge.

A hero is no braver than an ordinary man, but he is brave five minutes longer. ■ RALPH WALDO EMERSON

Athletes as Heroes

The terms *hero* and *celebrity* increasingly are being used interchangeably, but they are fundamentally different. According to Daniel Boorstin: "The celebrity is a person who is known for his well-knownness.... The hero was distinguished by his achievement; the celebrity by his image or trademark. The hero created himself; the celebrity is created by the media. The hero is a big man; the celebrity is a big name" (1992, 57, 61). Thus, there are some clear distinctions between the two concepts, and the challenge is to ascertain how and why they have become conflated. First, we must examine the meaning, significance, and types of heroes and why sport remains such an important site for their identification and development. In turn, we need to understand how changes in wider society have tended to shift attention, status, and rewards from heroes to celebrities.

What Is a Hero?

Heroes and heroines have existed throughout human history. From ancient Greece and Rome through the Middle Ages and the Renaissance to the twenty-first century, societies and cultures have created, defined, and otherwise recognized what is known as a hero (Klapp 1949). In Browne's (1990) view, heroes highlight the potential and possibility of humans by expanding and/or conquering the physical, psychological, social, spiritual, and altruistic limits of human beings.

There are many cultural arenas through which individuals have emerged as heroes, and sport has always been one of them. There are likely many reasons for this, but in particular sport as a cultural practice and institution offers the opportunity for the demonstration of physical superiority in a system with clear rankings and rewards; the display of courage, commitment, and sacrifice; and the chance to represent a particular group, community, or nation. In a contemporary commercial context, the last point is quite important given that "only sports has the nation, and sometimes the world,

watching the same thing at the same time, and if you have a message, that's a potent messenger" (Singer 1998).

Even a cursory look at the diversity of sport heroes, both historical and contemporary, indicates that they emerge from a wide range of personal achievements, social backgrounds, and cultural contexts. In effect there are different ways by which heroes emerge. Although the typology that follows is not exhaustive it may aid in understanding the process of how different individuals became heroes. Although the categories are not mutually exclusive, one becomes a hero in one of four ways (Ingham, Howell, and Swetman 1993). First, a person can perform an extraordinary superhuman feat. In ac-

Athletes as Heroes

Grave Inscription for Crescens

Crescens, a heroic charioteer who died at age 22, is remembered in this grave inscription:

With the four-horse chariot he won his first victory when L. Vipstanius and Messalla were the consuls [c. 115–116 CE] on the day of the races in honor of the birthday of the divine Nerva in the twenty-fourth race with the following horses: Circius, Acceptor, Delicatus, Cotynus. From the consulship of Messalla to the races for the birthday of the divine Claudius in the consulship of Glabrio [c. 124–125 CE] he started 686 times and won 47 times. In single races, he was victorious 19 times, in double races 23 times, in triple races 5 times. Once he overtook the entire field from behind. 8 times he won with a lead. 38 times he won by means of a final spurt. He won 130 second places and 111 third places. In prize money, he took in 1,558,346 sesterces.

tual fact heroes are often people who perform ordinary things but at a much higher level and with much greater consistency than the average. A few people who fit this category might include Sir Donald Bradman, Babe Didrikson, Jessie Owens, Paavo Nurmi, Pele, Nadia Comaneci, Michael Jordan, Wayne Gretzky, Carl Lewis, Tiger Woods, and Lance Armstrong.

Second, one can become a hero by being the first to achieve at a particular and unexpected level. Such a category would include people like Sir Roger Bannister who, in 1954, was the first person to break the four-minute mile; or Sir Edmund Hillary who, along with Tenzing Norgay, was the first to climb Mount Everest, the highest point on earth, in 1953.

Third, one can become a hero through risk taking, personal sacrifice, and/or saving a life. There may be no better example of this type of hero than Canadian Terry Fox. Diagnosed with cancer and with part of his right leg amputated, Fox set out to run across Canada in what he called "The Marathon of Hope." Sadly, his run ended after 3,339 miles because the cancer had spread to his lungs. Terry Fox died at age twenty-two on June 28, 1981. Still his life and mission are celebrated annually. Each September 13 marks the Terry Fox Run and to date his foundation has raised over $360 million.

Finally, a person can become a hero by virtue of a particular performance within a specific sociohistorical context: being the right person at the right time (see Ingham, Howell, and Swetman 1993). One example of this type is John Roosevelt (Jackie) Robinson, who, facing enormous racial discrimination and other social barriers, in 1947 became the first "black" athlete to play modern major league baseball.

Hero or Celebrity?

The world still has heroes, but something has changed in terms of the type of people that society celebrates and rewards. Increasingly, status appears to be something that is *manufactured* versus *achieved,* and heroes are being marginalized by celebrities, stars, and idols (cf. Andrews and Jackson 2001, Dyer 1979, Gamson 1994, Rojek, 2001). While there are no simple answers

A large painting of basketball player and coach Dawn Staley on a building in her hometown of Philadelphia, Pennsylvania.

to explain this transformation, consideration must be given to the emergence of the society of the individual, a greater scrutiny of private lives embodied in an exploitive tabloid culture, and a world driven by consumption, advertising, and marketing. As a consequence "everyone is involved in either producing or consuming celebrities" (Rein, Kotler, and Stoller 1997, x). Arguably, the most powerful vehicle in this shift are the media whom Leo Braudy (1997, 550) calls the "arbiters of celebrity." The media are global, immediate, and increasingly interconnected, resulting in a virtual saturation of celebrity culture linked to sport, music, fashion, movies, and reality television.

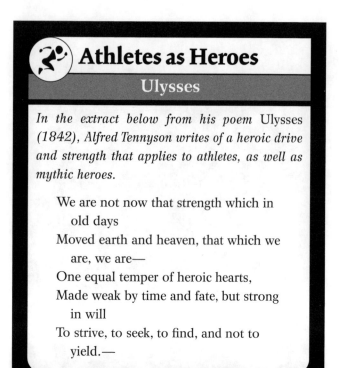

Athletes as Heroes

Ulysses

In the extract below from his poem Ulysses *(1842), Alfred Tennyson writes of a heroic drive and strength that applies to athletes, as well as mythic heroes.*

> We are not now that strength which in
>   old days
> Moved earth and heaven, that which we
>   are, we are—
> One equal temper of heroic hearts,
> Made weak by time and fate, but strong
>   in will
> To strive, to seek, to find, and not to
>   yield.—

Ultimately, we are left with a challenge to gain a better understanding of the social and political function of contemporary heroes and celebrities. In part this will require an examination of who has the power to define heroes and celebrities, under what conditions, and in whose interests.

Steven J. Jackson

Further Reading

Andrews, D., & Jackson, S. (2001). (Eds.). *Sport stars: The politics of sporting celebrity.* London: Routledge.

Boorstin, D. (1992). *The image: A guide to pseudo-events in America.* New York: Random House.

Braudy, L. (1997). *The frenzy of renown: Fame and its history.* New York: Vintage.

Browne, R. B. (1990). *Contemporary heroes and heroines.* Detroit, MI: Gale Research.

Carr, E. (1961). *What is history?* London: Penguin.

Dyer, R. (1979). *Stars.* London: BFI Publishing.

Gamson, J. (1994). *Claims to fame: Celebrity in contemporary America.* Berkeley: University of California Press.

Ingham, A., Howell, J., & Swetman, R. (1993). Evaluating sport hero/ines: Contents, forms and social relations. *Quest, 45,* 197–210.

Klapp, O. (1949). Hero worship in America. *American Sociological Review, 14* (1), 57–63.

Rein, I., Kotler, P., & Stoller, M. (1997). *High visibility: The making and marketing of professionals into celebrities.* Chicago: NTC Business Books.

Rojek, C. (2001). *Celebrity.* London: Reaktion Books.

Rowe, D. (1999). *Sport, culture and the media: The unruly trinity.* Buckingham, UK: Open University Press.

Singer, T. (1998, March). Not so remote control. *Sport, 36.*

Athletic Talent Migration

The migration of elite athletes within nations, between nations, and across continents has been of growing interest to many people during the past twenty years. Since the early 1990s discussion of the transcontinental migration of athletic talent in the context of globalization has especially increased. Although sports geographers may have been the first to monitor the geographical variations in migratory flows of athletes and the "brawn drain," sociologists and social historians, among others, have taken up the challenge of considering the implications of athletic talent migration for sports and society. The collection co-edited by Bale and Maguire systematically organized writing on the migration of athletic talent. The papers in the collection exhibited a range of conceptual tools and theoretical frameworks within which to study the migration of foreign-born athletes in sports such as track and field, baseball, cricket, ice hockey, rugby, and football (soccer). Subsequently, a growing number of studies have focused on such sports as football, rugby, and ice hockey.

Research Themes

Research has focused on three themes. First, research has focused on the impacts of athletic talent migration on both host countries and donor countries, on the role of intermediaries such as sports agents, and on the effect on sports fans and the athletes themselves. Second, research has considered the responses to athletic talent migration by the nationally based governing bodies of sports and sports associations. Third, researchers

People think baseball players make $3 million and $4 million a year.
They don't realize that most of us only make $500,000. ▪ PETE INCAVIGLIA

have been interested in the implications of athletic talent migration for conceptions of identity in regions and nations.

Impacts of the Migration of Sports Laborers

The social historians Lanfranchi and Taylor note that from "the very start of the game, men have moved across national borders and from city to city, to play football" (Lanfranchi and Taylor 2001, 1). Arguably Scottish professionals were the earliest "international" migrants as they were lured south to England by the professional contracts offered after 1885 (the Scottish Football Association did not permit professionalism until 1893). From their detailed historical survey Lanfranchi and Taylor discerned three main types of football migrant: itinerant, mercenary, and settler. Each has been stimulated to move by three main factors: economic crises and national financial weakness, the existence of semiprofessional or unpaid amateur opportunities only, and the attraction of European leagues that can offer unrivaled lucrative contracts. Other research has created typologies (classifications based on types) of six or even seven types of sports migrants but arguably without shedding a great deal more clarity on the phenomenon.

The sociologist Manuel Castells suggests that the impact of athletic talent migration in what he refers to as contemporary "network society" is particularly important:

On the light side an illustration of this double dynamic of local identity and European networking, which I consider to be extremely important, is the structuring of professional sports, such as football and basketball, in the past decade. As everybody knows, the local team is an essential rallying point for people's identity. While national competitions continue to be played, maximum attention is given to European competitions (of which there are three for football, for instance), so that the reward for teams in the national competition is to become "European," a goal that many teams can reach, in contrast with

only a few three decades ago. At the same time, the opening of labour markets for European players, and the mass migration to Europe of players from other countries, means that a significant proportion of players in the local team are foreigners. The result is that people mobilise around the identity of their city, as represented by a group of largely foreign professional players competing in various European leagues. It is through these kind of basic life mechanisms that the real Europe is coming into existence—by sharing experience on the basis of meaningful, palpable identity. (Castells 1998, 329)

Although conditions in European football have changed in recent years—two, not three, competitions now exist—Castells's argument draws attention to the socio-cultural impact of cosmopolitan teams representing particular cities. For example, during the 1999–2000 season Chelsea Football Club in the English Premiership fielded a team that consisted entirely of foreign players.

Note that these developments have been hastened by changes in the regulatory frameworks within which professional and elite-level sports are conducted and hence within which elite athletes can ply their trades. In 1995 the Belgian football player Jean-Marc Bosman won a court case that confirmed that a player is free to work anywhere in Europe when his contract with a club expires. The European Union wants to abolish transfer fees as part of its effort to remove all obstacles to the freedom of movement in European member countries. The problem for many European football clubs is that they had come to depend on transfer fees as compensation for the scouting, training, and development of junior players. The concern is that now leading players will gain more bargaining power and that local loyalties will diminish even further in importance for players. Homegrown talent will no longer be the key to success, with implications for coaching, training, and national sides. People have expressed similar concerns about the growth in the number of Japanese baseball players in the U.S. major leagues since Nomo Hideo joined the Los Angeles Dodgers.

Research Shortcomings

Much of the literature on athletic talent migration has focused on the cultural rather than the economic significance of labor mobility. An overwhelming interest in identities has developed in such a way as to occlude attention to the economic and organizational dynamics of labor mobility. A further shortcoming in the literature is methodological—the data used in analyses have often been derived, somewhat uncritically, from the print or other mass media. Additionally, to date researchers have done less sustained academic analysis of the mobility of non-Western sports stars, including those from Asia and Africa.

With only a few exceptions academic interest in athletic talent migration among professional baseball leagues in the Pacific rim countries has been quite limited. Specific interest in Japanese player migration into Major League Baseball (MLB) has largely been the preserve of journalists. In the case of Africa, researchers Bale, Bale and Sang, and Darby have made useful contributions to our understanding of the migration of football players and other athletes. In Australasia, Hall has discussed the impact of the sports "brawn drain" on football in Australia, and Obel has considered the response of the NZ Rugby Football Union (NZRFU) to player migration.

Football and Japan

Lanfranchi and Taylor acknowledge that the expansion of football in eastern and southeastern Asia has extended the football labor market in recent years. They write that "Indonesia, Malaysia, Singapore, Hong Kong, South Korea, and even China have all started to admit foreign players and have reciprocated by sending their best talent abroad" (Lanfranchi and Taylor 2001, 12). They state that Japan offers a particularly interesting case study in light of the government's opposition to foreign labor. They note that "Non-nationals had played as amateurs in Japanese football for some years but it was the acceptance of full-time professionals, and the creation of the J. League in 1993, which encouraged the influx of migrant footballers" (Lanfranchi and Taylor 2001, 12–13). Missing from their study, however, is more detailed consideration of the mobility of Japanese players themselves, especially because during the 1990s "Serie A, the Premier Liga and the [English] Premiership [became] the football equivalent of Silicon valley" (Lanfranchi and Taylor 2001, 5).

Recently Takahashi and Horne have analyzed the history of the migration of Japanese football players. Using Internet searches, and especially Japanese-language databases and players' webpages, autobiographies, and biographies, Takahashi and Horne found that during the past twenty years shifts have taken place in the geographical spread of Japanese football talent, corresponding to new opportunities, both in Japan and internationally, for football labor. South America has given way to diverse regions, including Europe. Both socio-cultural and structural-institutional factors can be used to explain these developments with respect to Japanese football players.

Takahashi and Horne identified three time periods: before the launch of the first professional football league in Japan (the J. League) in 1993, from then until the first appearance of the Japanese national team at the Football World Cup Finals in 1998, and since 1998. Takahashi and Horne suggest that seven factors have transformed the mobility of Japanese professional football players during the past three decades:

1. Technological improvements in transportation and communication
2. Growth of the numbers of actors and institutions facilitating mobility (agents and national and supranational football and nonfootball organizations)
3. Expansion of the Federation Internationale de Football Association (FIFA) to 204 members in 2004
4. Expansion of television coverage of football (as increasingly it becomes valuable "entertainment content")
5. The end of the Cold War and the collapse of state capitalism that led to the opening up of borders

Athletic Talent Migration

Foreign Talent and the National Basketball Association

The first non-U.S. born player drafted by an NBA team was Yasutaka Okayama of Japan by Golden State in 1981. Most foreign-born players did not have an impact until the late 1990s and by 2005 there were nearly 80 players not born in the United States playing in the NBA. This constituted nearly 20 percent of the players and some such as Dirk Nowitzki (Germany), Tony Parker (France), and Manu Ginobili (Argentina) are among the best players in the league. More important, this large number of international players has brought an international style of play to the NBA. More and more the emphasis is on teamwork, passing, and the three-point shot with less emphasis on one-on-one moves by a few superstars. There is more finesse and less reliance on sheer strength. Whether this new style replaces the old one more fully is yet to be seen.

David Levinson

6. In the European Union the Bosman Judgment, which laid the basis for greater internationalization of European league football

7. The "footballization" of eastern Asia (the growth in national professional football leagues—the J. League [Japan], the S. League [Singapore], the C. League [People's Republic of China], and before that the K. League [South Korea]—in eastern Asian societies)

Takahashi and Horne conclude that prior to 1993 and the launch of the J. League a weak football infrastructure existed in Japan. This infrastructure did not lead to widespread player migration, however, because of the influence of the amateur tradition in Japanese sports and the incorporation of football into the corporate sports system. More important, football was not the nation's culturally central team sport. Since 1993 Japanese football players have increasingly begun to follow Japanese sponsors (capital) to European and South American league clubs, and likewise Japanese capital has begun to follow players (through the emergent sports tourism business, for example). Increasingly football clubs in mature football cultures have recognized the economic benefits that Japanese (and, in some cases, Chinese) players can bring to them. However, most Japanese and other football players from eastern Asia are hired on loan rather than with full registration contracts. European football clubs operate risk-averse strategies. Rather than finding evidence of a global labor market in football, therefore, Takahashi and Horne found that employer strategies in national football labor markets, although internationalized, continue to determine who gets recruited by which clubs and why.

The Future

Most researchers agree that athletic talent migration involves processes that continue to develop. Athletic talent migration is a dynamic process involving countries, clubs, and athletes in a complex chain of negotiations over rights and responsibilities. People will continue to debate whether athletic talent migration is an example of heightened globalization, regionalization, or internationalization. National sports associations, unions, and governing bodies will continue to act in ways that secure the best athletes for their teams. Sometimes such action means securing the services of athletes and managers who are prepared to switch national allegiances at short notice. The International Olympic Committee rule on eligibility is straightforward: Anyone who has a passport can represent a country as long as he or she fulfills the residential qualification of the sport's governing body. In 2004, for example, Malachi Davis, a 400-meter runner born and educated in the United States, gained his British passport just months before he qualified for the British Olympic team. At other times selection will be based on national preferences about playing style and temperament.

People also will continue to debate the impact of athletic talent migration on the sense of national identity of fans and athletes. The researchers Wong and Trumper suggest that such migration can undermine *and* strengthen nationalism. Leading players seem able to move according to the attractions of money and their desire to compete with the best. We can see the ensuing "brawn drain" of the best athletes from the poorer countries to the West as a form of exploitation through dependent development. However, the mediated representations of these players abroad can also have a culturally affirmative impact on national identities. As the researcher Christian Bromberger (1994, 189) noted:

> The study of international migrations of sportsmen [sic] leads us to the heart of one of the major contradictions of our time: the tension between, on the one hand, local loyalties, spatial affiliation, cultural affinities, traditions and history, a world of ascriptions and, on the other hand, personal contracts, market laws, universal rationalism, space without boundaries, a world of achievement.

John Horne

Further Reading

Bale, J. (1984). *Sport and place: A geography of sport in England, Scotland and Wales.* London: Hurst.

Bale, J. (1991). *The brawn drain: Foreign student-athletes in American universities.* Urbana: University of Illinois Press.

Bale, J. (2004). Three geographies of African footballer migration: Patterns, problems and postcoloniality. In G. Armstrong & R. Giulianotti (Eds.), *Football in Africa* (pp. 229–246). London: Palgrave.

Bale, J., & Maguire, J. (Eds.). (1994). *The global sports arena: Athletic talent migration in an interdependent world.* London: Frank Cass.

Bale, J., & Maguire, J. (1994). Sports labour migration in the global arena. In J. Bale & J. Maguire (Eds.), *The global sports arena: Athletic talent migration in an interdependent world* (pp. 1–21). London: Frank Cass.

Bale, J., & Sang, J. (1996). *Kenyan running: Movement change, geography and global change.* London: Frank Cass.

Bromberger, C. (1994). Foreign footballers, cultural dreams and community identity in some northwestern Mediterranean cities. In J. Bale & J. Maguire (Eds.), *The global sports arena: Athletic talent migration in an interdependent world* (pp. 171–182). London: Frank Cass.

Castells, M. (1998). *End of millennium.* Oxford, UK: Blackwell.

Chiba, N. (2004). Pacific professional baseball leagues and migratory patterns and trends: 1995–1999. *Journal of Sport and Social Issues, 28*(2), 193–211.

Darby, P. (2000). The new scramble for Africa: African football labour migration to Europe. *European Sports History Review, 3,* 217–244.

Darby, P. (2001). *Africa, football and FIFA.* London: Frank Cass.

Gardiner, S., & Welch, R. (2000). "Show me the money": Regulation of the migration of professional sportsmen in post–Bosman Europe. In A. Caiger & S. Gardiner (Eds.), *Professional sport in the European Union: Regulation and reregulation* (pp. 107–126). The Hague, Netherlands: T. M. C. Asser Press.

Hall, M. (2000). *The away game: The inside story of Australian footballers in Europe.* Sydney, Australia: Harper Sports.

Hirai, H. (2001). Hideo Nomo: Pioneer or defector? In D. Andrews & S. Jackson (Eds.), *Sport stars* (pp. 187–200). London: Routledge.

Kidd, B., & Donnelly, P. (2000). Human rights in sports. *International Review for the Sociology of Sport, 35*(2), 131–148.

Klein, A. (1994). Trans-nationalism, labour migration and Latin American baseball. In J. Bale & J. Maguire (Eds.), *The global sports arena: Athletic talent migration in an interdependent world* (pp. 183–205). London: Frank Cass.

Lanfranchi, P., & Taylor, M. (2001). *Moving with the ball: The migration of professional footballers.* Oxford, UK: Berg.

Magee, J., & Sugden, J. (2002). "The world at their feet": Professional football and international labor migration. *Journal of Sport and Social Issues, 26*(4), 421–437.

Maguire, J. (1999). *Global sport.* Cambridge, UK: Polity Press.

McGovern, P. (2002). Globalization or internationalization? Foreign footballers in the English League, 1946–95. *Sociology, 36*(1), 23–42.

Obel, C. (2001). National responses to the migration of players and coaches in the sport of rugby union. In K. Eunha et al (Eds.), *Proceedings of the 1st World Congress of sociology of sport* (pp. 533–542). Seoul: Organizing Committee for the 1st World Congress of Sociology of Sport.

Takahashi, Y., & Horne, J. (2004). Japanese football players and the sport talent migration business. In W. Manzenreiter & J. Horne (Eds.), *Football goes east: Business, culture and the people's game in China, Japan and Korea* (pp. 69–86). London: Routledge.

Whiting, R. (2004). *The meaning of Ichiro: The new wave from Japan and the transformation of our national pastime.* New York: Warner.

Wong, L., & Trumper, R. (2002). Global celebrity athletes and nationalism: Futbol, hockey and the representation of nation. *Journal of Sport and Social Issues, 26*(2), 168–194.

Athletic Training

A thletic training is the process that athletes undergo to prepare to compete in a sport. Such training includes work on the sport itself and its components, as well as exercises that increase the strength, flexibility, and endurance that athletes need to achieve their potential. Athletic training also prevents injury.

Everyone has limits on the time they can devote to exercise, and cross-training simply gives you the best return on your investment—balanced fitness with minimum injury risk and maximum fun. ■ PAULA NEWBY-FRASER

The certified athletic trainer is a health-care professional who provides health and injury care to physically active people such as athletes. Working in cooperation with physicians and other health-care professionals, the certified athletic trainer is an integral part of the health-care team, providing skills in the recognition, immediate care, treatment, rehabilitation, and prevention of musculoskeletal injuries. A four-year degree program is offered at more than one hundred institutions throughout the United States. All certified athletic trainers have a bachelor's degree; 70 percent have a postgraduate degree. With a combination of classroom education and clinical experience athletic trainers are prepared to apply a variety of health-care skills and knowledge in a variety of settings.

Origins

In 1990 the American Medical Association recognized the profession of athletic trainer as an allied health profession. The history of athletic trainers, however, can be traced to the early 1900s, when athletic trainers provided health and injury care to athletes participating in organized athletics such as the Olympic Games. When football became a national sport in the United States, people realized that someone needed to care for players' inevitable injuries. The profession of athletic trainer grew from that need.

The National Athletic Trainers' Association (NATA), the professional association for certified athletic trainers, was founded in 1950. It is a worldwide association with more than thirty thousand members, primarily from the United States, Canada, and Japan. The mission of NATA and certified athletic trainers is to provide health and injury care to active people of all ages through the prevention, treatment, and rehabilitation of activity-related injury and illness. The National Athletic Trainers' Association Board of Certification, incorporated in 1989, provides a certification program for entry-level athletic trainers and continuing education standards for certified athletic trainers.

Studies of athletic training show that the methods that trainers use are effective in treating musculoskeletal injuries and that trainers return athletes quickly to their preinjury status. These methods also are used outside athletics. Studies have also shown that athletic training methods improve work-related disorders and that rehabilitation provided by certified athletic trainers improves the functional status of patients after reconstructive surgery of major joints.

Exactly what athletic trainers do—known as their "scope of practice"—is defined by specific competencies. These competencies, referred to as "athletic training competencies for health care for the physically active," define

Working out with weights.

Source: istockphoto/sandoclr.

In order to excel, you must be completely dedicated to your chosen sport.
You must also be prepared to work hard and be willing to accept destructive criticism.
Without 100 percent dedication, you won't be able to do this. ■ WILLIE MAYS

the areas of expertise of entry-level athletic trainers and are based on these educational areas: risk management, assessment-evaluation, acute care, general medical and disabilities, therapeutic exercise, therapeutic modalities, health-care administration, professional development and responsibilities, psychosocial intervention and referral, pathology of injury and illness, pharmacological aspects of injury and illness, nutritional aspects of injury and illness, and illness.

During earlier decades athletic trainers practiced primarily in scholastic, amateur, and professional athletic settings. However, during the last twenty years the number of certified athletic trainers working in sports medicine clinics, hospitals, and industrial settings has increased. Indeed some 40 percent of certified athletic trainers work outside of school athletic settings.

Athletic Training and Injury

One cannot overemphasize the role of physical training in the prevention of injury. The injury patterns and rates of male and female athletes are similar. Generally speaking, the injuries suffered in men's sports are suffered in comparable women's sports, and the management of these injuries by certified athletic trainers is also similar.

Athletic Training and Women

During the early years of women's participation in organized sports, people placed little emphasis on conditioning and strength training, both of which are important factors in mechanically correct performance and injury prevention. Sports, by their nature, invite injury. Women athletes are exposed to the same injury risks as are men athletes and therefore need the same injury prevention and management considerations.

However, many myths and misconceptions surrounded women's participation in sports. Apprehension and skepticism prevailed, based on fears of risk to women's musculoskeletal systems and reproductive capabilities. These fears were based on perceived differences in physiological and anatomical strength between the genders. After research dispelled such myths and

misconceptions, conditioning and strength programs gradually were implemented for women athletes.

However, implementation did not guarantee access. Previously men athletes had been the sole occupants of facilities such as conditioning areas and weight rooms. The availability of facilities became a deterrent to the newfound interest of women and to their conditioning goals. Through Title IX (the U.S. law passed in 1972 to prohibit sex discrimination in federally funded education programs and activities), this deterrent was gradually overcome, and training facilities were either added or made co-educational so that both men and women could use them.

Resolution of questions such as "Where can women train?" and "Is training appropriate for women?" did not settle all issues. Social issues arose, and many young women were prevented from reaching their performance potential because of the negative stereotype of the athletic woman's physique. However, through time these issues also were resolved. Today conditioning and strength are accepted as necessary prerequisites for sports participation by both genders.

Women as Athletic Trainers

Once dominated by men, the profession of athletic trainer now includes women. The increase in participation by girls and women in sports and other physical activity, encouraged by Title IX, created a need for health and injury care for these athletes. Initially serving only women athletes, women athletic trainers now provide health and injury care to athletes of both genders.

NATA has demonstrated its commitment to the needs of women. Since the early 1970s women certified athletic trainers have played an important role in the development of NATA and the profession of athletic trainer. More than 50 percent of the membership of NATA is female. Women are represented on all major NATA committees, chair several of those committees, and are members of NATA's board of directors. NATA also has awarded grants to women scientists who serve as principal investigators of issues of importance to ac-

tive women, such as anterior cruciate ligament injuries of the knee and eating disorders.

Marjorie J. Albohm

Further Reading

National Athletic Trainers' Association. (2004). The FACTS about certified athletic trainers. Retrieved December 6, 2004, from http://www.nata.org/publicinformation/files/FactsaboutATCS.pdf

Australia

A vast island continent sparsely populated with almost 20 million inhabitants, Australia has long had a reputation as a sports-loving nation, a notion that has contributed strongly to its sense of identity. Indeed, the physical geography of the country—an equable climate, relatively flat terrain, and proximity of most urban centers to the coastline—along with international sporting success and rates of spectator attendance often disproportionate to its small population base, has given currency to the description of Australia as a "paradise of sport."

History

Inhabited by Aborigines for at least 40,000 years, indigenous physical activities such as hunting, throwing, swimming, and dancing, unlike the games that Anglo-Celtic settlers imported during the late eighteenth century, were not separate from other ceremonies, rituals, or pursuits. Instead, they were an integral part of daily life, played for enjoyment and governed by few rules. It was only later that Aborigines became highly skilled participants in many of the popular European sports such as athletics, boxing, and the various forms of football (known as football "codes"), although racial discrimination often inhibited their success at the highest level.

From the beginning of white settlement—as a penal colony—in 1788, sports that could be played in conjunction with the complementary activities of gambling and drinking soon gained prominence. These activities included bare-knuckle boxing, wrestling, and cockfighting. Horse racing was well patronized, as were other recreational activities that required little or no equipment in the initially harsh and restrictive environment of a penal colony. The public hotel played an important role in the development of this sporting culture and also served to strengthen the links between masculinity and sport in a population where men outnumbered women by a ratio of three to one. In fact a wide range of sports such as cricket, foot-racing, billiards, bowling, quoits, skittles, and trotting all took place within close proximity of "pubs" during the first half of the nineteenth century. In essence the sporting values and preferences of European settlers molded the cultural practices of sport in Australia, fueling a cult of athleticism throughout the antipodes.

Sporting clubs were quick to form in the latter half of the nineteenth century, and local contests soon developed into regional competitions. With the advent of the Federation of six Australian states in 1901, national organizations in a range of sports gradually developed despite the tyranny of distance. Most sporting bodies were club-based, and by 1910 there were national governing bodies for sports such as Australian Rules football, cricket, cycling, golf, lawn bowls, and rifle shooting.

Throughout the first forty years of the twentieth century, local governments were an important contributor to the success of this club-based sport system. They traditionally provided playground facilities, which comprised slides, swings, hoops, and bars. These facilities were usually located in public parks and gave children the opportunity not just to play, but also to develop their confidence and motor skills. In addition local governments constructed sports grounds and pavilions. Australia's community sporting infrastructure was therefore dependent on local councils, particularly when large open space was required for the activity. In this respect the football codes, cricket, swimming, tennis, and

Australian cricketers at Lord's Cricket Ground in May, 1884.

grams at centers located across Australia and internationally.

The AIS was complemented by the formation of the Australian Sports Commission (ASC) in 1985. This organization was set up as an independent statutory authority to provide leadership and direction at the national level. In order to further streamline the decision-making and administrative functions of both bodies, the ASC and AIS were merged in 1989. The ASC is the peak sporting body in Australia, and since 2000 it has overseen an annual budget of approximately $130 million. This money is primarily used to fund the AIS and Australia's national sporting organizations, such as Australian Swimming, Cycling Australia, and Hockey Australia.

Participant and Spectator Sports

Australians are renowned for watching a lot of sport on television. The two most popular television sports are Australia Rules football and Rugby League, which also happen to be the strongest national sport leagues. Each sport is broadcast on both free and pay television networks over their entire seasons, which can last between twenty and twenty-five weeks. The grand finals for each league usually attract a nationwide audience of more than 2 million people. Cricket is the other dominant television sport, and over the summer period, it can regularly attract nationwide audiences of between 1.5 and 2 million fans, especially when a series against archrival England takes place.

Over the last thirty years there has been sustained growth in professional and spectator sport. The Melbourne Cup horse-racing carnival now attracts more than 500,000 visitors, while the Australian Open Tennis Championship has increased its annual aggregate tournament attendance to nearly 500,000. The Australian Football League (AFL), Australia's most popular

particularly netball benefited substantially from local government support.

Prior to the election of the Whitlam Labor government in 1972, federal government sport policy was limited to the selective assistance of Olympic Games teams, as well as physical fitness and surf lifesaving initiatives. However, the election of the Whitlam government was a watershed for Australian sport, a view supported by Prime Minister Whitlam's statement that "there was no greater social problem facing Australia than the good use of leisure." Contrary to the conservative Menzies government of the immediate postwar period, which regarded sport as an essentially private and individual pursuit, the Whitlam government acknowledged that sport could be used to improve the social conditions of outer-urban and regional Australia. Despite this rhetoric, since the 1970s the federal government, with the support of the states, has continued to take a leading role in developing a system to support elite-level sport, rather than grassroots participation. In particular, following Australia's poor performance at the Montreal Olympic Games in 1976, the federal government made a quantum leap with the establishment of the Australian Institute of Sport (AIS) in 1981. Modeled on the successful East German and Chinese sport academies, the AIS was a high-technology training center located in Canberra, the nation's capital. Originally targeting eight sports and situated in a central location, the AIS has since expanded and decentralized with specialized pro-

As harrowing occupations go, there can't be much to choose between the Australian cricket captaincy and social work on Skid Row. ▪ DOUG IBBOTOON

spectator sport, generated a total attendance of 6.5 million for its winter competition in 2003, while the National Rugby League (NRL) drew a cumulative attendance of nearly 3 million. Melbourne, the capital of Victoria, has a particular passion for professional sport and was recently judged to be the sporting capital of the world on the basis of its ability to attract a remarkable minimum average weekly spectator audience of more than 300,000, easily ahead of cities such as London. Overall, just over 7 million, or 47 percent, of adult Australians attend sporting events on a regular basis.

Australia has several world famous sporting venues. Regarded as one of the best sport stadiums in the world, the Melbourne Cricket Ground is located in a sporting precinct and is a major venue for the Australian Football League and Australian cricket team. Its record crowd stands at just over 120,000, but improvements to the ground and the introduction of corporate facilities have reduced the ground's capacity to approximately 95,000. Australia's other great stadium is a relatively new addition, built for the Sydney Olympic Games. Stadium Australia has a capacity of approximately 80,000 and is located in Sydney's western suburbs, which is also home to many other Olympic venues.

Australia is just one of only two countries that have taken part in every summer Olympic Games since 1896, a record enhanced by the fact that the International Olympic Committee awarded the right to host the Games to Melbourne (1956) and then Sydney (2000). Australian athletes performed exceptionally well at both events, and the nation's overall Olympic record is an enviable one. Dawn Fraser, Murray Rose, Marjorie Jackson, Ron Clarke, and Betty Cuthbert became household names around the world following their feats in 1956, while a new generation of athletes, including Ian Thorpe, Kieren Perkins, Susie O'Neill, and Cathy Freeman, ensured Olympic success continued at the end of the twentieth century. Australia has also dominated the Commonwealth Games since their inception in 1938, hosting the event on a number of occasions.

Nationwide surveys conducted at the turn of the twenty-first century found that 92 percent of respondents felt proud of Australia's international sport achievements, and seven of the ten most inspirational moments in Australian history were sport-related. These results indicated that as well as having a strong culture of sport participation and sport spectatorship, Australians also use sport to establish a sense of collective identity and self-respect. In an increasingly globalized world, sport has become a primary vehicle for expressing national legitimacy, pride, and independence. For a country that is geographically isolated from the rest of the world, sporting success at mega-events is a highly visible and potent way of achieving global media exposure and international awareness.

Women and Sport

Females have always had to struggle for resources and recognition in Australian sport, a fact partially recognized by the promulgation of the Sex Discrimination Act in 1984. Yet despite a lack of parity in terms of facilities, funding, and media exposure, Australian sportswomen have played an important role in the development of the national sporting ethos. For example, women staged the first national golf championship in 1894, and Australian Rules football boasts the highest percentage of female spectators of any form of football in the world. However, it is in the Olympic arena where women have outshone their male counterparts. In fact, between 1948 and 2000 women made up only 28 percent of Australian Olympic squads, and yet they have won 39 percent of all gold medals, despite being able to compete in fewer events. Their dominance in this area is reflected in the exponential increase given to women in media coverage whenever Olympic Games are staged.

Youth Sports

School sport associations have been established in some states for over one hundred years, and interstate school sporting competitions can be traced back to the 1920s. The Australian School Sports Council (ASC), formed in

Australia Olympics Results
2002 Winter Olympics: 2 Gold
2004 Summer Olympics: 17 Gold, 16 Silver, 16 Bronze

1981, now acts as the parent body for all school sport, and in 1992 a report by the Senate Standing Committee on Environment, Recreation, and the Arts confirmed the place of sport in the school curriculum, making positive recommendations concerning the funding of physical education and sport in schools. Government involvement in the delivery of sport has also been underpinned by the launch of the ASC's "Aussie Sports" program in 1986. The program was developed partly in response to concerns about the overly competitive nature of school sport, and modified games (minimizing height, weight, and gender differences) were offered to school children so that motor skills could be practiced in a nonthreatening sports environment. Many other sporting organizations also offer modified games, such as Auskick and Netta Netball, partly as a promotional exercise and partly to smooth the transition to senior, club-based sporting activities.

Organizations

In terms of sports organizations, the Australian Sports Commission (http://www.ausport.gov.au) is the top regulatory body for sport in Australia and is responsible for implementing federal government policy, managing the Australian Institute of Sport, and distributing funding to national sport organizations. The Australian Football League (www.afl.com.au) is the most popular national sport league in Australia. It began in 1897 as the Victorian Football League, and in the 1980s and 1990s, it added teams from most Australian states. The Australian Sports Drug Agency (http://www.asda.org.au/) is the peak body in Australia, set up to deter the use of banned doping practices in sport through education, testing, advocacy, and coordination of Australia's antidoping program, while Sport Industry Australia (www.sportforall.com.au), established originally as the Confederation of Australian Sport in 1976, represents the interests of Australia's national sport organizations and their members. Cricket Australia (aus.cricinfo.com/db/NATIONAL/AUS) is the governing body for Australia's national sport, which manages the Australian cricket team, the world leader

throughout the early part of the twentieth century and the 1990s.

Sports in Society

Australian sport has often been referred to as an industry, and there are good grounds for this claim. There are 14,000 playing fields and indoor sport centers, supported by 1.5 million volunteer administrators and officials, while the sport industry provides paid employment for 275,000 people. Households spend more than $7 billion a year on sport-related services and goods, while corporate sponsorship accounts for $300 million. When $430 million of sport exports are added to the national sport "accounts," the total contribution of the sport industry to gross domestic product (GDP) is approximately 1 percent. It is also a complex industry, since it comprises an array of government-owned facilities, not-for-profit clubs and associations, and privately owned businesses. It specifically includes sporting competitions that range from small rural amateur competitions to fully professional national sport leagues, commercial operators, consultants, and sport-product manufacturers and retailers.

The hyper-commercialization of Australian sport has been accompanied by an apparently insatiable need for sporting heroes. However, not all Australia's contemporary sporting champions fit the archetypal mold. Cathy Freeman does because she is unassuming, dedicated, courageous, and a great spokesperson for the Aboriginal community. Lleyton Hewitt did not fit the mold for a long time because he was seen to be too competitive and opinionated and not as modest as Australians like heroes to be. The player who best fitted the archetype was Pat Rafter. He was not only an outstanding tennis player, but also good looking, self-depreciating, every mother's ideal son, and also seen as one of the boys. Sporting heroes are an important part of Australia's sporting landscape and are used to not only promote their sport, but also to endorse all sorts of consumer products. A quarter of all people who have won the Australian of the Year award over the last thirty years were sportsmen and sportswomen, while the last three Australian cricket team captains have all become Australians of the Year. The two most widely acknowledged sporting icons from Australia's past are the recently deceased Sir Donald Bradman, far and away the nation's greatest cricketer, and Phar Lap, the New Zealand–born horse that was nigh unbeatable during the 1930s and died tragically after racing in the United States.

Australians also like their sporting heroes to be extraordinary in the sense that they should both win against the world's best and symbolize sport's working-class traditions and tribal relations. Australian sporting rowdies are revered for their indifference to authority, loud humor, and heavy drinking. There is however, a downside to this hypermasculine and "blokey" sporting ethos. In addition to its tendency to marginalize the participation of women, it can produce chronic displays of poor sportsmanship and crass behavior. While sporting larrikins are quintessentially Australian, they also reveal an ugly and anti-intellectual side of the Australian sporting culture, where boisterous good humor degenerates into personal abuse, racist taunts, and physical violence.

The Future

Despite Australia's sporting achievements and the willingness with which Australians consume both broadcast and live sporting events, Australia is the second most obese nation on the globe, second only to the United States. In many respects the increasing success of Australia's athletes has been paralleled by a difficulty in getting more people to participate in enough physical activity to provide mental and physical health benefits. Although it is often noted that in excess of 60 percent of Australians participate in physical activity, this figure can be misleading, for according to research done by the Australian Bureau of Statistics, only 10.5 percent participate in sport two or more times per week. At the same time people are moving subtly away from organized and competitive sport to more informal, time-compressed leisure activities. Of the 9 million people who participate in physical activity annually, approxi-

Australia

Vigoro

Similar to cricket, vigoro is an Australian women's sport invented around 1900. It became an organized sport in 1919 after the Vigoro Association was established. The sport is still based in Australia, played in leagues in New South Wales, Tasmania, and Queensland. The major difference between cricket and vigoro is that vigoro teams have twelve players with the extra player being a second bowler. There are no overs, and bowlers can use any type of throw as long as the ball is thrown overhand. It is faster-paced than cricket, and a game can be completed in two and a half hours.

Key organizations are the New South Wales Vigoro Association (www.vigoro.com.au) and the Townsville Ladies Vigoro Association (www.angelfire.com/va2/vigoro).

mately 3.7 million walk for exercise, 1.6 million swim, and another 1.6 million participate in aerobics or related fitness activities. Both the levels of physical activity and the shift to unstructured sport activities will present a challenge for the Australian sport system in years to come.

Since the early 1970s, Australia has grown to become one of the world's sporting powers. It has done so with a relatively small population and a geographic location that isolates it from most of the rest of the world. It used to be said that Australia rode on the sheep's back, a phrase that indicated that Australia was dependent on its agricultural and livestock industries for its economic success and broader reputation in the world. It is now fair to say that Australia rides on the back of its athletes. These athletes and their performances at a range of international events, most notably the Olympic Games, have ensured that Australia has a particularly strong global sporting profile.

Robert Hess and Matthew Nicholson

See also Bondi Beach

Further Reading

Bloomfield, J. (2003). *Australia's sporting success: The inside story.* Sydney, Australia: University of New South Wales Press.

Booth, D., & Tatz, C. (2000). *One-eyed: A view of Australian sport.* St. Leonards, Australia: Allen & Unwin.

Cashman, R. (1998). *Paradise of sport: The rise of organised sport in Australia.* Melbourne, Australia: Oxford University Press.

Gordon, H. (2000). *Australia and the Olympic Games.* St. Lucia, Australia: University of Queensland Press.

Mangan, J., & Nauright, J. (Eds.). (2000). *Sport in Australasian society: Past and present.* London: Frank Cass.

Shilbury, D., & Deane, J. (2001). *Sport management in Australia: An organisational overview.* Melbourne, Australia: Strategic Sport Management.

Stell, M. (1991). *Half the race: A history of Australian women in sport.* North Ryde, Australia: Angus and Robertson.

Stewart, B,. & Nicholson, M. (2003). Australia. In L. DaCosta & A. Miragaya (Eds.). *Worldwide experiences and trends in sport for all* (pp. 35–76). Oxford, UK: Meyer and Meyer.

Stewart, B., Nicholson, M., Smith, A., & Westerbeek, H. (2004). *Sport policy in Australia: Evolution and contemporary practice.* London: Routledge.

Vamplew, W. et al. (Eds.). (1997). *The Oxford companion to Australian sport.* Melbourne, Australia: Oxford University Press.

Australian Rules Football

Australian rules football, originally known as "Victorian rules football" because it was established in Melbourne in the state of Victoria, is a form of football that is popular particularly in southern and western Australia. Its first rules, dating from 1859, make it one of the world's oldest forms of football. A handwritten copy of these rules was discovered only in 1980.

Rules, Playing Surfaces, and Equipment

Australian rules football is played on a ground roughly oval in shape—although the size and shape can vary—between two teams of eighteen players. Four vertical goal posts—large central posts flanked on each side by smaller posts—are used. No horizontal bars are used. A goal (six points) is scored when the ball is kicked between the two central posts without being touched. If the ball is touched, hits the central posts, is rushed through by the defending side, or travels between the smaller posts, a behind (one point) is scored. No offside exists, and the sport is primarily a kicking, catching, running, and hand-passing game—players can run a maximum of 10 meters before they either pass or bounce the ball. A game is played over four quarters of approximately thirty minutes each and with intervals lasts almost three hours. A game begins when an umpire bounces the ball in the center circle, and players attempt to tap the ball to their side's advantage.

Australian rules football is a high-scoring and fast-moving sport with some similarities to basketball—play moves rapidly from one end to another, and scores frequently fluctuate. It is an expansive and crowd-pleasing sport with less measurement and standardization than other sports, making it closer to folk football. Margaret Lindley has noted that Australian footballers "run, dodge, leap, spin and slide; execute a variety of kicks which place their bodies in arabesques and attempt marks which see them in every conceivable airborne position."

Creation Myths

Some people believe that the sport was derived from an Aboriginal game played with stuffed opossum skins. Others have claimed an Irish origin, although Gaelic football was codified at a much later date. A more plausible and orthodox explanation is that seven men who were educated at British public schools created the 1859 rules in the absence of any agreed model of football. A letter from colonial sportsman Thomas Wills to a local newspaper, suggesting the need for a winter sport, some schoolboy games, and the formation of the Melbourne Football Club in 1858 added to a growing interest in football.

Although Victorian rules football combined the rules of various English public schools, it soon developed a distinctly Australian ethos (distinguishing character, sentiment, moral nature, or guiding beliefs) that valued improvisation and spontaneity. Initially played in the parklands of Melbourne the sport expressed the brash

Australian Rules Football

South Africa Embraces Australian Rules Football

The following transcript from a February 2005 radio broadcast makes clear that Australian Rules Football has found a new home in South Africa:

ELIZABETH JACKSON: The South African Government has declared Australian Rules Football the sport for "the new South Africa," and the league is ratcheting up its marketing to target a whole new market. Africa Correspondent Zoe Daniel reports.

ZOE DANIEL: In the townships outside rural Potchefstroom in South Africa's North West province soccer is the sport of choice. It's in line with the traditional demarcation of sport in a country where historical racial divisions are still strong. But the AFL thinks it may be the bridge between black and white.

STEVE HARRISON: Aussie Rules so far, has proven to be a very good way of bringing people together. We had a game, it was the Gauteng Province playing against the convicts and it was a half and half mix of black and white players, and that was absolutely fantastic, and they lined up, they sung the national anthem, playing Australian football and it was half black, half white and that's what we're going for.

ZOE DANIEL: Steve Harrison, Footy South Africa Coordinator.

Australian Rules was played here during the Boer war, but until recently, it had died out of the South African sporting scene. That was until the Government declared it the sport for the new South Africa because of its ability to embrace different races and cultures. Now the AFL is cranking up its push to get more people playing.

BRIAN CLARKE: They're using the north western province as sort of a trial run for the remaining eight provinces, identifying the sport as the new sport for the new South Africa in the sense that, traditionally they've had rugby as a sort of white domain, the blacks playing soccer, and this is a great way to combine the two in a new game. It's going to take some time to gel together, but it's really pleasing to see that they share one thing in common, they want to learn about this new game.

Source: South Africa embraces Australian rules football. (2005, February 5). Retrieved March 15, 2005, from http://www.abc.net.au/am/content/2005/s1296562.htm

self-confidence of the colonial culture of gold-rich Victoria. The founders of the Australian sport wanted to create a "game of our own."

History

The simplicity of the original rules allowed fluidity in the evolution of the sport. H. C. A. Harrison, a notable player and administrator, was prominent in revisions of the rules in 1866 and 1874. In 1877 eight Victorian teams joined to form the Victorian Football Association (VFA) to regulate the sport and to promote intercolonial contests. A similar association was formed in South Australia in 1877, and suburban football competitions also emerged in Hobart, Launceston, and Perth. Intercolonial rivalry and long distances were two reasons why the northeastern states of New South

Wales and Queensland eventually opted for the British sport of rugby.

With the onset of professionalism during the 1890s eight clubs split from the VFA in 1897 to form the Victorian Football League (VFL), which remained the dominant body in the sport for almost a century. In 1906 a national body, the Australian National Football Council (later the National Football League), was formed to control interstate player exchanges and to develop interstate competition. The first national carnival was held in August 1908 at the Melbourne Cricket Ground with teams from all the Australian states and New Zealand competing.

When a national competition emerged during the 1980s, it was under the aegis of Victorian rules football. The South Melbourne Swans relocated to Sydney (and

became the Sydney Swans) in 1982, the Brisbane Bears and the West Coast Eagles joined in 1987, followed by the Adelaide Crows (1991), the Fremantle Dockers (1995), and the Port Adelaide Power (1996). The VFL changed its name to the "Australian Football League" (AFL) at the end of 1989.

Key People

With the high mark a spectacular feature of Australian rules football, fans have admired full forwards such as Roy Cazaly, who played from 1910 to 1927. Cazaly gave rise to the phrase "Up there, Cazaly," which was reputedly the battle cry of Australian soldiers in World War II as they stormed trenches. The song "Up There, Cazaly" later became an anthem of the AFL. Some notable players, such as Norm Smith, Ron Barassi, and Leigh Matthews, have been equally prominent as coaches.

Although Australian rules football was a demonstration sport at the 1956 Melbourne Olympic Games, and although clubs were formed in New Zealand and South Africa, it remains almost exclusively an Australian sport. Similarities between Australian rules football and Gaelic football led to the development of a hybrid sport —international rules football—and occasional international contests between Australian and Irish teams from 1967. Since the 1980s a number of Irish footballers have been recruited to play for Australian clubs.

From its inception Australian rules football has been accessible to the community. The passionate attachment of Melburnians to their clubs is the subject of David Williamson's play and film, *The Club,* based on the Collingwood Football Club, with approximately forty thousand members. The community support for the battling Footscray (now Western) Bulldogs is the subject of another film, *The Year of the Dogs.* Women have comprised 30 to 50 percent of Australian rules football spectators since the late nineteenth century, a markedly higher proportion of spectators than those of other types of football. Women played football only sporadically during the twentieth century before formation of the Victorian Women's Football League in 1981. With seven thousand players by 2004, women's football is one of the fastest-growing sports in the Victorian school system.

An Aboriginal presence in Australian rules football became more notable during the 1960s, and by the 1980s clubs recruited Aboriginal players in larger numbers. Some became stars. A dramatic gesture against racism by Nicky Winmar at the end of a game in 1993, when he raised his jersey and pointed to the color of his skin, encouraged the AFL to develop a player code to reduce racial incidents.

The Future

Although the future of Australian rules football is secure in Australia because of its popularity, Matthew Nicholson noted that the AFL is "awkwardly perched between its Victorian suburban traditions and its national aspirations." The national competition of sixteen teams includes nine Melbourne suburban teams, one regional Victorian team, and six teams from four other states.

Richard Cashman

Further Reading

Blainey, G. (1990). *A game of our own: The origins of Australian football.* Melbourne, Australia: Information Australia.

Hess, R. (1996). Women and Australian rules football in colonial Melbourne. *International Journal of the History of Sport, 13*(3), 356–372.

Hess, R., & Stewart, B. (Eds.). (1998). *More than a game: The real story of Australian rules football.* Melbourne, Australia: Melbourne University Press.

Lindley, M. (2002). Taking a joke too far and footballers shorts. In D. Hemphill & C. Symons (Eds.), *Gender, sexuality and sport: A dangerous mix* (pp. 61–67). Sydney, Australia: Walla Walla Press.

Linnell, G. (1995). *Football Ltd: The inside story of the AFL.* Sydney, Australia: Ironbark.

Pascoe, R. (1996). *The winter games: Over 100 years of Australian football.* Melbourne, Australia: Mandarin.

Sandercock, L., & Turner, I. (1982). *Up where Cazaly?* Sydney, Australia: Granada.

Stewart, B. (1983). *The Australian football business: A spectator's guide to the VFL.* Kenthurst, Australia: Kangaroo Press.

Stewart, B., Hess, R., & Nicholson, M. (Eds.). (2004). *Football fever: Grassroots.* Melbourne, Australia: Maribyrnong Press.

Stremski, R. (1986). *Kill for Collingwood.* Sydney, Australia: Allen & Unwin.

Austria Olympics Results
2002 Winter Olympics: 2 Gold, 4 Silver, 11 Bronze
2004 Summer Olympics: 2 Gold, 4 Silver, 1 Bronze

Austria

Austria is a small country in central Europe and has a population of about 8 million. Its capital, Vienna, has about 1.5 million inhabitants.

Austria has a rich and famous athletic tradition, not only in competitive sports but also in physical education. Today, many Austrians engage in leisure sports (hiking, biking, skiing, swimming). In the field of elite sports, Austria has top athletes, especially in winter Alpine sports. There have also been some outstanding achievements in summer sports by individual athletes.

History

The beginnings of physical activities in Austria can be traced back to the early Iron Age through artifacts (700–300 BCE) that document riding, dance, wagon races, and wrestling. In the late Middle Ages and the eighteenth century, the first schools were created in which dance, riding, fencing, and ball games played an important role in tournament preparation. Nonprofessionals or specific professional groups practiced movement games for important occasions (Easter runs, for example). Required schooling was introduced during the reign of Maria Theresa in 1774. Physical education and calisthenics were increasingly included in normal school activity. The typical enthusiasm for sports emanating from England developed first in the universities and persisted despite strong political and cultural pressure after the 1860s. The evidence lies in the establishment of numerous clubs: Austrian Alpine Club 1863, Rowing Club 1867, Vienna Ice Skating Club 1887, First Vienna Amateur Swim Club 1892, Austrian Ski Club 1894, First Vienna Football Club 1896, and the like. Mountain climbing and Alpine skiing developed as widespread popular sports independently of the English example. Between the world wars Austria became famous for the natural gymnastics promoted by Gaulhofer and Streicher. But Austria's soccer teams also enjoyed renown and international success, as did Austrians competing in ice skating, Alpine skiing, and as part of the Austrian team at the 1936 Olympic Games.

During World War I, sport was employed as a specific political instrument. After 1945 three large umbrella organizations were reestablished: the Workers Association for Sport and Body Culture (ASKÖ), the Sport Union of Austria (Union), and the General Sport Association (ASVÖ). Since the 1960s Austrian soccer at the international level has suffered substantially, although it is still an important leisure sport for men. In various other sports, a few individual athletes have reached world-class status in track and field, shooting, judo, sailing, table tennis, and recently swimming.

Several umbrella organizations for leisure and competitive sports are financed using profits from soccer and other lottery games. Current government support is provided for elite sports to promote youth and women's sport development, "Top Sport Austria," sport coordinators in the federal sport organizations, sport infrastructure and federal sports facilities, and large sporting events. At the same time funding by private sponsors is both important and increasingly difficult given the penchant of these the sponsors to back only the very best athletes or teams.

Participant and Spectator Sports

Alpine sports are Austria's major elite sports. Level of participation and skill in these sports at national and international competitions is very high. The most famous regularly held events in Austria are the downhill skiing races in Kitzbühel: a victory there is comparable with a gold medal in Olympic games, and Austrian winners gain star status in their country. There is no comparable event in summer sports, although there are some significant tennis and track and field events. Several major winter sport events hosted in Austria over the last seventy-five years include two Olympic Games, a number of world championships, and a Paralympics and Special Olympics.

In summer sports the rate of participation is lower and the performance level generally is moderate, with a

A popular ski area in Austria.

Source: istockphoto/darklord_71.

hockey, in-line skating, skateboarding, and football (soccer) (levels of participation: boys 31.4 percent; girls: 2.6 percent). School competitions are offered in various games, orienteering, and Alpine and Nordic sports and are well attended. The programs for competitive youth sport are organized by the special federations (e.g., football [soccer] training centers run by the football federation). Noncompetitive youth sport is organized by the umbrella federations, which also initiate national and international activities.

few exceptional achievements. Marathon and long distance running as well as cycling, in-line skating, and mountain biking are sports that appear to be enjoying increasing popularity among weekend athletes as measured by the increasing number and variety of events and participation levels.

Women and Sport

The origins of women's participation in sports go back to about 1830, when girls were taught gymnastics for the first time. Early on, most women engaged in gymnastics, but from the 1880s women participated increasingly in sports like biking, swimming, skiing, ice hockey and ski jumping, football (soccer), tennis, and horseback riding. The Second World War reduced women's activities in sports dramatically and it took some time before Austrian women began to participate in sports again. At present women are at least as successful as men in the sports arena, but programs to develop leadership positions in and encourage media coverage of women's sports are still necessary. Austria has the chair of the European Women and Sport from 2004 to 2006 and will host the Congress 2006 in Vienna.

Youth Sports

Primary sports for children ten to nineteen years old include biking, swimming, downhill skiing, ice skating, ice

Organizations

In Austria sport is organized by government as well as by nongovernmental institutions. The Federal Chancellery (www.sport.austria.gv.at) is responsible for the allocation of grants to sports organizations, clubs, and municipalities; the promotion and organization of sports matters of national importance; and the awarding of medals and trophies. Due to the high value of sports in the Austrian society, a state secretary for sports exists. At the regional level each of the nine federal states deals with sports matters independently. They are responsible for general promotion of sport. Further, cooperation among the Ministry of Defense, the Ministry of Education, Science and Culture (for school sports and physical education), and the federal government rounds out the government support structure.

The central national body for voluntary sports activities is the Austrian Sports Federation (BSO: www.bso.or.at), whose main aim is to represent organized sport, to improve systematic cooperation between the members, and to promote collective interests in amateur sports. Under its umbrella the BSO unites fifty-three special federations, the three umbrella organizations for sport (ASKÖ: www.askoe.or.at, ASVÖ: www.asvoe.at, Union: www.sportunion.at) with about 3.9 mil-

Even if you are on the right track, you'll get run over if you just sit there. ■ WILL ROGERS

lion memberships, the organization for disabled sports (OeBSV: www.oebsv.or.at), and the Austrian Olympic Committee (OeOC: www.oeoc.at). Austria's interests also are widely represented in a variety of international sports associations.

Sports in Society

Media and active sport plays an important role in the society, and Austrians are very proud of the performances of top athletes in international competitions. Very famous Austrian sports "heroes" are Hermann Mayer and Annemarie Moser-Pröll (Alpine skiing), Thomas Muster (tennis), Stephanie Graf (track), Hans Krankl and Herbert Prohaska (soccer), Nikki Lauda (auto racing), and Werner Schlager (table tennis).

Future

Sport-related issues and topics of current interest in Austria include the innovation and modernization in sport clubs, projects for recruiting more elite athletes (especially in summer sports), sport for all, violence in sport, gender mainstreaming, and preparation of international events like the winter Universiade 2005 and the European Soccer Championship in 2008. On the occasion of the European Year of Education through Sports 2004 about eighty-eight projects were promoted, which attest to the relevance of and interest in sports in the Austrian society.

Rosa Diketmüller

Further Reading

Bruckmüller, E., & Strohmeyer, H. (Eds.). (1998). *Turnen und Sport in der Geschichte Österreichs*. Vienna: OBV.

Bundeskanzleramt, Sektion Sport. (2002). *Sportbericht 2001–2002*. Vienna: Eigenverlag.

Diketmüller, R. (2001). Austria. In K. Christensen, A. Guttmann, & G. Pfister (Eds.), *International encyclopedia of women and sports* (pp. 77–80). New York, London: Berkshire Publishing Group.

Kornexl, E. (1999). Are Austrian elite athletes given scientific support? In E. Müller, G. Zallinger, & F. Ludescher (Eds.), *Science in elite sport* (pp.74–81). London: Routledge.

Statistik Austria. (2001). *Freizeitaktivitäten. Ergebnisse des Mikrozensus September 1998*. Vienna: Verlag Österreich.

Auto Racing

Automobile racing began in France in 1894 when the magazine *Le Petit Journal* organized a point-to-point race to test performance. The first speed race came a year later when drivers raced from Paris to Bordeaux. Races were regularly run each year until 1903 when a series of fatalities caused the French government to ban open road racing. The first race in the United States was staged in Chicago in November 1895. Auto racing has since evolved into a wide variety of forms, including drag racing, Formula 1, Indy 500, stock car, off-road, vintage, hill climbing, and karting. All forms share the same goal of racing to the finish line in the fastest time. In all forms today there is also much concern over safety, and technological changes have sometimes been mandated that actually reduce speed.

To a significant extent each of the auto sports attracts its own legion of fans, and they are competitive as to which is the premier sport. For example, fans of Formula 1 see it as the highest form of racing and deride the relative lack of technological sophistication in stock car racing. But, stock car fans in the United States have little interest in European Formula 1 and little appreciation for the sophisticated design of the vehicles. There is some crossover among drivers in Formula 1 and Indy Racing.

Automobile racing is the major part of the larger sport of motor sports, which also includes truck, motorcycle, and powerboat racing. Revenues in the industry come mainly from admissions to races, sponsorship by corporations whose advertising is displayed on the cars and driver's clothing, and television and radio broadcast rights fees. A related industry is the recreational motor sports industry, which includes snowmobiling, ATV, and personal watercraft. Automobile racing is a leading spectator sport, and some events such as the Le Mans rally, Daytona 500 stock car race, and Indianapolis 500 are counted in the list of top sports events each year. Several leading drivers—Don Garlits, Richard Petty, Dale Earnhart, Jim Clark, Emerson Fittapaldi,

Michael Schumacher to name a few—have become national and international celebrities. While auto racing is a global sport, some locales have been especially important in its growth and development. For example, most of the British motor sports industry can be found within a 50-mile radius of Oxford in an area known as "Motor Sport Valley." In the United States, the Southeast has been the base of stock car racing—now best known to Americans by the acronym NASCAR (National Association for Stock Car Auto Racing)—with North Carolina especially serving as the home to many race teams, tracks, events, and associated industries.

Bringing Diversity to the Sport

Auto racing is mainly a male sport. Over its history there have been very few female drivers. Male drivers have usually resisted women's participation, and sponsors have been reluctant to take on female drivers. The most successful was Shirley Muldowney, the first woman licensed to drive top fuel dragsters. She won three NHRA top fuel world championships. Another leading drag racer was Agnes E. M. B. "Aggi" Hendricks of Canada, who won the International Hot Rod Association (IHRA) title of "Showman of the Year" three times and one Jet Car National championship. The first to drive at the Indianapolis 500 was Janet Guthrie in 1977, and she has been followed by Lynn St. James and Sarah Fisher, although none have come close to winning. Among women who raced in NASCAR events (although usually below the top level series) are Shawna Robinson, Angie Wilson, Patty Moise, and Tammy Jo Kirk. Women, do, however, make up a sizeable percentage of the fan base. Studies indicate that 40 percent of spectators at NASCAR events are women. Auto racing is also short on minority (non-white) drivers. Here the issue is the lack of lifelong involvement in the sport

(many racing teams are multigenerational family businesses) and lack of sponsorship, which makes it impossible to field a competitive car and hire a skilled and experienced crew. Efforts are underway in NASCAR to appeal to African-Americans and Latinos.

Drag Racing

Organized drag racing developed from street racing in southern California in the 1930s when young men raced souped-up cars against each other. Today drag racing involves all types of vehicles from street cars to motorcycles to highly engineered drag racers. The most highly engineered cars produce up to 1,500 horsepower. Several competition classes exist based on the type of fuel used (ordinary pump gas, methanol, nitromethane [top fuel]) or the type of car (an unmodified car off the assembly line or a modified car).

The pure dragster is a long chassis built of metal tubing with two small tires resembling bicycle tires in the front and two massive, treadless tires in the rear, all of which support an engine weighing 455–591 kilograms mounted behind the driver and between the rear wheels. A "funny car" is basically a dragster with a fiberglass body—made to resemble a flashy passenger car—that lowers over the cockpit, driver, and engine.

The drag racing track is a two-lane paved strip one-quarter-mile long with a shutdown area at the end. At the start of a race two competitors line up side by side on the starting line. The cars leave from a standing start, attempting to beat each other, or sometimes the clock, to the finish line. The first car to break the timing light beam on the finish line wins.

Formula 1 Racing

Formula 1 (F1, Grand Prix) cars are single-seat, open wheel vehicles that are built according to specifications developed by the Federation Internationale de l'Automobile (FIA) and used only for racing. All F1 races are held on specially constructed racecourses except the Grand Prix of Monaco, which is still held on public roads prepared for the race. Cars are associated with the manufacturers of their chassis and engines such as BRM, Honda, Ferrari, Mercedes, Maserati, Alfa Romeo, Porsche, Vanwall, and Matra. Most F1 cars are hybrids with a chassis constructed by one manufacturer fitted with an engine from another. F1 cars are technological and aerodynamic marvels with enormous amounts of expertise and money invested to make the vehicles hold the track and go as fast as possible. FIA regulations for F1 stipulate engine style and design.

For Europeans, Formula 1 is the pinnacle of auto racing and only the very best drivers compete in F1 races. It is a dangerous sport and several dozen drivers have been killed in races and practices since 1950. New rules, safer car and track designs, and better protective gear for drivers have made it somewhat safer since the 1970s. Formula 1 has experienced a period of spectator decline in the early twenty-first century due in part to continuing safety concerns but also the dominance of races by driver Michael Schumacher and Ferrari.

Indy Car Racing

Indy car racing is the major form of single-seat open-wheel racing in North America. To the general public it is usually associated with the Indianapolis 500 race held each Memorial Day weekend. In the past many racers moved up from stock car racing to Indy racing, but for the last few years it has been just as common for drivers to come from the Formula 1 circuit in Europe and South America and win Indy races. A major difference between Indy racing and Formula 1 is the effort by Indy officials to limit technological innovations in ways that maximize driver skill.

Indy racing began in the early twentieth century as road racing but by 1910 had begun to migrate to enclosed board and then dirt tracks. The Great Depression

---

Auto Racing
Horseless Carriage Races

Before the terms "automobile" and "car" came into use, the first motor vehicles were known as "horseless carriages." The 1896 extract below announces a race of these carriages on a track usually reserved for horses.

The Rhode Island State Fair Association announced that $5,000 will be given in prizes in a series of horseless carriage races to be held during its annual exposition week at Narragansett Park, Providence, R.I., in September. Racing of this kind has been attempted before, but never on so large a scale. The series of races will be held on a regulation trotting track, and the results promise to be interesting. One of the exhibition buildings will be set apart for a horseless carriage exposition. Certainly no "infant industry" was ever so coddled and fostered by the offer of large rewards; up to the present time the results in this country have not been worth the cost.

Source: A new horseless carriage race. (1896, May 23). *Scientific American*, p. 327.

---

and World War II brought a decline in racing but the sport rebounded in the 1950s with most major events now on enclosed, paved tracks with large grandstands. The sport has suffered from turf battles between competing sanctioning bodies including the one between CART (Championship Auto Racing Teams) and the Indy Racing League in the 1990s.

Stock Car Racing

A stock car is an automobile as it comes from the factory. The term "stock" was used early in racing history to distinguish those cars from others designed for racing. It has little meaning today as stock cars at the highest level of the sport bear little resemblance to cars coming off the dealer floor. They are modified for racing at high speeds on circular or oval tracks.

Stock car races are the most-attended professional spectator sports events in the United States. More than

A grid full of Minis in the Pit Lane at the Silverstone Pre Race. *Source: istockphoto/achundee.*

100,000 spectators attend major Nextel Cup (formerly Winston Cup) races held at major tracks such as the Daytona 500, the Michigan 400 and the California 500. The sport began and remains centered in the southeast United States but in the 1990s grew and expanded and now has a strong fan base across the United States. In 2005 a Busch series race was held in Mexico in a further attempt to expand the geographical boundaries of the sport.

There are two types of stock car racing. The highest level of competition is the Nextel Cup series and several lower series such as the Busch series, which attract the best racing teams and drivers, most wealthiest sponsors, media coverage, and fame. These series are circuits of races across the United States with drivers competing to win each race and the annual championship. The industry has a complex structure with NASCAR as the sanctioning organization, overall sponsorship by Nextel (formerly by the R. J. Reynolds Tobacco Company), and individual races sponsored by other companies. In Canada stock car racing is sanctioned by CASCAR (Canadian Association for Stock Car Racing).

The second form of stock car racing takes place in weekly competitions at short tracks in rural communities across the United States. The drivers (generally men) are local, and race part-time and semiprofessionally. The tracks are usually less than a mile around, and most are banked dirt ovals with grandstands on one or more sides and an interior pit area.

The popularity of stock car racing in the United States is the result of two developments. First, the successful effort by the industry itself in the 1970s and 1980s to make the sport safer and to change its reputation as a sport that appealed only to people who wanted to see wrecks and mayhem. Second, the role of ESPN, the cable television sports channel. Automobile racing was a natural for ESPN's largely male audience. Broadcast networks soon followed, and television contract money increased prize money and incentives for advertisers to sponsor cars and races.

Truck Racing

Truck racing is a motor sport in which utility and recreational vehicles race against each other. It includes many types of vehicles, including pickup trucks and sport-utility vehicles. These vehicles traditionally competed in off-road rallies and other events on unpaved roads and trails or over open countryside. Many vehicles in off-road races use four-wheel drive. Among these are the Baja series of desert races, the Pikes Peak Hillclimb in Colorado, and the Camel Trophy Mundo Maya, a grueling twenty-day race through Central America.

Trucks became a regular feature of closed-track stock car racing in 1994 when NASCAR established a Super Truck division. Super Trucks are modified pickups that adhere to guidelines for engines and body construction similar to those for NASCAR stock cars. Super Truck is organized much like NASCAR's stock car series and events. Trucks are also used in drag racing, with a National Hot Rod Association category for modified trucks.

Vintage Auto Racing

Vintage auto racing enthusiasts collect, restore and maintain historic high-performance cars and then drive

A 1929 Ford Roadster Street Rod.

Source: istockphoto/4allthingsweb.

them in races. Automobiles used in vintage auto racing include retired Formula 1 cars, classic sports cars, and other top-quality street and touring vehicles. The goal is to restore and maintain the vehicles exactly as they were built. Original parts are encouraged in repairs. If they are no longer available, substitution parts must be similar. Vintage auto races range from local, informal gatherings to large races that attract drivers and spectators from around the world. Major vintage races are held at historic and prominent racetracks such as Watkins Glen in New York, Lime Rock in Connecticut, and Sebring in Florida.

Karting

In karting (also known as "go-karting") people drive small four-wheeled vehicles powered by internal combustion engines. The frame of karts is often uncovered, and karts seat only one person. Most karts have small two- or four-stroke engines that resemble lawnmower engines. Karts and karting events are divided into several classes based on the age of the drivers or the specifications of the karts. Karts have sensitive steering; therefore, concentration and fast reflexes are important. In addition to using the steering wheel, the driver shifts his or her weight to assist in turning. The sense of speed often seems more intense to a driver in a kart than in a larger vehicle. Karting is the way many professional drivers begin to learn their sport.

David Levinson, Garry Chick,
Scott A. G. M. Crawford, Richard Pillsbury,
John Townes, and Suzanne Wise

See also Indianapolis 500; Karting; Le Mans; Nextel (Winston) Cup

Further Reading

Arlott, J. (1975). *The Oxford companion to sports and games.* London: Oxford University Press.

Benson, M. (1997). *Women in racing.* Philadelphia: Chelsea House Publishers.

Chimits, X., & Granet, F. (1994). *The Williams Renault Formula 1 motor racing book.* New York: Dorling Kindersley.

Fox, J. C. (1967). *The Indianapolis 500.* New York: World Publishing.

Georgano, G. N. (Ed.). (1971). *The encyclopedia of motor sport.* New York: Viking Press.

Griffiths, T. R. (1993). *Grand prix.* London: Bloomsbury Publishing.

Grimsley, W. (Ed.). (1971). *A century of sports.* New York: Associated Press.

Hagstrom, R. G. (1998). *The NASCAR way: The business that drives the sport.* New York: Wiley.

Hodges, D., Nye, D., & Roebuck, N. (1981). *Grand prix.* New York: St. Martin's Press.

McCart, J. (1976). Goodbye to the powder puffs: Women stake their claim in stock car racing. *Branching Out, 3*(2), 11–13.

Montville, L. (2001). *At the altar of speed: The fast life and tragic death of Dale Earnhardt.* New York: Doubleday.

Mull, E. (1958). *Women in sports car competition.* New York: Sports Car Press.

Nye, D. (1992). *The autocourse history of the grand prix car 1966–91.* Richmond, UK: Hazleton Publishing.

Phillips, D., (Ed.). (1997). *American Motorsports.* Edison, NJ: Chartwell Books.

Post, R. C. (1994). *High performance: The culture and technology of drag racing.* Baltimore: Johns Hopkins University Press.

Rosiniski, J. (1974). *Formula 1 racing: The modern era.* New York: Madison Square Press.

Smith, L. (1982). *Karting.* New York: Arco Publishing.

Stambler, I. (1984). *Off roading: Racing and riding.* Toronto, Canada: General Publishing.

Standridge, J. (1992). Making it in racing: How women are getting jobs in auto racing. *Stock Car Racing, 27*(2), 59–66.

Tremayne, D., & Hughes, M. (1999). *The concise encyclopedia of Formula One.* London: Parragon.

Badminton

Badminton, which some people call "the world's fastest racket sport," is played with shuttlecocks (lightweight conical objects with rounded noses) and rackets on a court divided by a net.

History

Researchers have found evidence of sports similar to badminton as early as the first century BCE in China, where *ti jian zi* (shuttlecock kicking) was popular. In *ti jian zi* players hit a shuttlecock with a foot or hand or occasionally a bat. The sport also was popular in India, Japan, and Siam (Thailand) and spread to Greece and Sumeria.

During the fourteenth century in England people played battledore shuttlecock with a racket or paddle and a shuttlecock. This sport used no nets or boundaries and was mainly a means of testing two players' skill at keeping the shuttlecock in play as long as possible. Battledore shuttlecock by the late sixteenth century had become a popular children's sport, the object of players still being to hit the shuttlecock to each other, or to oneself, and to keep it in the air as long as possible. The notions of using a net and of trying to prevent one's opponent from returning the shuttlecock were still a century away.

The social status of battledore shuttlecock increased during the seventeenth century as British royalty and the leisured classes played the sport. Early English settlers in the American colonies also played battledore

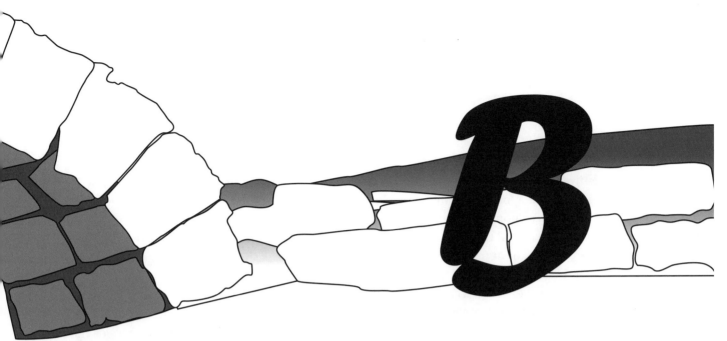

shuttlecock. During the 1800s the seventh duke of Beaufort and his family were keen players at his estate in Gloucester, called "Badminton House." There the "new game" of badminton battledore, using a net and boundaries, evolved; thus, the term *badminton*. By 1867 English officers and their families in India were playing a formal version of badminton and had developed the first set of rules.

Evolution

Badminton evolved into a competitive indoor sport during the last three decades of the 1800s, and clubs were formed throughout the British Isles to promote competition. The first tournaments were held in England during the 1890s, and the first All-England Badminton Championships were held in 1899. Until the 1920s the major badminton titles were played for by the English, Scots, and Irish. Rules varied from place to place until about 1905, when the Badminton Association of England adopted uniform rules that are similar to the official rules of the International Badminton Federation (IBF), which players observe today.

During the 1920s badminton spread from England to northern Europe (it was especially popular in Scandinavia) and North America. It also spread from India throughout the rest of Asia.

The International Badminton Federation, which governs international competition, was formed in 1934 with nine member countries. More than 125 countries now belong to the IBF. After World War II several international competitions for teams and individual players were established, and by 1979 badminton had

become professional. A year-around international grand prix circuit attracts the top players to a touring career similar to that of other professional athletes.

The acceptance of badminton into the Olympic Games in 1985—and its debut at the 1992 Olympics in Barcelona, Spain—solidified badminton's position as an international sport.

Rules of Play

Two features distinguish badminton from other racket sports, all of which use a ball: (1) the use of a shuttlecock and (2) the fact that the shuttlecock must not touch the ground. These features make badminton a fast sport that requires strong conditioning and quick reflexes. Indeed, top athletes can deliver smashes of more than 320 kilometers per hour.

Although badminton may be played indoors or outdoors, all officially sanctioned competitions around the world are played indoors. Competitive badminton is played in five events: men's singles, men's doubles, women's singles, women's doubles, and mixed doubles.

Keeping Score

A badminton game consists of fifteen points, except for women's singles, in which a game is eleven points. The best of three games constitutes a match. Only the serving side can score points. A game does not need to be won by two points. If the score becomes tied near the end of a game, the game may be lengthened by a procedure called "setting." For example, when the score becomes tied at thirteen in a fifteen-point game, the side that reached thirteen first has the option of setting the game to five (a total of eighteen points), so that the side that scores five points first wins. The score may be set in the same manner at a fourteen-point tie for three points (a total of seventeen points). In women's singles the eleven-point game may total twelve points by setting at nine-all for three points or at ten-all for two points. Only the side that reached the tied score first has the option of setting the score; if the side elects not to set, the conventional number of points completes the game.

Changing Sides

The two sides change ends at the beginning of the second game and at the beginning of the third if a third game is necessary. In a fifteen-point game sides change ends in the third game when the leading side reaches eight points; in an eleven-point third game, sides change ends when either side reaches six. The side that wins a game serves first in the next game.

Strategies

In singles play the goal is to move the opponent primarily up and back on the court, using deception and forcing errors by the opponent. In doubles play a team's goal is to repeatedly hit the shuttlecock down to its opponents and force the opponents to hit defensive shots up in return. The offensive doubles formation is one player playing at the net and the other player smashing from the backcourt. The defensive doubles formation is both players playing back, each defending his or her side of the court.

In singles play a typical rally consists of a serve and repeated high, deep shots hit to the baseline (clears), interspersed with dropshots. If a short clear or other type of "set-up" is forced, a smash wins the point. More often than not, an error (in which the shuttlecock is hit out of bounds or into the net), rather than a positive winning play, ends a rally. A player who is patient and commits few or no outright errors often wins by simply waiting for the opponent to err.

Doubles play has fewer clears and more low serves, drives, and net play. Again, a smash often ends the point. As in singles, having patience and avoiding unforced errors are important in winning.

Basic Shots

Strokes and striking techniques vary greatly from relatively slow shots to quick and deceptive shots. Basic shots consist of underhand strokes (serve, underhand clear, underhand dropshot), overhead strokes (clear, dropshot, smash), a sidearm stroke (drive), and the hairpin drop at the net.

Unlike a player serving in tennis, a player serving in badminton has only one attempt to put the shuttlecock into play. In doubles both players on a side have a turn at serving before the serve passes to the other side. A serve that hits the top of the net and goes into the correct service court is legal and in play.

In addition, the serve in badminton is a defensive shot: It must be underhand. The racket shaft must point downward at the point of contact, so that the entire racket head is below the server's hand and fingers.

Faults

Faults are violations of the rules in serving, receiving, or playing. If the receiving side faults, the serving side scores a point. If the serving side faults, no point is scored, and the serve passes to the next appropriate server.

Equipment

All major badminton competitions use the traditional feathered shuttlecock. It must weigh between 4.74 and 5.5 grams and have fourteen to sixteen feathers fixed in a cork base covered with a layer of leather or similar material. Shuttlecocks are humidified to prevent drying and becoming brittle. They are produced at different "speed" levels and weights to suit all playing environments. One shuttlecock usually lasts for only two games.

The badminton net is 1.524 meters high at the center of the court and 1.55 meters high at each end post. The badminton court measures 5.2 meters by 13.4 meters for singles play and 6.1 meters by 13.4 meters for doubles play. Badminton rackets were made of wood until the 1950s. Today's rackets are made of blends of boron, aluminum, carbon, and steel. They are light (around 98 grams) and can be strung tightly with natural gut or synthetic string. Dimensions cannot exceed

An early Chinese shuttlecock.

69 centimeters by 23 centimeters, and the head length cannot exceed 33 centimeters.

Competition at the Top

Major international competitions include the Olympic Games, the Thomas Cup and the Uber Cup, the World Badminton Championships, and the Sudirman Cup.

OLYMPICS

Although badminton was a demonstration sport at the Olympics in Munich, Germany, in 1972 and an exhibition sport at the Olympics in Seoul, South Korea, in 1988, its Olympic debut as a full-medal sport did not come until 1992 in Barcelona, Spain. Four events were played: men's singles, men's doubles, women's singles, and women's doubles. At the 1996 Olympic Games in Atlanta, Georgia mixed doubles were added.

THOMAS CUP AND UBER CUP

The Thomas Cup is the men's world team championship, similar to the Davis Cup in tennis. The competition began in 1949 and was held every three years until 1984, after which it has been held every even year. The Uber Cup is the women's world team championship, held with the Thomas Cup. The event began in 1957.

In the competitions for the Thomas and Uber Cups, each tie between two countries consists of five matches —three singles and two doubles. Regional playoffs are held in several locations around the world, and the winners of these playoffs, along with the defending champion nations, gather in one location for the final rounds.

WORLD BADMINTON CHAMPIONSHIPS

The World Badminton Championships were begun in 1977 to provide individual championships to complement the previously described team competitions. The World Badminton Championships are held every odd-numbered year. Prior to 1977 the prestigious All-England Badminton Championships were considered the unofficial individual world championships. The All-England Badminton Championships were founded in 1899 and are still staged annually. Since 1992 World Junior Badminton Championships have also been staged.

SUDIRMAN CUP

The Sudirman Cup, begun in 1989, is the world mixed team championship. Held in conjunction with the World Badminton Championships in odd-numbered years, the Sudirman Cup provides competition between teams consisting of men and women. In this competition each tie between two countries consists of five matches—one men's singles, one women's singles, one men's doubles, one women's doubles, and one mixed doubles.

Today China is at the top in international badminton competition. Chinese players won four medals at the 1996 Olympics in Atlanta, Georgia; South Korea and Malaysia won four and two, respectively. At the 2004 Olympics in Athens, Greece, China won the most medals: three gold, one silver, and one bronze. Gold medalists in badminton were: men's singles, Taufik Hidayat of Indonesia; men's doubles, Tae Kwon Ha and Dong Moon Kim of North Korea; women's singles, Ning Zhang of China; women's doubles, Wei Yang and Jiewen Zhang of China; and mixed doubles, Jun Zhang and Ling Gao of China.

The International Badminton Federation's top world rankings in late 2004 were: men's singles, Dan Lin of China; women's singles, Ning Zhang of China; men's doubles, Jens Eriksen and Martin Lundgaard Hansen of Denmark; women's doubles, Wei Yang and Jiewen Zhang of China; and mixed doubles, Nathan Robertson and Gail Emms of England.

Popularity

In most countries of Southeast Asia and northern Europe badminton is a major sport and virtually the national sport in Indonesia and several other countries.

I hate all sports as rabidly as a person who likes sports hates common sense. ■ H. L. MENCKEN

England, Denmark, Sweden, the Netherlands, and Germany lead Europe in their interest. The five nations with the most registered players, according to the IBF, are Denmark (180,977); Germany (142,253); Japan (115,682); China (110,550); and the Netherlands (94,815).

The International Badminton Federation lists the number of players registered with national badminton associations around the world at 1.4 million. The IBF estimates, however, that ten times that many people play badminton.

Kathleen M. Spence

Further Reading

Adams, B. (1980). *The badminton story.* London: British Broadcasting Publications.

Bloss, M. V., & Stanton Hales, R. (1994). *Badminton.* Dubuque, IA: Brown & Benchmark.

Davis, P. (1983). *Guinness book of badminton.* London: Guinness Superlatives.

Grice, T. (1994). *Badminton for the college student.* Boston: American Press.

Hales, D. (1979). *A history of badminton in the United States from 1878–1939.* Pomona: California State Polytechnic University.

Hashman, J. D. (1984). *Winning badminton.* London: Ward Lock.

International Badminton Federation. (1994). *IBF statute book.* Cheltenham, UK: Author.

United States Badminton Association. (1995). *Badminton '95.* Colorado Springs, CO: Author.

United States Badminton Association. (1996). *60 years: 1936–1996, 60th jubilee fact book.* Colorado Springs, CO: Author.

Balloooning

The sport of ballooning is a study in contrasts. The balloon simply drifts with the wind, but its pilot must understand the complex meteorological conditions that cause that wind. A balloon in flight floats literally lighter than air; but a typical four-person balloon rig can weigh as much as 363 kilograms. The speed of the wind determines the distance of a flight, but too much wind means that the pilot will probably elect not to fly at all.

To celebrate these contrasts, balloonists arise before dawn to prepare their craft. They may launch those craft from their own backyards or travel thousands of miles to participate in ballooning competition with others. They may cruise the treetops looking for leaves or soar aloft thousands of feet to find wind directions with which to steer to a competitive goal or suitable landing site.

Most balloonists enter the sport for the sheer beauty of flight, although some compete in championship events, fly paying passengers, or fly balloons as sky-high billboards.

Origins

Ballooning marked the beginning of human flight. The Montgolfier brothers of France are credited with inventing and developing lighter-than-air craft. Sons of a paper manufacturer near Annonay, Joseph (1740–1810) and Jacques Etienne (1745–1799) began building model balloons of paper laminated with taffeta. They believed that the lifting power came from smoke, based on their observations of cloth and paper floating up the chimney of their fireplace. Thus, they powered their early balloons with smoke from burning wet straw under a paper envelope. On 19 September 1783, the Montgolfiers launched a balloon carrying a sheep, a chicken, and a duck.

That same year J. A. C. Charles (1746–1823), working with Aíné and Cadet Robert, built an envelope of silk coated with varnish. They filled it with hydrogen, made by pouring sulfuric acid over iron filings.

On 21 November 1783, the first balloon to carry a person, built by the Montgolfiers, launched from Bois de Boulogne park in Paris. Pilatre de Rozier (1756–1785) and copilot Marquis d'Arlandes (1742–1809) became the first humans to fly. Their aircraft would later become known as a "hot air balloon." Ten days later, on 1 December, Charles and Aíné Robert launched in a hydrogen-filled balloon from the Tuilleries Gardens in Paris. Gas ballooning soon grew in popularity in Europe and the United States, with Jean Pierre François Blanchard (1153–1809) making the first balloon ascent in North America in 1793.

However, not until 1960 did hot air ballooning again capture the public imagination. On 10 October, Paul Edward Yost (b. 1919), an aeronautical engineer under contract to the U.S. Navy, launched a tiny aerostat (a lighter-than-air aircraft) from Bruning, Nebraska. Lift came from a small propane burner. Shortly thereafter Yost began building hot air balloons for sport flying. His contribution resulted in the explosive growth that ballooning has enjoyed since.

Practice

Hot air balloons and gas balloons operate on the same principle: Gas of a density lesser than the ambient air will lift until it attains equilibrium, with lift diminished by the weight of the container holding the gas. The lifting gas in a balloon may be air heated to make the air less dense than the ambient air, hydrogen, helium, cooking gas, or, in recent years, ammonia gas.

In a hot air balloon the pilot uses a propane burner to heat the air inside the envelope, making it less dense and providing lift. In a gas balloon the pilot releases ballast, usually water or sand, to allow the gas to lift the balloon rig. To descend, the hot air pilot allows the air in the envelope to cool or vents hot air out the top. The pilot of a gas balloon vents gas to descend.

Some balloon manufacturers in recent years have experimented with a hybrid balloon called a "Rozier," named for Pilatre de Rozier. This balloon is a gas balloon sphere surrounded on the bottom half by a hot air balloon cone. The pilot uses a propane burner to heat the air inside the cone, which then warms helium, expanding it and increasing lift. Rozier balloons have proven useful for long-distance flights such as transoceanic and transglobal attempts.

Hot air ballooning is by far the most popular form of balloon flight. Hot air rigs cost less to purchase than gas balloons and are less complex. The propane used to fuel

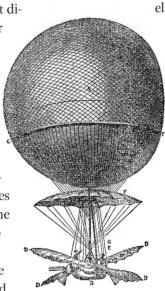

Blanchard's Balloon.

the burner costs a fraction of the price of gas needed to fill a gas balloon. In Europe most gas balloons use hydrogen, whereas in the United States most gas balloons use helium. A helium fill can cost more than $3,500. Propane for a typical one-hour hot air balloon flight costs between $10 and $30. A gas balloon flight, however, lasts many hours or even days, whereas a hot air balloon flight usually lasts about an hour.

In flight a balloon joins an air mass and goes wherever that air mass goes. Thus, balloons are called "aerostats," that is, they are static within the air. A pilot can vary the direction of flight somewhat by adjusting the altitude of the aircraft—air currents at different levels can differ by as much as 90 degrees of the compass, depending on prevailing weather conditions.

Flying with the wind, a balloon can rarely fly back to its launch site. For that reason a chase crew on the ground must follow the flight. After the balloon lands, the pilot and crew pack the equipment onto a trailer or truck for the trip back to the launch site. A hot air balloon flight may cover 40 kilometers or more, depending on wind speed at the altitudes chosen by the pilot. A gas balloon flight may cover much greater distances.

Hot air balloon rigs have three basic components. The envelope is the fabric "balloon" part that holds the hot air used for lift. The envelope is sewn together from panels of nylon or polyester cloth, which usually are coated with urethane or silicone to minimize porosity. The basket is the "cabin" that hangs from the envelope by aircraft cables connected to envelope cables. Most baskets are woven from wicker or rattan. The burner and fuel system are the "engine." The burner is attached to a frame over the pilot's head and is connected by fuel hoses to the fuel tanks stored in each corner of the basket.

Balloon pilots are trained in much the same manner as pilots of other aircraft: Instructors provide ground and flight training that covers equipment operation, weather, aviation regulations of the pilot's home country, emergencies, and launch, flight, and landing procedures. A student must complete a predetermined number of flight hours and perform an ascension to a given altitude (1,067 meters for a private pilot in the United States) and solo flight. Then the student takes a written exam, an oral exam, and a flight test from a government-designated examiner.

Ideal ballooning weather consists of high pressure, light winds at the surface, and moderate winds at higher elevations. Although balloons can fly in rain, packing away a wet envelope causes mildew and premature degradation of the envelope fabric and coating.

Balloons normally fly within three hours of sunrise or sunset. At dawn and dusk the air near the ground is most stable and the winds most predictable. As the sun heats the Earth's surface, thermals and higher winds often develop and are not conducive to ballooning. Balloons rarely fly during the middle of the day. A pilot has no brakes to slow the balloon's forward motion; thus, light winds make the most comfortable landings.

Terrain

A balloonist must learn to take advantage of various aspects of terrain that affect a flight in addition to weather systems. Winds flow differently in the wide, flat expanses of plains than they do in wooded, mountainous areas. Yet, both terrains can be good areas for ballooning.

The Federation Aeronautique Internationale (FAI), headquartered in Paris, oversees the worldwide sport aviation community. The FAI governs all world aviation records and all international aviation competitions, including world championships. The FAI has separate committees for each air sport, including one for ballooning.

Each FAI member country governs its own air sports through its National Aero Club (NAC). Separate air sport federations exist within each NAC. Thus, each country with a ballooning community has its own ballooning federation. The two most active are the British Balloon and Airship Club (BBAC) and the Balloon Fed-

eration of America (BFA). The BFA is the largest group of balloonists in the world.

Balloonists compete to win local, regional, national, and world championship flying events or to set world records. The FAI organizes ballooning records into categories (gas, hot air, or Rozier) and sizes of balloons. Within these categories are records for altitude, distance, and duration.

Ruth P. Ludwig

Further Reading

Crouch, T. (1983). *The eagle aloft.* Washington, DC: Smithsonian Institution Press.
Ludwig, R. (1995). *Balloon digest.* Indianola, IA: Balloon Federation of America.
Wirth, D. (1982). *Ballooning, the complete guide to riding the winds.* New York: Random House.

Baseball

Baseball most likely evolved from the British bat-and-ball games of cricket and rounders or perhaps from the more ancient English game of stool ball. Organized play of "base ball" began in the United States in 1845; in 1856 it was dubbed that country's "national pastime" (Ward and Burns 1994, 6), and by 1869, the amateur-only sport progressed into one including an openly professional component. Traveling teams spread the sport to locales around the world, with Latin American countries—including Cuba, the Dominican Republic, Nicaragua, Venezuela and Puerto Rico—as well as Japan, Taiwan, and Australia being the most receptive.

History

Traditionally, it was believed that Abner Doubleday, who later became a Civil War Union major general, transformed casual bat-and-ball games into the modern-day sport of baseball; this legend suggests that he cre-

You teach me baseball and I'll teach you relativity . . . No we must not.
You will learn about relativity faster than I learn baseball. ■ ALBERT EINSTEIN

ated its rules in Cooperstown, New York, in 1839, but no supporting historical evidence exists. Origins of the Doubleday myth trace back to Albert Spalding, an early scion of the sport and successful sporting goods entrepreneur, who publicized the story in 1907 to make baseball appear purely American (Spalding 1991).

As further proof that Doubleday did not "invent" baseball, a Pittsfield, Massachusetts, ordinance, dated 1791, referred to "base ball," prohibiting its play within 80 yards of the town meetinghouse. Moreover, it is highly probable that Alexander Cartwright Jr. created the first written rules in 1845, compiling them for the New York Knickerbockers, a team that played gentlemanly matches in Hoboken, New Jersey. These rules resemble modern-day play and established the foul line, distinguishing baseball from other bat-and-ball sports; there are, however, noteworthy differences when comparing Cartwright's rules with those of the modern-day game. Balls caught after one bounce constituted an "out" and, originally, the winning team was the first to score twenty-one runs. The pitcher threw underhanded, with the batter permitted to request a high or low pitch, and no strike zone existed. Furthermore, "New York ball" contrasted significantly with the rougher Massachusetts style of play; in those games, players were out after being "soaked"—or hit—by the ball.

ORGANIZING THE SPORT

By 1858 the National Association of Base Ball Players was codifying rules and charging a fifty-cent game admission; James Creighton served as the first star player. Enthusiasm for the sport was growing when the Civil War began; instead of slowing its progress, the war actually spread the game when it was played at battle encampments and prison grounds, extending baseball to southern states and other regions of the country.

In 1869, four years after the war's end, the Cincinnati Red Stockings shed all pretense of amateur sport and openly began paying players. As the sport turned professional, though, there came the taint of gambling and purposefully lost games, and the National Association

of Base Ball Players could not control these undesirable elements. A new organization, the National Association of Professional Base Ball Players, formed in 1871, but it struggled with similar issues. To simultaneously solve this dilemma and further his own career goals, coal magnate William A. Hulbert lured the best players —against association policy—to form a new team; in a more drastic move, he also formed his own league in 1876: the National League of Professional Base Ball Clubs (NL).

Although it may sound similar to previous organizations, it was radically different. In this league players were, for the first time, employees of team owners. Because of the "reserve clause" included in contracts, players lost their ability to choose where to play; this clause was formulated to prevent the frequent "revolving"—or team jumping—of players in search of a better deal, but it also drastically shifted the balance of power from the players to team owners. Ball clubs, for their part, were also now committed to playing all scheduled games, rather than choosing the most lucrative.

Attempts to challenge the National League's monopoly on professional baseball ensued, most notably by the American Association, a league that played in uneasy tandem with the NL for ten seasons (1882–1891); less successful attempts included the Union Association (1884) and the Players League (1890), both of which focused on the needs and wants of the players, partly as an attempt to lure quality players to their organizations and partly because of genuine intentions to improve their circumstances.

It wasn't until 1901, when Byron Bancroft Johnson renamed the Western League the American League (AL) and decided to pursue major league status, that changes were effected. Johnson saw the problems caused by alcohol and gambling in the NL and, spotting an opportunity for a rival major league that could be extremely profitable, he vowed to create and run a clean association. He directly challenged the NL by putting teams in some of the same cities, and for three years the NL struggled with accepting the equal status that the AL desired;

My motto was always to keep swinging. Whether I was in a slump or feeling badly or having trouble off the field, the only thing to do was keep swinging ■ HANK AARON

in 1903 a truce was called, solidifying the two-league system that exists today.

The last significant attempt at creating a third league occurred in 1914–1915 when the Federal League, which was created in 1913 but did not announce its major league aspirations until 1914, directly challenged the monopolistic nature of major league baseball in court. They ultimately failed, in large part because the judge, Kenesaw Mountain Landis, procrastinated in giving his ruling. Landis was a passionate fan, and he feared that ruling against the current structure would destroy the sport; and yet, as a judge who traditionally ruled against reigning monopolies, he could not in good conscience rule for the major league system. Therefore, he stalled and allowed the Federal League's increasingly difficult financial situation to cause the league's collapse.

While the National League and the American League were developing, other teams were also participating in amateur games and minor leagues, and the term *minor league* had a different connotation then. Now, minor league teams are farm teams for the major leagues, but in this era they were often high-quality teams playing in smaller towns; and they were, without exception, independent of the major league system. Moreover, mill-town teams and other teams in the southern states were highly competitive, and black teams were developing their own leagues. Teams were also forming in Latin America.

RACIAL ISSUES EMERGE

As early as 1911 baseball pundits were pointing out that premium players were being banned from the major league system because of the darkness of their skin. After a series of games between major league and Cuban ballplayers that year in which the Cubans often outplayed their opponents, Johnson, the AL president, banned future matchups. This ban led some reporters to point out that top-notch players were being "elbowed off the diamond" because of racial prejudice (Cottrell 2002, 8).

Blacks nevertheless played ball; the National Colored League appeared briefly in the mid-1840s, and black players participated in racially integrated teams or on all-black clubs. During the Civil War era, a significant number of black teams formed in northern states, but in 1867 the National Association of Base Ball Players banned any team containing "one or more colored persons," presumably to avoid racial tensions (Cottrell 2002, 60).

In 1878 John "Bud" Fowler pitched for the International League, breaking the minor league color barrier. Many white teammates would not accept his presence, and he spent the next ten seasons playing second base for various minor league teams. In 1883 Fowler was playing in the Northwestern League; then the Toledo team in this league signed catcher Moses Fleetwood "Fleet" Walker, a black man who had played integrated baseball for Oberlin College. The following year, Walker's team merged with the American Association, a major league system, thereby making Walker—who was soon joined by his brother, Welday—the first black player on a major league ball club.

During the 1880s thirteen black players—including Fowler, the Walker brothers, Bob Higgins, Andy Jackson, William Renfro, Richard Johnson, George Stovey, Sol White, Frank Grant, and Jack Frye—participated on minor leagues teams populated by white players, with 1887 being their peak year. Moreover, there were successful all-black professional teams, most notably the Cuban Giants. Those players were, however, neither giants nor Cuban; the United States was currently on good terms with Cuba, so players felt that white spectators would be drawn to a team dubbed Cuban; the name "Giants" cued fans that players were black.

Although all-black teams were finding some successes, integrated play was not harmonious, with fans hollering death threats at black players. Moreover, some ballplayers intentionally made errors when a black teammate pitched, while others would refuse to pose for racially integrated team photos. The worst blow to integrated play occurred on July 14, 1887, when NL star

Baseball the national sport on par with the American flag and apple pie.

Source: istockphoto/LizV.

Williams, Josh Gibson, John "Buck" O'Neil, Oscar Charleston, "Bullet" Joe Rogan, and James "Cool Papa" Bell—played with skill and power equal to their major league counterparts. They never became as well known as Jackie Robinson, the player who broke the color line by joining the Brooklyn Dodgers—and who won the Rookie of the Year Award—in 1947, or Larry Doby, who broke the American League color barrier later the same year by joining Bill Veeck's Cleveland Indians team and who participated in All-Star games from 1949 to 1954. There was also Leroy "Satchel" Paige who, after pitching in the Negro leagues for twenty-two years, finished his illustrious career in the major league system, joining the Cleveland Indians in 1948 and pitching well into his fifties. Another well-known player who started in the Negro leagues but finished his career in the major leagues was catcher Roy Campanella, who also played for Branch Rickey's Dodgers.

Cap Anson demanded that George Stovey be banned from exhibition play, for racial reasons. The following day, the International League agreed to "approve no more contracts with colored men" (Dixon and Hannigan 1992, 51). Although Grant and Higgins continued to play through 1888, and Fleet Walker through 1889, by the mid-1890s, the only integrated play occurred during unofficial contests in the off-season (Jackie Robinson being the first player to break the color barrier of the National League in 1947).

From the 1840s until 1919, entrepreneurs struggled to form all-black leagues. They often lacked sufficient financial backing, so players' wages were uncertain. The better-situated leagues did follow predetermined schedules, but teams also "barnstormed"—or traveled across a region—in search of quality local teams to challenge; game receipts were divided according to prearranged plans. In 1920 a more successful and stable league—the Negro National League—was created by outstanding pitcher, Andrew "Rube" Foster.

Foster's league continued until 1930, and a second version ran from 1933 until 1948, the year after major league baseball finally became integrated. There was also a Negro American League from 1937 until some time in the 1950s; because of integration occurring in the major leagues, this league also folded.

During those years of "blackball," Foster and many other nonwhite players—including "Smokey" Joe

Development of the Sport

In the 1860s–1870s, when professional leagues were first organizing, rules were becoming more standardized; significant credit goes to journalist Henry Chadwick, who later developed the modern box score, and who created two important statistics: batting average and earned-run average. He also edited numerous baseball guides and served on rules committees.

When individuals began to invest their funds into teams in the 1870s, teams became more financially stable; prior to that time, teams used gate receipts to cover expenses and, if applicable, to pay their players. This was the beginning of many decades whereby players had little control over their careers, and team owners made nearly all decisions. During this decade players

Baseball

Henry Chadwick on New Pitching Rules

Henry Chadwick (1824–1908) holds a legendary place in early baseball for his dedication to setting out rules for the game as chairman of the National League Rules Committee. In an article for Outing, *a sports magazine of the late nineteenth and early twentieth century, he explains new rules for baseball pitching.*

The changes made in the rules governing the delivery of the ball to the bat are decidedly of a radical nature in many respects. In the first place, the pitcher is now allowed to send in but five unfair balls to the bat before he is subjected to the penalty of giving the batsman a base on called balls. Last year he could deliver six such unfair balls. Moreover, the penalty for such unfair balls has been increased by adding the charge of a base hit against the pitcher for every base given on balls. Secondly, the penalty of giving a batsman a base is inflected every time the pitcher hits the batsman with a pitched ball, provided that the batsman has made all due effort to avoid being hit by the ball. Thirdly, whenever the pitcher makes a balk-as defined in the new code the batsman, as well as base runners occupying bases, is also given a base as a penalty for

the unfair delivery... This largely increased responsibility attached to the position, however, is offset by an important advantage which the new code grants to the pitcher, and this advantage lies in the throwing out of the code the clause in the rules which required the pitcher to send in balls to the bat "high" or "low," as the batsman might choose to designate, thereby relieving the pitcher from the difficulty of delivering the class of balls known as "waist" balls, viz., balls just above or below the waist. Not only was it quite a task of the pitcher to measure high or low balls in his delivery, but it was one of the most difficult parts of the umpire's duties to judge such balls accurately, and the apparent mistakes of judgment made in this respect were fruitful of disputes by players as to the soundness of the decisions rendered. Under the new code, therefore, the pitcher is now only required to send in balls between the designated height of the batsman's knee and shoulder, all such balls being regarded as fair balls, provided that, at the same time, they pass over the home base...

focused more heavily on defensive strategies, backing up one another during plays; equipment such as the catcher's mask and fielding gloves were also introduced. Schedules were still unpredictable and rules often changed. Stars of the era included Adrian "Cap" Anson, Albert Spalding, Charles Comiskey, and Michael "King" Kelly.

During the 1880s teams were first required to announce batting orders before the game started; this negated the strategy employed by some, which was to keep the opposing team wondering when a power hitter would appear at the plate. Meanwhile, owners continued to gain control over their teams and began to build their own stadiums. The first night game was played in Massachusetts on 2 September 1880, under dim electric lights.

Mitts and chest protectors were introduced for catch-

ers, along with a rubber home plate; previous home plates had been stone, iron, or wood, causing injuries. The sport was still rough, with players and owners arguing fiercely; to add to the difficulties, players often arrived obviously drunk, and brawls would often ensue.

The following decade saw quality play by William "Dummy" Hoy, "Wee" Willie Keeler, and Denton True "Cy" Young, but there was also much violence on the field, especially by John McGraw's Baltimore Orioles. Players spiked one another and shoved, spat on, and punched umpires.

Catchers began signaling pitchers more frequently, letting them know which type of pitch to throw, and this led the Philadelphia team to create the first system to intercept an opponent's signals. Two percent of minor league teams were no longer independent; they were now associated with a major league team.

Slump? I ain't in no slump.
I just ain't hittin. ▪ YOGI BERRA

THE TWENTIETH CENTURY

At the turn of the century, attendance skyrocketed, in part because unruly behavior on the field was better controlled, in part because of publicity given the sport by newspaper syndicates, and in part because the stable two-league system allowed for an exciting postseason competition, the World Series. Significantly fewer runs were scored because foul balls were now strikes; this change, according to baseball historian Harold Seymour, "fortified pitchers further"(Seymour 1989, 123). Star pitchers included George "Rube" Waddell, Christy Mathewson, Walter Johnson, and Mordecai "Three Finger" Brown; they faced challenges from talented hitters such as Nap Lajoie and Honus Wagner.

1910-1929

During the 1910s, baseball was seriously disrupted when many players left to fight in World War I or to work in shipbuilding plants. Earlier in the decade, though, young players such as George Herman "Babe" Ruth, "Shoeless Joe" Jackson, Eddie Collins, "Smokey" Joe Wood, Tris Speaker, Ty Cobb, and Pete Alexander piqued the interest of fans. Owners were hiring coaches, who were starting to use relief pitchers and pinch runners.

The 1920s brought renewed interest to postwar baseball, with over nine million people attending games in 1920 alone. The spitball pitch had been banned and a better quality of baseball introduced, ending the "dead ball era" and ushering in the "lively ball." Babe Ruth and Rogers Hornsby dominated the offense, with Ruth hitting a record sixty home runs in 1927, for a total of 467 from 1920 to 1929; Hornsby batted .424 in 1924, still the highest batting average, post–1900. Quality pitchers included Grover Cleveland Alexander, Red Faber, and Dazzy Vance. By this point, 50 percent of minor leagues were part of the major league system.

1930s and 1940s

During the 1930s night baseball games were scheduled, and Sunday games became more acceptable; ironically, attendance was down, due to the Great Depression. Offensive stars included Lou Gehrig, Babe Ruth, and Joe DiMaggio, while Lefty Grove and Dizzy Dean excelled as pitchers. During this era pitchers were increasingly specializing as starters or relievers.

World War II affected major league baseball: Many players fought overseas, and as the quality of the ball itself declined due to a shortage of raw material. Major league teams culled new talent, offering high school students lucrative signing bonuses, and the farm system became firmly entrenched, with 80 percent of the minor league teams now part of the major league system. Stars included Bob Feller, Stan Musial—and Ted Williams, baseball's most recent (and last) .400 hitter.

1950s and 1960s

During the 1950s attendance dropped. Rather than attend games in aging stadiums often located in declining urban neighborhoods, with poor public transportation systems and inadequate parking, fans watched an expanded schedule of games on television. Team franchises were switching locations, and fans in abandoned cities often resented the changes and did not support baseball; team owners began building new stadiums to replace obsolete ones and gain fans in their new locations, but team loyalty could not be rushed. Batting helmets became mandatory in the NL (1955) and in the AL (1956); games were longer, and fans were restless. New stars of the era included Mickey Mantle, Willie Mays, and Hank Aaron, the last of whom holds the record for the most career home runs (755).

Players were rediscovering speed an as offensive strategy, and in 1962 Maury Wills stole 104 bases. Roger Maris broke Babe Ruth's home run record in 1961 with 61. It seemed likely that offensive performance would dominate the game, as it had in the 1920s. In 1963, though, the strike zone was increased, causing home runs to decrease by 10 percent and overall runs by 12 percent, and so the anticipated offensive explosion did not occur. What did happen was expansion. Each league increased from eight teams to twelve, which made domination by any one team more difficult. Outstanding pitchers included Warren Spahn, Sandy Koufax,

Never bet on baseball. ■ PETE ROSE

Bob Gibson, and Tom Seaver; Frank Robinson, Roberto Clemente, and Carl Yastrzemski also offered fans stellar performances to applaud.

1970s-1990s

A player's strike occurred in 1972, and a landmark court decision in 1975 revolutionized owner-player disputes. For nearly one hundred years, players had been bound to owners, by means of the reserve clause contained in their contracts. In 1975, though, a baseball arbitrator ruled in favor of two players, Andy Messersmith and Dave McNally, who challenged that interpretation —and the advent of "free agency" occurred. This gave players significantly more control over their careers.

In 1973 the American League approved the designated hitter rule, which permitted another player to bat in place of the pitcher, who was almost invariably the worst hitter in the lineup. This freed pitchers to focus on their pitching and allowed managers to add another powerful hitter to their batting order. The AL expanded to fourteen teams in 1977. Stars of the era included Nolan Ryan, Rod Carew, Reggie Jackson, Joe Morgan, Pete Rose, and Johnny Bench.

The free-agency ruling of the 1970s segued into a decade of contract arbitration; players could now earn salaries in the millions. Strikes occurred again in 1981 and 1985. By the 1990s players were moving from team to team in greater numbers, and contractual disputes increased. To encourage fan interest, baseball administrators approved interleague play. The National League expanded to fourteen teams in 1993, but a strike during the 1994–1995 seasons canceled a World Series for the first time in ninety-two years, and caused some of the most loyal fans to question the direction that professional baseball was heading.

LEAGUES IN THE TWENTY-FIRST CENTURY

Current East Division AL teams include the Baltimore Orioles, Boston Red Sox, New York Yankees, Tampa Bay Devil Rays, and Toronto Blue Jays. In the Central Division, there are the Chicago White Sox, Cleveland Indians, Detroit Tigers, Kansas City Royals and

Minnesota Twins; the Anaheim Angels, Oakland Athletics, Seattle Mariners, and Texas Rangers make up the West Division.

East Division NL teams include the Atlanta Braves, Florida Marlins, Montreal Expos, New York Mets, and Philadelphia Phillies; in the Central Division, there are the Chicago Cubs, Cincinnati Reds, Houston Astros, Milwaukee Brewers, Pittsburgh Pirates, and St. Louis Cardinals. West Division teams are the Arizona Diamondbacks, Colorado Rockies, Los Angeles Dodgers, San Diego Padres, and San Francisco Giants.

Overall major league attendance totals approximately 70 million annually; this includes repeat attendees, of course, but it does not include attendance at minor league games or any other amateur or professional baseball leagues around the world. Early in the game's evolution, the majority of baseball's fans were men; today, people of both genders and all ages enjoy the sport, and team management promotes family friendly events and atmospheres.

SCANDAL IN THE NATIONAL PASTIME

Although baseball teams and players have been much revered by fans, the game has had its share of scandals. Most scandals have centered on gambling and/or game throwing in exchange for pay, with an early example occurring in 1865 when the New York Mutuals were accused of accepting money to deliberately lose games; something similar occurred with the Louisville Grays in 1877. Dead-ball era first baseman Hal Chase was especially noted for being involved in illicit schemes, and one of the greatest disgraces of baseball history—the Black Sox Scandal—emerged in 1920.

Eight White Sox players were accused of having collaborated with notorious gamblers to "fix" the 1919 World Series against the Cincinnati Reds and deliberately lose the Series in exchange for payoffs. This scandal served as the impetus to replace baseball's three-person ruling body, the National Commission, with a baseball commissioner. Owners chose Kenesaw Mountain Landis, the judge who had stalled on the Federal League rulings five years before. Landis's first significant

Fans watching the Red Sox play at Fenway Park, Boston.

act as commissioner was to ban permanently the accused players from professional baseball, although they had not been found guilty in the courtroom.

No scandal of magnitude occurred again until the banishment of Pete Rose in 1989. Rose, the career leader in hits, singles, at-bats, and games played, had retired from playing and was managing the Cincinnati Reds. He was reportedly deeply in debt and accused of betting on his own team—an act that became illegal after the Black Sox Scandal of 1920. Rose has requested reinstatement to professional baseball, not to participate in the sport again, but to gain Hall of Fame eligibility. All requests, to date, have been denied.

In 2004, a federal investigation uncovered evidence that a lab had been supplying certain well-known professional baseball players with banned performance-enhancing drugs; some players admitted to using these substances. This series of events has caused great debate in the baseball world and the media at large. These drugs enhance muscle mass at a faster rate and allow fatigued muscles to recover more quickly, thus permitting the athlete to engage in a much more rigorous training regime. These substances are banned for two reasons: one, it is illegal to distribute and/or use them; and two, the side effects, especially after long-time use, may be significant. Moreover, these drugs are deliberately designed to avoid detection, opening players who use them to charges of cheating and deception. How the commissioner of baseball will ultimately address this issue and what the legal consequences may be to players who have been using these drugs are still open to question.

Nature of the Sport

Two teams alternate between playing offense (batting) and defense (fielding) for nine innings, with the home team batting last. If a batter reaches first base on a hit, that is a single; second base is a double; and third base a triple. Runners generally advance on the base paths

Baseball

Baseball in Finland

Although baseball is typically thought of as an American sport, a version was being played by the Saami (Lapp) people of northern Finland in the nineteenth century. The following are descriptions of the game provided by anthropologists.

. . . In the Inari winter village, in February 1820, the youths attending confirmation school handled the ball and bat with great skill in spite of the snow and cold. They marked two parallel lines in the snow about 15 or 20 fathoms apart. Two equal groups took up positions behind each line, while one boy remained halfway between the lines. One boy of each group was positioned on his line and had to serve the ball, while the others tried, by turns, to strike it towards the opposite line. At the same time one player of the same group had to run to the opposite line. The boy standing halfway between tried to catch the ball and hit the runner before he had reached the goal. If he succeeded, the "burned" runner took his place. The ball players had all been fishing by the Arctic Ocean and had probably learned the game on the coast, where it was common.

The Kolt-Lapps have the most highly developed ball-game, which they practice almost every day during certain periods (not, however, during Lent), in their winter villages as well as in summer in Kolt-taköngäs. The "one-hit"-game (*oy'tes-t sas'k'em-pál'l a*), which corresponds to the Finnish "cantor's ball," is less common. Usually each player has three hits (*kol'me s-t sas'k'em-pál'l a*). This game needs at least four participants. Before starting they cast lots: Some-

one spits on the bat and one group chooses the "wet" side, the other the dry one. Then the bat is thrown in the air and the group whose side falls upwards will begin the game as batters, the other group as "guardians." The children cast lots in the following way: Two of them throw the bat to each other three times. From the point where one of their hands was the third time, they will remove their grip alternately upwards; the one whose hand grips the top will become batter, the other guardian. The other children proceed by turns in the same way, until each one has his place. In the beginning only the children play but later on they are joined by grown-ups, men and women. The game is very similar to the Finnish "king" or "castle-game." Each player may hit three times and he is served by one of the opposite group. He may run immediately after a hit, or later. If one of the guardians catches the ball in the air or "burns" the runner with the ball, his group will get a turn to hit. In the course of the game there is a change: During the first round one ball has to be caught, during the second two, and during the third round three balls. The ball-games prove that at least the most highly developed types were adopted from neighbor peoples. The original names for the ball and the bat, as well as the verb *tuos'tuh* [meaning] "catch the ball" ([in] Finnish *tastia*), which appear in certain dialects indicate, however, that the Lapps already at an early period practiced their own primitive ball-games.

Source: Itkonen, T. I. (1948). *The Lapps in Finland up to 1945* (pp. 855–858). Porvoo, Helsinki: Werner Sderstrm Osakeyhti.

when teammates hit the ball, but they can also "steal"— or advance to the next base—when the pitcher is preparing to pitch. If the pitcher tosses four "balls"— nonstrikes—to a batter, that qualifies as a "walk," and the runner automatically goes to first base; if a pitch hits the batter, he goes to first base. A run is scored whenever an offensive player successively and safely lands on first, second, and third base—and then home plate. If

a ball is hit directly over the outfield fence in fair territory, that is a home run; if it bounces and then goes over the fence, a ground-rule double. If someone reaches base after a defensive mistake, that is a fielding error. The team that scores the most runs, wins; a tie is resolved by playing extra innings until one team secures the lead. Baseball is the only game in which the defense controls the ball.

I don't feel right unless I have a sport to play
or at least a way to work up a sweat. ▪ HANK AARON

Defensive positions are the pitcher; catcher; first, second, and third basemen; shortstop; and right, left, and center fielders. Their goal is to cause the offensive players to become "out" via three strikes—a "strikeout," or by a tag, cleanly played ground ball, caught fly ball, or force out at the base. Once three outs are obtained, the two teams switch sides.

In amateur play, for youth or adults, rules may be modified. In some leagues, for example, steals are not permitted. In softball leagues, a game increasing in popularity, the ball is pitched underhanded. In leagues for the youngest players, pitching is sometimes eliminated entirely, and batters are permitted to hit the ball from a stand—or tee—for training purposes.

FACILITIES AND EQUIPMENT

Baseball facilities have ranged from park space with no permanent seating to those with bleachers and dugouts. As the game developed and increased in stature, full-fledged stadiums were built—first wooden, then steel—complete with rest rooms, restaurants, and gift shops. Throughout most of baseball's history, the game was played on grass or dirt; in 1965 artificial turf was introduced and used throughout many stadiums. Domed stadiums, which allow games to be played in inclement weather, have also surfaced in modern-day play. Basic equipment—bat, ball, gloves, and batting helmets—has remained constant for decades, although technological improvements have altered the appearance and quality of all items.

Opening Up the Game

Originally, the sport was a gentleman's game, but rougher elements entered the equation when salaries were first paid. The *New York Times* called baseball players of that era "worthless, dissipated gladiators; not much above the professional pugilist in morality and respectability" (Ward and Burns 1994, 51). Many immigrants—most notably the Irish—dominated early teams; when the American League formed, Germans settling in the Midwest flooded the league. College baseball programs became more competitive around 1905;

when those graduates entered the major league system, well-educated men played beside the illiterate. In the 1930s, baseball "offered mill hands, plowboys, high school kids a better way of life. They rose on sandlots to big city diamonds," according to the resident "mastermind" of the St. Louis Cardinals, Branch Rickey (James 2001, 146).

BREAKING THE COLOR BARRIER

By the 1950s the color barrier was broken, and 8 percent of major league players were black. Polish-American participation was at an all-time high, and Latin/Hispanic players were joining the major leagues in greater numbers. Latin/Hispanic players continue to play an expanding role, and college-educated players are in greater demand.

WOMEN AND THE GAME

Although nowhere near as extensively as men, women have played baseball almost since its inception. A collegiate female baseball team briefly existed as early as 1866 at Vassar College, but women's teams did not survive for long. Novelty acts such as the "Blondes and Brunettes" lasted only a short time, while late nineteenth-century professional ball clubs with both men and women on their rosters—known as "Bloomer Girl" teams—challenged all-male teams, an activity often deemed improper. When, in 1904, five female students joined a men's baseball game in progress at the University of Pennsylvania, campus administrators contacted the police to prevent any such games in the future.

In 1931 pitcher Jackie Mitchell was signed to a minor league contract, the first female to play professional ball since Lizzie Arlington's brief foray in 1898. In 1934 Babe Didrikson—a star athlete who also excelled in track, basketball, and golf—pitched two scoreless innings for a Cleveland Indians minor league team.

The notion of women playing baseball became more acceptable in the World War II era, when "Rosie the Riveter" was leaving domesticity behind to support the war effort, doing factory work. In 1943 the owner of the Chicago Cubs, Philip Wrigley, proposed a professional

*In the great department store of life,
baseball is the toy department.* ■ UNKNOWN

women's league, intended to fill the void in case World War II caused a major league hiatus. Even though the hiatus didn't occur, the result was the All-American Girls Baseball League, which lasted until 1954. In 1974 young females began participating in Little League.

Female pioneers include pitcher Maud Nelson—who played, scouted, and managed in baseball from 1897 to 1935, and was called the "the greatest: the reliable starter and the keeper of the flame" (Gregorich 1993, 10)—and Alta Weiss, the "Girl Wonder," who took the mound in Cleveland's major league stadium in 1907 to successfully pitch against a roster of semiprofessional male players. Many women currently umpire games; one of the earliest female umpires was Amanda Clement, who started professionally in about 1904.

Baseball Goes Global

Although baseball first gained strength in the United States, the game quickly spread to other locales, most notably Japan and countries in Latin America.

JAPAN

The sport of baseball was introduced in Japan as early as 1873; taught by teachers and professors, early Japanese baseball was seen primarily as a method to strengthen oneself, both physically and mentally, much like the philosophy undergirding martial arts. Because baseball was used as a teaching tool, amateur ball—in high schools and colleges—predominated. In 1915 Japanese educators formed the National High School Baseball Tournament; even today, Japan is at the forefront of amateur baseball.

In the early 1930s, Matsutaro Shoriki sponsored a tour during which major league players from the United States—including Babe Ruth and Lou Gehrig—played against Japanese college all-stars. Inspired by the interest in this matchup, Shoriki formed the Great Japan Tokyo Baseball Club in 1934; this led to the formation of the Japan Pro-Baseball League in 1936. Seven teams were in the original league, with the Kyojin team most prominent. They won six titles from 1936 to 1944, along with two half-season titles; star players included

pitchers Eiji Sawamura, Victor Starfin and Hideo Fujimoto.

Teams were sponsored by newspapers that wanted to increase circulation or by train lines wishing to increase the number of people using their mode of transportation. During World War II, though, baseball was chaotic; teams were formed, merged and disbanded, and English names of teams were forbidden. In 1946, though, baseball resumed in a more orderly fashion with eight established teams; and English names began to be used again by all teams.

English nicknames of teams returned after the war; in 1950 seven teams were added, forming today's Nippon Professional Baseball League, consisting of the Central League and the Pacific League. The winner of each league—each of which currently has six teams—meets in the Japan Series to determine the year's overall champion.

In 1965, to counteract the imbalance of player talent on teams—with the Central League Giants being the most powerful—the player draft was introduced. Nevertheless, the Kyojin Giants remained a powerhouse; media has paid significant attention to its players, and even when Japan's baseball commissioner ruled against a contract the owners had signed, the Giants won the dispute after threatening to withdraw from the league. Interest was also strong in the Giants because of Sadaharu Oh, who hit 868 home runs from 1958 to 1980.

The Pacific League, which has received less media attention, has tried to garner some of the spotlight by using a designated hitter, hiring flamboyant mascots, and designing neon uniforms. They also hosted an intraleague playoff from 1973 to 1982, whereby the first half leader challenged the leader of the second half of the season. The Pacific League's most popular team, the Lions, won eleven pennants and eight Japan Series titles from 1982 to 1994.

Baseball continues to be popular in Japan and is currently one of the country's favorite forms of athletics. In recent years some of the better players—including Hideo Nomo, Kazuhiro Sasaki, Ichiro Suzuki, and Hideki Matsui—have been choosing to enter the major

A night baseball game at the Pan American Games. Baseball is a major sport in Latin America.

league system in the United States. Nevertheless, Japan's quality performances in the Olympics and other international championships demonstrate that a significant number of quality players are still participating in Japan's leagues.

LATIN AMERICA

Known as "el beisbol," baseball is also an integral part of Latin American athletics; Cuba, in particular, gained early predominance as a baseball powerhouse, winning twenty-four world championships and two Olympic gold medals. Moreover, off-season matchups between Cuban players and major league players from the United States created exciting games to watch.

Sailors from the United States introduced baseball to Cubans in the 1860s. After that Cubans spread the game to other countries, most notably Mexico (1890), Puerto Rico (1890), Dominican Republic (1891) and Venezuela (1895). In 1900 a United States team of color barnstormed against Cuban teams; by 1904 there were Cuban teams in the Negro Leagues in the United States.

In 1908, during an off-season barnstorming challenge, Cuban Jose Mendez threw a one-hitter against the Cincinnati Reds; in 1909 Eustaquio Pedroso tossed an eleven-inning no-hitter against the Detroit Tigers, who were without their strongest players, Ty Cobb and Sam Crawford. In 1910 Cobb and Crawford did play against Cuban ballplayers; although Cobb batted .369, three of his opponents had a better batting average that series, and Cobb—a renowned base stealer—stole no bases; he vowed not to play against nonwhite players again. When the New York Giants challenged the Cubans in 1911, each team won a few games, but then Mendez and Pedroso outpitched the great Christy Mathewson. This challenge to United States superiority led the American League president, Ban Johnson, to ban fu-

ture barnstorming matches between the United States and Cuba. Lighter skinned Cubans, such as Adolfo Luque, found their way into the major leagues; once the color ban was lifted in the United States in 1947, greater number of Cuban players began participating in major league ball.

Currently, in Cuba there are fourteen teams divided into two zones; each zone is further subdivided into two groups. At the end of a ninety-game season, there is a championship playoff. Players can only play for the team located in the area in which they live.

There is also a Caribbean World Series, with four countries or commonwealths—Puerto Rico, Venezuela, the Dominican Republic, and Mexico—currently participating in this event. The series, which was founded in 1949, is usually played in February; in the past Panama and Cuba have also participated.

Competition at the Top

In the United States pennant-winning teams from the American League and the National League compete in the World Series, a best-of-seven postseason series that determines the championship. The highest honor that a retired player or manager can receive is induction to the National Baseball Hall of Fame and Museum, located in Cooperstown, New York. In Japan, the Japan Series is comparable to the World Series in the United States.

Baseball first appeared as a full-medal Olympic sport in 1992, but it served as a demonstration sport as early

A well-run restaurant is like a winning baseball team. It makes the most of every crew member's talent and takes advantage of every split-second opportunity to speed up service. ■ DAVID OGILVY

as 1912. That year, a Swedish team challenged competitors from the United States track and field team in Stockholm. The U.S. team won, 13–3, but needed to borrow teammates from Sweden to fill its roster. A second game was played with American decathlon star Jim Thorpe playing right field. The Americans won, 6–3.

In 1936 the United States intended to play an exhibition game against Japan in Berlin, Germany. When Japan withdrew, the United States sent two teams. In 1952 *pesapallo*—a Finnish version of baseball—was played in Helsinki; in 1956 United States servicemen played against the Australians in Melbourne. It is believed that 114,000 spectators observed, possibly the largest baseball audience ever. The United States won, 11–5. In 1964 the Americans challenged the Japanese team in Tokyo; the United States won, 6–2.

OLYMPIC BASEBALL
In 1981 the sport of baseball was officially granted the status of a demonstration sport and several teams—the Unites States, Japan, South Korea, the Dominican Republic, Canada, Taiwan, Italy, and Nicaragua—competed in Los Angeles in 1984; because of a difficult political situation in the Soviet Union, Cuba boycotted the games. Japan won the event, beating the United States in the final game, 6–3.

In 1988 baseball was played in the Olympics in Seoul, South Korea; Cuba again boycotted the games. Teams included the United States, Japan, South Korea, Puerto Rico, Canada, Taiwan, the Netherlands, and Australia. The two finalists were again the United States and Japan; this time, the American team won, 5–3.

In 1992, in Barcelona, Spain, baseball was first played as a full medal sport. Cuba did compete in these Olympics and won the gold medal. Taiwan earned silver; and Japan, bronze. The United States ended up in fourth place.

Softball was added as an Olympic sport in 1996, when games were played in Atlanta, Georgia. In baseball Cuba again earned Olympic gold; Japan won the silver, and the United States notched bronze. In Sydney,

Australia in 2000, professional players were permitted to participate, but no major league players were on the United States team that won the gold. Cuba earned silver; South Korea, bronze.

In 2004, in Athens, Greece, Cuba regained its predominance in the Olympics; Australia won the silver medal and Japan earned the bronze, while the United States didn't make the final eight teams.

Governing Body
The primary governing body for baseball in the United States is Major League Baseball (MLB; www.mlb.com).

Kelly Boyer Sagert

See also Astrodome; Baseball Stadium Life; Baseball Wives; Fenway Park; Franchise Relocation; World Series; Wrigley Field; Yankee Stadium

Further Reading
Baseball in Cuba. (2005). Retrieved March 14, 2005, from http://baseballguru.com/bbcuba1.html

Bouton, J. (1970). *Ball Four.* New York: Wiley.

Cottrell, R. (2002). *Blackball, the Black Sox and the Babe: Baseball's crucial 1920 season.* Jefferson, NC: McFarland & Company.

Dixon, P. with Hannigan, P. (1992). *The Negro Baseball Leagues: A photographic history.* Mattituck, NY: Amereon, Ltd.

Golenbock, P., & Bacon, P. (1990). *Teammates.* San Diego, CA: Harcourt Brace Jovanovich.

Gregorich, B. (1993). *Women at play: The story of women in baseball.* San Diego, CA: Harcourt Brace & Company.

Halberstam, D. (2003). *The teammates.* New York: Hyperion.

James, B. (2001). *The new Bill James historical baseball abstract.* NY: The Free Press.

Japanese baseball history. (2004). Retrieved December 14, 2004, from http://ww1.baywell.ne.jp/fpweb/drlatham/history/history.htm

Johnson, S. (1994). *When women played hardball.* Emeryville, CA: Seal Press.

Kahn, R. (1971). *The boys of summer.* New York: Harper.

Latino baseball history. (2004). Retrieved December 16, 2004, from http://latinobaseball.com/cwb-history.html

Lewis, M. (2003). *Moneyball.* New York: W. W. Norton.

Malamud, B. (2003). *The natural.* New York: Farrar, Straus, and Giroux. (Original work published 1952)

Rader, B. G. *Baseball:* (2002). *A history of America's game.* Urbana and Chicago: University of Illinois Press.

Seymour, H. (1989). *Baseball: The golden age.* NY: Oxford University Press.

Spalding, A. (1991). *Base ball: America's national game: 1839–1915.*

(S. Coombs & B. West, Eds.). San Francisco: Halo Books. (Original work published 1915)

Veeck, B., &. Linn, E. (1962). *Veeck as in wreck.* New York: Simon & Schuster.

Ward, G., & Burns, K. (1994). *Baseball: An illustrated history.* NY: Alfred Knopf.

White, S., with Malloy, J. (1995). *Sol White's history of colored base ball, with other documents on the early black game 1886–1936.* Lincoln: University of Nebraska Press.

Baseball Nicknames

Nicknames are more common in childhood than later in life—except in sports. In no other sport are nicknames more pervasive than baseball. Who hasn't heard of "Slammin' Sammy" or the "Rocket" or the "Big Unit"?

A nickname often tells us something about a player. Nicknames such as "Penguin," "Pee Wee," "Stretch," "Red," "Whitey," "Bones," "Moose," "Baby Bull," and "Pudge" all reveal attributes of appearance or physique. Having hardly anything between his chin and his chest, Walt Williams was called "No Neck," and Ken Harrelson's prominent nose caused him to be called "Hawk." "Wee" Willie Keeler was just five-foot-four. Occasionally a nickname relates to personality, such as "Goofy," "Space Man," "Bulldog," "Daffy," and "Blue." Some nicknames are based on unusual mannerisms, such as the "Human Rain Delay" for former Cleveland first baseman Mike Hargrove because of his time-consuming batting rituals or the "Hat" for Harry Walker, who took his cap off between every pitch when batting.

Some nicknames, such as "Charlie Hustle," "Mr. October," "Hammerin' Hank," "Wizard," and "Sudden Sam," often stem from performance. Less often they stem from a player's weakness, such as the nickname "Wild Thing" for Phillies pitcher Mitch Williams, who sometimes couldn't find the strike zone; he walked the bases loaded and caused his team to lose the 1992 World Series.

Geographical origin is the source of other nicknames, such as the "Georgia Peach," "Mex," and "Oil Can." "Wahoo" Sam Crawford, Wilmer "Vinegar Bend" Mizell, and "Hondo" Clint Hartung were all nicknamed after their hometowns. During the late 1960s and early 1970s a few players had their nicknames, instead of their surnames, stitched on the back of their jerseys. "Hawk" Harrelson was the first to do so, followed by Jim "Mudcat" Grant, Ralph "Roadrunner" Garr, and others. The trend declined around the time Atlanta Braves owner Ted Turner asked his newly acquired free-agent pitcher Andy Messersmith to have "channel" stitched above his jersey number 17, looking for some free advertising for his cable network with that same channel number.

Elaborate, multiword nicknames coined by sportswriters and broadcasters are known to fans but never used by the players themselves. Can you imagine the Boston Red Sox players calling teammate Ted Williams the "Splendid Splinter," or the Giants calling Willie Mays the "Say Hey Kid," or the Pirates calling Honus Wagner the "Flying Dutchman"?

Authentic or not, nicknames have been good for baseball. Fans feel closer to individuals when they can use a nickname, and such memorable monikers as the "Sultan of Swat" (Babe Ruth), the "Iron Horse" (Lou Gehrig), or the "Yankee Clipper" (Joe DiMaggio) probably increase a star player's potential of becoming a household name.

Time is required for a player to acquire a genuine nickname. When players are starting out in pro ball, most are called by simple diminutives of their surnames, such as "Ash" for Ashford, "Topper" for Topham, "Doobie" for Duboise. Although these are not very original, they do imply an intimacy lacking with given names. A few rookies retain the nicknames they had while playing amateur baseball when those names are known to one or more of their new teammates.

What's in a Name?

"Acquiring a nickname is part of arriving," said Chicago Cubs infielder Mark Grudzielanek. "If you are worth giving a name to, it means your teammates think you're okay and that you're going to be around for a while." Players who are not well liked usually do not have nicknames, or such nicknames are seldom used. When former Mets pitcher Rick Reed was called up to the big leagues after having been a replacement player—a scab—during the 1995 strike, he was snubbed by his teammates. Two seasons later he knew that he had redeemed himself when his teammates began to use his nickname "Reeder."

However, nicknames may not always be positive. As Jack Fitzpatrick, a former minor leaguer and now psycho-historian, notes during a phone interview, "Nicknames can sometimes also be used to express derision or even hostility toward a player. Penguin may be cute, but it can be derisive too if teammates are making fun of the deformity that produces an odd appearance or strange way of walking and running."

Sociologist James Skipper found that baseball nicknames have been declining since the 1920s. Skipper measured the frequency of nicknames among major league players over the decades, using the *Baseball Encyclopedia* as his database (The encyclopedia includes all players who have appeared in the major leagues since 1871 along with their statistics and any nicknames known to the public.) From 1871 to 1979, when Skipper did his analysis, 25 percent of the 11,351 players listed had nicknames unrelated to their surnames. The actual figure is likely to be higher because nicknames used by teammates but not known to the public were not recorded. More telling, Skipper found that nicknames declined most sharply after 1950 (the 1950s had a 50 percent drop). He attributed this drop to the more impersonal manner in which major league players were perceived by the public and a diminished belief in folk heroes generally.

Skipper also believed that the first franchise relocations in more than fifty years (i.e., Boston Braves moving to Milwaukee in 1953, St. Louis Browns to Baltimore in 1954, the Philadelphia Athletics to Kansas City in 1955, and the Giants and Dodgers to the West Coast in 1958), which were all done for strictly mone-

tary reasons, shattered the fans' illusion that teams have an enduring loyalty to their cities. It also contributed to the fans' growing realization, said Skipper, that baseball is foremost a business. Nicknames continued to decline during the 1960s but took their sharpest nosedive during the 1970s, the decade of the first players' strike, the beginning of arbitration, free agency, and multimillion-dollar salaries. In short, fans have become less inclined to use nicknames as their image of ballplayers has changed from larger-than-life heroes to money-hungry entrepreneurs—a change that implies being impersonal and putting self before team. The more detached style of today's sportswriters has probably meant fewer names being coined in the press box or in the sport pages.

The Future

Team nicknames also are less popular today. During the 1920s St. Louis fans often called their Cardinals the "Gashouse Gang," the 1940s Dodgers were affectionately known as "Bums," the 1950 pennant-winning Phillies were the "Whiz Kids," the 1970s Reds were the "Big Red Machine," and the Oakland As of the same period were the "Mustache Gang," to name a few. Today we have only the "Bronx Bombers," which is a carryover from the 1920s.

We cannot say whether real nicknames are gone forever. Some aspects of the game have moved in cycles, and in recent years we have seen the return of belts and button-down uniforms and old-style ballparks with character. Perhaps we will see the return of nicknames, too.

George Gmelch

Further Reading

Light, J. F. (1997). *The cultural encyclopedia of baseball.* Jefferson, NC: McFarland & Company.

Pruyne, T. W. (2002). *Sports nicknames: 20,000 professionals worldwide.* Jefferson, NC: McFarland & Company.

Skipper, J. (1992). *Baseball nicknames: A dictionary of origins and meanings.* Jefferson, NC: McFarland & Company.

Zminda, D., Callis, J., & Miller, C. (1999). *From Abba Dabba to Zorro: The world of baseball nicknames.* Morton Grove, IL: Stats Pub.

Baseball Stadium Life

Baseball stadiums or "ballparks" are magical places for players and fans alike. They have an aesthetic all their own—the sweep of the grandstands, the rainbow of color in the different seating sections, and the emerald green field crisply outlined in chalk. Baseball fans have a closer attachment to their ballparks than fans in any other sport. Fans speak with reverence about Fenway Park, Yankee Stadium, and Wrigley Field, and with admiration of a different sort for new ballparks such as Safeco Field and Camden Yards. Phillip Lowry called his book on ballparks *Green Cathedrals* because the more he studied ballparks, the more he thought they resembled mosques, synagogues, churches, and similar places of worship. Many Americans, Lowry states, have a "spiritual reverence for ballparks, because they hold treasured memories and serve as a sanctuary for the spirit" (Lowry 1992, 52). In no other sport do fans plan vacations around visiting ballparks. Certainly, we never hear of football fans making pilgrimages to all the NFL stadiums or basketball fans bragging about all the NBA arenas they've been to (Wright and House 1989).

The First Ballparks

The earliest ballparks were built in the 1850s; they were multipurpose, often used for cricket as well as baseball. They were open, without fences. Efforts to enclose them, known as "the enclosure movement," were done so that owners could more easily charge admission and bring order by preventing fans, who sometimes encroached on the field, from simply sitting wherever they pleased. The earliest parks accommodated just a few thousand fans on wooden benches, close to the action.

Squeezed into long city blocks, most parks were rectangular in shape, often resulting in a short right field that favored left-handed hitters. Constructed of wood, the parks were often in need of repair, and sometimes burned to the ground. Cincinnati's Redland Park collapsed in 1892, killing a spectator.

The first concrete and steel park, Shibe Park in Philadelphia, wasn't built until 1909, and the first triple-decked ballpark, Yankee Stadium, didn't appear until 1923 (it seated 57,545). It was thirty years later before the first major league park had lights—County Stadium in Milwaukee in 1953. In the 1960s baseball began leaving the inner city, and the old ballparks were replaced with new, concrete multisport ovals, some of which had artificial turf. Their design and uniform dimensions made them impersonal and soulless, with no suggestion of history, tradition, or sense of place. So similar to one another, they were called "cookie cutter" stadiums, and they blighted baseball's landscape for over two decades. During the 1990s most of them were pulled down and replaced with new ballparks with a retro feel. Oriole Park at Camden Yards began the trend and so far has spawned the construction of ten other postmodern ballparks with frills and loads of character. Domed or indoor stadiums are also out of fashion, as is the artificial turf that has proved hard on players, shortening their careers. At its peak, ten teams played on artificial turf; in 2004 only three are left. Some of the newest stadiums (e.g., in Seattle, Houston, Milwaukee, Arizona) have retractable roofs, eliminating rainouts, allowing real grass to grow, and giving fans the comfort of a controlled climate.

Ballpark Spectators

The crowds at nineteenth-century ballparks were small compared with those of today. During the 1871–1875 National Association seasons, for example, teams averaged less than 3,000 spectators per game. The Boston Red Stockings drew only 1,750 per game in 1875 when they finished first.

Attendance fluctuated, depending on the health of the economy and pennant races, in the early years of the twentieth century. But ballpark attendance boomed after the end of the World War I and on through the 1920s as prosperity returned to the country and the home run became common with the arrival of larger-than-life Babe Ruth, and a "livelier" baseball. Attendance then declined during the Great Depression and

During the seventh inning stretch, a crew rakes out the infield.

didn't recover until after World War II. At bottom, in 1934 the National League averaged just 5,200 fans per game, while in the first year after the war attendance averaged 15,000 per game. Crowds grew larger in the 1950s, slipped in the 1960s when the major leagues expanded, and grew again after 1975. Some experts say the exciting 1975 World Series between the Boston Red Sox and the Cincinnati Reds reignited interest. Crowds increased steadily from 1975 until 1991 when labor strife between the club owners and the players union alienated many fans. When a strike ended the 1994 season in August, many unhappy fans turned to minor league baseball, sparking a renaissance and record attendance all across the country. After the 1994 strike, which also led to canceling the World Series, attendance declined by 29 percent. Major league baseball won back some but not all of its disaffected fans after

a thrilling home run race in 1998 between the Cardinals Mark McGwire and the Cubs Sammy Sosa.

The Field

One way to understand stadium life is to think in terms of a "front stage" (the field where the game is played and the stands where the spectators watch from) and a "backstage" (where the preparations and business takes place, such as clubhouse, equipment rooms, press box, and front office).

On the field are the players, along with a supporting cast of coaches, managers, trainers, batboys, ball girls, mascots, groundskeepers, and the umpires, the arbiters of the game. For all of them, the playing field is their work place—the stage on which they perform their jobs. Their roles are easily identified by dress—the white baseball uniform of the home team players and

It ain't over till it's over. ▪ YOGI BERRA

coaches, the nonwhite (usually with some element of gray) uniform of the visitors, the black or dark blue blazers and pants worn by the umpires, and the usually khaki, forest green, or brown trousers and white shirts of the groundskeepers.

For spectators, the field is the focal point of the ballpark. Their gaze is usually fixed on the field even as they talk, drink, and eat. The field's expanse of emerald green turf and the dirt insets of the batter's box, pitcher's mound, and infield, all outlined in white chalk, is the aesthetic center of the ballpark. Whoever walks on the field, even during pregame activities, is noticed. Even batboys and ball girls may become fan favorites.

The field is protected, separated from the grandstands and spectators by a wall or railing. It is secured by ushers and security guards who defend the "boundary," maintaining order and preventing trespass onto the field. For the groundskeepers, the field is the showcase of their skills, a visible indicator of how well they do their work. The condition of the field—turf and dirt—is of vital importance to the players, as it can influence their performance. Infield dirt that is too sandy or damp will slow a base runner, an uneven surface in the infield can cause a bad hop, grass that is only slightly longer than usual will slow down ground balls and potential base hits going through the infield.

In baseball, unlike basketball, football, and hockey, there are several hours of activity on the field before the game begins, and much of it is enjoyable for fans to watch. By 4:00 P.M. (for a 7:00 P.M. game), players are in the outfield loosening up—running and then stretching, which is led by the team's trainer. Next, they play catch—slow toss from close range, gradually lengthening the distance. But batting practice, better known as "BP," is the centerpiece of pregame activities. Players hit in groups of four. Waiting their turn, other players banter and tease. Fans enjoy the scene—the pitch, swing, crack of the wooden bat, and the flight of the ball to the outfield. Those that land in the seats trigger a scramble among fans for a souvenir. In the outfield, pitchers run and others "shag" fly balls.

Hidden from view is the clubhouse, the area where the teams and the umpires, who are in separate quarters, dress, eat, relax, and mentally prepare for the game. Clubhouses in the major leagues are spacious and well appointed, with carpeting, sofas, televisions, and oversized lockers. Food is plentiful, spread on large tables. Near or attached to the locker room is the training room and video room where players view their own performances and that of the pitcher they are about to face. Finally, there are batting cages with pitching machines. The clubhouse is a sanctuary, a place where the players are sheltered from autograph requests and the other demands an adoring public makes on them.

The Stands

Activity in the stands starts long before the sun comes up. Cleaners armed with backpack leaf blowers move through each row, blowing trash from the night before into the aisles and then bagging it to be taken away. Every seat is wiped down, the concourse is scoured with pressure hoses, and the toilets are scrubbed and sanitized.

Once cleaned, the cavernous stands sit silent, except for an occasional worker eating lunch or jogging on the concourse. The stands slowly come alive again after the gates open up two hours before game time. The players are already on the field taking batting practice as the first fans trickle in. Despite the rock 'n' roll music blaring from the sound system, the crack of the bat from the batting cage can be heard everywhere in the stadium. "Pregame" is a time when fans are allowed to move close to the field and get a good view of the players. Some seek autographs from the players, "Hey, Nomar . . . over here, over here." Part of the job of being a big leaguer is dealing with an admiring public, such as the fans who want a close look and an autograph to take away—a memento or proof of their brief encounter with "fame."

As the stands fill up, the bold, uniform bands of brightly colored seats disappear beneath the throng of spectators in multicolored dress. The stands are the workplace of ushers, security personnel, food vendors, and mascots. Known as "game-day staff," they only

A hot dog at the ballpark is better than steak at the Ritz. ■ HUMPHREY BOGART

work when the team is playing at home. Ushers and security maintain order among the spectators, whether it be helping people find their seats or keeping drunks off the field. City police are also present to deter would-be lawbreakers and to make arrests when necessary (most stadiums even have a holding pen where serious offenders can be detained). Vendors, with their rhythmic refrains, like "Ice-cold beer here," and their quick pace provide ambience and the convenience of a hot dog, beer, peanuts, Cracker Jack, cotton candy, or ice cream without leaving your seat. Mascots, who mock everyone from umpires to fans, entertain.

Stand workers, like field personnel, are uniformed to make their roles clear to the public. Ushers and security personnel are attired in blazers and matching slacks, while vendors usually wear vests and caps and a large button announcing their product and its price. Most mascots wear oversized animal costumes with exaggerated features—gigantic heads, bulging midsections, big feet. To broaden ballpark appeal to younger fans, most teams have had mascots since the 1970s–1980s. Some of the best known are the (former) San Diego Chicken, the Cardinals' Fred Bird, the Pirate Parrot, the Mariner Moose, and especially the Phillie Phanatic. (Early in the twentieth century, it was not uncommon for teams to use dwarves, hunchbacks, or mentally challenged adults as mascots.) Mascots are the only ballpark personnel to work both in the stands and on the field.

The stands in major league stadiums sit on multiple decks of concrete and are divided into bleachers, grandstands, loge, and box seats, with the price of the seats in each section determined by its proximity to the field and view of the action. While most fans sit in the open air, an affluent few, often corporate executives and their clients and friends, sit in air-conditioned skyboxes, furnished with couches, wet bars, and television. Beneath and behind the stands are the wide concourses where one can find souvenir shops, fast-food outlets, and toilets. Television sets hang from the concourse walls and in the concession areas to insure that no one misses any of the action while buying a team cap, T-shirt, pennant, miniature bat, or a hot dog and drink.

The stands in minor league ballparks, of course, are smaller; rarely do they have an upper deck. In place of seats that wrap entirely around the field, as in major league parks, along the foul lines they have picnic areas for groups and play areas for children. With virtually every seat close to the action, minor league parks have an intimacy not often found in the big leagues.

But the stands, whether in the majors or minors, are always more than a collection of seats. There is activity in the stands that contributes to a fan's experience and enjoyment of being at a ballpark—the eccentricities of individual vendors hawking their products; video replays, jingles, and games played on the scoreboard (Diamondvision or Jumbotron); and in the minor leagues, between-inning competitions involving children. Fans sometimes create their own diversions such as the *wave* —in which thousands of spectators join together in rising to their feet in sequence to produce a human ripple across the stadium. Also, fans may bat beach balls around the stands, directing them from one section of seats to another. Throughout the game, fans follow developments elsewhere in the major leagues on the scoreboard, noting how division rivals are faring.

Fans enjoy being part of the crowd, looking at the people around them, overhearing conversations in front and behind, and watching the antics of a boisterous fan razzing the opposing team or a disliked player. They watch foul balls hit into the stands, following their trajectory, waiting to see what happens—who catches it, the occasional scramble for a muffed or loose ball, the reaction of the person who gets possession of the ball, especially the elation of kids who snag one.

The changing light is also part of the ballpark experience: the typical three-hour "night" game begins when the sun is still up, progresses through sundown and the gathering dusk in which the visibility temporarily worsens, and then into real darkness when the powerful stadium lights take full effect.

Sound is an important element of the ballpark experience. Some of the sounds are programmed, such as the announcements over the public-address system, the organ music between innings, and the special effects

A view from outside Boston's historic Fenway Park reveals an architectural design intended to entice onlookers. The narrow passageway visible in the center of the image leads the eye past the food and clothing vendors and up to the large scoreboard.

sounds, such as glass shattering after a foul ball is hit into the parking lot. In one of the venerable rituals of the game, all spectators stand to stretch in the seventh inning and often sing a chorus or two of "Take Me Out to the Ball Game," the most popular song ever associated with a particular sport. In the post–September 11 era, "God Bless America" has been added to the seventh-inning break. Other sound comes from the crowd itself, the din of a thousand conversations periodically interrupted by cheers for good plays by the home team and groans of disappointment for setbacks. Ballparks have gotten noisier as fans have taken up inflatable "Thunder Sticks" to root for their home team. Probably the favorite sound of all still is the crack of the wooden bat striking the baseball. There are Americans who can't bear to sit through an inning of televised baseball but relish spending hours in the bleachers or grandstands.

The Press Box

Anyone who has been to an older minor league ballpark has noticed the elongated, shoe-box-shaped wooden structure above the stadium roof or suspended from it. This is the press box. In the multitiered major league stadiums, the press box is usually located in the loge level between the first and second deck. But in all ballparks, the press box is always behind and above home plate to give the press the best possible view.

The term *press box* is a holdover from the days before radio and television when newspapers were the only medium covering professional baseball. Today, television and radio broadcasters, public-address announcers, scoreboard operators, and others work there as well as print journalists. As radio, and later television, began to cover baseball, the press box expanded in size and then became internally divided into separate areas or rooms. Those who perform live and require a quiet environment, notably radio and TV broadcasters and the PA announcer, work in booths. The booth with the best location from which to observe the game—directly in line with the batter and pitcher—is usually given to television broadcasters.

The number of people in the press box can vary from a dozen in the low minors to upwards of seventy in the major leagues. In the small, single newspaper towns of the Class A leagues, there is often only one writer and one radio broadcaster there to cover the game. In the major leagues, there can be several dozen beat writers alone covering the game for different city and suburban papers, writers from the wire services and national papers like *USA Today,* as well as correspondents and freelancers for a variety of other publications, such as *Baseball America,* the *Sporting News,* and *Baseball Digest.* The front row seats, with the best view of the field, are reserved for the regulars. Their nameplates—the New York Times, the Daily News, and so on—are fixed to the countertop. At one end of the front row are the home team's media relations staff. Open seating in the back rows is taken up by writers from the suburban papers and other irregulars. Major league baseball is televised, so in addition to the radio and print people, there is also a TV crew, with a play-by-play announcer and a color commentator doing the game live, often with pregame and postgame shows.

There is always a table full of handouts of statistics on the home and visiting teams and players available in the press box. These "media notes," which often run to five pages of small type, are compiled by the home team's media relations staff for distribution to writers and broadcasters. They contain every imaginable statistic and trend, plus odd bits of information and reports from the club's minor league teams. The press box is governed by the home team's director of media relations. The director and media relations staff determine who shall be issued a pass or "credential," for access to the press box, field, and clubhouse.

The media people who work in the press box can be divided into those who cover the game live (TV and radio broadcasters) and those who don't (the print journalists): instantaneous electronic media versus print journalism. For writers the press box is a pretty relaxed work environment. They need only to observe and make occasional notes when something significant happens in the game, and should they be gone for a few minutes in the bathroom or getting a hot dog when a key play is made, they can watch the replay on the television monitors that are suspended from the ceiling in major league press boxes. The work of writing an account of the game for the next day's newspaper readers is mostly done after the game is over. Broadcasters, on the other hand, report the play as it happens. There is no room for mistakes; mangled syntax, mispronunciations, or stupid observations cannot be retrieved, unlike those of the writer who can always delete an awkward passage from the computer screen. Broadcasters must concentrate, not unlike the players on the field; in fact some broadcasters talk about getting mentally prepared for the game and "putting on their game face."

In the press box, one can often distinguish the writers from the broadcasters by their dress. In television, appearances are important; the field cameras sometimes scan the broadcast booth and broadcasters often do on-air pregame and postgame interviews. Therefore, broadcasters are usually well dressed and well groomed. Radio announcers are somewhat less concerned with appearance, but they still are generally neater than most writers. Writers, more inclined to see themselves as having intellectual qualities, tend to be less conservative, and less careful about dress and appearance.

Front Office

The term *front office* first appeared around the turn of the century when it was used by the New York City underworld to refer to police headquarters. Today, it is a synonym for the main office of any company; however, many people also use it when talking specifically about the business operations of professional sports teams. In baseball the front office is almost always housed in the ballpark itself, although in the low minors the lack of space may result in the front office spilling over into an outside trailer or two.

As one ascends from the low minors to the big leagues, the number of front-office employees rises markedly. Major league teams in big media markets (e.g., New York, Los Angeles) have staffs of over one hundred full-time, year-round employees, while their affiliates in the small towns of the low minors may have fewer than a half dozen.

In the minor leagues, members of the front office staff routinely have contact with the team's fans. Some team owners and general managers even greet arriving fans at the gate. The location of minor league front offices reflect this greater accessibility to the public, as most are at ground level and open onto the park's main concourse. Major league offices, in contrast, are high above the field, on the mezzanine level, near the press area and skyboxes, their entrances guarded by security so that only those with credentials may pass. Major league front-office staff rarely venture into the stands to mingle with fans.

In sum, ballparks are complex and varied places—sites of work, entertainment, and even tourism.

George Gmelch and Patricia San Antonio

Further Reading

Gmelch, G., & Weiner, J.J. (1998). *In the ballpark: The working lives of baseball people.* Washington, DC: Smithsonian Institution Press.

Koppett, L. (1998). *Koppett's oncise istory of Major League Baseball.* Philadelphia, PA: Temple University Press.

Light, J. F. (1997). *The cultural encyclopedia of baseball.* Jefferson, NC, and London: McFarland and Company, Inc., Publishers.

Lowry, P. (1992). *Green cathedrals.* Reading, MA.: Addison-Wesley.

Rader, B. G. (1991). *American sports.* Englewood Cliffs, NJ: Prentice Hall.

Rader, B. G. (2002). *Baseball: A history of America's game.* Urbana and Chicago: University of Illinois Press.

Rossi, J. P. (2000). *The national game.* Chicago: Ivan R. Dee.

Seymour, H. (1960). *Baseball: The early years.* New York: Oxford University Press.

Skolnik, R. (1994). *Baseball and the pursuit of innocence.* College Station: Texas A&M University Press.

Smith, C. (2001). *Storied stadiums.* New York: Carroll & Graf Publishers.

Tygiel, J. (2000). *Past time.* New York: Oxford University Press.

Wright, C., & House, T. (1989). *The Diamond appraised.* New York: Simon and Schuster.

Baseball Wives

Not surprisingly, most of what is written about baseball is about the men who play the game, with little attention given to life at home or to their wives and families. The baseball fan's image of players' wives—based on televised glimpses of them in the stands—is that they are pretty, wear stylish clothes, and lead a life of privilege. The reality is far different, as the demands of their husbands' occupation have a large impact on their lives.

A Transient Life

Mobility is the feature of pro ball that exerts the greatest influence on the wives and families of ballplayers. In the minor leagues the men play in a different town almost every season. If they make it to the major leagues, trades and free agency make them almost as transient there. Because ballplayers rarely play in their hometowns, their wives and children must move every year, not once but several times. In March many wives follow their husbands to Florida or Arizona for spring training; six weeks later, when spring camp breaks, they relocate to the city where their husband's team plays; finally when the season ends in September, they return to their hometown. If their husbands play "winter ball," they may move yet again, usually to the Caribbean or Latin America. Every trade, promotion, or demotion during the season means an additional move. One baseball wife who moved twenty-three times during her husband's ten-year career said, "We could probably stop in any state in the country and know someone from baseball" (Gmelch and San Antonio 2001, 338).

When a husband is traded or moved within the organization, he gets a plane ticket and a ride to the airport; his wife is left with the burden of moving—disconnecting the utilities, closing the bank account, removing the kids from school or camp, and then reestablishing the household in a new locality. It is she who packs the household possessions, loads the U-Haul, and transports the kids to the new town. Some wives enjoy being nomads, especially in the early years before they have children. As one wife put it, "You do get to see a lot of the world. . . . There are only a few states we haven't been in or lived in, and a lot of people can't even say that at the age of fifty or sixty" (Gmelch and San Antonio 2001, 339). But the appeal wears off pretty quickly for most wives, and the frequent changes of place cause many baseball families to postpone buying homes.

Baseball Wife or Baseball Widow?

Because every team plays half of its games on the road, husbands are away a good deal during the season. Inevitably, baseball wives spend a great deal of time alone; from April through September, they are without husbands about half the time. Some women jokingly refer

to themselves not as baseball wives but as baseball widows. Young wives, who may be only a few years out of high school, are not just lonely, they feel vulnerable and insecure being on their own. Fran Kalafatis watched her husband and teammates pull away on the team bus for a road trip as a hurricane approached, leaving her and the children in the parking lot to deal with the approaching storm. As the bus pulled away, the players yelled out warnings and instructions to their wives.

Even when the team is at home, husbands are not around the house much. Ballplayers may spend late mornings at home, but they typically leave for the ballpark by early afternoon, and by the time the game has ended and they have showered and changed, it is after eleven o'clock before they leave. Even then, many players like to go out to eat and unwind before going home. In short, a player's schedule does not mesh well with the needs of a family. Children are in school when he is home in the mornings, and they are asleep by the time he arrives home at night. The children's school summer vacations fall in the middle of the season, when their father is most occupied. Nor do the men have weekends free like most other workers. What little time off ballplayers do have (about two days per month) never falls on a weekend. Even when they are home, the physical grind of the baseball schedule can leave husbands with little energy for family life.

The husband's absence means the baseball wife cares for the children by herself—supervising homework, preparing meals, setting standards, enforcing discipline —acting as both a father and mother for much of the baseball year. With husbands away so much, and the operation of the household and its decisions left to her, it is not surprising that the baseball life requires a wife to be independent. Some of the things women learn to do for themselves are often reserved for men in more conventional households, such as repairing the car, fixing the plumbing, or disciplining the children. Former major leaguer and now baseball analyst Tom House (1989) thinks that baseball wives grow up faster than their husbands do because they have to stay at home to

"anchor" the relationship and deal with the real world, while their husbands are off living in a fantasy world.

The Roles of a Baseball Wife

The baseball wife's primary role is to support her husband and his career. The men depend on their wives as baseball careers are demanding, high pressured, and unfortunately, often short—an average of just four years if they make it to the major leagues. Competition from other players, trades, injuries, and prolonged slumps can end a career at any time. Given the uncertainty, husbands and wives want to do everything to maximize his chances of success. To this end husbands want to be able to focus on baseball, which means wives are expected to shield husbands from distractions. Sharon Hargrove (1989) and Cyndy Garvey (1989) describe in their memoirs how they screened calls, fielded requests for tickets, and dealt with the demands of unreasonable fans. Wives arrange household and children's schedules to suit their husbands. "I am both the mother and the father until September," explained Megan Donovan (Gmelch and San Antonio 2001, 343). Wives are expected not to trouble their husbands with domestic problems, except for crises, while the men were at the ballpark. The ballpark is sacrosanct. Beverly Crute (1981) quotes one baseball wife: "You just don't call at the ballpark unless they're [the children] on their deathbed or something. I mean, there are girls that have babies while their husbands are at the ballpark, and they don't call them." A wife may even support her husband by participating in his superstitions, such as by preparing certain foods, wearing particular clothes to the ballpark, and following other ritualized behaviors her husband deems important to playing well. The enormous financial rewards for those who make it to the major leagues, and the brevity of the average career, justify in the minds of most wives the sacrifices required. Also, the baseball life is not completely burdensome. Many wives say they feel fortunate to be able to go to the games and watch their husbands at work and that ballgames are usually enjoyable affairs. By providing

free tickets, child care, family lounges, and special sections in the stands for wives and children, the teams encourage family attendance.

How Important Is Appearance?

Baseball wives and girlfriends are expected to look attractive. In the words of a San Francisco Giants official: "When you see them all sitting together, it's like a fashion show. They don't come out to the ballpark like other folks, just to have a good time. They are here to watch their husbands play, but they also know they are being looked at and that they have to put their best foot forward. Their appearance is very important to them and to their husbands" (Gmelch and San Antonio 2001, 346). Such comments reveal another aspect of the role of the baseball wife—she is viewed in large measure as a player's property, part of the assets he brings to the game. A wife's looks and behavior, some wives claim, can even affect her husband's baseball career. "You're part of the package, and if you don't look the part, well, some are going to notice," said Sherry Fox (Gmelch 2001, 346).

His Status and Her Identity

Baseball wives enjoy a measure of status by virtue of being married to professional ballplayers. When they are with their husbands in public, they also receive attention. TV cameras focus on them at games, they are asked to participate in community and charity events, and they may meet celebrities outside baseball. But their identities are always tied to their husband's. Marilyn Monroe aside, the baseball wife's identity is hidden under that of her husband. He is seen as the breadwinner, and if he is in the major leagues, he probably earns more in a year than she will in a lifetime. He is in the limelight; he is in demand. To the public, baseball wives are not known by their names, rather they are always Mrs. Curt Schilling, Mrs. Roger Clemens, and so on. We came across an ironic illustration of the subservient status of wives on the dust jacket of Sharon Hargrove's (1989) memoir *Safe at Home.* Despite having written

the book, in which she discusses the identities of baseball wives as being ancillary to their husbands', the biographical blurb about the author on the dust jacket reads: "Sharon Hargrove is the wife of Mike Hargrove, formerly a big league baseball player and presently a minor league manager . . . ." Nothing else is said about the author, other than her having four children.

Transience is partially to blame for the wives' dependent identity in that it makes it next to impossible for women to pursue their own careers. Even those who have the credentials or degrees have difficulty finding work as they are only in town for the six-month baseball season. Wives postpone starting careers of their own until their husbands leave baseball.

Another dimension of the wife's dependency is that her status among the other baseball wives is influenced by her husband's status. In the major leagues there is usually a loose pecking order among the wives in which their individual standing is swayed by their husband's salary, performance, and standing on the team. The wives of star players bask in the glow of their husbands' fame, while wives of lesser players, no matter how talented the women themselves may be, enjoy less prestige. Children may confound the pecking order a bit in that wives caring for young children are often drawn to other wives with young kids, overriding other considerations. Team hierarchy also influences relationships in that the spouses of players and the spouses of coaches don't mingle much, even when they are of similar age. They may sit together at the ballpark, but rarely do they fraternize on the outside, just as in the business world the wives of management do not socialize with the wives of workers. The anomaly in baseball is that the workers and their wives are usually much wealthier than the managers and their wives.

Uncertainties of the Baseball Life

Baseball wives contend with more uncertainty than do many American women. In addition to having to move without notice, an injury to her husband can suddenly end his career and their livelihood at any time. The vagaries of baseball performance in which bad times or slumps inevitably follow good times make the baseball life an emotional roller coaster—highs when husband and team are playing well and lows when he and they are not. One day you are the toast of the town, the next day you're invisible. And all of it is beyond the wife's control.

Wives may also worry about their husbands' faithfulness, especially while they are on the road. Wives are aware that there is temptation in every town: groupies, those often scantily clad, overly made-up young women who pursue ballplayers. While many players don't indulge, groupies are successful often enough to make some wives uneasy about what their husbands do while away from home. Bobbie Bouton and Nancy Marshall devoted an entire section to the groupie problem in their joint memoir, *Home Games* (1983). Wives often cope by excusing their husbands' behavior—"boys will be boys" or "what he does on the road is his business, what he does at home is my concern." Overall, the wives have little choice but to accept the insecurity, though some say they try to keep their husbands happy at home in the belief that a contented husband is less tempted to fool around.

Clearly, there are both significant rewards and costs to being the wife of a professional baseball player. Baseball wives are fortunate to have the prestige and financial security if their husband reaches the major leagues, but they must also deal with isolation, heavy responsibility in daily life and parenting, and the postponement of their own career plans. It is no wonder that some people refer to the baseball wife as "the fifth base," an anchor point outside of the field, but inextricably bound to the game itself.

Patricia San Antonio and George Gmelch

Further Reading

Bouton, B., & Marshall, N. (1983). *Home games.* New York: St. Martin's Press.

Bouton, J. (1970). *Ball four.* New York: World.

Crute, B. (1981). *Wives of professional athletes: An inquiry into the impact of professional sport on the home and family.* Unpublished doctoral dissertation, Boston College.

Garvey, C. (1989). *The secret life of Cyndy Garvey.* New York: Doubleday.

Gmelch, G. (2001). *Inside pitch: Life in professional baseball.* Washington, DC: Smithsonian Press.

Gmelch, G., & San Antonio, P. (1998). Groupies in American baseball. *Journal of Sport and Social Issues, 22*(1), 32–45.

Gmelch, G., & San Antonio, P. (2001). Baseball wives: Work and gender in professional baseball. *Journal of Contemporary Ethnography, 30*(3),335–356.

Hargrove, S., & Costa, R. H. (1989). *Safe at home: A baseball wife's story.* College Station: Texas A&M University Press.

House, T. (1989). *The jock's itch.* Chicago: Contemporary Books.

Torrez, D. G. (1983). *High inside: Memoirs of a baseball wife.* New York: G.P. Putnam's Sons.

Basketball

The sport of "basket ball" was first played in December 1891 in a Young Men's Christian Association (YMCA) gymnasium located in Springfield, Massachusetts; eighteen players were involved in the initial game. Basketball has since evolved into a sport played worldwide, with an estimated 300 million people participating, either at an amateur or professional level, in over 170 countries.

History

Unlike other sports—such as football or baseball—that developed from already-established games, basketball was deliberately created at a specific point in time to address a particular situation. In the autumn of 1891, Dr. Luther H. Gulick asked his employee, James Naismith, to provide quality physical education for eighteen adult males who were attending the School for Christian Workers in Springfield, Massachusetts (renamed International YMCA Training School and then Springfield College). This was to further the YMCA's goal of "muscular Christianity," whereby a sound mind was housed in a healthy body. Although the games of football and baseball would work well for much of the year, options were more limited for winter recreation in

*You can't win unless you learn how
to lose.* ■ KAREEM ABDUL-JABBAR

New England, and gymnastic activities did not interest these men.

Naismith tried indoor versions of rugby, soccer, and lacrosse, but the modifications weren't successful. In his frustration he described the students as "incorrigible." Naismith also realized, though, that these men would benefit from a simple and interesting game that would be easy to play in wintertime's artificial light. He had been given two weeks to solve this dilemma. During that time he analyzed popular sports and determined that most used a ball; furthermore, sports featuring a larger ball didn't need equipment such as a bat or racket. He decided that passing would be a key element of his game. Remembering his Canadian childhood, he incorporated a component from "duck on the rock," which involved tossing a stone in the air in an arc.

As he was developing his game strategy, he asked the school's janitor for two boxes, intending to nail one up at each end of the gymnasium. The janitor did not have boxes, but he did provide peach baskets to Naismith, who attached them to the bottom of a balcony located in the gymnasium. The ledge was located 10 feet from the ground.

Naismith then tacked thirteen simple rules on the wall. Players would use a soccer ball, and the goal of the offense was to pass the ball (the person possessing the ball could not run) to teammates until it was successfully thrown into the appropriate peach basket. Meanwhile, the goal of the defense was to prevent that from happening and to regain possession of the ball for its team. Whenever a basket was made, one point was awarded. If the ball went out of bounds, either the last person touching the ball—or the umpire, in case of disputed possession—would throw it back and the person who touched the ball first was now in possession. Fouls would be called for rough play, striking at the ball with a fist, running with the ball, or holding it against the body. Players with two fouls could be temporarily banned from the game, and if a team garnered three consecutive fouls, then their opponents were awarded one point. Games consisted of two fifteen-minute halves,

with a five-minute break in between, and the team with the highest score won.

Years later, Naismith recalled that several points—or goals—were scored that first game, but others remember a game with a score of only 1–0. In either case the game was an immediate success and basketball spread rapidly from the YMCA in Springfield to other YMCAs, and then to other venues around the country. Naismith did not receive—nor did he seek—any compensation for creating this sport. Naismith, who would later become a Presbyterian minister and who wanted basketball to improve the mental, physical, and spiritual well-being of those who played the sport, was pleased by the rapid expansion of the game that he'd invented. That was reward enough.

There have been intermittent claims that Naismith was not the person who invented the game of basketball. Proponents of this alternate theory suggest that a friend of Naismith, Dr. George Gabler, actually created the sport in the Holyoke (Massachusetts) YMCA in either 1885 or 1890. Gabler presumably then showed Naismith the game, and Naismith taught the game at the YMCA in Springfield. Gabler, however, never challenged claims that Naismith invented the sport, and it seems unlikely that this alternate scenario occurred. Nevertheless, details appeared in the *Holyoke Daily Transcript* in the 1940s.

Throughout the early days, rules fluctuated. Naismith, who was respected for his innovation, influenced the evolution of these rules for several years; for example, he stipulated that an equal number of men, anywhere from three to forty, could play on the court for each team, with nine per side being the optimum. In 1893 the YMCA rules offered more specific guidelines, stating that venues that were less than 1,800 square feet were suitable for teams of five men each; if the gym was up to 3,000 square feet, teams could have seven players. Larger facilities could handle teams of nine. In 1897 five players per team became standard.

Games were played in gymnasiums, social halls, and National Guard armories. By 1895 better gymnasiums had 18-inch iron-hooped basketball rims with closed nets hanging from them, while less elaborate setups included wire cylinders or other suitable—and available —materials. After a point was scored, referees either climbed a ladder to retrieve the ball or used a pole to knock it out. The Narragansett Machine Company created a net with a drawstring; when pulled, the net lifted up and the ball was forced out. By 1912 open-bottomed nets were used, increasing the pace of the game.

Early basketballs were imperfect spheres, larger in diameter (between 30 and 32 inches) than modern-day (29.5-inch) counterparts, with a rubber core and a sewn leather covering. Backboards were first used in 1895 to discourage spectators from deflecting balls tossed by the opposing team. At first the backboards were wire mesh; as they dented, though, home teams gained a significant advantage because they knew how to "play" the dents. Therefore, wooden backboards became standard.

Naismith had considered and then discarded the notion of a free throw as a penalty for rough play; there is, however, no question that rough play existed. In a record of an 1890s game, the reporter spoke of several simultaneous wrestling matches on the court, fingernail scratches, and the fact that, if someone did get possession of the ball, it might take several minutes to dislodge him from the mob that charged him.

In these early games, there was a sideline jump ball after every basket made, as well as one at the beginning of each half. The referee handled these jump balls and ruled when a ball was out of bounds. He also kept time and scores. The umpire called the "violations" or fouls. For a short time the court was divided into three sections, with forwards, centers, and guards required to remain in designated areas. Innovative players began to roll or bounce the ball to get it away from opponents. They also tapped the ball over their heads. Shots were generally underhanded throws or two-handed presses from the chest. Although the YMCA banned two-handed dribbles as early as 1898, professional leagues permitted them into the 1930s. The first professional game most likely occurred five years after the sport's inception. Although one promoter insisted that select players had received a small amount of money in 1893 in Herkimer, New York, most basketball experts believe that an 1896 game in Trenton, New Jersey, was the first professional competition.

The Trenton team had traveled throughout New York, New Jersey, Connecticut, and Pennsylvania, playing and beating teams, and then self-proclaiming themselves as national champions. On 7 November 1896, the team challenged the Brooklyn YMCA in their Masonic Temple. Home-team players were paid for this game. Seven hundred fans attended, paying a quarter for a seat or garnering standing room only space for fifteen cents. The Masonic Temple had newly built risers, with portable baskets on each end of their social hall. There was also a wire mesh cage that separated playing space from the spectators, a practice that was initially derided but soon incorporated in other venues. (Although this mesh helped prevent fans from becoming injured, players used the netting to trap their opponents who were in possession of the ball.) The Trenton-Brooklyn game was scoreless for the first seven minutes, and the final score was Trenton 16, Brooklyn 1.

The Amateur Athletic Union (AAU) held its first national basketball championship tournament in New York in 1887. The National Collegiate Athletics Association (NCAA) was formed in 1906, and by 1910 nearly two hundred colleges fielded teams. The sport was becoming increasingly popular in high schools, as well.

Professional Leagues

The first professional league, the National Basketball League (NBL), was founded in 1898; ironically for a league self-described as "national," all teams were located in either Philadelphia or New Jersey. Court sizes were standardized at 65 feet by 35 feet, with a wire cage at least 10 feet high required. Illumination, either electric or gas, was mandatory, and backboards were 4 feet by 4 feet. The basket's rim jutted out 12 inches. This particular league lasted for six seasons and was challenged, briefly, by the Interstate League (1899–1900) and the American League (1901–1903). From this period until

**This diagram from a 1930s
instructional manual shows how to
"Fool 'em with Your Offense."**

World War I, there was always at least one professional league in existence in the eastern states, and sometimes more than one. Semiprofessional teams flourished. The Eastern League, which existed from 1909–1923, with a break during World War I, was a relatively stable organization.

Teams switched locations frequently, game commitments were not always fulfilled, and players jumped teams. In 1909, for example, some players were playing on five different teams. Although an attempt to form a National Commission—a body that would oversee leagues—occurred in 1920, this particular commission never came to fruition.

Barnstorming, even across state lines, was common. This meant that instead of playing for an organized league, teams would travel in search of competition. One of the most successful examples was the Original Celtics, a team formed for teenagers living in a settlement house in Manhattan, New York. The 1920s were their glory years, and they earned such a national reputation that team members were even featured in newspapers, a rare feat for basketball players at that time.

BREAKING THE RACIAL BARRIERS

Basketball teams were almost entirely segregated by color, and the Renaissance Big Five—an all-black team formed in 1922 in Harlem, New York—served as the premiere African-American team in this era, barnstorming throughout the 1920s and reaching its full potential in the 1930s. They played against teams comprised of white players, as well, providing opportunities for quality, racially integrated play. In 1926 another all-black team formed, playing their first game on 7 January 1927 in Hinckley, Illinois. Because they were constantly on the road, traveling in among other vehicles a Model T Ford owned by their promoter, Abe Saperstein, the team eventually became known as the Harlem Globetrotters. By 1934 the Globetrotters had played 1,000 games. In 1939 they competed in their first professional tournament. That same year, players began "clowning around" during a game, making the crowd laugh; Saperstein approved of this side entertainment as long as the team had already established a safe lead.

Although this team continued to have a highly talented roster, the Harlem Globetrotters became as well known for their ability to entertain the crowd with skillfully orchestrated slapstick routines. In 1937, while the Globetrotters were dazzling audiences, the National Basketball League (NBL) was formed. That year, the center tip-off after each basket was officially eliminated, significantly increasing the pace of the games. Although the NBL was more organized than earlier leagues, as could be expected, World War II disrupted this league's play appreciably.

In 1946 owners of sports arenas—particularly Walter Brown of Boston—chartered a new organization, the Basketball Association of America (BAA), with teams located in Boston, Toronto, Providence, New York, Philadelphia, Washington, Pittsburgh, Cleveland, Detroit, Chicago and St. Louis. On 6 June 1946, the BAA chose attorney Maurice Podoloff, the president of

Basketball

Intramural Basketball at Smith College, 1893

Northampton, March 26 (Special).—On Wednesday evening an exciting game of "basket Ball" was played by the sophomore and freshmen teams. The running track of the gymnasium was crowded with spectators, and gay with the colors of the two classes. One side was occupied by sophomores and seniors, the other by juniors and freshmen, and a lively rivalry between the two parties was maintained throughout the contest. The game consists in the two sides trying to get the ball into their respective baskets, which are suspended at opposite sides of the gymnasium, and each tries to prevent the other from accomplishing that. Every time the ball is put in it counts one point. All the playing must be done by throwing, as no running while the ball is in the hands is permissible. In spite of the fact that the sophomore captain was disabled at the beginning of the game, the score was 5 to 4, in favor of the sophomores after a close contest of fifteen minute halves. The winning side gained a gold and white banner, which will be handed over to the next victorious team. . . .

Source: Smith College. (1893, March 27). *New York Herald Tribune*, p. 4.

the American Hockey League, as commissioner. On 3 August 1949, Podoloff negotiated a merger between the BAA and NBL and the result was the National Basketball Association (NBA).

Podoloff served as commissioner until 1963. By the time that he retired, the NBA had seventeen teams in three different divisions; collectively they played 557 games a season. Podoloff had also negotiated the sport's first television contract, and today's most valuable player award is named after him.

Meanwhile, basketball was slowly being desegregated. In 1950 the New York Knicks purchased Nathaniel "Sweetwater" Clifton from the Harlem Globetrotters, the Boston Celtics signed Chuck Cooper, and the Washington Capitols signed Earl Lloyd. These three men were the first black players in the NBA. Desegregation, however, did not signal the end of the Harlem Globetrotters. That same year, Abe Saperstein organized an international basketball tour, visiting Portugal, Switzerland, England, Belgium, France, Germany, Italy, Morocco, and Algeria. In 1954 Meadowlark Lemon became one of the Globetrotters star attractions and remained a member of the team for twenty-four years. In 1958 the team signed Wilt "The Stilt" Chamberlain for one season. Chamberlain then signed with the NBA, playing for fourteen years and setting many records (including scoring 100 points against the New York Knicks on 2 March 1962).

New Rules, New Era

Although the Globetrotters continued to provide excitement for fans, the game of basketball during the 1950s was stagnating. Play was rough, and one team could maintain possession of the ball as long as the players were able. If offensive players handled the ball well, there could be long periods with no scoring, and the opposing team's only viable action was to force a foul. The offensive team would then toss a free throw. This scenario would be played out over and over again in the course of a game. The year 1954, then, proved to be a benchmark for basketball: The twenty-four second rule was instituted, which meant that if a team did not shoot the basketball in that time span, ball possession went to the opponent. This greatly increased the pace of the games, and the average number of points scored skyrocketed from 79.5 per game to 93.1. That same season, the NBA limited the number of team fouls permitted each quarter: For the seventh—and all subsequent—personal fouls, the opposing team would be given an extra free throw, greatly reducing the strategic value of deliberate fouls. These changes favored players who were quick and athletic and who used innovative methods to obtain possession of the ball.

From 1967 until 1976, the NBA was challenged by the American Basketball Association (ABA). The ABA was known for its "outlaw" style of play, and players such as Julius "Dr. J" Erving added a new level of ex-

Basketball is like war in that offensive weapons are developed first,
and it always takes a while for the defense to catch up. ■ RED AUERBACH

citement to the sport. In June of 1976, the financially troubled league dissolved as the four strongest ABA teams—the New York Nets, Denver Nuggets, Indiana Pacers, and San Antonio Spurs—merged with the NBA.

Exceptional NBA play occurred during the 1980s, most notably with the Boston Celtics—a team with Larry Bird, Kevin McHale, and Robert Parrish—and the Los Angeles Lakers, with Kareem Abdul-Jabbar, Ervin "Magic" Johnson, and James Worthy on their roster. Arguably two of the best teams ever, they are joined in basketball annals by the Chicago Bulls of the 1990s, a team led by Michael Jordan and coached by Phil Jackson. All-time leading NBA scorers include Abdul-Jabbar, Karl Malone, Jordan, Chamberlain and Moses Malone. Coaches with the most wins include Lenny Wilkins, Pat Riley, Don Nelson, Bill Fitch, and Red Auerbach.

The Current Game

The current NBA consists of two conferences, each containing three divisions. The Eastern Conference has the Atlantic Division, the Central Division, and the Southeast Division. The Atlantic Division includes the Boston Celtics, New Jersey Nets, New York Knicks, Philadelphia 76ers, and Toronto Raptors. The Central Division consists of the Chicago Bulls, Cleveland Cavaliers, Detroit Pistons, Indiana Pacers, and Milwaukee Bucks. The Southeast Division has the Atlantic Hawks, Charlotte Bobcats, Miami Heat, Orlando Magic, and Washington Wizards.

The Western Conference is divided into the Southwest, Northwest, and Pacific Divisions. The Southwest Division includes the Dallas Mavericks, Houston Rockets, Memphis Grizzlies, New Orleans Hornets, and San Antonio Spurs. The Northwest Division consists of the Denver Nuggets, Minnesota Timberwolves, Portland Trail Blazers, Seattle SuperSonics, and Utah Jazz. The Pacific Division includes the Golden State Warriors, Los Angeles Clippers, Los Angeles Lakers, Phoenix Suns, and Sacramento Kings.

The United States has, without question, served as the leader in the sport of the basketball, but other counties, especially since the 1930s, have formed strong teams of their own. The World Basketball Championships, sponsored by the Federation Internationale de Basketball Amateur (FIBA) and initially played by amateur players, have existed since 1950. In its initial tournament, Argentina beat the United States for the title. The United States won in 1954, but came in second to Brazil in 1959 and 1963. Other winners include the Soviet Union (1967, 1974, 1982) and Yugoslavia (1970, 1978, 1990). In the 1994 tournament professional players were allowed to participate for the first time, and the United States, with its roster of NBA stars, won that year. Russia took the gold medal in 1998; Yugoslavia in 2002.

In women's basketball the United States won the World Basketball Championship in 1953 and 1957. The team boycotted the 1959 event that was held in Moscow, and the Soviet Union team won easily. The Soviet team won again in 1964, 1967, 1971, and 1975. In 1979 it was the Soviet team that boycotted the event, and the United States won its first medal since 1957. In 1983 it was a Soviet win; in 1986 and 1990, the United States took the gold. In 1994, for the first time since the inception of the women's tournament, a team other than the United States or the Soviet Union won the gold: Brazil took first place honors, while China garnered the silver. The United States reclaimed first place in 1998 and then repeated the feat in 2002.

Nature of the Sport

Although outdoor versions of the sport exist—such as three-on-three tournaments and forms of "street" ball—basketball is generally played indoors. NBA games are played on courts that are 94 feet by 50 feet (29 meters by 15 meters). Points are scored whenever a ball is successfully thrown through the appropriate basket, which is suspended 10 feet above the floor with a backboard behind the rim. The team that scores the most points, either by field goals or free throw shots, wins the game. A field goal is a basket that is scored during competitive action of the game; a free throw is tossed from the foul line, which is 15 feet from the backboard and is awarded because of a violation. When a free throw is taken, no

I know that I'm never as good or bad as any single performance. I've never believed my critics or my worshippers, and I've always been able to leave the game at the arena. ■ CHARLES BARKLEY

defensive action can occur until the shooter releases the ball from his hands. If a game is tied at the end of regulation play, "overtime" is played to break the tie.

Teams play with two forwards, two guards, and one center. The forecourt, for a particular team, is where their basket is located. The backcourt is where the team's opponent's basket is found. The center, generally the tallest person on the team, participates in a center court jump ball, whereby the referee tosses the ball in the air to start the game. Each center attempts to tap the ball to teammates, who then try to gain possession and score a basket. A field goal may be worth two or three points, depending on which side of the three-point line the ball is on when it left the hands of the shooter. In professional games the three-point line is located 23 feet, 9 inches from the basket. In college games it is located 19 feet, 9 inches from the basket; in international play, 20 feet, 6 inches.

The ball can be moved toward a basket by passing or dribbling. After a basket is scored, the opposing team passes the ball back into play from an out-of-bounds position; the offense continues to attempt to score, while the defense attempts to thwart that action. Professional games consist of four twelve-minute quarters; college games, two twenty-minute halves. The game clock stops when fouls are committed. Fouls are called for inappropriate blocking or stealing, which involves making contact with the player rather than with the ball. In this instance the opposing team gets the opportunity to shoot free throws, and each successful free throw is worth one point. If a player receives six personal fouls, that player is eliminated from play for the rest of the game. The offense loses possession for traveling, which is running with the ball without steady dribbling; double (two-handed, or stop-and-start) dribbling; and other illegal moves. Rule modifications exist for amateur play and for women's basketball.

The Women's Game

Early on, some believed that the competitive nature of basketball made it an inappropriate activity for females. Nevertheless, women began playing basketball shortly after their male counterparts. Senda Berenson pioneered the women's version of the sport at Smith's College in 1892, modifying the rules so as to reduce the need for endurance. In 1895 Clara Gregory Baer introduced the game to students at Sophie Newcomb College in New Orleans, also publishing "Basquette," the first set of basketball rules written specifically for women. Furthermore, bloomers first replaced long skirts on the basketball court at this educational institution in 1896.

The International Women's Sports Federation formed in 1924. In 1926 the AAU sponsored the first national women's basketball championship, using men's rules. Nevertheless, women's rules continued to fluctuate over the upcoming decades, mirroring what was occurring in men's basketball.

In 1972 the Association for Intercollegiate Athletics for Women held its first basketball championship; two years later, these games had television and radio coverage. In 1978 the eight-team Women's Professional Basketball League (WBL) debuted, lasting three seasons. In 1992 the Women's World Basketball Association (WWBA) was founded with six teams, but the league quickly folded. The Women's National Basketball Association (WBNA) began play in June 1997. The first players signed were Sheryl Swoopes, Rebecca Lobo, and Lisa Leslie. Initially, there were eight teams. Rules differ little from men's play, although the shot clock is thirty seconds, rather than twenty-four, and the game consists of two twenty-minute halves. The ball is 28.5 inches in circumference, an inch smaller than the ball currently used in the NBA.

Competition at the Top

Men and women across the United States compete in collegiate (NCAA) basketball, and championship tournaments have existed since 1939. Initially, the teams in the United States were divided into eight NCAA districts, and games were arranged accordingly. Through a series of playoffs, teams competed for titles. Even today, the basic structure remains the same, although the criteria for creating divisions have evolved. The semifinal

A basketball game at the Pan American Games.

sity of Tennessee's Lady Vols with six championships and the University of Connecticut's Huskies with five NCAA tournament wins.

Olympic Play

Basketball served as an Olympic demonstration sport in 1904, and was first played as a full medal sport in Berlin in 1936. The National Association of Basketball Coaches (NABC) sponsored Naismith's trip to Germany so that he could witness his invention become an Olympic sport. He also tossed the opening jump ball. The United States was the powerhouse team from 1936 through 1968, winning all Olympic gold. The streak ended when the United States lost a controversial game against the Soviet Union in 1972 wherein the clock was reset twice with only three seconds left. The United States team voted to reject the silver medal, believing that they had, in fact, won another gold. In 1980 the United States boycotted the Olympics, held in Moscow, because of the Soviet foray into Afghanistan.

In 1984 the Soviet Union returned the favor and boycotted the Olympics that were held in Los Angeles. The United States team subsequently won Olympic gold. In 1988 the Soviet Union won gold, Yugoslavia earned silver, and the United States won the bronze.

In 1992 professional players competed in Olympic basketball for the first time. The United States team, which consisted mostly of NBA stars, won the gold that year, as well as in 1996 and 2000. In 2004, however, the United States finished third, behind Argentina (gold) and Italy (silver.) Throughout Olympic basketball history, the Soviet Union has won a significant number of medals, including the gold in 1972 and 1988; four silver medals, in 1952, 1956, 1960 and 1964; and three bronze medals, in 1968, 1976, and 1980. Yugoslavia won the gold in 1980, along with the silver medal in 1968, 1976, 1988, and 1996. They also won

and final games—that narrow teams down to the "Final Four"—are a television extravaganza. This time on the college basketball calendar has come to be known as "March Madness." The greatest men's NCAA teams, according to ESPN, have included the 1968 UCLA Bruins, led by Lew Alcindor (later Kareem Abdul-Jabbar) and coached by John Wooden who led UCLA to ten titles. Other teams lauded were the 1996 Kentucky Wildcats; the 1976 Indiana Hoosiers, coached by the controversial Bob Knight; the 1972 UCLA Bruins, with future NBA star Bill Walton on the team; and the 1992 Duke Blue Devils.

According to *Total Basketball*, the top five collegiate basketball programs in the United States, historically speaking, are the Kentucky Wildcats, North Carolina Tar Heels, Kansas Jayhawks, UCLA Bruins, and the Indiana Hoosiers. The top five coaches are John Wooden, Dean Smith, Adolph Rupp, Clair Bee, and Hank Iba. Top players include Lew Alcindor (Kareem Abdul-Jabbar), Oscar Robertson, Jerry Lucas, Larry Bird, and Bill Walton.

For women the National Women's Invitational Tournament (NWIT) served as the championship sponsor from 1969 through 1996. There was no tournament in 1997. In 1998 the Women's National Invitation Tournament (WNIT) began and continues to be played today.

Women's NCAA play began in 1982. Between 1982 and 2004, the clear standout teams have been Univer-

the bronze in 1984. Lithuania is an up-and-coming contender, having won bronze medals in 1992, 1996, and 2000.

Women's basketball was added to Olympic competitions in Montreal in 1976. The Soviet Union won the gold that year. and in 1980 as well. The United States women's team has won the gold medal from 1984 until 2004, except in 1992, when the multinational Unified Team won the gold. That year, China won the silver medal; the United States, the bronze.

In the NBA a series of playoff games determines who will play in the championship series. Division winners from the Eastern and Western Conferences play one another until only two teams—one from each conference—remain. These teams then play a seven-game series to establish the overall NBA championship title for that season. During the 1940s and 1950s, the Minnesota Lakers, Philadelphia Warriors, and Boston Celtics won multiple titles. The Celtics dominated the 1960s, while no one particular team stood out during the 1970s. During the 1980s, Los Angeles Lakers and Boston Celtics rivalry was a highlight; the Detroit Pistons also won two titles. The Houston Rockets and Chicago Bulls were the powerhouse teams of the 1990s, and during the past few years, the Los Angeles Lakers have regained their prominence.

Although, in some ways, the game of basketball has evolved beyond the scope of what James Naismith could have imagined, in many others it retains the original essence. A memorial to its founder was proposed as early as 1936, shortly after the Berlin Olympics ended. The idea was revived in 1941, but then put on hiatus because of World War II. In 1948 a hall of fame was proposed to house exhibits and artifacts and to honor players of merit. Fund-raising began for such a structure, but then this project ran into snags that spanned two decades. In 1959, nine years before a hall of fame existed, the first roster of players was honored, and the Naismith Memorial Hall of Fame was finally completed and dedicated on the campus of Springfield College in Massachusetts on 17 February 1968. In 1985 this building was closed, and a new state-of-the-art facility was opened in the business district of Springfield.

Governing Bodies

Basketball's governing organizations include Eurobasket, for European basketball (www.eurobasket.com); the National Basketball Association (NBA) (www.nba.com); and the Women's National Basketball Association (WNBA) (www.wnba.com).

Further Reading

Axthelm, P. (1970). *The city game.* New York: Harper's Magazine Press.
Bradley, B. (1995). *Life on the run.* New York: Vintage. (Original work published 1976)
Feinstein, J. (1986). *A season on the brink.* New York: Simon & Schuster.
George, N. (1992). *Elevating the game: Black men and baseball.* New York: HarperCollins.
Hult, J. S., & Trekel, M. (1991). *A century of women's basketball.* Reston, VA: National Association for Girls and Women in Sports.
Krause, J. (2002). *Coaching basketball.* New York: McGraw-Hill.
Naismith, J. (1996). *Basketball: Its origin and development.* Lincoln: University of Nebraska Press. (Original work published 1946)
Neft, D. S. (1992). *The sports encyclopedia: Pro basketball* (5th ed.). New York: St. Martin's Press.
Peterson, R.W. (1990). *Cages to jumpshots: Pro basketball's early years.* New York: Oxford University Press.
Shouler, K., et al. (2003). *Total basketball: The ultimate basketball encyclopedia.* Wilmington, DE: Sports Media Publishing.
Wooden, J. (1991). *They call me coach.* New York: Contemporary Books.

Baton Twirling

Baton twirling is the sport of manipulating metal rods to create choreographed routines incorporating diverse patterns of movement. Routines typically include jumps, lunges, twists, and other body movements in combination with baton movements such as tosses, flips, spins, and slides. Baton twirlers perform alone, in pairs, and in larger groups. Although this recreational and competitive sport includes events for men, most participants are women.

Baton twirling developed as a sport in the United States, with its most rapid growth occurring during the

The rewards are going to come, but my happiness is just loving the sport and having fun performing. ■ JACKIE JOYNER KERSEE

1950s and 1960s. However, although baton twirling is considered "American," it was influenced by both Asian and European practices.

History

People have practiced the formalized waving of sticks, torches, and swords in various countries and cultures for centuries. In Europe twirling originated with military drum directors who were called "drum majors." They used elongated drumsticks known as "batons" (a French word meaning "stick") to make their directions more visible for guiding soldiers' marching maneuvers and for changing music to which the soldiers marched. From the 1600s records indicate a commanding "master drummer" leading marching soldiers for England's King Edward VI (reigned 1547–1553) and accounts of "drummer majors." The "twirling drum majors" who led the British Army's Janissary Band were influenced by Turkish marching troops and Roman jugglers.

In the Pacific Rim Samoan sword and knife twirlers spun their weapons in mock duels and military and religious ceremonies. In the Hawaiian Islands people twirled flaming torches as they danced to drumbeats. Chinese performing artists incorporated stick twirling into elaborate dances. European travelers who witnessed these practices may have adapted them to their own cultures.

Men dominated early baton twirling, being physically able to handle the heavy drum-major batons. The transformation of the baton from an instrument of band direction to an instrument of performance and competition may be related to the practice of flag signaling, by swinging the flag, in Switzerland to communicate from one mountaintop to the next. Flag swinging evolved into parade performances, incorporating such twirling maneuvers as high pitches, circles, and flashes to accompany marching. Eventually festivals sponsored events in which flag swingers performed competitively. German and Swiss immigrants brought the tradition to Pennsylvania, most likely influencing modern baton twirling.

In the United States, Major Reuben Webster Millsaps, founder of Millsaps College in Mississippi after the Civil War, probably coined the baton-twirling term *majorette*. Millsaps used the term for his women athletes. By the early 1930s women baton twirlers adopted the term as their presence added grace and color to civic, military, and school marching units. Because the majorette role was based on traditionally feminine attributes, men, with their battle-oriented image, did not commonly practice baton twirling. Baton twirling was one of the few sports viewed as acceptable for women. This acceptance contributed to baton twirling's popularity. Twirling remained dominated by women even as more sports opened to women. Participation increased through the 1950s as twirlers commonly performed with college bands, marched in parades, and participated in community recreation programs.

Baton twirling more recently has expanded internationally. The Starline Baton Company sponsored the International Twirling Teachers Institute (ITTI) throughout the United States and Europe during the 1950s and 1960s. This effort to promote baton twirling led in 1977 to creation of the World Baton Twirling Federation (WBTF). Baton twirling gained international recognition as a sport at the World Games in the Netherlands, where it was included as a "promotional sport." Twirling was an exhibition sport at the World Games held in Cleveland, Ohio, in 1999. Twirling also was included in the 1999 Junior Olympic Games, sponsored by the Amateur Athletic Union (AAU).

Play and Rules

Original baton twirling included such basic movements as horizontal and vertical patterns spiced with finger twirls, rolls, tosses, slides, and swings. As twirling evolved the movements became more complex, with twists, spins, lunges, and leaps combined with strenuous twirling. As twirling became more popular, in 1956 Don Sartell of Janesville, Wisconsin, founded the first baton twirling organization, the National Baton Twirling Association (NBTA). The United States Twirling Association (USTA) was established in 1958 as a democratic, not-for-profit enterprise. Founders of the USTA included Nick Michalares, Fred Miller, John Kirkendale,

Bobbie Mae, and George Walbridge. USTA—a member of the AAU and the National Council of Youth Sports (NCYS)—fosters development of twirling throughout the world and represents the United States in the WBTF, whose mission is to standardize and develop the sport internationally.

Since its founding the NBTA has sponsored the Miss Majorette of America twirling competition. Contestants are judged on twirling, strutting (marching with intricate baton maneuvers), modeling, and interviews. The competition has age divisions that allow participation through college levels. NBTA also stages local, state, and national competitions, allowing participation through age twenty-one. Events include men's and women's solo, two-baton, super-x strut, flag, hoop, show baton, duet, trio twirling, twirling team, dance team, and corps. America's Youth on Parade, which is NBTA's national competition, is staged annually in July at Notre Dame University in Indiana. Qualifying competitions for the NBTA-sponsored world championships, which began in the Netherlands in 1990, are staged every three years at America's Youth on Parade. The championships were held in France and Italy, respectively, in 1993 and 1996. Most participants came from North America or Europe.

At national and regional conventions the USTA presents clinics on baton twirling, dance, sports psychology, sports medicine, and related topics for athletes, coaches, judges, and parents. The USTA National Baton Twirling Championships and Festival of the Future (a national open competition for developing athletes) are held each year at different locations. Events are similar to those of the NBTA. A qualifying competition for the annual WBTF-sponsored world championships is held at the nationals.

The WBTF designed regulations for baton twirling routines. Beginning at the 1980 world championships in Seattle, Washington, these regulations revolutionized twirling. The regulations—including performance of compulsory movement sequences, mandatory exclusive use of one baton, and selection of optional music for free-style performance—created dramatic shifts in twirling competition. Athletes and coaches began to incorporate into their routines artistic, innovative movements in addition to dynamic, intricate twirling maneuvers. The regulations also influenced team and duet competitions (added in 1981 and 1993, respectively). The WBTF hosts the world championships each summer in alternating member countries. Member countries include the United States, Australia, Norway, Scotland, Spain, Belgium, Canada, England, France, Germany, Ireland, Italy, Japan, the Netherlands, and Switzerland. As more countries have participated, the competitive domination of the United States has lessened. From 1980 through 1988 the United States captured the World Cup award for overall performance. However, since then Japan has won the award each year except 1990 and 1991, when Canada won.

The Future

Several social changes have lessened women's interest in baton twirling. In the United States, Title IX legislation of 1972, which mandated equal opportunity for women in sports, opened new doors for women, drawing women away from twirling into other sports. At the same time twirling was excluded from increasingly popular indoor drill competitions, which decreased band-related opportunities for twirlers. Also, as more women worked full-time, they had less interest in earning the modest income to be earned by teaching twirling. Another factor that inhibited teachers and athletes alike was the increased liability insurance required for practice facilities. However, perhaps the biggest reason why fewer women were interested in twirling was inaccurate media portrayal of twirling as an exhibitionist circus act.

Nevertheless, baton twirling survives. Recreation programs, amateur competitions, and schools continue to provide opportunities. Opportunities for professional involvement exist in judging, coaching, and administrating. New developments include the potential for a baton twirler to win the Presidential Sports Award. Twirling is an officially recognized, government-subsidized sport in Canada and several other countries.

In Japan some schools include twirling in their curriculum. The inclusion of twirling in the Junior Olympics is a step toward establishing the legitimacy of the sport. As it evolves internationally, twirling may eventually be included in the Olympic Games. Educational and scholarship opportunities may also evolve as baton twirling becomes more prominent.

Valerie J. Ludwick Willman

Further Reading

Atwater, C. (1964). *Baton twirling; The fundamentals of an art and a skill.* North Clarendon, VT: Charles E. Tuttle.

Miller, F. J., Smith, G., & Ardman, P. (1978). *The complete book of baton twirling.* New York: Doubleday.

Robinson, N. L. (1980). *Baton twirling.* New York: Harvey House Publishers.

Smith, S. R. (1985). *Cheerleader-baton twirler: Try out & win.* New York: Tom Doherty Associates.

Wheelus, D. (1975). *Baton twirling: A complete illustrated guide.* New York: Sayre Publishing.

Beauty

The human body is the basis of one's physical existence, the interface of the individual with society, the means to present oneself and interact with one's environment. But the body is also a site of social control and a product of social construction; thus norms, rules, ideals, and rituals connected with the body, its ethos and its techniques, and the regulation and control of body functions depend on the social structures and conditions, cultural patterns, and ideological orientations of a given society, its order, and its gender order. In every society, ideas and theories about the forms, functions, and competencies of male and female bodies are closely intertwined with gendered bodily practices as well as with norms and ideals of male and female beauty. The body, the body ideals, and the body culture contribute to the development and maintenance of dichotomous and hierarchical gender relations. The gender order engraves its traces into the bodies of women and men: The human body becomes gendered and gender becomes embodied. The body has also served and continues to serve to legitimize male dominance and female subordination, which is, at least in Western societies, closely connected with myths of male strength and female beauty.

Bodies and Beauty: Developments and Trends

Despite the focus on male strength, men's body ideals and the enactment of male beauty changed according to social conditions and culture-specific tastes:

- In medieval tournaments, physical skills and prowess of the knights were enacted.
- In the seventeenth century, the "homme gallant" of court society displayed grace, elegance, and refinement.
- Since the nineteenth century, men's bodies disappeared behind uniform suits, and physical strength increasingly lost its importance, at least among the middle and upper classes. Men were evaluated according to their social status, their professions, and their income rather than according to their beauty.

Since the end of the nineteenth century, different forms of body culture, among them strength training and nudism, developed in the Western world, and beauty contests for men were organized that demonstrated more or less muscular bodies. However, the physical culture movement was a subculture that did not gain attention and acceptance among the mainstream society. In most cultures and periods, the male body ideals derived from the tasks and functions of men, whereas the ideal female body underwent radical and cyclical changes. In many cultures and periods, female attractiveness was connected with fertility; broad hips and a full bust were considered beautiful. However, there are numerous exceptions. In Western societies, women's bodies and beauty ideals changed continuously, which was enforced but also supported by the changing fashion.

A French woman on a bicycle plays a hoop and pole game, c. 1900.

and sexual attractiveness became the credo of modern society and the leading values of everyday culture. The new body ideal demanded tautness, demonstrative good health, and youth, showing no traces of work, illness, age, giving birth, or living life in general.

A basic assumption of this cult of body, beauty, and health is the conviction that bodies can be manipulated without any restriction. The body is no longer destiny; form and function of the body are products of individual work in which money, time, and strength have to be invested to create a work of art independent from time and material. Health and beauty are goods that have, therefore, reached an incredibly high value in the modern economy and generated entire industry sectors that serve the demands of an increasingly aging society.

Female Body and Beauty Trap

Today, the female body is restricted by social norms and social control to a much higher degree than is the male body. Whereas society tends to evaluate the male body primarily according to its functions, society regards the body of women primarily as a medium for social and sexual attractiveness. Girls and women are evaluated to a high degree according to their appearance. Because girls and women are defined and judged by their appearance, an aesthetic styling of the body is incredibly important. This is shown by the time and the large amount of money that is spent for clothes, diets, cosmetics, and plastic surgery. Beauty ideals are continuously reproduced and modified by the mass media and especially by advertisements. Striving to satisfy the dreams and desires of their target groups, advertisements create and enact fantasy women, the beauty queens with traditional signals of femininity such as long blond hair, a slender body, and a flat stomach. The fantasy woman shows fanny and breasts, does not have too many muscles, and is shaved, smooth, and tanned. Her outfit signals femininity, her image, posture, and clothes (or missing clothes) make her a sexual object. The fantasy woman who promotes nearly all products from cars to cosmetics is offered to the male gaze: "Men act and women appear. Men look at women. Women

- During the Gothic period, long limbs, a slender body, and a protruding belly were considered attractive.
- In the seventeenth century, the court fashion, especially in France, focused on a large bosom, which was supported by the corset and made visible through the large décolleté.
- The "Empire clothes" worn at the high society of the Napoleonic area demanded again slimness.
- In the nineteenth century, the corset enforced the hourglass shape of the female body.
- In the 1920s, the New Woman had long legs, small hips, and small breasts and loved sport.

After World War II, the range of beauty ideals reached from Marilyn Monroe to Twiggy and to Barbie. These female idols had one feature in common, however: They had no visible muscles.

Revival of the Body Since the 1970s

The "revival" of the body in the 1970s signaled a crisis of the modern industrial society. Increasing society-wide demands for identity, authenticity, and social distinction led to a revaluation and even a fetishization of the body. Fitness and health, thinness, youthfulness,

Beauty

"The Pursuit of Beauty" (1932)

I saw an aged, aged man
One morning near the Row,
Who sat, dejected and forlorn,
Till it was time to go.

It made me quite depressed and bad
To see a man so wholly sad—
I went and told him so.

I asked him why he sat and stared
At all the passers-by,
And why on ladies young and fair
He turned his watery eye.

He looked at me without a word,
And then—it really was absurd—
The man began to cry.

But when his rugged sobs were stayed—
It made my heart rejoice—
He said that of the young and fair
He sought to make a choice.

He was an artist, it appeared—
I might have guessed it by his beard,
Or by his gurgling voice.

His aim in life was to procure
A model fit to paint
As "Beauty on a Pedestal,"
Or "Figure of a Saint,"

But every woman seemed to be
As crooked as a willow tree—
His metaphors were quaint.

"And have you not observed," he asked
"That all the girls you meet
Have either 'Hockey elbows' or
Ungainly 'Cycling feet'?
Their backs are bent, their faces red,
From 'Cricket stoop,' or 'Football head.'"
He spoke to me with heat.

"But have you never found," I said,
"Some girl without a fault?
Are all the women in the world
Misshapen, lame or halt?"

He gazed at me with eyes aglow,
And, though the tears had ceased to flow.
His beard was fringed with salt.

"There was a day, I mind it well,
A lady passed me by
In whose physique my searching glance
no blemish could descry.
I followed her at headlong pace,
But when I saw her, face to face,
She had the 'Billiard eye'!"

Source: *Mr. Punch's Book of Sports* (1910). London: Educational Book Company.

watch themselves being looked at" (Berger 1977, 47). Thus, women turn themselves into objects, whereas men are imagined as spectators and owners of the pictures. The fantasy woman appeals also to women who assume the role of the model and can thus imagine that they are attractive and desirable.

In recent decades, female beauty has been inextricably connected with slimness; to be thin is the foremost ingredient of good looks, and the slimness norms have become nearly unreachable. Female models weigh more than 20 percent less than women with "normal" weights.

For example, the "ideal" size of clothes in Germany is 36 or 38, but most women wear clothes in size 40 or larger. Results of studies show that women who do not reach the slimness norms have decisive disadvantages, such as in the labor market. Not surprisingly, the initiatives to lose weight reaching from diets to exercises are endemic. Today, slim women can proudly present tough and muscular bodies, but they should not surpass the always newly defined borderlines between the sexes.

The slimness and beauty ideals are out of reach for "normal" women, especially because the ideals are

Beauty

Body Outlaws

In her book Body Outlaws, *Ophira Edut, a columnist for* Teen People, *gathered essays by women (and a few men) that take aim at traditional notions of beauty. The extract below is from Erin J. Aubry's essay "The Butt: Its Politics, Its Profanity, Its Power":*

I have a big butt. Not wide hips, not a preening, weightlifting-enhanced butt thrust up like a chin, not an occasionally saucy rear that throws coquettish glances at strangers when it's in a good mood and withdraws like a turtle when it's not. Every day, my butt wears me—tolerably well, I'd like to think—and has ever since I came full up on puberty about 20 years ago and had to wrestle it back into the Levi's 501s it had barely put up with anyway.

Source: Dizon, K. (2004, February 19). Breaking the laws of beauty. *Seattle Post-Intelligencer Reporter.* Retrieved March 1, 2005 from: http://seattlepi.nwsource.com/lifestyle/161108_bodyoutlaws19.html

constantly changing. The discrepancy between ideal and reality frequently leads to the feeling that body and appearance have deficits that demand continuous activities and a strict regime and management of the body. Therefore, the arrangement and the presentation of the body, from makeup to body styling and exercises, are important parts of the everyday life of women. Women seem to use stricter methods for the disciplining of the body and to apply higher standards to the female body than men do. For example, in a survey women tended to judge thinner women more beautiful than men did (Pfannenschwanz 1992).

As a consequence of this beauty trap, women develop different and more ambivalent relationships to their bodies than men do. Adult women report more often than men to be not satisfied with their health and their appearance, but even at an early age, when there are no differences in abilities and performances, girls tend to evaluate their sporting achievements and their competencies and their appearance more negatively than boys do theirs. Adolescent girls suffer especially from the dictatorship of beauty and slimness. High demands on appearance and pressures of peer groups have many negative consequences for the self-concept and self-esteem of girls.

This ambivalent and problematic relationship to the body can contribute to the development of eating disorders (anorexia or bulimia) and misuse of drugs, especially of psychophysiological drugs. Many girls have been or are currently on diets; many even plan beauty operations. For numerous girls, looks are more important than intellectual or sporting performances.

Beauty, Body, Physical Activity

The described "ecology of the female body" and the body and beauty management are connected with specific needs and expectations for physical education and sport. Surveys that asked for motives of sports engagement in various countries showed similarities, but also some decisive differences between women and men:

- In a German study, for example, four times as many women than men wanted to be active in sports to "do something for the figure."
- Men more often than women reported that they play sports because they wanted to improve their condition.

Girls and women tend to choose physical activities that fit their bodies and their beauty ideals, which do not surpass their imaginary performance standards, and which do not provoke conflicts with their identity. Being attractive requires a well-formed body and a feminine movement culture, which means, at least in Western countries, gracious, soft, harmonious, and rhythmical movements. Therefore, women focus on those sporting activities that allow an aesthetical presentation and a styling of the body according to ruling ideals that are connected with well-being. Despite the growing integration of women in formerly male sports from soccer to boxing, most women are active in different forms of gymnastics and fitness or in common activities such as hiking, cycling, or swimming.

A Veracruz, Mexico, carnival beauty queen.

Source: istockphoto/palmera.

Studies have shown conclusively that these physical activities can have various benefits, for instance, a positive body concept and increased well-being. But physical activities can also be connected with negative consequences because it is often impossible, or at least very difficult, to reach the promised ideal body. Many women become frustrated and quit, as evidenced by the high rate of fluctuation in fitness studios. In addition, the typical feminine sports convey one-sided body and movement experiences. They produce a specific way of dealing with the body, and some promote a strong focus on appearance that is closely connected with the female role and its restrictions and exclusions.

Current developments signal a change of the trend, however, at least in the United States, where women and female athletes are becoming increasingly assertive. In their book, *Built to Win,* third-wave feminists Leslie Heywood and Shari Dworkin described the fascination with strong and androgynous athletes such as Mia Hamm whose fame is based on high performances, often in formerly male sports, and who present proudly their muscular bodies. To be a woman and a powerful athlete is no longer a contradiction; on the contrary, strong women seem to be the new idols, at least among young women.

At the same time, we can observe another tendency, the increasing sexualization of female athletes. For a decade, the Kournikova-syndrome has been spreading. Anna Kournikova's fame and popularity is based largely on her appearance and her image. She is the fantasy woman of numerous men and a role model for girls and women. Even though Kournikova could not win a single tournament of the Women's Tennis Association, by the time she reached age eighteen in 1999, she had endorsement deals worth millions, and in 2000, she was dubbed the most photographed woman on the planet. Numerous other female athletes used their appearance and their erotic attractiveness as marketing tools. Like the stars and starlets in the entertainment field, they presented themselves nude or scarcely clothed in sexy poses in the mass media. Very successful athletes—such as Brandi Chastain, a member of the U.S. world cham-

pion soccer team, or Anni Friesinger, the German ice skater, gold medalist, and several times world champion —tried to get additional public attention with sex and beauty. Increasingly, the slogan holds true: Appearance is at least as important as performance.

The ways boys and men deal with their bodies, their images, and how they "do gender" also leads to problems and conflicts. The demand that young males excel at sports can be as oppressive and as destructive to self-esteem as the demand that young women conform to the ruling ideal of female attractiveness. The ritualized image of hard masculinity that is typical for some subcultures as well as the high standard of risk-taking are symptomatic of the difficulties men have with their masculinity.

Men are increasingly affected by body and beauty ideals. Broad shoulders, six packs (well-defined abdominal muscles), small hips, and bulging muscles are the new challenges for men, whereby the ideal difference between hips and shoulders has increased enormously in recent decades. The number of young men who try to reach these ideals by taking drugs is increasing.

Whereas numerous girls, even those dying from undernourishment, are convinced that they are not thin

Models are like baseball players. We make a lot of money quickly, but all of a sudden we're 30 years old, we don't have a college education, we're qualified for nothing, and we're used to a very nice lifestyle. The best thing is to marry a movie star. ■ CINDY CRAWFORD

enough, the distorted relation of young men to their bodies gives them the impression that they are not big enough. Men can also be infected by the slimness virus, especially if their sport demands light bodies. Thus, several ski jumpers developed anorexia with the connected problems for bodily and psychological health. Another current trend is the marketing of body, beauty, and erotic attractiveness of male athletes. Today, athletes like David Beckham or David Coulthard are like the members of boy music groups—the objects of girls' and women's desires. But athletes can also present ambiguous images; they play with gender or they bend gender.

Beauty ideals lead to a continuation of gender arrangements and the gender hierarchy. The cult of beauty seems to be the one of the last means to prevent the emancipation of women. The mass media play a central role in the production and reproduction of beauty ideals. The sports news also propagates the idea of the strong sex and the beautiful sex. On the one hand, women are marginalized in sport reports. On the other hand, as many studies in different countries have shown, female athletes are often defined by their looks and are sometimes even presented primarily as sexual objects.

In the 1990s—from football to boxing, from ski jumping to ice hockey—women participated in sports not fitting the traditional myths of femininity. As women entered the new century, many anticipated that ideals of beauty would change and that perhaps even the pressure to be beautiful would vanish.

Gertrud Pfister

See also Aesthetics; Art

Further Reading

Berger, J., et al. (1977). *Ways of seeing.* London: Penguin.
Bordo, S. R. (1993). *Unbearable weight: Feminism, Western culture, and the body.* Berkeley: University of California Press.
Brownmiller, S. (1984). *Femininity.* New York: Simon & Schuster.
Davis, K. (Ed.). (1997). *Embodied practices: Feminist perspectives on the body.* London: Sage.
Drolshagen, E. D. (1995). *Des Körpers neue Kleider: Die Herstellung weiblicher Schönheit.* Frankfurt, Germany: Fischer.
Falk, P. (1994). *The consuming body.* London: Routledge.
Freedman, R. (1986). *Beauty bound.* Lexington, KY: Lexington Books.
Guttmann, A. (1996). *The erotic in sports.* New York: Columbia University Press.
Hall, A. (1996). *Feminism and sporting bodies: Essays on theory and practice.* Champaign, IL: Human Kinetics.
Heywood, L., & Dworkin, S. (2003). *Built to win: The female athlete as cultural icon.* Minneapolis: University of Minnesota Press.
Jaggar, A. M., & Bordo, S. R. (Eds.) (1989). *Gender–body–knowledge: Feminist reconstructions of being and knowing,* New Brunswick, NJ: Rutgers University Press.
Luciano, L. (2001). *Looking good: Male body image in modern America.* New York: Hill and Wang.
Nuber, U. (Ed.) (1995). *Spieglein, Spieglein an der Wand: Der Schönheitskult und die Frauen.* Munich, Germany: Heyne.
Neimark, J. (1994). The beefcaking of America. *Psychology Today.* Retrieved January 12, 2005, from http://cms.psychologytoday.com/articles/pto-19941101-000021.html
Pfannenschwanz, C. (1992) Schön und gut. *Psychologie heute, 4,* 36–43
Pfister, G. (Ed.) (1996). *Frauen in Bewegung: Fit und gesund mit Sport.* Berlin, Germany: Orlanda.
Pope, H. G., Phillips, K., & Olivardia, R. (2001). *Der Adonis-Komplex: Schönheitswahn und Körperkult bei Männern.* Munich: DTV.
Ussher, J. M. (1989). *The psychology of the female body.* New York: Routledge.
Wolf, N. (1992). *The beauty myth.* New York: Morrow.

Belgium

Belgium, with a population of about 10 million, is situated at the cultural crossroads of Europe. The frontier between Germanic and Latin languages divides the country into Flanders, the Flemish-speaking North (58 percent of the population), and Wallonia, the French-speaking South. There is also a small German-speaking enclave. At the core lies Brussels, the bilingual capital, which is also the seat of the European Community and NATO headquarters. Having served both as buffer state and battlefield between France and Germany, Belgium also borders the Netherlands to the north and Luxembourg to the south. Moreover, Great Britain is only fifty sea-miles away from its northern shore.

Under the reign of the Spanish Habsburgs, the Low Countries (the region now comprised of Belgium, the Netherlands, and Luxembourg) had already split up in 1585 into the southern Catholic part of the Low

Countries (later to become Belgium) and the northern Protestant part (later to become the Netherlands). Belgium broke away as an independent state in 1830. The Low Countries had thus been reunited again only shortly from 1815 to 1830, after Napoleon's defeat at Waterloo (located south of Brussels).

A Great Ludodiversity of Folk Games

Belgium's sports history reflects the nation's social and cultural development. The country has a long tradition and a rich variety of folk games (the term *ludodiversity* is often used in connection with the preservation of these folk games). The Saint Georges crossbow guilds, the Saint Sebastian archery guilds, the Saint Barbara arquebuse guilds, and the Saint Michael swordsmen guilds were products of medieval civic pride especially in Bruges, Ghent, Antwerp, Leuven (Louvain) and Brussels. Many of these guilds still exist and thus belong to the oldest sporting relics in Europe. The crossbowmen and archers whose guilds date back to the fourteenth and fifteenth centuries still have their popinjay shooting contests. This type of archery where one shoots at "jays" fixed on top of a tall pole, was for the last time practiced as an Olympic sport at the 1920 Antwerp Olympics. The fencers of the Saint Michael guild of Ghent still practice in the same premises, where their guild was founded in 1613. *Kaatsen* (in Flemish) or *Balle Pelote* (in French) is a five-a-side handball game also with medieval roots. The same holds true for bowling games such as *closh* (province of Limburg), *curl bowls* (provinces of East and West Flanders), nine pins (Brabant, Antwerp, Limburg, and in the Germanophone East Canton). Cock fighting, though illegal in Belgium, is still practiced near the French border (where it is still legal) and in a few pockets in Brabant, Limburg, and Liège. Throwing games come in many variants: throwing small discs to a target (a line, a hole in a table as in "toad in a hole" etc.), throwing darts or *javelots* at a board, throwing clubs at a tripod etc. Traditionally women have played only a minor role in these games, which were linked with the local pubs, typical male preserves. In 1973 the Flemish Folk Games File re-

search project was launched at the Catholic University of Leuven. In order to preserve the rich but endangered ludodiversity of Flanders, the Flemish Folk Games Central was founded in 1980 and the Traditional Sports Federation (VLAS) in 1988. A recent survey comparing the situation of traditional games in Flanders over the 1982–2002 period has shown that during these twenty years the mean age of the practitioners has continued to increase, their already low social status has dropped even further and their location was now more rural than before. The only good news was that the participation of women in traditional games had slightly increased (from 11 percent to 22 percent).

Struggle Between German and Swedish Gymnastics

Gymnastics was first promoted in the new Kingdom of Belgium (1830) by the French "gymnasiarch" Hippolyte Triat in his private gymnasium in Brussels, and by Joseph Isenbaert in Antwerp and August De Krijger in Ghent. Isenbaert founded the first gymnastics society in 1839 in Antwerp. German *Turnen* (gymnastics) was introduced in 1857 when Johann Jacob Happel was imported from Germany to teach in Antwerp. Another German teacher, Carl Euler, did the same in Brussels from 1870 onwards. Although the Belgian Turner Federation (based on the German system) was founded in 1865, the country would eventually become a stronghold of the Swedish gymnastics system of Per Henrik Ling. The strong political polarization of the country lies at the origin of the creation of a separate Catholic Turner Federation in 1865 and a Socialist Turner Federation in 1904. Colonel Charles Lefébure first officially introduced Swedish gymnastics at the Military Normal School for Fencing and Gymnastics in Brussels in 1904. He also managed (with the help of Cyrille Van Overbergh) to create the very first university Higher Institute of Physical Education in Europe—and in the world—at the State University of Ghent in 1908. The Institute was linked to the Faculty of Medicine and fully based on the Swedish method. It offered candidate, licentiate and doctoral degrees. Female participation in gymnastics was hampered during the Belle Epoque period by bourgeois conservatism on the one hand and Catholic prudery on the other. The State University of Ghent appointed Irène Van der Bracht as the first female university professor in Belgium's history in 1925. The rationale was that female physical education students should be taught by a female instructor. Female gymnastics was organized in similar fashion to the Girl Guides, operating in parallel with but independently from the Boy Scouts. This gender "apartheid" was taken very seriously. In 1932, for instance, the Flemish nationalist Turner leader Maurits Verdonck (1879–1968) was banned from the Catholic Gymnastics Federation, because he trained and coached both male and female members in his Ganda Turnverein in Ghent. This "heresy" led to the creation of a separate Catholic Ladies Gymnastics Federation. German *Turnen* flourished in the many turnverein both in Flanders and Wallonia. Swedish gymnastics, on the contrary, would invade and monopolize physical education in Belgian schools until 1968. From then onwards the Swedish pedagogical spell was broken and replaced by a pluralist physical education concept of sports, games and other physical activities. Belgium was, however, not the very last country in Europe to give up Swedish gymnastics for its school physical education. That record went to Portugal (in 1973), which had been lured into Swedish gymnastics via Leal d'Olivera, a Portuguese army officer who had obtained his PhD in physical education in Ghent in 1929.

Infiltration from Albion: Modern Sports

Thoroughbred horse racing and rowing are generally considered as the precursors of the sports "anglomania," which affected Belgium as one of the first countries on the European continent. The very first thoroughbred horse races on the continent were held in the thermal city of Spa in the Belgian Ardennes in 1773. They took place before the eyes of the aristocratic *fine fleur,* who had gathered there for their yearly thermal cure and other more amorous *liaisons dangereuses.* The Society

for Fostering the Amelioration of Horse Races and the Development of Horse Races in Belgium was founded in 1833, three years after the creation of an independent Belgium. It is important not to confuse *horse races* with *horse racing* in the title of this very exquisite association. The second wave of English sports import consisted of the creation of Nautic Clubs both in Ostend and Ghent in 1946. Antwerp followed with the Société des Régates De Schelde in 1851, founded by Englishman Georges Collins. The very few, but wealthy aficionados of rowing and sailing had their first *moment de gloire* when amateur oarsmen from Ghent won the famous Henley Regatta in 1906. What the local organizers probably did not know was that the Ghent crew was composed of oarsman from two rival clubs: Royal Club Nautique de Gand on the one "oar" and Royal Sport Nautique de Gand on the other. Maybe the fact that they were both Royal and both from Ghent fooled the English organizers. This "mixed" crew repeated its rowing exploit in 1907 and 1909.

Cycling has always fascinated the Belgians. In the year 1869 cycling races were organized for the first time in Brussels, Charleroi, Ghent, and the Veurne-Adinkerke race was won by Justin Vander Meeren. The very first *velodrome* was opened in 1886 in Antwerp and many others would follow. The great breakthrough of Belgian road cycling came with the victory of Cyrille Van Hauwaert in Bordeaux–Paris in 1907 and Odiel Defraeye's victory in the Tour de France in 1912.

It is generally accepted that football took off in Belgium in 1863 when an Irish pupil from Killarney first kicked his ball on the playground of the Catholic boarding school of Melle near Ghent. "The great old" Antwerp Football club was founded in 1880 by British residents in the harbour city. Originally they played cricket and rugby football. The second club, Football Club Liégeois, made its appearance only twelve years later in 1892. In 1895 the Belgian Union of Societies of Athletic Sports (UBSSA) was created, which reunited sportsmen of diverging disciplines. This temporary "Union" would split in 1912 into separate football and track and field associations.

Belgium

The Play Forms of Our Forefathers and the Sport of Our Children

This sad call to readers appeared in the very first issue of the first volume of the Flemish weekly Ons Land *(Our Country) of 1919. This newspaper report illustrates the problematic relationship between traditional games and modern sport at the crucial turning point in the history of physical culture in Europe, namely the end of World War I. These traditional games were described as at risk of being ousted by the introduction of modern sports. The next issues of the magazine included six reader responses describing a number of traditional games, especially local bowl games. There was no trace, however, of the prize that was promised.*

The Olympic Games, which stem from a modern invention, occupy the place of honor in our popular recreations. They are controlled by an official international regulation.

Although we fully approve of this, we want to point at the disdain which is shown—unjustifiedly—towards the games of strength and agility, which have contributed so much to the physical development of our forefathers and which were for them such a pleasant delight.

Here we have to safeguard a respectable tradition, as these games are deeply rooted in the inner life of our peasantry and cannot be extracted from it without grieve.

Our soccer players should not forget the game of handball or the longbow or any other games, too many to enumerate, because they all require the exercise of the eye and the hand and because they all develop dexterity, precision, nervous strengthening and body flexibility.

We call upon all our readers to inform us as completely as possible on the local forms of play and amusements which are still in use in their region, and especially those which are typical for a specific province or which are linked with the natural characteristics of the area.

We will offer a price to the fifty correspondents who will provide the best information by sending in photographic pictures and short descriptions. These results will then be published in "Ons Land" in order to contribute in this way to the revival of traditional folk games.

The Belgian Olympic Committee was only founded in 1906. Belgian athletes had, however, already participated in the 1900 Paris Games where Léon de Lunden had for instance won the gold medal in live pigeon shooting, the famous archer Hubert van Innis won two gold and one silver medal, and the four oarsmen of Royal Club Nautique de Gand (Ghent) also won their race on the Seine river. The fact that the VII Olympic Games were given to the city of Antwerp in 1920 can be seen as a recognition of and recompensation for "Brave little Belgium," which had withstood the German invasion of 1914–1918 with great magnanimity. The Antwerp Olympics were certainly not the best organized nor most spectacular Games, but they symbolized the revival of the Olympic Movement and they put the Games back on track. The Olympic flag with five rings was for the first time shown at Olympic Games and Olympic water polo player and fencer Victor Boin took the Olympic oath for the first time. He would later become president of the Belgian Olympic Committee from 1955 to 1965.

One of the first important victories of the Flemish movement after the Great War was the *flemishization* of the State University of Ghent. This led to the creation of a Francophone Higher Institute of Physical Education at the State University of Liège in 1931. The Catholic University of Leuven, founded in 1425, opened its own Physical Education Institute in 1942 with separate Flemish and Francophone sections. The Free University of Brussels followed this example in 1946.

Pierre de Coubertin's successor as IOC President, the Belgian count Henri de Baillet-Latour died in 1942

Belgium Olympics Results
2004 Summer Olympics: 1 Gold, 2 Bronze

during the German occupation of the country. The German occupants together with their collaborators decided to create a General Commissariat for Physical Education and Sports, which would take over control of sport and physical education from the existing National Committee of Physical Education and Belgian Olympic Committee. This new General Commissariat established separate sport structures for Flanders and Wallonia, but this bifurcation of Belgian sport was strongly contested by the unitary sport federations and culminated in a protest letter published in the weekly magazine of the Royal Belgian Football Association. The German military command was afraid of such rebellious acts that might disturb their imposed "pax Germanica" and worked out a modus vivendi between the collaborating General Commissariat on the one hand and the independent National Committee. The end of the war instigated a patriotic and unitarist revival in Belgium, which also led to a reinforcement of the unitary sport structures and an abdication of the regionalist tendencies.

The incipient democratization of sport that had slowly started in the interwar period continued and resulted in higher sport participation among the population. Cycling, especially road races, and football which had not been stopped during the war, drew large crowds of enthusiasts who wanted to support their local heroes. Very popular were the track cyclist Jef "Poeske" Scherens and the road cyclists Rik Van Steenbergen and Rik Van Looy. And then came Eddy Merckx, who dominated international cycling in the 1960s and 1970s and became Belgium's best-known sportsman worldwide. The country also produced a lineage of medal-winning track athletes in the Olympic Games during the decades after World War II: Gaston Reiff (gold; 5000m, 1948), Roger Moens (silver, 800m, 1960), Gaston Roelants (gold, 3000m steeple 1964), Emiel Puttemans (silver, 10,000m, 1972), Karel Lismont (silver, marathon,1972), and Ivo Van Damme (silver, 800m and 1500m, 1976).

The unitary organization of Belgian sport split in 1969 as a logical consequence of the introduction of the cultural autonomy of the Flemish and the Francophone communities in Belgium. Two separate sport administrations were created, the Francophone sport department (ADEPS) and the Flemish (BLOSO). Now "sport for all" became a priority and, especially in Flanders under the dynamic leadership of Armand Lams, all kind of initiatives were taken to lower the threshold for sport participation. This has since then resulted in a continuously increasing degree of sport participation and, synchronically, the construction of a new sport infrastructure. Physical education programmes also radically changed in 1968–1969 when the monopoly of the Swedish gymnastics system was finally replaced by the introduction of sports and games. This new approach aims to initiate and socialize pupils in sport participation, which they would hopefully continue after leaving school. Some critics claim though that this *sportization* of physical education has gone too far and that more emphasis should be laid again on general physical fitness and motor skills.

Two sports in which Belgians have dominated the world and European championships have a lot to do with mud: motor cross and cycling cross. The motor crosser René Baeten excelled in the 1950s, Joël Robert and Roger De Coster in the 1960s, Harry Everts, André Malherbe and Gaston Rahier in the 1970s, Eric Geboers in the 1980s, and Stefan Everts (Harry Everts' son) and Joël Smets in the 1990s. Eric De Vlaeminck won seven world championships in cycling cross between 1966 and 1973, Roland Liboton won four in the 1980s and from the 1990s onwards the international success was divided among Danny De Bie, Bart Wellens and Sven Nijs. Belgian judo has gained world-class status through Olympic medallists such as Robert Van de Walle and Harry Vanbarneveld and their female colleagues Ingrid Berghmans, Ulla Werbrouck, Gella Vandecaveye, Heidi Rakels, Marie-Isabelle Lomba and Ilse Heylen.

In 2005 female sprinter Kim Gevaert excelled in the 60m, 100m and 200m at the European indoor athletic championships in Madrid, but probably the most astonishing international sport breakthrough was realized by two female tennis players: the Walloon Justine Henin (who won gold at the Athens 2004 Olympic Games) and the Flemish Kim Clijsters, who succeeded each other as No. 1 in the World Tennis Association ranking in 2003.

The highlights of Belgian football have been the 1920 Olympic gold, reaching the World Cup semifinals in Mexico 1986, and, on the club level, Sporting Club Anderlecht having won the European Cup in 1976 and 1978 and the UEFA Cup in 1883.

Two International Olympic Committee Presidents

After Count Henri de Baillet-Latour had been IOC president from 1925 to 1942, another Belgian was elected in this office in 2001: the Flemish orthopedic surgeon Jacques Rogge. This alumnus of the University of Ghent competed in the yachting competitions at the Games of Mexico 1968, Munich 1972 and Montreal 1976. He was president of the Belgian Olympic and Interfederal Committee from 1989 to 1992 and became IOC member in 1991. The profile and career of these two men can be seen as a "pocket" history of Belgium. The first was a diplomat and member of the Francophone aristocracy of Brussels; his father had been governor of the province of Antwerp. Baillet-Latour was a keen horseman (polo, hunting and steeple chasing) and President of the Jockey Club of Belgium. The second is a polyglot medical doctor from the province of East Flanders, who sailed and played rugby and still practiced surgery until the day he was elected IOC President. Trained to make vital decisions about the quality and quantity of the life of his patients, he now faces the political, economic, and medical problems of the world's top sport trust. Let us hope that he can also cure them.

Roland Renson

Further Reading

Delheye, P., & Renson, R. (2004). Belgique. In J. Riordan, A. Krüger, & T. Terret (Eds.), *Histoire du sport en Europe* (pp. 113–145). Paris: L'Harmattan.

D'hoker, M., Renson, R., & Tolleneer, J. (Eds.). (1994). *Voor lichaam en geest.* Leuven, Belgium: Universitaire Pers Leuven.

Mathy, T., & Mathy, C. (1982). *Dictionnaire des sports et des sportifs belges.* Brussels, Belgium: Legrain.

Renson, R. (1996). *The Games reborn: The seventh Olympiad Antwerp 1920.* Antwerp, Belgium: Pandora.

Renson, R. (1998). Sport and the Flemish movement: Resistance and accommodation 1868–1914. In K. Deprez & L. Vos (Eds.), *Nationalism in Belgium: Shifting identities, 1780–1995* (pp. 119–126). London: Macmillan.

Renson, R., De Cramer, E., & De Vroede, E. (1997). Local heroes. *International Review Sociology of Sport, 32*(1), 59–68.

Vandeweghe, H., Hereng, J., & De Veene, C. (2000). *Keizers koninginnen en kampioenen.* Tielt, Belgium: Lannoo.

Biathlon and Triathlon

Biathlon and triathlon are multisport endurance races. Biathlon combines cross-country skiing and target shooting; triathlon combines swimming, bicycling, and running.

Biathlon

In biathlon a competitor skis a loop with a .22-caliber rifle harnessed on his or her back, pausing to shoot at ranges along the loop. At each shooting range the competitor must switch from the exertion of skiing to the concentration of target shooting. Thus, biathlon requires athletes to master the physical and mental demands of two conflicting disciplines. Athletes need physical strength and stamina to ski a course that can be as long as 20 kilometers for the individual event, yet athletes need great self-control to quiet the body and concentrate the mind to fire with accuracy at the shooting range.

Origins

The origins of biathlon may be revealed in rock carvings in Norway that date from 2000 BCE and show two hunters on skis stalking animals. Biathlon, like many other activities we now regard as sport, may have evolved from activities our ancestors performed to survive—in this case, travel across deep snow and hunt for food.

Modern biathlon has military origins in Scandinavia, where the climate and terrain required troops to be trained and equipped for combat in winter conditions. The earliest recorded biathlon event occurred in 1767 between "ski-runner companies" who guarded the border between Sweden and Norway. The first international biathlon competition was held as a demonstration event at the 1924 Winter Olympics in Chamonix, France, and was continued at the Winter Olympics of 1928, 1936, and 1948. Biathlon was dropped from the Olympic program after 1948 in response to antimilitary sentiment that followed World War II. Biathlon again became an Olympic event for men in 1960. Women's biathlon events were added at the 1992 winter Olympics in Albertville, France.

The Union Internationale de Pentathlon Moderne et Biathlon (UIPMB) was founded in 1948 to promote the development of modern pentathlon and biathlon as Olympic events. (In modern pentathlon contestants compete in a 300-meter freestyle swim, a 4,000-meter cross-country run, a 5,000-meter equestrian steeplechase, fencing, and target shooting at 25 meters.) The UIPMB instituted annual World Championships for biathlon in 1957, and biathlon was added as an individual event for male athletes at the Winter Olympics in Squaw Valley, California, in 1960. In 1966 the biathlon relay was introduced at the World Biathlon Championships and added to the Olympic program in 1968. The first Women's World Championships were held in Chamonix, France, in 1984.

EVENTS

Biathlon has three race events—individual, sprint, and relay. Each event has different distances, rules, and penalties. Competitors ski a set number of loops of the course depending on the event, making four stops to shoot. The five metal targets at each stop are 50 meters away. The targets can be reset mechanically after each shooting bout and can be set for prone or standing positions. A hit is registered immediately by a white plate that flips up to cover the black target. For prone shooting the hit must strike a circle 45 millimeters in di-

ameter in the center of the target. A standing shot can hit anywhere in the 115-millimeter diameter circle. Competitors who miss shots must ski penalty loops, which add to the overall time and lower a competitor's score.

Range time is the time required for a competitor to enter the firing range, unsling the rifle, shoot five rounds, resling the rifle, and exit the range. Cross-country skiing requires intense physical effort; while competitors are on the course, their heart rates increase to 170–190 beats per minute. Thus, when they approach each shooting range, competitors must reduce skiing speed to slow their breathing in preparation for shooting. World-class range times average 30–40 seconds for the prone position and 25–30 seconds for the standing position.

The individual competition demands more endurance during skiing and greater body control at the range than do the shorter distances of the other events. In the individual competition men ski a total of 20 kilometers, and women ski 15 kilometers. The athletes start at one-minute intervals and ski five loops ranging from 2.5 kilometers to 5 kilometers, shooting five shots at each of four stages for a total of twenty shots. A one-minute penalty is levied for every missed shot and is added to the competitor's ski time at the end of the race for a total of twenty possible penalty minutes if all shots were missed. The winner is the competitor who had the lowest combined ski time and penalty minutes.

In sprint competition men ski a total of 10 kilometers, and women ski 7.5 kilometers, starting at one-minute intervals. Athletes ski one loop, shoot five rounds in the prone position, ski a 150-meter penalty loop for each missed shot, and then ski another loop. They then shoot five rounds in the standing position, ski a 150-meter penalty for each shot missed, and ski a final loop to the finish. Thus, they ski a total of three loops ranging from 1.75 kilometers to 3.75 kilometers and shoot two shooting stages for a total of ten shots. All penalties are skied during the race; thus, penalty time (about thirty seconds for each penalty) is already included in the time when athletes cross the finish line.

Man competing in the cycling leg of a Seattle-area triathlon.

Source: istockphoto/robh.

In the relay competition all teams start simultaneously in a mass start and ski the same course. Both men's and women's courses are 4×7.5 kilometers, that is, each member of a four-person team skis a 7.5-kilometer leg of the race. Each leg is skied in the same way as the sprint race except that racers can use "extra rounds" at the range. Each competitor has eight bullets with which to hit five targets at both the prone stage and standing stage. When racers ski into the range they place three extra rounds from their magazines into a small cup before they begin shooting. They then attempt to hit all five targets with five shots. If they miss any, they then load rounds from the cup and shoot until they have hit all five targets or used up all three extra rounds, whichever comes first. If, after shooting all eight rounds, the competitors still have not hit all five targets, they must ski a penalty loop for each missed target.

On completion of his or her leg of the relay, in a tag zone each skier touches the next teammate, who then starts out on the course. The winning team is the one whose last competitor crosses the finish line first.

At the 2002 Winter Olympics at Salt Lake City, Utah, Ole Einar Bjorndalen of Norway won the 10-kilometer men's sprint, the 12.5-kilometer men's pursuit event, and the 20-kilometer men's event; Norway won the 4×7.5-kilometer men's event; Kati Wilhelm of Germany won the 7.5-kilometer women's sprint; Olga Pyleva of Russia won the 10-kilometer women's pursuit; Andrea Henkel of Germany won the 15-kilometer women's event; and Germany won the 4×7.5-kilometer team event.

Triathlon

The best-known triathlon is the Hawaii Ironman Triathlon (HIT), which consists of a 3.9-kilometer swim, a 180-kilometer bicycle race, and a 42-kilometer marathon run. As is true in the majority of triathlons, a competitor completes the events sequentially with only brief stops or slowdowns (known as "transitions") to change equipment and clothes. These transitions count against the competitor's total race time. Thus, because minutes or only seconds can separate competitors, many triathletes train for the transitions as well as for the three sports of the triathlon.

Most competitions among triathletes occur at shorter distances than those in other ironman contests. Still, all triathlons are endurance events taking nearly an hour to complete for the best athletes in even the shortest races. Several distances exist. For example, as the name implies, a half-ironman (or long course) triathlon usually

involves a swim of about 2 kilometers, a bicycle race of 88 to 95 kilometers, and a run of 15 to 21 kilometers. About three-quarters of triathlons in recent years have occurred at the popular international distance. These triathlons involve a 1.5-kilometer swim, a 40-kilometer bike race, and a 10-kilometer run. Finally, the misnamed sprint-distance triathlon ranges about 400 meters for the swim, 15–32 kilometers for the bicycle race, and 3.2 kilometers for the run.

Considering that the International Olympic Committee (IOC) has been inclined to remove sports from the games and only reluctantly to add new sports, the quick rise of triathlon in the Olympics is remarkable. The sport moved from a first formal event in the mid-1970s to a full-fledged Olympic event in just more than twenty-five years.

At the 2004 Olympics in Athens, Kate Allen of Austria won the women's triathlon; Hamish Carter of New Zealand won the men's triathlon. New Zealand won first overall, followed by Austria, Australia, Switzerland, and the United States.

Origins

Triathlon emerged in California during the early 1970s. However, as International Triathlon Union President Les McDonald noted, triathlon is no longer the sport practiced by carefree California kids of the 1970s and 1980s. Early multisport athletes were, indeed, carefree young men who sought to combine some common elements of their lifestyle into a single race event. Those men might be amused at the current high-tech sport that focuses on every aspect of triathlon with a single concern—to increase the speed at which triathletes can complete an event. They also might be agog at their sport's compiling a 134-page rulebook.

Practice

The initial multisport event was only a variant of a common beach occurrence. One boy in the water says to another, "I'll race you to the refreshment stand." The two boys quickly are off, first swimming to the shore

and then running to the food vendor, perhaps eventually racing home on their bikes. Slight formalization of that common occurrence produced an early multisport —and quintessentially amateur—event. Now triathlon is moving along the path toward incorporation into the dominant sport culture. Triathlon appeared in the 2000 Olympics, only eleven years after the formation of an international governing body. A professional tour allows both men and women to compete in triathlons at various distances throughout the world. Corporations sponsor popular triathlons and triathletes. One can see testimony to the intimate involvement of triathlon and commerce at Nike-town in Chicago: A store in the chain of the international sporting goods giant closes in the evening at 8:07:45—Mark Allen's record time for the HIT. Allen was triathlon world champion six times.

Perspectives

Residual components of earlier sports culture are visible in triathlon in several aspects. One residual component is visible among the many triathletes who never join their national governing boards but instead pay a one-day licensing fee to participate in events sanctioned by the bureaucracy. Another residual derives from triathlon as a somewhat expensive and time-consuming pursuit. As such, it is mostly an activity of the middle class (and probably the upper middle class at that).

Triathlon, generalist by nature, is also nurturant to athletes such as the elderly and the physically challenged. Thus, for example, older competitors (in their seventies) have been among the featured triathletes. In 1989 Dick Hoyt completed the grueling HIT with his son Rick (who had cerebral palsy) in tow (literally, during the swim). Rick rode in a specially constructed "basket" on the bike race and a racing wheelchair on the run.

Despite the relative youth of triathlon, the emergence of mountain bike and ultraendurance (e.g., double-ironman) triathlons may reflect a nostalgic search for authenticity in the sport. Many triathletes believe that the raison d'etre of triathlon is the personal struggle to overcome the myriad sources of self-doubt. It emphasizes fortitude and dedication that place the greatest premium on individual effort. The increasing technological orientation, bureaucratization, and commercialization of triathlon detract from that emphasis.

GOVERNING BODY

In terms of bureaucracy, the International Triathlon Union (ITU, www.triathlon.org) has a membership that includes nearly 120 national governing boards for triathlon, representing 2 million or more affiliated triathletes worldwide. In some cases national governing boards further differentiate into regional bureaucracies.

Michaela Czech and Bonnie Dyer-Bennet

Further Reading

Almekinders, L., Almekinders, S., & Roberts, T. (1991). *Triathlon training.* Winston-Salem, NC: Hunter Textbooks.

Ballesteros, J. (1987). *El libro del triatlon.* Madrid, Spain: Arthax.

Blanchard, K., & Cheska, A. (1985). *The anthropology of sport: An introduction.* South Hadley, MA: Bergin & Garvey.

Cedaro, R. (Ed.). (1993). *Triathlon: Achieving your personal best.* New York: Facts on File.

Cook, J. S. (1992). *The triathletes: A season in the life of four women in the toughest sport of all.* New York: St. Martin's Press.

Edwards, S. (1983). *Triathlon, a triple fitness sport: The first complete guide to challenge you to a new total fitness.* Chicago: Contemporary Books.

Habernicht, J. (1991). *Triathlon Sportgeschichte.* Bochum, Germany: N. Brockmeyer.

Heimann, F. (1997). *Kurze geschichtliche Darstellung des Biathlonsports.* Wals-Himmelreich, Austria: International Biathlon Union.

Hilliard, D. C. (1988). Finishers, competitors, and pros: A description and speculative interpretation of the triathlon scene. *Play and Culture, 1,* 300–313.

Horning, D., & Couzens, G. (1985). *Triathlon, lifestyle of fitness: Swim! Bike! Run!* New York: Pocket Books.

Ingham, A. G., & Loy, J. W. (Eds.). (1993). *Sport in social development: Traditions, transitions, and transformations.* Champaign, IL: Human Kinetics.

Jonas, S. (1986). *Triathloning for ordinary mortals.* New York: W. W. Norton.

Lehenaff, D. D. A. (1987). *Votre Sport le Triathlon.* Paris: Bertrand.

Niinimaa, V. M. J. (1998). *Double contest: Biathlon history and development.* Wals-Himmelreich, Austria: International Biathlon Union.

Plant, M. (1987). *Iron will: The heart and soul of triathlon's ultimate challenge.* Chicago: Contemporary Books.

Scott, G. P. (Ed.). (1991). *The 1991 triathlon competition guide.* Colorado Springs, CO: Triathlon Federation USA.

Tinley, S., & Plant, M. (1986). *Winning triathlon.* Chicago: Contemporary Books.

Billiards

Billiards is descended from a fourteenth- or early fifteenth-century northern European lawn game played with balls. By the middle of the fifteenth century the game was moved indoors to a raised table, sometimes covered in green cloth to simulate grass, with a low sideboard to keep the balls from falling off. Like the outdoor game, the indoor game had one or more "ports" (hoops) and "kings" (upright pegs) as targets. The player shoved balls across the table with a wooden stick (mace) that had a flat face on an enlarged end. When executing a shot, the player held the handle end of the mace approximately at shoulder height with the enlarged end resting on the table.

Two types of tables became standard by the late eighteenth century. A pocket billiards table is rectangular and has six pockets, one in each corner and one on either long side. Scoring is accomplished by pocketing balls. A carom billiards table has no pockets. Players score points by propelling one of the balls (the cue ball) into other balls in some rule-governed fashion.

Equipment

Early billiard tables were constructed of wood. Some were square, whereas others were rectangular, and sizes were not standard. Modern tables range from 1.8 to 3.6 meters long and are twice as long as wide. A problem with wooden tables is that the playing surface is prone to warping. In 1826 John Thurston of England constructed a billiards table with a slate surface. Slate is inexpensive, readily available, and very resistant to warping. Today's quality tables have tops (beds) of slate 2.54 to 5 centimeters thick.

Players found that shots could be played by bouncing balls off the sideboards. Because the sideboards were often called "banks," these shots are referred to as "bank shots." Such shots were made easier when padded rails replaced the wooden sideboards. The earliest billiard balls were made of wood. Later the best

A woman lining up a shot.

balls were made of ivory. However, ivory was extremely expensive, prone to cracking and warping, and its use led to the slaughter of thousands of elephants during the early nineteenth century. In 1878 a U.S. chemist, John Wesley Hyatt, discovered that a compound of nitrocellulose, camphor, and alcohol could be molded into balls that are not affected by temperature and humidity. In 1870 Hyatt and his brother patented the process for making his compound, which they named "celluloid," the world's first commercial plastic.

The cue stick, a slender wooden rod, had largely replaced the mace by the end of the eighteenth century. By the early nineteenth century leather tips were applied to the cue sticks so that an off-center strike on a ball did not result in a "miscue," wherein the ball skids off to the side rather than in the intended direction. Players also found that putting chalk on the tip of the cue lessened the chance of a miscue. With these innovations, players

could purposely strike the cue ball slightly off center, thus imparting combinations of sidespin, topspin, or underspin, permitting more precise control of both the cue ball and the object balls.

Games

Modern billiards games come in four basic types. Carom billiards is played on a pocketless table with one red ball, one white ball, and one yellow (or white with two red or black spots on opposite sides) ball. Players score points by propelling their cue ball (either the white ball or the yellow or spotted ball) into the other two balls. By the late 1940s carom billiards faded in popularity in the United States in favor of pocket billiards games.

Snooker is played with twenty-two balls: the white cue ball, fifteen red balls worth one point each, and six numbered balls of different colors worth two through seven points. A player first attempts to pocket one of the red balls and then a numbered ball, which is then replaced on the table. If successful, the player shoots another red ball and so on. English billiards is played with a red ball, a white ball, and a white spotted ball and combines aspects of carom billiards with those of pocket billiards. The tables for these games are normally larger (up to 3.6 meters long) than other tables, and the balls, in turn, are smaller. Both games are much more common in Europe than in the United States.

Common varieties of pocket billiards include straight pool, 8-ball, and 9-ball. Straight pool is played with one white cue ball and fifteen numbered balls. Players attempt to pocket some agreed-upon number of balls (150 for tournament play). The first player reaching that number is the winner. Players must indicate where they intend to pocket a ball before shooting. Improperly pocketed balls are replaced on the table, and the player loses a turn. In 9-ball the balls are racked at one end of the table in a diamond shape with the 9 ball in the center of the diamond. The object balls must be pocketed in numerical rotation, with the player who pockets the 9 ball winning the game. The game of 8-ball is the most popular billiards game in the world and is played with a cue ball and fifteen object balls, numbered 1 through 15. One player must pocket balls of the group numbered 1 through 7, whereas the other player must pocket 9 through 15. The player who first pockets all of the balls in his or her group and then the 8 ball wins the game.

Status of the Game

The term *pool* is often used interchangeably with *billiards,* but during the nineteenth century, a "pool" was a group bet made on horse races in off-track betting parlors known as "poolrooms." Billiards tables were often installed in poolrooms so that patrons could play between races. The term *pool* now refers to any of the several versions of pocket billiards.

World championships in billiards began in 1870. Now both men and women vie for national and world championships in several varieties of billiards. In the past people often stigmatized billiards as a pursuit of lowlifes, but now, with televised tournaments and tables in many homes, billiards is more popular than ever.

Garry Chick

Further Reading

Billiard Congress of America. (1995). *Billiards: The official rules & records book.* Iowa City, IA: Author.
Chick, G. (1996). Billiards. In D. Levinson & K. Christensen (Eds.), *Encyclopedia of world sport: From ancient times to the present* (pp. 109–119). Santa Barbara, CA: ABC-CLIO.
Pool Player Billiard Accessories. (n.d.). The history of billiards. Retrieved April 27, 2004, from http://cuecare.com/history.htm
Shamos, M. (1995). A brief history of the noble game of billiards. In *Billiards: The official rules & records book* (pp. 1–5). Iowa City, IA: Billiard Congress of America.
Stein, V., & Rubino, P. (1996). *The billiard encyclopedia: An illustrated history of the sport* (2nd ed.). Minneapolis, MN: Blue Book Publications.

Biomechanics

Muscles govern range and speed of movement in all complex animals. To power movement, muscles must exert forces to support, forces to accelerate or decelerate, and forces to overcome inertia and the resistance of air or water through which movement occurs. The action of forces is studied in mechanics whereas the action of forces in living things is examined in biomechanics.

Biomechanics is a relatively new subdiscipline of kinesiology, although some people use the terms *biomechanics* and *kinesiology* interchangeably. *Kinesiology* means "the study of motion," which has a broad focus. In contrast, according to the American Society of Biomechanics, *biomechanics* means "the application of the principles of mechanics to the study of biological systems." Biomechanics views the human body as a machine—a mechanical system subject to the restrictions of the laws of physics. The body is divided into a collection of body segments connected to one another and pivoting at the joints, moved by muscular and/or externally applied forces.

Biomechanics

The Biomechanics of a Cricketer

In the extract below, from Badminton—*a sports publication of the late nineteenth and early twentieth century—the form and movement of the English cricketer David Harris is extolled.*

It would be difficult, perhaps impossible, to convey in writing an accurate idea of the grand effect of Harris's bowling; they only who have played against him can fully appreciate it. His attitude, when preparing for his run previously to delivering the ball, would have made a beautiful study for the sculptor. Phidias would certainly have taken him for a model. First of all, he stood erect like a soldier at drill; then, with a graceful curve of the arm, he raised the ball to his forehead, and drawing back his right foot, started off with his left. The calm look and general air of the man were uncommonly striking, and from this series of preparations he never deviated. I am sure that from this simple account of his manner, all my countrymen who were acquainted with his play will recall him to their minds. His mode of delivering the ball was very singular. He would bring it from under the arm by a twist, and nearly as high as his arm-pit, and with this action push it, as it were, from him. How it was that the balls acquired the velocity they did by this mode of delivery, I never could comprehend.

The subdiscipline of biomechanics has grown rapidly and steadily during the past fifteen to twenty years because of, in large part, improvements in instrumentation in general and in high-speed computers in specific. Pennsylvania State University and Indiana University were perhaps the first two universities to design a laboratory for biomechanics during the 1960s. Today, however, biomechanics is a part of every curriculum, and almost all departments of kinesiology have biomechanics laboratories.

Although biomechanics is a relatively new subdiscipline, the first "biomechanic" was probably the Italian painter, sculptor, architect, and engineer Leonardo da Vinci (1452–1519). Leonardo's works demonstrated his knowledge of the musculoskeletal system as he described the mechanics of movement. During the nineteenth century the photographer Edward Muybridge used a system of multiple cameras to document the movement of racehorses. During the 1990s high-speed cinematography became a cornerstone of data collection and analysis of many athletic activities.

Biomechanics incorporates many other fields (physics, engineering, biology, computer science, zoology, and physical and occupational therapy), and human biomechanics can be divided into many areas of study. For example, some biomechanics experts are interested in the elderly and mobility impairments. Others are interested in the development patterns of children. Clinical biomechanics experts might study the gait of people with cerebral palsy or the daily living activities of people with disabilities, whereas occupational biomechanics experts focus on work-related injuries and the prevention of those injuries and are particularly interested in safety factors in the workplace.

Biomechanics in Sport

In sport biomechanics is especially concerned with how the human body applies forces to itself and to other bodies with which it comes into contact and, in turn, how the body is affected by external forces. A sound knowledge of biomechanics equips the physical educator, the coach, and the athlete to choose appropriate training techniques and to detect and understand faults that may arise in their use. Joseph Hamill, a professor at the University of Massachusetts, listed the major categories of interest for the sport-biomechanics expert as improvement of health and physical fitness, injury prevention, equipment design, and improvement of athletic performance.

During recent years the number of girls and women participating in competitive sport, fitness activities, and recreational activities has grown rapidly. Women's de-

A golfer on the course.

Source: istockphoto/Skashkin.

mand for more information about new performance techniques and exercise regimens, accompanied by a willingness to spend money on scientifically designed running shoes, tennis rackets, exercise equipment, or health-promoting foods and diets, has brought even more support to sports research. Once considered the weaker sex, women are playing with speed, precision, explosiveness, and power.

Perhaps because of women's increased involvement in sports, people are beginning to rely less on the male body as a medical norm or athletic-performance yardstick. Biomechanical and physiological factors relative to women should be a primary concern for people who teach, coach, and participate in exercise and sports. However, although much has been said about the woman athlete, little research has addressed her performance. With the increasing number of women participating in sports and other physical activities, the need for such research is paramount. Concepts of biomechanics particularly relevant to women include the following.

CENTER OF GRAVITY

Perhaps the most important concept in biomechanics is equilibrium and stability. People often use the terms *equilibrium* and *stability* synonymously. However, *equilibrium* is that point around which the body freely rotates in any direction with all the opposing forces equal, whereas *stability* is the resistance to the disruption of equilibrium. *Balance* is the ability to control movements. Many factors affect stability and balance. For example, when the line of gravity is within the base of support, the body is more stable. Because of a slightly wider pelvic girdle and narrower shoulders, women have a lower center of gravity than men and are, therefore, more stable. In balance-related activities women have an advantage because of their lower center of gravity.

OVERUSE INJURIES

Overuse injuries result from repetitive stress and/or microtrauma (injury at the miscroscopic level) and can result from both intrinsic and extrinsic factors. Intrinsic factors are those biomechanical aspects specific to each athlete and include bone structure, muscle imbalance and/or weakness, and lack of flexibility. Extrinsic factors are usually specific to a sport, including faulty equipment, incorrect shoes, changes in running surfaces, and improper training. Overuse injuries usually begin as mild or moderate nagging soft-tissue injuries and advance to more severe problems if the person does not receive proper care. Common overuse injuries particular to women who exercise and participate in athletics are Achilles tendonitis, chondromalacia (abnormal softening of cartilage), iliotibial band syndrome, stress fractures, carpal tunnel syndrome, and plantar fascitis. Stress fractures are the most common type of injury for women in sports and occur most frequently with an increase in training. In addition, stress fractures are associated with girls or women who have irregular or no menstrual cycles because of heavy exercise routines.

Biomechanics

"Muscle Memory" by Grantland Rice

("... Golf is mainly a matter of muscle memory, where through play of practice the response from each muscle is instinctive a matter of habit."— From an expert.)

Regardless of its shape or size,
Or any other variation,
I made each muscle memorize
The part best suited for its station.
I taught each one to slice and hook,
To do the stuff that I intended,
From phrases in a copybook
By leading experts recommended.

The ball is teed—the road is clear.
With young hope glowing like an ember,
I whisper in each muscle's ear
"Here goes a hook—do you remember?"
And when I slice one from the lot,
As helpless as a ship that's sinking,
Some muscle murmurs: "I forgot,
I'm sorry—but I wasn't thinking."

In wrath I've cursed them to a turn,
Loud epithets I've kept on raining,
And yet they never seem to learn
In spite of all my careful training.
Just yesterday, through aches and pains,
One snarled at me amid the tussle:
"See here—if I had any brains,
You sap, I wouldn't be a muscle."

Source: Rice, G. (1924). *Badminton*, p. 147–148.

PREGNANCY

Every pregnancy is unique, but all pregnant women undergo significant and multiple physiological and biomechanical changes that affect the body. Some of these changes start as early as conception, but most occur during the third trimester. In particular, musculoskeletal changes occur as a result of the hormone relaxin. Relaxin causes a progressive relaxation of the joints, which include the ligaments that hold the sacroiliac joint and the symphysis pubis. Women often experience lower back pain as a result of an increase in lordosis (spinal curvature) and upper spine extension. These changes occur to accommodate the enlarged abdomen as the fetus grows. To compensate for this exaggerated lumbar curve, the center of gravity shifts. The woman must, in essence, lean backward to maintain a sense of stability. During the third trimester most women need to modify some of their movement patterns. An outward rotation (toeing out) of the feet and almost a shuffle gait usually occur.

KNEES

The knees are the largest and most vulnerable joints in the body. The combined functions of bearing weight and providing locomotion place considerable stress and strain on the knees. According to several studies, women athletes experience twice the knee injuries of men. This fact seems particularly true in such sports as basketball, soccer, and volleyball, all of which require constant pivoting. As with overuse injuries, the predisposition to a knee injury may fall under either intrinsic or extrinsic factors. Intrinsic factors include ligament size and intercondylar notch width (the distance between the lateral and medial condyle of the femur), joint laxity, and the quadricep angle (Q-angle), which is the angle made by the tendons of the quadriceps femoris and the ligamentum patella with the center of the patella, which is the thick, flat triangular movable bone that forms the anterior point of the knee. Extrinsic factors include motor skill, level of conditioning, muscular strength and coordination, and individual mechanics. Common knee injuries among women are patella femoral pain syndrome, chondromalacia, patella tendonitis, meniscal or cartilage injuries, and ligament injuries. In particular, a disproportionate number of anterior cruciate ligament (ACL) injuries occur in women's athletics. The anterior cruciate ligaments provide stability to the knee, particularly for forward-backward movement. The greater incidence of ACL injuries stems from interrelated factors, including hamstring-quadriceps strength imbalances, wider Q-angle, and joint laxity. These factors do not necessarily cause the problem together—hamstring-quadriceps strength imbalances may add to joint instability.

Athletic Equipment Design and Apparel

For many years women and girls participating in sports and fitness activities have had to use equipment designed for men. Recently, however, some companies have responded to the enormous number of women who are now physically active. Shoe companies and sporting goods and athletic-wear companies are making functional design adaptations to meet the needs of women. In addition, more businesses owned and operated by women are making design changes in athletic equipment for women. Compared to the average man, the average woman is shorter and has longer legs, shorter arms, and a shorter torso. Women also have smaller hands and feet, narrower shoulders, and wider hips. Women have a higher percentage of body fat and less lean muscle mass.

Biomechanical differences also apply to athletic shoes for women. Whereas most men's athletic shoes are designed on a standard athletic last (mold), many women's shoes are designed on a special last. Lasts come in two shapes: A straight-lasted shoe is filled in under the medial arch, whereas a curved-lasted shoe is flared medially at the ball of the foot. Also, women's shoes usually have narrower heels. Although a number of sport-specific athletic-shoe designs exist, all incorporate biomechanical factors such as heel counters, midsoles, and lateral forefoot support.

In summary, biomechanical factors are critical in analyzing and improving the way women execute particular movements. Some factors may also cause an increased predisposition to specific injuries. Therefore, people should understand the principles of biomechanics as they relate to care and prevention of injuries and to the enhancement of motor performance of people.

Rosalie DiBrezzo and Inza Fort

See also Human Movement Studies; Kinesiology; Sport Science

Further Reading

Adrian, M., & Cooper, J. (1995). *Biomechanics of human movement* (2nd ed.). Madison, WI: WCB Brown and Benchmark.

Hall, S. (1995). *Basic biomechanics* (2nd ed.). St. Louis, MO: Mosby-Year Book.

Hamill, J., & Knutzen, K. (1995). *Biomechanical basis of human movement.* Baltimore: Williams and Wilkins.

Hatze, H. (1974). The meaning of the term "biomechanics." *Journal of Biomechanics, 7,* 189.

Hay, J. (1993). *The biomechanics of sports techniques* (4th ed.). Englewood Cliffs, NJ: Prentice Hall.

Wade, M., & Baker, J. (1995). *Introduction of kinesiology.* Madison, WI: WCB Brown and Benchmark.

Biotechnology

In 1953 the English biophysicist Francis Crick and the U.S. geneticist James Watson presented the structure of deoxyribonucleic acid (DNA). Half a century later the HUGO (Human Genome Organization) project completed the mapping of the human genome (one haploid set of chromosomes with the genes they contain). Expectations of biotechnology have grown enormously ever since. These expectations concern not only the mapping and sequencing of many organisms, but also the modification of genes to cure diseases or to enhance human features. During the next few decades sports will be confronted with a variety of more or less realistic promises, varying from preventive screening to the genetic selection of talent and the enhancement of athletic performance with gene doping.

Basic Biology

The human body is made up of sixty trillion (6×10^{13}) cells of 320 types (muscle cells or blood cells, for example). The nucleus of each cell contains twenty-three pairs of chromosomes. These chromosomes carry most of our genetic material. This material, DNA, is made up of a chain of nucleotide (compounds that consist of a ribose or deoxyribose sugar joined to a purine or pyrimidine base and to a phosphate group and that are the basic structural units of nucleic acids) bases: adenine (A), guanine (G), thymine (T), and cytosine (C). These bases are grouped into two pairs: Adenine binds to thymine, and guanine binds to cytosine.

In 1953 Watson and Crick discovered the double helix, the structure of DNA. DNA carries our genes and almost all hereditary information. DNA passes information to proteins via ribonucleic acid (RNA). RNA and proteins play a crucial role in reproducing DNA and in life processes in general (instead of thymine, RNA has uracil, and RNA is not structured as a double helix but rather is single stranded). DNA is passed on from one generation to the next generation.

The human body is made up of 3 billion base pairs and probably thirty thousand genes. A gene is a distinct unit of DNA, a particular string of A, T, G, and C. Each particular string of bases may stand for a piece of information that is used to produce amino acids and proteins (proteins are chains of twenty types of amino acids).

Molecular biologists are gaining insights into these genetic building blocks of life. Meanwhile, genetic engineering (genetic transfer technology) of DNA is developing rapidly, and the applications of gene therapy seem promising. Gene technology also has resulted in controversial applications. After scientists began cloning animals (such as the sheep Dolly), many people were concerned about what would follow. People expressed even greater concern when gene doping entered the news. Big, muscled, genetically modified mice —named after the former bodybuilding champion Arnold Schwarzenegger—created many worries about the future of elite sports.

Sports

Genes are crucial for sports talent. Research on performances of identical (monozygotic—derived from a single egg) twin athletes has provided some clues to the heritability and the dominant role of genes that are related to sports performance. Empirical evidence that shows the genetic component for human performance has grown quickly during the last few decades. Genes determine to a large extent anthropometrical (relating to the study of human body measurements, especially on a comparative basis) features such as height and the length of arms and legs. Features such as muscle size, muscle fiber composition, heart size, lung size and volume, resting heart rate, muscular strength, flexibility of joints, and aerobic endurance are all in some respect trainable, but the influence of genes dominates.

Several large research programs are searching for the location of crucial genes that are related to elite sports performance. Researchers are scrutinizing several genes that might have a critical influence on specific sports talents. Genes that regulate muscle tissue and blood flow, for example, are associated with elite endurance athletes. More complex than establishing the relative contribution of genes, as opposed to nongenetic factors, is the search for specific genes, their location, and their specific influence on athletic performance.

Some researchers think that the human gene map is still in its infancy and that little has been accomplished thus far. However, several research programs reinforce the suggestion that in the long run sports-relevant features can be localized in our genes. After researchers localize these genes, the next step of modification—using knowledge for enhancement—might be imminent.

Developments in molecular biology hold several promises that might have spectacular influences on modern sports. Three of these promises are preventing risks related to sports, genetically screening to maximize selection processes in elite sports, and genetically modifying athletes (gene doping).

Preventing Risks

Knowledge about our genetic makeup and its relation with health risks raises possibilities for prevention. The emergence of "sports genetic passports" could have consequences for the ideology of "sports for all." Insights into genetic makeup can contribute to a restriction of choices. A genetic predisposition for sickle cell anemia can be life threatening, for example, in combination with certain types of sports.

There are one hundred and ninety nine ways to beat,
but only one way to win; get there first. ▪ WILLIE SHOEMAKER

Evidence indicates the risks of brain damage when engaging in contact sports such as boxing or even soccer. Information about genetic makeup can radically change the discussion about compulsory testing and preventive measurements in boxing. Besides factors such as the length of a person's boxing career, the number of knockouts, and the number of punches to the head, genetic predisposition clearly seems to play an important role in the prevalence of Parkinson's disease, Alzheimer's disease, and dementia pugilistica. Professional boxers who are homozygotic (having the two genes at corresponding loci on homologous chromosomes identical for one or more loci) for the Apo-E4 gene have a great risk of suffering Parkinson's or Alzheimer's at a young age: One out of six boxers will suffer Parkinson's or Alzheimer's by the fiftieth birthday. Although no curative therapy is available, people must make decisions about preventive options such as medical examination, waiting times for the next match, or restriction of a boxing career (temporary or definitively). People also face the question of what preventive options are available for young children who practice contact sports, either on a recreational basis or with the intention of becoming an elite athlete.

With preventive screening and advice people can gain clear health benefits. Negative advice ("it is better not to box") is not uncontroversial. However, it does seem less complex than the situation in which genetic testing is translated into positive advice, such as when a favorable genetic blueprint with respect to athletic features leads a person to a forced predestination to become an elite athlete.

Maximizing Athletic Potential

Genetic screening might be applied to children whose genetic makeup would allow them to perform a certain sport. This screening might be the next step in "talent scouting." The application of gene technology as a selective tool would be one tool among others, but it would advance the moment of selection and the efficiency of scouting.

Coaches have already expressed their interest in these possibilities of gene technology. Hartmut Buschbacher, a native of East Germany, has been coach of the U.S. national women's rowing team for nine years. Of genetic screening he said, "As a coach, I'm interested in performance, and if this information would give me a better opportunity to select the athletes for my team, I would like to use that. That way you're not going to waste so much time and energy on athletes who may not be as successful" (Farrey 2002).

However, such an increased level of knowledge might decrease sports participation in general, especially among people who have a less favorable genetic profile for high performance. Early insight into "objective" standards of talent can have a discouraging effect on children who don't have enough talent for elite sports. Genetic screening might also contribute to a widening gap between sports as an educational and cultural phenomenon and sports as a merely selective and performance-driven practice in which the matching of the "right child to the right sport" becomes a central objective.

On the other hand, parents and children who are willing to spend their time and money to achieve sports success have a right to insights. In any case, the interests of children need to be carefully weighed against those of ambitious parents, coaches, and countries. Knowledge about genetic makeup may even enhance autonomy and contribute to the prevention of harm. A parent's decision to exploit the athletic talent of a child is potentially a more restricting decision (given the relative uncertainty about the talent) than a decision that is based on a genetic profile. This practice of early selection does, however, raise moral and pedagogical (relating to a teacher or education) questions about the threat of autonomy of selected children. A child's knowledge that he or she has genetic variants associated with a higher probability of success in sports may be a source of problems. People may have to balance the right to know with the right not to know.

On the other hand, one can imagine that the nonselected will be spared grief because they will not fail to match their high ambitions. In any case (with or without genetic screening) people must cope with alternative

People are so busy lengthening their lives with exercise
they don't have time to live them. ■ JONATHAN MILLER

scenarios when the talent cannot live up to the expectations. That means, if necessary, a flexible readjustment of the athletic blueprint. That also means considering the social, ethical, pedagogical, and commercial limits of "athletic predestination."

Enhancing Performance

One can think of several biotechnological applications to enhance athletic performance. Genetic information might be used, for example, to fine-tune training and nutrition in relation to an athlete's genetic makeup. One of the prospects that appeals most to the imagination is that of gene doping. Gene doping is the nontherapeutic use of genes, genetic elements, and/or cells that have the capacity to enhance athletic performance.

The insertion of artificial genes is already possible, although the problem of controlling the activity of the artificial genes so they don't produce too little or too much of the required substance remains. The artificial gene can be inserted into a patient in three ways. The simplest way is to inject the DNA directly into the muscles. Some of the muscle fibers will then take up the DNA. Alternatively, one could introduce the DNA into cells in the laboratory and then inject these cells back into the body. Finally, one could use viruses to introduce foreign DNA into human cells. Sports performance could be increased by increasing red blood cells by inserting an EPO (erythropoietin, a synthetic hormone that stimulates production of oxygen-carrying red blood cells) gene and by building muscle mass by inactivating the myostatin gene (successfully applied to mice). After a synthetic gene was injected into the muscles of so-called Schwarzenegger mice (to produce more insulin-like growth factor 1), their muscle force increased 60 percent after a month. The injection of EPO genes into monkeys made the level of red blood cells rise from forty to seventy (fifty is a "health limit" within elite sports).

These experiments seem to be preparation for the first genetically modified athlete. Indeed, some people expect the first genetically modified athlete to enter the sports arena in the near future. Some researchers think that as soon as gene therapy becomes a well-established

technique, gene doping of elite athletes will become routine. Other researchers temper such high expectations and do not think that in the near future the genetically modified athlete will become reality. Many genes are involved in athletic performance, especially in sports that do not merely measure force or speed. Complex interactions exist among genes, and complex interactions exist among genes and the environment. No one crucial gene for sports talent can be identified, inserted, or modified at will.

Notwithstanding these diverging interpretations of future scenarios, no doubt biotechnological developments will raise and stimulate a broad spectrum of ethical and social-political questions.

Sports, Biotechnology, and Ethics

People have applied general principles, such as autonomy, privacy, justice, equity, and human dignity, to reach an international consensus and to harmonize national regulations on biotechnology. However, we can question whether conventional human rights meet all the dilemmas that will arise from biotechnology. Ideas that come into play include the Kantian (referring to the German philosopher Immanuel Kant) maxim of not treating a person as a means to an end, a right to a unique genotype (all or part of the genetic constitution of a person or group), harm done to an unborn person, discrimination, the right to privacy, and an equal availability to new technology. People who oppose the use of molecular biology to enhance human beings think this new technology will endanger the "intrinsic value of diversity" or is a reprehensible way of "playing God."

The discussions about the ethics of genetic enhancement in sports are more specific. The purpose of the World Anti-Doping Program, as written in the code of the World Anti-Doping Agency (WADA), is to protect athletes' fundamental right to participate in doping-free sports and thus to promote health, fairness, and equality for athletes worldwide. While repeating its militant statement, "For once, we want to be ahead, not behind," WADA has tried to keep up with the latest developments in gene technology. International regula-

tion and harmonization of the antidoping policy remain the primary aim. The representation of "pure and honest sport" is also related to the possibilities of public identification and to the protection of commercial interests.

Although a long history of the use and detection of performance-enhancing substances exists in sports, the use of biotechnology seems to raise new and complex issues. A major issue is the moral and practical implications of control and detection. Although WADA initiated genetic research to stay ahead of the athlete, anti-doping authorities face serious problems in their search for a useful test to detect gene-doped athletes. The protein produced by the artificial gene will be identical to the endogenous (caused by factors inside the organism or system) protein because the human body itself produces it. If pure DNA cells are used, this DNA will be present only at the site of injection. That means that a muscle biopsy of the injected site would be required. However, what if athletes do not consent to a biopsy from the muscle in order to control for the "naturalness" of the DNA? What is considered an autonomous decision in a clinical context is considered fraud in the context of elite sports. The implications of control for "pure genes" ask for a careful consideration of the principle of informed consent in elite sports. Controlling practices also raise questions about the privacy of the screened athlete. WADA aims at an insight into the medical passports of all athletes to be able to screen the relevant medical parameters for a longer period of time. The question is, "Who will 'own' and protect the genetic information of the athletes?" Besides moral and practical questions about detection, people also are concerned about how these developments will influence sports and athletes themselves.

Another complex issue is the distinction between therapy and nontherapy. We can only with difficulty draw a clear line between a therapeutic and an enhancing use of genetics. Why do people condemn the healthy athlete who wants to become better but not the ill patient who wants to become better? Does a difference really exist between therapy to replace defective genes with healthy genes and therapy to enhance healthy genes? Although this difference is often difficult to see, it remains one of the most important fundaments of the international policy on sports and doping.

The discussion of sports and genetics clearly is about more than just protecting the health of the athlete or protecting the idea of a fair competition. What happens when talent is not something that is "just given" but rather is a feature we can modify or choose for? High-performance sports might have to adopt a new ethics that is adapted to changing times and technologies. For the time being good genes do not suffice for success in sports. Dedication remains an important factor that composes one of the relevant inequalities we want to measure for in sports. Sports are about measuring performances with the aim of comparing differences in talent and dedication. To be competitive within modern elite sports requires talent and dedication in extreme quantities. This requirement will not change with biotechnology. Biotechnology cannot replace training effort. Biotechnology can, however, change our perception of a fair and human way of practicing sports.

Ivo van Hilvoorde

See also Technology

Further Reading

Andersen, J. L., Schjerling, P., & Saltin, B. (2000). Muscle, genes and athletic performance. *Scientific American, 283,* 30–37.
Bouchard, C., Malina, R. M., & Perusse, L. (1997). *Genetics of fitness and physical performance.* Champaign, IL: Human Kinetics.
Buchanan, A., Brock, D. W., Daniels, N., & Wikler, D. (2000). *From chance to choice: Genetics and justice.* Cambridge, UK: Cambridge University Press.
Burley, J. (Ed.). (1999). *The genetic revolution and human rights: The Oxford Amnesty Lectures 1998.* Oxford, UK: Oxford University Press.
Davis, D. S. (2001). *Genetic dilemmas: Reproductive technology, parental choices, and children's futures.* New York: Routledge.
Farrey, T. (2002). *Genetic testing beckons.* Retrieved March 11, 2005, from http://espn.go.com/otl/athlete/monday.html
Hartmann, W. (Ed.). (2003). *Gendoping: Die Dopingbekampfung rustet sich.* Cologne, Germany: Sport und Buch Straub.
Jordan, B. D. (1997). Apolipoprotein E epsilon4 associated with chronic traumatic brain injury in boxing. *Journal of the American Medical Association, 278,* 136–140.
Lamsam, C., Fu, F. H., Robbins, P. D., & Evans, C. H. (1997). Gene therapy in sports medicine. *Sports Medicine, 25*(2), 73–77.

McGee, G. (2000). *The perfect baby: Parenthood in the new world of cloning and genetics.* Lanham, MD: Rowman & Littlefield.

Miah, A. (2004). *Genetically modified athletes: Biomedical ethics, gene doping and sport.* New York: Routledge.

Montgomery, H. E. (1998). Human gene for physical performance. *Nature, 393,* 221–222.

Munthe, C. (2000). Selected champions: Making winners in the age of genetic technology. In T. Tannsjo & C. Tamburrini (Eds.), *Values in sport: Elitism, nationalism, gender equality and the scientific manufacture of winners* (pp. 217–231). London: E & FN Spon.

Perusse, L., Rankinen, T., Rauramaa, R., Rivera, M. A., Wolfarth, B., & Bouchard, C. (2003). The human gene map for performance and health-related fitness phenotypes: The 2002 update. *Medicine & Science in Sports & Exercise, 35*(8), 1248–1264.

President's Council of Bioethics. (2003). *Beyond therapy: Biotechnology and the pursuit of happiness.* New York: HarperCollins.

Schuelke, M. (2004). Myostatin mutation associated with gross muscle hypertrophy in a child. *New England Journal of Medicine, 350,* 2682–2688.

Skinner, J. S. (2001). Do genes determine champions? *Sports Science Exchange, 14*(4).

Van Hilvoorde, I. (2005). Sport and genetics: Moral and educational considerations on "athletic predestination." In T. Torbjorn & C. Tamburrini (Eds.), *The genetic design of winners.* New York: Routledge.

Bislett Stadium

Bislett Stadium is located in Oslo, Norway. The stadium, known simply as "Bislett," for decades hosted speed skating in the winter and track and field and football (soccer) in the summer. In its heyday Bislett was known for its world records, its spectators, and its ambience.

Development

In 1898 the Oslo city council purchased an area belonging to a local brickworks to be developed as a sports ground and playground. The development was gradual, however. The initiative of one man, Martinius Lordahl, was decisive when the Bislett sports ground was opened in 1908. It was then a skating rink in the winter and a rather lacking athletic ground in the summer. In 1917 the city council took over responsibility for Bislett and invested enough to enable Bislett Stadium to be built and to open in 1922 with covered stands, indoor training facilities for boxing and wrestling, cafe, and changing rooms. Both the track and the infield were cindered. This opening meant that Oslo, at last had a modern stadium for the eastern, working-class parts of the city. During the latter part of the 1930s the stadium was modernized, cinders on the infield were replaced with grass, and stands to accommodate thirty-two thousand spectators were erected. The track kept its cinders until 1971, when a synthetic surface was installed. The track surface was renewed again in 1984–1985 during a long-overdue modernization that also improved stands and changing rooms. However, people proclaimed these improvements "too little, too late." The stadium had, for example, never more than six running lanes and needed dispensations from the International Association of Athletics Federations (IAAF) to arrange international track meets during its last years.

Social and Political Meanings

Bislett, however, was where Norwegian sports history and international sports history were made. After 1922 the stadium became Oslo's biggest communal sports ground, with a broad scale of uses and users. Bislett's political meaning between the two world wars, when Norwegian and European workers' sport was powerful, is also apparent. Its location made it the home venue of workers' sports competitions. Because it was a municipal stadium, access was open, and Bislett's reputation as a popular sports arena grew. In football this reputation was evident after 1945 as the top teams from the eastern districts with no grounds of their own gladly used Bislett as their own ground. The Norwegian national football team played one game there—in 1913. The only track and field championship staged there was the European track and field championship of 1946. Only one year after the end of World War II this event had political implications because the Soviet Union participated, six years before the Soviet Union entered the Olympic Games.

World Record Arena

Bislett's reputation also grew from its status as a world record arena. The first record was set in 1924 when the

*Think big, believe big, act big, and the
results will be big.* ■ ANONYMOUS

future IAAF president, Adrian Paulen, ran the 500-meter race. More records followed by athletes such as Jack Torrance, Forrest Towns, Ron Clarke, Roger Moens, Grete Waitz, Anders Garderud, John Walker, Henry Rono, Sebastian Coe, Steve Ovett, Ingrid Kristiansen, Steve Cram, Said Aouita, Jan Zelezny, and Haile Gebreselassie. Sixty-two world records in track and field were set at Bislett between 1924 and 2000, the majority of them in track's middle and long distances. Because the track was not particularly fast, other factors—such as the mild temperature, pure air, and usually windless conditions of Scandinavian summer evenings; the intimacy and ambience of the stadium; and the tightly packed crowd's enthusiasm and knowledge—were more decisive. The crowd's ability to carry athletes to their supreme levels of performance was shown in 1965 in perhaps the most overwhelming demonstration of running ability the world had seen: Australian Ron Clarke's world record-breaking run in the 10,000-meter race. On the cinders of Bislett he recorded a time of 27 minutes 39.4 seconds, smashing the record with 34.6 seconds.

Speed Skating and Ambience

"Only the greatest speed skating heroes are met with such enthusiasm," someone said after Ron Clarke's historic run in 1965, illustrating the place that speed skating held in Norwegian sports and culture. As a speed-skating arena Bislett attracted large crowds who nearly always created the "Bislett ambience" including the "Bislett roar." Bislett represented the utmost in the premodern sport of speed skating: an outdoor venue with natural ice. Being located in the lowlands near sea level, it could never compete with the high-altitude venues for ice conditions, times, and records. It nevertheless attracted tens of thousands of people who came to stand in the cold for hours to watch pairs of skaters glide loop after loop. Bislett was the setting for ten European and thirteen world championships, the 1986 European championship being the last. The Olympic speed and figure-skating competitions of 1952 also took place at Bislett. People such as Oscar Mathiesen,

Clas Thunberg, Hjalmar Andersen, Knut Johannessen, Ard Schenk, and Eric Heiden were celebrated there. Fourteen world records in speed skating were set at Bislett during the period 1963–1982. The Bislett ambience made the stadium popular among both spectators and competitors. Norwegian, Finnish, Swedish, Dutch, U.S., and Soviet skaters were all celebrated at Bislett.

The Future

The transition of speed skating to indoor arenas with artificial ice became unavoidable after the 1980s and especially after the 1990s. This transition meant that Bislett had seen its day, especially because it had not been designed for artificial ice. The stadium's use as a multisports facility made such a design difficult. Increasing demands for the quality of grass for football, ice for skating, and running lanes for track and field made a combined solution for all seasons impossible.

Bislett continued to host athletic events as world stars returned year after year to the rather primitive, old-fashioned stadium. However, after 2003 no more international events were staged at Bislett. After having been granted dispensations for lacking facilities for years, the stadium was finally declared too old. The debate over who was to blame for this dejected development was heated and involved some of Norway's most distinguished voices. However, being labelled "conservative nostalgics," they were on the losing side of the debate. The Oslo city council in 2004 decided to tear down Bislett Stadium, and to erect a new stadium at the same place, ending eighty years of sports history.

Matti Goksøyr

Further Reading

Bakke, S. (1989). *Verdensrekordbanen Bislett/The world record track.* Oslo, Norway: Verdens Gang.

Hauge-Moe, P. (1992). *Sølv var nederlag. Norges Skøyteforbund 100 ar, 1893–1993.* Oslo, Norway: Norges Skøyteforbund.

Olstad, F. (1987). *Norsk idrettshistorie, b.1, 1861–1939: Forsvar, sport, klassekamp.* Oslo, Norway: Aschehoug.

Blood Doping

See Performance Enhancement

Boat Race (Cambridge vs. Oxford)

A rowing competition is held annually in late March or early April between the boat clubs of Oxford and Cambridge, two of England's oldest and most prestigious universities. First held in 1829, and held annually since 1856 (except for war years), the race is considered a symbol of British sport and is one of the world's oldest surviving sporting events. The 2004 race was both the 150th race and the 175th anniversary of the first race. Part of the worldwide appeal of the event is that one needs to know nothing about the sport to follow the race.

Origins

The idea for the boat race came from Oxford student Charles Wordsworth (nephew of the famous poet) and his Cambridge friend Charles Merivale, who staged an interuniversity cricket match in 1827. They extended the interuniversity sport idea to a rowing competition, when Cambridge formally challenged Oxford to the first race on 10 June 1829, at Henley-on-Thames. This also started the tradition whereby the previous year's loser must formally challenge the other university each year. Cambridge leads the series 78-71-1 through 2004. The Henley Boat Races are a tradition that started in 1975; they are held about a week before the men's race and include races between the main and reserve all-women's teams and women's and men's lightweight team races.

Race and Course

The 4.25-mile course, used every year since 1849, follows the River Thames between Putney and Mortlake.

This course is three times longer than a regular modern rowing course. Traditionally, the races are won and lost in the "battle of the bends" on the three main bends in the course. The race takes less than twenty minutes to complete, with the current course record at 16:19, set by Cambridge in 1998, in a year when both teams broke the previous course record. Approximately 250,000 spectators line the course to watch the race live each year, while 8.9 million watched the race on the BBC in 2004, and about 400 million were in the international television audience.

The start of the race is usually about ninety minutes before high tide, when water is running at its fastest. The hoopla surrounding the race has turned into a week-long celebration, known as "Tideway Week," which coincides with the beginning of England's "social season." The boats have sunk on more than one occasion, which used to mean an automatic forfeit but now causes a restart of the race. Weather can often be a factor in the event, with high winds or heavy rain affecting the race. A coin toss determines who chooses the side of the river to row on, which can make a big difference, depending on the weather.

Teams

To compete, a rower must be a currently enrolled student at either Oxford or Cambridge. Competitors in the early years of the race were often "muscular gentlemen of the cloth." Family members of previous team members often end up in the boats. The race is not limited to men—women occasionally make the teams. In 1981, Susan Brown, a member of the British Olympic team, was the first woman to steer in the men's boat race, leading the winning Oxford team. The naming of some "students" in the past to teams was a bit more suspect, as international rowing stars were recruited to take one-year courses at the university and qualify for the team.

History

Cambridge dominated the race overall during the early to mid-twentieth century; they won a record thirteen in a row (1924–1936), took seventeen out of eighteen from 1914–1936, and won all but twelve from 1914–1973. Oxford's longest winning streak was ten in a row from 1976–1985 and sixteen of seventeen from 1976–1992, followed by another streak by Cambridge of seven years from 1993–1999. The winning margin is often small (indeed, 1877 was a dead heat), and the history of the race is marked with accusations on both sides of errant oars, ramming of boats, shady recruiting of team members, and bad sportsmanship.

The race was first broadcast as a running commentary by BBC radio in 1927 and was first televised on the BBC in 1938. John Snagge, the BBC commentator for the race from 1931–1980, considered the "voice of the boat race," is famous for his 1949 pronouncement, "I can't see who's ahead, but it's either Oxford or Cambridge." Sponsorship of the race began in 1976. One of the more famous stories out of the race was the "Oxford Mutiny" of 1987, when the Americans chosen for the team refused to row in the race after one of their countrymen was dropped in favor of the English president of the club. The Oxford coach, Dan Topolski, cobbled together a new young team of reserves that still won the race by four lengths. Many previous races can be viewed or listened to online at the official boat race website, http://www.theboatrace.org.

The Future

Technology has finally come to the traditional boat race, with large viewing screens on the banks of the Thames, in-boat cameras, and microphones on the coxes, bringing fans closer to the experience. The boat race will be leaving the BBC, its long-standing broadcast partner, in 2005 and moving to new broadcast partner ITV. Although the race itself is sponsored, the boats and individual competitors are not yet, but that is inevitable in the future. With all the sponsorship

Rowers on the Thames. *Source: istockphoto.com/RuudVNR.*

Boat Race (Cambridge vs. Oxford)

Team Building through Boat Racing

This 1915 account of a boat race on the Thames River stresses the value of teamwork on the water:

As an instance of that physical perseverance which wins, two pictures come up before me as I write. They are connected with a contest between Cambridge and Oxford on the Thames River. The first scene shows the start; the rowers are in their places, —every one alert and strong,—while cheering thousands encourage their respective teams. The second picture is the finish of the race. The winning crew,— that of Cambridge,—comes in with only two of the rowers able to pull their oars, while the others evidence by their hanging heads and bowed bodies their completely fagged condition. The honor goes to Cambridge; and it all depended on the two men who were able to hold their own. Some day in the race of life their exploit will be duplicated, and the training of the days of school life will be responsible for their again proving themselves superior to their fellows.

The spirit which enabled those two to win out for their team, as well as the spirit which carried the other to the point of complete exhaustion, is highly beneficial factor to society. A distinctive element of the team-game is the sacrifice of the individual's personal interest for the benefit of the clan. One day, during the progress of a football game, a young quarter-back said to his coach, "Take me out; I've forgotten the signals." The personal privilege of being in the game was nothing to him compared with the success of his team.

Similar self-sacrifice is the constant need of social life. The team athletic contest has been the means of making the individual player realize that he is not an isolated factor in life's problem, but that he stands related to the other factors. In Public School 30, New York City, the champion broad-jumper was ineligible to compete on account of low grades in his studies. The boy-editor of the school-paper remarked, "It's a pity he can't jump as well with his lessons."

Source: Character through recreation in the field of athletics. (1915). *Badminton*, p. 160–161.

money coming into the race, teams are better funded and use professional coaches who were not available to them in the past, making the races much more competitive during the last several years.

Christina L. Hennessey

Further Reading

Andrews, J. (2004) *What it takes to earn your place: Celebrating rowing through the 150th Oxford v. Cambridge boat race.* London: Third Millennium Publishing Company.

Burnell, R. D. (1979). *One hundred and fifty years of the Oxford and Cambridge boat race: An official history.* Marlow, England: Precision Press.

Burnell, R. D. (1954). *The Oxford & Cambridge boat race, 1829–1953.* London: Oxford University Press.

Dodd, C. (1983). *The Oxford & Cambridge boat race.* London: Stanley Paul.

Dodd, C., and Marks, J. (2004). *Battle of the blues: The Oxford & Cambridge boat race from 1829.* London: P to M Ltd/Midway House.

Gill, A. (1991). *The Yanks at Oxford: The 1987 boat race controversy.* Sussex, UK: The Book Guild, Ltd.

Ross, G. (1954). *The boat race: the story of the first hundred races between Oxford and Cambridge.* London: Hodder and Stoughton.

Topolski, D. (1985). *Boat race: The Oxford revival.* London: Willow Books.

Topolski, D., with P. Robinson. (1989). *True blue: The Oxford boat race mutiny.* New York: Doubleday.

Boating, Ice

Ice boating (also called "ice yachting") is a fast-paced winter sport that uses a boat propelled by wind. An ice boat resembles a sailboat, with a hull, mast, and sails, but also has runners on its flat-bottomed hull to allow it to glide along the ice. An iceboat can cruise at 50 to 100 kilometers per hour and in strong winds can accelerate to 225 kilometers per hour or more. Ice boaters sail on frozen rivers, lakes, or bays, primarily in northern regions of Europe and North America where weather conditions freeze the water but keep the ice clear of snow.

Origins

People in early northern cultures used a variety of objects to glide over snow and ice. Historians often cite eighteenth-century Netherlands, where people sailed wind-powered boats on winter ice, as the birthplace of modern ice boating. Other European countries also practiced ice boating. In the United States during the nineteenth century the communities of Long Branch and Red Bank in New Jersey and the region around the Hudson River in New York State were early centers for the sport. It subsequently became popular in the upper midwestern United States and in Canada and other chilly regions.

Early ice boats were basic, having crude skatelike runners and simple sails and rigging. Some ice boats were just conventional sailboats with runners attached to them. However, during the mid-nineteenth century people began to build larger and more complex ice boats. In the United States people often called these boats "Hudson River ice yachts," and, not surprisingly, they were usually owned by wealthy people. One prominent early ice boater, for example, was John E. Roosevelt (member of a prominent New York family and an ancestor of President Franklin D. Roosevelt), whose boat, the *Icicle*, had more than 93 square meters of sail. Such large ice boats were among the fastest vehicles in the world at the time.

Ice boating gained wider popularity during the twentieth century with the tread toward small boats that were inexpensive and portable. This trend began in 1931 in Milwaukee, Wisconsin, when the ice boater Starke Meyer designed a boat that was steered by a pivoted runner in the bow (front) instead of the stern (rear), which had previously been more common. The Joys family, whose members were professional sailmakers in Milwaukee, devised a similar ice boat. This design allowed people to build small ice boats known

as "Skeeters" that are both fast and stable. Other ice boat builders created variations on this design. Among the most popular modern ice boat designs is the DN, which was created at the *Detroit News* in 1937.

During the years ice boaters have formed organizations to sponsor races and other activities. The Poughkeepsie, New York, Ice Yacht Club, founded in 1869, was the first formal ice boating organization in the United States. Some organizations are geographically oriented, and some, such as the International DN Ice Yacht Racing Association, are oriented to specific types of boats. Important competitions have included the Hearst Cup, the Ford Cup, and the Ice Yacht Pennant.

Practice

Ice boaters, like other sailors, steer their craft and pull in or let out their sails to take best advantage of the direction and speed of the wind. An ice boat also has a tiller in the bow or stern that is turned to steer the boat (similar to turning the rudder on a sailboat). Ice boats also heel (tip to one side) when sailing fast.

Ice boating requires unique skills and conditions. Ice boats are not slowed by the resistance that slows sailboats as they move through the water. A fast-moving ice boat also generates a separate wind, which increases its speed to three or four times that of the natural wind. Ice boats have unique steering characteristics, and the skipper must be careful to avoid spinning out of control on slippery ice. Safety is a crucial consideration, and sailors wear helmets and other protective gear.

Today's ice boats come in many sizes and designs. Some ice sailors build their own boats to standard specifications. The hulls of ice boats are usually narrow, with parallel runners attached to perpendicular crossplanks extending out to the sides. Ice boaters sit either in a small cockpit in the hull or on a seat attached to its surface. Most small ice boats are built to accommodate one person, but some types, such as the Yankee, carry two or more persons.

People classify ice boats by the size of their sail area. Sail area sizes are divided into classes, which range from boats with a sail area of 23 square meters or more to boats with a sail area of less than 7 square meters. These boats are usually designated from Class A (large) to Class E (small). People also classify ice boats by their design. The DN design, for example, usually has a 3.7-meter-long hull, 2.4-meter runners, and 5.5 square meters of sail. The larger Skeeter design has a hull about 6 meters long or longer and 7 square meters of sail.

Ice sailors compete in local and regional races and in national and international championships. (As in sailing, races are called "regattas.") Some races are open to all boats with similar sail sizes. One-design competitions are open only to boats of a specific design. In the United States the National Iceboat Authority establishes basic racing guidelines.

The direction of the wind determines the courses for ice boat racing. Courses are marked by buoys set some distance apart, commonly a mile. Racers line up at an angle to the buoys and start simultaneously. They circle the buoys and must tack on a course that takes them into the wind at different angles, finishing at a predetermined location. Judging is based on a combination of speed and the ability of the sailor to control the boat and follow the course as closely as possible.

John Townes

Further Reading

Roberts, L., & St. Clair, W. (1989). *Think ice! The DN ice boating book.* Burlington, VT: International DN Ice Yacht Racing Association.

Bobsledding

The history of bobsledding as an organized and identifiable sport stretches back for over a hundred years. Emerging from the Alpine areas of Europe, the sport now has a regular worldwide platform as an event of the Winter Olympics. Bobsledding, despite its being very expensive, requiring specific climatic conditions, and having facilities that are available in only a small number of countries, has an increasingly global appeal.

At present over thirty nations are affiliated with the Federation Internationale de Bobsleigh et de Tobogganning (FIBT). The spectacle of two or four racers traveling down a 1,600-meter (1,744-yard) course at speeds approaching 130 kilometers (78 miles) per hour, thereby suffering a centrifugal force of up to 4 g's as they approach a bend, makes bobsledding one of the most fascinating winter sports for participant and spectator alike. Bobsledding is growing and increasing in popularity, especially, and in many ways surprisingly, in countries where snow is seldom, if ever, seen.

Origins of Bobsledding

The sled and the luge were common sights in the mountainous regions of Europe and North America throughout the nineteenth century. Developing from local forms of transportation, the sled and the luge had increasingly been used as part of the pursuit of leisure by visitors to mountain areas seeking new thrills and new ways of traveling down mountainsides at great speed.

At the forefront of this search for new thrills were the British, and in 1875 a group of tourists were responsible for the invention of the "Skeleton." The Skeleton took the basic form of a sled with the addition of a sliding seat that would enable the rider to travel down a slope while lying on his or her stomach. The sled could be controlled by shifting the rider's weight on the seat. The Skeleton took the old sled and luge to new speeds, while opening minds to the possibility of new and future forms of downhill travel that would be used primarily for sport.

The first identifiable bobsled was designed in 1886 by Wilson Smith, an Englishman. This idea was advanced by Christian Mathias, a St. Moritz, Switzerland, blacksmith. The bobsled was taking on definite form.

In the early days those brave enough to board these early contraptions had to restrict their runs to the high frozen banks of roads in the Alpine regions. Foremost among these were the Swiss areas surrounding Davos, St. Moritz, Les-Avants-sur-Montreux, Leysin, Murren, and Engelberg. As the bobsled became a more frequent sight, and specific roads were used on a more regular

Success without honor is an unseasoned dish; it will satisfy your hunger, but it won't taste good. ■ JOE PATERNO

basis, organized clubs grew up in the various localities. The first of these was founded in 1896 at St. Moritz, the spiritual home of the bobsled, by Lord Francis Helmsley of Britain.

The use of roads as bobsled runs was far from ideal, and the clubs began to think in terms of purpose-built runs. The first was built by the St. Moritz club in 1903. This first run was 1,600 meters (1,750 yards) long and linked le Parc Badrutt with Celerina. A second run, the Schatzalp, was built in Davos in 1907 and included fifty-one bends. The first national championships were held in Germany at Oberhof, also in 1907, with the winning team receiving a trophy donated by Crown Prince William of Prussia. From these beginnings bobsled clubs grew up in Germany, Romania, and France, as well as Switzerland.

During the early 1920s, there were international moves to organize a winter sports week recognized by the International Olympic Committee as the Winter Olympics. These first Winter Olympics were held at Chamonix in France in 1924 and played host to the first four-man bobsled event. The staging of the games was of vital importance to bobsled as a sport; the International Olympic Committee was the catalyst for the formation of the FIBT, which in turn introduced standardized rules and regulations for bobsledding. The meeting in Chamonix on 31 January 1924, attended by six delegates from six countries, is central to the history of bobsled as it heralded the birth of a modern, regulated, and centrally organized sport.

Growth of Bobsledding

To understand the origins of bobsledding as an organized sport, it is centrally important to understanding the cultural context from which it grew. Essentially, as pointed out earlier, bobsledding emerged from the activities of thrill-seeking Alpine tourists who were searching for a new form of amusement in the snow. This group of people primarily was made up of those wealthy enough to spend part of the winter in places such as St. Moritz. This shows up in the background of those key figures who established bobsled clubs, brought about

the standardization of rules, and established the FIBT. The fact that Count Renaud de la Fregeoliere, Lord Francis Helmsey, and Crown Prince William of Prussia are key figures in the evolution of the sport demonstrates its origins as the pastime of the aristocratic and the wealthy. Equally, the distribution of the seven founding nations of the FIBT—Austria, Belgium, Canada, France, Great Britain, Switzerland, and the United States—says much about its cultural context. These are nations with the social groups who have traditionally wintered in Alpine regions, or they are nations with a tradition of Alpine sports and access to snow, thereby able to host bobsled events. Until World War II, the adoption of bobsled by other nations followed a similar pattern. The nations joining the FIBT were either those with traveling wealthy elites—or those with snow. By 1945 only Argentina, Spain, Italy, Japan, Liechtenstein, Holland, Poland, Romania, and Czechoslovakia had been added to the list of members, and the active participation of some of these nations was at best limited.

Bobsledding as a competitive sport has been dominated by the Winter Olympics. For most spectators who enjoy the sport, the Winter Olympics are the only time it enters their consciousness. Although the FIBT has held World Bobsled Championships every year since 1930, these do not reach the same global audience as do the Olympics. In many ways this reliance on the Winter Olympics has stunted the growth of bobsledding by comparison with other winter sports such as skiing or ice skating, both of which have regular media coverage of their annual national and international championships. The more fundamental problems that have held back wider growth of bobsledding have continued to be the high cost of participation and the limited availability of runs. By 1988 the FIBT recognized nineteen official runs, only three of which, Calgary (Canada), Lake Placid (New York), and Sapporo (Japan) were outside the European Alpine area.

The limited number of bobsled runs, which obviously restricts the chances of training for those competitors who do not have a national run, adds further

to the cost of the sport. At present even a second-hand bobsled will cost up to $25,000. For these reasons the development and spread of the sport has been slowed. In the post–World War II period, the coverage of bobsled events has improved as the media coverage of the Winter Olympics has grown, and it is a highly popular event when it is screened, with its combination of speed, ice, and danger. Despite this popularity, it is not a sport that the viewer or spectator can then go out and try. Therefore, the nations that have joined the FIBT and who have competed in the Winter Olympics over the last are years are, in the main, those nations with access to snow who have come late to the event, or those with a political agenda. Nations such as Andorra, Bulgaria, Sweden, Taipei, Venezuela, and the former Yugoslavia have joined the ranks of bobsled nations as a result of their wider cultural and sporting links with Alpine sports events. The participation of the former German Democratic Republic (since 1973), the former Soviet Union (since 1980), and China (since 1984) has its roots in the sporting agendas of these Communist nations. The competitors from these nations were usually members of the armed forces, and their successes were seen as the glorification of sponsoring Communist regimes. A quirkier spread of bobsled has taken place in the last ten years among nations supporting the Olympic movement but with no background in winter sports, including Australia, Mexico, and Jamaica in recent winter games. These nations have been reliant on private funding, foreign coaches, and huge amounts of travel, as they do not have domestic training facilities.

The sport of bobsledding is still dominated by those nations with a wider cultural background in winter sports. Although the sport has spread and its basic principles are understood worldwide, the bulk of competing nations are still drawn from Western and Central Europe and North America, essentially those nations responsible for the early development of the sport. The picture is much the same with respect to Olympic medals. Of the seven leading medal-winning nations to date, four, Switzerland, the United States, Italy, and

Britain, can date their membership in the FIBT to within three years of its foundation. Of the other three, the former German Democratic Republic, the Federal Republic of Germany, and the former Soviet Union, political considerations were more important than cultural context.

BOBSLEDDING CHANGES ITS RULES

Bobsledding, from an organizational perspective, has been equally dominated by its traditional member nations. Since the foundation of the FIBT in 1923, all the rule changes and sled design alterations have been centrally controlled and agreed on.

The meeting in 1923 to formulate commonly agreed standards formed the basis on which bobsled would operate as a competitive sport. In the first instance, the standard international rules were based on those used by the St. Moritz club and were aimed solely at a four-man bobsled. The four-man bobsled was abandoned in 1928 in favor of one with a five-man team. This experiment only lasted for two years, and the four-man bobsled has existed ever since. The two-man bobsled competition was introduced in 1932, and with the four-man bobsled, it forms the basis of all bobsled competitions. Over the years the rules changed to include new technological developments and to encourage greater safety. These changes included the adoption of amateur status in 1927; the introduction of maximum weight limits for bobsled teams in 1939, 1952, 1966, and 1978; the introduction of a uniform and standard bobsled for all competitors in 1984; and inclusion of women in world competition in the 1990s.

As the FIBT was an all-powerful body that completely controlled the rules of bobsledding since the sport's earliest days, there has been a near total absence of different rules or strategies springing from local cultural or national conditions. All nations that have ever attempted to develop bobsledding as a sport in their own locality have always done so under the aegis of the FIBT. Even those nations (e.g., the United States, Romania, and Italy) that did not have the natural climatic conditions to develop a run, and thus had to turn to artificial runs, did so only after consultation with the FIBT. Likewise, in 1979, when the French Federation was seeking to encourage the growth of bobsledding by going back to the nineteenth-century idea of racing on the road, thereby avoiding the heavy cost of building a run, it did so with the full knowledge and approval of the FIBT.

The first bobsled competition at the Winter Olympics was staged in 1924, as a four-man competition. In 1932 a two-man competition was added. The format of the competition has remained the same. Each bobsled team makes four runs down the course. The course, a chute of packed ice, twists and turns down an incline. The team with the lowest aggregate time is the winner. All internationally recognized runs are between 1,200 and 1,600 meters (1,313 and 1,750 yards) long and the journey to the finish line will be down a gradient of between 8 and 15 percent. The first section of the run lasts for 50 meters and allows team members to push the bob from the start to build up momentum before jumping in. Once the crew is in the bob, the frontman takes control and attempts to keep the bob on the straightest course. The other members sit as low as possible in the bob to offer the least wind resistance, thereby increasing the speed of the bob.

Since the 1950s the weight limits for both competition have been standardized. The four-man bob must not weigh in excess of 630 kilograms (1,389 pounds), and the two-man bob no more than 375 kilograms (827 pounds). By making the weights standard, the rules removed the unfair advantage that heavy teams were having over their lighter competitors. The bob itself is a sectionalized steel structure that is positioned on four blades. The front of the bob is covered with a streamlined plastic cowling, and the whole machine is steered by cables attached to the blades. In 1988 the winning bobsled team at the Winter Olympics covered the four runs over the 1,600-meter course in an aggregate time of 3 minutes, 47.51 seconds. Since the introduction of the bobsled to the Olympics, teams from Germany have won the most medals (27), followed by Switzerland (23) and the United States (16).

Women's Participation

In today's women's races, bobsled teams consist of two people: a brake and a pilot. Although women competed in bobsledding's earliest days, prior to the 1924 inauguration of the sport at the Olympic Games at Chamonix, the FIBT banned women from competing in bobsled. No longer just an enjoyable winter sport for both genders, bobsled now was viewed as an elite sport for men that was too dangerous for women. After Chamonix, women were slowly but surely excluded from all European bobsled events, although they continued, for a time, to compete in the less socially exclusive atmosphere of North America. However, in 1938, after Katherine Dewey had driven her way to victory in the U.S. national championships, women were banned from subsequent bobsled championships by the U.S. Amateur Athletic Union (AAU). In AAU's view, Dewey's win was improper: bobsled was "a man's sport."

For nearly sixty years, women were excluded from organized bobsled racing, denied recognition by FIBT and the organizers of the Olympic Games. They only began competing again on an organized basis in bobsled events during the 1990s. In 1995 women's bobsled was finally recognized by the FIBT, which, with the support of different national bodies, is now campaigning for women's bobsled to be included in the Winter Olympics. It was a demonstration sport at the 2002 Winter Olympics in Salt Lake City, Utah and will become a full Olympic event in the 2006 games at Torino, Italy.

At present an average of twenty women's crews from twelve different nations take part in the FIBT six-race world cup series. The races are held at venues across North America and Europe. The season is a ten-race series at five venues: Calgary, Canada; Salt Lake City, Utah; Igls, Austria; La Plange, France; and Winterberg, Germany.

Bobsledding is expensive. Without the lure of Olympic competition, it has been difficult for many aspiring women's teams to gain the necessary sponsorship to get a bobsled up and running. The combination of the high cost of bobsledding and the discrimination that has kept women out of the Olympics has resulted in a sport with low numbers of women competitors that can survive only through the intervention of state bodies. In Britain, the women's bobsled team is run under the auspices of the Royal Air Force and has charitable status. The women on the team are all serving as members of the air force, without whose help and organization the team would probably not survive.

In many ways the history of women's bobsled has turned full circle. It began as a winter pastime of the social elite. Within such an elite women were allowed to take part, indeed, they were encouraged. Once bobsled was caught up in the machinery of modern sporting organization, women were, as was so often the case with all sports, excluded. The last few years have seen the reintroduction of organized women's bobsled, but the prohibitive costs make it once more socially exclusive or charity-dependent. Although it is an immensely popular television spectacle during the Winter Olympics, bobsled is most unlikely to become a mass participation sport. Within such a rarefied and elite context, women will have to continue the fight for an equal right to compete . It is hoped that the first Winter Olympiads of the twenty-first century will make it possible for women bobsledders to compete equally with men, as they did late in the nineteenth century.

Outlook

Bobsledding is an excellent example of a sport that grew from rudimentary forms of travel and leisure, the sled and the luge. Its growth was initially inspired by specific climatic conditions and patronized by a wealthy elite searching for new forms of entertainment. Once the sport had taken a definable form, its organization, regulation, and growth were centrally controlled by a single international body that has never been challenged by other cultural practices or traditions. Bobsledding, due to its expense and its climatic requirements has, despite some growth, remained dominated by the countries of the original areas where the sport was taken up and by athletes from a similar class as its inventors. One chal-

lenge to this had come in the Cold War era as political concerns led some former Soviet bloc nations to take to the sport by entering athletes drawn from their armed services. Additionally, there has been some participation by non-Alpine nations. The spectator base for bobsledding is still primarily drawn from those who have an interest in Alpine sports, but because of the thrill of the sport, the high speeds, the potential for accidents, and the romance of snow and ice, bobsledding, especially during the Winter Olympics, always attracts a large television audience.

Mike Cronin

Further Reading

Federation Internationale de Bobsleigh et de Tobaganning. (1984). Bobsleigh and Olympism. *Olympic Review, 206,* 1003–1030.

Kotter, K. (1984, June). Le bobsleigh et la federation internationale de bobsleigh et de tobogganing. *Message-Olympique,* 59–66.

Mallon, B. (1992). On two blades and a few prayers. *Olympian, 18*(6), 54–55.

O'Brien, A., & O'Bryan, M. (1976). *Bobsled and luge.* Toronto, Canada: Colban.

Body Image

Body image is the perception that an individual has of what he or she looks like. An individual's body image is a response to his or her own physical features and personal experiences and to the social values that form standards of appearance against which one evaluates the body. Sport and exercise affect body image in a number of ways:

- The sportsperson's body is often viewed as the standard of appearance to which the greater population should aspire. This may result in the belief that marked muscularity in men, or thinness in women, is a reasonable expectation for nonathletic individuals.
- Sports and physical activity may be credited with helping to achieve the perfect body and thus are an

I like thinking big. If you're going to be thinking anything,
you might as well think big. ■ DONALD TRUMP

important component of people's beliefs about self-discipline and its affect on the body. Carried to excess, however, this can result in unhealthy approaches to exercise that are related to oppressive standards of normative appearance.

■ By engaging in sports and wearing sporting gear, individuals are commonly required to reveal parts of their bodies that are otherwise hidden. This means that the sportsperson's body is on display, subjected to the gaze of others, which potentially provides social control over that person's behavior.

Body Image and Social Control

Standards of appearance and critical self-scrutiny are pivotal elements of social control in Western society because of the importance of sight in making sense of the world. Vision gives us the power to assess far more than simple physique; Western culture credits vision with being able to uncover truths about the moral fiber or the true nature of those things we see. This creates the notion that appearance reflects inner truths and is strongly grounded in both religious and popular texts. The Greek New Testament, for example, uses the words *beauty* and *goodness* interchangeably. Similarly, Baldassar Castiglione, the author of a sixteenth-century courtesy book, wrote,

Whereupon doth very seldom an ill soule dwell in a beautifull bodie. And therefore is the outwarde beautie a true signe of the inwarde goodnesse, and in bodies this comeliness is imprinted more and lesse (as it were) for a marke of the soule, whereby she is outwardly known. (1561/1948, 309)

This historical link between appearance and inner values is also apparent in educational treatises that advise parents to choose a governess on the basis of her looks: "If a teacher's face reflects in her traits the character of a pure and virtuous heart, the child in her turn will reflect this as well, and a simple glance at the teacher will suffice to fulfill her and produce the happiest of impressions," wrote the Abbé Balme-Frézol in 1859. The emphasis on visual truths was present in

physiognomic work, which linked character traits to body features; in anthropometry, which attempted to find racial, criminal, and psychiatric trends in the size and proportion of bodies; in portraiture, where mottos and captions associated moral values with physical representations; and remains present, particularly in health discourses, where aesthetics (body size, hair and skin color and tone, and a certain degree of muscularity) are often indicators of well-being, fitness, and happiness.

Appearance becomes an important mechanism of social control because of the presumed link between the outward show of the body and the inner nature of an individual. The idea that we can be seen and that people can make assumptions about who we are by looking at us is the foundation for the importance that people give to their body images.

In describing the panopticon, Michel Foucault theorized that the concept of being seen, or the possibility of being seen, is an important controlling factor in social behavior. The panopticon was an architectural design for prisons, in which prisoners would be housed in a circular edifice with cells on the outside that created shadows on the internal tower where the guard was stationed. Because of the shadows cast by their own cells, prisoners could not determine whether a guard was actually in the tower. As a result, the prisoners would moderate their behavior as if they were being guarded, without a guard necessarily being present. Applied to appearance, the panopticon principle captures the idea that people internalize standards of physical presentation and looks and discipline themselves to attain these standards. Contemporary standards of body size, shape, feature, and dress are formulated through technologically and socially mediated representations of elusive perfection, which can be difficult, if not impossible to attain. Thus, appearance can serve as an oppressive and constraining form of social control.

Body of the Sportsperson

Today, the ideal body is often projected to be that of the sportsperson. Muscle development, sun-exposed skin, and leanness are valued as evidence of disciplined and

The muscled back of a bodybuilder.
Source: istockphoto/blende64.

organizational feature of Western society, and traditionally gendered sporting bodies are held in the highest esteem. Traditional gender values cast men as strong and muscular and women as slight and malleable. Both of these images, however, may be cultivated in, and maintained by, a range of sporting practices.

Sport has been, and continues to be, considered a proving ground for teaching male social values. Ball games, as we know them today, were introduced in Great Britain in nineteenth-century boys' public schools, which rationalized sport as a means for instilling muscular Christianity and for teaching young men from the new industrial middle class how to be gentlemen. Sport was also projected as an antidote to the perceived feminization of sedentary urban lifestyles—thus, a sporting body confirmed masculinity. Exercise rejuvenates virility, wrote early twentieth-century physical and exercise culturists. Hence, the male sporting body chosen as a normative standard is one that demonstrates muscularity and strength.

In contrast, sport served a different role in female gender identity for classifying sport and integrating physical activity in the educational setting. Woman's role as nurturer and domestic partner resulted in sport emphasizing grace and malleability. Today, this is evidenced in a standard of femininity that suggests a prepubescent form. The endurance athlete model of runner or aerobics instructor embodies social values about how women should appear: slight yet disciplined. This image of slenderness also includes, as Carol Spitzack describes, appropriate skin coloring, muscle conditioning, facial structure, and an absence of facial lines or "defective" features.

healthy virtue. The body resembling that of the sportsperson is thus endowed with values of virtuous self-care and discipline, conveying important messages about the potential for self-improvement and inner control. This is not unproblematic, however. Although physical activity is appropriately touted as an important component of health, sporting activity seeks more than just health; it seeks athletic performance. Thus, the amount of physical activity required to enhance health does not normally affect the body's appearance in the same manner as does the intensity of sport training.

Not all sporting bodies are considered the standard to which people should aspire. Gender remains a strong

The traditionally gendered sporting bodies result in a particular form of tension. Sportspeople are successful, and their bodies held as the normative standard because they do not challenge the traditional order. The body of the strong and muscular sportswoman is not coveted in the same manner as is that of her endurance-sport counterpart. The male body with highly developed muscles and bulk is selectively highlighted as the masculine standard rather than the frame of the small male dancer, gymnast, or jockey. Cultural fears about strong and independent women and graceful and sensitive men can translate into both healthy and unhealthy activities that focus on creating an appearance aligned with traditional gender expectations. This may result in women engaging in dieting and endurance aerobic activities to cultivate a slender feminine body and in men focusing on weights and power-development exercises.

Both men and women may flock to sport as a means for cultivating the perfect body, but this can also result in a state of angst relative to the elusive goal. Sports practices mandate unveiling the body, by wearing sports clothes, and the assimilation of sporting practices. Weight and aerobics training often takes place in front of full-length wall mirrors, with sleeveless jerseys, skin tight Lycra, and short pants. Skin-fold calipers, scales, and measuring tapes are used in the gym environment to assess progress toward fitness goals, and the sportsperson subjects himself or herself to the public gaze in sporting events and to self-scrutiny in training. The result of this focus on the external can result in destructive behaviors, especially when there is a misfit between how a person perceives his or her body and the normative standards of appearance.

This can be seen in the training methods and eating patterns known as the female triad—young women engage in restrictive and controlled eating patterns while engaging in excessive endurance training. The result of this behavior is seriously reduced bone density, which significantly affects the women's future health. Risk factors for this inordinate focus on the control and management of body weight by these young women include many of the frequent practices associated with sport, including weigh-ins, punishment by coaches for weight gain, the presumed association of performance and leanness, and social isolation.

Sportswomen are not alone in suffering from body image pressures in the sporting environment. The popularity displaying the muscular male body creates a hypermasculine aesthetic that affects general male attitudes toward appearance and self-culture. Hypermasculinity is the exaggeration of those traits thought to be associated with masculine identity, such as determination, energy, and independence. The pursuit of the hypermasculine body is often associated with insecurity about sex-role identity. An increase in dissatisfaction with the shape or size of the body has resulted in practices including body obsession, eating disorders, and steroid use. Contemporary consumer capitalism is also driving the new preoccupation with male appearance. In late twentieth century, men's fitness and beauty culture has blossomed with fashion magazines and representations of the eroticized male body. Images of the male body are skillfully used for consumer appeal and are featured in a range of advertisements, from underwear to sound systems, cologne to beer, that highlight the muscular male body as a strong and challenging individual. Male insecurity about appearance is a new goldmine for the diet, exercise, cosmetic surgery, and drug industries, which previously targeted an exclusively female clientele.

Body image need not relate only to oppression and constraint, however. The idea that the body can betray the inner self, revealing deeply grounded deficiencies, sits in uneasy disharmony with the idea that the self can control the body and make it conform to an appearance that fairly represents the self, but other meanings can be associated with the body. As third-wave feminists point out, understanding is empowering. The image of, and search for, the perfect body is not innately oppressive; rather, the power relations embodied within these images have the potential to subjugate people. Exercise culture and its discourses do not have only one unique, fixed, and essential meaning. Exercise practices can focus on choice and enjoyment rather than on fine-tuning inner virtue with appearance and, thus, can simultaneously contain the potential to be fulfilling, fun, and liberating. Exercise can also offer important health and psychological benefits, some of which may indeed be incidentally associated with changes in appearance. Ultimately, exercise, like many other contemporary practices has, through its potential to transform, the ability to both liberate and to constrain.

Annemarie Jutel

See also Beauty; Feminist Perspective

Further Reading

Bordo, S. (2000). Beauty (re)discovers the male body. In Peg Zeglin Brand (Ed.), *Beauty matters.* Bloomington: Indiana University Press.

Castiglione, B. (1561/1948). *The book of the courtier.* Trans. Sir Thomas Hoby. London: J.M Dent.

Klein, A. (1993). *Little big men: Bodybuilding subculture and gender construction.* Albany: State University of New York Press.

Spitzack, C. (1990). *Confessing excess: Women and the politics of body reduction.* Albany: State University of New York Press, 1990.

Bodybuilding

Bodybuilding is exercising with weights to reshape the physique including the addition of muscle mass along with separating and defining the various muscle groups. Male and female bodybuilders display their physiques on the competitive stage in a series of mandatory poses and through a routine of poses choreographed to music; they are judged on their symmetry, muscle density, and definition. Whether practiced by men or women, bodybuilding is both a competitive performance sport and a lifestyle. Women began entering the male-defined spaces of gyms in the 1970s as a result of the health and fitness movement of the era that subsequently snowballed into a huge industry in the 1980s. By 1990, *Time Magazine* proclaimed: "Work that Body! Fewer curves, more muscles: a sweat-soaked revolution redefines the shape of beauty... Across the country, women are working out, ... even pumping iron" (Donnelly 1990, 68).

Female bodybuilders differ from women who resistance train by the subcultural context of their experience that includes competition as a significant self-identifying feature. Robert Duff and Lawrence Hong conducted a study of 205 women bodybuilders registered with the International Federation of Bodybuilders (one of several bodybuilding organizations), and found that 74 percent were active competitors, while many of the others were either anticipating their first competition or were temporarily sidelined due to injury.

Bodybuilding competitions for men and women may look fairly similar in format, but the process, the competition, and the milieu, represent different cultural domains in Euro-American society. Men's bodybuilding is a sport that reproduces and amplifies Western beliefs about the differences between men and women. Muscles signify masculinity in Western culture, and they testify to the belief that these differences are primarily based on biology.

A different cultural agenda is represented by women's bodybuilding. The female bodybuilder is in a position to do just the opposite, to challenge bioreductivist views that place biology at the center of male–female differences. The female competitor's body is a statement of rebellion against this view, a way of contributing to the wider redefinition of womanhood and femininity underway in Euro-American society. Women who are bodybuilders challenge the Western view of women as the weaker sex; instead they live and embody a femininity that includes strength and muscularity.

History

The first bodybuilding competition for men was staged in 1901 and established a history with unbroken continuity. Although women's bodybuilding followed closely in 1903; it was discontinued in 1905 and did not reappear in its modern form until 1975. The physique exhibitions of the music halls and theaters of the "strongman era" of the 1800s are, however, part of the ancestry of modern competitive bodybuilding for both women and men.

The mid to late 1800s were a period in which strongmen and muscular display provided the roots for the physical culture movement that branched out into various sports. This variety notwithstanding, the movement maintained some continuity through the late 1930s, when men's physique contests started to become their own distinctive form of athletic contest. As discussed below, it was not until forty-five years later that modern women's competitions were initiated.

MEN'S HISTORY AND DEVELOPMENT OF MEN'S COMPETITIONS

The mid-nineteenth century health-reform movement with its emphasis on exercise was the springboard for the physical-culture movement. This was initially expressed in American and European popular culture as the strongman and physique showman era, buttressed by a developing industry associated with resistance and weight training, including equipment, programs, and the expertise of professionals. The growth of the fitness industry was linked with broader trends of an emerging middle class, increasing urbanism, and attendant concerns regarding the effects of increasing sendentarism. The strength and health elements of physical culture also appealed to the flood of immigrants to America in the early 1900s. Many occupied blue-collar positions that demanded sheer physical wherewithal as well. Into this milieu stepped Eugene Sandow, who first displayed his well-sculpted physique to Americans at the 1893 Chicago World's Fair after training with his mentor, former strongman Professor Attila Brussels. Sandow was able to capitalize and give impetus to a new Euro-American cult of masculinity that emphasized exercise, weight training, and an embodied health and physicality. Having gained British acclaim, his career skyrocketed in America and he became the masculine ideal for American men. His good looks, muscular physique, and great strength were coupled with an entrepreneurial genius that flourished in America and upon his subsequent return to England. He not only operated an active mail-order business and physical culture studios, but he invented and sold exercise equipment, published and founded the first bodybuilding magazine *Physical Culture* (1898), and promoted exercise for women. In 1901, he promoted the first bodybuilding competition,

---

🏃 Bodybuilding

Don't Give Up

In his book Brother Iron, Sister Steel, *Dave Draper—a former Mr. America, Mr. Universe and Mr. World—offers the following caution to other bodybuilders:*

The uncomfortable truth is too many of those who venture to the fields of iron and steel give up, quit, abandon the glorious task too soon to realize the sub-surface bounty of exercise, good eating and training. The qualities they lacked to keep them going were amongst the qualities they were about to discover.

Source: Draper, D. (2001). *Brother iron, sister steel.* Aptos, CA: On Target Publications.

---

called the Great Competition in the Royal Albert Hall in London. His criterion for judging was remarkably modern, emphasizing balanced muscularity over total muscular size (Bolin 1996, Chapman 1994; Todd 1991).

In America, Bernarr Macfadden, a contemporary of Sandow who was, in fact, greatly inspired by him, was also extremely successful in translating physical culture into a successful business. He published magazines on physical culture, including *Physical Development* (1898), and like Sandow, his business flourished though an array of enterprises including health studios, physical culture clubs, personal appearances, lectures, books, the sales of home exercise equipment, and the promotion of strength and physique exhibitions and contests. He also was an advocate for women's physical fitness. Macfadden may be credited with sponsoring the first major American bodybuilding contest in 1903 that was undoubtedly modeled on Sandow's 1901 Great Competition. His contest gained notoriety in that it also included the world's first women's bodybuilding contests from 1903–1905.

Macfadden's contest was based on a system of qualification through regional contests as a prelude to a national competition selecting the most perfect man in the United States. It became an annual event that continued through the 1920s and 1930s. Following Sandow, his contests emphasized that the winner's physiques were selected on the basis of a balanced, proportional and symmetrical muscular development. It was Macfadden's 1921 physique contest that gave America a glimpse of its first American bodybuilding media personality, Charles Atlas, aka Angelo Siciliano, who was hailed as the "Most Perfectly Developed Man in America" (Klein 1993).

Through the efforts of Macfadden and those who followed him, by the 1930s physique contests had gained in popularity so that the Amateur Athletic Union began integrating bodybuilding as a part of its weight-lifting competitions. The first Amateur Athletic Union (AAU) national contest titled "America's Best Built Man" was held in 1939 and subsequently became known as the "Mr. America." Despite the popularity of associating physique competitions with demonstration of athletic expertise and strength, this was a period in which the idea of the physique competitor as a distinctive form became emergent.

As more national contests followed, men's bodybuilding grew economically and in the consciousness of the American imagination, attracting a unique athlete whose interests were in celebration of the muscular physique. The development of physique competition was given impetus through the Californian Muscle Beach phenomenon. From the 1930s through the 1950s Muscle Beach thrived in its original location in Santa Monica but in the 1950s it relocated to Venice Beach. Muscle Beach included some of the most famous names in bodybuilding and fitness history, including Jack La Lanne, Joe Gold, John Grimek and Pudy and Les Stockton among many others.

The history of bodybuilding from the 1940s through the 1960s is intimately tied to the incremental hegemony of the International Federation of Bodybuilders (IFBB) controlled by Joe and Ben Weider over the AAU's incipient domination of the sport of bodybuilding, spearheaded by Bob Hoffman. The 1960s has come to be regarded as the Golden Age of bodybuilding. This is attributed in part to the flourishing of Venice Beach bodybuilding culture as well as the creation of the first professional bodybuilding title in 1965: the IFBB Mr. Olympia. The last twenty years have witnessed the continued professionalization of the sport, the full incorporation of women's bodybuilding and the development of "natural bodybuilding" as a distinctive venue. Bodybuilding however, still remains a somewhat specialized sport with a following of beloved female and male "muscleheads" and gym rats.

Women's Bodybuilding History

Health reform in the mid-nineteenth century combined with early feminism to promote the novel idea that exercise was healthful for women and that women's muscles could be beautiful. This was contrary to the dominant white middle-class notion of femininity as fragile and ethereal, the embodiment of which was enhanced by the custom of tightly laced corsets that continued through the turn of the century. Health reform and feminism made some inroads, but women remained hesitant to exercise for fear of losing their "natural" curves (created by tight lacing) and developing muscular bodies. Then, in the late nineteenth century and early twentieth century, beauty standards evolved to include the athletic aesthetic of the "Gibson Girl."

It was in this milieu in the first part of the twentieth century that Eugene Sandow began to bring women into his physical culture enterprises. Sandow challenged prevailing views of the passive and frail woman, and he was extremely critical of corsets. He promoted an idea of a femininity that included strength and exercise for all women to bring them good health and cure illness. Similarly Bernarr MacFadden saw an opportunity to include women in his enterprises. In 1889 MacFadden began to publish *Physical Culture*, a periodical, in the United States and his second issue contained his first articles on women's health and exercise.

Macfadden was a strong advocate for the benefits of exercise for women. He founded the first women's magazine, *Women's Physical Development,* in 1900, and changed the name in 1903 to *Beauty and Health: Women's Physical Development.* In addition, Macfadden may have been the first to sponsor a women's physique

Cheryl Sumner is a national-level competitor with aspirations to turn professional.

Source: Cheryl Sumner.

competition, a precedent to modern women's body-building competitions: From 1903 to 1905 he held local and regional physique competitions that finished with a grand competition, where the "best and most perfectly formed woman" won a prize.

Macfadden, however, fell prey to his own success. His cultivation of women's physique competitions inadvertently stopped the sport until the 1970s. In 1905, shortly before his Madison Square Garden Mammoth Physical Culture Exhibition that included the finale of the women's competition, Macfadden's office was raided by Anthony Comstock of the Society for the Suppression of Vice. Comstock accused Macfadden of pandering pornography. Included among the alleged pornographic materials that Comstock acquired in his raid were posters of the finalists of the women's physique competition who were dressed in white form-fitting leotard-like exercise wear.

Publicity about Macfadden's subsequent arrest and the decision that he was indeed dealing in pornography was an advertisement that attracted even more specta-

tors. The Mammoth Physical Culture Exhibition had an audience of 20,000 and turned away 5,000 more. That was, however, the end of his enterprise.

Music halls and circuses of the late nineteenth century and early twentieth century were also venues for displays of women's physiques. This was the era in which very large and muscular strongwomen displayed their strength. One muscular diva was Sandwina, who performed with the Barnum and Bailey Circus in 1910. Standing six feet one inch, and weighing 209 pounds, she could jerk 280 pounds over her head and was able to carry her husband over her head using one arm. Another strongwoman, Vulcana (Katie Roberts) continued to perform through the 1940s, but no real audience for strongwomen developed until the final two decades of the nineteenth century and first two of the twentieth century.

According to Jan Todd, the 1920s and 1930s brought in wider societal acceptance of a new fit and slender physical ideal for women in contrast to the sheer size and mass of the "Amazon-like" strongwomen such as Sandwina, Minerva, Madame Montagna and others who weighed in at over two hundred pounds. It is Santa Monica's Abbye ("Pudgy") Eville Stockton who may be given credit as a central figure in popularizing a new embodiment of femininity as strong and fit dovetailing with America's war effort. She was a regular in the developing Muscle Beach mecca of physical culture displaying her strength and athleticism through weightlifting and acrobatics. Her athletic figure coupled with her striking looks made her a national figure. She may be seen as America's first fitness model. She promoted products and graced the covers of forty-two magazines. In 1944 she began writing a regular column for women on the benefits of weightlifting for Bob Hoffman's *Strength and Health* magazine that appeared for just under a decade. Indeed Bob Hoffman was one of the first promoters of women's weightlifting in the 1930s. John D. Fair maintains that he did more "than any other promoter to advance the concept of weight training for women" throughout his career as physical culture

business maven and Olympic coach. However as a sport, women's bodybuilding is distinct from weight lifting and power lifting.

Two major influences in the development of women's bodybuilding were the 1950s reintroduction of resistance training for women athletes and the feminist movement of the 1960s. Throughout the 1940s weight training by women athletes was at the individual level; however the 1950s ushered in an era in which national and Olympic athletic teams began using weight training in their respective sports. Resistance training for women in general gained a large following in the 1970s, as the fitness industry exploded. Health clubs and spas enticed women by offering aerobics classes, selling fashionable athletic attire, and providing color-coordinated locker rooms with amenities such as blow dryers and curling irons.

Hardcore bodybuilding gyms distinguished themselves symbolically from these health clubs and spas in the 1970s and 1980s through cultural features associated with the masculine such as a "no frills" atmosphere. In its infancy in the 1970s to early 1980s, women's bodybuilding began to find a home in the hardcore gyms where men trained, and became part of the history of bodybuilding as it moved from these gyms into the scientific and contemporary pavilions of nutrition and training of today. As Tom Platz, Mr. Universe 1978, reminisces, "Prior to 1983, the gym was a man's sanctuary...[t]here was also just a handful of girls who trained in those days." In the new millennium, few of these "hard core" bastions of bodybuilding survive, having been replaced by contemporary chains such as Gold's Gym.

Development of Women's Bodybuilding Competitions

Since its inception in the 1970s, the sport of women's bodybuilding has been transformed from one in which the competitors wore high heels and rarely performed muscular poses such as the iconic front double biceps with closed fists, which were discouraged. These bodybuilding contests were accused of being nothing more than beauty pageants. The seeds of early women's bodybuilding lie in the occasional beauty body contest held during men's bodybuilding events. For example, a Ms. Body Beautiful competition was held during the 1973 World Bodybuilding Guild Mr. America Championships, and the Miss America was held during the Mr. Olympia at the Brooklyn Academy of Music. It was not until the 1980s that women's bodybuilding contests were legitimized as competitions in their own right, not just as auxiliaries for male competitions. The first Miss (now Ms.) Olympia, regarded as the zenith of women's bodybuilding titles, was held in 1980 and set the standard for women's international and professional titles that continues today.

Through the 1980s, 1990s and the new millennium bodybuilding continues to grow as a sport and as big business. The women competitors have, over time, achieved degrees of muscularity, symmetry, and definition once believed impossible for women to achieve. Nevertheless, since its beginnings, women bodybuilders have been involved in a debate over the issue of muscularity and femininity.

Bodybuilding Organizations

Women's competitive bodybuilding is entrenched in men's bodybuilding organizationally. No separate women's organizations exist today, although in the early 1980s, Doris Barrilleaux founded and was president of the American Federation of Women Bodybuilders. Barrilleaux may be credited as the parent of women's bodybuilding. At the age of forty-seven Barrilleaux began competing in what purported to be women's physique contests, but were in reality beauty pageants. Her disaffection with these contests and her vision of women's bodybuilding, which featured muscular development, led her to establish the Superior Physique Association and to publish the *SPA News*, a newsletter for women bodybuilders in 1979. As early as 1983, Barrilleaux lobbied the International Federation of Bodybuilders to test the women competitors for illicit performance-enhancing drugs. Currently, the NPC and

The mind is the limit. As long as the mind can envision the fact that you can do something,
you can do it as long as you really believe 100 percent. ■ ARNOLD SCHWARZENEGGER

the IFBB have women's representatives as do some of the self-identified natural bodybuilding organizations such as the Organization of Competitive Bodybuilders.

Prominent organizations are the International Federation of Bodybuilders (IFBB, www.ifbb.com) and the National Physique Committee (NPC, www.getbig.com), founded by Ben and Joe Weider. The Amateur Athletic Union (AAU, www.aausports.org) was involved early on in bodybuilding, holding its first Mr. America Contest in 1939. Bob Hoffman played a major role in the development of American bodybuilding through his influence on the AAU. For nearly two decades, the AAU and the IFBB competed for control of muscledom. By the 1990s, the IFBB was able to claim hegemony over the sport although other organizations continue to hold competitions such as the National Amateur Bodybuilders Association (NABBA, www.nabba.com), an international organization with fifty active nations, making it the second largest organization for bodybuilders worldwide. The AAU dropped the physique competitions from their venue at the end of 1999, although some AAU competitions have been revived.

The 1990s also brought the establishment of organizations targeted to drug-free athletes, as well as the promotion of drug-free shows by existing organizations, such as the NPC (amateur), and IFBB (international and professional), from the local to the international level. Since the 1980s, a burgeoning of natural/drug-tested organizations has occurred in part because the public has become more aware of anabolic steroid use among athletes in general. There are over twenty extant natural drug-tested organizations such as the World Natural Bodybuilding Federation (WNBF, www.wnbf.net), which sponsors professional-level bodybuilding shows with affiliates at the amateur level including the International Natural Bodybuilding and Fitness Federation and the North American Natural Bodybuilding Federation, NABBA International and its affiliates, the United States Bodybuilding Federation, and Natural Bodybuilding Incorporated, among others. The drug-tested organizations and competitions are international

in scope. The WNBF includes a number of country affiliates including South Africa, Great Britain, Japan, Switzerland, and Germany. In 2002, the IFBB has formulated its anti-doping program for the Amateur Division following International Olympic Committee and World Anti-Doping Agency banned substances and methods protocols (IFBB 2002). The NPC also offers specified competitions that require drug tests.

This anti-doping program is part of a broader IFBB strategy to eventually gain Olympic status for bodybuilding. According it the IFBB president Ben Weider, "the overall goal of the IFBB is to gain Olympic participation." In 1986 and 1987 doping controls were implemented at the World Amateur Bodybuilding Championships for men and women respectively and subsequently at all IFBB amateur events. Currently, the General Association of International Sports Federations (GAISF) recognizes the IFBB as the only International Sport Governing Body (ISGB) for the sport of bodybuilding.

Muscularity/Femininity Debate

The debate over masculinity and femininity continues in women's bodybuilding. The basic question is: how muscular can a woman be and still be feminine? From the beginning of women's bodybuilding in the late 1970s the women athletes were confronted with this dilemma. They wanted to be taken seriously as athletes and despite their muscularity, they wanted to maintain their femininity. In 1979, after winning the first major women's bodybuilding competition, Lisa Lyon stated, "women can be strong, muscular and at the same time feminine." And female bodybuilders today still echo this concern. Kim Chizevsky, the 1998 Ms. Olympia, declared that "People need to start changing their views about women bodybuilders. We're strong muscular women, but we're beautiful feminine women too."

Although the debate over femininity and muscularity was inflamed by anabolic steroid use among women competitors, this debate actually existed prior to the reported use of steroids among competitors. This debate

Bodybuilding

Anne Bolin, Bodybuilder

I have been competing in bodybuilding since 1988 when I started at the tender age of 39. When I saw the movie in 1987 by Gains and Butler, *Pumping Iron II: the Women,* I knew I wanted to study bodybuilding because I have an academic interest in gender transgression; and at that time, what could be more subversive, than women with muscles. Bev Francis particularly captured my imagination through her magnificent musculature (way ahead of her time), athletic determination and her spirit for adventure. I had never lifted weights much less ever entered a gym in my whole life. I started lifting weights because I am an anthropologist, and our primary method is participant-observation also known as ethnography. Shortly after watching *Pumping Iron II,* I began the process of immersion in the subculture of bodybuilding in order to research it. You might say I have "gone native," that is, I became who I studied. I think this just adds to my anthropological understanding of the phenomenon of bodybuilding. I love training and competing and I have no intention of retiring from competition any time soon.

My titles include:

- First Place Lightweight. The 1989 Colorado State Championships
- Overall Champion and First Place Short Class in the Women's Grand Masters Division (50 and over). North Carolina State Bodybuilding Championships, 1999, AAU
- First Place Senior Grand Masters (50 and Over) and Best Senior Grand Masters Poser. The American Natural Bodybuilding Association North Carolina Supernatural 2000, ANBA
- First Place Senior Masters Over 50. The SI-Flex 2001 Masters Universe Bodybuilding Championships, NPA
- Second Place Quincy Roberts NPC North Carolina Junior and Masters State Bodybuilding Championships Women's Masters 45 and older

I am a mature competitor. What I love about the performance sport of bodybuilding is its democracy, anyone at any age with the determination and love of training can compete in a bodybuilding show. If you have the desire to compete, age need not be a barrier.

Anne Bolin

surfaced in the infancy of women's bodybuilding when Gloria Miller Fudge first kicked off her high heels. It arose again when Cammie Lusko, in the 1980 Miss Olympia, presented a "hardcore muscular routine," using poses associated with men's bodybuilding in displaying her muscularity; she drove the audience wild, but didn't even place in the competition.

That women bodybuilders at elite levels have been becoming more muscular has been attributed by some to the increasing sophistication of anabolic steroid use and other doping technologies. In the early days, however, women did not commonly use steroids, yet the debate over muscles and femininity was well underway as a discourse.

Between 1980 and 1989, the sport of bodybuilding as epitomized in the Ms. Olympia contest deferred to

society's view of femininity. The judges selected athletic, slim, and graceful women, reflected in the embodiments of Rachel McLish and Cory Everson, as opposed to the more muscular physiques of competitors such as Bev Francis. The debate over the direction the sport would take was resolved with the retirement of Cory Everson in 1989. Cory Everson, six-time Ms. Olympia champion, was not known for having a great deal of muscle mass but was said to embody the perfect combination of symmetry, muscularity, and femininity.

In 1990 Lenda Murray won the Ms. Olympia over Bev Francis, known as a woman whose muscle mass had been way ahead of its time. Francis, who had the year before trimmed her physique down to be competitive with Everson, lost to the heavily muscled Murray because she was not muscular enough. The following year Francis muscled up again but came in second to Murray in the 1991 Olympia because this time the judges felt she was too muscular. Francis subsequently retired, and the 1992 Olympia became the stage on which the debate was resolved in favor of muscularity. Lenda Murray won yet again and remained undefeated until the even more muscular but also ultra-ripped (lean) and hard, Kim Chizevsky claimed the title in 1996 and continued to hold through 1998; retiring in that year from bodybuilding to go into fitness competitions. This trend for increasing muscle mass is illustrated in the increasing body weights of the competitors: In 1983 the average weight of the Ms. Olympia contenders was 121 pounds while in 1997 it was 155 pounds.

Although steroids and other doping techniques may play a role in enhanced muscularity, other factors have accelerated progress in both men and women bodybuilders. The competitors have been training over a longer period of time; their muscles have matured, and the sport has enjoyed an explosion in scientific research on training techniques, nutrition, and supplements.

Also caught in the muscularity/femininity debate are judging standards, known in the bodybuilding community to be unstable; even as the emphasis on muscularity seemed to be predominant, the female bodybuilder was often required to maintain a seemingly ineffable quality of femininity that was never defined or clearly articulated in the judging criteria.

During the period of Kim Chizevsky's reign, professional women bodybuilders have shown they were willing to take their physiques up a notch, getting bigger and harder in the course of two years in the Ms. Olympia. However in 2000, after the near cancellation of the Ms. Olympia in 1999 and reduction in prize money at 1998 Ms. Olympia, the IFBB offered new rules in January 2000 for judging that would include the women's face and makeup. In addition, women would be judged on "symmetry, presentation, separations and muscularity, but not to the extreme." Bill Dobbins, bodybuilding journalist, social critic, and advocate of women's bodybuilding, argues that women body-

builders are victims of their own success; that is, they are just too good at building muscle. Chizevsky set what could be perceived by the IFBB as a dangerous precedent achieving a size and harness that had never been equaled on a bodybuilding stage.

To buttress the new direction for women's bodybuilding, the IFBB reorganized the Ms. Olympia to include both a lightweight and a heavy weight title in 2000 and in 2001 introduced an overall title pitting the light and heavy weight winners against one another. From 2000 to present, the impact of the new judging standards has been represented in the physiques of the winners. In the 2001 Ms. Olympia, Juliette Bergmann came out of retirement after her last competition in 1989 to win the overall title with an aesthetic and softer look than her competition. And in 2002 Lenda Murray returned to the Ms. Olympia stage after a five-year hiatus to capture the crown and win her seventh Ms. Olympia against Juliette Bergmann, with a repeat performance in 2003. Murray is known for having the complete package of symmetry and proportion as well as the "cover girl" beauty that guarantees the endorsement success of so many women athletes in the contemporary world of commodification.

As a sport, women's bodybuilding rebels against traditional notions of femininity and in doing so, contributes to a broader, ongoing redefinition of femininity and womanhood in society today. Bodybuilding as a sport symbolically sustains traditional images of masculinity as associated with strength and power embodied in the ideal of the male bodybuilder. Images of this body type signify youth, health, sexual virility, and power. Arnold Schwarzenegger illustrated this in his dialogue in the movie *Pumping Iron*, where he directly links pumping up the muscles to male sexual arousal and orgasm. Competitive women's bodybuilding blurs gender differences. This occurs not only through the muscularity of the competitive women bodybuilder, but also in the subculture of bodybuilding itself where gender is enacted in the gym. In these less public spheres, serious athletes are serious athletes regardless of gender.

Bodybuilding Rules and Play

Women and men are judged by the same criteria, although femininity is an issue in the judging process for women. In assessing competitors' physiques, judges rely on three primary criteria. These include the depth and development of muscularity; symmetry, or the proportions of the body parts/muscle groups in relation to one another (for example, shoulder width and muscularity in relationship to waist and thighs); and definition generally characterized as the degree of visibility of muscle striations and separation, leanness, and general hardness of the body. Related to this is the visibility of veins and the thinness or transparency of the skin, called vascularity.

Bodybuilders strive to achieve muscular size and density as well as make their body more symmetrical through development of various muscle groups. To do so, they follows a rigorous training plan and a strategy for continual improvement. Preparation for contests includes disciplined dieting, training, attention to nutrition, posing practice, and the preparation of a choreographed posing routine.

In the subculture of bodybuilding, muscular development and definition are not regarded as qualities that belong exclusively to men or women. The difference between the two genders is one of degree, not kind. Thus, bodybuilders do not consider muscles a physical symbol of masculinity, but rather a generic quality available to humans. Seriousness and training hard are the badges of those who are members of the subculture.

At the local, state, and national levels, competitions consist of two segments. In the morning or pre-judging portion, the majority of the judging decisions are made. The judges rank the competitors in each class usually from first to third and sometimes fifth place for trophies. In the evening show, usually the first five bodybuilders in each class are judged again and these scores are added into prejudging scores. Following this, the winners of each class compete against each for the overall title. The overall winners are selected in night shows (bodybuilding contests are also referred to as shows because of their performance aspect) as the winner of each class competes for the overall title. The trophies are given in the evening show. National and international competitions, both professional and amateur, may have different agendas. For example, professionals in the International Federation of Bodybuilders are typically judged in three rounds based on symmetry, muscularity, and posing ability, as displayed in the choreographed posing routine and a "posedown" round. Posing ability is not usually a factor in the amateur contests, although it is significant in couples-posing competitions. Best posing-routine trophies are given out at some contests. Breaking a judging tradition, the 2004 Mr. Olympia has established a new approach to judging. A callout venue has been added wherein the top six competitors will be allowed to challenge one another on a bodypart/pose basis to establish the final ranking and winner of the Mr. Olympia (Perine 2004, 82–95).

Competitors are usually placed in weight categories, although some organizations include height categories. Master's categories for women and men are also included at various shows. The age requirements vary among organizations; some begin the master's category at age thirty and others at thirty-five years of age. The general trend has been for the competitions to offer more age categories for masters men than for women, with some competitions only offering master's categories for men. Recently organizations and promoters have begun to offer more age categories for women at the local and regional level. Several organizations, among them the NPC and various national organizations, have national master's competitions. At the international level, the International Federation of Bodybuilders' Mr. Olympia contest includes the men's masters Olympia, although the Ms. Olympia does not yet have a women's masters Olympia.

Since 1995, with the inaugural Ms. Fitness Olympia and the increasing popularity of Ms. Fitness competitions (a competition that combines elements of beauty pageants with those of an aerobics competition), various bodybuilding writers have pronounced the death knell of women's bodybuilding. More recently figure

How am I to know what I can achieve
if I quit? ■ JASON BISHOP

competitions have also been added to the bodybuilding venue. Figure competitions are similar to fitness competitions without the required fitness routine wherein competitors demonstrated flexibility and strength with the most successful women having gymnastic ability. Figure competitions, introduced at the national level in 2001 and the professional level in 2003 with the inaugural Figure Olympia are arguably the fastest growing segment with the most number of competitors among the three women's physique sports (Bolin 2004).

Despite the competition for attention and resources (e.g. sponsors) by fitness and figure competitors whose physiques represent more traditional ideals of feminine embodiment, women's bodybuilding continues to survive, although its growth is more gradual than that of the figure competitions with some evidence suggesting the numbers have peaked but stabilized. Data from the USA Bodybuilding competition are indicative. The USA Bodybuilding contest is a very competitive national amateur-level arena. In 1999, there were thirteen women competitors. However, this increased to fifty-three in 2000, escalating to sixty-six (an increase over the prior three years) in 2002 and dropping back down to fifty-two in 2003. The Ms. Olympia indicates a similar trend with peaks and valleys that stabilize at a threshold level over the twenty-four competitions since 1980. The Ms. Olympia went from a high of thirty-two women in 1993 to a low of twelve in 1996, 1999, and 2000. Numbers of competitors oscillated at a threshold level of fourteen to eighteen in half the competitions, but these numbers must be viewed in the context of the number of pro cards available within a given year and the special invitations offered by the IFBB to certain women.

Perspectives

Competitive bodybuilding is a sport that spans all age groups, from teen to masters. For either gender, bodybuilding requires no special skills except determination, although at the elite levels, those who are genetically predisposed with a symmetrical body shape, full muscle bellies, small joints, and muscle that grows readily,

will have an advantage. Those not so endowed can compensate and successfully compete through discipline, the acquisition of bodybuilding lore, scientific training techniques, and good nutrition. There is a diversity of organizations at the local, regional, national, international and professional levels. Bodybuilding may be regarded as a very democratic sport, spanning all age groups and ethnicities. It can be a rewarding hobby or an exciting professional career.

Anne Bolin

See also Venice Beach

Further Reading

Bolin, A. (1992). Vandalized vanity: Feminine physiques betrayed and portrayed. In F. Mascia-Lees (Ed.), *Tattoo. torture. adornment and disfigurement: the denaturalization of the body in culture and text* (pp. 79–80). Albany, NY: State University of New York Press.

Bolin, A. (1997). Flex appeal, food and fat: Competitive bodybuilding, gender and diet. In P. L. Moore (Ed.), *Building bodies* (pp. 184–208). New Brunswick, NJ: Rutgers University Press.

Bolin, A. (2004). *Testy and docile bodies: Her-stories of compliance and defiance in women's bodybuilding.* Plenary Address, The International Super Slim Conference on Sexual Politics Center for the Studies of Sexualities. National Central University. November 27, 2004, Chungli, Taiwan.

Chapman, D. L. (1994). *Sandow the Magnificent: Eugene Sandow and the beginnings of bodybuilding.* Urbana: University of Illinois Press.

Dobbins, B. (1999). *Professional Bodybuilding for Women: A Victim of Its Own Success.* Retrieved March 16, 2005, from http://billdobbins.com/PUBLIC/pages/coolfree/mso_canc.html

Donnelly, S. B. (1990). Work that body. *Time, 136*(19), 68.

Duff, R. W., & Hong, L. K. (1984). Self images of women bodybuilders. *Sociology of Sport Journal, 1,* 374–380.

Gaines, C., & Butler, G. (1974). *Pumping iron.* New York: Simon and Schuster.

Gaines, C., & Butler, G. (1984). *Pumping iron II: The unprecedented women.* New York: Simon and Schuster.

Klein, A. (1993). *Little big men: Gender construction and bodybuilding subculture.* Albany, NY: State University of New York Press.

McLish, R. (1984). *Flex appeal.* New York: Warner Books.

Perine, S. (2004). Putting the 'O' in the Olympia. *Flex Magazine, 22*(8), 82–95.

Rose, M. M. (2001). *Muscle Beach.* New York: St. Martin's Press.

Schwarzenegger, A. (1985). *Encyclopedia of modern bodybuilding.* New York: Simon and Schuster.

Todd, J. (1991). Bernarr MacFadden: Reformer of feminine form. *Iron Game History, 1*(4/5), 3–8.

Todd, J. (1992). The origins of weight training for female athletes in North America. *Iron Game History 2*(2), 4–14.

Todd, J. (1992). The legacy of Pudgy Stockton. *Iron Game History, 2*(1), 5–7.

Tyler, Dick. (2004). *West Coast bodybuilding scene: The golden era.* Santa Cruz, CA: On Target Publications.

Vertinsky, P. (1990). *The eternally wounded woman: Women, doctors and exercise in the late nineteenth century.* Manchester, UK: Manchester University Press.

Wilkins, R. (2004). *Ben Weider: The driving force behind the IFBB.* http://www.ifbb.com/reports/BenWeider2004.htm

Weider, B., & Weider, J. (1981). *The Weider book of bodybuilding for women.* Chicago: Contemporary Books.

Wennerstrom, S. (2000). The bashing of women's bodybuilding...so what else is new? *Women's Physique World, 70,* 5.

Bondi Beach

As well known internationally as the beaches of Waikiki, Acapulco, and Miami, Bondi Beach in Sydney, Australia, embodies a sense of place and a way of life synonymous with a hedonistic culture of sun, sand, and surf. Befitting the beach's iconic cultural status, the Australian Heritage Council lists Bondi Beach, Bondi Pavilion, Bondi Pool, and the adjacent Campbell Parade streetscape on its Register of the National Estate. The primary appeal of Bondi Beach lies in its natural amenities as an open stretch of golden sand approximately 1 kilometer long and 50–100 meters wide, guarded in the north and south by rugged sandstone cliffs and lapped in the east by the Pacific Ocean.

The original Aboriginal inhabitants of the region occupied the Bondi basin during summer, living in *gunya*s (temporary shelters made from bark sheets) that they built near the northern headland. They caught fish using spears and clubs and swam in the natural rock pools beneath the two headlands. Whether they were Darug or Eora people is the subject of debate, as is the meaning of the word *Bondi,* which is variously given as "the sound of falling water" or "a heavy Aboriginal club."

The governor of New South Wales, Lachlan Macquarie, granted William Roberts, a road builder, 80 hectares at Bondi in 1810. By the mid-nineteenth century Bondi, then also known as "Boondye" or "Boondi," as the closest ocean beach to Sydney Town, was popular among European settlers as a picnic and fishing site. Edward Hall, a newspaper publisher, bought the Bondi Estate in 1851 and four years later opened the beach and adjacent foreshore to the public. In 1856 Francis O'Brien, a land developer and farm manager, bought the estate and began the process of subdivision. Finally, Waverley Municipal Council took over as trustee of 10 hectares of public recreation land known as "Bondi Park" in the mid-1880s.

Bondi had become a popular place for bathers during the last quarter of the nineteenth century, with the natural rock pool at the southern end of the beach a favorite attraction. Government legislation at the time restricted bathing to either enclosed baths or to waters open to public view at dusk and dawn. At issue was exposure of the human body, a practice deemed offensive and subversive by moralists. To cater to the burgeoning bathing community Waverley Municipal Council built the first baths around the rock pool at the southern end of Bondi Beach in 1884. Early the next decade a group of young men who swam regularly at the baths formed the Bondi Amateur Swimming Club.

A surfbathing movement coalesced in Sydney during the last decade of the nineteenth century. The movement challenged the laws that forbade bathing in daylight hours, and in 1903 it forced the government to rescind restrictions. During the next two decades a distinctly Australian beach culture emerged, and Bondi Beach was at the forefront.

Waverley Municipal Council and the New South Wales state government initiated a foreshore improvement program that included dressing sheds and fencing before the legalization of daylight bathing. After 1903 the Public Works Department accelerated its building program, constructing changing rooms and a kiosk (1906), the Castle Pavilion (1911), and a sea wall (1911–1920). In 1923 the council and state government embarked on a grand development scheme. The cornerstones were reconstruction of Bondi Pool and construction of the monumental Bondi Pavilion. Offering changing rooms for swimmers, food outlets, Turkish baths, a courtyard, and ballroom, the pavilion was officially opened in 1929. Bondi Beach, Bondi

People playing beach volleyball on Bondi Beach, Sydney, Australia. *Source: istockphoto.com/davidf.*

Pavilion, and Bondi Pool (home of the Bondi Icebergs Swimming Club, whose members swim all year around) were the best-known emblems of Australia's beach and leisure culture. On warm summer Saturdays, Sundays, and public holidays during the 1930s upward of fifty thousand people frolicked in the surf, played and relaxed on the sand, or promenaded behind the beach.

Safety First

Safety in the surf was a major issue for surfbathers and municipal and state governments. At beaches across Sydney local surfbathing clubs assumed responsibility for providing safety services. These clubs helped surfbathers legitimize their pastime. Well into the last quarter of the twentieth century conservative moralists still railed against sun and surfbathers, whom they accused of abandoning public decency in pursuit of their pleasures. As well as offering safety services, lifesaving clubs disciplined their members and the bathing public.

The lifesaving movement debates which club was the first established. Bondi, Bronte, and Manly have all claimed the status of being Australia's first surf lifesaving club. Bronte cites its foundation year as 1903; until recently a sign above the main entrance to the Bondi clubhouse gave its foundation year as 1906. The best primary historical evidence discovered by historian Sean Brawley awards the title to Bondi. Brawley dates the official formation of the club as 21 February 1907.

By the 1930s the surf lifesaver was the paragon of Australian national manhood. Surf lifesavers at Bondi made significant contributions to that status. In one legendary exploit in 1938, Bondi surf lifesavers performed a mass rescue of three hundred swimmers. Around 3 P.M. on 6 February, a set of large waves generated a powerful backwash. The backwash swept several hundred swimmers, many of whom panicked, off a sand bar. Three teams of lifesavers were preparing for a race at the time, and a relieving patrol was about to come on duty. Among those rescued were thirty-five

Bondi Beach

Bondi Beach Tram

Memories of the Bondi Tram are recorded on the Bondi Beach website:

One hundred years ago the tram line was extended from the Bondi Aquarium terminus at Fletcher Street to a balloon loop at the southern end of Bondi Beach. Early morning tram journeys were particularly popular with bathers, as it was then forbidden to swim at Bondi Beach between the hours of 8am and 8pm.

[. . .]

The first of the popular O class trams entered service on the Bondi and Waverley lines in March 1908 and they were in general use by 1911. Nicknamed "toast-rack" trams, they successfully carried passengers until 1957 and are remembered with nostalgic affections.

- The conductor on the running boards crying "fez pliz,"
- The segregated smoking sections, usually occupied by men.
- The canvas blind which was pulled down to keep out the rain.
- Strap-hangers jostling for seats as passengers departed.
- The paper boys who jumped on and off calling "pa-yur."

The Bondi tram loop was demolished as part of Waverley Council's Bondi Improvement Scheme in the 1920s and the trams re-routed along Campbell Parade to a new terminus at North Bondi, the site still used today by buses.

Source: The Bondi Beach Home Page (2003). Retrieved February 24, 2005, from http://www.voyeurmagic.com.au/thennow.htm#tram

swimmers who were brought back to the beach unconscious; five people drowned.

Notwithstanding the broad social appeal of its beach, Bondi the suburb has been traditionally working class with a high proportion of transient residents. Most of the contemporary housing was constructed in the interwar period and consists of dreary squat apartments. Suburban Bondi spiraled into a state of decline during the 1950s. Promenading rituals vanished when Returned Services League and other clubs granted free admission and the offer of dancing, cheap meals, and gaming machines. Television and movie theaters further hastened the demise of these public rituals. Similarly, the wider availability of cars opened up new picnic and bathing areas and drew the population away from what were now inner-city beaches.

Urban Renewal

During the mid-1970s Waverley Municipal Council initiated an urban renewal program. The program included converting the pavilion into a community center. Among the facilities offered by the new center were a theater, art gallery, rehearsal, meeting, and function rooms, music workshops, art workshops, pottery studios, and a recording studio. Today staff members at the Bondi Community Centre organize a variety of classes, workshops, exhibitions, and concerts. One of the biggest events staged by the center is the annual Festival of the Winds.

During the 1990s Australians discovered the beach as the place to live. Bondi, and especially the southern headland with its views of the beach and protection from prevailing winds, attracted an unprecedented influx of wealth. However, the moneyed set did not simply expel the economically weaker from Bondi. The beach attracts tens of thousands of foreign backpackers each year, and to meet their demands for cheap accommodation many residents have turned their houses into illegal (substandard) hostels.

The social composition of visitors to Bondi Beach has changed during the last quarter of a century. Local surf lifesavers and police report an upsurge in gangs of antisocial young men from Sydney's poorer western suburbs. They come to provoke trouble; they start sand fights and play soccer and tackle football to force sunbathers to surrender beach space. Lifesavers, once figures of high authority on the beach, now tell of being spat at, assaulted, and abused. However, social tension has a long tradition at Bondi: As far back as 1877 Francis O'Brien threatened to close the beach to "rowdy larrikins."

Yet, regardless of their intentions or interests, visitors and residents alike remain as captivated by Bondi's sun, sand, and surf as they have always been.

Douglas Booth

Further Reading

Booth, D. (2001). *Australian beach cultures: The history of sun, sand and surf.* London: Frank Cass.

Cass, C., & Cass, L. (2003). *Bondi: The best of the Bondi view.* Bondi Beach, Australia: Boondye Books.

Game, A. (1989). *Australian national identity and Bondi* (Working Paper No. 48). London: Sir Robert Menzies Centre for Australian Studies, University of London.

Huntsman, L. (2001). *Sand in our souls: The beach in Australian history.* Melbourne, Australia: Melbourne University Press.

Kent, J. (Ed.). (1993). *Bondi.* St. Leonards, Australia: Allen & Unwin.

Taussig, M. (2000). The beach (A fantasy). *Critical Inquiry, 26*(2), 252–253.

Boomerang Throwing

Boomerang throwing is a recreational and competitive sport in which participants try to achieve specified effects in their throws: accuracy, speed, distance, tricks, extended time aloft, and the like. Although usually linked with Australian culture, modern-day competitive boomerang throwing owes much to grassroots efforts in the United States during the latter part of the twentieth century.

History

Long believed to be of Australian origin, boomerangs from other parts of the world may predate those depicted in 15,000-year-old cave paintings of Australian Aborigines. In 1987, a 20,300-year-old throw stick (a throw stick generally travels in a relatively straight line, unlike a boomerang, which returns) carved from a mammoth's tusk was discovered in Poland. Boomerangs and throw sticks were found in King Tutankhamen's tomb (1350 BCE) in Egypt, where they were perhaps used as early as 2000 BCE.

Boomerangs were used as a hunting decoy for birds. Ducks might see a boomerang and believe it to be an eagle. They would huddle under the "eagle," making them an easy target for a hunter with a net. Throw sticks were used for hunting ground game.

Aboriginal tribes in Australia held competitions with both returning boomerangs and nonreturning throw sticks, focusing on accuracy and distance as goals. A 1968 *Scientific American* article on boomerangs stimulated interest in them in the United States. Yearly workshops by the Smithsonian Institute on making and throwing boomerangs fueled this interest, and in 1981, the United States Boomerang Association (USBA) was formed. That same year, a U.S. boomerang team challenged and beat an Australian team in the first international competition; its success sparked today's multinational tournaments.

The United States and Australia have defined the sport of competitive boomerang throwing in their respective rule handbooks. However, most nations follow the European standard for competition, at least for scoring and ranking, and countries such as Germany, France, and Japan are now fielding successful boomerang teams.

The atmosphere at boomerang tournaments is informal and filled with camaraderie. Friends and family members often make up the audience; they observe from folding chairs and frequently share a picnic lunch with participants.

What Is Boomerang Throwing?

In a boomerang competition, standard events include the following:

- *Accuracy.* The competitor throws the boomerang in hopes of landing it in the accuracy target, which is a circle 10 meters (11 yards) in diameter outlined on a grass field. Within this circle are five concentric circles laid out in the same fashion as an archery target. A

A hand holding a boomerang.

Source: istockphoto.com/calving.

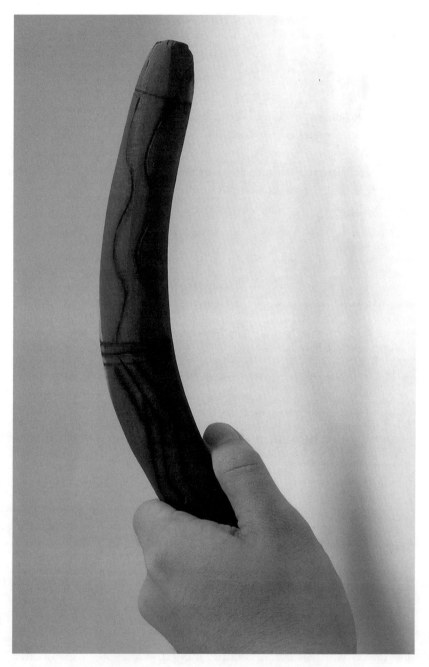

boomerang landing in the bull's-eye is worth 10 points. Subsequent larger circles award points on a declining scale of 8, 6, 4, and 2, respectively.

- *Australian Round.* This event expands on Accuracy by also factoring in points for distance and catching.
- *Fast Catch.* The thrower makes five throws and catches with the same boomerang as rapidly as possible.
- *Endurance.* The goal is to catch as many boomerangs as possible in five minutes.
- *Maximum Time Aloft.* The competitor tries to keep the boomerang in the air for the longest time possible.
- *Trick Catch.* The event requires making difficult catches—one-handed, under the leg, and with the feet—in the attempt to accumulate points.
- *Doubling.* Two boomerangs are thrown by one person and then caught on return in quick succession.

One might also see juggling or long-distance throwing at a competition.

In this sport, participants are separated by skill levels and then compete accordingly. Once placed in a particular category, there are no handicaps granted, and men, women, and youth compete on an even playing field.

Boomerang tournaments take place outdoors, in parks and other venues with the appropriate amount of wide-open space; the only equipment needed is a set of boomerangs. Competitors make or purchase differently crafted boomerangs for different events and wind conditions, and they tape coins and other objects onto their boomerangs to weight them for varying conditions of wind.

Participants range from the very small number of people who make their living from boomerang throwing, mostly through demonstrating the sport to schools and other audiences, to those who work full-time jobs in other vocations and then compete on the weekends.

Competition at the Top

Presently twenty-five countries have national boomerang organizations, each of which schedule their own tournaments, and there is an official international competition held every two years. In most—if not all—instances, boomerang associations hold both individual and team events.

Effort is a measure of a man. ■ WILLIAM JAMES

Cultural attitudes toward the boomerang vary. The Australians, generally speaking, favor preserving the original materials and shape of the boomerang and maintaining the nature of the tournaments as they stand, while the French seek world-record performances and hold competitions intended to achieve new records; they prefer more technologically advanced boomerang designs to traditional shapes and colors. The Germans hold artisanship and successful performance in high regard. German and Swedish engineers create boomerangs with intricate inlaid patterns and use high-tech materials in their crafting, and in the United States, the favored boomerang is the one that will win a tournament rather than one that is aesthetically pleasing or designed to break world records.

Boomerang throwing has never been an Olympic sport, although the sport was demonstrated at the 2000 Olympics in Sydney, Australia. Likewise, few boomerang champions would be recognized except by those who participate in or follow the sport. One notable exception might be Chet Snouffer of Delaware, Ohio, who competed on the United States team in the first international competition, held in Australia. Snouffer has since won twelve national championships and three world titles.

Governing Body
There is no international governing organization; however, clubs and associations exist around the world. Key organizations include the following: Boomerang Association of Australia (www.boomerang.org.au); Boomerang World (www.flight-toys.com/boomerangs.htm); France Boomerang Association (franceboomerang.free.fr/); German Boomerang Club (www.bumerangclub.de); United States Boomerang Association (www.usba.org).

The Future
Referred to as the "ancient sport of the future" by the United States Boomerang Association, it seems likely that the United States, France, Germany, and Japan will remain powerhouses in the sport, and that additional

countries will join them in domestic and international competitions. Throwers and crafters will continue to refine the technology of their boomerangs, tailoring them to specific events such as long distance, fast catch, and MTA, and records will, most likely, continue to be broken. It is doubtful that the niche sport of boomerang throwing will ever become popular with a large number of people or that quality boomerangs will become mass-produced items, but it does seem plausible that a slow and quiet growth of the sport will occur.

Kelly Boyer Sagert

Additional information was provided by Ted Bailey.

Further Reading
Mason, B. S. (1974). *Boomerangs: How to make and throw them.* New York: Dover.
Ruhe, B. (1977). *Many happy returns: The art and sport of boomeranging.* New York: Viking Press.
Sagert, K. B. (1996). *About boomerangs: America's silent sport.* North Ridgeville, OH: PlantSpeak.

Boston Marathon

The Boston Athletic Association's Boston Marathon, inaugurated just one year after the modern marathon was introduced at the 1896 Olympics, arguably remains the most prestigious running event in North America, and one of the most celebrated in the world. Held the third Monday in April on Patriot's Day, the regional holiday commemorating Paul Revere's ride, the race takes a winding course from the small town of Hopkinton eastward to Boston, passing through seven other communities along the way. Over its century-plus history, participation has grown from the first group of fifteen (of whom ten were certified finishers) to the current field maximum of 20,000 spots filled by qualifying times and lottery, as crowds en route have swelled to number an estimated 1.5 million spectators each year. It is one of the most lucrative races as well, with the

total purse for 2004 amounting to $525,000, including $80,000 each for top men's and women's finishers.

Legendary Marathoners

The litany of legendary characters begat or confirmed in Boston would have to start with the spunky Clarence H. DeMar, a printer who trained by running to and from work and whose 1937 autobiography *Marathon* provides reminders of what genuine amateurism was like. DeMar first ran the race in 1910, won it an astonishing seven times between 1911 and 1930, and ran it for the last time in 1954 at age sixty-six. Bill Rogers won Boston four times in the 1970s—and is remembered especially for stopping five times during his 1975 victory, once to tie a shoelace as well as four times for water. It is a mark of Boston's distinction that nonwinners also belong to the lore: one is two-time Olympic champion Abebe Bikila, who ran but did not win Boston in 1963, between his Olympic golds; another is Frank Shorter, gold and silver Olympic medalist of the 1970s, who did not run Boston until 1978 when he was past his prime, having stayed away before because he deemed the prize money too minimal.

By the mid-1940s, the Boston race was undergoing transformation from a parochial New England affair to a marquee event reflecting the globalization of competitive distance running. A string of top finishes by Finns, Japanese and Koreans—including a sweep of the top three spots by Koreans in 1950—marked an end to U.S. domination; between 1946 and 1967 an American won the race just once. The 1960s saw a surge in home participation, however, reflecting the U.S. running boom of the period; the number of runners surpassed 1,000 for the first time in 1969. To control entries qualifying times were steadily lowered and, after some adjustments, now start at 3:10 for men and 3:40 for women, with additional time allowed for ascending age groups.

Boston's was the first major marathon to include a wheelchair division when it recognized Bob Hall as an official finisher in 1975, with a time just under three hours; the first acknowledged wheelchair completer, however, was Eugene Roberts of Baltimore, who took seven hours to finish in 1970. Money prizes were first awarded in 1986, when Boston-based insurance company John Hancock assumed financial sponsorship.

Women Participate

The 1960s also saw women break into the ranks—at first surreptitiously, since not until 1972 was entry officially opened to them. For the first time in 2004, elite women runners got their own start, twenty-nine minutes ahead of the rest of the field, a move aimed at heightening attention to the women's race. Roberta "Bobbi" Gibb had been the pioneer, hiding in the bushes at the 1966 start and jumping in to become the first woman to successfully complete the race. In 1967 Kathrine Switzer entered as "K. Switzer," and a race official attempting to intercept her mid-race made embarrassing news all over the world. Joan Benoit Samuelson, who shredded a world record at Boston in 1983, went on to take the gold medal in the first women's Olympic marathon the next year. In 1994–1996, German Uta Pippig won three times in a row—the third time with severe menstrual cramps and diarrhea; other three-time women winners are Rosa Mota of Portugal, Fatuma Roba of Ethiopia, and Catherine Ndereba of Kenya. Ibrahim Hussein's win in 1998 already had ushered in the preeminence of Kenyan runners on the men's side; South Korean Li Bong-ju's 2001 win has been the only break in a Kenyan men's streak from 1991 to 2004.

How Long Is a Marathon?

The original Boston course fell about 2 miles short of marathon length; the original start in the town of Ashland was moved 2 miles west to Hopkinton when Boston became the qualifying race for the 1924 Paris Olympics—at which DeMar took bronze. After closer remeasurement in 1927, the course was lengthened a bit more to conform to the exact official marathon length of 26 miles and 385 yards. To this day different portions of the race maintain their own character as runners pass from relatively rural areas through small

towns and suburbs before arriving at the city for which the race is named. At about the halfway point, Wellesley College students recreate a ritual "sound tunnel" of screaming and shouting. A few miles farther, runners begin one of the most famous stretches of punishment in contemporary marathon racing, a chain of hills offering a steep rise and then abrupt fall in elevation, culminating in the so-called Heartbreak Hill in Newton, a nickname affixed by a longtime *Boston Globe* sports editor. The marathon's overall downhill trajectory makes the course fast, so Boston times that make records now receive an asterisk.

Boston's Legacy

In sum, many elements make the Boston Marathon special, from its status as the first annual U.S. race of its kind, subsequently replicated by rival New York and other cities to its association with Revolutionary War history, highlighted at the first running by an entourage of infantry soldiers, and from its important place in the careers of many outstanding runners to its many adaptations to larger trends in competitive national and global sports—sometimes ahead of the curve, sometimes behind.

Judy Polumbaum

Further Reading

Atkin, R. (1996, April). "100 years of multitudes: Boston Marathon spurs the sport's resurgence." *Christian Science Monitor, 88*(97).

Connelly, M. (2003). *26 miles to Boston: The Boston Marathon experience from Hopkinton to Copley Square.* Guilford, CT: Lyons Press.

DeMar, C. (1937). *Marathon.* Brattleboro, VT: Stephen Daye Press.

Derderian, T. (1996). *Boston Marathon: The first century of the world's premier running event.* Champaign, IL: Human Kinetics.

Derderian, T. (2003). *The Boston Marathon: A century of blood, sweat, and cheers.* Chicago: Triumph Books.

Higdon, H. (1995). *Boston: A century ofrRunning.* Emmaus, PA: Rodale.

Layden, T. (2004, April 19). "The long run." *Sports Illustrated, 100*(16).

Rodgers, B., & Concannon, J. (1980). *Marathoning.* New York: Simon and Schuster.

Samuelson, J., with Baker, S. (1987). *Running tide.* New York: Alfred A. Knopf.

Wulf, S., & Allis, S. (1996, April 15). "A long running show: Boston, the marathon of marathons, is bracing for its 100th start." *Time, 147*(16).

Bowls and Bowling

Bowls and bowling include a group of activities that involve rolling or throwing balls at targets with the intent of hitting or knocking them over. The term "bowls" generally refers to variants of the game played in Europe and the United Kingdom, and "bowling" is the Americanized version of the sport played in the United States. Long dominated by men, bowls and bowling have fairly recently accepted the full participation of women.

Bowls and bowling claim their origins in antiquity. Rolling or throwing small balls at various targets is said to be portrayed in carvings from ancient Mediterranean civilizations, but there are very long gaps in the evidence. Bocce claims to have been played in Italy since the days of classical Rome, with distinctive regional variations. Bocce (literally, "bowls") and petanque/ boules, played in Italy and France, respectively, are traditional peasant games that were long played exclusively by men.

Peasant Recreations: Bocce and Petanque/Boule

In the Mediterranean countries of Italy and France, these broadly similar games emerged primarily as agents for male bonding. Men took over the sandy or gravel spaces of village squares for play, which was often associated with drinking during the warmer months from April to October. The games have common elements: the small and relatively heavy balls are tossed from a fixed line toward a target. Both have been codified only relatively recently, as they have been adapted to wider usage and urban play.

Bowls, as with many medieval and Renaissance European folk customs, is quite difficult to reconstruct in terms of whether both men and women took part. Only as the game began to be played with formal rules in the late nineteenth century has the role of women been given an occasionally controversial prominence. Many clubs remained all-male in membership.

Bowls and Bowling

Bowling in Lappland

In the beginning of the 19th century the Utsjoki-Lapps practiced a kind of bowling. They used one rather small pin which was placed upright on a board, and they chose a "caretaker" by casting lots. Each player had a stick which he bowled on the pin, and every time the pin fell the caretaker put it upright again. When all the players had thrown their sticks, these were picked up as fast as possible, as the caretaker had a long switch in his hand with which he hastened to strike the players. If the last bowler hit the pin, the caretaker was not allowed to pursue the players before he had placed the pin upright again; therefore the last bowler was usually the strongest and the most skillful. If the caretaker managed to strike a player before the latter had found his stick, he was freed from his task and replaced by the stricken bowler.

Source: Itkonen, T. I. (1948). *The Lapps in Finland up to 1945* (pp. 861). Porvoo, Helsinki: Werner Sderstrm Osakeyhti.

Significant differences remain between women's playing as part of family recreation in these sports deeply rooted in European masculine peasant cultures and their part in those games that have been developed in the wider contexts of the white-dominated sections of the former British Empire and North America. That women are confined to amateur status is also an issue; this is perhaps a remnant of the social and religious purity they have long been supposed to represent.

Since the 1980s, however, urbanization has started to break down bocce's traditional maleness. This has been even more the case in the United States, the country to which it has been most successfully exported along with other aspects of Italian migrant culture. Here it has developed increasingly as a means of family bonding in suburbia; women tend to play within extended domestic teams rather than in separate organizations, but the situation remains very fluid.

Petanque/boule is broadly similar in history, although its spread outside the former French colonial empire owes more to tourists taking the game home to Britain than to ethnic migration. It has been codified since about 1910, having emerged from older games played in southern France.

Bowls, rolling a heavy wooden ball biased with a metal weight toward a small jack, has been played in Britain since at least the Middle Ages, and little-changed versions are still played by exclusively male clubs in a few places, including Lewes and Southampton. A limited amount of evidence shows occasional female participation in more domestic versions during the Tudor and Stuart periods—the great diarist Samuel Pepys played with his wife in the 1660s. But it was with the reemergence and popularization of the masculine game at the end of the nineteenth century that women appeared both as serious, and segregated, contenders.

Bocce and Petanque: Rules and Play

Bocce uses an "alley" or "rink" 18.3 meters long and 2.4 meters wide. As it has become more popular in cities, more indoor facilities have been constructed, which often house several such pitches. Each player tosses a bowl to get as close as possible to a smaller target bowl, the pallino, which has already been thrown to lie at least 1.4 meters beyond a central regulator peg. The player usually walks up to do this within a separate area. Competitors may play either as singles with two shots each or in teams of up to six people with four shots each. Bocce is organized into various regional and national federations but, until recently, had no organized international competition because it was played largely in Italy.

The name *petanque* means, literally, "feet tied together." This refers to the standing position from which the metal boule ("bowl") is thrown at the small wooden target, the *cochonnet,* which has been tossed some 6 to 10 meters into a space roughly 12 meters by 1.3 meters. Scoring depends on the player's skill in getting a bowl closer to the target than the opponent's bowl. In the 1980s indoor urban arenas extended the playing season to year-round. Codification led in 1945 to the organization of a national body, the Federation

Boys playing boules outside a pub in England.

Francaise de Petanque et Jeu Provencal and eventually to world championships as visitors from neighboring countries, as well as those in the former French empire, took up the game.

One major factor in opening play up to women came with the formation of a British Petanque Association in 1974 (now with 320 clubs and 4,000 members), at a time when they were being admitted more readily, in southern England at least, to pubs. While some women play independently in league games, their partners are drawn largely from their families and both sexes, reflecting the domestication of a previously singularly masculine preserve. This domestication is even more pronounced when it is remembered that most games are recreational and played on family space in gardens or vacation sites.

Bowls: Rules and Play

There are two main versions of the modern game, both played seasonally out of doors, with broad similarities. The "lawn" version is played on level grass greens. These are squares of between 31 and 41 meters that are usually divided into rinks of up to 5.5 meters wide, to allow several matches to be played side by side. The green is surrounded by a shallow ditch and a bank at least 23 centimeters high.

The second version, called the "crown" version, may be played on either a square or a rectangular area, but it must be a minimum of 25 meters wide. It usually rises to a central crown up to 35 centimeters high. Both games use "woods," now usually made of artificial materials, which are "biased," weighted to one side, so that a direct line is virtually impossible. These are bowled at a smaller "jack" up to 6.4 centimeters in diameter. Players, grouped in various combinations, usually play with up to four bowls each, the winner being the player those wood comes closest to the jack.

Participation in Bowls

Bowls was frequently and inaccurately portrayed as a semisedentary game for the middle-aged. At the beginning of the twentieth century, male clubs were recognized, in a semipublic and partly humorous way, as a refuge from both overdomestication and feminine domination. The first national organization, the English Bowling Association (EBA), was founded for men in 1903, dominated initially by the aging and irascible cricket hero, Dr. W. G. Grace. It was followed in 1926 by the rival English Bowling Federation (EBF) and by the British Crown Green Association, first begun in 1903 but reorganized in 1932. For flat green players national championships are provided by the EBA in southern England and by the EBF in the Midlands. Crown Green players have had a national championship since 1878, reorganized in 1907 as the Waterloo Cup, held in the northern seaside resort of Blackpool.

Eventually a case was advanced that play would benefit women in two ways. It would improve the health of women who were excluded from more active pursuits by age and convention, and it would also extend the women's role from the more traditional one of making teas for visiting teams. The "ladies" became "women" players. Playing was also promoted as an additional means of inculcating graceful movement. Such pressures led the London authorities to make limited separate playing facilities in public parks available for women in 1906.

Most developments since then have seen an uneasy coexistence with men's clubs on both private and public spaces. Women have progressed more rapidly in the "lawn" game, with its flat greens, in the predominantly southern and middle-class areas, than in the "crown" game, with its uneven greens and semiprofessionalism, in more northern and working-class towns. The latter has often been associated with gambling, supposedly a male activity. The first specifically female club was probably founded in 1910 in Kingston Canbury, near London. The great boom came in the decade after the end of World War I, when bowls became a somewhat unlikely tool in the growth of women's independence.

Although British women moved steadily toward greater playing organization, this was one area where the island's power did not automatically cause it to lead in imperial developments. The slightly freer culture of white groups in some of the colonies had already led South Africa and Australia to form women's bowls associations and England's leading women lawn bowls players followed suit, opting for the purposeful-sounding English Women's Bowling Association, or EWBA (a rival Ladies' Association was very short-lived).

The EWBA was founded in 1931 (twenty-eight years after the men's), with the support of many male players, and grew rapidly thereafter, pulling many existing county associations together and prompting the formation of new ones. Eventually it grew to have almost 2,000 affiliated clubs. It was matched, on a smaller scale, by the emergence in 1957 of the English Women's Bowling Federation, for the crown green game. The two bodies' regional influence has closely matched the distribution and the social cachet of their parallel sports. Their most significant role has been in organizing ladders of championships up to international level. Perhaps the peak of recognition for the lawn game came with its inclusion in the Commonwealth Games in 1982. The full age range is now well represented, and the playing of matches has had to adapt to the sharply changing women's employment patterns of Britain since

the 1960s. Weekday play still favors those who are retired.

Although there are honorific prizes in the women-only lawn tournaments—culminating in the annual championships held for years in the Sussex seaside resort of Worthing—any hint of professionalism has been firmly resisted in women's lawn bowls. By comparison, the crown variant has developed a women's version of the male semi- and fully professional sponsored tournaments firmly located in the north of England. Early competition prizes in the 1930s consisted largely of useful domestic goods.

After World War II, financial incentives began to appear, although at a level much below the male equivalents. With sponsorship, the top champions could win thousands of pounds by the 1980s, although they were still a long way from the more obviously glamorous women's sports, even when their matches were televised. The key change came with the organization in 1977 of a women's annual Waterloo Championship, named after the long-established male one. Several thousand women now take part in this circuit, but few are fully professional.

Indoor Variants

Women players have also found a new outlet in the late-twentieth-century development of a previously eccentric minority version of the sport, indoor bowls, usually played on special carpets up to 46 meters long in shared multipurpose halls. Over 250 clubs in England have emerged to follow this winter game, often with membership drawn largely from the seasonally restricted outdoor game. It has its own hierarchy of tournaments, largely under the auspices of the National Indoor Bowls Council, formed in 1964, but a great deal of the play is between older husbands and wives, another extension of domestic bonding.

International Play

As with a number of other quintessentially British sports, women's bowls has spread among Anglophiles

Bowls and Bowling

"The Hat and Blazer Brigade": British Bowling Dress

Few issues have aroused more controversy and offered more targets for ridicule than the dress code adopted since the 1920s by women playing bowls. Whereas women participating in bocce/pentanque or bowling have opted largely for the practical informality of trousers and similar leisurewear, bowls players have a very limited and regulated choice. The emphasis is on a uniform which seems to be a mixture derived from the lawn tennis wear of the early 1920s and male cricketing dress. It is best suited for the fine weather of the summer months. Jewelry, such as earrings and brooches, has long been forbidden; wedding rings and watches are acceptable. A white, cream or gray skirt with a hem well below the knees and a white/cream blouse are compulsory, as are formal stockings, usually brown; the bare legs made fashionable by Princess Diana in other circumstances are respectably covered on the lawns. Flat-heeled brown, white, or gray leather shoes, soft-soled to protect the green, are mandatory; there is no market for the ambitious and fashion-changing trainer manufacturers here. Cream or navy blue blazers may be worn, and soft white or cream rainwear made of artificial fabrics has slowly crept in. By far the most distinctive, and much-ridiculed, item is the hat. Although a few now play bare-headed, the norm is still a white soft-brimmed hat which is a mixture of the male Panama and solid women's styles of the early 1920s. A colored band may indicated the player's team allegiance, but that is the only adornment. The eye shades or colored baseball hats beloved by women golfers have no place in women's bowls. Not surprisingly, there has been a number of attempts to throw off the staid and conservative image the uniform suggests, which some critics have likened to the older uniforms of the Salvation Army. These moves have largely failed. Divided skirts (culottes) were eventually allowed after much debate, but Australian attempts in the early 1990s to introduce brightly striped colored garb, bringing the game "out of the Dark Ages," were soon squashed at a local level. The uniform remains, only slightly modified. As such, it is usually worn with great pride by players of all ages, a central sign of another "unchanging" tradition which the British have exported so successfully. Its survival is seen as another sign of just how serious ("fanatic," according to some observers) women are about the game and about its perceived purity and order.

in the United States as well as throughout the former British Empire. As with cricket, its following in the United States is limited and strongest among the eastern seaboard states, where women play as part of the approximately 7,000 players affiliated with the American Lawn Bowls Association, formed in 1915. But it is deeply rooted in the dominant white suburban cultures of South Africa, New Zealand, and Australia. In Australia, in particular, it is often an arena for sharp clashes between women themselves over issues such as dress and apparent cultural dependency on Britain's former power. It is also a major target of semiaffectionate male criticism because of Australia's uneasy history of macho male cultural dominance. The formidable dedication of many female bowlers is often portrayed as more of a threat to male power than the more traditional restrictions expected from domesticity.

Bowling in North America

The various games that bowl at skittles or pins grew largely as an Americanization of European men's play linked with taverns and pubs, more often played indoors than outside. As such, they had a distinctly working-class following tied to a culture formed around recreational alcohol consumption. In this setting, views on the role of women in these games have been ambivalent. It was with the popularization in the United States of tenpin bowling (and its Canadian variations)

Candlepin bowling. *Source: istockphoto/gmnicholas.*

that women emerged more significantly, although some historians have pointed out that the greatest female following is blue-collar in its origins. When bowling became a respectable family activity in the 1950s, women usually entered it as wives or daughters playing alongside their menfolk in friendly games—it had become another wholesome prop to suburban lifestyles, an image it has largely retained. That move had accompanied its mechanization and the shift to larger, specialist premises that attracted larger groups. As a way of meeting high investment costs, promoters set out to popularize bowling among women.

Women have gradually emerged as independent players, and it is no accident that a number of the standard rule manuals are written by women. When local leagues emerged to play, women were quick to organize. The overall rules were standardized by the essentially male American Bowling Congress, founded in 1895, and the Women's International Bowling Congress, a women's organization that emerged in 1916, well before the game assumed its mantle of suburban respectability—although it is said that their presence led to a rapid

cleanup of the alleys. The 1950s brought an increasing professionalism with commercial sponsorship. A Professional Women's Bowling Association (later changed to "Tour") was formed in 1959, a year after its male equivalent, the Professional Bowlers' Association, which had 2,000 members.

At this level of the sport, women's participation is relatively small and sparsely funded by male standards, although play is vibrant and important as one aspect of career development in sport and as a source of models for playing performance. The four major events on the women's tour are the Bowling Proprietor's Association of America U.S. Open, the Women's International Bowling Congress Queens, Sam's Town Invitational, and the WPBA National Championship. The leading women bowlers earn only about 60 percent of that earned by the leading men. For example, in 1997 the earnings of the top ten men ranged from $75,000 to $166,000, while for women the figure fell between $44,000 and $117,000. Altogether 7 million men and women play in organized U.S. leagues. The various alley games have largely involved women at local amateur and domestic recreational levels, particularly when exported overseas to such places as Britain.

The Future

For both sexes, bowling offers various advantages that make its continued growth likely, on both professional and recreational levels. Many communities have bowling alleys, and casual play requires no serious investment of time or money. Provided prize money keeps pace with interest, more women may take up professional bowling. In the 1990s the sport became a symbol of the supposed decline of family recreational activities as well as reflecting a less sociable work culture, but there has recently been a resurgence. Whether the North American form of bowling will spread further abroad remains an open question.

John Lowerson

Further Reading

Collins, M. F., & Logue, C. S. (1976). *Indoor bowls.* London: Sports Council.

Dunstan, K. (1987). *The bowls dictionary.* Newton Abbot, UK: David & Charles.

Freeman, G. (1987). *Pentanque: The French game of bowls.* Leatherhead, UK: Carreau.

Harrison, J. M., & Maxey, R. (1987). *Bowling.* Glenview, IL: Scott, Freeman.

Marchiano, A. (1980). *Bocce, che passione!* Padua, Italy: Casa Editrice.

Martin, L. L., Tandy, R. E., & Agne-Traub, C. (1994). *Bowling.* Madison, WI: William C. Brown & Benchmark.

Newby, D. (1991). *Bowls year book.* London: Pan.

Philips, K. (Ed.). (1990). *The new BBC book of bowls.* London: BBC.

Pognani, M. (1995). *The joy of bocce.* Indianapolis, IN: Masters.

Boxing

Boxing means fighting with one's fists. Up until the twentieth century, the sport based on boxing was prizefighting in which two men fought bare knuckled for money. The modern sport of boxing is a sport rather than a form of entertainment or simply physical violence because it follows a set of predetermined rules that shape the nature of the fight and set forth criteria for determining the winner. The most important rule is the classification of fighters according to weight that helps ensure that fights will be fair. Professional boxing is now a global, multibillion-dollar industry centered in the United States. Amateur boxing, which both exists on its own and to prepare boxers for a professional career is also a worldwide sport, although it centers are in Russia, Cuba, and Eastern Europe.

Boxing has long been criticized for various ills including the level of violence, corruption, and racism. Nonetheless, it has remained extremely popular with its appeal crossing social class, gender, and ethnic lines. Perhaps its appeal is in the primordial nature of boxing. It is, in some sense, the basic sport. Two men, almost naked, use their strength, speed, agility, stamina, and courage to fight it out until one is too beaten to continue or gives up.

Although the attention of the public is on the boxers in the ring, there are other significant players in the boxing industry. Most important are the trainer, manager, and promoter. The trainer is responsible for getting the fighter physically and mentally ready for the bout, mapping out strategy and offering advice and encouragement from the corner during the bout. The manager is the fighter's representative and as such negotiates contracts with promoters, seeks endorsement and other deals, and acts as the fighter's press agent. The manager has a legal responsibility to act in the fighter's best interest. The promoter is the fight producer. He or she arranges the fight, secures the venue, raises the money to pay the fighters and other expenses, and arranges for media coverage. The promoter's interest is making money off the fight.

Despite the physical danger, boxing and training for boxing is unsurpassed at developing and maintaining physical fitness. In recent years some women have appreciated this and taken to the sport. Boxing feints, the movement of the feet, the skill in a rally, are all elements that can be appreciated by the aesthete, inside or

 Boxing

outside the ring. Many boxing fans believe that the sport should be about hitting, stopping blows, and avoiding being hit. Today, however, the focus is more often on power and knockouts.

History

The roots of modern boxing are found in ancient Greece and Rome. Prizefighting emerged in Great Britain in the seventeenth century. The first written rules were published by Jack Broughton (1704–1789) in London in 1743 although most people learned the rules from personal involvement. In 1841 the editors of *Bells Life in London and Sporting Chronicle* began publishing a boxing yearbook called *Fistiana,* which soon modified Broughton's Rules. Under the revised rules prizefighting could take the form of upright wrestling until either or both men went down. What we now would call a round might last a few seconds or forty minutes. The rest between rounds was thirty seconds. The fight continued until one contestant gave in or his second gave in for him. Fighters invariably bled, and spectators commonly laid bets on "first blood." In the late eighteenth century the notion of science or "scientific boxing" entered the sport. It emphasized foot and hand speed and stopping or avoiding punches and made smaller men competitive with heaver and stronger men. It quickly became popular outside Britain. Its best-know practitioner was the British champion Daniel Mendoza (1764–1836).

Boxing became popular in Paris in the early twentieth century and replaced savate, which allowed blows with the feet. British and African-American boxers fought in France including the world heavyweight champion, Jack Johnson (1878–1946). The first major French fighter was Georges Carpentier (1894–1975). He switched from savate in 1908 and boxed up to heavyweight division. In 1921 he lost to Jack Dempsey (1895–1983) before 90,000 fans in Jersey City, New Jersey.

Boxing, as opposed to prizefighting, used rules written by a Cambridge University athlete, John Graham Chambers (1843–1883) and published by Sir John Sholto Douglas (1844–1900), who was the eighth Marquis of Queensberry in 1867. These rules came to be known as the Queensberry Rules and distinguished between boxing competitions and contests. Competitions were for amateurs as well as professionals. These bouts were limited to three rounds in about ten minutes and were usually decided on points. Contests, on the other hand, were tests of endurance that continued until one man could no longer fight; they were confined strictly to professionals. Only in the latter code was it specified that new gloves of fair size and best quality be used, so Queensberry Rules assumed the superiority of

I coulda been a contender. ▪ MARLON BRANDO AS
TERRY MALLOY IN *ON THE WATERFRONT* (1954)

contests over competitions. Amateurs sparred, professionals fought, and both boxed sportingly according to Queensberry. In both forms timed rounds were timed with a one-minute rest between rounds; gloves were to be used, and wrestling was prohibited.

Between the two world wars, boxing expanded—professional boxing became very profitable and both amateur and professional boxing became popular in Europe and the United States. At the same time, boxing started to become integrated. Joe Louis (1914–1981), an African-American, won the world heavyweight title in Chicago in 1937. But, black men were not permitted to win British professional championships until 1948.

Professional Boxing

Domination of early professional boxing moved back and forth across the Atlantic between Britain and the United States. By the early twentieth century, the United States had become the center of professional boxing with it ranks of fighters filled by poor immigrant men including Irish, Jews, and Italians, and African-Americans. Among the leading fighters as the century moved on were John Sullivan, Jack Dempsey, Benny Leonard, Willie Pep, Sugar Ray Robinson, Joe Louis, and Rocky Marciano. By the 1960s the upper weight divisions were dominated by African-American men, most notably Sonny Liston, Joe Frazier, Muhammad Ali, George Forman, and Mike Tyson. Poverty was and is what brings many athletes into professional boxing. From the mid-twentieth century, boxers from less-developed countries began to replace white men, whose generally improved living conditions allowed them to choose less painful work and pastimes. From Mexico to South Korea, poorer countries have produced more and more boxers, especially at the lighter weights. And, in the United States, Latino boxers have entered the sport in significant numbers.

Central to the rise of boxing in the twentieth century has been the promoter—the person responsible for signing the fighters and officials, paying them, renting a suitable venue, attracting spectators, controlling betting, and generally maintaining order. The leading promoter

in the history of boxing was George L. "Tex" Rickard (1871–1929), who with the help of leading sportswriters turned New York City's Madison Square Garden into the "mecca" of professional boxing in the 1920s. Radio and then television increased the popularity of boxing even more and in the twenty-first century boxing is a staple of premium and pay-per-view television.

Amateur Boxing

The first championships for amateurs were contested in western London. The Queensberry Rules were written for this occasion, but boxing was only part of a two-day open-air program of general athletics, bicycling, and wrestling for gentlemen from newly formed London sports clubs and the universities of Oxford and Cambridge. A shortage of quality boxers led six of the boxers and the editor of a weekly newspaper, the *Referee,* to form the Amateur Boxing Association (ABA), which allowed workingmen to enter its annual championships each spring. The real amateur sport then developed, not among the comfortably off, but in boys' clubs near factories, docks, and railway arches.

In the United States the integration of wealthy clubs with the hoi polloi came much later. The Golden Gloves tournament was started by the *Chicago Tribune* in 1926 and became annual a few years later. Boxing first appeared at the Olympics in 1904, was dropped for the 1912 Games, but returned in 1920 and has been on the program since. International amateur boxing was organized in 1920 with the formation in Paris of the Federation Internationale de Boxe Amateur. The 1932 results say much about the internationalization of amateur boxing with titles won by boxers from Hungary, Canada, and Argentina (two), South Africa (two), and the United States (two). The European titles (awarded to the European who placed best at the Olympics) went to men from Hungary, Sweden, France, Italy (two), and Germany (three).

When amateur boxing resumed after the war, the world was split into two hostile camps: capitalist and communist. Amateur boxing flourished in Communist nations, which rejected professional sport and supported

I'll be floating like a butterfly and stinging like a bee. ■ MUHAMMAD ALI

their amateurs with state funds. Amateur boxing in capitalist countries largely lacked government support, but compensated with television fees and sponsorship from industry and business. In both systems excellence at sport was linked to national prestige. In market economies, professional boxing siphoned off gifted amateurs. Communist nations like Poland, the Soviet Union, and Cuba had an advantage in keeping fighters in the amateur ranks for their entire careers, as in the examples of the Cuban heavyweights Teofilo Stevenson and Felix Savon.

Africa, Asia, and the Middle East became involved in boxing through the amateur version of the sport. The International Amateur Boxing Association was formed in London in 1946. Its congresses, held every four years, indicate the widening interest in boxing: the first congress outside Europe was held in Tanzania in 1974, followed by Madrid, Spain; Colorado Springs, Colorado; and Bangkok, Thailand. Between the International Amateur Boxing Association World Amateur Boxing Championships and the Olympics, boxing produced winners worldwide. Tournaments organized by the Arab Boxing Union involve associations from Iraq to Algeria; and the Oceanic Federation, which includes Australia, has successfully staged its championships in Tahiti.

The sport was, however, disgraced at the 1988 Olympics, held in Seoul, South Korea, by chauvinistic judging and some crowd misbehavior. This led directly to changes in the scoring at all major international tournaments. Five ringside judges, equipped with computers for the first time, had to register points as they saw them scored, but only those points signified by a majority within a second of each other were counted toward the final result. The new system has rapidly gained devotees since it was used at the Barcelona Olympics in 1992, and the increased impartiality, with its low, measured scores is adjudged a triumph in the management of amateur boxing.

Women's Boxing

Women's boxing at the organized, professional level is a recent development. It began on 16 March 1996 when Christy Martin and Deidre Gogarty stole the show on the otherwise boring Mike Tyson–Frank Bruno heavyweight championship card in Las Vegas. The Martin–Gogarty fight however, proved to the 1.1 million people watching on pay-per-view television that women could actually fight with skill, bleed, "get rocked," and come back for more. Martin became the first woman boxer to appear on the cover of *Sports Illustrated*.

Women's boxing differs from men's in several ways. Breast protectors are mandatory for women, but groin protectors are optional. The woman must not be pregnant. Rounds in women's fights are two rather than three minutes long; and women officials must be in charge of pre-fight weigh-ins, although the paucity of such officials means that male officials sometimes must be used.

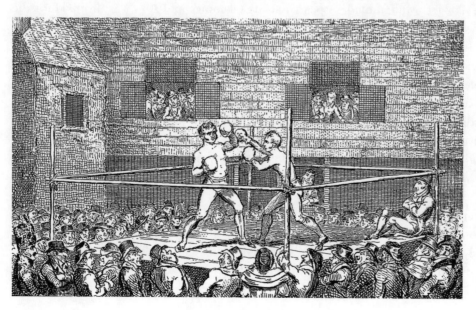

A boxing match at Five Courts, London, in the early nineteenth century.

A boxer ready for action.

Source: istockphoto/lisegagne.

Little is known about women's boxing in the past. Most information comes from newspaper or magazine accounts of bouts in Britain, France, United States, and Australia that were usually more a form of entertainment than sport. These bouts seem to have been a working class entertainment frowned upon although ignored by the middle and upper classes. For example, in 1807 the *Times* of London described a fight between Mary Mahoney and Betty Dyson, commenting that at the end of forty minutes, both "Amazons" were "hideously disfigured by hard blows." Part of the appeal and perhaps much of the appeal for spectators was that the women were sometimes bare to the waist or wore revealing clothing. During the 1890s women's boxing was a popular form of entertainment in saloons and the vaudeville circuit in the United States despite calls in the 1880s to ban women's boxing.

Women's boxing enjoyed a brief period of popularity in Germany of the 1920s and 1930s. In the United States women's boxing continued as a variety act. Still, there was more opposition than support and in 1933 Pope Pius XI condemned women who attended a boxing match as not helping to preserve "the dignity and grace peculiar to women."

For fifteen years in the 1940s and 1950s, the best-known female boxer Barbara Buttrick, from Yorkshire, England who stood but 4 feet 11 inches, weighed in at about 100 pounds. Buttrick latter founded the Women's International Boxing Association (WIBF).

A major impediment to the development of women's boxing in the United States was the state boxing commissions, controlled by white men, who refused to license women. In the 1970s women brought legal challenges and women were licensed in Nevada, California and then New York. Women also won the right to enter the all-male Golden Gloves tournament. Women fighters during this period were a mix of a few with talent and many with little or none.

The 1980s saw a decline in serious women's boxing with far more spectator interest in entertainment provided by partially nude "boxers" and tough women in brawls. At the same, legal challenges to restrictions con- tinued and court rulings and Michigan and then Massachusetts created more opportunities for female fighters. In 1992 the Amateur International Boxing Association (AIBA) officially recognized women's boxing. Boxing training also became a form of exercise and fitness training for women with "boxercise" classes becoming popular in the 1990s.

Since 1996, however, not all has gone smoothly for professional women's boxing. The biggest problem has been a lack of quality boxers that often produces matches that are embarrassing mismatches and which create a serious injury risk for the weaker boxer. This situation is not likely to change until there is a functioning amateur circuit for women boxers so they can learn to box and gain experience before turning professional.

Boxing and Society

Boxing has always been criticized and at times banned. The criticisms are many, some more serious than others. The great boxing writer, A. J. Liebling, is often cited as undoubtedly correct when he called boxing "the red light district of the sports world."

PHYSICAL DANGERS

One major criticism is of the physical dangers—short and long term—to the boxers. At least fifty boxers have died from injuries suffered during a bout since the

Boxing

"The Knock-Out" by Grantland Rice

"A clean knock-out blow to the chin is painless. One may have visions or even hear birds singing before recovering consciousness."—Scientific report.

Hit me, dear heart, upon the chin;
Massage me in the good old way;
Hit me as if you meant to win
The crown that Dempsey holds today.
For lately I have felt the stab
Of dull routine in endless range;
Yea, I have found existence drab
And I am yearning for a change.

I'd like to hear the brown thrush pipe
His melody, well known thrush pipe
His melody, well known of old;
Out where the blooms of May are ripe
In sprays of scarlet, blue and gold;
I'd like to watch the rivers run,
Rock-fretted, as they whirl and pass
Between tall cliffs that hide the sun,
Where vagrant shadows streak the grass.

And somewhere out beyond the walls,
With all their driving, hurried bands,
I'd like to hear the rainbirds call
Through gray days on the meadowlands;
Or, by the marshes and the bog,
Where swallows wheel in restless flight,
I'd like to hear the fluting frogs
In earnest chorus greet the night.

Soak me, dear heart, upon the jaw,
Unfettered with the block and feint;
Nor let the province of the law
Hold you to any light restraint;
For lately I have felt the lure
Of stream and mountain, bird and bough;
My soul is craving for a cure,
But travel's too expensive now.

Source: Rice, G. (1924). *Badminton*, p. 132–133.

1950s and many others have been seriously injured. And the long-term neurological effects of taking repeated blows to the head over the years are well-documented by medicine. Champions such as Joe Louis, Sugar Ray Robinson, and Muhammad Ali all suffered from serious neurological impairment later in life. The greatest risk is sustained by overmatched fighters who take a brutal beating over the course of a bout. A well-known example is heavyweight Chuck Wepner, known as the "Bayonne Bleeder," who fought many of the leading heavyweights of the latter twentieth century and sustained considerable brain damage as a result.

Amateur fights have produced far fewer deaths, presumably because their bouts are shorter. And damage tends to be worse in the heavier divisions because the fighters hit with more force. Since the 1980s, head guards have been required in amateur fights, although they are unpopular with both boxers and spectators. It is not clear if the guards reduce brain injuries, but they do reduce the risk of facial cuts and detached retinas. Also significant is that fighters have no union and no health benefits and no pension.

CORRUPTION IN THE SPORT

Another major issue is corruption. One major appeal of boxing for fans is betting on their fighter. In the past the fixing of matches was a serious issue, although since the crackdown on organized crime's control of boxing in the 1950s it is now less common. The issue now is the fixing of rankings by the competing boxing associations. Professional boxing matches are sanctioned and boxers ranked by three competing organizations—The World Boxing Association, the World Boxing Council, and the International Boxing Federation. Observers charge that these organizations corrupt the sport by ranking fighters and arranging fights on the basis of how much profit the federations can make. Fighters are forced to pay sanctioning fees and boxers who don't pay are lowered in the ranking. Promoters play the role of both promoter and manager and look out for their financial interests first. All this produces a system where the best fighters may never have the chance to reach the top honestly, through victories in the ring.

Tough times don't last.
Tough people do. ▪ Anonymous

Critics charge that corruption flourishes in the sport in the United States because there is no national control of boxing. Rather, boxing is governed by independent state boxing commissions which, except for Nevada and Pennsylvania, critics describe as ranging from incompetent to corrupt. Many state boxing officials are political appointees with limited knowledge of the management of the sport. Critics charge that it is their lack of oversight that leads to mismatches and the risk of serious injury and allows the exploitation of poor black and Latino fighters. There is currently an effort led by Sen. John McCain (R. Arizona) in the U.S. Congress to create central government control over boxing.

RACISM

The third major criticism is racism. It is well-documented that in the nineteenth and first few decades of the twentieth century black men were either banned or discriminated against in professional boxing. Only toward the middle of the century when the number of white fighters coming out of immigrant communities declined were black fighters allowed in large numbers. However, racism did not end. Some commentators believe that racism entered into the decision of state boxing commissions to strip Muhammad Ali of his title when he declared himself a conscientious objector in 1968. And, since the 1960s when blacks and Latinos began their dominance in the ring, there has a search for the "Great White Hope"—the white boxer (like the fictional Rocky) who would win the heavyweight title. Several who have failed are Chuck Wepner, Frans Botha, and Gerry Cooney. Although professional boxing is now dominated by African-American and Latino fighters, many still feel that these fighters are not given their due. For example, the city of Philadelphia erected a statue to Rocky, the fictional white fighter, since the film takes place in the city. However, no such honor was given to the real-life world champion Joe Frazier who has spent most of his life in Philadelphia. Critics charge that racism today comes in the form of the exploitation of some of these fighters by managers, promoters, and sanctioning bodies.

Boxing in Popular Culture

Because of its broad appeal, boxing has spawned a large literature of novels, magazines, films, and several fights described as the "fight of the century." Many experts agree that if there was a fight of the twentieth century it was Joe Frazier's fifteen-round decision over Muhammad Ali at Madison Square Garden in 1971. Among the greatest boxing films are *Golden Boy* (1939), *The Harder They Fall* (1956), *Somebody Up There Likes Me* (1956), *Requiem for a Heavyweight* (1962), *Rocky* (1976), *Raging Bull* (1980), *The Hurricane* (2000), *Girlfight* (2000), and *Million Dollar Baby* (2004). And among literary figures drawn to boxing are Albert Camus, Ernest Hemingway, Jack London, Norman Mailer, and Joyce Carol Oates.

The Future

Despite these issues and the large number of prominent critics of boxing in general or professional boxing today, boxing continues to flourish. It remains a popular amateur and Olympic sport around the world. Professional boxing also remains extremely popular with bouts shown regularly on television. Efforts to control corruption have usually failed, and current efforts seem to have little chance of long-term success. Boxing brings out a basic instinct in many and remains a path out of poverty for some.

David Levinson, Stan Shipley, and
Edward R. Beauchamp

See also Madison Square Garden; Mixed Martial Arts

Further Reading

Berger, P. (1989). *Blood season: Tyson and the world of boxing.* New York: Morrow.

Bodner, A. (1997). *When boxing was a Jewish sport.* New York: Praeger.

Cahn, S. K. (1994). *Coming on strong: Gender and sexuality in twentieth-century women's sports.* Cambridge, MA: Harvard University Press.

Denfeld, R. (1997). *Kill the body, the head will fall: A closer look at women, violence, and aggression.* New York: Warner Books.

Fleischer, N. (1929). *Jack Dempsey: The idol of fistiana.* New York: Ring Athletic Library.

Fried, R. K. (1991). *Corner men: Great boxing trainers.* New York: Four Walls, Eight Windows.

Gorn, E. J. (1986). *The manly art: Bare-knuckle prize fighting in America.* Ithaca, NY: Cornell University Press.

Guttmann, A. (1991). *The erotic in sport.* New York: Columbia University Press.

Hartley, R. A. (1988). *History & bibliography of boxing books.* Alton, UK: Nimrod Press.

Hauser, T. (1991). *Muhammad Ali: His life and times.* New York: Simon and Schuster.

Heller, P. (1974). *In this corne: Forty world champions tell their stories.* New York: Dell.

Isenberg, M. T. (1994). *John L. Sullivan and his America.* Champaign/Urbana: University of Illinois Press.

Johnson, J. (1977). *Jack Johnson: In the ring and out.* London: Proteus.

Magriel, P. (Ed.). (1951). *Memoirs of the life of Daniel Mendoza.* London: Batsford.

Mason, T. (Ed.). (1989). *Sport in Britain: A social history.* Cambridge, UK: Cambridge University Press.

Miles, H. D. (1906). *Pugilistica.* Edinburgh, UK: John Grant.

Newfield, J. (1995). *Only In America: The life and crimes of Don King.* New York: Morrow.

Reid, J. C. (1971). *Bucks and bruisers: Pierce Egan and Regency England.* London: Routledge.

Roberts, R. (1979). *Jack Dempsey: The Manassa Mauler.* Baton Rouge: Louisiana State University Press.

Salmonson, J. A. (1991). *The Encyclopedia of amazons: Women warriors from antiquity to the modern era.* New York: Paragon House.

Sammon, J. T. (1990). *Beyond the ring.* Champaign/Urbana: University of Illinois Press.

Shipley, S. (1993). *Bombardier Billy Wells: The life and times of a boxing hero.* Tyne and Wear, UK: Bewick.

Brand Management

*S*ports organizations, such as professional teams, college athletic departments, health clubs and even athletes, increasingly view themselves as brands to be managed. In addition, corporations spend billions of dollars every year to sponsor sporting events in an attempt to further their brands. To understand brand management, we must start with a definition of *brand*. According to David Aaker, "a brand is a distinguishing name and/or symbol (such as a logo, trademark, or package design) intended to identify the goods or services of either one seller or a group of sellers, and to differentiate those goods or services from those of competitors" (Aaker 1991, 7). As the branding concept relates to sports, the most noticeable application is to team names and related nicknames. For example, the New York Yankees of Major League Baseball and Man-

chester United of the English Premiere soccer league are strong professional sports brands. Coca-Cola and Nike are companies that regularly associate their brand names with sports entities to sell more products.

Brand management starts with the brand name but entails much more. Successful brand management creates brand equity or "a set of assets and liabilities linked to a brand, its name and symbol, that add to or subtract from the value provided by a product or service to a firm and/or that firm's customers" (Aaker 1991, 15). In the examples of the New York Yankees and Manchester United, both teams have long histories of success in competition. This success can be viewed as a strong asset linked to their respective brands. Nike paid Manchester United $473 million in a ten-year sponsorship agreement. A significant benefit of this agreement for Nike is that Nike products will be worn by the team when it plays. The agreement could also link the Manchester United brand name (and all of its assets such as success and tradition) to the Nike brand name.

Brand Equity

Brand equity is created through the development of brand awareness and a brand image. Brand awareness is the ability of a consumer to recall the brand name of a product when the industry in which that product competes is mentioned. If a consumer is unaware of the brand, then the brand cannot have equity in the consumer's mind. Brand awareness is easy to achieve for some sports entities. For example, most U.S. fans would name the Dallas Cowboys, Miami Dolphins, or New England Patriots when asked to name professional U.S. football teams. For other sports entities, achieving brand awareness is not as easy. New events and programs, such as the Dew Action Sports Tour (the first tour for action-sports athletes), must create awareness to be successful. Similarly, some corporations use sponsorships to create brand awareness. Nextel's sponsorship of the National Association for Stock Car Auto Racing (NASCAR) points championship is an attempt to build greater awareness of Nextel in the technology industries in which it competes.

The brand image of an organization must be devel-

When basketball is spoken, no translation is needed. It has become an independent international language. ▪ DAVID STERN

oped in order for the organization to have brand equity. *Brand image* is defined as "perceptions about a brand as reflected by the brand associations held in consumer memory" (Keller 1998, 93). Brand associations are the links in someone's memory to the brand name. Put another way, brand associations represent anything that exists in someone's memory with respect to a particular brand. For example, when asked about the Wimbledon tennis tournament, a tennis fan might mention words or phrases such as *tradition, grass playing surface, all-white uniforms,* and *great tennis.* These words or phrases are brand associations. Keller argues that in order to create brand equity, brand associations must be strong, unique, and favorable. One of the strong, unique, and favorable associations with the Wimbledon tennis tournament is the grass playing surface. One of the strong, unique, and favorable brand associations associated with Major League Baseball's Boston Red Sox is the stadium the team plays in—Fenway Park.

Benefits of Brand Equity

Brand equity provides a number of benefits for a sports entity, including strong loyalty to the brand. For example, the Chicago Cubs team of Major League Baseball, despite not winning a world championship in nearly one hundred years, regularly draws capacity crowds to its stadium, Wrigley Field. Why? The Cubs draw fans because the team has strong brand equity. Thus, having a strong brand enables a sports organization to retain fans even though the organization does not perform well. Brand equity provides other benefits, such as the ability to create and/or expand licensing (creation of products with the team name, logos, and colors) opportunities. Manchester United sells millions of dollars in merchandise worldwide because the team has such a strong brand. A sports organization that has brand equity is also more likely to not lose fans when it raises prices because fan loyalty to the brand is so high.

Unique Aspects of Branding

Because the outcome of sports competition is difficult to control and because the outcome affects a fan's enjoyment of the competition, branding of a sports product is more challenging. As a result, many teams focus on providing the best possible experience for their fans in order to create brand associations. Unlike most consumer goods and services, sports have the ability to engender strong emotional reactions in their consumers. In some cases this ability can be advantageous in creating brand associations. For example, when a team such as the Chicago Bulls of the National Basketball Association has a history of success (that translates into a strong, unique, and favorable association tied to the past) but is not successful currently, the team can promote its future by reminding its fans of the joy they experienced when the team was successful. These reminders trigger associations of what they felt as they followed a championship team. Because sports are often consumed in a social setting, fans also can have the strong, unique, and favorable brand association of sharing good times with friends or family. For this reason many sports marketers facilitate social interaction through the development of website chat rooms and bars and restaurants at stadiums and arenas.

Professional Sports

Brand management in professional sports typically occurs at three levels: the league or governing body, the team, and the athlete. David Stern, commissioner of the National Basketball Association (NBA), is a master of branding at the league level. Stern assumed the helm of the NBA in 1984 and developed widespread popularity for the league by creating strong, unique, and favorable brand associations relating to star players such as Michael Jordan, Larry Bird, and Magic Johnson. He also created strong associations tied to the NBA as an entertaining product. Using advertising taglines and positioning statements such as "I Love this Game," Stern oversaw the promotion of NBA action as exciting, fun, and entertaining.

At the team level teams create strong, unique, and favorable brand associations in a variety of ways. In addition to promoting star players, a team can make its head coach a source of brand equity. For example, Phil Jackson, former coach of the Chicago Bulls and Los Angeles Lakers of the NBA; and Bill Parcells, former coach of the New York Jets and Giants and New England Patriots and current coach of the Dallas Cowboys of the National Football League, are sources of strong, unique, and favorable brand associations with a sports team. Logos and team names can also be sources of brand associations. For example, the National Football League's team in Pittsburgh, Pennsylvania, has a name—"Steelers"—that is representative of the city's historically rooted major industry, the production of steel. The name provides an identity (hard working, blue collar) for the team that resonates with the community. Another source of brand awareness is the stadium in which a team plays. For example, given their historical significance, Old Trafford, where Manchester United plays its home soccer matches, and Santiago Bernabeu, where Spanish professional club Real Madrid plays, create strong, unique, and favorable brand associations.

The athlete can also be a brand. Did a more recognizable figure than Michael Jordan exist worldwide during his playing days? Similarly, athletes with global appeal, such as U.S. golfer Tiger Woods, British soccer player David Beckham, and race car driver Michael Schumacher of Germany, are brands unto themselves, as evidenced by the large sums of money that corporations pay them to endorse their products. Since about 1990 female professional athletes have increasingly become sports brands as well. In the United States soccer player Mia Hamm and tennis players (and sisters) Venus and Serena Williams have developed strong associations for themselves and the companies that endorse them.

College Sports

Brand management in major U.S. college athletic programs is similar to brand management in professional sports setting in some ways. For example, players, coaches, and stadiums can contribute to the creation of brand equity. However, some differences exist in the overall influence of each of these factors on the sports brand. Whereas star collegiate athletes are at college for only four to five years, star professional athletes may play their entire career of ten or more years with the same team. As a result, the head coach, who could be at one college for twenty or more years, may be a more influential source of strong, unique, and favorable brand associations than are athletes. For example, Joe Paterno has been head football coach at Pennsylvania State University since 1966 and has donated millions of dollars to the educational side of the university. Because of such donations and the success of his teams, he is a strong source of positive brand associations.

Other factors can create strong, unique, and favorable brand associations in the college setting. For example, the athletic reputation of a college is tied to the overall reputation of the college. For example, beyond its athletic prowess, the University of Michigan athletic program is tied to a university with a history of academic prestige. Additionally, the experience of watching (either in person or on television) a college sports event is different than watching a professional sports event. Most notably, marching bands play before, during, and after the event, adding to the experience and perhaps adding to the associations with a college's athletic program.

Corporations' Use of Teams and Athletes

The most common means by which corporations build their brands is sponsorship agreements with leagues, teams, events, and athletes. Corporations that sponsor events seek a variety of benefits, two of which are building brand awareness and enhancing or reinforcing brand image. Under Armor, a company that makes performance-based sports apparel products, created awareness for its products when famous athletes were seen wearing Under Armor apparel under uniforms and in practice settings. Presence on the playing field or in the arena is often a key strategy that makers of sports-related products use to create awareness. For example, Gatorade wants to be on the sidelines at athletic contests so that attendees and viewers see athletes drinking Gatorade. Similarly, Spalding pays the National Basketball Association for the right to produce the "official basketball of the NBA." From such exposures sports-related products gain not only awareness, but also cred-

Brand Management

Amateurism as the Brand

In Great Britain well into the twentieth century, making sure that all competitors were amateurs was a key element of the "sport" brand. The following rules, established by the Amateur Athletic Association (A.A.A.) in 1887, defines an amateur.

1. All competitions must be limited to amateurs.

   "An amateur is one who has never competed for a money prize or staked bet, or with or against a professional for any prize, or who has never taught, pursued, or assisted in the practice of athletic exercises as a means of obtaining a livelihood."

2. No person must be allowed to compete while under a sentence of suspension passed by either the A.A.A., National Cyclists Union, Swimming Association of Great Britain, Scottish A.A.A.

3. No "value" prize (i.e. a cheque on a tradesman) must be offered.

4. No prize must be offered in a handicap of greater value than 10*l*.10*s*.

5. Every prize of the value of 5*l* or upwards must be engraved with the name and date of the meeting.

6. In no case must a prize and money be offered as alternatives.

7. All prizes shall be publicly presented on the grounds on the day of the sports.

8. All open betting must be put down.

9. All clubs holding and advertising their sports 'under the laws of the Amateur Athletic Association must have printed on their entry forms "the definition of an Amateur" as adopted by the Amateur Athletic Association.

Source: *Badminton.* (1887). p. 222–223.

---

ibility because people can reason that if the product is used by athletes or coaches in competition, the product is one of the best.

Corporations also sponsor athletes, teams, and events to generate strong, unique, and favorable brand associations. For example, Nike became well known for sponsoring athletes who wore its products. Some people argued that Nike focused on identifying athletes who fit the image that Nike attempts to project: "Nike-endorsed athletes continued to embody the athletic ideals of determination, individuality, self-sacrifice, and winning through their continued successes on and off the playing field" (Keller 1998, E-9). Nike's sponsorship of Michael Jordan starting in 1984 is a perfect example of how Nike enhanced the image of its basketball shoes. Building on the shoes' "air" technology (air pockets in the soles), Nike partnered with Jordan, who was known for his ability to jump and remain airborne while shooting a basketball. One advertisement for Air Jordan shoes was described as a "testimonial comprised of nothing more than Jordan's ability to fly like a bird and the implication that the padded [air] technologies

bound to his feet had something to do with his agility and grace" (Katz 1995, 7).

Air Jordan shoes are an example of how a corporation enhances or reinforces brand associations through its involvement with athletes, teams, or leagues. Some researchers argue that a potential sponsor should consider the image of a sports entity. The image of an athlete, team, or event can help a sponsor reshape its image as well. For example, in an attempt to become the leading sponsor in soccer, a sport traditionally dominated by rival Adidas, Nike entered into two enormous sponsorship agreements with teams considered among the best in the world—the Brazilian national team and Manchester United. Mountain Dew is another example of a company that has borrowed brand associations from a sports organization. Mountain Dew has sponsored many action sports (snowboarding, BMX motorcycling, skateboarding, etc.) since such games began to become popular through cable TV network ESPN's X-Games. Through its sponsorship of these alternative sports, Mountain Dew has repositioned its brand as edgy, rebellious, and irreverent.

The Future

Leagues, events, teams, and athletes increasingly attempt to develop brand associations that portray them as being charitable or concerned about the community. Such "cause-related" sports-marketing efforts strive to create yet another strong, unique, and favorable brand association. Judging by the popularity of these efforts, they will become more important to brand management in the future.

Jay Gladden

See also Franchise Relocation; Sponsorship

Further Reading

Aaker, D. A. (1991). *Managing brand equity.* New York: Free Press.
Aaker, D. A. (1995). *Building strong brands.* New York: Free Press.
Aaker, D. A., & Joachimstahler, E. (2000). *Brand leadership: The next level of the brand revolution.* New York: Free Press.
Bedbury, S. (2002). *A new brand world: 8 principles for achieving brand leadership in the 21st century.* New York: Penguin Books.
Gladden, J. M., & Funk, D. C. (2001). Understanding brand loyalty in professional sport: Examining the link between brand associations and brand loyalty. *The International Journal of Sports Marketing and Sponsorship, 3*(1), 45–69.
Gladden, J. M., & Funk, D. C. (2002). Developing an understanding of brand associations in team sport: Empirical evidence from consumers of professional sport. *Journal of Sport Management, 16*(1), 54–81.
Gladden, J. M., Irwin, R. L., & Sutton, W. A. (2001). Managing North American major professional sport teams in the new millennium: Building, sharing, and maintaining equity. *Journal of Sport Management, 15*(4), 297–317.
Gladden, J. M., & McDonald, M. A. (1999). The brand management efforts of a niche specialist: New balance in the athletic footwear industry. *The International Journal of Sports Marketing and Sponsorship, 1*(2), 168–184.
Gladden, J. M., & Milne, G. R. (1999). Examining the importance of brand equity in professional sport. *Sport Marketing Quarterly, 8*(1), 21–29.
Gladden, J. M., Milne, G. R., & Sutton, W. A. (1998). A conceptual framework for assessing brand equity in Division I college athletics. *Journal of Sport Management, 12*(1), 1–19.
Gladden, J. M., & Wolfe, R. (2001). Sponsorship and image matching: The case of intercollegiate athletics. *The International Journal of Sports Marketing and Sponsorship, 3*(1), 71–98.
Kapferer, J. N. (1992). *Strategic brand management: New approaches to creating and evaluating brand equity.* New York: Free Press.
Katz, D. (1995). *Just do it: The Nike spirit in the corporate world.* Avon, MA: Adams Media.
Keller, K. L. (1998). *Strategic brand management: Building, measuring, and managing brand equity.* Upper Saddle River, NJ: Prentice Hall.
Pringle, H., & Thompson, M. (2001). *How cause related marketing builds brands.* Chichester, UK: Wiley.
Strasser, J. B. (1993). *Swoosh: The unauthorized story of Nike and the men who played there.* New York: Harper Business.
Travis, D. (2000). *Emotional branding.* Roseville, CA: Prima Venture.

Brazil

Foreigners—first the colonizing Portuguese and then British, French, Italian, and German immigrants and black slaves—played an important role in the development of sports in Brazil. The Europeans, for example, brought the practices of establishing sports clubs, setting up competitions, and teaching physical activities.

However, in spite of these European influences, sports did not develop in Brazil as they did in Europe. Brazilian culture, sports included, was formed as an eclectic amalgam from many sources.

Horse Racing: The First Sport

Although sports associations had existed in Brazil since the beginning of the nineteenth century, the first club dedicated to sports was established in the city of Rio de Janeiro in 1849. The Racing Club was dedicated to horse racing. People, generally Englishmen, had begun racing horses in Brazil in 1810, but only after establishment of the Racing Club did the sport become organized. The organization, form of competitions, and rules were based on those of clubs in England and France. Even the technical terms used were British. Until the middle of the twentieth century no Portuguese terms were used for sports in Brazil.

When horse racing began in Brazil, people began to include sports as part of the modernization of Brazilian society, which had begun in 1808 when the Portuguese royal family transferred the imperial court from Portugal to Brazil because of the Napoleonic Wars in Europe. This modernization was accelerated in 1822 when Brazil won its independence from Portugal.

A Brazilian Indian with archery gear. The woodcut is by Jacopus Sluperius, Antwerp, c. 1570. *Source: Sport Museum Flanders.*

Members of the upper classes, mainly people involved in the production and export of agricultural products, were instrumental in the introduction of horse racing, but they had many difficulties to overcome. Only after 1860 did horse racing become better organized and slowly find its way to Rio de Janeiro.

By 1870 horse racing was quite popular. By 1890 Rio de Janeiro had five horse racing clubs, each with its own turf. Horse racing was organized in cities such as Salvador, Recife, and Sao Paulo. Horse racing became not only a major entertainment option, but also an influence on customs.

Rowing

In the middle of the nineteenth century the national economy diversified, and industry began to develop. A new sector of the upper classes began to organize with urban characteristics. With slavery abolished in 1888 and the republic proclaimed in 1889, the urban sector of the upper classes became more powerful. Under the influence of positivism, the aim of the upper classes was to modernize Brazil at any cost. Tensions arose in the upper classes when people began to question the ethos (distinguishing character, sentiment, moral nature, or guiding beliefs) of the agricultural upper class. In this context of tensions many people began to criticize horse racing, saying that it was old-fashioned, tied to monarchy and rural ways of thinking. Even though such criticisms did not eliminate horse racing in Rio de Janeiro, by the end of the nineteenth century and into the twentieth century, the popularity of horse racing clubs was reduced because the city had new sports and new amusements.

In the second quarter of the nineteenth century people became concerned about the sanitation of their cities and took action to make cities more inhabitable. In this context seashore bathing became more popular —not for amusement but rather for health. Such bathing was regulated by the owners of scientific knowledge: physicians. Seashore bathing created a new sociability on the beaches and helped bring ocean sports to cities. The first boat races were held, creating a sense of competition against opponents, against oneself, and against the sea.

Although boat racing attracted large crowds from the beginning, time passed before it was well organized. People also had to accept a new body aesthetic. During the last quarter of the nineteenth century, influenced by Europe, Brazilians slowly began to value the strong physical body aesthetic. During the 1860s people began to accept the exposition of the human body, a healthy life standard, urban culture, and leisure time. In this context boat racing developed. By the end of the nineteenth century Brazil had fifteen boat racing clubs that held competitions. Boat racing became popular, taking the place of horse racing, although horse racing influenced the development of other sports, which used horse racing's structure of clubs, competition, and language.

A New Sports Standard

By the last quarter of the nineteenth century many gymnasiums had been built in cities. Such gymnasiums had

Brazil Olympics Results
2004 Summer Olympics: 4 Gold, 3 Silver, 3 Bronze

Brazil

Key Events in Brazil Sports History

1790s Capoeira is popular in Afro-Brazilian communities.

1849 The Racing Club dedicated to horse racing is founded in Rio de Janeiro.

1894 Soccer is brought to Brazil from England.

1900 Boat racing is popular.

1914 The Brazilian Olympic Committee is established.

1920 Brazil competes in the Olympics for the first time and Guilherme Paraense wins Brazil's first gold medal, in shooting.

1930s Sports are placed under government administration.

1939 Swimmer Maria Lenk is Brazil's first internationally famous athlete.

1950 Maracana Stadium is built in Rio de Janeiro.

1958 Brazil wins the Football World Championship for the first time.

1970s Capoeira becomes an international sport.

1980s Volleyball becomes a highly popular sport.

2003 The Ministry of Sports is established.

boat racing departments and competed in races. Gymnastics and swimming developed in colleges.

After boat racing began sports took on a new meaning and brought a new style of living to Brazilians. The boat racing clubs supported the concept of physical education; boat racing was acknowledged as one of the most complete forms of physical activity. Other sports (bicycle racing, fencing, shooting, swimming) also were being developed and guided by the concept of physical education.

Boat racing helped establish the values of Brazilian sports: the challenge, the connection with physical activities important for health, and a new body aesthetic of beauty and muscles. People active in sports were seen to be of good moral behavior.

The sport of rowing exemplified the modern values that Brazilians were embracing: open air, illumination, and nature (races were held outdoors), cleanliness (races were held in ocean water), wealth (the urban upper classes joined and lent their approval), health (rowers were strong and brawny), harmony (rowers worked as a team), organization (clubs were efficient), beauty (beautiful bodies competed in beautiful seashore landscapes), humanity (men, not horses, were the athletes), and challenge (rowers faced the dangers of the sea).

Football

The arrival of a new sport—football (soccer)—threatened the popularity of rowing. Charles Miller, a Scotsman working for the Sao Paulo Railway, had returned to England to attend college and in 1894 returned to Brazil with footballs, shoes, team shirts, and the game rules. He began to develop football in Brazil, where it was almost unknown. The sport quickly became popular in Sao Paulo.

The popularity of football, with its opportunity of direct participation, grew quickly. During the first decade of the twentieth century football fever swept Brazil as football clubs were founded and as rowing clubs and clubs of other sports began to create their own football teams. Championships were organized, and matches attracted more and more fans.

During the following decades football would be the subject of literature (Jose Lins do Rego, Vinicius de Moraes, Joao do Rio, Paulo Mendes Campos, and Carlos Drumond de Andrade), theater (Oduvaldo Viana Filho, and Nelson Rodrigues), plastic arts (Gerschmann and Portinari), music (Noel Rosa, Geraldo Pereira, and Chico Buarque), and movies (Nelson Pereira dos Santos and Joaquim Manuel Macedo).

The dynamics of football contributed to its popularity: Football can be played in many spaces, does not require expensive equipment, has simple rules, and allows

A lifeguard on duty in Brazil. Salva-Vidas means lifeguard in Portuguese.

Source: istockphoto/lucato.

physical contact and the participation of many persons. Football can be played not only on club grounds, but also on fields, yards, and improvised tracts of land: any place where the goals can be set. It can be played with a ball made of many materials: socks, paper, plastic, leather, and so forth.

1920–1970

During the 1920s sports in Brazil became more organized and diversified, with more clubs and competitions. After the 1930s government organizations became responsible for the rules governing sports. However, a ministry of sports was not established until 2003.

The Brazilian Olympic Committee was set up in 1914 but became effective only in 1935. Brazil first participated in the Olympic Games in 1920 (Antwerp, Belgium), when Guilherme Paraense won Brazil's first gold medal (in shooting). In 1939 Brazil produced its first athlete with international fame: The swimmer Maria Lenk broke the world record in the 400- and 200-meter breast stroke.

During the period 1950–1970 Brazil won interna-

tional recognition in two types of sports: (1) In track and field Adhemar Ferreira da Silva won gold medals in the triple jump at the Olympic Games in Helsinki, Finland (1952), and Melbourne, Australia (1956), and Joao Carlos da Silva broke the world record for that event; (2) in football Brazil won second place in the Football World Championship competition in 1950 and won the world championship in 1958 (Sweden), 1962 (Chile), and 1970 (Mexico).

Because of the quality of its players, Brazil became known as "the football country," and football became its most important sport. Brazil has five times been the world football champion. In addition to the years 1958, 1962, and 1970, Brazil won in 1994 (United States) and 2002 (Seoul/Tokyo) and was co-champion in 1998 with France.

1980–2004

During the 1980s Brazil's sports became more popular. Volleyball in particular became more popular, second only to football, as teams performed well in international contests in gymnasiums and on beaches. Sports

I've come to accept that the life of a frontrunner is a hard one, that he will suffer more injuries than most men and that many of these injuries will not be accidental. ▪ PELE

also became more professional as a growing number of athletes and teams began to gain notice in international competitions and as Brazil hosted important international competitions.

Brazilian athletes performed well in swimming (Gustavo Borges), yachting (Roberto Scheidt and Torben Grael), tennis (Gustavo Kuerten), judo (Aurelio Miguel), track and field (Joaquim Cruz and Ronaldo Costa), and artistic gymnastics (Daiane dos Santos). Their successes contributed to the popularization of sports in Brazil.

In addition, some Brazilian national sports, such as body attack and *futsal,* were becoming known in other countries.

The Future

Sports in Brazil lack the organization that sports have in other countries, but the Brazilian Olympic Committee now has better financial resources to make investments because of national legislation that provides incentives to sports. Rio de Janeiro has been chosen to host the Pan American Games of 2007 and is preparing to become a candidate to host the Olympic Games in 2012.

Victor Andrade de Melo

See also Capoeira; Maracana Stadium

Further Reading

Costa, C. (1961). *The turf of the past.* Rio de Janeiro, Brazil: Vida Turfista.
De Araujo, R. M. B. (1993). *Vocation to pleasure: City and family in republican Rio de Janeiro.* Rio de Janeiro, Brazil: Rocco.
De Melo, V. A. (2001). *Sporting city: First moments of sport in Rio de Janeiro (1849–1903).* Rio de Janeiro, Brazil: Relume Dumara.
Edmundo, L. (1957). *Rio de Janeiro of my time.* Rio de Janeiro, Brazil: Conquista.
Licht, H. (1986). *Rowing in the history.* Porto Alegre, Brazil: Corag.
Marinho, I. P. (1943). *Contributions to history of physical education in Brazil.* Rio de Janeiro, Brazil: Imprensa Oficial.
Mendonca, A. B. (1909). *History of the nautical sport in Brazil.* Rio de Janeiro, Brazil: Federacao Brazileira de Sociedades de Remo.
Needell, J. D. (1993). *Tropical belle epoque.* Sao Paulo, Brazil: Companhia das Letras.
Pereira, L. A. M. (2000). *Football mania: A social history of football in Rio de Janeiro (1902–1938).* Sao Paulo, Brazil: Nova Fronteira.
Rabello, T. (1901). *History of turf in Brazil.* Rio de Janeiro, Brazil: Leuzinger.
Renault, D. (1978). *Rio de Janeiro: The life of the city in newspapers—1850–1870.* Rio de Janeiro, Brazil: Civilizacao Brasileira/MEC.
Sevcenko, N. (1998). *History of the private life in Brazil.* Sao Paulo, Brazil: Companhia das Letras.

British Open

The 2004 Open Championship of the Royal and Ancient Golf Club (R&A) marked the 133rd time the contest was held since its inception on Prestwick's twelve-hole course on 17 October 1860. The first "Open" contestants were actually eight caddies—the first "professional golfers"—responding to an invitation sent to six area clubs to send their best, respectable caddies, to prepare the course for the Grand Tournament (first held in 1854) pairing gentleman golfers from the twelve established clubs. These caddie/professionals spent their days playing with and assisting the "gentleman" (amateur) golfers, often making balls or golf clubs at their home courses, and preparing the courses for the gentlemen's matches. The Amateur Championship consisted of a week of match play, and the first Open was actually a one-day Challenge event for the professionals at the end of the Amateur week. The first Challenge winner was Willie Park of Musselburgh, who beat "Old" Tom Morris by two strokes with a score of 174 over three rounds played on the same day. The winner received only the title—The Champion Golfer of the Year—and the Challenge Belt, but no money, whereas the runner up received the sum of 3 pounds. To increase the participation for the next year, the event was opened to amateurs and professionals alike. Ten professionals and eight amateurs entered the 1861 Open. The highest placed amateur was Colonel J. O. Fairlie in eighth place, twenty-one strokes behind the champion, Tom Morris Senior, who outscored Park to claim the victory, and later won an additional three (1862, 1864, and 1867) times. In 1864, a monetary prize was first awarded to the champion (6 pounds). Morris's win in 1867, at the age of 46 years 99 days, remains the record for oldest winner of the event. His son, "Young" Tom Morris, won the event four consecutive outings, with his 1868 victory setting the record for the youngest victor to date—17 years 5 months 8 days.

The tournament continued the format of three rounds of thirty-six holes of golf on one day, at one of the three host club courses (Prestwick, St. Andrews, or Musselburgh) until 1892, when Muirfield was introduced as a new venue. This signaled the change of the Open format, as the clubs established more entry regulations, higher fees (10 shillings), played the event as four rounds over two days, and opened it internationally to include two English Clubs (St. George's at Sandwich and Royal Liverpool at Hoylake). The Open Championship was governed by delegates of the five affiliated clubs, each contributing 15 pounds annually. The prize money totaled 100 pounds. This format remained until World War I, when play was suspended. After the war, the championship reemerged under the governance of the R&A, which assumed the responsibility every year since 1920. Today, there are qualifying events on five continents, and the contest is played over four days with as many as 160 players teeing off in the first round. The prize purse exceeds 1.5 million pounds, and the winner takes home more than 200,000 pounds, yet the greatest prize remains the title and the Claret Jug.

Prizes

From 1860 until 1870, the winner was awarded a Moroccan leather belt bejeweled by a silver buckle engraved with a golf scene. The Open champion could only gain permanent possession of the Challenge belt by winning three years in succession. In 1870, Tom Morris Junior was the first to complete the requisite three consecutive victories, which left the Open without a trophy to present. To ease the burden of hosting the event, Prestwick invited R&A and the Honourable Company of Edinburgh Golfers to co-host the championship beginning in 1871. However, a lack of urgency and coordination by the three clubs resulted in no contest being held that year. In May 1872, the clubs reached agreement, and the event was held at the R&A (St. Andrews) in 1873, and at the Honourable Company of Edinburgh Golfers (Musselburgh) in 1874. In 1872, the winner, Tom Morris Junior, was awarded a metal, and Mackay Cunningham & Company of Edinburgh was commissioned to cast the future trophy—the famous Claret Jug, which was presented to the winner, along with a medal, until 1927. Following Bobby Jones's win at St. Andrews, the Championship Committee of the R&A decided that "in future the original Open Championship Cup be retained in possession of the Royal and Ancient Golf Club and . . . a duplicate be obtained for presentation to the winners." Today, the trophy is presented to each new champion, but many winners privately commission copies of the ancient jug for their personal collections.

Venues

The Challenge Trophy event was held at Prestwick from 1860 until 1870, played for the first time on the Old Course at St. Andrews in 1873, and played only in Scotland, at Prestwick, St. Andrews, or Musselburgh until 1894. In 1894, Royal St. George's became the first English (non-Scottish) club to host the Open (at Sandwich in Kent). In 1897, the Royal Liverpool Golf Club (Hoylake, in Cheshire) was the second English venue to be added. Since then, the championships have been held at fourteen different venues in the British Isles, with the home course of the R&A, St. Andrews, hosting the most, twenty-six events.

Champions

The British Open continues to perpetuate periods of dominance, just as Tom Morris Senior and Junior dominated the early days (1860–1872). Notably, from 1894 to 1914, the trio of Harry Vardon, J. H. Taylor, and James Braid became known as the Great Triumvirate, winning the championship sixteen times, with Braid and Taylor posting five victories each, and Vardon remaining the only man to win the title six times.

The first overseas champion was Frenchman Arnaud Massey in 1907.

Golf. Trying to knock a tiny ball into an even smaller hole with implements ill suited to the purpose. ■ WINSTON CHURCHILL.

In 1921, just after World War I, the championship became truly a worldwide challenge following the victory of Jock Hutchison, an American citizen and immigrant from St. Andrews. Although Hutchison was the first American citizen to win, every Open champion from 1924 until 1933 was an American. Most notable was the young lawyer and amateur from Atlanta, Bobby Jones. Playing against professionals such as Walter Hagen (the first American-born champion, 1922, and four-time winner) and Gene Sarazen (who set the low aggregate record score of 283 in 1932), Jones won the Open three times—his final in 1930, the year he won the grand slam, then immediately retired from the game at only 30 years of age. Jones joins Harold Hilton and John Ball as the only amateur champions through 2004. Henry Cotton's 1934 victory included a record-setting second-day low score of 65, a tie with Sarazen's overall 283, and an end to the string of American wins—Cotton won three Opens in his career and brought pride back to Britain. British pride and dominance prevailed until World War II; however, in postwar years South African Bobby Locke and Australian Peter Thomson regularly led the field, capturing the title four times each in a ten-year period, starting in 1949. Thomson added a fifth championship win in 1965. Only two other players, Max Faulkner for England and Ben Hogan for America, won during the Locke and Thomson era. Among modern-era champions are Arnold Palmer, Gary Player, Jack Nicklaus, Seve Ballesteros, Nick Faldo, Nick Price, Greg Norman, Lee Trevino, Johnny Miller, and finally Tom Watson (who joined Braid, Taylor and Thomson as a five-time champion); most of them have won multiple times.

Significance

The British Open is considered one of the four major or grand slam championships for male golfers around the world (the PGA, the U.S. Open, and the Master's Championships are the others).

Debra A. Ballinger

Further Reading

Frost, M. (2002). *The greatest game ever played: Harry Vardon, Francis Ouimet, & the birth of modern golf.* New York: Hyperion.
Glover, J. (1998). *Golf: A celebration of 100 years of the rules of play.* Chicago: Triumph Books.
Joy, D. (1999). *St. Andrews & the open championship: The official history.* Chelsea, MI: Sleeping Bear Press.
The Official Site of The Open Championships. Retrieved May 4, 2004, from http://www.opengolf.com/history/default.sps
British Open Golf Championship. Retrieved July 20, 2004, from http://golf.about.com/library/weekly/blbritishopen.htm
The Official Site of the Royal and Ancient Golf Club. Retrieved July 20, 2004, from http://www.randa.org
Golf Europe.com. Retrieved July 20, 2004, from http://www.golfeurope.com/almanac/majors/the_open.htm

Bulgaria

Bulgarians take pride in the antiquity and diversity of their sports, which include football (soccer), rugby, gymnastics, weightlifting, bowling, ice-skating, and swimming. Sports have uplifted Bulgaria during centuries of foreign domination. Bulgaria occupies 110,910 square kilometers on the west coast of the Black Sea. In addition to its eastern border along the sea, Bulgaria extends north to Romania, south to Greece and Turkey, and west to Serbia, Montenegro, and Macedonia. Sofia, the Bulgarian capital, is home to 1,088,700 of the country's 7.5 million inhabitants.

Religious Festivals to Olympic Championships

Polish philosopher Jerzy Kosiewicz traces the origin of Bulgarian sports to Thrace, a region of Bulgaria inhabited since 7000 BCE.

■ In the thirteenth century BCE, Thracian king Orpheus organized religious festivals that included contests of strength and speed. These contests inspired the Greeks to found the Olympic Games in 776 BCE, contends Kosiewicz.

■ In the first century BCE, the Romans used Thracians in gladiatorial combat, a mix of sport and savagery.

Bulgaria

Key Events in Bulgaria Sports History

13th century BCE	Religious festivals in Thrace include sports competitions.
1880s	The first ice rink is opened.
1896	Bulgaria competes in the first modern Olympics.
1920	The first swimming competition is held.
1922	A rhythmic gymnastics team for women is formed.
1944	The Committee of Physical Culture and Sports and the National Sports Academy are established.
1959	The first rugby club is formed.
1959	Bulgaria wins for the first time the European Junior Football Championship.
1962	Bulgaria competes in its first soccer World Cup.
2000	The Bulgarian Bowling Federation is established.
2000	The Bulgarian weightlifting team is banned from the Olympics for the use of performance-enhancing drugs.

■ In the second century CE, the amphitheater in Plovdiv, Bulgaria, hosted gladiators and charioteers.

In the 1880s, Alexander of Battenberg, ruler of the Third Bulgarian Kingdom, fashioned the first ice rink. In 1944, the Soviet Union created the Committee of Physical Culture and Sports to fund sports in Bulgaria. That year, the Committee founded the National Sports Academy in Sofia to train athletes. The Academy and other Bulgarian schools control access to sports, holding entrance exams for children as young as age five. Instructors supervise training and diet to a degree uncommon in American schools.

Participant and Spectator Sports

In 1920, the Bulgarian People's Marine Agreement hosted the first swimming competition in Varna. In 1931, the Dianabad, an Olympic pool in Sofia, convened the first swim meet of the Balkan Games. Bulgarian swimmers have entered the following contents:

■ Balkan Championships in 1946
■ European Championships in 1958
■ Olympic Games in 1968

■ Fédération Internationale de Natation Amateur World Championships in 1973

Bulgarian swimmers hold 136 men's and 95 women's titles in the Balkan Championships.

Bulgaria has fielded a football team for international competition since 1924 and for seven World Cups since 1962, posting 4 wins, 6 ties, 14 losses, and a fourth place finish, the best to date, in 1994. In 1956, the Bulgarian Olympic team won a bronze medal and in 1968 a silver. In May 2003, the Fédération Internationale de Football ranked Bulgaria thirty-fourth in the world.

In 1959, the National Sports Academy founded its first rugby club. The sport is transnational—Murphy's Misfits, an amateur team in Sofia, recruits players from Bulgaria, England, Ireland, Scotland, Wales, France, the United States, Romania, Canada, Zimbabwe, and New Zealand. The International Rugby Board ranked Bulgaria eighty-eighth in the world in 2004. Bulgaria qualified 30 September 2004 for Round 2 of the Rugby World Cup by beating Finland 50 to 3.

In 2000, the Ministry of Youth and Sports, successor to the Committee of Physical Culture and Sports,

Bulgaria Olympics Results
2002 Winter Olympics: 1 Silver, 2 Bronze
2004 Summer Olympics: 2 Gold, 1 Silver, 9 Bronze

established the Bulgarian Bowling Federation, which hosts more than 50 tournaments in Bulgaria, the most prestigious being the National Individual and Team Bowling Championships. Bulgaria competes in the European Cup, the Bowling World Cup, and the World Tenpin Bowling Championships.

Since resumption of the Olympic Games in 1896, Bulgaria has won 195 medals in the Summer Games and 5 in the Winter Games, ranking eighteenth of 146 countries and twenty-fourth of 43, respectively.

Women and Sport

In 1922, Bulgarian women joined the first rhythmic gymnastics team in Plovdiv and in 1944 took the first course in rhythmic gymnastics at the National Sports Academy. In 1964, the Bulgarian Rhythmic Gymnastics Federation organized the first national women's team. Since that year, Bulgarian women have won 157 gold, 180 silver, and 78 bronze world championship and Olympic medals. In 2004, the Federation numbered 40 clubs and more than 5,000 women ages four to twenty.

In 2004, the National Sports Academy fielded women's teams in football, skiing, track and field, swimming, handball, fencing, volleyball, basketball, rugby, tennis, judo, boxing, weightlifting, gymnastics, archery, and windsurfing.

Youth Sports

Girls begin training for rhythmic gymnastics at age four with school entrance exams at five. Girls younger than age ten compete in the children's division, between ages ten and twelve in the junior division, between thirteen and fourteen in the senior division, and older than fourteen in the adult division. Most girls end their career by eighteen.

In 1959, 1969, and 1974, Bulgaria won the European Junior Football Championships. Since 1976, Bulgaria has competed at the World Junior Figure Skating Championships and, since 1997, at the Junior Figure Skating Grand Prix Series of the International Skating

Union. The Arpezos Swimming Complex in Kardjali, Bulgaria, hosts youth meets. The Bulgarian Bowling Federation also has a children's league.

Sports in Society

Sports in Bulgaria have provided cohesion during periods of foreign domination. The importance of sports to national identity presses athletes to succeed, instilling a win-at-all-costs mentality.

This mentality tarnished Bulgaria in 1988 when the International Olympic Committee rescinded gold medals from two Bulgarian weightlifters for using furosemide, a diuretic that masks the presence of anabolic steroids in blood and urine. In 2000, the Committee stripped three weightlifters of medals for the same offence and banned Bulgaria's weightlifting teams from the rest of the Games. The infraction prompted the International Weightlifting Federation to suspend Bulgaria from international competition for twelve months.

The Future

Sports, a constant for 3,300 years, promises to shape Bulgaria's future. Fresh from its victory in Round 1 of the Rugby World Cup, Bulgaria is poised to improve its ranking, an ascent that should attract new players to rugby. Bowling may likewise recruit new participants, thanks to an influx of U.S. and European sponsors. Foreign investment may strengthen the role of private enterprise in Bulgarian sports, making them less dependent on government.

Governing Bodies

The Bulgarian Football Union (www.bfunion.bg) is an affiliate of the Federation Internationale de Football, the Bulgarian Rugby Federation is an affiliate of the International Rugby Board, and the Bulgarian Skating Federation (www.bsf.sof.bg) is an affiliate of the International Skating Union. The Bulgarian Rhythmic Gymnastics Federation (www.olympic.bg/rgym) and the Bulgarian Bowling Federation (www.bulgarian

bowlingf.com) have guided the development of their sports since 1964 and 2000 respectively.

Christopher Cumo

Further Reading

Freeman, S., & Boyes, R. (1980). *Sports behind the Iron Curtain.* New York: Lippincott & Crowell.
Hickok, B. (2004). *Everything you wanted to know about sports.* Retrieved November 12, 2004, from http://www.hickoksports.com
Ivanova, D., & Boyes, R. (2004). *Art gymnastics in Bulgaria.* Retrieved November 12, 2004, from http://library.thinkquest.org/29171
National sports academy. (2004). Retrieved November 12, 2004, from http://www.nsa.bg

Bullfighting

Bullfighting is a spectacle in which men ceremonially fight with—and in Hispanic tradition—kill bulls in an arena for public entertainment. Bullfighting is practiced primarily in Spain and to a lesser extent in Mexico, Central America, South America, southern France, and Portugal.

The sport depends on five elements:

1. A large and constant supply of "noble" or "brave" bulls (i.e., bulls specially bred to charge aggressively in a straight line)
2. A large and constant supply of young poor men
3. Large numbers of hero-worshipping people addicted to thrilling displays of raw physical courage
4. A smaller number of aficionados obsessed with technical and historical details
5. Generations of writers and intellectuals who consider bullfighting a fine art rather than a sport

In any given year approximately ten thousand bullfights are held worldwide, usually in the context of a local religious fiesta that may also include running bulls or cows through the town streets, as in the famous festival of Pamplona, Spain.

Although bullfighting possesses many ritualistic aspects, we should not call it a "ritual." In a true ritual, such as the Catholic Mass, the officiate and communicants are engaged in deliberately symbolic activity; their every word and every action have an agreed-on spiritual referent; everything is rigidly predetermined, nothing is left to chance. None of these qualities can be found in a bullfight. Bullfighting has no deliberately symbolic activity, only simple signals such as handkerchief waving and clarion calls. The bullfighter's actions do not "stand for" anything beyond themselves, and the spectators are always entitled to disagree about the actions. A great deal is left to chance because one cannot predict the behavior of bulls, crowds, or matadors. A fair chance always exists that the performance will turn sour and anticlimactic or tragic and ugly.

The rules of a typical bullfight call for a four- or five-year-old bull to be "picced" in his withers with a long lance, further weakened by banderillas (decorated darts) and risky or flashy cape passes, then killed with a sword thrust by a man wearing decorative rather than protective clothing. Because the horses of picadors (mounted riders who pierce the bull with lances during the first stage of the fight) now wear thick padding, the element of cruelty to animals is incidental rather than central to the actual mechanics of the bullfight, more apparent than real. Bullfighting has been an ecological preserve for the Iberian *toro bravo* (brave bull), a species as rare and unique as the American buffalo, cherished and pampered by ranchers. The archaic concept of manhood that animates the spectacle requires a worthy opponent at all times. That is why Hispanic fans always shout out their disapproval if they perceive that a bull is being mishandled and mistreated. Nevertheless, the psychology of both bullfight performers and spectators is thoroughly sado-masochistic, as could hardly be otherwise in a show that features public killing and needless risk of human life. For the thoughtful student of world sports, bullfighting raises questions of a moral or ethical nature much more serious than the ones raised by animal rights activists.

Origins

A predatory species of mammal known as Homo sapiens and a herbivorous mammal species known as *bos taurus* had gone forth and multiplied with particular success in the Iberian peninsula (Spain and Portugal). Mythology tells us that when Hercules had to steal bulls, he went to what is now the province of Cadiz in southern Spain. Apart from being used as food, the bull was in all likelihood a totemic figure and/or sacrificial victim for the races that populated Iberia during the Bronze Age (c. 2500 BCE). Local cults were later blended with beliefs and practices common to the entire Mediterranean area—chief among them the cult of Tauromorphic Bacchus, or Dionysus, firmly entrenched in the Hispania of Roman days. However, the Visigothic barbarians who occupied Hispania when Rome fell had no interest in animal baiting, and the grand amphitheaters were abandoned and never used again.

In the hinterlands, however, the bull continued to play the role of magical agent of sexual fertility, especially in wedding customs that called for the bride and groom to stick darts into a bull tied to a rope. The object was not to fight the beast—certainly not to kill him—but rather to evoke his fecundating power by "arousing" him, then ritually staining their garments with his blood. This nuptial custom evolved into the rural *capea* (bull-baiting fiesta), which in turn led to grandiose urban spectacles organized to celebrate military victories or royal weddings. The common people were permitted to crowd into gaily decorated plazas (one in Madrid had room for sixty thousand spectators) and watch their lords, mounted on gallant steeds, lancing bulls.

Until the eighteenth century vast herds of aggressive Iberian bulls roamed freely and bred themselves with no interference from the human species. When knightly bullfighting was in flower, the elite sent their peons into the wilds to round up as many bulls as they could. However, not every wild bull had the right amount of *bravura* (focused aggressiveness) to make the aristocrat look good with his lance; thus, large numbers of bulls were supplied in the hope that enough of them would act out their roles convincingly.

Hostility on the Hoof

As bullfighting on foot became more popular during the 1700s, the demand for bulls increased accordingly, specifically for bulls that could be counted on to charge and not to flee. So the landed blue bloods did the same thing with the bulls that they had done with themselves in earlier epochs: They developed techniques for testing *bravura*, then perpetuated the blood of the bravest through consanguineous (descended from the same ancestor) mating. Whether or not we think that aristocrats were a superior species, the animals they bred unquestionably were and are amazingly consistent in their power, size, and aggressiveness. Hundreds of cattle ranches supply the roughly twenty-five thousand bulls killed every year by Spanish matadors. The many brands of brave bulls that constitute the indispensable raw material for today's corridas (programs of bullfights for one day, usually six) descend from only five *castas* or bloodlines, all developed during the eighteenth century. The prestige of a particular brand of bulls was traditionally based on the number of horses, toreros (matadors or members of the attending team), or innocent bystanders they had killed or maimed. On several occasions bulls being shipped to a bullfight by train escaped from their railroad crates to wreak havoc.

Practice

In a rural fiesta no one is in a hurry to see the bull dead; when the time comes to kill him, any method will do, from a shotgun to a mass assault with knives. In the urban corrida, however, showing efficiency and know-how is crucial; the bull is to be dispatched cleanly (at least in theory) and in three timed *suertes* (acts)—picador, banderillas, and matador. Daily experience in the slaughterhouse gave certain ambitious plebeians the necessary knowledge and skill, and the boldest discovered they could earn more money by doing their jobs in public in the manner of a duel: man against monster. The guild system then dominant in the workaday world served as the model for turning bullfighting into a true profession with rules, regulations, hierarchism, apprenticeship, and seniority.

Bullfighting

Excerpt from Ernest Hemingway's *Death in The Afternoon* (1932)

Although underappreciated by early critics, Hemingway's account of bullfighting in Spain is now considered one of the most important works on the topic. Hemingway came to see bullfighting as a tragedy, not a sport.

The three phases of the bull's condition in the fight are called in Spanish, levantado, parado, and aplomado. He is called levantado, or lofty, when he first comes out, carries his head high, charges without fixing any object closely and, in general, tries, confident in his power, to sweep the ring clear of his enemies.

[. . .]

When the bull is prado he is slowed and at bay. At this time he no longer charges freely and wildly in the general direction of any movement or disturbance; he is disillusioned about his power to destroy or drive out of the ring anything that seems to challenge him and, his initial ardor calmed, he recognizes his enemy, or sees the lure that his enemy presents him instead of his body, and charges that with full aim and intention to kill and destroy.

[. . .]

When he is aplomado he has been made heavy, he is like lead; he has usually lost his wind, and while his strength is still intact, his speed is gone. He no longer carries his head high; he will charge if provoked; but whoever cites him must be closer and closer. For in this state the bull does not want to charge unless he is sure of his objective, since he has obviously been beaten, to himself as well as the spectator, in everything he has attempted up to that time; but he is still supremely dangerous.

Source: Hemingway, E. (1932). *Death in the Afternoon* (pp. 145147). New York: Charles Scribner's Sons.

The first professional bullfighters were men completely immersed in the ethos (distinguishing character, sentiment, moral nature, or guiding beliefs) of the eighteenth-century urban slum. They detested the effeminate aristocratic fashions imported from France and proudly affirmed "pure" native concepts of male honor, along with bold and insolent styles of dressing, walking, talking, and killing. Among the rank and file of the down and outs, the readiness to kill or die with a maximum of nonchalance was the only route to prestige. Bullfighting on foot appealed chiefly to violent men who had nothing to lose and something to prove. Ironically, the sport has always enjoyed enthusiastic support among the same poor masses who would never have chosen bullfighting as a way to escape poverty—masses who, in other words, were either resigned to their lowly fate or hopeful that through hard work and daily sacrifice they could somehow find a better life but who were willing, all the same, to deify those few who were neither resigned nor inclined to hard work. Bullfighters were rebels in a rigidly stratified society, violators of the general law of submission to circumstances. However, the violation of one value system implies adherence to another.

The code that matadors lived by was called *"verguenza torera"* or *"pundonor"* (point of honor). Both terms possess a certain connotation of "touchiness" that descends quite directly from the oldest, most benighted tradition of Spanish honor obsessions. Simply put, the colloquial term *verguenza torera* means a bullfighter's willingness to place his reputation ahead of his own life. This is not a mythical or romantic notion but rather a genuine code of conduct. Flashy flirtation with death has both financial and psychological rewards: By all accounts the heady delusion of omnipotence and heroism that matadors experience is quite addictive. A retired bullfighter is like a reformed alcoholic, always on the verge of a relapse into his favorite vice. Sometimes death is the only sure cure. Those bullfighters who best embody the imprudent honor code receive positive reinforcement from the crowds—rewarded, as it were, for their appetite for punishment. Toreros who stray

A matador in Quito, Ecuador. *Source: istockphoto/sweef.*

from the code are negatively reinforced in the form of jeers, taunts, thrown objects, and malicious reviews. Readers of *Death in the Afternoon* may recall the U.S. writer Ernest Hemingway's witty, catty, and often vicious disparagement of the bullfighters of his day.

Throughout the nineteenth century the popular concept of bullfighting was that of a martial art. Matadors were considered to be warriors; their "suits of light" were a kind of super-uniform, and their performances were so many episodes of a grandiose national saga. Unlike other European nations during this period, Spain saw its colonial possessions shrinking instead of expanding. For many Spaniards the corrida may have been a gratifying fantasy of national potency to make up for the less-than-glorious reality.

The military origins of bullfight music have been firmly established by scholars. Every change of *suerte* in a bullfight was, and is, signaled by a bugle call; the melodies are much the same as those used in infantry and cavalry barracks. The *pasodoble*, the stirring music played even today by bullring bands, descends directly from the military march. More than five hundred of them were composed, and the band was always on hand

to set the right tone of militancy. After the loss of Spain's colonies to the United States in 1898, numerous bullfights were organized in which people wore the national colors, and bullfighters made inflammatory speeches. During the Spanish Civil War (1936–1939) both sides sponsored corridas; bullfighters would parade with clenched fists or fascist salutes, whichever was appropriate. During the darkest days of their country's isolation under General Francisco Franco, Spaniards flocked to bullrings to reaffirm their identity with something that they knew was their own and that they took to represent their finest qualities. However barbarous its origins, however sordid some of its practices, the *fiesta de toros* (festival of the bulls) had truly become Spain's Fiesta Nacional.

Process of Elimination

For every successful matador paraded around the bullring on the shoulders of ecstatic fans, an invisible army of forgotten young men tried and failed. Like certain marine species that give birth to thousands of young so that a few will reach maturity, the overwhelming majority of would-be matadors has been eliminated by environmental factors, each harsher than the last. The bull's horns are the most basic, physical agent of this process of natural selection. For many Spanish youth the beginning was the end. Since the mid-1700s at least 170 young aspirants were killed by goring, along with 142 banderilleros (persons who thrust in the banderillas), 70 picadors, 59 full matadors, and 4 comic bullfighters. These statistics do not include toreros killed during ranch tests or private parties, nor do they include *capeas* (amateur bullfights), which have arguably been festal Spain's major device for maiming young bodies and crushing hopes. Doctors specializing in *taurotraumatologia* (horn-wound surgery) are accustomed to working on the pierced thighs, ruptured rectums, and eviscerated scrota of bullfighters. When an apprentice torero recovers from his first goring and reappears in the ring, his manager anxiously watches for any sign that his valor or his determination has been compromised. The all-powerful element of luck will still preside over his career. To be successful, a man must meet a noble and cooperative bull at the right moment; he must also have *padrinos* (godfathers), a good manager, opportunities, a crowd-pleasing personality, grace, flair, and a whole series of other qualities that is difficult to isolate but nevertheless means the difference between glory and mediocrity.

In view of this brutal selection process, one might well ask why any young man in his right mind would want to be a bullfighter. Poverty is the answer most often given to this question. Many portions of the Spanish populace have been condemned to misery, illiteracy, and lack of opportunity. Harsh as they have been, however, these social conditions are not sufficient in themselves to explain matador motivation. They obviously do not tell us why bullfighters who were already immensely wealthy—such as Espartero or Belmonte or Paquirri—remained in the plazas, or why so many men who had actually found good jobs wanted only to fight bulls. Additional motivational factors include self-destructive tendencies and unusually powerful oedipal conflicts. With an activity that has been one of the only means of advancement in a rigidly stratified society, whose wellspring is passion and whose lifeblood is the ritual combat between two animal species, where a lucky and skillful few succeed where so many hundreds fail, where so many frustrated men hound their sons into bullrings to avenge their own defeats, where critics dip their pens in poison and crowds go from adulation to mockery in a second, we cannot help but find sadomasochistic behavior patterns. In general, matadors are men obsessed with insurmountable violent masculine role models and rivals; their ambition is directly correlated with the obstacles placed in their path. Violence becomes identified with fullness of being; winning or losing, brutalizing or arranging to be brutalized, the bullfighter keeps his buried fantasies of omnipotence alive. Hemingway idolized masochistic matadors with adolescent enthusiasm, but in many ways they are like compulsive gamblers who throw caution to the winds and unconsciously play to lose all. Unlike gamblers, bullfighters go for broke in front of huge crowds of people egging them on; so, in the last analysis, the taurine (relating to bulls) honor code is a matter of mass cultural psychology. Countless bullfighters have confessed to fearing the crowd's reactions more than the bulls themselves. Mass desire is as potentially sadomasochistic as individual desire: It will polarize around any expert manipulator of violence, seemingly autosufficient and untouchable in his charisma. The dramatic death of a matador in the line of duty (caused most often by his socially sanctioned suicidal honor) and his subsequent deification in popular lore simply carry the whole idolatrous process to its logical conclusion.

Women in Bullfighting

The bullfight has been transformed by the entry of women performers to its professional leagues as matadors. The presence of women in the ring remains an issue with some aficionados, but more and more are coming to accept women as the equals of their male counterparts.

The most respected woman performer of the early twentieth century was Juanita Cruz (b. 1917), of whom ex-bullfighter Domingo Ortega declared "she was the pure bullfight represented in the body of a woman." Juanita Cruz's debut public performance was in 1932, and her career was at its peak when in 1934 the dictatorship of General Franco banned women from performing on foot in public. His ban cut short the ambition of a whole generation of women bullfighters. Unable to continue her career in Spain, Cruz went to Latin America, where she graduated to professional status.

Juanita Cruz was not the only woman performer to have her career in Spain halted by Franco's ban, although some, like Cruz, managed to continue elsewhere. Under his rule women were allowed to participate in *rejoneo* (horseback bullfighting). During this period the *rejoneadora* Conchita Cintron, born in Chile in 1922, developed an outstanding career in Latin America and later in Spain as a horseback performer. However, in Spain women did not legally perform in public on foot until 1974, when a campaign led by the woman bullfighter Angela Hernandez (b. 1946) ended the ban.

Since the reentry of women, such as Angela Hernandez and Maribel Atienza (b. 1959), into bullfighting during the 1970s, the number of women taking part has gradually increased in what is now a media-dominated and structured and regulated amateur and professional bullfighting league. The women performers of the 1970s and 1980s participated at the amateur *novillero* (novice bullfighter) stage but were never referred to by the masculine title of *novillero* or torero; they were instead referred to as *novilleras*. Like their predecessors they faced fierce criticism, and their careers were usually short-lived. Only in the 1990s did women foot performers become fully established as bullfighters.

The career of Cristina Sanchez has come to symbolize a new status for women in bullfighting. Sanchez, born near Madrid in 1971, graduated as the top student from the Madrid bullfighting school in 1989. She continued on to become one of the most successful young *novilleros* of her time. Sanchez maintained her place at the top of the *novillero* leagues until 1996, when she became the first woman to take the alternative, graduating

to professional torero status in Nimes, France, one of the bullrings included in the Spanish circuit. Unlike her predecessors, Sanchez insists on being called a "torero" rather than the feminized "torera." Although she rejects the label of "feminist," she argues that as performers, men and women should be treated as equals. Her success during the early 1990s was followed by several other hopeful young women performers, such as the *novilleros* Yolanda Caravajal (b. 1968), Laura Valencia (b. 1971), and Mari Paz Vega (b. 1974), who was granted professional torero status in 1997.

Microcosm of Spain

From a historical point of view, bullfighting has been nothing less than a microcosm of Spain, a nation built not on individuals but on quasi-familial factions, where a "strong man" ultimately derived his strength from the debility of his supporters, and the weak got nowhere without patriarchs, godfathers, political bosses, and other men who bestowed rewards and punishments in accordance with their mood swings. Until recently the Spanish political system served to keep most Spaniards out of politics altogether, instilling in them a fatalistic attitude regarding the whims of authority. The office of president of a bullfight still represents this legacy of arbitrary despotism. Fraud and influence peddling were once endemic on the "planet of the bulls." Horns were shaved, half-ton sandbags were dropped on bulls' shoulders, critics were bribed. (One of the cruel ironies of bullfighting is that the most honest and reputable critics are also the ones most determined to preserve the authentic risk of human life upon which the whole enterprise is founded.)

Beyond tricks and corruption, we can see that bullfighting's personalistic patronage system mirrors that of the larger society. The provincial *fiesta de toros* was a cautionary tale about what could happen to people without connections or friends; small-town mayors anxious to please their supporters had no qualms about acquiring the largest, most fearsome bulls for penniless apprentice toreros to struggle with and occasionally succumb to. Sooner or later a would-be bullfighter must

There are only three sports—mountain climbing, bullfighting, and motor racing—all the rest being games. ■ ERNEST HEMINGWAY

find protectors-exploiters, the more the better, or he will get nowhere. El Cordobes wandered for years without such connections, and when he finally found them they were desperate gambling types much like himself who were willing to take a chance on a brash newcomer. The other side of this coin of unfair exclusion is unfair inclusion, young men from the right families, prodigies favored from the beginning by cattle breeders, impresarios, and critics. Traditionally the whole point of a matador's career was to go from being a dependent, a client, a receiver of favors in a more-or-less corrupt system of personalistic patronage to being a dispenser of favors and patronage—the boss of his *cuadrilla* (team), a landowner, a big man in his community, a pillar of the status quo, idolized by impoverished and oppressed people. A whole web of complicities makes bullfighting possible—including local religious belief systems. The *fiesta de toros* is always held in honor of a patron saint, a kind of supernatural protector in touch with an arbitrary central authority who can be cajoled into doing favors for his "clients."

Like old-fashioned Spanish political oratory, bullfighting can be seen as a series of dramatic public gestures. Every bullfighter is a potential demagogue, a man who stirs up the emotions of a crowd to become a leader and to achieve his own ends. A bullfighter gains power and wealth only when he learns how to sway the masses, to mesmerize them, to harness their passion for his private profit. The matador rides to the top of society on the backs of mass enthusiasm. However, no bullfighter could sway the masses if they were not disposed to be swayed. As soon as we become spectators of the spectators, we find their mobile and emotional disposition to be intimately related to popular concepts of power, authority, justice, and masculinity. Without heed to experts or critics, bullfight spectators evaluate artistic merit or bravery on their own and express their views instantly and unself-consciously. The downside of this refreshing spontaneity, however, is that popular value judgments tend to be arbitrary, impulsive, and unreflexive. The impulsive evaluations of bullfight crowds rattle and unnerve bullfighters, sometimes leading them

to commit acts that result in serious injury or death. At the Almaria Fair in 1981, for example, the normally cautious Curro Romero was gored in an attempt to appease a hastily judgmental crowd. Afterward the public was sorry, of course, as sorry as it had been in 1920 after hounding Joselito into fatal temerity at Talavera and in 1947 when it drove Manolete to impale himself on the horns of Islero. *Blood and Sand,* the famous bullfighting novel by Blasco Ibanez, ends with this description of the public: "The beast roared: the real one, the only one."

Cheers and Jeers

At the very least the public judges the taurine performance in an arbitrary, capricious, and personalistic manner. Because the decisions of the bullring president form part of the entire affair, they, too, fall under the scrutiny —and often the vociferous condemnation—of the spectators. Like old Spain itself, the bullfight is a mise-en-scene (stage setting) of an authoritarian power in an uneasy relationship with a blasphemous and rebellious underclass. For many Spanish writers the crowd's impulsive style of reacting to duly constituted authority was the worst evil of bullfighting, one that reconfirmed Spaniards in their submission to the despotic whims of the powerful. As the embodiment of arbitrary might, the president possesses total immunity, and his decisions cannot be appealed. The public's only recourse is to whistle, hoot, or insult. Thus, in much the same manner as the old African monarchies described by anthropologists, the corrida permits a ritualistic contestation of power that is momentarily gratifying but essentially without consequence. In his own way, of course, the matador polarizes the crowd's criteria of dominance and submission: Whatever power he has must be seen in terms of popular concepts of power (who deserves to have it and who doesn't) worked out long ago during Spain's traumatic history of civil conflicts. We can picture the bullfight—and its appear to spectators—as a dramatization of machismo as long as we remember that machismo is primarily a psychological mechanism of compensation that provides a fantasy image of superiority in the absence of real sociopolitical power. Perhaps a bullfighter's manly hyperbole serves to mediate between personal and national inferiority complexes. In any event the evidence would seem to support people who argue that bullfighting is the legacy of obscurantism (opposition to the spread of knowledge), that it is emblematic of the manipulability of the people, their gullibility, their irrational hero worship, their civic immaturity. One would surely exaggerate to see bullfighting as the "cause" of Spain's former political backwardness, but it was certainly no cure.

Bullfighting is a spectacle of killing and gratuitous risk of life. Only with difficulty can people watch such violent spectacle without being aroused in some way. Even reactions of horror confirm that such spectacle is inherently erotic. Properly defined, disgust is just negative arousal, caused by the fear of degradation that accompanies the desire to give way to the instincts and violate all taboos. Most Spaniards and many foreigners enjoy the violent spectacle without guilt or other moral qualms. The group norms that hold sway at a bullfight enable each spectator to feel his or her physiological arousal as entirely appropriate. Intense stimulation actually increases commitment to the group's rationalization of it. This socio-psychological mechanism has permitted Spaniards to experience titillation at bullfights and associate it, at a conscious level, with patriotism, manly ideals, integrity, honor, art, and so on. What happens to this group consensus when a goring occurs and the transgressive nature of bullfighting is fully manifested? Community norms are already in place to provide cognitions appropriate to the intense arousal that spectators experience. These norms forge a new group consensus whose conscious elements are grief, forbearance, pity, resignation, and ultimately, reaffirmation of all the heroic qualities that led the matador to risk his life in the first place. The normative emotionality that forms around the fallen matador persists for many years after the tragedy and, in its sociocultural implications, goes far beyond the blood and sand.

Timothy Mitchell

Further Reading

Arauz de Robles, S. (1974). *Sociologia del toreo.* Madrid, Spain: Prensa Espanola.

Arevalo, J. C., & del Moral, J. (1985). *Nacido para morir.* Madrid, Spain: Espasa-Calpe.

Blasco Ibanez, V. (1911). *The blood of the arena.* Chicago: McClurg.

Chaves Nogales, M. (1937). *Juan Belmonte, killer of bulls.* New York: Doubleday.

Claramunt, F. (1989). *Historia ilustrada de la tauromaquia.* Madrid, Spain: Espasa-Calpe.

Conrad, J. R. (1957). *The horn and the sword: The history of the bull as a symbol of power and fertility.* New York: E. P. Dutton.

Fernandez Suarez, A. (1961). *Espana, arbol vivo.* Madrid, Spain: Aguilar.

Hemingway, E. (1932). *Death in the afternoon.* New York: Charles Scribner's Sons.

Levers de Miranda, A. (1962). *Ritos y juegos del toro.* Madrid, Spain: Taurus.

Mitchell, T. (1991). *Blood sport: A social history of Spanish bullfighting.* Philadelphia: University of Pennsylvania Press.

Noel, E. (1914). *Escritos antitaurinos.* Madrid, Spain: Taurus.

Pink, S. (1997). *Women and bullfighting: Gender, sex and the consumption of tradition.* Oxford, UK: Berg.

Tynan, K. (1955). *Bull fever.* New York: Harper & Bros.

Burnout

Athletes withdraw from sport for many different reasons: one potential reason is burnout. Burnout occurs when the rewards from sport participation (e.g., confidence, improving skills, teammate relationships) are no longer greater than the sacrifices of participation (e.g., pain, stress, excessive pressure). As a psychological condition, burnout in the sport arena is associated with fatigue, a decreased sense of personal accomplishment, and a lack of caring about one's sport or personal performance. Although burnout can occur in athletes, coaches, athletic trainers, and officials, this entry will focus on athletes.

Precursors of Burnout

Two burnout models have been proposed. The first explains burnout as a response to chronic stress. In this model, athletes withdraw from sport when they do not think they can meet the demands of sport. The second model asserts that burnout occurs when athletes do

Why did I lose? No reason, though you might like to know that I got tired, my ears started popping, the rubber came off my shoes, I got cramp, and I lost one of my contact lenses. Other than that I was in great shape. ■ BOB LUTZ

not develop identities outside the realm of sport and when they perceive a lack of personal control. In both models, environmental and individual factors interact to produce burnout.

Specialization in one sport at an early age and year-round training, both environmental factors, may lead to burnout, especially in young athletes. Many believe that specialization in one sport must occur in order for athletes to reach their maximum potential and achievement. Within this environment, athletes may experience chronic stress due to excessive practice, time demands, and overuse injuries. Additionally, specialization limits athletes in their ability to create social relationships outside their sport, often resulting in a self-identity focused only on one's sport involvement. Athletes may also experience tremendous pressure to practice and win from significant others in their lives. Pressure and high expectations from parents and coaches may result in stress, anxiety, and fear and is a potential predictor of burnout.

Perfectionism, often resulting in self-pressure or inappropriate expectations for success, is an individual factor that may lead athletes to experience burnout. Athletes who strive for perfection are at risk for burnout because they set unrealistic standards for themselves and devote large quantities of time to trying to achieve their high standards. Athletes who focus on the needs of others and lack assertiveness are susceptible to burnout: these athletes are often sensitive to criticism and ignore their own needs. Finally, athletes who experience high levels of anxiety are also at risk for burnout.

Signs and Symptoms

Because there are many different signs and symptoms of burnout, it is often difficult to detect in athletes. Physical signs of burnout include sleep disturbances, physical exhaustion, increased muscle soreness, decreased body weight, low energy, and overuse injuries (e.g., shin splints, stress fractures, "tennis" elbow). These physical signs of burnout are often the result of excessive training demands. Psychological signs of burnout

include concentration problems, lack of caring, mood changes, negative affect or depression, emotional isolation, and increased anxiety.

Prevention

Because of the psychological and physical consequences of burnout, it is important to take prevention measures. Athletes themselves need to maintain an optimistic outlook and focus on what they can control about their sport and their performance. This optimistic outlook can be created by setting short-term goals and learning self-regulation skills. By setting realistic yet challenging short-term goals, athletes receive feedback about their progress and maintain their motivation to continue striving for their goals. Self-regulation skills, including relaxation techniques, imagery, and positive self-talk, are important in dealing with the stress and pressures of sport participation. Proper communication is necessary among the social network (e.g., coaches, parents, teammates) of athletes. Within their social network, athletes should be able to express their feelings and frustrations about practice demands and competitions. Athletes also must take breaks during the season to ensure that they preserve their psychological and physical health.

The Role of Others

Parents and coaches can also work to prevent burnout in athletes. Both parents and coaches should allow athletes to be involved in decision-making opportunities—this helps athletes feel that they have control of their sporting experience. Parental and coach support should be given for all the athlete's hard work and effort, not just for winning. Parents should help children prepare for competitions without putting excessive pressure or stress on them. It is also important that parents leave the coaching of their child to the coach. Additionally, parents should encourage their child to participate in a range of activities that they enjoy, instead of specializing in one sport at an early age. Coaches should maintain positive coaching standards and should avoid excessive use of punishment. Coaches should also have personal involvement with the athlete and work to understand his or her feelings and perspective.

The Future

Burnout is an important issue to consider in sport because it results in psychological and physical symptoms and may eventually lead to athletes withdrawing from sport. At present, the pervasiveness of burnout in the athletic population and the percentage of athletes who withdraw from sport due to burnout are unknown. As the rewards of sport—money, fame, medals—increase, it is likely that more athletes will specialize in one sport at earlier ages. Specialization often results in overtraining and an inability to form relationships outside of sport, thus increasing the likelihood of burnout to occur. Athletes, coaches, and parents should all take strategies to prevent burnout in athletes.

Jennifer J. Waldron

See also Psychology

Further Reading

Committee on Sports Medicine and Fitness. (2000). Intensive training and sports specialization in young athletes. *Pediatrics, 106*(1), 154–157. Retrieved September 21, 2004, from http://aappolicy.aappublications.org/cgi/content/full/pediatrics;106/1/154

Cox, R. H. (2002). Burnout in athletes. *Sport psychology: Concepts and applications* (pp. 393–406). Boston: McGraw-Hill.

Donnelly, P. (1993). Problems associated with youth involvement in high-performance sport. In B. R. Cahill & A. J. Pearl (Eds.), *Intensive participation in children's sports* (pp. 95–126). Champaign, IL: Human Kinetics.

Gould, D. (1993). Intensive sport participation and the prepubescent athlete: Competitive stress and burnout. In B. R. Cahill & A. J. Pearl (Eds.), *Intensive participation in children's sports* (pp. 19–38). Champaign, IL: Human Kinetics.

Henschen, K. P. (2001). Athletic staleness and burnout: Diagnosis, prevention, and treatment. In J. M. Williams (Ed.), *Applied sport psychology: Personal growth to peak performance* (pp. 445–455). Mountain View, CA: Mayfield Publishing.

Raedeke, T. D., & Smith, A. L. (2001). Development and preliminary validation of an athlete burnout measure. *Journal of Sport and Exercise Psychology, 23,* 281–300.

Waldron, J. J. (2000, Summer). Stress, overtraining, and burnout associated with participation in sport: Is your child at risk? *Spotlight on Youth Sports, 24*(2), 4–5. Retrieved September 21, 2004, from http://ed-web3.educ.msu.edu/ysi/Spotlights.htm

Weinberg, R. S., & Gould, D. (2003). Burnout and overtraining. In *Foundations of sport and exercise psychology* (pp. 468–487). Champaign, IL: Human Kinetics.

Buzkashi

Buzkashi (goat dragging) is an equestrian game played primarily by Turkic peoples of northern Afghanistan and by people in the Muslim republics of the former Soviet Union north of the Oxus River and in China's Xinjiang Province. During the 1980s and early 1990s Afghan refugees played *buzkashi* near Chitral and Peshawar in Pakistan; however, it bears no cultural relationship to Pakistani polo. In both of its main forms—a traditional game *(tudabarai)* and a modern sport *(qarajai)*—the central action is similar: Riders on horses gather above the carcass of a goat or calf, lean from their saddles, grapple with each other to grab the carcass from the ground, and then attempt to keep sole control of the carcass while riding away at full speed.

Although regarded primarily as fun, both forms of *buzkashi* also are political in that patron-sponsors try to demonstrate and thus enhance their ability to control events.

Origins

As with most folk games, we cannot precisely trace the origins of *buzkashi*, but no doubt it sprang from ancestors of the Turkic peoples who are its core players today: Uzbeks, Kirghiz, Turkmen, and Kazakhs. These equestrian nomads spread westward from China and Mongolia between the tenth and fifteenth centuries. *Buzkashi* probably developed, much like U.S. rodeo, as a recreational form of everyday herding or raiding activity. No evidence supports the sensational notion, circulated for tourism purposes during the 1960s and 1970s, that *buzkashi* was originally played with live human prisoners instead of dead livestock.

Other ethnic groups in northern Afghanistan in recent generations have embraced the culture of *buzkashi*: Tajiks, Hazaras, and even Pushtun migrants from south of the Hindu Kush. Another key development came in 1953 when the federal government, based in Kabul, hosted its first *buzkashi* tournament on the birthday of King Mohammed Zahir. Successive national regimes hosted similar *buzkashi* tournaments from the mid-

*If you run into a wall, don't turn around and give up. Figure out
how to climb it, go through it, or work around it.* ■ MICHAEL JORDAN

1950s to the early 1980s. With the collapse of the federal government during the Afghan-Soviet War (1979–1989), the tournaments ceased. During the 1990s, amid the ongoing political chaos, *buzkashi* largely reverted to its original status as a local pastime north of the Hindu Kush. By the winter of 2003-2004, post-Taliban Kabul featured weekly matches, hosted by the politically ambitious defense minister. But no prewar scale national tournaments had been resumed, in part because the new central government was as yet unable to command team attendance.

Practice

Buzkashi depends on sponsorship of both the horses and riders and of the ceremonial event in which it is played. In the rural context of northern Afghanistan, khans exercise both types of sponsorship. Khans are men of political, social, and economic importance who constitute the informal, ever-shifting power elite of local life. They breed, raise, and own the horses, whose bloodlines are proudly chronicled and whose success in *buzkashi* enhances the status of their owners. Khans likewise employ special riders (*chapandazan*) for their special horses. Most important of all is their sponsorship of *toois*—the celebratory events at which *buzkashi* is played. *Toois* are staged during the winter, both because winter is the agricultural slack season and because horses and riders can play then without becoming overheated.

Khans stage *toois* to celebrate ritual events such as a son's marriage or circumcision. Although the event is generally a private family affair, it is also the occasion for much wider gatherings whose focus is a day or several days of *buzkashi*. The event also is a status-oriented initiative during which the political, social, and economic resources of the sponsor (*tooi-wala*) are tested in public. If these resources are sufficient and the *tooi* is deemed a success, its sponsor's reputation will rise. If not, the sponsor's reputation may be ruined. Preparations for the event include amassing funds for prize money and food and recruiting nearby hosts for the hundreds of guests. The sponsor hopes that the guests will bring cash gifts to help defray the costs of the *tooi*.

After a ceremonial lunch on the first day, everyone rides to the *buzkashi* field: sponsor, closest associates, invited khans, their sizable entourages (including prize horses, *chapandazan*, and associates who have come in friendship but who can be mobilized in case of serious conflict), and the local populace. The field usually is a barren plain, undemarcated and unbounded, on the edge of the village. The carcass of a goat or calf lies in the middle. (Although the word *buzkashi* refers to a goat, calf carcasses are often used instead because, it is said, they last longer.) Without ceremony but in accordance with Muslim law *(hallal)*, the animal has been bled to death, dehooved, and decapitated to protect the hands of contestants. A carcass that has been disemboweled makes for faster play, but purists favor a heavier, ungutted animal so that only power, rather than quickness, will prevail.

Most *buzkashi*s commence without fanfare and gain in intensity as more participants arrive. Any number of riders may participate, and a game may involve hundreds of riders. A session consists of several dozen play cycles. Each cycle begins as riders form an equestrian scrum over the carcass. As their horses lurch, rear, and try to hold position, riders lean down from the saddle and grab at the carcass. More horses and riders maneuver their way toward the center of a mass of wild movement that is ever growing, ever more fiercely contested. One rider, lunging half-blind in the melee, manages to grab the carcass briefly, but, as a saying goes, "Every calf has four legs," and other riders quickly wrench it away from him. The carcass is trampled, tugged, dragged, lifted, and lost again as one rider after another seeks to gain sole control. Riders do not play in teams, although friendly riders (or the riders of friendly khans) may sometimes help each other. Everyone has the right to try, but *chapandazan* in their distinctive fur-trimmed headgear monopolize play. Meanwhile the *jorchi* (town crier) shouts the amount of prize money offered. The longer a play cycle is contested, the greater that amount grows and the fiercer the competition becomes.

One rider and horse finally emerge from the mass *(tudabarai)*, take control of the carcass free and clear, and drop it in triumph. Play stops briefly as the town crier begins a stylized chant to praise the rider, the horse, and—most of all—the horse owner:

> Oh, the horse of Hajji Ali,
> On him rode Ahmad Gul.
> He leapt like a deer.
> He glared like a leopard.
> How he took it away.
> How he showed what he is.
> How the name of Hajji Ali rose.
> How we all hear his name.
> How his pride is complete.

Prizes for the winning rider once were carpets, rifles, and even horses. Today almost all prizes are cash. Amounts depend on the generosity of the *tooi* sponsor and sometimes exceed $100. Post-Taliban *buzkashis* (2003–2004) featured cell phones as prizes. The horse owner's sole prize is prestige or "name," that intangible but most important currency of traditional Afghan life.

Soon after the chant has finished the next play cycle begins. Cycle follows cycle without any sense of cumulative score. However, the last cycle of each day, typically played with a carcass now in shreds, has special value, and the winning rider proudly departs with the tattered carcass dangling across his saddle. The visiting khans and their entourages then retire for dinner and sleep at nearby host houses, where guests review every event of the day in conversation: which horse did well, whether the prize money was sufficient, and—most of all—what happened if a serious dispute arose. Disputes and the issue of who can control them are the darker, less readily admitted core of interest in *buzkashi*.

Disputes

In traditional *buzkashi* three factors contribute to disputes: (1) The game itself is full of physically brutal contact. (2) The question of a rider being sufficiently "free and clear" for a score is notoriously subjective. (3) The khans, whose horses and riders compete, often are rivals in local politics. Indeed, during *buzkashi* such rivalries, otherwise hidden by the diplomatic niceties of day-to-day existence, are revealed in all their disruptive potential.

A dispute can be easily triggered. Had a rider claiming victory really gotten the carcass "free and clear" before dropping it? Was one rider guilty of whipping another rider in the face or grabbing another's bridle? Did the *chapandaz* of Mujib Khan hide a rope in his sleeve to improve his grasp of the carcass? Suddenly the violent pushing and shoving, hitherto "for fun," become "for real." Each khan's entourage closes ranks around him. Riders abandon the play cycle, and the air is full of angry shouting as everyone attempts to gain control of an increasingly uncontrollable situation.

Although outright fighting is rare, an aggrieved group may leave the *buzkashi* and return home rather than stay and suffer what it perceives as injustice. Such a defection lessens the reputation of a *tooi* and thus of its *tooi-wala*. More commonly the jostling and shouting subside gradually as one of the khans emerges as peacemaker and makes himself heard. Much prestige thereby attaches to him because he has, after all, shown an ability to control volatile events, to exert his will over a dynamic that had changed from playful to political. Now his "name will rise" in repeated tellings and retellings of this *buzkashi*. Such a gain in reputation can be important as potential followers weigh the benefits of attaching themselves to a patron or of taking sides in a dispute over water, land, livestock, or women.

Afghanistan's federal government, beginning in the mid-1950s, likewise began to enlist *buzkashi* in an effort at political impression management. The Afghan National Olympic Committee was charged with staging a national *buzkashi* tournament in Kabul each year on the birthday of King Zahir. Provincial contingents were organized in the North (as yet unlinked by all-weather roads to the rest of the country), and the game was transformed into a codified sport with authorized referees, uniformed teams, a demarcated playing field, a cumulative scoring system, and severe penalties (including arrest) for any form of dispute during play. Only players (typically ten or twelve per team) and referees (usually military officers) were allowed on the playing field. Horse-owner khans, their *tooi*-sponsorship role now taken over by the government, had to sit on the sidelines. Also, instead of having the vague "free-and-clear" objective, riders had to carry the carcass around a flag and drop it in a clearly marked circle *(daiwra)*. The king took the role of national *tooi-wala*, hosting the tournament banquet and presenting the medals to winners. The tournament allowed urban Kabul residents to rub elbows with rustic horsemen from the distant North. The northerners returned home with tales of a broader Afghanistan and strong impressions of the federal government's capacity for control.

By the time King Zahir fell from power in 1973, the Kabul *buzkashi* tournament had become a fixture in the national calendar. Subsequent nonroyalist regimes kept the October date but shifted the event first (under President Mohammed Daoud, 1973–1977) to United Nations Day and then (under Communist rule) to the anniversary of the Bolshevik Revolution in 1917. Always staged in the name of mere fun, Kabul *buzkashi* tournaments continued to serve as a symbol of both Afghan national unity and the government's capacity for dispute-free control. The collapse of federal government control during the early 1980s was reflected in the year-by-year disintegration of Kabul *buzkashi*. During Daoud's era the tournament had lasted twelve days and had featured ten provincial teams in a precisely orchestrated round-robin. After 1980 fewer teams participated each year. By 1983 the Soviet puppet government had abandoned all pretense of staging *buzkashi*.

During the Afghan-Soviet War (1979–1989) refugees based in Peshawar and Chitral in Pakistan's northwestern frontier province played *buzkashi*. Many of the riders and khans who had dominated the game in prewar Afghanistan now formed the core of competitions played on Fridays during the winter. Now, however, the main *tooi-wala* role shifted to men whose new renown rested on their leadership of local refugee relief efforts. As usual, all was done in the name of fun, but soon the new breed of sponsor-entrepreneurs was competing for resource-rich spectators from the fast-growing expatriate community: United Nations personnel, diplomats, and directors of nongovernmental aid organizations. These *tooi-walas* in exile, thus ingratiated with their "guests," promoted themselves as conduits for international aid to the refugee community.

By the mid-1990s the federal government in post-Soviet Afghanistan was still too weak to resume the national tournament. The main locus of *buzkashi* reverted to the northern provinces. Some traditional khans still sponsored *toois*, but militia commanders and local warlords were replacing them as sponsors.

This pattern continued in post-Taliban times. By 2004 a new National Buzkashi Federation was dominated by a militarily powerful clique from Panjsher province, where the game had scant prewar legacy. Leading this regional group was the Defense Minister who, despite that title, maintained his own militia and often blocked the growth of central government authority. He had imported many of the top horses and riders from other provinces, claimed Panisher as *buzkashi's* new homeland, and used the game—like so many before him—to enhance his personal prestige.

G. Whitney Azoy

Further Reading

Azoy, G. W. (2003). *Buzkashi: Game and power in Afghanistan* (2nd ed.). Prospect Heights, IL: Waveland Press.
Balikci, A. (1978). Buzkashi. *Natural History, 87*(2), 54–63.
Balikci, A. (1978). Village buzkashi. *Afghanistan Journal, 5*(1), 11–21.
Michaud, R., & Michaud, S. (1988). *Horsemen of Afghanistan*. London: Thames and Hudson.

Cameroon

The Republic of Cameroon is a coastal country in Equatorial Africa with an area of 475,650 square kilometers, (183,569 square miles). Its two largest metropolitan growth centers are the administrative capital, Yaoundé, and the economic capital, Douala. The population of Cameroon is estimated at about 16.5 million inhabitants. About half of these are rural; two-thirds are under the age of twenty-four. The country was a German protectorate from 1884 to 1919. The League of Nations placed Cameroon under British and French control in 1919, and it remained under their mandates until it became independent in 1960. In view of the more than 200 different ethnic groups and as many dialects, the quest for national unity since then has been a leitmotiv of successive governments. Sports have proved to be a valuable aid in that quest.

History

In precolonial Cameroon, traditional dances and games were essential activities. Mbonji (1992) has shown that such practices perform three functions: (1) a warrior function in terms of preparation for combat; (2) a socioeducational and cultural function in terms of preparing young people for their entry into the adult world (social integration, comprehending the environment, physical training, abstract and logical skills, learning to work together, etc.); and (3) a symbolic function as a repository for group culture. There are considerable dif-

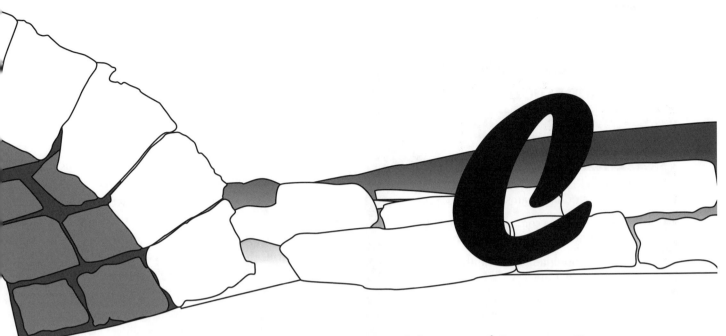

ferences from one ethnic group to the next, although some dances and games have spanned the entire twentieth century and are present in most of the populations. Games of skill that involve throwing assegais (javelins) at moving targets are common, as are wrestling games. Some ethnic groups even organize their social life around these activities, for example, the Tuburi in the far north of Cameroon.

New cultural models emerged with the colonial period, but until the interwar period (in the 1920s and 1930s between the two World Wars) was over, sports were just something that colonists did. One exception was soccer, which was being played by organized indigenous teams as early as the turn of the twentieth century. In the 80 percent of the country under French mandate, physical education in school was the preferred method of diffusing a sports culture. A few activities, such as gymnastics or track and field, were promoted as being more educational.

The development of associations and the training of sport managers, such as coaches, technicians, and Physical Education teachers, accelerated, especially after the Brazzaville Conference in 1944 and during the 1950s, and then even more after independence in 1960. Sports were considerably helped out—although often selectively—by company sponsorship (Coca-Cola, the Cameroonian Breweries, Elf, etc.). The state also provided subsidies to the extent of 0.5 percent to 1 percent of its operating budget. The commitment was not sufficient to allow setting up an ambitious national sports program or building infrastructures, however.

Participant and Spectator Sports

After Cameroonian independence in 1960, soccer powered its way in about twenty years to become by far the most popular sport—played, watched, or covered by the media—in the country. A player like Roger Milla, the best player during the 1980s and 1990s, is a genuine national hero. The Douala and Yaoundé teams have monopolized victories in the national championships. The only other sports to achieve some degree of popularity are handball, volleyball, basketball, track and field, basketball, weight lifting, and combat sports. Tennis and bicycling are less popular.

Although Cameroon has participated in all the Olympic Games since 1964, it only started to do really well in international competitions in the 1980s, particularly in soccer. Cameroon's "Indomitable Lions" team has played in the finals of five World Cup championships, even reaching the quarterfinals once in 1990. The team also has won four African Cup of Nations championships (in 1984, 1988, 2000, and 2002), and became an Olympic champion in 2000. Cameroonian soccer clubs have also had frequent success in Club World Cup championships (victories in 1965, 1971, 1978, 1979, and 1980).

Aside from the African Athletics Confederation's first Central African championships in 1973, Cameroon has not organized any major sports events. The main international event is the annual Mount Cameroon race, created by Guinness, also in 1973. The Supreme Council of Sport in Africa (SCSA), created in 1966, has its headquarters in Yaoundé.

275

Cameroon Olympics Results
2004 Summer Olympics: 1 Gold

representative of the considerable economic and scholastic inequalities still existing between the sexes. Moreover, when colonial sports practices were first adapted for Cameroonians, they were adapted exclusively by men. From a cultural point of view, the traditions surrounding a woman's place in the home (polygamy is official) and the influence of Islam in northern Cameroon are not particularly favorable to her entering sports. Sports are also strongly associated with the state that, until women's political awakening in the 1990s, always made it difficult for them to access sports. And, while there has been unquestionable progress in terms of the number of women participating in sports since then, sport does still remain the fief of men—whether in media coverage, sponsorship, the events, or actual participation.

Organizations

Structurally speaking, the administration of Cameroonian sports is largely based on the French colonial model. Since 1970, it has depended on a relatively powerful Youth and Sports Ministry, aided by ten provincial delegations. Fourteen federations manage the country's main sports, which are soccer, boxing, tennis, volleyball, track and field, swimming, handball, judo, basketball, bicycling, table tennis, wrestling, water sports, and weightlifting. The federations are empowered by the Youth and Sports Ministry, which is responsible for the three separate sectors of sports, physical education, and youth. The higher executive body for sports, the National Sports Committee, liaises between the ministry and the federations. The government depends on the National Olympic Committee, however, to accurately reflect its sports policy. The National Institute of Youth and Sports created in 1961 is in charge of training managers and helps out with preparing the national teams.

At the local level, sports clubs are subject to the 12 June 1967 Freedom of Association Act (modified in 1990). A sports charter specifying the operating rules for the clubs places them under state control.

Cameroon has been an IOC member since October

Cameroon was first a state and then a nation. As a result successive governments have always sought to achieve national unity. They have consistently supported the national soccer team, promoting its success and enhancing its public exposure as much as possible. As Mbengalak (1995) states, soccer is becoming a veritable state sport, one that plays a major role in the country's domestic and foreign politics. In the 1980s, a point was made of showing an explicit relationship between the success of Cameroonian soccer and the ambitions of the country's only party, the Cameroon People's Democratic Movement.

In Cameroon a sports event often becomes a pretext for dancing and music, which are essential aspects of society; it is also readily an occasion for traditional fetishistic practices.

Women and Sport

Women's sports, which began in Cameroon during the 1950s, are repeatedly confronted with obstacles that are

1963, and it belongs to most of the international sports federations. It is a member of the Union of African Sports Confederations (UCSA), the technical agency for the SCSA, which reports to the Organization for African Unity (OAU).

Sport in Society

Sports may appear to be a preferred instrument of the strategy to detribalize Cameroonian society, but it actually continues to reflect the ethnic divisions in the country. The Bamilekes predominate in soccer, for example, while the Betis are more present in track and field. In some sports the national team is made up of members mostly from a single ethnic group, although strictly anthropological arguments cannot account for such success. This situation provokes interethnic tensions, even more so that the push for democracy in the 1990s and a multiparty system that rather paradoxically have produced a withdrawal into ethnic identity.

Several times, Cameroonian participation in international sports events has brought to light political interference in the selection or rejection of certain players. Major financial problems are recurrent, tarnishing the image of the Cameroonian soccer delegation.

The Future

The best athletes often have trouble making a living from their sport in Cameroon. In sports like tennis, volleyball, track and field, and soccer, many athletes move to France or elsewhere in Europe. Cameroon's economic problems are still compromising any significant progress in sports participation there.

Thierry Terret

Further Reading

Kemo Keimbo, D. C. (1999). *Représentations politiques et pratiques corporelles au Cameroun (1920–1996). Enjeux et paradoxes du sport et de l'éducation physique en Afrique noire.* Doctoral dissertation, University of Strasbourg.

Mbengalak, E. (1995). *La gouvernementalité du sport en Afrique. Le sport et le politique au Cameroun.* Lausanne, Switzerland: Centre d'Etudes et de Recherches Olympiques.

Mbonji. (1992). *Le jeu dans l'univers culturel camerounais. Contribution à une analyse des pratiques traditionnelles comme exercices initiatiques.* Doctoral dissertation, University of Paris.

Paul, S. (1987). The wrestling tradition and its social functions. In W. J. Baker & J. A. Mangan (Eds.), *Sport in Africa: Essays in social history* (pp. 23–46). New York: Africana.

Paul, S. (1992). Afrikanische Spiele und ihre Dokumentation. In G. G. Bauer (Ed.), *Homo ludens: der spielende Mensch* (pp. 143–200). München: Emil Katzbichler.

Camogie

Camogie is a game of Irish origin and remains predominantly a game of Ireland. It is quite clearly a women's derivative of hurling, the national sport of Ireland, a fast and forcefully played ball-and-stick game played by two teams of fifteen players each. As a distinct sport, hurling has origins that stretch back nearly two thousand years. It became widely played across Ireland in its modern form after the leaders of the Gaelic Athletic Association (GAA) drew up the rules in 1884. Camogie is played elsewhere across the globe by members of the Irish Diaspora, those Irish men and women who live outside their native land.

Camogie and Irish Nationalism

Camogie is a sport born of Irish women's nationalist sentiments. The GAA had strong links with the nationalist movements that formed the backbone of the Irish revolution against British rule that began in the late 1890s. The revolution would culminate in the War of Independence fought between the British and the Irish Republican Army (IRA) and the division of Ireland between the independent South and the British North.

Women played a key role in the revolutionary period as soldiers, organizers, fund-raisers, and ideologues. Because the GAA played such a key role in revolutionary activity, it was natural that nationalist-minded women would turn their attention to the Gaelic sports. These sports, Gaelic football and hurling, were viewed as representative of good Irish values, such as morality and strength, and had ancient Irish origins. They were also a complete counterbalance to what the Irish saw as the "corrupt" sports of the British imperialists, such as soccer (association football) and cricket, both closely associated with the British Army.

That camogie was, indeed, a political statement as well as a game became clear in 1917. The strong links between the GAA and the activities of political nationalists were demonstrated that year at the funeral of Thomas Ashe. Arrested by the British for inciting the civil population, Ashe had gone on a hunger strike in prison in an attempt to secure political status for nationalist prisoners. He died as a result of force-feeding, and his funeral became a showpiece for the aspirations of nationalist politics. Because Ashe had been a leading member of the GAA, a large number of GAA members attended his funeral. At the core of this group were scores of women in full mourning dress carrying their camogie sticks (*camog*). At the outbreak of the modern troubles in Northern Ireland in the late 1960s, nationalist women regularly paraded in Belfast carrying their *camog* as a marker of their affiliation to the nationalist cause.

History of the Game

Hurling was a game that was deemed too violent and masculine for women in the late nineteenth and early twentieth centuries, and thus women developed their own game. The first camogie club was formed in 1898 in Navan, County Meath, specifically to play one match as part of the centenary celebrations of the 1798 Rising against the British presence in Ireland. The first modern games of what can be identified as formally organized camogie were apparently played in 1902 by members of the Gaelic League, a radical Irish language and cultural organization. In these early days, the game was heavily based on the rules and spirit of hurling. In 1904 the first formal rules of camogie were drawn up. The term *camogie* was dreamed up by the Cork language scholar Tadhg O Donnchadha. As with many other Irish terms that originated in the late nineteenth and early twentieth centuries, "camogie" was a word for a

game whose invented traditions were representative of Irish characteristics, but that had no actual roots in Irish folklore or history, and thus had no traditional name. The first game under the new rules was organized in Craobh a' Chéitinnigh, the Keating branch of the Gaelic League, and was played on 17 July 1904 in Navan, near Dublin, between two Dublin-based clubs; Craobh a' Chéitinnigh defeated Cúchulaoinns 1–0.

Cumann Camógaíochta, the Camogie Association of Ireland (CAA), was founded on 25 February 1905 by the women who played the sport, and Máire Ní Chinnéide was elected the first president. By 1913 the first-ever college club was formed by Professor Una Ní Fhaircheallaigh, a lecturer in Modern Irish and eventually chair of Modern Irish Poetry, at University College Dublin. Ní Fhaircheallaigh's role in the sport was so important that she remained president of the university's club from 1914 until 1951, and was president of the Camogie Association of Ireland in 1941–1942. She was also instrumental in convincing William Gibson, the second Lord Ashbourne, to donate the Ashbourne Cup as the prize for the winners of the annual intervarsity camogie championship in 1915. This trophy is played for to this day. By the start of World War I, camogie was being played in seventeen of Ireland's thirty-two counties. By then it had also spread to London and New York, and each city had some six teams. It was in New York City that the American Camogie Association (ACA) was founded in 1930. Although a distinct body responsible for the administration of camogie, the CAA works with the recognition of the GAA. The women's association is organized in the same way as the GAA, and its tournaments are run on a similar basis.

The local parish is the base for all Gaelic games. It is here that teams are organized on the local level and the games enjoy the widest participation. The parish teams play in league tournaments, and over the course of the season (March to September), the best players are selected to play at the county level. The thirty-two counties play knockout matches in four separate groupings, based on the four provinces of Ireland (Ulster, Con-

Two women playing camogie.

naught, Leinster, and Munster). The county winners of the four provincial titles play off in semifinals for the privilege of playing in the All-Ireland final. The first official inter-county games were played on 12 July 1912 between Dublin and Louth at Croke Park, the Dubliners winning 2–1. In 1932 an All-Ireland championship was formally started and was won by Dublin. The game had spread to such an extent by the 1930s that every one of the thirty-two counties of Ireland had representative teams. The respectability of the game in the eyes of the male custodians of the GAA and its attraction to supporters was such that by 1934 the All-Ireland final was allowed to be played at the GAA's headquarters in Croke Park. The final approval of the GAA-camogie relationship came in 1980 when the women's sport appointed its first full-time paid official, who was provided with an office at Croke Park paid for by the GAA.

Camogie has been fortunate in that, since its early years, it is has attracted committed and long-serving administrators who have done much to promote the game, including such legendary figures as Una Bean Úi Phuirséach and Shelia McNulty, both of whom served as president and general secretary of the association. Men have also been centrally important in the promotion of the game. Unlike other sports and cultures in which men appear to hold back and discourage the growth of women's sport, the committeemen and promoters of Gaelic games have worked well with the women who organized camogie. Camogie is seen as part of the cultural and nationalistic crusade to promote an independent sense of Irishness that is the ultimate function of Gaelic games. As such, men have been keen advocates of camogie and view it as an equally valid and important expression of Irish sporting and nationalistic cul-

ture as either hurling or Gaelic football. These men included Séan O'Duffy, who worked for seventy-five years promoting camogie, and Pádraig Puirséal, the legendary Gaelic games correspondent of the *Irish Press,* who did his utmost to promote the game in his columns. In 1966, when the first National Training Programme for Coaches was instigated, the majority of participants in the courses were men. Since 1999 the spirit of camogie as a game has moved closer to that of hurling. While certain rule differences remain, the game is now played by two sides of fifteen, and on the full-size GAA pitch.

In the last two decades, the game of camogie, while remaining strictly amateur at the playing level, has developed into a modern commercial organization. From 1986 annual courses in administration, refereeing, and public relations have been held, and the association became an official member of the government-funded National Coaching and Training Centre Programme. In 1995 the association signed its first-ever national sponsorship deal. In keeping with the national spirit of the organization, the agreement was signed with the governmental body charged with promoting the use of the Irish language, Bord na Gaelige. The need for such sponsorship to support an amateur game was highlighted in

You miss 100% of the shots you never take. ■ WAYNE GRETZKY

2003 when the association appointed its first full-time sponsorship and finance manager.

Rules and Play

Camogie is played by two teams, each with fifteen women. The field is the same as that which is used for hurling. The standard measurements are 110 meters long and 68 meters wide. The stick (*camog*) is based on the hurley (*caman*) of the men's game, although it usually made to a lighter weight specification. The stick is used to advance the ball, pass to a teammate, shoot at the goal, or take the ball from the other team. At either end of the pitch are H-shaped goalposts in the same style as the posts in Rugby Union. The bottom sections of the posts are netted as in soccer. To score a player must hit the ball (*sliothar*) over the top section of the uprights for one point, or else hit the ball into the bottom net for three points. The winner of the game is the team with the highest total score. Players wear footwear, shorts, and shirts bearing the colors of their team or county, and some players will choose to wear headgear to protect them from injuries caused by the ball or stick. Matches last 70 minutes; two halves of 35 minutes each.

Given the GAA's dominant role in the new Irish State that was formed in 1922, Gaelic games became the officially sanctioned sports in Ireland and were encouraged at the school level. As the foremost women's game, camogie was positioned as the main game for girls in schools, a tradition that continues to the present. As the main school sport for girls, camogie has a huge pool of players, supporters, and organizers for its adult competitions. It currently has 78,000 playing members: 14,000 at the under-13 age level, 40,000 between 13 and 18, 20,000 between 19 and 35, and 4,000 players in the over-35 category. Until the 1990s, camogie was unchallenged as the most popular sport for women in Ireland. It now faces serious challenges from the growth in support for women's Gaelic football.

In 2004 the association celebrated its centenary. A yearlong series of events was staged across Ireland, including a banquet, a historical exhibition at the GAA museum, and the naming of the camogie team of the century.

Further Afield

All the Gaelic games have been taken overseas by those millions of Irish men and women who have left Ireland's shores over the centuries. Other aspects of Irish culture, such as music, have survived transplantation to other nations better than have the games, but pockets of activity remain. Irish emigrants apparently prefer sporting assimilation to sporting separation and have thus more readily adapted to sports such as baseball and Australian Rules football, rather than continuing Gaelic games on foreign fields. Nevertheless, the GAA is an international organization, and GAA clubs can be found across the globe in nations such as the United States, Canada, China, South Africa, Argentina, Australia, and the United Kingdom. Camogie is usually found in all those clubs. It may not be as buoyant as Gaelic football or hurling, but it has its core of women adherents who play camogie in the same way, with the same rules, and with the same enthusiasm as they do on the playing fields of Clare or Roscommon.

Mike Cronin

Further Reading

Camogie Association of Ireland. (1984). *Scéal na Camógaíochta* (History of camogie). Dublin: Author.

Camogie Association of Ireland. (1990). *Playing rules and constitution.* Dublin: Author.

Camogie Association of Ireland. (1996). *Control of matches and playing rules.* Dublin: Author.

Cronin, Mike. (1999). *Sport and nationalism in Ireland: Gaelic games, soccer and Irish national identity since 1884.* Dublin: Four Courts Press.

Cumann Lúthchleas Gael. (1984). *A century of service, 1884–1984.* Dublin: Author.

De Búrca, Marcus. (1980). *The GAA: A history of the Gaelic Athletic Association.* Dublin: Cumann Lúthchleas Gael.

Hughes, Anthony. (1997). The Irish community. In P. A. Mosely, R. Cashman, J. O'Hara, & H. Weatherburn (Eds.), *Sporting immigrants* (pp. 73–87). Crow's Nest, NSW: Walla Walla Press.

Mandle, W. F. (1987). *The Gaelic Athletic Association and Irish nationalist politics 1884–1924.* London: Christopher Helm.

O'Hogartaigh, M. (2003, July). "Shedding their reserve: Camogie and the origins of women's sport in Ireland." *High Ball,* 29–30.

Canada

As the northernmost country in the Americas, Canada is home to 32 million people. It is officially bilingual (with federal government services provided in both English and French) and multicultural. Competitive sports have been essential to the Canadian economy, culture, and identity since the beginning of the modern nation in 1867.

Sports in Canada are currently organized, financed, and followed in two distinct sectors. The most visible is the masculinist and corporate professional sector, which is closely integrated with United States–based leagues and what scholars call "the sports-media complex." The second is the network of public, private, and voluntary organizations in the amateur and Olympic sports known as "the Canadian sport system." It is increasingly state-driven and financed, and committed to gender equity. It focuses on the participation in and the staging of national and international competitions, especially the Olympic and Paralympic, Commonwealth, Pan American, and Canada Games.

In 1998, nearly 37 percent of Canadians over fifteen years of age reported that they were active in physical activity, including organized sports. Soccer is the most widely played sport with 900,000 registered participants, 40 percent of whom are women. The overall impact of the sport and recreation sector upon the Canadian Gross Domestic Product (GDP) was calculated to have been CAN$8.9 billion, or 1.1 percent of the Canadian GDP, bigger than the mining and papers industries. It provided 262,325 jobs, or 2 percent of the total employment in Canada.

History

Canada is home to both indigenous peoples and those who have arrived from other parts of the world during the last four hundred years. Although there is a lack of recorded (and undistorted) history about aboriginal Canadians, those who arrived from elsewhere—European explorers, fur traders, settlers, and more recently, southern Canadian bush pilots and geologists in the far Arctic—readily engaged with them in various forms of physical activity and sport. Some aboriginal sports and games served as the basis for the popular sports we know today. Lacrosse, Canada's official summer sport, is based on George Beers's 1860 codification of the aboriginal stickball game *teewarathon,* which he learned from the Mohawk at Kahnawake across the St. Lawrence River from Montreal.

ABORIGINAL ATHLETES

Throughout Canadian history, aboriginal athletes have been prominent in both integrated and native-only associations and sporting events. Early in the twentieth century, marathon runner Tom Longboat from the Six Nations Reserve near Brantford, Ontario, became a sporting icon across North America for his spectacular national and international achievements. Today, kayaker Alwyn Morris from Kahnawake is remembered fondly for his gold medal victory (with Hugh Fisher) at the 1984 Olympics.

That said, like indigenous peoples in many other immigrant societies, indigenous Canadians have faced and continue to face many forms of overt and systemic discrimination in mainstream Canadian sports. In response, they have developed the Northern Games, the North American Indigenous Games, special events in the Arctic Winter Games, and organizations like the Aboriginal Sport Circle to revitalize opportunities for themselves and their children and showcase their achievements and culture.

MIDDLE-CLASS MEN

Sports in Canada were codified, played, elaborated, and promoted in the context of rapid nineteenth-century urbanization and industrialization and similar developments in the British Empire and the United States. The most influential early clubs and organizations were located in Montreal, at the head of the "National Policy" economy of railroads, staple exports, protective tariffs for manufacturing, and the promotion of immigration. The Montreal Amateur Athletic Association, formed in 1881,

Canada

First Annual Report of the Montreal Base-Ball Club, 1886

GENTLEMEN:—

I have the honor of presenting you with the first annual report of the above club.

We were formerly organized and officers elected July 29, 1886.

Our season began so late and the difficulty of obtaining special days for practice has been so great that the first year of the club has not been marked by any special feature.

We made our debut Saturday, August 21st, when we met the Gordon B.B. Club, of Point St. Charles, in a practice match of 7 innings and were defeated by a score of 24 to 17.

Nothing daunted we accepted a challenge from the Clippers, and met them on the grounds of the M.L.C. September 4th, winning the match and our first ball by a score of 15 to 14, with an innings [sic] to spare. Time of Game 1h, 50 min.

The following players donned their new uniforms to meet the Clippers:—

Jos. Bruce, Jno. Heenan, T.S. Brophy, A.G. Walker, E.A. Cowley, W.G. Slack, J.A. Walker, E.S. Putman, J.G. Cornell, Captain.

September 11th, we met the Gordons and through want of practice sustained a defeat, the score standing 24 to 17 at the end of the 7th innings when game was called to allow the M.J.L.C. the use of the grounds. This match was advertised and netted us a small balance.

When it is taken into consideration that practice was limited to August and the first half of September, our practices were fairly well attended.

Our membership now numbers over 70 and should be tripled by the middle of the coming season.

For the coming season we will have the pick of a very large number of men and should become the possessors of the championship pennant of the City League just formed.

We have purchased 9 uniforms [$26.10], 9 caps, a mask [$1.50], catcher's gloves [$5.75], & c. [for a total of $38.75] and with the exception of, perhaps, a new mask, and bats and bases, we should begin the season of 1887 fully equipped. . . .

Source: Cowley, E. A. (1886). *First annual report of the Montreal Base-Ball Club, season 1886*. National Archives of Canada.

---

created eight of the first Canadian national governing bodies, including the Amateur Athletic Union of Canada (AAU), which governed other sports and won many of the first Canadian championships, including the first Stanley Cup, emblematic of supremacy in ice hockey, Canada's official winter sport.

These early clubs, leagues, and organizations were invariably restricted to the white, English-speaking, middle-class males who formed them, and they expressed and required adherence to the Victorian ideology of amateurism. Sports were quickly taken up in other cities and regions, and by those who had been excluded (often in their own clubs) especially Francophones, girls and women, immigrants, and the working class. They were assisted by the spirit of "rational recreation," which developed out of the late nineteenth-century urban reform movement, which inspired universities and schools, municipal recreation departments, voluntary associations such as the YMCA, and the Christian churches to organize teams and leagues. By the 1920s, sports were played and watched at some point by most Canadians, even if it was in organizations that were separated by class, gender, region, and ethnicity.

THE NHL

Growing urban densities, the popularization of sports by the mass media, and the growing marketing of sports to symbolize collective identities, especially among males, also enabled the growth of capitalist professional sports in baseball, lacrosse, ice hockey, and Canadian football. The most established of these has been the

I wouldn't say it's cold, but every year Winnipeg's athlete of the year is an ice fisherman. ■ DALE TALLON

National Hockey League (NHL). Formed in 1917, it grew significantly during the years between World War I and World War II through expansion to the United States and the development of a pan-Canadian radio network, Hockey Night in Canada, in the 1930s. Today there are six Canadian franchises—in Montreal, Ottawa, Toronto, Calgary, Edmonton, and Vancouver—in the thirty-team NHL.

THE CFL

The Canadian Football League (CFL), created in 1958 out of long-established community-based clubs and leagues, is the only professional league to operate on a pan-Canadian basis, although it briefly experimented with expansion to the United States during the 1990s. Today, there are CFL teams in Montreal, Ottawa, Toronto, Hamilton, Winnipeg, Regina, Calgary, Edmonton, and Vancouver. The National Basketball Association entered Canada in 1946 with the short-lived Toronto franchise, the Huskies. In 1995, the NBA returned to Canada with the Toronto Raptors and the Vancouver Grizzlies.

BASEBALL AND LACROSSE

Major League Baseball entered Canada in 1967 with a franchise in Montreal, the Expos. In 1977, it added the Toronto Blue Jays. Today, only the Toronto franchises remain in these leagues. Professional lacrosse has had a much rockier history, with leagues and teams being formed and disbanded with almost every season. The National Lacrosse League currently has two Canadian franchises—in Calgary, and Toronto—in the ten-team circuit.

Government and Sport

In 1961, amateur sport received a significant boost with the passage of the Fitness and Amateur Sport Act (FAS) by the federal Parliament. The FAS Program initially supported broadly based fitness and recreation initiatives as well as high performance. After 1970, in the face of threats to national unity from Quebec separatism, the Americanization of culture, and the dis-

affection of the western provinces from the federal government, embittered by what they perceived to be its domination by the central Canadian provinces of Ontario and Quebec, the Liberal government of Prime Minister Pierre Trudeau stepped up its investments in elite sport, believing that successful Canadian performances in international competition strengthened pan-Canadian unity and gave Canadians a better sense of themselves. A new federal agency, Sport Canada, transformed the voluntary amateur governing bodies into fully professionalized enterprises, with paid coaches, technical and administrative staff, and living and training stipends for top athletes.

To assist and promote elite sport development, Sport Canada also created new institutions, such as the National Sport and Recreation Centre, the National Coaching Certification Program, and the Athlete Information Bureau, and encouraged Canadian cities to bid for international games. Most provincial and territorial governments followed suit. The wisdom of these policies seemed to be borne out at the 1978 Commonwealth Games in Edmonton. For the first time ever, Canadian athletes fared better than those of any other team, and the new Canadian sport system caused so much envy that critics dubbed Canada "the GDR of the Commonwealth."

Subsequent governments allowed the Canadian sport system to fall into decline. However, early in the twenty-first century, sorry overall performances at the Atlanta and Sydney Olympics, growing concerns about physical inactivity among young people, and a decline in sports participation stimulated an effort to revitalize federal legislation. In 2003, the FAS Act was replaced by the Physical Activity and Sport Act.

Women and Sport

The 1920s and 1930s were a period of such rapid growth and achievement in women's sports that some scholars refer to it as the "Golden Age." Led by famous teams such as the Edmonton Grads, which won seventeen straight North American basketball championships and four straight "Olympic" titles (in the tournaments

Canada Olympics Results
2002 Winter Olympics: 6 Gold, 3 Silver, 8 Bronze
2004 Summer Olympics: 3 Gold, 6 Silver, 3 Bronze

organized at the time of the Olympic Games by the Féderation Sportive Feminine Internationale), and the "matchless six," who returned from the 1928 Olympics with more medals than any other track and field team, Canadian women excelled in virtually every competition they entered. They created their own clubs, leagues, and governing bodies, coordinated by the Women's Amateur Athletic Federation, attracted considerable spectatorship and won widespread coverage in the mass media, spearheaded in many cities by daily women's sports columnists. These breakthroughs were short-lived, however, and by the 1950s Canadian sportswomen once again faced closed doors, bad science (the specious "moral physiology" that claimed that active physical activity would harm their reproductive organs), and the social expectation that sports were properly a male domain.

During the last four decades, second-wave feminists also sought to win opportunities in sports and physical activity. But unlike their predecessors, who sought as much as possible to develop women's sport within women's organizations, they sought for the most part to do so within integrated organizations. Employing a range of tactics, from quiet lobbying to political demonstrations and human rights legislation, encouraged by feminist advances elsewhere in society, they won opportunities to participate and compete at every level. Today, while overall male participation rates remain higher than those of females, most national sports organizations provide as many national and international opportunities for women to compete as they do for men. Approximately the same number of women as men competed on the Canadian Olympic Teams in Atlanta, Sydney, and Athens. But Canadian women still continue to be woefully underrepresented in sport leadership and administrative and coaching positions.

The most significant voice for women in sports has been the Canadian Association for the Advancement of Women and Sport (CAAWS), formed in 1981 by an alliance of academics, athletes, and movement activists. CAAWS has become a powerful advocate for gender equity and a strong voice against sexual harassment and homophobia in the Canadian sport system.

Youth and Sport

Young women and men are the most physically active of all Canadians, with national surveys consistently showing that more than 50 percent of youth between the ages of five and fourteen years are active in sport. Sport and physical activity are a recognized part of the educational curriculum, and many municipal recreation departments privilege children and youth in their programming. The nature, extent, and provision of opportunities vary significantly from place to place, however. Increasingly, shrinking school and municipal budgets, deteriorating or closed facilities, and a shortage of qualified teachers and leaders contribute to the difficulties of delivering sport and physical activity.

Outside the public school and recreation systems, there is an extensive community-based organized sport system, especially among the middle to upper classes. But these are increasingly inaccessible for those facing economic hardship because participant fees continue to rise. Moreover, community sport continues to face the challenges of undertrained volunteer leaders and some of the darker aspects of youth sports, including the increasing preoccupation with performance rather than pleasure and participation, the intensification of training, and sexual harassment and abuse. A number of "made in Canada" strategies have been developed to address and resolve these problems, including a renewed emphasis upon coaching certification, the development of "fair play" leagues in hockey, and the introduction of child protection policies and programs.

With respect to colleges and universities, sport and physical activity are recognized as integral parts of a student's cocurricular educational experience. All Canadian postsecondary institutions offer a variety of recreational and competitive sporting opportunities to their students, including intramural and intercollegiate or interuniversity competition. The Canadian Colleges Athletic Association (CCAA) and Canadian Interuniversity Sport (CIS) are the governing bodies for postsecondary sport in Canada, and both organizations work in concert with other national and provincial sport organizations to further equitable and accessible sport for

The Saddle Dome in downtown Calgary.

Source: istockphoto/crescott.

Canadians. The CIS has taken significant steps to promote gender equity in sport and currently recognizes ten women's sports and nine men's sports.

Organizations

Framed under the umbrella of Sport Canada (http://www.pch.gc.ca/sportcanada), the Canadian sport system is comprised of numerous national and provincial-territorial sport organizations. Some organizations of note include the following:

Aboriginal Sport Circle (aboriginalsportcircle.ca); Arctic Winter Games (www.awg.ca); Canada Games Council (www.canadagames.ca); Canadian Colleges Athletic Association (www.ccaa.ca); Canadian Olympic Committee (www.olympic.ca); North American Indigenous Games (www.internationalgames.net/namindig.htm).

The Future

Sports are a recognized and valued part of Canadian social and cultural life. That said, there remain several challenges. The first challenge involves an age-old issue that has garnered public attention at different times and in different ways. This is the extent to which Canadian sport remains fair and Canadian athletes, especially those representing Canada in international competitions, exhibit ethical behavior. ("The team that marches behind the flag must represent the values of that flag,"

as one federal sports minister put it.) In recent years, many Canadian athletes and their leaders have internalized these expectations, and in coalition with others have contributed to the push toward gender equity, doping-free sport, and the fair treatment of high performance athletes (an "athlete-centered system").

As a result of the tireless lobbying of such organizations as Athletes CAN (the association of national team members in the amateur and Olympic sports) and the Canadian Centre for Ethics in Sport (CCES), the 2003 Physical Activity and Sport Act declared that Canadian sport policy "is founded on the highest ethical standards and values, including doping-free sport, the treatment of all persons with fairness and respect (and) the full and fair participation of all persons." That legislation also created the Sport Dispute Resolution Centre of Canada to ensure the "fair, equitable, transparent and timely resolution of disputes." Canadians have also been vocal and influential proponents of ethical sport internationally. Canadians were integrally involved in the development and establishment of the World Anti-Doping Agency (WADA), now located in Montreal.

A second challenge concerns the mass media, which are essential to Canadians' understanding of sports. Most newspapers devote entire sections to sports. The Canadian Broadcasting Corporation devotes 11 percent of its entire television schedule to sports, and specialized cable channels like the Sports Network (TSN), CTV Sportsnet, and Réseau des Sports (RDS) in Quebec broadcast 4,300 hours of programming annually. For almost eight months of the year, CBC's flagship *Hockey Night in Canada* attracts 5 to 6 million viewers every Saturday. But except for the commercial-free CBC radio and during major games such as the Olympics, the sports media distorts the landscape of Canadian sports,

Canada

Key Events in Canada Sports History

1860	The Native American game that becomes lacrosse is codified.
1881	The Montreal Amateur Athletic Association is formed.
1917	The National Hockey league is formed.
1920s	Sport is popular across Canada.
1920s–1930s	The Golden Era for women's sports in Canada.
1930s	Hockey Night in Canada on the radio is popular across Canada.
1958	The Canadian Football League is founded.
1961	The Fitness and Amateur Sport Act is passed.
1967	The Montreal Expos join Major League Baseball.
1977	The Toronto Blue Jays join Major League Baseball.
1978	The Commonwealth Games are held in Edmonton and Canada wins more medals than any other team.
1981	The Canadian Association for the Advancement of Women and Sport is founded.
2003	The Physical Activity and Sport Act is passed.

giving the bulk of coverage to the men's professional leagues while marginalizing women and athletes in the Canadian sports system. They are constrained by the basic economics of the sports media complex to marshal affluent male audiences for advertisers. In radio and television, the media are contractually bound to the leagues they cover. While many sports reporters provide brilliant, even incisive, commentary and coverage, they can be considered "embedded" journalists, with considerable limits on their autonomy. Policy makers have long struggled with this challenge in the context of the freedom of the press. A recent parliament committee recommended that the federal regulatory agency, the Canadian Radio Television Commission, direct the CBC to broadcast more events involving Canada's national teams, and not authorize any more foreign programming services with strong United States sports components.

A final challenge is the uneven and inconsistent support for sport as an institution by federal, provincial-territorial, and municipal governments. While the Canadian government is signatory to numerous international conventions and charters that proclaim sport and physical education to be basic human rights, and the health benefits of sport and physical activity are regularly touted during major games and elections, in practice, sport and physical activity programs, services, and facilities are often on the frontline of budget cutbacks and spending curtailments. Part of this is a result of the continued perception among Canadian government officials that sport and physical activity are low priorities. The consequence, however, has been declining participation rates, especially among the economically challenged.

Hopefully, the new federal legislation and the 2002 Canadian Sport Policy, signed by federal, provincial, and territorial governments as part of the same process, will contribute to a revitalization of public opportunities. With the 2010 Winter Olympic Games to be held in Vancouver, British Columbia, there is renewed energy for strengthening Canada's sport system, with regard to both elite sport and mass recreation, to ensure for all present and future Canadians accessible, ethical, and equitable sport.

Bruce Kidd

See also Football, Canadian; Maple Leaf Gardens; Stanley Cup

Further Reading

Coakley, J., & Donnelly, P. (2004). *Sports in society: Issues and controversies.* Toronto, Canada: McGraw-Hill Ryerson.
Donnelly, P. (Ed.). (2000). *Taking sport seriously: Social issues in Canadian sport.* Toronto, Canada: Thompson Educational Publishing.

Gruneau, R., & Whitson, D. (1993). *Hockey night in Canada: Sport, identities and cultural politics.* Toronto, Canada: Garamond Press.

Hall, A. (2002). *The girl and the game: A history of women's sport in Canada.* Peterborough, Canada: Broadview Press.

Kidd, B. (1997). *The struggle for Canadian sport.* Toronto, Canada: University of Toronto Press.

Macintosh, D., & Whitson, D. (1990). *The game planners: Transforming Canada's sport system.* Kingston and Montreal, Canada: McGill-Queen's University Press.

Macintosh, D., with Bedecki, T., & Franks, C. (1987). *Sport and politics in Canada: Federal government involvement since 1961.* Kingston and Montreal, Canada: McGill-Queen's University Press.

Standing Committee on Canadian Heritage, Sub-Committee on the Study of Sport in Canada. (1998). *Sport in Canada: Leadership, partnership and accountability.* Ottawa, Canada: Public Works and Government Services.

White, P., & Young, K. (Eds.). (1999). *Sport and gender in Canada.* Toronto, Canada: Oxford University Press.

Canoeing and Kayaking

Canoeing and kayaking are sports that have a variety of disciplines. Canoeing, in which participants sit or kneel on seats and use single-bladed paddles, is often called "Canadian canoeing" because of Canada's early promotion of international racing. Kayaking, in which participants use double-bladed paddles, is known as *kanusport* in some countries and is one of the fastest-growing activities globally.

History

Canoes and kayaks still show the traditional lines of a Greenland Inuit kayak or Aleutian umiak, a Maori (relating to a Polynesian people native to New Zealand) dugout, or a Native American birch-bark canoe because the designs that allowed paddlers to handle challenging conditions more than five thousand years ago are still relevant today. The traditional lines bring a sense of tradition to paddle sports, appreciated by many modern paddlers regardless of whether they are racing in sleek, modern craft or touring inland waterways in more stable designs.

The peoples of indigenous cultures in North America, Greenland, Scandinavia, and the former Soviet Union used canoes and kayaks. Builders stretched the skins of seal, walrus, or caribou around wooden frames and fastened them with sinew, baleen (a substance found in plates that hang from the upper jaws of baleen whales), bones, or antlers. Later, the presence of metal tools and toggles in North American boat construction indicated contact with European explorers. Ingenious crafters, the Inuit peoples used local materials to develop a variety of functional designs for different conditions, each of which could handle different types of water and activities.

Kayaks (from the Inuit word *qayak*) were traditionally used to hunt sea animals, including large mammals such as walruses and whales. The kayaks were relatively small, often ranging from 3.6 meters to 4.8 meters, which made them highly maneuverable for chasing prey. Because only men hunted in these societies, the kayak has been associated primarily with men until recent history.

The Inuit umiak (canoe) was a large, undecked skin boat of 7.6 meters to 12.1 meters used to carry large groups of people and heavy loads of cargo. Sometimes also used for hunting, it could be paddled, rowed, or sailed long distances. In Greenland the umiak came to be defined as the women's boat because women used them when they handled the transport of communities of people to new settlements. The umiak is believed to be the oldest working boat. Rock paintings in Norway from 5000 BCE show illustrations of what some archaeologists conclude to be open skin boats, although this conclusion is controversial. Some experts believe that the elk figureheads etched onto these boats were a link between land and sea and provided a means for humans to entire the lower spirit world. Similar seaworthy craft are also believed to have aided Asian peoples in their migration to the New World.

New World Exploration

When European explorers arrived in the New World during the 1600s, the original dugout or hollowed-out log of native peoples had given way to the birch-bark canoe used by woodland Native Americans. These lighter, more versatile craft enabled explorers to navigate the thousands of miles of inland lakes and rivers, portaging (carrying overland) over land divides to reach new watersheds. As early as the 1700s traders or voyagers penetrated the Canadian wilderness by canoe to send furs back out for shipment to Europe.

Meanwhile, when European explorers reached Polynesia in the 1600s, they discovered that the indigenous fishermen's skill with dugout canoes and outrigger canoes had allowed them to travel treacherous southern seas for thousands of years. These canoes, built with tools of stone, bone, and coral, were seaworthy enough to complete voyages of more than 3,200 kilometers and to settle Oceania (lands of the central and southern Pacific) in an area of 16 million square kilometers. Double-hull construction created a catamaran-style canoe capable of traveling faster by wind than the English navigator James Cook's ships.

By the mid-1850s canoeing and kayaking were no longer predominantly a means of subsistence, exploration, or commerce. The earliest recreational paddling was probably races by indigenous people, but the development of canoeing as a more formal activity began around 1850 in the Peterborough region of Ontario, Canada. Craftsmen began to develop plank-style canoes that, by the end of the century, led to an explosion in building boats at more affordable prices, an explosion welcomed by the general public, especially in Great Britain. Then the English barrister John MacGregor brought an oak "canoe" home to Europe from Canada. It was propelled by sail and had a double-bladed paddle similar to the one that kayakers use today. MacGregor recorded his exploits in 1866 in the popular *A Thousand Miles in the Rob Roy Canoe on the Rivers and Lakes of Europe,* which fueled an amazing rise in canoe travel for pleasure on both continents. Two years later he toured the eastern Mediterranean, including the Red Sea and the Nile River, to publish *Rob Roy on the Jordan.*

Interest by the General Public

The popularity of canoeing as an egalitarian (relating to a belief in equality) activity during the late 1800s came at a time when the public interest in recreation in general, including bicycling, was rising. Increasingly industrialized nations could produce sporting goods more cheaply, and Victorian attitudes that treated recreation as a frivolous activity were changing. A change in work weeks created more leisure time, and the rise of tourism around the globe prompted a surge in the poor man's yacht—a canoe. Guiding "sports" on notable fishing streams in North America and Europe became a cottage industry and encouraged the construction of specialized guide boats. The canoe became a popular vehicle for cruising, camping, and courting, and canoeing was considered an acceptable activity for women.

Colleges in the United States, including such women's schools as Smith and Wellesley, added canoeing as healthful activity for its students. Not only did general publications such as *Outing* feature gentlemanly wilderness excursions by canoe, but also women's periodicals such as *Cosmopolitan* began to laud the health-enhancing virtues of canoeing. No longer a wilderness endeavor, canoeing expanded in popularity when canoe liveries began renting boats in urban parks by the 1890s. The establishment of local canoe clubs in North America and Europe continued to promote canoeing after the turn of the century, but despite the popularity of races and regattas, no women appeared in American Canoe Association (ACA) race results from that period. Racing was still considered a gentleman's province, although women were actively involved in the social and recreational activities of the clubs. Not until 1944 did women became full voting members of the national association.

Rise of Recreational Racing

Scholars generally believe that canoe races and regattas predate recorded history and figured prominently in the rituals of ancient cultures. Thanks to John MacGregor modern racing emerged in Great Britain with royal

A kayaker on a man-made race course.

Source: istockphoto/groweb.

approval in the 1870s, and the military used canoe racing for training throughout the British empire. The American Canoe Association formed in 1880 as an international organization and awarded three honorary memberships to important non-American men such as John MacGregor and Worrington Baden-Powell, the brother of the Boy Scout founder, Robert Baden-Powell. Many ACA members preferred canoe sailing races in decked boats, which looked more like kayaks, rather than the open Canadian canoe. War canoes created a new class of racing in which teams of twenty people or more propelled a large boat, and boys and girls at summer camps quickly embraced this team event. Outrigger canoe racing, initially for men, began in the Hawaiian islands and quickly grew more competitive.

By the turn of the twentieth century racers experimented with the high kneel position of modern "sprint" canoeing for greater leverage against the paddle, and the greater speed made the high kneel the favorite racing position for flatwater despite its instability. After World War I canoeing and kayaking expanded so greatly that the era has been called their "golden age." Men first competed in sprint canoeing and kayaking as demonstration sports in the Olympics in 1924 in Paris and as full medal events in 1936 in Berlin. The onset of World War II stalled the expansion of international racing, but later manufacturers converted the war technologies of aluminum and fiberglass to create a wealth of new canoe and kayak designs. The post–World War II popularity of whitewater paddling in western and eastern Europe and former Soviet bloc countries contributed to the 1972 entry of slalom racing at the Munich Olympics, but it has appeared in only four subsequent Olympics because of the expense of creating artificial whitewater facilities.

The International Canoe Federation (ICF), the international governing body for paddle sports, recently approved canoe water polo for men and women as an international event. In this event two teams of kayakers in highly maneuverable boats attempt to score goals by passing a ball. National governing bodies within each country develop training and racing opportunities for athletes, often in conjunction with local clubs and private schools that have traditionally supported the development of canoe and kayak racing.

However, other forms of racing continue to emerge, often as non-Olympic events. Marathon racing in kayaks and open canoes tests paddlers on 8-kilometer to multiday courses. Whitewater freestyle or rodeo competitions require paddlers to execute technically difficult moves on holes and waves. Flatwater freestyle is sometimes called "canoe ballet." In it competitors create a dance choreography set to music. Dragon boat racing, similar to war canoe racing, involves teams of twenty-two people. The colorful nature of competition is a reflection of canoeing's and kayaking's enduring popularity among a variety of nations and cultures.

The principle is competing against yourself. It's about self-improvement, about being better than you were the day before. ■ STEVE YOUNG

Nature of the Sports

Many variations of canoeing and kayaking have emerged to offer many opportunities to paddle. Some variations have been accepted as Olympic sports, and many countries have local, regional, or national championships that allow many levels of competition. The International Canoe Federation recognizes the following six disciplines.

FLATWATER

In flatwater sprint racing athletes compete head to head on calm bodies of water in 500- and 1,000-meter distances. The events require speed, strength, and endurance. In the Olympics, women's events were added at London in 1948. However, women compete only in kayaking, not in canoeing, in single, double, and four-woman kayaks in 500-meter races. The four-woman kayak event was added in 1984.

Olypmic sprint races begin with qualifying heats, and the eight fastest qualifiers advance directly to the semifinals. The rest compete in a second-chance round known as a *"repechage"* (French for "fishing again"), and the four fastest boats advance to the semifinals. The top six semifinalists take part in the final, whereas the other six take part in a petit-final to determine seventh through twelfth places. Soviet and German women dominated in the early years, whereas more recently a variety of nations has been represented at the winner's podium.

SLALOM

In the slalom single kayakers negotiate a course of twenty-five hanging poles called "gates" over stretches of whitewater rapids 300 to 600 meters long. Kayakers attempt to negotiate as quickly as possible the gates in designated upstream-facing or downstream-facing positions. Kayakers try to complete the course without accruing penalties from touching gates (two seconds) or missing gates (fifty seconds). Only men compete in the canoe classes, kneeling in decked boats that resemble kayaks. C-1 (singles) and C-2 (doubles) races are challenging because each canoeist uses only one blade.

The challenge is to be fast and clean through the gates in frothy whitewater, creating an exciting spectator sport. Paddlers take two runs down the course, and both runs are added together for the final score. Women paddle the same whitewater stretch as men in kayaking classes, although the gates may be placed differently. Development of a slalom site can be difficult and expensive if a natural whitewater site is unavailable. However, the sport has spread beyond hosts in mountainous countries known for their steep rivers to urban hosts that have invested in artificial whitewater parks. Slalom is an intermittent demonstration sport in the Olympics.

WILDWATER

Wildwater racing is downriver sprinting in either kayaks or decked canoes through whitewater. One of the smallest disciplines, wildwater racing requires that paddlers find the fastest current and negotiate challenging obstacles on a sharply descending river in a race against the clock. The first world championship in France in 1959 featured long races of fifty minutes or more, and the trend through the years has been to shorten distances to enhance spectator interest and reduce the expense of managing long river courses. In 1988 the ICF created two racing classes: classic and sprint. The classic race distances are 4 to 6 kilometers, and the sprint race distances are 500 to 1,000 meters. Men's classes include K-1, C-1, and C-2; women race in K-1; mixed teams (man-woman) compete in C-2. Wildwater racing is currently a non-Olympic event.

MARATHON

Canoeing over long flatwater distances is known as "marathon racing" and has enjoyed popularity in Europe with the Kronberg race in Denmark, the Devises in Great Britain, the Sella Descent in Spain, the Liffey Descent in Ireland, and the Tour du Gudena in Denmark. More than twenty national federations sponsored national championships by 1976, and they proposed to the ICF that marathon racing become a sanctioned event, initially for K-1 and K-2 men. With international interest in marathon racing continuing to build, the

ICF finally approved the first world championship in 1988 with trophies for K-I and K-2 men, K-1 and K-2 women, and C-1 and C-2 men. Interest surged in the United States, Canada, Australia, and South Africa, and now marathon racing exists on all seven continents. It is currently a non-Olympic event.

Canoe Polo

Europeans began kayaking and throwing balls to each other during the 1930s, but international canoe polo rules did not resolve national differences in play until 1990. The game is played in an area that is 30 by 20 meters with goals of 1 by 1.5 meters that hang 2 meters above the water. Playing time is two ten-minute periods. The game begins with each team on its goal line and the ball in the center of the playing field. Every player tries to get to the ball, which can be moved by throwing or hitting it with a paddle. Players are not allowed to keep possession of the ball longer than five seconds, which creates fast turnovers. Players are allowed to attack and push over the opponent in possession of the ball. The first world championship—a biennial event—was held in Great Britain in 1994. Japan introduced the first junior world championship in 2004 as part of the ICF's plan to expand the base of support for canoe polo. Canoe polo competition is not yet an Olympic sport, but there are world and continental championships.

Canoe Sailing

With roots in Polynesian exploration, canoe sailing emerged as a racing discipline in Great Britain through John MacGregor's efforts in 1866 to establish the Canoe Club, which later became the Royal Club. Within twenty years the New York Canoe Club had established an international sailing cup, and U.S. participants had experimented with sliding seats and hiking boards to sit outside the canoe to control the rudder and sails, much to the disdain of British sailors who did not allow such practices. Scandinavians and Germans created entirely different specifications before World War II, and the ICF was challenged to establish hull, sail, and rigging designs acceptable to many countries for the first world championship in 1961. Canoe sailing is currently a non-Olympic sport.

Dragon Boat Racing

A dragon boat resembles the classic Chinese vision of a dragon: At the bow are an oxen's head, deer antlers, and the mane of a horse; the body has the scales of a python; a hawk's claws are represented by canoeists with single-bladed paddles; and at the stern are the fins and tail of a fish. Usually twenty paddlers propel the large dragon boat with a drummer and helmsman. They often race head to head with another boat over various distances where strength and endurance must be married with team unity and spirit to paddle well to the rhythm of the drum. The ancient Chinese originally used the dragon boat in religious events and later in honor of a beloved patriotic poet. Dragon boat races were a symbol of patriotism long before a 1976 festival in Hong Kong began a new era of modern competition. Now more than 20 million Chinese compete in dragon boat racing, which has spread to western and eastern Europe, where fifty thousand people compete. Dragon boat racing is not yet an Olympic sport, but it organizes world and continental championships.

Competition at the Top

Sprint canoeing and kayaking racers compete each year in world championships as well as in the summer Olympic Games every four years in: kayak singles (K-1), kayak tandem (K-2), kayak fours (K-4), and Canadian singles (C-1), Canadian tandem (C-2), and Canadian fours (C-4). The Olympic performance of Germany's athletes was important to the Nazi leader Adolf Hitler, and Germany had a top-three medalist in eight of the ten canoeing and kayaking events in the 1936 Olympics. Other strong contenders in the early years were Austria, France, Sweden, Canada, and Czechoslovakia. Women were allowed to compete in 500-meter sprints in the Olympics in London in 1948, and in the 1956 Olympics in Melbourne, Australia, the Soviet Union made the medals list.

In 1972 slalom racing entered the Munich Olympics as a demonstration sport but had made only its third appearance during the 1996 Olympics in Atlanta, Georgia, because many host countries cannot offer a whitewater venue.

Australia's Danielle Woodward won a silver medal in slalom racing at the Olympics in Barcelona, Spain, in 1992. Then the 2000 Olympics in Sydney further inspired Australia to build a multimillion-dollar slalom course, the only facility of its kind in the Southern Hemisphere. This course has enhanced the training of canoeists and kayakers in the surrounding countries and made them a more dominant force in competition.

Governing Body

The ICF, formed in 1924, has governed international canoe and kayak racing since World War II and has 117 national associations as members. Europe leads the way with forty-three associations, Asia has twenty-nine, the United States has twenty-four, Africa has fifteen, and Oceania has six. The ICF is located in Madrid, Spain.

The ICF formed to provide a link between national associations, to organize international competitions in three flatwater events (kayak racing, Canadian canoe racing, and canoe sailing), to promote foreign touring through river guides and tourism materials, and to share educational materials about the disciplines. Now millions of people are involved in a variety of competitive events globally.

The Future

Whereas at one time paddling appealed to only people who also hiked and backpacked, paddling has a much broader appeal today, and women in particular often see it as a way to gain outdoor skills. In Europe and mountainous countries such as New Zealand, kayaking was once the province of competitors and hard-core adventurers who could handle the rigors of steep, alpine rivers. However, more recreational paddlers are discovering the joys of learning to negotiate whitewater. River kayaks are shorter and highly maneuverable boats, and new paddlers require instruction to paddle them safely

in swift water. Whitewater schools have joined paddling clubs as important developmental programs for recreational paddlers as well as would-be racers.

An analysis of canoeing and kayaking participants reveals some trends. In the United States the Sporting Goods Manufacturers Association Internationale (SGMAI) tracked explosive growth in kayaking between 1998 and 2001 to 4.7 million people, a 34.3 percent increase. That increase makes kayaking one of the top three fastest-growing activities behind artificial wall climbing and snowboarding. More than half of the participants—2.5 million—are women. The average age of participants is thirty-one years, and they participate an average of seven days each year. Canoeing declined slightly in participation during the same period, but canoeists still outnumber kayakers with 12 million participants. Of that total, 5.9 million are women who average twenty-six years of age. The 6.1 million men who canoe average thirty years of age. About half of those who canoe also fish, and the average number of days in which they canoe is six. The most active age group for either activity is children from twelve to seventeen years of age. Surprisingly, members of the next most active group of kayakers are ages forty-five to fifty-four, and in canoeing members of the next most active group are ages thirty-five to forty-four.

Most people paddle on vacations, at summer camps, and on adventure travel excursions. Sea kayaking is experiencing a surge in growth internationally as the result of a general growing interest in adventure travel. The longer, sleeker sea kayaks are easy to paddle and stable and thus offer a secure and rewarding introduction to an outdoor experience. They also allow people to explore such beautiful and exotic locations as sea caves in Thailand, the rocky shores around Great Britain and Norway, the dolphin-filled bays and straits of New Zealand, and the island chains within the United States' Great Lakes.

People who fear being enclosed in a kayak can try sit-on-top kayaks, which seem like modified surfboards and have their origins in surfing cultures along the Pacific Ocean. These kayaks look like the bottom half of a kayak with a seat and foot supports that allow paddlers to control the kayak. Canoes continue to be a sensible option for families, and the larger size of canoes allows people a greater opportunity for wilderness travel for extended periods of time.

The ICF moved sharply away from its original promotion of paddling tourism, but the public has continued to be attracted to the wealth of opportunities internationally and fascinated by the many designs of canoes and kayaks.

Laurie Gullion

Further Reading

Arina, E. Y. (1987). *Inuit kayaks in Canada: A review of historical records and construction.* Ottawa: National Museums of Canada.

Bond, H. (1995). *Boats and boating in the Adirondacks.* Blue Mountain Lake, NH: Adirondack Museum/Syracuse University Press.

Endicott, W. T. (1980). *To win the worlds: A textbook for elite slalomists and their coaches.* Baltimore: Reese Press.

Ford, K. (1995). *Kayaking.* Champaign, IL: Human Kinetics Publishers.

Gullion, L. (1994). *Canoeing.* Champaign, IL: Human Kinetics Publishers.

Gullion, L. (1999). *A Ragged Mountain Press guide: Canoeing.* Camden, ME: Ragged Mountain Press/McGraw-Hill.

Heed, P., & Mansfield, D. (1992). *Canoe racing.* Syracuse, NY: Acorn Publishing.

Kawaharanda, D. (n.d.). The settlement of Polynesia, part I. Retrieved May 22, 2004, from http://leahi.kcc.hawaii.edu/org/pvs/migrations part1.html

Jennings, J. (2002). *The canoe: A living tradition.* Buffalo, NY: Firefly Books.

Snaith, S. (1997) *Umiak: An illustrated guide.* Eastsound, WA: Walrose & Hyde.

Capoeira

Capoeira is an Afro-Brazilian game with more than two hundred years of history. Often called a "dance fight," it incorporates martial arts, gymnastics, improvisation, music, and ritual. Together these elements form a cultural practice that is a physically exuberant—and at times slightly dangerous—game. To play, two *capoeiristas* approach a *roda* (circle). At the discretion of the *mestre* (master), who generally plays the lead *berim-bau* (a percussive, tonal bow of African origin), the *capoeiristas* squat in front of the area where musical instruments are played and, after greeting each other, cartwheel into the *roda* and begin to play. The game consists of infinite variations on a number of movements. The most important movement is the *jinga*, a rhythmic, swinging, side-to-side back step. From the *jinga* the *capoeiristas* unleash sweeping, circular kicks that are evaded or ducked but never blocked. These evasions flow seamlessly into counterattacks and counterevasions, creating a current of intertwined movement, a mesmerizing, improvised spectacle. As a game and a martial art capoeira inverts normal assumptions; *capoeiristas* are as comfortable on their hands as on their feet, and they use the appearance of weakness to lure opponents into foolish attacks. Instead of rules players observe customs and conventions. Players use no hand strikes, but plenty of head butts, sweeps, and sly feints. Only a player's hands, feet, or head should touch the ground. No one wins, no one loses. Success is judged by one's skill, wit, physical bravado, and creativity. Speed, strength, balance, and flexibility are admired only as part of a creative approach. *Malicia* and *malandragan,* essentially untranslatable adjectives of praise for someone's capacity for deceptive play, creative sneakiness and even well-timed treachery, are admired and encouraged.

Early History

Scholars disagree on the cultural and geographic origins of capoeira, although the combination of playfulness and deceit clearly were an elegant solution for enslaved Africans who wished to pursue martial training undetected by their oppressors. Some scholars, pointing to similar practices in Martinique, Cuba, and elsewhere, argue that capoeira originated in central Africa and was brought to the Americas fully formed. Others scholars argue that capoeira was created in Brazil by Africans, who, although building on existing traditions, were responding to the conditions of New World slavery.

The first written records of capoeira are in newspaper articles from the late eighteenth century, when Brazil was still a Portuguese colony. Later records, after Brazilian independence in 1822, describe capoeira at festivals and parades. Illustrations show a combative game played in a social setting, and traveler's reports describe an effective form of self-defense unleashed in moments of apparent weakness. Court records from Rio de Janeiro document people imprisoned simply for being identified with capoeira. At other times *capoeiristas* served as bully boys for politicians and headed patriotic crowds confronting rioting foreign soldiers. According to legend they acquitted themselves with honor during the disastrous War of the Triple Alliance during the 1870s.

As the free black population increased in Brazil, particularly after the abolition of slavery in 1888, and as urban centers expanded, capoeira was seen by the government as even more threatening. Capoeira was repressed during the empire (1822–1889), and it was formally outlawed during Brazil's first republic (1889–1930). Although a few elite thinkers saw capoeira as an authentically Brazilian product to be celebrated, the campaign of repression was largely successful.

Twentieth Century

Capoeira survived mainly in the city of Salvador da Bahia, the historic center of African Brazil. To avoid the watchful eye of the republican state, *capoeiristas* further disguised the game's martial qualities by emphasizing its playful nature. The *berimbau* emerged as the conductor of the *roda*, able to slow down an angry game or warn of approaching police with a subtle change in rhythm. After this era of repression, the history of capoeira turns on the work of two *mestres:* Bimba (Manoel dos Reis Machado) and Pastinha (Vicente Ferreira Pastinha). Bimba introduced substantial modifications to capoeira, adding some elements and de-emphasizing others, highlighting the art's combative nature, creating a style now called capoeira regional. He also opened an academy, the Academia-Escola de Capoeira Regional, taking the game off the street, making it accessible to white and middle-class students. Capoeira regional was praised by the government of Gertulio Vargas as a prod-

uct of the Brazilian racial democracy that his authoritarian, populist regime championed. Pastinha, who was taught by an African master, responded by opening an academy where he emphasized and refined traditional capoeira, which in tribute to its roots he named "capoeira Angola." To this day capoeira Angola is deemed traditional, playful, African, and "blacker," whereas by reputation capoeira regional is aggressive, "whiter," and, critics say, less authentic. Capoeira regional spread throughout Brazil during the 1960s and 1970s, and capoeira Angola, after a time when interest waned, also thrives. Capoeira classes are now offered at Brazilian colleges and elite fitness centers, yet it retains its historic link to street culture and blackness.

Attempts to form national federations and to institute formal competitions with scoring and points systems, sometimes led by government ministries, have not proved successful. Factionalism and disagreements on the merits of different styles made uniform judging impossible, and to some people such efforts miss the point. Capoeira remains informally organized around groups, affiliations, academies, and charismatic *mestres*, usually, although not always, defining themselves as regional or Angola.

Capoeira in a Globalized World

During the 1970s capoeira went international. Young *mestres* began to teach classes and open academies in the United States and then Europe. Today it is taught and played around the world. Although this growth has brought many benefits, one cannot know what the ultimate impact will be and what challenges will arise. For example, the U.S. conception of racial identity and the meaning of African cultural practice in the Americas have added new perspectives and heightened the tension in the debate over historic origins. How will this debate proceed in the future? Will capoeira spread until as many academies as tae kwon do (a Korean art of unarmed self-defense) studios exist, or will its growth level off? How will capoeira maintain its distinctiveness in a world where people borrow bits of culture with only a slight understanding? At present one cannot imagine

Losing is the great American sin. ■ JEROME HOLTZMAN

capoeira not rooted in Brazilian culture and Brazilian Portuguese, but the game will have to overcome the challenges brought on by its success. In the meantime capoeira reigns, in the words of Robert Farris Thompson, supreme "of all the martial arts of the black Atlantic world," funky, intoxicating, spiritual, slightly dangerous, profound, and beautiful, like jazz, samba, pickup ball in the park, or Pelé playing soccer on the beach.

Joshua M. Rosenthal

Further Reading

Almeida, B. (1986). *Capoeira, a Brazilian art form.* Berkeley, CA: North Atlantic Books.

Browning, B. (1995). *Samba: Resistance in motion.* Bloomington: Indiana University Press.

Capoeira, N. (1995). *The little capoeira book.* Berkeley, CA: North Atlantic Books.

Capoeira, N. (2002). *Capoeira: Roots of the dance-fight game.* Berkeley, CA: North Atlantic Books.

Chvaicer, M. T. (2002). The criminalization of capoeira in nineteenth-century Brazil. *Hispanic American Historical Review, 82*(3), 525–547.

Desch-Obi, T. J. (2002). Combat and the crossing of the Kalunga. In L. M. Heywood (Ed.), *Central Africans and cultural transformations in the American diaspora.* (pp. 353–370). Cambridge, UK: Cambridge University Press.

Downey, G. (2002). Domesticating an urban menace: Efforts to reform capoeira as a Brazilian national sport. *International Journal of the History of Sport, 19*(4), 1–32.

Downey, G. (2005). *Learning capoeira: Lessons in cunning from an Afro-Brazilian art.* New York: Oxford University Press.

Holloway, T. (1989). A healthy terror: Police repression of capoeiras in nineteenth-century Rio de Janeiro. *Hispanic American Historical Review, 69*(4), 637–676.

Lewis, J. L. (1992). *Ring of liberation: Deceptive discourse in Brazilian capoeira.* Chicago: University of Chicago Press.

Carnegie Report

The Carnegie Report—a report by the Carnegie Foundation for the Advancement of Teaching in 1929 and formally entitled "American College Athletics"—is often considered the most significant historical document on intercollegiate athletics in North America. It is basically a condemnation of the professionalized and commercialized athletics that had developed during the previous eight decades in U.S. colleges. Its findings mirror the problems that exist into the twenty-first century.

Background

College sports have been commercialized since the first U.S. intercollegiate contest: a rowing contest between Harvard and Yale in 1852. A railroad sponsored the contest at Lake Winnipesaukee, New Hampshire. About a decade later Yale hired the first professional coach to beat Harvard in rowing. By the 1870s and 1880s other forms of professionalism and commercialism existed in college sports, including contending for valuable noncash and cash prizes, competing against professionals, collecting gate money, providing training tables, paying for tutors of athletes, and recruiting and paying athletes.

Students in nearly all colleges organized athletic associations from the 1870s to 1900, principally to give moral and financial support to the teams they supported—often crew, baseball, football, and track and field. Amateur ideals were often violated because the desire to win was far more important to the students than how the sports fit into general educational goals. In contrast, faculty athletic committees on campuses were established to limit the extent that extracurricular sports would overshadow the educational curriculum.

However, restrictive legislation by a faculty athletic committee lessened the ability of that college to compete against other colleges in sports. Therefore, interinstitutional regulations were needed to "level the playing field" between colleges. Thus, a small group of colleges, such as the four colleges that formed the first Intercollegiate Football Association in 1876—Harvard, Yale, Princeton, and Columbia—joined to create common rules. From the 1890s to the 1920s dozens of conferences, such as the Big 10 in 1895, were created in an attempt to set standards, including limiting the number of years of participation, setting minimum academic achievement standards, and allowing no payment of players.

Carnegie Report

Pritchett on College Sports

The president of the Carnegie Foundation for the Advancement of Teaching, Henry S. Pritchett, offered the strongest condemnation of college athletics in his preface to American College Athletics:

The paid coach, the gate receipts, the special training tables, the costly sweaters and extensive journeys in special Pullman cars, the recruiting from the high school, the demoralizing publicity showered on the players, the devotion of an undue proportion of time to training, the devices for putting a desirable athlete, but a weak scholar, across the hurdles of the examinations-—these ought to stop . . . .

Source: Savage, H. J. (1929). *American College Athletics* (pp. xxi). New York: The Carnegie Foundation for the Advancement of Teaching.

Calls for National Standards

By the twentieth century people were calling for common rules of various sports and creating common standards of amateurism. Football, which had become the most important college sport by the 1890s, came to a crisis during the early 1900s because of the charge of brutality and the evasion of amateur standards. The 1905 football crisis, involving President Theodore Roosevelt, led to creation of the National Collegiate Athletic Association (NCAA) at the end of that year. The NCAA was a faculty-controlled organization that created common rules for football and other sports and set standards, although only advisory, for honorable conduct of athletes. Yet, individual colleges still had their own eligibility rules, and the evasion of those rules created continual controversy.

Even before the United States entered World War I, the University of Chicago football coach Amos Alonzo Stagg (1862–1965) called for the Carnegie Foundation for the Advancement of Teaching, the Sage Foundation, or the General Educational Board to conduct a survey to establish standards for college athletics. In

1916 the Amateur Athletic Union, the principal amateur athletic organization outside of colleges, and the NCAA agreed in principle on the definition of an amateur as one who competes "only for the pleasure, and the physical, mental, moral, and social benefits derived therefrom." The NCAA then resolved to petition a foundation to survey intercollegiate athletics. This action was not taken for another decade.

By the early 1920s, as commercialism intensified, people again called for reform of intercollegiate athletics. The NCAA's Edgar Fauver suggested that a large foundation, such as the Rockefeller Foundation or Carnegie Foundation, conduct a thorough study of intercollegiate athletics. He wanted facts, not sentiment, on which future college athletics could be conducted. In January 1926, the Carnegie Foundation for the Advancement of Teaching announced that it would carry out the study.

Carnegie Survey

The Carnegie study team little doubted that its survey would uncover corruption in intercollegiate athletics. The team was careful, though, to quantify the degree of corruption. The team, led by Howard J. Savage, visited more than one hundred U.S. and Canadian schools, including seventy-two private and forty public colleges and ten secondary schools, after questionnaires sent to colleges were found to be untrustworthy. Yet, the team trusted the interviews that raised questions about recruiting by schools and alumni, part-time employment and subsidies for athletes, provision for professional tutoring of athletes, the degree of faculty or alumni control of athletics, the salaries and hiring practices of coaches, and athletic "slush funds." Those schools that were honest in their answers were lampooned in the final report, whereas those that either lied or concealed data were let off generally unscathed.

The 350-page report, published on 24 October 1929, attacked practices in intercollegiate athletics. It criticized recruiting and subsidization, the hiring of professional coaches, the abandonment of amateurism, and the lack of student involvement in decision making.

More than anything it condemned the rampant commercialism in intercollegiate athletics. Nevertheless, the Carnegie Report did little to change the direction taken by intercollegiate athletics. Although some schools were influenced to get out of big-time athletics, most major schools continued to promote athletics by recruiting the best athletes possible, to try to fill giant stadiums and arenas, and to reap whatever prestige they could from winning athletic teams.

The Future

The commercialization and professionalization of big-time intercollegiate athletics increased when radio, and then television, added to the commercial possibilities of intercollegiate athletics. However, the Carnegie Report had a lasting impact in one respect. Foundation studies of college sports, such as the Knight Foundation Commission on Intercollegiate Athletics of 1989, used the Carnegie Report as a starting point for reform. However, later studies influenced by the Carnegie Report had little effect on the direction taken by big-time intercollegiate athletics.

Ronald A. Smith

Further Reading

American Council on Education. (1952). *Report of the Special Committee on Athletic Policy of the American Council on Education, February 16, 1952*. Washington, DC: Author.

Falla, J. (1981). *NCAA: The voice of college sports: A diamond anniversary history, 1906–1981*. Mission, KS: National Collegiate Athletic Association.

Fauver, E. (1922, June). The place of intercollegiate athletics in a physical education program. *American Physical Education Review, 27*, 1–5.

Friday, W. C., & Hesburgh, T. M. (1991). Keeping faith with the student-athlete: A new model for intercollegiate athletics. *Report of the Knight Foundation Commission on Intercollegiate Athletics*. Charlotte, NC: Knight Foundation.

Hanford, G. H. (1974). *A report to the American Council on Education on an inquiry into the need for and feasibility of a national study of intercollegiate athletics*. Washington, DC: American Council on Education.

Sack, A. L., & Staurowsky, E. J. (1998). *College athletes for hire: The evolution and legacy of the NCAA's amateur myth*. Westport, CN: Praeger.

Savage, H. J. (1929). *American college athletics*. New York: Carnegie Foundation for the Advancement of Teaching.

Smith, R. A. (1988). *Sports and freedom: The rise of big-time college athletics*. New York: Oxford University Press.

Watterson, J. S. (2000). *College football: History, spectacle, controversy*. Baltimore: Johns Hopkins University Press.

Carriage Driving

People domesticated the horse at least five thousand years ago and used it as a major source of transport until the early twentieth century, when the internal combustion engine reduced the importance of the horse to its current role in recreation and equestrian sports.

Origins

The development of equestrian sports incorporating vehicles such as carriages lagged far behind those equestrian sports in which the horse is ridden under saddle, such as polo, flat racing, and hunting. The amount of equipment required for carriage sports and the additional personnel required for harnessing and handling restricted their development to the most affluent equestrians. Likewise, the creation of breeds suitable for carriage sports was slower than creation of breeds for flat racing and polo. Cold-blooded draft horse breeds, which are sturdier, heavier, and more powerful, were bred to include lines from the faster, lighter-boned, and more high-strung hot-blooded breeds, such as the Thoroughbred, to produce "warmbloods" suitable for driving. The result was carriage horses with the power of cold bloods and the competitiveness and speed of hot bloods.

Driving clubs, such as the Benson Driving Club (1807–1854), the Whip (founded 1808), and the Richmond Driving Club (1838–1845), first developed in England. The British Driving Society has operated since 1958, and the Coaching Club has operated for more than 125 years.

Organized carriage driving competitions have existed in central Europe and Germany for a hundred years, primarily because of the efforts of Benno von Achenbach

(1861–1936) of Germany. He was trained by Edwin Howlett of England, who is considered the father of modern four-in-hand driving (four horses under harness, two in front and two behind). What had been the vocation of coachmen became a pastime of the leisure class.

Four-in-hand driving as a sport declined greatly after World War I. Organized carriage driving competitions did not revive until after World War II, and multinational contests in Europe began during the 1950s. Competitions of the time generally included two phases: dressage and marathon.

A ridden version of three standard military tests for horses (dressage, cross-country, and stadium jumping, known collectively as "three-day eventing" because each phase was tested on a different day) had been an Olympic sport since 1912. Adaptations were dictated by the presence of the carriage and the fact that a driver's only control over the horses is through the voice, the whip, and the reins that attach to each side of a metal bit through the horses' mouth. Whereas use of the voice is not allowed in ridden dressage, it is allowed in driven dressage. Jumps used in the cross-country phase of a ridden three-day competition are replaced by a marathon section with hazards—water-filled ditches or narrow gates—and, in place of stadium jumping, a precision driving test known as the "cones phase."

Dressage is an equestrian discipline based on military training in which a horse must demonstrate obedience, flexibility, and strength as its driver directs it through a routine of movements. Ridden dressage has been a staple of classical equestrian training since the seventeenth century.

Marathon driving, also based on military training, requires the horse to be driven across open country and through water and to negotiate obstacles such as an orchard of narrowly spaced trees or a combination of gates.

Practice

In 1969 Prince Philip of Great Britain was president of the Federation Equestre Internationale (FEI, www.horsesport.org), the governing body for show jumping, dressage, three-day eventing, and other international equestrian competitions. At an FEI meeting, Polish delegate Eric Brabec suggested to Prince Philip that the FEI establish standardized rules for carriage driving competitions. Brabec's suggestion was acted on almost immediately. With the help of Sir Michael Ansell of Great Britain, European drivers convened in Bern, Switzerland, and produced a set of rules based on ridden three-day tests. The first test, dressage, includes two parts: presentation and the driven dressage test. Presentation requires that horses, driver, grooms, and equipment be cleanly turned out and correctly outfitted.

The dressage test takes place in a large arena with at least three judges (five for important international contests) scoring the test from different vantage points. Scores are based on the accuracy of the driven test and the quality of the horses' performance. The test is driven at two gaits—the walk and trot—with halts and backing included. Movements include circles and serpentines down the length of the arena. Scoring is based on how close a driver and team come to achieving the ideal; penalties are levied for deviation from the ideal, based on a high score of ten points per movement. Thus, the lowest dressage score wins.

The second phase is known as the "marathon," although the distance covered is usually about 27 kilometers. This phase tests the stamina and fitness of the horses and the ability of the driver to maneuver the horses through obstacles and complete the distances within a prescribed pace. Three to five sections are included, with the obstacles course as the final section. A full, five-sectioned marathon would be driven as follows: section A driven at a trot; section B driven at a walk, at the end of which is a compulsory ten-minute halt when horses are inspected for fitness to continue; section C driven at a fast trot; section D again driven at a walk with a compulsory ten-minute halt; and section E, the obstacles course, driven at a trot. Eight obstacles usually are included in this course. Obstacles might be a series of gates, a sloped, wooded area, or a shallow pool of water.

The greatest spectator appeal of carriage driving occurs during the final phase of the marathon. Drivers, belted onto their carriage seats, must drive with enough speed not to incur penalty points as their grooms—

serving as navigators—shout reminders from their posts on the back of the carriages to keep the drivers on course through the maze of gates. Grooms often throw their weight to one side or the other around a turn to shift the carriage on the track, freeing a wheel or avoiding its entrapment on a gatepost or tree. As in dressage, penalties are scored, and the low score wins. Time penalties are scored on each phase and through each obstacle in the final section.

The obstacle phase is usually staged in the same arena as the first day's events—presentation and dressage. The course consists of gates, which are pairs of plastic cones similar to traffic cones, with a ball atop each. The goal is to drive one's horses and carriage between each set of cones without dislodging any balls. The cones are spaced just a few inches wider apart than the wheels of the carriage passing between them, and courses are complicated, twisting back and forth across the arena.

The first international competition driven under the new FEI-created rules was held in 1970 in Lucerne, Switzerland. In 2004 Michael Freund of Germany won the FEI World Cup Driving Championship for the third time in a row. At the 2004 International Paralympic Committee's Carriage Driving World Championships in Edinburgh, Scotland, twenty-nine equestrians from eight nations (Austria, Germany, Great Britain, Hungary, Ireland, the Netherlands, Sweden, and the United States) competed in dressage, marathon, and obstacle driving. Karl Bernd Kasgen of Germany won first place in grade 1; Elek Taczman of Hungary won grade 2; Brenda Hodgson of England won the pairs; and Germany won the team event.

Kate Lincoln

Further Reading

Duke of Edinburgh. (1982). *Competition carriage horse driving.* Macclesfield, UK: Horse Drawn Carriages Limited.

Jung, E. B. (1980). *Combined driving.* New York: Author.

Pape, M. (1982). *The art of driving.* New York: J. A. Allen.

Rogers, F. (1900). *Manual of coaching.* Philadelphia: J. B. Lippincott.

Von Achenbach, B. (1922). *Anspannen und Fahren.* Berlin, Germany: Fn Publishing House.

Watney, B. M. I. (1981). *The British Driving Society book of driving.* London: British Driving Society.

Central American and Caribbean Games

On 4 July 1924, during the Paris Olympic Games, representatives from Mexico, Cuba, Colombia, and Venezuela met to establish a gathering to be called the Central American Games, beginning in 1926 and being held every four years. The goal was to create a competition in which athletes could participate for the sole pleasure of taking part in it and for the physical, mental, social, and moral benefits that result from such participation. These games are now the world's oldest continuous regional games.

History

The first two editions of the games were called the Central American Games, but in 1934 the title "Central American and Caribbean Games" was adopted to reflect the participation of the Caribbean nations.

EARLY GAMES

At the first games Cuba and Guatemala visited Mexico City, and 269 athletes participated in eight sports. Guatemala's president died on the eve of the games, but Guatemala still decided to send a team.

The U.S. ambassador to Cuba, Harry F. Guggenheim, insisted that Puerto Rico be included in the second games in Havana in 1930. A last-minute effort was needed to pull together a team of four athletes, and money was raised by donations from Puerto Rican citizens to fly them by plane, a rarity at that time, to Havana. That year, also, women competed in the games for the first time, in tennis.

San Salvador, El Salvador, hosted the next edition of the games, which were held early in 1935, having been postponed for a year due to an earthquake that hit El Salvador in 1934.

The fourth games were held in Panama City, Panama, from 4–24 February 1938. Jamaica participated for the first time, becoming the first English-speaking nation to join in the games. Unruly crowds led to the cancellation of both the men's and women's basketball final games because the safety of the visiting teams could not be guaranteed.

POSTWAR GAMES

The 1942 edition of the games was cancelled due to World War II, but the games were revived in 1946 in Baranquilla, Columbia, with the next games held in 1950 in Guatemala City, Guatemala. The 1954 games were scheduled to be held in Panama City, but because of the country's economic problems at the time, Panama had to forego the games. Mexico City volunteered to host the events.

The eighth edition was postponed one year, to 1959, due to political unrest in Venezuela. Cuba did not attend, because of the unrest associated with their revolution.

Jamaica became the first English-speaking host nation when it sponsored the games in 1962 in Kingston. Athletes from the Bahamas and Barbados competed for the first time.

THE BATTLE OF CERRO PELADO

The 1966 games in San Juan, Puerto Rico, are significant for "the battle of Cerro Pelado." Many factions wanted to ban Cuba from the games for political reasons after Castro's rise to power, but Don German Rieckehoff, president of the organizing committee, stood alone in his insistence that Cuba be allowed to compete in the games. While the argument raged, the Cubans' boat, the "Cerro Pelado," was not allowed into Puerto Rican waters. Though under intense pressure, Rieckehoff stood firm and finally convinced the governor of Puerto Rico to change his mind. The governor agreed to allow the Cubans into the country, but they had to leave their boat and be picked up and brought to shore on a ship of Puerto Rican ownership, which they did, and Cuba was able to participate in the games.

CUBAN DOMINATION

Mexico, until that point, had been the dominant sports nation, finishing atop the medals standings in nine of the previous ten games (the exception was Havana in 1930). In Panama City in 1970, Cuba took over and become the dominant athletic nation in the region. The Cubans won medals in every team sport and dominated in gymnastics athletics, wrestling, boxing, fencing, and judo. Cuba won ninety-nine gold medals; all other nations combined just eighty-two gold medals.

Cuba continued their domination in the 1974 games, held in Santo Domingo, and in the 1978 games in Medellin, but they broke all their previous records when they hosted the games in Havana in 1982 (originally awarded to Mayaguez, Puerto Rico) and took 173 of the total of 248 available gold medals.

The sixteenth games were scheduled to be held in Guatemala, until the Guatemalan government pulled its financial support early in 1990. Mexico fortunately stepped in and hastily organized the games for later that year, the second time that Mexico had rescued the games. Carlos Salinas de Gortari, president of Mexico, opened the games on the anniversary of Mexico's revolution.

The seventeenth edition of the games was held a bit early, in November of 1993, in Ponce, Puerto Rico. At least forty-two Cubans defected over the course of the games, but Cuba set another record, taking 180 gold medals.

The eighteenth edition of the games, held in August 1998 in Maracaibo, Venezuela, broke records for participation with 1,827 female and 3,487 male athletes, for a total of 5,314.

CUBAN WITHDRAWAL

Cuba surprised everyone in 2002 when it announced that it would not be participating in the games in El Salvador. The two nations have not had diplomatic relations since 1961. Cuba cited concerns about security, possible coercions to defect, kidnappings, and even the possibility that Vice President Jose Ramon Fernandez, the president of the Cuban Olympic Committee, might be assassinated. It was only the second time that Cuba had missed the games, and several nations took advantage of Cuba's absence by winning more medals than they ever had at the games. One member of Venezuela's rowing team drowned after their rowing shell capsized during practice on Lake Coatepeque before the games.

THE FUTURE

The 2006 games are scheduled to be held in Cartagena, Colombia. Mayagüez, Puerto Rico, has been chosen over Guatemala City to host the 2010 games.

Daniel Bell

Further Reading

Bell, D. (2003). Central American and Caribbean Games. *Encyclopedia of International Games.* Jefferson, NC: McFarland Publishing.

Beracasa, José. (1976). From 1926 to 1976: Twelve Central American and Caribbean Games. *Olympic Review, Vol. 109–110,* 626–629, 659.

Days of glory in Santiago (DOM) and Mexico. (1986, August). *Olympic Review, No. 226.* Retrieved February 16, 2005, from http://www.aafla.org/OlympicInformationCenter/OlympicReview/1986/ore226/ore226g.pdf

14th Central American and Caribbean Sports Games. (1982, July). *Olympic Revue.* Retrieved February 16, 2005, from http://www.aafla.org/OlympicInformationCenter/OlympicReview/1982/ore177/ORE177za.pdf

McGehee, R. (1994). Revolution, democracy and sport. The Guatemalan Olympics of 1950. *Olympika, The International Journal,* 49–81.

McGehee, R. (1994). Los juegos de las Americas: Four inter-American multisport competitions. In R. C. Wilcox (Ed.), *Sport in the Global Village* (pp. 377–387). Morgantown, WV: Fitness Information Technology, Inc.

Cheerleading

Cheerleading is a sport that combines stunts, tumbles, dance, cheers, and crowd psychology. Although cheerleading has flourished in the United States since the late 1800s, women have participated only since the 1920s. Although the sport did not spread beyond the United States until the 1980s, it has been transformed into a multibillion-dollar industry.

History

During the 1840s, prior to the creation of cheerleaders, organized cheering was part of military tradition in the U.S. Army and Navy. Cheerleading began with a male "yell leader" who would single-handedly rouse a crowd to motivate its team on the field. The first documented cheering at a sporting event occurred at the 1869 Rutgers-Princeton football game as cheering sections cheered, "Siss, boom, ahhh!" Initially, cheers were led by substitute or injured players on the bench who would seek fan support at critical points of the game. By the late 1890s yell leaders who were captains of baseball, track, and other sports teams were designated as cheerleaders. Johnny Campbell of the University of Minnesota became the first cheerleader in 1898. During the early 1900s the position of yell leader was nearly as prestigious as that of quarterback of the football team. After nearly three decades of having sports captains as yell leaders, noncaptain lettermen began to join the ranks of cheerleading as captains opted to spend their Saturday afternoons in the stands. Eventually cheerleading squads of four or more members replaced individual yell leaders. Women became cheerleaders during the 1920s, although in a limited way and with some opposition.

Growth of the Spirit Industry

Cheerleading associations emerged in 1948 in Dallas, Texas, when Larry Herkimer started the National Cheerleading Association (NCA). Herkimer, the "father of cheerleading," wrote books on cheerleading, created jumps and cheers, and published the first cheerleading magazine *(The Megaphone).* A year after forming the NCA Herkimer held the first cheerleading camp in Huntsville, Texas, at Sam Houston State University.

The NCA provided cheerleading camps and clinics and helped cheerleading to become nationally organized. Cheerleading competitions were held during the early 1950s in New York's Westchester County. Twenty-five high school squads competed annually in front of large crowds. Participants held a roundtable discussion after these competitions to develop recommendations for cheerleader selection, types of cheers, precision and timing in cheerleading, uniform problems, and sportsmanship. Herkimer also invented the pom-pom to add color and to attract more people to television. Herkimer has sold more than 1.5 million pom-poms through his company, Cheerleader&DanzTeam. In 1990 he had a gross income of $60 million.

Growth in the interest in cheerleading and growth in the profit in cheerleading were ignited by a former employee of Herkimer. Jeff Webb left the NCA in 1974 and started Universal Cheerleading Association (UCA) because he wanted to modernize cheerleading by showcasing athleticism. In 1979 he created Varsity Spirit Fashion and Supplies to sell cheerleading equipment, camp gear, accessories, and uniforms. Today the company claims almost 60 percent of the revenue in the cheerleading business, and in 2001 the company's revenue was $147.5 million. In 1994 *American Cheerleading* magazine was created to cater to high school and college squads. In 2002 *American Cheerleader Junior* magazine was created to attract younger cheer-

leaders. These two magazines have a combined readership of 1 million. Cheerleading camps generate revenue of more than $100 million a year.

Women Cheerleaders

Documentation of women's early participation in cheerleading is sketchy, but scholars say the University of Minnesota appointed the first woman cheerleader. In general educators initially resisted the notion of women cheerleaders, fearing that women would become "masculinized." Some people thought that the loud and deep yelling causes women cheerleaders to develop manly voices. Some people also thought that women are less capable of performing the acrobatic stunts that men cheerleaders had introduced.

After World War II, as young men returned home, they reclaimed their cheerleading positions. During the 1950s several colleges (e.g., University of Tennessee) and many high schools prohibited women from cheerleading. In fact, Harvard University did not allow women to be cheerleaders until 1971.

Cheerleading increased in popularity among women throughout the 1940s and 1950s despite the occasional ban. In 1946 Bruce Turvold of Northwood, Iowa, began the first cheerleading clinic. In 1950 the University of Minnesota hosted a cheerleading clinic for two hundred cheerleaders. The University of Michigan's cheerleading squad conducted clinics in five locations with two thousand to twenty-five hundred participants per clinic.

College courses in cheerleading emerged during the 1940s and 1950s. In 1942 Purdue University offered a course in which thirty students learned about crowd psychology and tumbling. The University of Michigan offered a course for cheerleading advisers in 1952; it was limited to senior women physical education majors. During the 1950s and 1960s cheerleaders often served as class representatives. Many high school students tried out in front of the student body or faculty. These tryouts often drew between ninety and one hundred aspirants. During this time most high school cheerleading squads were composed of women, and most college squads were co-ed. During the 1960s African-

Cheerleading

From Cheerleading to Fame

Over recent years, movies such as *Bring It On* and *Sugar and Spice* have raised the profile and popularity of cheerleaders. However, numerous female celebrities were also former cheerleaders during their high school or collegiate years including Halle Berry, Katie Couric, Sandra Bullock, and Jamie Lee Curtis. Interestingly, many notable male celebrities (and several U.S. presidents) cheered in their formative years, such as George W. Bush, Michael Douglas, Dwight D. Eisenhower, Samuel L. Jackson, Steve Martin, Franklin D Roosevelt, and Jimmy Stewart.

American and hippie yell leaders were elected to squads, reflecting the civil rights and antiwar sentiments of the time. In 1969 a yell leader at the University of California at Berkeley was elected on an antiwar platform and yelled, "End the war! End the war!" during football games. African-American athletes in Oklahoma fought to elect an African-American cheerleader. During the 1960s some of the first African-American cheerleaders introduced soul-dance movements that involved stomping and clapping more than traditional cheers with straight-arm motions.

Competitive Cheerleading

Prior to the enactment of federal Title IX, which banned sex discrimination in schools, cheerleading was often one of the few sports opportunities for women. When schools deemed cheerleading a varsity sport for funding purposes, feminists were, perhaps understandably, outraged, and many women who were trying to promote what they viewed as more serious women's athletics resented cheerleading. After enactment of Title IX in 1972, people began to see cheerleaders not only as motivators on the sidelines but also as competitive athletes who perform complex gymnastics and stunts. These gymnastics and stunts showcased women cheerleaders' strength, coordination, agility, and athletic prowess.

Since the 1950s cheerleading competitions in the United States have increased in number and have often been televised by cable sports channels. Many high school and college cheerleading teams enter regional, state, and national competitions. In 1978 the Collegiate Cheerleading Championships were nationally televised on CBS-TV, initiated by the International Cheerleading Foundation. The first national high school cheerleading competition was held in 1981, and cable TV channel ESPN began televising the event in 1983. The competition separates women's squads from coed squads (equal representation of males and females) and small squads from large squads into different categories. Typically routines last two and a half minutes and include a combination of music, cheers, stunts, pyramids, and dance.

A high school cheerleader.

Source: istockphoto/kickstand.

Tumbling has reemerged as a crowd-pleasing and competitive element of cheerleading. Since the 1980s many former gymnasts have joined high school and college cheerleading squads as back handsprings and other gymnastic skills have increasingly become tryout requirements. Competitive-only squads (called "All-Stars") were formed in the 1990s. These squads compete for themselves and do not represent any school or sports team. The increased popularity of cheerleading, despite the limited number of school squad slots, led to the growth of All-Stars. In addition, the decrease in interest in gymnastics led private gyms to recruit cheerleaders. At first private gyms provided training for

Cheerleading

Cheerleading on Fiji

A race (*rova*) was then held. The whole of Lakemba took part; there might be as many as three hundred runners, a custom still observed. When the new provincial cutter was brought to Lakemba the race started from a point about half to three quarters of a mile from Tumbou along the beach toward Tarukua; the ladies stood at the goal with bark cloth tied on sticks like flags. The runners are placed in several rows, each man pleasing himself except that none is allowed to stand too far in advance, and the man who won the last race is placed hindmost "to keep guard on the beach" (*vakatawa nuku*). One man stands about half way with a conch; when he blows the conch the signal is given: "Stamp once, stamp twice, stamp thrice, stamp four times, run." The man with the conch runs and blows as he runs; if the others catch him up he is trodden upon. Sometimes a man will hide in the bush and join in near the goal; in the old days if he was caught he was hit by the nobles; nowadays he is stamped upon, the common method of "ragging." While the men run the ladies wave their flags and sing:

> Ure, ure wi, urea.   Shake, shake the plum tree, shake.
> Laki kau mai a i sulu loaloa,   Bring the black cloth,
> A ondra i suai a ngone sokoa.   A rag for the sailor boys.
> Ure, ure wi urea.   Shake, shake the plum tree, shake.
> Laki kau mai a masi volavola.   Bring the variegated tapa,
> A ondra i suai a ngone ni Tonga.   A rag for the boys from Tonga.

Another runs:

> Niu lele ki Tonga, lele mai,   Coconut that crossed to Tonga, crossed back,
> Tou sa veithoka, niu lele.   Let us cast spears, floating nut.

The man who gets in first is said to salute the race (*tamaka a rova*). A piece of bark cloth is wrapped round his legs, and is called "the burying of his legs" (*a i mbulu ni yavana*). If a man is present who does not belong to Lau the winner hands him the bark cloth, otherwise he keeps it. The remainder of the stuff is divided among the carpenters and the crew; these gifts are called *i rova*. Unlike the race for a new garden, this race has no ulterior motive (*vakaimbalembale*), but is merely a matter of kinship.

Source: Hocart, A. M. (1929). Lau Islands, Fiji. *Bulletin of the Bernice P. Bishop Museum* (62), 130.

middle and high school cheerleaders, but then they formed their own competitive-only squads for girls ages five to eighteen. More than fifteen hundred private gyms or clubs charge $100 or more a month for training. According to the National Federation of State High School Associations, about 111,200 girls and 3,200 boys participated in competitive cheerleading during the 2002–2003 school year. The introduction of competitive-only squads has lured males back to cheerleading, especially at the high school level.

Professional Cheerleading

During the late 1960s and early 1970s professional cheerleading squads emerged to support U.S. football and basketball teams and to add entertainment. Although the Baltimore Colts was the first team to have a professional cheerleading squad, the Dallas Cowboys cheerleaders were the first to perform a dance routine with pom-poms. In 1976 they performed at Super Bowl X and started an evolution of "dancing cheerleaders." Professional cheerleaders cheer at games, promote their team in the community, make public appearances for charity, and entertain crowds. Professional cheerleading is not lucrative (less than minimum wage), and most professional cheerleaders have another job.

Cheerleading by Country and Region

Cheerleading remained a U.S. phenomenon until 1982, when the introduction of U.S. football in Great Britain led to the parallel establishment of cheerleading in that nation. The creation of the World Football League in 1991 led to an international expansion of both U.S. football and cheerleading. The style of cheerleading across the world is modeled on the style developed in the United States. Today cheerleading associations, camps, and competitions are organized in fifty countries outside of the United States (i.e., Canada, Sweden, Germany, Japan, Russia). The World Cheerleading Association (WCA) was established in 1995 and held its 2002 WCA Europe Cheerleading and Dance Championship in Scotland.

People in nations that are unfamiliar with the history of cheerleading, however, do not always view it as a sport. Instead, they view cheerleaders as sex symbols rather than as athletes. Cheerleading squads are not affiliated with or sponsored or funded by schools or clubs. They have to raise money to pay for uniforms and other expenses and often have more than one hundred cheerleaders per squad. In Japan company cheerleaders cheer at football games of the Japanese-based X League. They also promote sponsoring corporations such as Fujitsu and Japanese Airlines.

The Future

Controversy is still rife in cheerleading. People debate the legitimacy of cheerleading as a sport, particularly in professional sports, where cheerleaders are often portrayed as glamorous and sexy entertainment complimentary to the game. However, at the high school and college levels cheerleading is gaining respect for its athletic demands. Cheerleaders must try out, dedicate much time to practice and "spirit-raising" activities, rep-

resent their school or team at nonathletic events, and recover from injuries, all in addition to their academic obligations. A growing number of universities (e.g., University of Kentucky, Penn State, University of Memphis) now recognize the contributions made by cheerleaders and offer full and partial athletic scholarships. People do not universally accept cheerleaders as athletes, but many people are campaigning cheerleading to be accepted as a sport because such acceptance would make cheerleading subject to the safety regulations that govern other high school and college sports. Advocates hope that such regulations would reduce the increased prevalence of injuries to cheerleaders. Several universities—San Jose State University, Duke University, and University of Nebraska, for example—have prohibited aerial stunts because of the high risk of injury and litigation that might follow.

The UCA and the National Federation of State High School Associations in 2002 tried to regulate cheerleading and to increase safety standards by educating coaches and organizers of cheerleading events. The National Council for Spirit Safety and Education (NCSSE) helped by providing uniform safety regulations, workshops, and certification programs to increase awareness of the demands of cheerleading as well as by emphasizing the need for safer practices and new guidelines regarding stunts and equipment. Within the cheerleading world people are apprehensive also about issues of adolescent development and body image. More research is needed to fully understand the prevalence and impact of these issues.

Sonya SooHoo, Katie Sell, and Justine J. Reel

Further Reading

Adams, N. G., & Bettis, P. J. (2003). *Cheerleader! An American icon.* New York: Palgrave Macmillan.

Birrell, S., & Cole, C. (1994). *Women, sport, and culture.* Champaign, IL: Human Kinetics.

Brady, E. (2002, April 26–28). Cheerleading in the USA: A sport and an industry. *USA Today,* p. B1.

Evans, M. (1982). *A decade of dreams.* Dallas, TX: Taylor.

When I was young, I never wanted to leave the court until I got things exactly correct. My dream was to become a pro. ■ LARRY BIRD

Gach, J. (1938). The case for and against girl cheerleaders. *School Activities, 9*(7), 301–302.

Gonzales, A. (1956). The first college cheer. *American Mercury, 83,* 101–104.

Hanson, M. E. (1995). *Go! Fight! Win! Cheerleading in American culture.* Bowling Green, OH: Bowling Green State University Press.

Hatton, C., & Hatton, R. W. (1978). The sideline show. *Journal of the National Association for Women Deans, Administrators, & Counselors, 42*(1), 23–28.

Herkimer, L., & Hollander, P. (1975). *The complete book of cheerleading.* Garden City, NY: Doubleday.

Kurman, G. (1986). What does girls' cheerleading communicate? *Journal of Popular Culture, 20*(2), 57–64.

Loken, N., & Dypwich, O. (1945). *Cheerleading and marching bands.* New York: A. S. Barnes.

Manfredi, J. (1983). Peptalk: The history of cheerleading. *Seventeen, 42,* 94.

National Federation of State High School Associations. (2003). 2002–2003 participation survey. Retrieved July 26, 2004, from http://www.nfhs.org/scriptcontent/VA_Custom/SurveyResources/2002_03_Participation.pdf

Reel, J., & Gill, D. (1996). Psychosocial factors related to eating disorders among high school and college female cheerleaders. *Sport Psychologist, 10,* 195–206.

Schmid, S. (1995). Safe cheering. *Athletic Business, 19*(7), 20.

Thompson, R. A. (2003). The last word: Cheerleader weight standards. *Eating Disorders, 11,* 87–90.

Webb, G. (1984). Cheerleaders—Spirit leaders and then some. *Interscholastic Athletic Administration, 11*(1), 18–19.

Child Sport Stars

Success at the highest levels in many sports depends on early entry, early specialization, year-round training, and frequent competition. Achievement in sport at elite levels and in professional sport may often be accompanied by lucrative financial rewards, college scholarships, and celebrity, and the drive toward such ends often means children are committed to intense training, with a singular focus on one sport at a young age. National and international media coverage of superior accomplishment by other young athletes often serves as a powerful incentive for parents to enroll young children in competitive programs; efforts to outdo predecessors and outperform contemporaries reflect the ethos of competitive sport. When children are identified as future champions, specialized training soon follows in a systematic, intensive approach to training regimens and competitions, even when the probability of reaching the highest levels of athletic achievement is exceedingly low.

Early Preparation and Training

Preparation for careers in elite sport, as for those in dance or music, begins in childhood, often long before athletes are able to make decisions for themselves. Decisions are made by parents and coaches when children remain entirely under their control. The selection processes for most Olympic sports attempt to identify future champions at the earliest possible age, so that the young athletes may begin specialized training in organized programs as soon as possible. For sports such as women's gymnastics and figure skating, where world and Olympic champions are generally crowned in their teens, rigorous training begins at the first opportunity, even in toddlerhood.

Early experiences are crucial to the development of children in sport. When such experiences are positive, children will likely continue involvement. In organized, competitive sport, children are introduced to adult-controlled, structured sport with formalized rules, uniforms, and an environment governed by winning. Many parents view such experiences not only as necessary for the development of future world champions, but also for the instrumental objectives of teaching their children values and skills that may help them later in life.

Organized, competitive sports emphasize winning. Experiences with winning and losing may be seen as valuable learning opportunities for children, and certainly, some children thrive in competitive environments, finding such experiences exciting and rewarding. Organized sport may fulfill many important needs for children, such as affiliation, challenge, skill development, success, status, as well as fitness.

Demands Made on Young Athletes

While the benefits of organized, competitive sport serve as positive experiences for some children, the pressures inherent in highly competitive environments may have adverse effects on children's growth and development and may hinder even potential world champions and professional athletes from developing their talents. The demanding commitment, intensive training, and early and frequent competition of talented young athletes necessarily requires schedules that would be extreme for most adults. There are physical, psychological, and social pressures on young athletes that raise concerns about their health and safety both during childhood and later on in adulthood. Negative experiences early on in sport also may lead to burnout and a complete loss of interest in physical activity, sometimes for a lifetime.

Heavy training loads, early sport-specific training, inadequate rest periods, and the pressure to train and compete while injured increase the risk of impaired skeletal development and permanent deformity. The risks of injury rise as training increases in frequency, duration, intensity, and technical difficulty; they may also be attributed to the age-related vulnerability of the immature skeletal system. Children are poor thermoregulators and are highly susceptible to dehydration and heat-related illnesses. Growth itself may increase children's susceptibility to injury, since growth spurts may interfere with balance and coordination and decrease flexibility. Training for judged sports such as gymnastics and figure skating, as well as those sports with weight classes such as wrestling and rowing, involve severe caloric restrictions in attempts to improve performance. Paradoxically, in an attempt to gain a competitive advantage, such limited nutritional intake may result in muscle weakness, compromised bone density, iron deficiency, and menstrual irregularities.

Despite assertions by organizations such as the International Federation of Sport and the American Academy of Pediatrics that intensive training of children has no physiological or educational justification, and that diversity of movement and all-round physical conditioning should have priority over later specialization, promising young athletes continue to be inducted into high-performance sport. While advocates of children's organized sport promote peer socialization as one of the benefits, not all sports provide such opportunity, at least

---

Child Sport Stars

Omo Grüpe on Children in Elite Sport

Sport scientist Omo Grüpe has written that children in top-level sport:

- Are not permitted to be children
- Are denied important social contacts and experiences
- Are victims of disrupted family life
- Are exposed to excessive psychological and physiological stress
- May experience impaired intellectual development
- Are detached from larger society
- Face a type of abandonment upon exiting their athletic careers

Source: Grüpe, O. (1988). Top-level sports for children from an education viewpoint. *International Journal of Physical Education, 22*(1): 225–226.

---

not during training itself. One young swimmer spoke of the sensory deprivation experienced while he was training: "You can neither hear not [*sic*] see while you swim. You can see next to nothing and the only taste is chlorine! In truth, to the outsider, the only social side to swimming training is a shared mutual discomfort" (Juba 1986, 174). Juba calls the pressure ambitious parents place on their children "parental projection," since such parents view their children as extensions of themselves and perhaps their own missed opportunities. Tofler et al. (1996) refer to this as "achievement by proxy." The importance parents place on swimming within the framework of their lives—both in terms of time and financially—turns into pressure on the children, for example.

What Is the Degree of Risk?

Experience suggests that some degree of harm is an inevitable component of almost all activities. However, in some environments harm appears to be more prevalent than in others. Competitive sport, particularly at the highest levels of performance, seems to involve significant risk of injury—significant in both frequency and degree. Young athletes suffer a wide array of injuries while training and in competition. In high-performance sport, elements such as injuries, fatigue, and even bad weather rarely interfere with an athlete's participation except in extreme circumstances. Given the intense demands of high-performance sport and the vulnerable nature of children's developing bodies and minds, such excessive cognitive and physiological demands may overburden a child, resulting in harm. The effects of this harm on the shaping of a child's identity and on the child's future are difficult to predict.

Young Female Superstars

There are a number of examples of young female athletes who reached the heights of stardom and of athletic success at very young ages. Athletes such as tennis players Martina Hingis and Jennifer Capriati, gymnasts Dominique Moceanu and her predecessors Nadia Comaneci and Olga Korbut, figure skaters Tara Lipinski, Michelle Qwan, and Sarah Hughes are or have been household names around the world. While many of these athletes have achieved remarkable success at exceedingly young ages, many of their careers are known also for their personal struggles.

Olympic gold medallist Dominique Moceanu began her gymnastics training as a toddler. With both parents former elite-level gymnasts, there seemed to be no doubt that she would follow in their footsteps. Before the age of five, her parents had already asked renowned coach Bela Karolyi to take Dominique on as a pupil, which he did not long thereafter. Dominique's life was focused on gymnastics throughout childhood. By the age of ten, and the youngest qualifier at the United States Nationals, she won a gold medal on the balance beam. That early success continued as she went on to win more gold medals at the Nationals in future years, including becoming the youngest national champion in gymnastics history. At fourteen, Dominique won an Olympic gold medal in the team competition, and finished eight all-around. After the Olympics, Dominique spent time outside the sport for the first time in her life, making the rounds of the talk show circuit, dabbling briefly in modeling, and living under intense media scrutiny. This combination, along with coping with lingering injuries, her sudden growth spurt of six inches, as well as dealing with significant parental problems, left Dominique struggling to continue her career in gymnastics. She sued her parents for squandering her trust fund, money earned in her professional career from the age of ten. A restraining order against her parents was put in place, and Dominique told the world that she had never had a childhood. Following those events, Dominique never regained her top form.

Perspectives

Child sport stars live, train, and compete in a world that is demanding and ruthlessly competitive. They dedicate, if not sacrifice, one of the most crucial phases of their lives in the quest for success as world or Olympic champion or for a career as a professional athlete. It is essential to remember that while they may be highly competent and talented in the specialized requirements of their sport, as children they remain unaware of their own limitations, susceptibility to injury, and the long-term consequences of injuries to their futures. They should be treated and protected as children first—and as athletes second.

Gabriela Tymowski

See also Academies and Camps, Sports; Elite Sports Parents; Play vs. Organized Sport; Youth Sports

Further Reading

American Academy of Pediatrics: Committee on Sports Medicine and Fitness. (2000). Policy statement: Intensive training and sports specialization in young athletes. *Pediatrics, 106* (1), 154–157.

Bompa, T. (1995). *From childhood to champion athlete. Toronto, Canada: Veritas Publishing.*

Coakley, J. (2003). *Sport in society* (8th ed.) New York: McGraw-Hill.

Juba, N. (1986). The requirements of competitive swimming—the effect on children: A coach's perspective. In G. Gleeson (Ed.), *The growing child in competitive sport* (pp. 173–178). London: Hodder & Stoughton.

Rowland, T. (1990). Risks of sport participation during childhood. In *Exercise and children's health* (pp. 235–254). Champaign, IL: Human Kinetics.

Ryan, J. (1995). Little girls in pretty boxes: The making and breaking of elite gymnasts and figure skaters. *New York: Warner Books.*

*If you must play, decide on three things at the start:
the rules of the game, the stakes, and the quitting time.* ■ CHINESE PROVERB

Tofler, I., Knapp, P. , & Drell, M. (1998). The achievement by proxy spectrum in youth sports: Historical perspective and clinical approach to pressured and high-achieving children and adolescents. *Child and Adolescent Psychiatric Clinics of North America, 7* (4), 803–820.

Tofler, I. , Stryer, B. , Micheli, L. , & Herman, L. (1996). Physical and emotional problems of elite female gymnasts. *New England Journal of Medicine, 335*(4), 281–283.

Tymowski G. (2001a). Pain, children, and high-performance sport: A justification of paternalism. *Journal of Professional Ethics, 9* (3–4), 121–152.

Tymowski, G. (2001b). Rights and wrongs: Children's participation in high-performance sport. In I. R. Berson, M. J. Berson, B. C. Cruz. (Eds.), *Cross-cultural perspectives in child advocacy* (pp 55–93). Greenwich, CT: Information Age Publishing.

China

China has one-fourth of the world's population and a heritage of more than five thousand years of history and civilization. The history of China's sport can be divided into three periods: Ancient (2100 BCE–1911 CE), Modern (1911–1949), and the People's Republic (1949 to the present).

Ancient Chinese Physical Education and Sport

In over five thousand years of feudal history, the Chinese people have created some traditional forms of physical exercise and activities and embraced others. Among them were archery, *chuju* (Chinese football), polo, *guiyouci* (long-distance running), wrestling, and *wushu* (martial arts), all with a distinct Chinese character.

Archery was a competitive contest with well-established rules and regulations. It was also called "Archery Ceremony." It was included in the six elements of Confucius's education theory and practice: ritual, music, archery, charioteering, literature, and math. It emphasized social status rather than the performance of the participants. Distinctive bows, arrows, and accompanying music were strictly allocated according to the social status of the participants.

Chuju was Chinese classic football. It started during the Warrior States (475–221 BCE). It was originally an aggressive, competitive game and was played by two opposing sides, each with goals. During the Han (206 BCE–220 CE) and Tang (618–907 CE) dynasties, due to its competitiveness, the game was often used by military mandarins to train soldiers in order to cultivate their fighting spirit and improve their physical conditioning. However, as time passed, two goals merged into one in the Song (960–1279 CE) and Yuan (1260–1368) dynasties. Vigorous competition was replaced by a much gentler phenomenon: a less competitive and primarily exhibitive game. Gracefulness and harmony of movement were given priority.

Polo was not a game indigenous to China. It came by way of the Silk Road, which began in northeastern Iran and reached northwestern China by way of Turkistan and Tibet. The game reached China about 641 CE and was a very popular throughout the Tang (618–907 CE) and Song (960–1179 CE) dynasties. Most of the twenty-two Tang Dynasty emperors enjoyed playing polo. There was a national polo tournament, which attracted hundreds and thousands of spectators. The first international polo match took place between the Tang palace team and the Tibetan prince's team around 708 CE. Polo was also used to train soldiers in the Tang army. Polo declined during the Ming (1368–1644) and Qing dynasties (1644–1911).

Guiyouci means "fast runner." It was a popular long-distance race in China during the Yuan dynasty (1206–1368). It took place once a year in Dadu (Beijing), the capital of Yuan dynasty. The whole distance was 180 li (about 90 meters), which is longer than today's marathon (42.195 meters), and it required participants to finish the distance in six hours. The fastest runner would receive an award from emperor himself.

Wrestling started in West Zhong (eleventh century–771 BCE), and it became popular in the Qin dynasty (221–206 BCE). During the Song Dynasty (960–1179 CE), wrestling became a profession, with professional wrestling organizations and tournaments. Women wrestlers appeared during the Song dynasty, but they were entertainers rather than competitors and some of them wrestled naked to attract spectators. Women's

Women hurdlers at the 5th National Games in Shanghai in 1933.

Source: Fan Hong.

wrestling was banned in late Song due to criticism from orthodox Confucianism.

Wushu is the Chinese term usually translated as "martial arts" or "kung fu" in the West. *Wu* is associated with warfare; *shu* with the skill, way, or methods of doing an activity. As a term, wushu covers a wide variety of martially inspired practices. Its entire offensive and defensive repertoire was based on the fighting methods of certain animals and adapted to form the basis of a martial arts system. As Chinese society came to place more and more emphasis on warfare, weapons such as the sword, spear, or knife were employed. Martial arts system and methods became more and more complicated, and they were a specialized profession for many. As a product of feudal society, martial arts were closely linked to feudal culture. The ethical code of martial arts required absolute loyalty and obedience of students to masters and of sons to fathers. The organizational system had tribal characteristics. Each tribe had its own rules and martial-arts style.

In general, during the ancient period, Chinese sports developed very rich forms. However, its development was limited by the traditional Confucian-dominated culture. In Confucianism exercise was an educative tool. Its purpose was to achieve a morally well-developed society through noncompetitive physical activity and to serve as a cohesive ritual helping maintain the social status quo. In Confucianism appreciation of the beauty of the human body was simply nonexistent. It was forbidden for men to show large parts of the body or even to talk about the human physique. Physical culture was adapted to reinforce moral values. As a result Chinese sport lost its earlier degree of competitiveness, which was replaced by an emphasis on harmony of movement, representing cohesion. Therefore, many forms of traditional Chinese sport, such as polo, chuju, archery, swimming, and wrestling, all of which could have easily developed into competitive sports as did their Western counterparts, ceased to evolve and remained essentially forms of recreation.

Modern Chinese Sport and Physical Education

In 1911 the Nationalist Chinese overthrew the Qing government, finally ended the feudal social system, and established a republic. China began to change from a feudal to a modern society. In order to create a new culture for the new society, Western concepts, especially "science" and "democracy'" were introduced, and modern education and physical education systems were advocated in order to push aside feudal traditions. On 1 November 1922, the republic government issued "The

Great souls have wills; feeble ones have only wishes. ▪ CHINESE PROVERB

Decree of the Reformation of the School System." The new school system drew heavily on American ideas about education. It emphasized that education must suit the needs of social evolution and pay attention to developing individualism. The result was a complete transformation of Chinese education. In 1923 a new curriculum was issued. In the new curriculum one to two hours of exercise a day became common, and male and female students took part in modern sports activities including basketball, volleyball, tennis, and swimming.

In December 1927, a National Physical Education and Sports Committee was established under the Education Ministry of the Nationalist government. It was the first time that the Chinese had a national government body to supervise exercise throughout the country. To promote exercise the government issued the "Law of Sport for Citizens" on 16 April 1929. It was the first sports law in Chinese history. It laid a foundation for the systematic organization of exercise throughout Nationalist China. It stated that: "Boys and girls must take part in physical education and sport.... They should participate in physical activity in which scientific sports methods are applied.... The aim of physical education and sport is to develop men and women's bodies for the good of the country." Four months later, the "Curriculum of Middle Schools and Primary Schools" was issued. It stated that physical education and sport were compulsory. The curriculum was revised over 1931 and 1932, but most of the original remained in force. Primary school pupils were to have 150–180 minutes physical education classes in their timetable per week, and middle school pupils 85–135 minutes. In addition they should have some activities after school. Activities in and after classes were almost all modern ones, including games, athletics, dance, mountain climbing, football, basketball, volleyball, and tennis.

These developments urgently required professional physical education specialists, and so more than twenty new physical education colleges and departments of universities were opened to train teachers of physical education. The students learned several subjects, including

China

Key Events in Modern China Sports History

1923	A new school curriculum is enacted which requires exercise and sports for boys and girls.
1924	The China National Amateur Athletic Federation is founded.
1927	The National Physical Education and Sports Committee is established.
1929	The Law of Sport for Citizens is promulgated.
1932	China competes in the Far-East Athletic Championships and the Olympics for the first time.
1952	A central Sports Ministry is established.
1956	The Competitive Sports System of the PRC is established.
1979	China renews it seat on the International Olympic Committee.
1980s	Competitive Olympics sports are emphasized.
1984	China participates in the Olympics for the first time since 1952.
1993	The government encourages the commercialization of sports.
2008	The Summer Olympics are to be held in Beijing.

Chinese language and literature, English, history, education, psychology, physiology, gymnastics, athletics, dance, games, and swimming.

Provincial and regional sports meetings now took place, organized by provincial and regional sports associations. There were five regional sports associations in China in 1915: the North, South, East, West, and Central. Each region included several provinces and was responsible for organizing its own athletic competitions. For example, the North China Regional Association held ten sports meetings from 1913 to 1934. The Central Region had six sports meetings from 1923 to 1936.

China

China in the Asian Games

Results of China's Participation in the Asia Games, 1974–2002

Number	Year	Place	Total Medals	Note
1st	1951	New Dehli		China sent a delegation to observe. After the Games China declined to attend subsequent games due to the "Two China" issue.
2nd	1954	Manila		Taiwan attended
3rd	1958	Tokyo		Taiwan attended
4th	1962	Jakarta		Taiwan did not attend
5th	1966	Bangkok		Taiwan attended
6th	1970	Bangkok		Taiwan attended
7th	1974	Tehran	33	China renewed its seat at the Asian Games Federation in 1973.
8th	1978	Bangkok	51	
9th	1982	New Dehli	61	
10th	1986	Seoul	94	
11th	1990	Beijing	341	
12th	1994	Hiroshima	266	
13th	1998	Bangkok	274	
14th	2002	Busan	308	

In 1924 a nongovernmental national sports orgaization, the China National Amateur Athletic Federation (*Zhonghua quanguo yeyu tiyu xiejinhui*) was founded in Nanjing. The aim of the federation was to supervise and organize all national and international athletic competitions. It was also the official national representative organization in all international athletic organizations, such as the IOC. Under the leadership of the federation, national games took place four times between 1924 and 1948. The Chinese athletes took part in the Far-East Athletic Championships four times and the Olympic Games three times between 1932 and 1948. All the sports events followed the Olympic model. The pattern of organization was copied from the Olympics, and the rules and regulations also were copied from Western competitions. There were two reasons for this. First, initially most of the games were organized by YMCA sports secretaries. Referees spoke English, and even the rules and regulations of competitions were written in English. Second, traditional Chinese sports could not be used in these newly established sports events. Therefore, modern sport and the Olympic

Games readily furnished Chinese sports with both forms and rules. It was this complete imitation that provided a solid foundation for the development of modern Chinese sport. Hence, the period between 1911 and 1949 saw the country advance from a traditional sports system to a modern one. Modern sport became a major part of the Chinese cultural domain and a new physical culture was born.

Sport and Physical Education in the People's Republic of China

In 1949 the Communist Party defeated the Nationalist government and founded the People's Republic of China. The new state was built on Marxist ideology and established a highly centralized government. Chinese Communist leaders showed no hesitation in realizing the importance of sports in state political life. They believed in the superiority of the socialist system and sport provided a stage on which to display this superiority. A centralized organization, the Sports Ministry, was established in 1952 to administer and supervise sport activities throughout China. Physical education

The only expectation I have of myself is to play well. ▪ YAO MING

was made compulsory in schools and universities. More than ten sports and physical education institutes and colleges were established. A national official sports daily newspaper, *Tiyu bao*, was published to carry sports propaganda.

During the early years of the People's Republic, in order to guard the young republic against possible invasion from outside and to develop its own socialist identity, the party's slogan became "develop sport in order to build and defend the motherland." Sport in the 1950s and 1960s, on one hand, was focused on exercise for the masses, because the New China needed healthy labor to build the socialist country. On the other hand, the government saw the need to establish a competitive sports system. The ministry issued "The Competitive Sports System of the PRC" in 1956. Rules and regulations were implemented and professional sports teams were established at national and provincial levels. In order to train and advance athletes from young age, the Soviet Union's sports school system (half-day study and half-day training) was copied. National Games took place every four years.

The Cultural Revolution started in 1966 and lasted until 1976. During this period, in order to purify the prevailing ideology elite sport was attacked as capitalist and revisionist. However, mass sport and exercise remained

People in China participate in a group exercise program.

China

Chinese *Disike:* A New Folk Sport for the Young at Heart

In the extract below, the anthropologist Susan Brownell recounts how older Chinese have retooled disco for their own generation.

Disike is a phonetic approximation of "disco." As a fitness activity it emerged around 1985 and became very popular over the next few years. It bore a little resemblance to aerobic dancing or jazzercize and a lot of resemblance to the radio broadcast exercises it had supposedly replaced. The types of body movements characteristic of disco were Western-inspired. Hip-swiveling and shoulder-rolling, hand-clapping and cross step. The music tended to be slightly outdated Western pop music, which was lively by Chinese standards of the time. "Old people's disco" was said to be one of the "Three Hots," or three biggest crazes, in China along with billiards and *qigong*.

Handfuls of older disco dancers could be found in almost every Beijing park in the early morning hours, and the same was true in other cities. It seems that the women usually outnumber the men by quite a bit.

Elderly female disco dancers often put on brightly colored, red, or shiny beaded or silk blouses to dance, sometimes borrowing them from their daughters-in-law. When an older woman wears a bright blouse, she is breaking a taboo by adopting the trappings of the youth, and this is regarded with much amusement by the spectators who laugh and comment on the brightly colored clothes of the dancers. [. . .]

A few years prior, disco was viewed askance by the authorities and banned as decadent, bourgeois, and Western. But in 1987, old people's disco was even broadcast by the national television station on the eve of the Chinese New Year, during the most-watched television program of the year. It featured the disco performance of a Shanghai club founded by a 70-year-old woman.

Source: Brownell, S. (1995). *Training the body for China: Sports in the moral order of the People's Republic* (p. 277ff). Chicago: University of Chicago Press.

China

China in the Olympic Games

Results of China's Participation in the Summer Olympic Games, 1932–2004

Number	Year	Place	Total Medals	Note
11th	1932	Los Angeles	0	
12th	1936	Berlin	0	
14th	1948	London	0	
15th	1952	Helsinki	0	After the Games China declined to attend subsequent Games due to the "Two China" issue.
23th	1984	Los Angeles	15	China renewed its seat at the IOC in 1979.
24th	1988	Seoul	27	
25th	1992	Barcelona	54	
26th	1996	Atlanta	50	
27th	2000	Sydney	59	
28th	2004	Athens	63	

untouched. In many schools and universities, physical education was often carried out in factories, on farms, and in military barracks. It was regarded as Karl Marx's and Mao Zedong's ideal of physical education. Later, when China wanted to escape its long isolation from the international community, competitive sport was brought back into foreground and served as means of diplomatic communication. The "Ping-Pong diplomacy" and "friendship first, competition second" were strategies used to open up new diplomatic channels with the West.

After the Cultural Revolution, at the end of the 1970s and into the early 1980s, China finally emerged from its economic stagnation and isolation. New Communist leaders initiated profound economic reformation in 1981. Their ambitions were to open up China, accelerate China's development, and catch up with the Western capitalist world through "controlled" emulation. China was changing from a centralized state-planned economy to a market economy. After its long period of international isolation, China was eager to be recognized by the outside world. Sport was used as a shop window in which to display the progress and the greatness of China. Therefore, during the 1980s the emphasis of the government was on competitive sport, in particular, the Olympics. China renewed its seat at

the International Olympic Committee in 1979. In 1984 China sent a delegation (of 225 athletes) to the Olympic Games, which were held in Los Angeles, for the first time since 1952. At the games China won fifteen gold medals. These victories provoked a "sports fever" and "gold medal craze" throughout the country. An "Olympic strategy" was formulated:, The whole country was to channel its limited resources to convert China to a sports superpower by the end of the twentieth century. The strategy worked very well. Between 1985 and 1998, China won 1,047 world championships and broke world records 674 times. At the 2000 Sydney Olympics, China came third overall.

However, the rapid development of the economy and the commercialization of China, in general, have influenced the development of the sports system. In 1993 the national sports management system developed under Communism more than forty years earlier was reformed. Now, the concern of the government was to promote the commercial development of the sports industry. Sport was expected to stand on its own feet and not only rely on the state for support. The new strategy was to commercialize all aspects of sport, including sponsorship and investment, the club system, advertising, lottery tickets, and participation fees. Chinese sport

China Olympics Results
2002 Winter Olympics: 2 Gold, 2 Silver, 2 Bronze
2004 Summer Olympics: 32 Gold, 17 Silver, 14 Bronze

today has been turned into a money-making proposition. Gradually, the government also shifted its emphasis from elite sport to mass fitness and health while still trying to cater to both elements.

With the approach of the Beijing Olympic Games in 2008, the Chinese government began to focus on elite sports again. It expects that Chinese athletes will win more medals and the Beijing Olympic Games will be the best ever in the history of the Olympics.

Fan Hong

Further Reading

Chehabi, H. E., & Guttmann, A. (2002). From Iran to all of Asia: The origin and diffusion of polo. *The International Journal of History of Sport, 2–3*(19), 384–400.

Chinese Society for History of PE and Sport. (Ed.). (1989). *Zhongguo jindai tiyu shi* [Modern Chinese sports history]. Beijing: Beijing tiyu xueyuan chubanshe.

Chinese Society for History of PE and Sport. (Ed.). (1990). *Zhongguo gudai tiyu shi* [Physical education and sport in ancient China]. Beijing: Beijing tiyu xueyuan chubanshe.

Gu, S., & Lin B. (1989). *Zhingguo tiyu shi* [History of Chinese physical education and sport]. Beijing: Beijing tiyu xueyuan chubanshe.

Guomin tiyu fa (The Law for Sports for Citizens) 16 April 1929. (1933). *Diyichi Zhongguo jiaoyu nianjian* (The First Chinese Educational Annual Book). Nanking: Education Ministry

Hong, F. (1997). Commercialism and sport in China: Present situation and future expectations. *Journal of Sport Management, 4,* 343–354.

Hong, F. (1997). *Footbinding, feminism and freedom: The liberation of women's bodies in modern China.* London: Cass.

Hong, F. (1998). The Olympic movement in China: Ideals, realities and ambitions. *Culture, Sport, Society, 1*(1), 149–168.

Hong, F. (2001). Two roads to China: The inadequate and the adequate. *The International Journal of the History of Sport, 2*(18), 148–167.

Hong, F., & Tan, H. (2002). Sport in China: Conflict between tradition and modernity, 1840s to 1930s. *The International Journal for the History of Sport, 2–3*(19), 187–210.

Hong, F., & Xiong, X. (2002). Communist China: Sport, politics and diplomacy. *The International Journal for the History of Sport, 2–3*(19), 317–340.

Lews, P. (1988). *The martial arts.* London: Apple Press.

Research Centre of Sports History, Chengdu Physical Education Institute. (Ed.). (1989). *Zhongguo jindai tiyu shi zhiliao* [Historical archives of modern China]. Chengdu, PRC: Sichuan jiaoyu chubanshe.

Rong, G., et al. (Eds.). (1987). *Dangdai Zhongguo tiyu* (Contemporary Chinese sport). Beijing: Zhongguo kexue chubanshe.

Wang, D., & Hong, F. (1990). *Tiyu shihua* (Sport: A social history). Beijing: kexue puji chubanshe.

Wu, Shaozu, et al. (Eds.). (1999). *Zhonghua renmin gongheguo tiyu shi* [Sports history of the People's Republic of China 1949–1999]. Beijing: Zhongguo shuju chubanshe.

Clubsports

Clubsports are usually considered amateur sports under the aegis of sports organizations, primarily staffed by volunteers and providing participation opportunities in local or community sport at a range of levels. Clubsports (at this amateur level) provide two major elements of the sport experience that are part of the overall performance but not necessarily core elements of the sport event. These elements are the sport's club structures and the ethos of amateur or community sport that may be concerned more with participation than with performance.

The full spectrum of clubsport structures, however, includes those engaged with amateur sport through to the professional sport organization. McConnell (2003) offers a core classification of clubsports that assists in considering their range and characteristics. This includes:

- *Professional clubs,* with teams competing in professional sport-specific environments. These clubs are each associated with only one sport;
- *Pro-am clubs,* which have professional sport-specific participation and may also have lower-level participation in community or amateur competition in the one sport;
- *Amateur clubs,* which are sport-specific and compete mainly, or solely, in amateur competitions;
- *Community clubs,* which offer a range of sport-participation opportunities, usually across various clubsports, under the aegis of a community sports organization;
- *Clubs in nonsport organizations,* found in organizations whose primary operational goals are not necessarily community-based or sport-centered; and

■ *Governance clubs,* which are mainly engaged in the governance and/or administration of a specific sport or sport facility.

Professional Clubs

A club operating in a professional "paid-to-play" environment may be owned by an individual, a group of investors, or a commercial organization. Such clubs are usually based around one sport and may have "feeder levels" below that of the elite. The feeder levels offer a step up to the top team, opportunities for athlete assessment, and induction to the club culture. Realities of player transfers, purchasing of players, and draft systems in fully professional clubsports influence formation of only one squad that exists at the elite level. Examples of such clubs are the Dallas Cowboys Football Club and the Real Madrid football team.

Professional clubsports are associated with paid athletes, salaried or contract administration staff paid by the club, media focus, and a highly paid coach (known as the "manager" in many sports). Such clubs have facilities and infrastructures oriented to performance, an emphasis upon winning, low tolerance for underachieving coaches and athletes, require financial support from wealthy backers, and engage in competition characterized by high media attention and a play-off or finals system of competition. The club has substantial financial investments in its athletes, in comparison with athletes engaged in other categories of clubsports.

NEW YORK YACHT CLUB

The New York Yacht Club is a contemporary professional sports club that, historically, has not had a focus on annual competition. Inaugurated in 1851 with the New York Yacht Club, the America's Cup competition asks the winning yacht club to set the rules and conditions for the next challenge it hosts. Clubs in the United States, England, Australia, New Zealand, and Switzerland have held the America's Cup. Each country's association is characterized by a small, committed group of backers; high costs of participation (including boat construction); intense media attention upon each every-fourth-year competition; an increasingly mobile pool of sailors who move beyond their original club allegiance; and an undercurrent of legality and laws issues governing yachts and racing.

Pro-Am Clubs

Pro-am clubs clubs have participation up to the elite level, with some or all athletes at that level being paid professionals. Club administrators include some paid officials, but lower-level teams participate in amateur levels of the sport with unpaid managers and coaches.

Such clubs must balance resources between professional and amateur levels of the club, face incremental professionalization of some sports (as in demands on players' time), and engage in competition with clubs of differing athlete populations or financial resources.

STUDIES DONE

Tensions arising in clubs that encompass amateur and professional sport or in clubs facing increasing professionalization have been studied by researchers in New Zealand (McConnell, 1998) and in Australia. The *Kicking Goals in Community Football* research in Victoria was carried out by an RMIT University research group headed by Peter Kell and Scott Phillips and Mark Penaluna of the Western Region Football League.

They explored recruitment training, volunteer retention, contemporary club management, and tensions between professionalizing clubs, as well as the complexities of developing a professional dimension with volunteers. An overriding dimension of the research was the need for a sport club to operate in a manner that recognized the cultural and linguistic diversity of its community. The complex challenges of commercialization, professionalism, inclusion, and perpetuation of a volunteer ethos in the face of increasing professionalization were features of the research findings.

Amateur Clubs

The "amateur clubs" category is the usual focus for persons examining clubsport. Clubsport is traditionally

Clubsports

Letter from Thomas Wentworth Wills

Thomas Wentworth Wills (1835–1880) is considered one of the founders of Australian Rules Football. In the letter below to the sporting paper Bell's Life, *Wills suggests forming a "foot-ball club" to keep cricketers fit in the off-season.*

Sir,—Now that cricket has been put aside for some months to come, and cricketers have assumed somewhat of the chrysalis nature (for a time only 'tis true), but at length will again burst forth in all their varied hues, rather than allow this state of torpor to creep over them, and stifle their now supple limbs, why can they not, I say, form a foot-ball club, and form a committee of three or more to draw up a code of laws? If a club of this sort were got up it would be of vast benefit to any cricket-ground to be trampled upon, and would make the turf quite firm and durable; besides which, it would keep those who are inclined to be stout from having their joints encased in useless superabundant flesh. If it is not possible to form a foot-ball club, why should not these young men who have adopted this new-born country for their mother land, why I say, do they not form themselves into a rifle club, so as at any rate they may some day be called upon to aid their adopted land against a tyrant's band, that may some day 'pop' upon us when we least expect a foe at our very doors. Surely our young cricketers are not afraid of the crack of the rifle, when they face so courageously the leather sphere, and it would disgrace no one to learn in time how to defend his country and his hearth. A firm heart, a steady hand, a quick eye, are all that are requisite, and with practice, all these may be attained. Trusting that some one will take up the matter, and form either of the above clubs, or at any rate, some athletic games.

I remain, yours truly, T. W. Wills.

---

regarded as any amateur sport organization that is primarily staffed by volunteers and existing to provide participation opportunities in local or community sport over various levels of competition. Amateur clubsport competition is usually officiated by volunteers. Administrators in these clubs are volunteers, although some amateur clubs may pay executive officer and clerical assistant salaries. Such clubs, despite engaging in "amateur sport," may overtly or covertly pay certain players or assist them financially (known as "shamateurism"), but the majority of participants are amateurs. Some clubs engaged in "shamateurism" in certain sports before they became professional, rugby union being an example. In sports such as Gaelic football in Ireland, the clubs engaging in a national amateur competition face challenges in trying to retain an amateur ethos or structure in contemporary environments that have expectations of professional or pro-am commitment, media focus upon achievement in elite competition, high levels of skills mastery, and player time committed to club training and practice.

Consett Rugby Club

The innovative Consett Rugby Club of County Durham in northeast England is an example of an amateur sport club with a strong community base and entrepreneurial development of facilities and operations. The area once encapsulated the experience of northern England rugby clubs, whose players sought payment for broken time when away from their workplace playing club rugby and met antagonism from administrators and lawmakers of more traditional or affluent clubs in the south of England. This dissonance eventually led to the separate sports of rugby league and rugby union and the establishment of famous rugby league clubs such as Bradford and Wigan.

Today, the Consett Rugby Club has revamped its playing headquarters and successfully obtained major financial assistance of some £800,000 (U.K.) to install ground lighting and develop facilities for players and club supporters. Club administrators generated private funding to purchase a local hotel, which has become a valuable investment in terms of developing a club social

I don't believe in team motivation. I believe in getting a team prepared so it knows it will have the necessary confidence when it steps on a field and be prepared to play a good game. ■ TOM LANDRY

center, generating approximately £70,000 annually for the club. In a significant political move affecting club-sport, the British government in 2003 created tax relief in the category of "Community Amateur Sports Clubs" (CASC), which provides relief to amateur sport clubs, like Consett, similar to that granted charitable trusts. In a soccer-oriented town of thirty thousand persons, the rugby club has 150 playing members and three thousand social members. Club playing strength has risen, with four senior teams and teams at each age from Under-7s to Under-16s participating in minirugby and fifteen-a-side rugby union. The club's development officers work with local secondary schools and educational institutions and received external funding support over the past ten years of £250,000. A feature of the club is the off-season arrangement of activities for their club members.

BIRKENHEAD BOWLS CLUB

On the other side of the sporting globe, the Birkenhead Bowls Club in Auckland, New Zealand, elects a voluntary governance committee, in the structure of an incorporated society. Subcommittees work in the areas of match organization, tournaments, grounds and maintenance, and dealing within fractions of discipline. Competition is at various levels from juniors to Champion of Champion events, and coaching is provided by club coaches every Tuesday evening, at no charge. Revenue comes from the amateur club's bar, open each evening and all day on weekends; from gambling machines; and from funding agencies. Most tournaments are sponsored, so entry fees for such competitions go to club funds. Prize money is provided at tournaments, but the club has no paid professionals or salaried employees, although the greenkeeper is contracted to maintain the club's greens. As with many amateur sport clubs, the secretary and treasurer receive modest honoraria annually.

Community Clubs

There are many clubs or community organizations that offer participation in community sport through sport clubs operating within their structure. These are found across the socioeconomic spectrum, ranging from country clubs that offer relatively select sport club membership to community service organizations reliant upon limited budgets and volunteers.

VAST DIFFERENCES

The Meadowood Country Club in the Napa Valley of California has an "introduction fee" of $25,000. At Meadowood members can play a number of sports, one of which is the flourishing sport of croquet. In the 1980s there were fewer than fifty croquet clubs in the United States, but by 2004 the number had increased dramatically to over four hundred clubs.

In contrast, the Brentwood YMCA in Nashville, Tennessee, is an example of a community-oriented organization that offers sport-club involvement at minimal costs for young people. It has a youth soccer league with up to 130 teams and a youth winter basketball league with 120 to 140 teams involving children from ages three to fourteen.

An amateur sport club formed by a particular sector of the community is seen in the Spears Sports Club of Bankstown City, Sydney, Australia, a not-for-profit organization founded by the Islamic Charity Projects Association in 1999. The club participates in soccer, netball, karate, and table-tennis competitions run locally or statewide.

Clubs in Nonsport Organizations

Many social, commercial, educational, and other types of organizations not formed for sporting purposes have sport clubs operating within their structures. They offer opportunities for their members, followers, or employees to participate in organized clubsports formed within the organization, and offer social or informal sport (for example, weekly baseball matches between different divisions of a company) up to countrywide competitions (such as national university tournaments). Factories in nineteenth-century England, arguably, formed such sport clubs or teams to facilitate control over and allegiance from their workers. Historically, examples of clubs were found within railway companies in South

America, churches in Ireland, aboriginal tribes in Australia, and branches of the armed services in many countries.

The University of Massachusetts (UMass) is an educational organization with clubsport in various sports and competition levels. At UMass, clubs include bicycle racing, fencing, ice hockey, baseball, lacrosse, rugby, volleyball, water polo, wrestling, tennis, and disk Frisbee sport. All athletic department sport clubs at UMass are recognized student organizations. Competition exists at intercollegiate or interuniversity, club and intramural, and internal-university levels, offering opportunities for students to participate at several levels.

Governance Clubs

The final category of clubsport, governance clubs, is markedly different from those discussed above. In certain sports, over time, prestigious clubs have become recognized as special bodies shaping a particular sport's laws and assuming responsibilities for the sport's governance. The Royal and Ancient Golf Club of St. Andrews, established in 1754 by twenty-two "Noblemen and Gentlemen" as the Society of St. Andrews Golfers, has had responsibility for the rules of golf and major facets of the sport. The club has been recognized in all countries except the United States as the governing authority of golf, despite having been a private sport club. In 2004, on its 250th anniversary, the Club devolved authority for golf's administration to a group of companies known as the R&A. The Royal and Ancient Golf Club of St. Andrews had two thousand four hundred members worldwide in 2004 and retained its identity as a private sports club.

CRICKET CLUBS

The Marylebone Cricket Club (MCC), based in London, has had a similar role in cricket, influencing the international development of the sport.

In Australia the Melbourne Cricket Club is, arguably, the largest sport club in the world. It is responsible for the administration and operation of the Melbourne Cricket Ground, popularly known as the MCG, and

has some eighty-five thousand members, of whom fifty-three thousand are full members and thirty-two thousand are in restricted membership. Such governance clubs may offer members the opportunity to engage in social sport under the club's name.

Development of Clubsport

A study of sports such as lacrosse and cricket in North America reveals historical trends and macroinfluences on clubsport, globalization, and diffusion of sport. In lacrosse, such factors as the indigenous influence, the 1850s–1860s Canadian-club foundations, formalized competition, a national body for governance of the sport, the rise of clubs in the late nineteenth century, and introduction of night games are illustrative signposts of the shaping of clubsport.

The introduction of cricket by the British into North America illustrates the impact of settlers on clubsport. West Indians in the latter half of the twentieth century spread the game, and rising numbers of nonimmigrant Americans have joined cricket clubs. In 2004 there were ten thousand registered players from five hundred clubs in twenty-nine regional leagues.

Contemporary Challenges

The twenty-first-century development of sport continues to be influenced by myriad factors affecting local and national sport bodies and community organizations in decision making and implementation of clubsport. These include:

- local and national government support for community sport
- attitudes of national sport structures towards local sport
- participation opportunities
- sport promotion
- media attention and support
- sport in schools
- cultural, gender, religious, and political considerations
- quality of sport administration

- influence of significant individuals and clubs
- opportunities for special populations and persons of varied abilities
- limited funds sought by rival community interests
- personal costs of sport, as in subscriptions, travel, equipment, fees, and time off work
- competitive opportunities appropriate for the age and ability of participants
- possible mergers, amalgamations, and ventures of common interest between clubs
- sponsorship, revenue generation, and grant applications
- equity in participation opportunities
- policies and organizational culture of clubs
- recognition of minority and special population groups
- building a youth or school-age base
- participant retention
- differences between sport opportunities in schools and those provided by local clubs
- transfer from secondary school participation to clubsport participation
- funding sought by elite sport levels and community or amateur sport within a club
- forces for professionalization of amateur sport
- social attitudes toward sport for participation and sport for performance
- volunteer training
- child protection and legal aspects of clubsport participation

A range of perspectives is covered in sporting-body publications. Guides for clubs and further information are published by bodies such as Sport England, and a New Zealand report (Genet, 2000) notes barriers to participation that are found in virtually all clubsport systems.

The Future

Sport clubs have a range of shapes, as noted above. Clubsport has existed, in various forms, for some two centuries and continues to be the base of much community sport, as outlined in the section called "Amateur Clubs" in this article. Historically shaped by factors as noted across the globe, clubsport continues to be subject to forces, both social and sport specific, into the twenty-first century. Significant among such challenges are the tensions between amateur and professional sport, often within the one sport, and the competition for allocation of resources to performance sport as against supporting the widening of participation opportunities. The opportunities for young people of particular social classes or special populations to engage in certain clubsports continue to be restricted by cost and perceived social attitudes in some sports.

Robin C. McConnell

Further Reading

Genet, G. (2000). *Barriers to participation in active recreation and sport: A study to identify constraints and solutions for specified Christchurch subgroups.* Christchurch, New Zealand: Christchurch City Council.

Hylton, K., Branham, P., & Jackson, D. (Eds.) (2001). *Sports development: Policy, processes and practice.* London: Taylor & Francis.

McConnell, C. D. (1998). *The Changing Face of Sports Management.* Unpublished Master of Business Studies thesis. Massey University, Albany, New Zealand.

McConnell, R. C. (2003). *Sport management: The case for a typology of sports clubs.* Jordanstown, Northern Ireland: School of Applied Medical Sciences and Sports Studies, University of Ulster.

Coaching

Teacher, facilitator, manager, counselor, recruiter, leader, role model—coaching involves wearing many hats. A coach directs activity during practice and competition, chooses and implements training regimens and competitive strategies, organizes practices, and schedules competitive events. Sometimes coaching involves the orchestration of a staff of assistants and the teamwork of additional professionals—for example,

To be prepared is half the victory. ■ MIGUEL CERVANTES

trainers, physicians, and sport psychologists. Many coaches spend time recruiting. But at some point, and usually on a regular basis, all coaches undergo a test for effectiveness. A coach prepares athletes to do their best, and when they experience success, however it is defined, so does the coach.

Essential Attitudes

Scholars have identified a number of attitudes that distinguish effective coaching and studied the relationships between those attitudes and other variables such as performance, safety, and athlete development. Among other qualities, effective coaching demands a flexible leadership style, a positive approach, and a focus on process rather than outcome.

FLEXIBLE LEADERSHIP STYLE

Scholarly work in the area of leadership styles has found that no single leadership style fits all situations. An effective style depends on many factors, such as the environment, the characteristics of the athletes, and team objectives. For example, a more authoritative style works better when a large number of athletes are trying to accomplish an immediate goal—for example, leading a two-hour practice with ninety-five football players or changing the lineup of a swim team during a meet. A more democratic style works best when intrinsic motivation, not time, is the primary concern—for example, leading a goal-setting session or deciding whether to practice on a Saturday or Sunday. Because a coach will most likely be called upon to use many different styles, effective coaching demands a flexible leadership style.

POSITIVE APPROACH

Coaches tend to be more successful when they provide positive feedback and reinforcement rather than negative remarks and punishment. A simple three-step strategy is often used to keep an athlete listening and learning, particularly in the moment after a mistake. The strategy includes (1) a positive statement, (2) positive feedback and instruction, and (3) another positive statement. An example might be: "Nice try, Chris. Lower your glove closer to the ground next time. Way to hustle to the ball."

The desire for mastery, a fundamental human motivation, drives many athletes to want to excel, and the coach is an athlete's most important source of information and guidance. Effective coaches practice their craft, just as athletes do, until their teaching methods become second nature.

FOCUS ON EFFORT

Effective coaching involves a focus on effort and process rather than on outcome and winning. An athlete's amount of effort is controllable, and to a large extent the training process is also controllable. Attributing mistakes and failure to a lack of effort or an inadequate training method allows athletes to see the opportunity to succeed in the future by increasing their effort or changing their methods. Focusing on the outcome might fire up a team momentarily, but focusing on the process creates a more lasting approach to success.

Essential Characteristics

Effective coaches have five important characteristics. They must be skilled in both verbal and nonverbal communication, must know themselves well enough to change if they need to, must be able to gain the trust of those they work with, must be able to entertain several perspectives on one situation, and must know when to rely on their instincts.

GOOD AT COMMUNICATING

An effective coach uses verbal skills such as active listening, immediate feedback, and clear, direct, and repetitive messages. An effective coach also needs nonverbal skills such as confident postures, appropriate touching, and eye contact.

SELF-AWARE

A self-aware coach can avoid the dangers of burnout. For example, a tendency to be athlete-oriented versus

The fewer rules a coach has, the fewer rules there are for players to break. ■ JOHN MADDEN

task-oriented will make a coach more vulnerable to exhaustion and burnout, but a coach who is aware of this tendency can change it.

TRUSTWORTHY

Relationships between coaches and others, including athletes, parents, and administrators, are built on trust. Demonstrating trustworthiness through consistency, honesty, and reliability, creates peak moments when athletes look to a coach with a complete readiness to learn and perform.

PERCEPTIVE

Effective coaching involves looking at a situation that might appear completely hopeless or anxiety-provoking to an athlete and turning it into a perfect picture of challenge and opportunity.

ARTISTIC

It is difficult to know where science stops and art begins in coaching. Sometimes decisions are made after contemplating concrete factors. Other times they are made with no such contemplation. Like an artist's stroke of the brush or choice of color, a coach puts in a substitute, changes a strategy, chooses this play or that, is patient or quick-acting, or uses humor or seriousness. Most experts agree that effective coaching is both a science and an art.

Mind and Body

Research in the twentieth century made it imperative to include mental training in an athlete's preparation. Coaching involves a greater understanding of team-building, goal-setting, motivation, thought processes, team dynamics, and the specific mental demands on each and every athlete in changing situations. Coaches are expected to understand the developmental differences in a young athlete's mental and physical abilities. As athletes mature, they themselves place greater importance on the mental aspect of training and performance. To a certain extent, a good coach is also a good sport psychologist.

NEW KNOWLEDGE

Coaches must continually update their knowledge of the physical and mental skills they teach. An increasing amount of research in the sport sciences—for example, biomechanics, exercise physiology, sport psychology, and motor learning—has fueled the organization of conferences and workshops and the creation of journals, books, newsletters, videos, and CDs. A pre-1970s instructional book on sport might have included advice on technique, nutrition, drills, games, and exercises to make practice more efficient and motivating. By the turn of the century, however, publishers were offering numerous books on each of these topics for a multitude of sports.

New knowledge gave birth to multiple industries that produce equipment and instructional aids, all of which a coach has to evaluate. Therefore, coaches need to understand the language of physics and chemistry, and effective coaching involves keeping abreast of current findings and applications.

WORKABLE PHILOSOPHY

A philosophy of coaching to a coach is like a goal-setting program to an athlete. Developing and adhering to it enhances confidence and decreases anxiety; attention is focused appropriately, and ultimately, performance improves. A well-thought-out philosophy is the foundation of an effective coach's daily and long-term success.

Ethics

Whenever a profession involves huge gains and losses, financial or otherwise, key players can become targets of negative influence and pressure. If a coach succumbs to this pressure, the result is conduct outside the rules—for instance, cheating, recruiting violations, or forming inappropriate relationships with players—or possibly outside the law—blackmail, fraud, or sexual harassment.

Negative influence can also be subtle, such as the pressure of conformity. Allowing aggressive behavior, illegal substance use, remarks or jokes that demean others, or eating behaviors that appear to enhance per-

Coaching

Creating Unity

At the same time, the plays are drawn with the greatest care, the men are taught to start quickly and run hard and to know their signals. This can be done by a good coach, and there are many teams even among the most successful which are trained on what has often been called the "One Man" system. Here the strategy, the play of the individual and the marshaling of the men on the field are all in the hands of one man, who is apt to rank above the captain.

This state of affairs is partly brought about by choice and partly by stress of circumstances. Colleges which are not situated near large business centers find great difficulty in persuading their graduates to come back and coach.

It has been the uniform policy among the larger colleges not to pay more than one man to supervise the coaching, and without offering inducements of a financial sort it is next to impossible to obtain the time of the best men. Accordingly, the smaller colleges, particularly those situated in more or less remote places, have to employ some one man to act as coach and take full charge of the whole development of the team. The advantage of this method is that the men are coached uniformly, and it is an axiom that a worse policy, well carried out, is more effective than a better one badly carried out.

These "One Man" teams have unity; they work as a team; they know what they are out for, move in a business-like way, and unless something much better is supplied by the many coaches of teams which they meet, they are apt to win on the very fact of their precision and dash.

Harvard is peculiarly favorably situated for obtaining the services of the largest possible number of coaches, owing to the large body of graduates living in Boston and vicinity, and the extensive graduate schools which tend to keep men on after their playing days are over.

Each season opens with an abundance of material and a multitude of coaches, and it becomes necessary to have a head coach, whose business it shall be to get the unity, without which no team can hope to win.

Source: Forber, W. C. (1899, December). The football coach's relation to the players. *Outing*, 3, 337.

formance but jeopardize health, are all results of a subtle, but powerful, pressure to conform.

The pressure on a coach to win can be tremendous. It comes from many sources, including parents, media, spectators, administrators, and other coaches, and from within the coaches themselves. But regardless of why it happens, unethical behavior is the kind of behavior that ends careers. It undermines another fundamental goal of coaching: influencing the development of athletes in a positive way. Regardless of the statistics, coaching integrity is a building block for all other goals and purposes, although coach education does not necessarily include ethics. The pressure is great, but coaches are in a powerful position to influence a great number of minds, young and old. If they choose to exhibit the highest level of integrity, they promote the integrity of sport and the positive development of participants, not only as athletes, but also as members of society.

Stress

Intense competition, little control once the contest begins, media attention, and a continual test of personal ethics are major sources of stress for all coaches. Coaches lead the charge for a limited number of positive tangible results, results that are used to measure their professional effectiveness and value. But in a zero-sum game, there can be only one winner and one loser. Not many professionals face the possibility of losing as publicly and as often as a coach does.

Exhaustion from long hours and emotional strain can bring on chronic frustration and irritability. Less enthusiasm, less energy, and an overall inability to reach

Pat Summitt, coach of the University of Tennessee women's basketball team.
Source: University of Tennessee Lady Vols Media Relations Department.

previous standards of effectiveness for an extended period of time despite short rests define staleness, an early stage of burnout. A persistent sense of failure, low self-esteem, depression, and ambivalence about a job that once evoked great passion can follow. For those in the final stage of burnout, a three-day weekend isn't sufficient for revitalization. Relationships with athletes, assistant coaches, administrators, family members, and friends suffer. Coaching effectiveness wanes. In some cases, recovery may not be possible.

Sometimes coaches choose to sacrifice many things with the knowledge that they are limiting the years they can spend coaching. But if a coach ignores the symptoms of staleness and burnout and continues to push without taking needed breaks, the result can be chronic failure, unhappiness, and possibly tragedy. A position that attracted a bright, enthusiastic, and effective leader becomes a place of despair.

Burnout can be avoided by using a number of strategies that most coaches are very familiar with: pacing oneself, maintaining perspective, using stress management skills such as relaxation and positive self-talk, surrounding oneself with supportive people, finding constructive ways to express frustration, laughing and having fun, and in general, making choices that promote health and happiness.

History

At the end of the nineteenth century, sport teams tended to be coached by one or more players on the team. In fact, until entrepreneurs and investors became aware of the entertainment value of sport, control of sport activity rested primarily with the athletes. However, by the 1920s a sport contest had more at stake than a win or a loss, and the organizational, technical, and managerial demands of teams grew in number and importance. People were needed to organize, teach, and prepare athletes and teams to perform to their highest potential.

The institutionalization of modern sport in the United States reflects the social environment in which

If at first you don't succeed, you are running about average. ■ M.H. ALDERSON

sport exists. In the early years, racial, ethnic, gender, and socioeconomic biases placed pressure on organizations of white athletes to be coached by white coaches, black by black, women by women, and so forth. Since greater financial reward was available within the white male sport arena, nonwhite and female coaches were not offered equal professional opportunities and salaries. Few or no opportunities to train, compete, and coach were available for people with disabilities, Native Americans, and other disenfranchised groups.

Social Context

As social contexts changed, so did opportunities for coaches from various oppressed groups. But today, many years after civil rights laws were passed, the number of minorities in head coach positions is still not representative of the number of minority athletes participating. For example, in 2002 there were four African-American head coaches in Division I-A football of the National Collegiate Athletic Association (NCAA.) In the fall of 2004, that number dropped to two. During this period there were no African-American head coaches in Division I-AA, if historically black colleges were not included.

In 2004, 10 percent of head coaches in the National Football League (NFL) were black, although 65 percent of players were black. Even though NFL teams led by black coaches performed better (won more games and went to the playoffs more often) than teams coached by white coaches, black coaches were hired less often and fired more quickly.

Title IX, which mandated that schools receiving federal aid had to provide equal opportunities for girls and women in sport, and the feminist movement of the 1970s sparked social change, making it more socially acceptable and financially feasible for females to train, compete, and coach. The development of the Special Olympics, the Senior Olympics, and Gay Games suggests a shifting away from prejudices of the past. But these changes did not bring more coaching positions to women and other minorities in sport.

When Title IX passed in 1972, women held approx-imately 90 percent of the coaching positions for women's teams. In 2002 women coached approximately 44 percent of women's teams. Ninety percent of new opportunities to coach women's teams between 2000 and 2002 went to men. The decline in the number of women coaches has been greatest at the highest level of sport and with the highest paying jobs.

Small changes have appeared on the global level as well. There were no women on the International Olympic Committee (IOC) until the 1980s. In 2004 the committee consisted of 10 women and 127 men. The IOC did not meet their goal of 10 percent women by the year 2000, and it is not likely that they will reach their goal of 20 percent by 2005. Over 90 percent of all national team coaches are men.

Despite legal advances, the prejudice and power structure of white males in sport worldwide continues to suppress efforts to equalize opportunities for women, nonwhite men and women, and other minorities. Increased efforts on the part of major governing organizations such as the IOC, the NCAA, and the NFL will be necessary if positive and enduring changes are to occur.

Throughout the twentieth century competition between teams became more popular and intense; schools developed mascots, uniforms, traditions, and rivalries; clubs, leagues, conferences, national teams, and other sport organizations formed. The IOC, the national Olympic committees, and numerous national governing bodies for each sport at the youth, adult, amateur, and professional levels formed to administer to the needs of these groups. Ever-increasing media attention inspired young and old to participate in sport. The number of girls and women playing interscholastic and intercollegiate sport increased as much as tenfold. The need for coaches at all levels, from volunteer parents to million-dollar professionals, grew concurrently.

The demand for coaches grew throughout the twentieth century as winning became more important and the belief grew that sport programs built character. Governing organizations and institutions established guidelines for professional competency and ethical conduct,

Coaching

Knute Rockne: Miracle Man of Athletics

In the extract below from a 1921 volume of sports stories, the legendary Knute Rockne is celebrated.

In the football world Mr. Knute K. Rockne, director of athletics at Notre Dame, is entitled "the Miracle Man of 1920"; by the student-body of the University he is considered "the greatest coach of all times."

To his football men on the field he is known simply and affectionately as "Rock."

As a student-athlete, as assistant-coach, and finally a head coach, he has a record of ten successful years at Notre Dame without a break.

With not a little reason has he been called the "Victory Builder." In his first three years at Notre Dame [1911–1913], the football team did not suffer a single defeat in twenty-two games.

In his last year as player he captained the great Western eleven that startled the East, West, and South.

As assistant-coach from 1914 to 1917 his linemen did more than their share in the remarkable victories of that period.

When as successor to Coach Jesse Harper he took full charge of Notre Dame athletics in the war year of 1918 the football conditions were hopeless, but Rockne would not see them so. He drilled a squad of men averaging only 160 pounds and made of them one of the most heroic of Notre Dame's fighting teams.

This midget Varsity fought the heavy Nebraska to a tie in the mud, won from Purdue, Wabash, and Case, and for a surprise climax tied the team of the Great Lakes Training Station, the national champions of that year.

In 1919 Rockne's squad of veterans romped home without a defeat or a tie—in such an impressive way as to disconcert most of the adverse critics.

If any further success was needed to prove Coach Rockne and his Notre Dame system, it has been superabundantly provided this year. The success which has so uniformly attended his work Coach Rockne modestly and sincerely attributes to the quality of the material provided him, to the unmatched morale of the squad, to the superb leadership of such captains as Frank Coughlin, to the natural football instinct of such players as Gipp, Brandy, and Smith—summarily to the clean living, clear thinking, and hard fighting of his men.

These no doubt have been important elements in Notre Dame's football successes, but we believe that they would have been of little consequence without the coaching of Rockne. His great elevens have on every occasion, and especially in the more trying ones, reflected the keenness, determination, and sportsmanship of their great coach—showing themselves true "Rockmen."

Source: Spink, A. L. (Volume No. 2). (1921). Knute K. Rockne, athletic coach at Notre Dame College, called the miracle man of athletics. *One thousand sport stories* (Vol. 2, pp. 353–354). Chicago: The Martin Company

and created opportunities for continuing education. More and more coaches with little or no training beyond their own sport or on-the-job coaching experience led a growing number of athletes. Thus the need grew for coach education and credentialing.

Training

Even if they are surrounded by assistants, few coaches today are able to succeed without formal training of some kind. Most high school and collegiate-level coaches have an undergraduate degree, and many have an advanced degree. In some educational institutions coaches are members of the faculty and are asked to teach courses and coach multiple sports.

Organizations

In the 1950 and 1960s, the American Association for Health, Physical Education, Recreation, and Dance (AAHPERD) set standards for training high school coaches and determining ethical conduct. A task force

Show me a good and gracious loser and I'll show you a failure. ■ KNUTE ROCKNE

from AAHPERD recommended the establishment of minimal competency certification standards. In 1970 the Task Force on Sport for Canadians issued similar recommendations, which resulted in the creation of the Coaching Association of Canada (CAC), an organization charged with the responsibility of improving coaching effectiveness for all sports at all levels. The CAC has become a world leader with regard to coach education and training.

The American Coaching Effectiveness Program (ACEP) was certifying approximately 63,000 coaches per year by 2004. Since 1971, the CAC has trained more than 900,000 coaches. They train over 50,000 per year. Many other coach-education programs have emerged—for example, the Coalition of Americans to Protect Sport (CAPS), the National Youth Sports Coaches Association (NYSCA), and the Program for Athletic Coaches Education (PACE). There are also countless certification programs designed for specific sports at different levels—for example, soccer coaches through the American Youth Soccer Organization, cross-country coaches through the Road Runners Club of America, and youth softball coaches through the ACE program of the Amateur Softball Association.

The International Council for Coach Education, established in 1997 with fifteen countries participating, now has thirty members. The European Athletic Association, the International Association of Athletics Federations, and sport-specific organizations such as the Union of European Football Association and the International Tennis Federation are examples of organizations that sponsor educational opportunities and training for coaches on an international level.

Educational websites for coaches have been growing on the Internet. In fact, websites serving the training and continuing education needs of coaches might be the way of the twenty-first century. Some examples of these include the following: Sports Coach (www.brian mac.demon.co.uk), Athletic Insight (www.athleticin sight.com), United States Sports Academy (www.ussa. edu), and the Institute for Sport Coaching (www.insti tuteforsportcoaching.org).

The Future

Sport in the twenty-first century is a major industry characterized by a network of local, regional, national, and international competitions. It is defined by the need for a positive outcome—to some extent, the job security of all coaches depends on their ability to win. But sport is also defined by the process, the competition, and the striving toward a goal. The process is a test of integrity, determination, teamwork, endurance, intelligence, patience, wit, and coping skills. Good character is not inherent in athletes any more than it is inherent in salespeople or musicians. Athletes build character through the choices they make, and coaches are in a powerful position to influence those choices. As long as coaching enhances the probability of winning and builds character, coaches will have a secure and valued place in the sport arena.

Barbara Teetor Waite

Further Reading

Acosta, R. V., & Carpenter, L. (1985). Status of women in athletics: Causes and concerns. *Journal of Physical Education, Recreation and Dance, 55(5),* 38–39, 53.

Anshel, M. (1994). *Sport psychology: From theory to practice* (4th ed.). San Francisco: Benjamin Cummings.

Bompa, T. (1994). *Theory and methodology of training: The key to athletic performance* (3rd ed.). Dubuque, IA: Kendall/Hunt.

Bompa, T. (1996). *Power training for sport: Plyometrics for maximum power development.* Gloucester, Ontario, & Oakville, Ontario: Coaching Association of Canada & Mosaic Press.

Brancazio, P. (1984). *Sport science: Physical laws and optimum performance.* New York: Simon & Schuster.

Bunker, L., et al. (2000). *Check it out: Is the playing field level for women and girls at your school?* Washington, DC: National Women's Law Center.

Burke, E., & Berning, J. (1996). *Training nutrition: The diet and nutrition guide for peak performance.* Carmel, IN: Cooper.

Carron, A. (1984). *Motivation: Implications for coaching and teaching.* London, Ontario: Sports Dynamics.

Coakley, J. (2004). *Sports in society: Issues and controversies* (8th ed.). Boston: McGraw Hill.

Coleman, E., & Steen, S. (1996). *The ultimate sports nutrition handbook.* Palo Alto, CA: Bull.

Cox, R. (1994). *Sport psychology: Concepts and applications* (3rd ed.). Dubuque, IA: Wm. C. Brown & Benchmark.

DiCicco, T., & Hacker, C. (2002). *Catch them being good.* New York: Penguin.

Eitzen, D. S. (1999). *Fair and foul: Beyond the myths and paradoxes of sport.* Lanham, MD: Rowman & Littlefield.

Figone, A. (1991). *Teaching the mental aspects of baseball: A coach's handbook.* Dubuque, IA: Wm. C. Brown.

Groppel, J., Loehr, J., Melville, D. S., & Quinn, A. (1989). *Science of coaching tennis.* Champaign, IL: Leisure Press.

Hanson, T., & Ravizza, K. (1995). *Heads-up baseball: Playing the game one pitch at a time.* Indianapolis, IN: Masters Press.

Horn, T. (Ed.). (1992). *Advances in sport psychology.* Champaign, IL: Human Kinetics.

Janssen, J. (1996). *The mental makings of champions: How to win the mental game* (workbook). Tucson, AZ: Winning the Mental Game.

Janssen, J. (1996). *Winning the mental game: How you can develop the motivation, confidence, and focus of champions* (video). Tucson, AZ: Winning the Mental Game.

Janssen, J. (2000). *Championship team building: What every coach needs to know to build a motivated, committed and cohesive team.* Tucson, AZ: Winning the Mental Game.

Janssen, J. (2001). *The seven secrets of successful coaches.* Tucson, AZ: Janssen Peak Performance.

Janssen, P. (2001). *Lactate threshold training.* Champaign, IL: Human Kinetics.

Jeffrey, A. (1988). *Fundamentals of coaching and understanding sport.* Ottawa, Ontario: Coaching Association of Canada.

Klavora, P., & Daniels, J. (Eds.). (1979). *Coach, athlete, and the sport psychologist.* Toronto, Ontario: University of Toronto.

Maglischo, E. (2003). *Swimming fastest.* Champaign, IL: Human Kinetics.

Mechikoff, R., & Kozar, B. (1983). *Sport psychology: The coaches' perspective.* Springfield, IL: Charles C. Thomas.

Moran, M. (2002, October 11). Success fails to open college doors for black football coaches. *USA Today.* Retrieved December 4, 2004, from http://www.usatoday.com/sports/college/football/2002-10-11-acover-black-coaches_x.htm

Nakamura, R. (1996). *The power of positive coaching.* Sudbury, MA: Jones and Bartlett.

National Fastpitch Coaches Association. (2002). *The softball coaching bible.* Champaign, IL: Human Kinetics.

National Soccer Coaches Association of America. (2004). *The soccer coaching bible.* Champaign, IL: Human Kinetics.

Noble, L., & Sigle, G. (1980). Minimum requirements for interscholastic coaches. *Journal of Physical Education, Recreation and Dance, 52*(9), 32–33. EJ 241455.

Orlick, T. (1986). *Coaches training manual for psyching for sport.* Champaign, IL: Leisure Press.

Orlick, T. (1997). *In pursuit of excellence: How to win in sport and life through mental training* (cassette recording). Champaign, IL: Human Kinetics.

Orlick, T. (2000). *In pursuit of excellence: How to win in sport and life through mental training.* Champaign, IL: Human Kinetics.

Orlick, T., & Botterill, C. (1975). *Every kid can win.* Lanham, MD: Rowman & Littlefield.

Pate, R., McClenaghan, B., & Rotella, R. (1984). *Scientific foundations of coaching.* Philadelphia: Saunders College Publishing.

Roberts, G. C. (Ed.). (1992). *Motivation in sport and exercise.* Champaign, IL: Human Kinetics.

Rushall, B. (1979). *Psyching in sport.* London: Pelham Books.

Rushall, B. (1992). *Mental skills training for sports: A manual for athletes, coaches, and sport psychologists.* San Diego, CA: Sport Science Associates.

Sabock, R. (1981). Professional preparation for coaching. *Journal of Physical Education, Recreation and Dance, 52*(8), 10.

Sabock, R. (2004). *Coaching: A realistic perspective* (8th ed.). Lanham, MD: Rowman & Littlefield.

Sabock, R., & Chandler-Garvin, P. (1986). Coaching certification: United States requirements. *Journal of Physical Education, Recreation and Dance, 57*(6), 57–59. EJ 340704.

Salmela, J. (1994). *Enhancing coaching performance.* Ottawa, Ontario: Basketball Canada and the National Coaching Certification Program.

Salmela, J. (Ed.). (1996). *Great job coach: Getting the edge from proven winners.* Ottawa, Ontario: Potentium.

Schmidt, R., & Wrisberg, C. (2000). *Motor learning and performance: From principles to practice.* Champaign, IL: Human Kinetics.

Schum, T. (Ed.). (1996). *Coaching Soccer.* Indianapolis, IN: Masters Press.

Silva, J., & Weinberg, R. (Eds.). (1984). *Psychological foundations of sport.* Champaign, IL: Human Kinetics.

Singer, R., Murphey, M., & Tennant, L. (1993). *Handbook of sport psychology.* New York: Macmillan.

Sisley, B., & Wiese, D. M. (1987). Current status: Requirements for interscholastic coaches. Results of NAGWS/NASPE coaching certification survey. *Journal of Physical Education, Recreation and Dance, 58*(7), 73–85. EJ 360109.

Smoll, F., & Smith, R. (Eds.). (1978). *Psychological perspectives in youth sports.* Washington, DC: Hemisphere.

Sweetenham, B., & Atkinson, J. (2003). *Championship swim training.* Champaign, IL: Human Kinetics.

Thompson, J. (2003). *The double-goal coach: Positive coaching tools for honoring the game and developing winners in sports and life.* New York: HarperResource.

United State Tennis Association. (1995). *Coaching tennis successfully.* Champaign, IL: Human Kinetics.

Veroni, K. (1998). *Coaching fastpitch softball successfully.* Champaign, IL: Human Kinetics.

Weinberg, R., & Gould, D. (2003). *Foundations of sport and exercise psychology* (4th ed.). Mountain View, CA: Mayfield.

Williams, J. (Ed.). (2001). *Applied sport psychology: Personal growth to peak performance* (4th ed.). New York: McGraw-Hill.

Wooden, J. (1991). *They call me coach.* New York: Contemporary Books.

Coeducational Sport

Originally, coeducation meant the integrated instruction of girls and boys with pedagogical intentions, but the term is often used, as in this article, for mixed classes. Throughout the nineteenth century,

coeducation was not an issue in schools for lower classes and schools in the countryside; on the contrary, big classes without age and sex segregation were the only way to provide at least a basic education for the poor, at least in Europe. Further education was reserved for children whose parents could afford to pay the tuition, and here coeducation was unthinkable. In the United States, girls and boys in the so-called common schools were in the same classes, and most high schools were also coeducational.

Following the modernization processes and social changes at the end of the nineteenth century, a reformation of girls' higher education became necessary in many Western countries. Despite the resistance from various sides—especially from men who were afraid of the potential competition from women in the labor market—after the turn of the century girls were even allowed to enter universities. This led to the question whether girls could be accepted in boys' schools. In many European countries, universities were a men's domain where women were first excluded, then later slowly and reluctantly accepted, but in the United States, women's colleges have been founded since the 1830s, and since the mid-1800s, female students have been admitted to some formerly all-male colleges and universities. However, numerous all-male colleges continued to exclude females until the 1960s.

ARGUMENTS FOR AND AGAINST COEDUCATION

For sixty to seventy years the pros and cons have repeated themselves in a relatively consistent fashion. Coeducational advocates placed economic arguments in the foreground: Many communities could not afford to establish girls' schools. Coeducation opponents based their arguments mainly on the theory of polarity, that is, on the differences in the nature and purpose of women and men and on the resulting differences in attributes, behavior patterns, interests, and competences. Views about the achievement potentials and natural gifts of men and women synthesized to form the myth of female weakness and male strength, in which the sup-

posed intellectual deficiencies of girls were emphasized. There were also fears of men and women becoming equals, which would have shaken the foundations of the prevailing gender order. Schools were expected to prepare boys for their roles as breadwinners and guardians of the family, and girls were to be prepared for their roles as wives and mothers. Coeducation, it was felt, would jeopardize this division of labor, partly because girls would be able to qualify for the professions. (It was precisely this improvement in educational opportunities for girls that the advocates of coeducation put forward as an argument for mixed classes.) Further arguments frequently used against coeducation were that girls would be overtaxed, that boys would become effeminate, and that coeducation represented a threat to decorum and propriety. The discourse on education before World War II was generally characterized by stereotypical and sometimes contradictory assertions that were not based on valid and reliable empirical findings.

However, the numerous arguments put forward against the teaching of mixed classes were unable to prevent the spread of coeducation in actual educational practice.

Coeducation in PE Developments

When the debate on the implications of coeducation flared up at the end of the nineteenth century, physical education (PE) was completely omitted from the discussion. It was not thought necessary to make any special mention of this issue because even the advocates of coeducation, both male and female, took separate physical education for boys and girls for granted. The manifest differences in athletic achievement, the dangers that seemed to threaten morals and decency, the different contents and goals of physical education—aimed at educating boys to become proficient soldiers and girls to become healthy mothers—all were arguments that made it impossible to even imagine coeducation in school sports. More than the lessons in the classroom, PE lessons emphasized gender differences, delineated the borders between the two sexes, and formed distinct, gender-specific bodies and characters that, in turn, were used as evidence to legitimize the gender order.

Controversial Mixed PE Classes—1970s

Coeducation in the classroom spread swiftly after World War II without causing controversy, but separate PE classes were still taken for granted, not least because different "male" and "female" sports dominated the curricula for girls and boys. Through women's integration in 'men's sports' such as football in the 1970s, among other things, the curricula and guidelines for girls' and boys' physical education began to adapt to each other. At the same time, though, educators and sports scientists started to question the whole concept of gender segregation in sports lessons. This was the era of the new women's movement, anti-authoritarian education, the criticism of competitive sports, and, generally, manifold reform initiatives; against this background, aims, contents, and teaching methods—including mixed PE classes—were scrutinized. Empirical studies of mixed PE lessons were carried out, particularly interviews and observations, lessons were evaluated, and pedagogic pilot projects devised. Extensive pupil surveys and numerous test lessons revealed that mixed PE lessons are possible and effective, depending on the aims of the lesson, but that they can also create specific problems.

In discussions of coeducation in the 1970s and 1980s, however, scientific results and arguments were often only ostensibly placed in the foreground while the real issues were the underlying political orientations and ideologies.

Opposition to mixed sports lessons came from various directions: not only from sport educators and administration officials who emphasized the traditional men's and women's roles but also from teachers with a traditional understanding of PE who wanted homogeneous groups because they wanted to concentrate on improving pupils' motor skills and performances.

The opposition to coeducation, which often came from conservative quarters in the 1970s, could call on a long and established tradition, thus meeting with broad support outside the sports movement, too. Coeducation seemed to challenge the gender order, and opponents considered this a danger but its advocates considered it a hope.

Very popular during this period were anthropological and phenomenological considerations that revolved around the "natures" and the naturally determined roles of men and women as well as around male and female movement patterns. The Dutchman F. J. J. Buytendijk was the most widely read representative (at least among European physical education specialists) of a gender anthropology based on the theory of polarity. He, for instance, regarded the game of soccer (known as football in Europe) as a demonstration of masculinity: "All attempts to make women play football have so far been unsuccessful." Based on the premises of Buytendijk and those of his followers, girls and boys should be taught separately in different sporting disciplines, according to their "natural" motor skills. Feminist scholars refuted this approach with the argument that it has apparently been proved possible after all "to make women play football" and that it has been demonstrated furthermore that the same basic principles of movement apply to both men and women.

Coeducation opponents also focused their arguments on the physical differences, the different performance levels, and the different needs, interests, and behavior patterns of the two sexes.

Supporters of mixed PE lessons, among them reform-oriented educators and sport scientists, warned against overemphasizing gender differences in sports performances because there are no significant discrepancies in basic motor properties and skills before the onset of puberty, and even afterward most pupils, irrespective of sex, can be classed in the same, middle band of achievement. According to these supporters, the different sporting interests of boys and girls were the result of processes of socialization. Sport scientists in favor of coeducation emphasized the significance of social learning processes and wanted to convey a wide variety of bodily and social experiences in PE lessons. They saw mixed PE classes as a chance of furthering empathy and

An otherwise happily married couple may turn a mixed doubles game into a scene from "Who's Afraid of Virginia Woolf." ■ ROD LAVER

cooperation skills as well as, generally, equal opportunity between the sexes.

In addition to the gender issue, mixed PE lessons brought up fundamental questions about the purpose of physical education:

- What should be learned and what should be taught in PE lessons and how?
- Is it sufficient to teach motor skills?
- Should competition and striving for the improvement of performances play a central role?

The debate about mixed PE classes petered out in the 1980s. A consensus could only be reached for primary schools, where coeducation in PE had already been practiced since the 1960s.

Spread of Coeducation

It is very difficult to get any information about the diffusion of mixed classes in PE in the different countries. In various developing countries and in Islamic cultures, PE is not even a subject in girls' schools, but in many western countries coeducation is the norm in the classroom and the gym hall. Often the choice of mixed or single-sex education depends on the age of the children; coeducation is widespread in elementary schools. For example:

- In the secondary schools of most German federal states, mixed PE lessons are possible if they appear beneficial from an educational point of view. In middle school (Grades 5 to 10), coeducation is regarded as particularly problematic, so mixed classes for girls and boys are likely to be the exception rather than the rule.
- In Australia, after an upswing of coeducation, many schools now choose to provide single-sex PE to avoid the problems in mixed classes.

Attitudes and Evaluations

Results of empirical studies show that most students are in favor of coeducation in the classroom. They would only accept a separation of the girls and boys in certain subjects, and PE is one of these subjects named in this debate. Research about the attitude of pupils toward mixed classes in PE has been conducted in various countries with different results. Whereas in an American study, most girls voted for single-sex PE, PE lessons in mixed groups seemed to be largely accepted by German pupils. However, their statements depended on their gender and their age and varied by grade and the type of sport. Those confronted with this form of teaching had a more positive attitude than did other students. The attitude toward coeducation in sports is particularly ambivalent among girls, although they support mixed lessons more often than boys do. Girls have more anxiety about high standards, about making fools of themselves, and about being taunted by the boys, but they also hope to be acknowledged, win more esteem from the boys, and have more fun.

Coeducation that is more than an organizational measurement can only succeed if both pupils and teachers are willing to make the best of this form of teaching. Studies of the attitudes of PE teachers reveal that the readiness to teach sports in mixed groups and to connect this with pedagogical purposes depends on many factors, including the age of the pupils and the age and sex of the teachers.

Interviews with male and female PE teachers in the United States and Germany revealed fundamental attitudes toward coeducation in sports that were marked by skepticism. The main difficulties seen were:

- The types of sports identified with one or other of the sexes
- The corresponding differences in the motor skills required
- The hierarchy of sporting values, with those of the boys at the top

In concrete terms, the teachers were concerned about the girls' deficiencies in the ball games that were most popular among the boys and the boys' refusal to participate in "unmanly" activities such as gymnastics and dance. One aspect of mixed PE lessons especially noted by women teachers was the aggressive behavior of (some) boys and the difficulty of keeping discipline. Both male and female teachers seem to feel that their training has not prepared them sufficiently for coeducation.

CRITIQUE OF COEDUCATION TO "REFLECTED" COEDUCATION

Interest in mixed PE lessons faded in the 1980s, as coeducation in classrooms as a whole was attacked and the "equal opportunity" approach was challenged. The criticism was that girls were not able to follow their success at school with successful careers. Good academic achievement did nothing to boost the little self-confidence that girls have compared with boys, and mixed lessons seemed to exercise a negative influence on girls' interests and opportunities. Empirical studies revealed that boys dominated the lessons, especially in science subjects, and that teachers gave considerably more attention to boys than to girls, not least because of disciplinary problems. Women education researchers demanded—from a position of "bias toward girls"—the abolition of coeducation or at least separate lessons in science subjects and PE. Whereas in the 1970s, coeducation opponents had feared that boys would be limited in their possibilities of athletic development, feminist sports scientists justified their rejection of coeducation by arguing that girls were marginalized in mixed PE classes.

Their arguments are based on the different "physical" culture of boys and girls resulting from specific male or female attitudes toward the body, body and beauty ideals, rituals, and techniques and practices of the body as well as from the gendered interests, experiences, competencies, wishes, and needs in the area of sports. Thus, both sexes have different strengths and different expectations for school sports, which reinforces, produces, and reproduces these gender differences. Generally speaking, the male values dominate in sports, so it follows that in school sports, the boys' strengths are taken as the norm, whereas the girls' strengths, which often lie in the gymnastic and rhythmical fields, are not valued very highly, either at school or in society as a whole. Moreover, as in the classroom, boys are more fre-

quently noticed in mixed PE classes, thus boys, or at least some boys, dominate the class and control the environment, whereas girls and their needs are not taken seriously. Aggressive behavior of male pupils against girls, teachers, and other boys was a further argument against coeducation. Both male and female teachers tend to accommodate the interests of the boys, partly in an attempt to make them conform before they become troublemakers. Finally, among the arguments against coeducation in sports is the focus on the body. In sports, one has to present the body constantly; it is perceived, judged, compared, and talked about. This could be a major problem for girls, who tend to develop negative body concepts in the confrontation with the beauty and slimness ideals of Western societies.

PE teachers commonly find that many girls respond to their marginalization in mixed classes with disinterest, with resistance, and by dropping out.

This critique of coeducation led to numerous projects being carried out with separate classes for girls and boys in PE, but also in other subjects. As surveys have shown, however, such projects, especially the sex segregation in scientific subjects, did not meet with an entirely favorable response, either from boys or from girls. In addition, there are benefits connected with coeducation. Thus, in recent years, a reassessment of coeducation was initiated; the magic formula is now the concept of "reflected coeducation," Reflected coeducation means teaching based on a reflection of gender issues and gender relations that takes differences seriously between the sexes and between other groups and individual students. Focusing on the specific needs of people, it aims at improving the potentials of individuals and groups. Reflected coeducation does not mean that girls are simply participating in the physical education of boys, but that the strengths of both sexes are cultivated while the weaknesses are accepted and compensated for. Strength and stamina as well as the self-confidence deriving from these must be imparted especially to girls, who are confronted with body and beauty ideals that focus on their appearance rather than on the capacities of the body. Creativity and rhythmic skills belong, as a rule, not to the strengths of the boys who have been afraid to be marginalized in the boys' groups as "sissies" if they participate in a typically girls' activity. These fears have to be taken seriously, but a "degendering" of dance in new dance styles makes a reconciliation of masculinity and rhythmic abilities possible.

This new approach to coeducation allows choices between mixed and (temporary) separate classes depending on pedagogic considerations and the circumstances in a particular class or at a particular school.

In the 1990s, a further paradigm shift occurred when attention was turned to boys and problems such as difficulties in concentrating, hyperactivity, and aggressive behavior. Unrealistic ideals of masculinity, violence in peer groups, and the "feminization" of education seemed to have an unfavorable effect on boys' intellectual and mental developments. The discrepancy between the norm of male superiority and boys' own inadequacies seemed to become especially evident in mixed classes with girls. This is also true for PE especially where those boys who are not skilled are marginalized or even bullied. When this happens in front of the girls, the humiliation is even worse.

The Future

Coeducation in PE is still a contested area, and its success or failure depends on numerous and various factors. Coeducation—not only in school sports—can only succeed under certain conditions. If basic prerequisites are lacking, such as a good understanding between the pupils of a class, a safe and supportive environment, especially for girls, and a positive attitude among the teachers, then coeducation is a liability for both sexes, especially for girls. The chances of mixed school sports increase when intentional and reflected coeducation begins at primary school because the course is set for later development of "doing gender." In addition, teachers must be sensitive toward gender issues and committed to and prepared for coeducation in their training.

The aim of coeducational school sports should be that boys and girls are given the opportunity to learn more about themselves and others, to understand gender and gender constructions in and through sports, and to act, interact, and participate in sports in a world that is not sex-segregated.

PE plays an important role in sports socialization and can thus contribute to the construction but also to the deconstruction of gender differences. Socialization means the appropriation of the social and ecological environment and self-training in and through cultural practices. Gender-specific sports engagement and the gender of a sport are social constructions and social arrangements. Sports can change their gender, and football is a good example: Whereas soccer (football) was viewed as an unfeminine sport until the 1960s, today it is one of the fastest growing sports for women in many countries of the world. Coeducation as a pedagogical means aims at providing equal opportunities, at transforming gender constructions, and, hence, at changing the hierarchical gender arrangements. This is especially difficult and challenging in PE lessons because they focus on bodies and, thus, on the basis and "markers" of masculinity and femininity. Moreover, sports is the arena in which masculinity and femininity can be convincingly enacted, "doing sport" is always "doing gender" with more or less emphasis on gender differences. It is not surprising, then, that mixed physical education lessons are connected with so many fears and so many hopes.

Gertrud Pfister

Further Reading

Derry, J. (2002, Fall-Winter). Single-sex and coeducational physical education: Perspectives of adolescent girls and female physical education teachers. *Melpomene Journal.*

Frohn, J. (2004). Reflexive Koedukation auch im Sportunterricht der Grundschule? *Sportunterricht 53*(6), 163–168.

Green, K., & Scraton, S. (1998). Gender, coeducation and secondary physical education. In K. Green & K. Hardman (Eds.), *Physical education: A reader.* Aachen, Germany: Meyer and Meyer Verlag.

Pfister, G. (1983). *Geschlechtsspezifische Sozialisation und Koedukationi im Sport.* Berlin, Germany: Bartels & Wernitz

Riordan, C. (1990). *Girls and boys in school, together or separate?* New York: Teachers College Press.

Wright, J. (1999). Changing gendered practices in physical education: Working with teachers. *European Physical Education Review, 5*(3), 181–197.

Coliseum (Rome)

The Coliseum is the first permanent and the largest amphitheater built in ancient Rome. Construction of the Coliseum began during the reign of Vespasian (Roman emperor 69–79 CE) in around 72 CE, and it was dedicated by Vespasian's son Titus (Roman emperor 79–81 CE) in 80 CE. The Coliseum was originally called the "Flavian Amphitheater" in honor of the Flavian dynasty. The popular name "Coliseum" came into existence because the amphitheater was situated next to a colossal statue of Nero (Roman emperor 54–68 CE).

Architectural Marvel

When it was built, the Coliseum was an architectural marvel, with a capacity of more than fifty thousand seats and an efficient system for producing spectacles and managing large crowds. It was a four-story oval structure, with the walls of its outer ring rising to about 55 meters above ground, the height of a modern building twelve to fifteen stories high. The major axis of the Coliseum's elliptical plan was 188 meters long, and the minor axis was 156 meters long. Eighty walls of arches at ground level supported vaults for passageways, stairways, and tiers of seats. Circumferential arcades at the outer edge linked each level and the stairways between levels. The arches were progressively numbered and led via a system of internal corridors to the outlets that took spectators to their seats. The construction utilized a combination of materials: concrete for the foundations, travertine (a mineral consisting of a massive, usually layered calcium carbonate) for the piers and arcades, and tufa (a porous rock) and brick for the walls and most of the vaults. More than 100,000 cubic meters of travertine were used in the construction, and the metal pins that held the blocks together were estimated to weigh more than 272 metric tons.

The interior of the Coliseum consisted of the arena, a wooden floor bearing a bed of sand and covering an area of about 76 by 46 meters. The stands were subdivided into four superimposed stories. At the top of the amphitheater masts fastened in brackets and sockets held a giant canvas canopy to protect the spectators from the heat of the sun. Toward the end of the first century CE (after mock naval battles were abolished), a complex system of subterranean tunnels was constructed underneath the wooden flooring, where gladiators and animals were kept prior to their performance. Elevators employing counterweights were built to transport cages of animals and other stage equipment to the arena floor. The gladiators would reach the arena directly from their "barracks" by the side of the Coliseum, using a passage leading to the amphitheater's underground spaces. During shows a metal mesh surrounding the arena would be set up to protect spectators from the danger of enraged wild animals. Archers were also placed inside the amphitheater at the foot of the steps, ready to intervene should an animal get out of control.

"Bread and Circuses"

The construction of the Coliseum was part of Vespasian's plan to restore the capitol, which had burned down during civil wars, and to improve the infrastructure of Rome and the empire. The project was also seen as a way to increase political stability by providing the people with "bread and circuses," as the poet Juvenal put it. The main function of the Coliseum was to provide public events such as gladiator fights, wild animal hunts, and mock naval battles. In many of these events

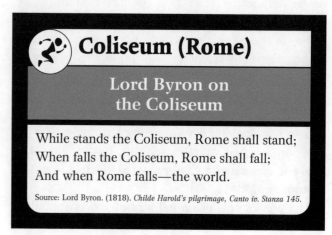

Coliseum (Rome)

Lord Byron on the Coliseum

While stands the Coliseum, Rome shall stand;
When falls the Coliseum, Rome shall fall;
And when Rome falls—the world.

Source: Lord Byron. (1818). *Childe Harold's pilgrimage, Canto iv. Stanza 145.*

animals, gladiators, condemned criminals, and slaves fought each other until death. The events were open to all people, free of charge, although the social elites were entitled to seats of marble at the lower level, whereas commoners, slaves, and foreigners were seated right under the canvas roof, which was the hottest area during summer. The grand opening of the Coliseum included one hundred days of ceremonies and games, which took the lives of five thousand wild animals in combats. Gladiator fights were abolished in the early fifth century CE. The last event on record, which consisted of only animal combats, was held in 523 CE under Theodoric, king of the Ostrogoths (471–526 CE).

Square of the Coliseum

Overshadowed by its imposing amphitheater, the Square of the Coliseum received a monumental addition with the building of the Temple of Venus and Rome, designed by Hadrian (Roman emperor 117–138 CE). The layout of the square has been substantially preserved to the present time. Beside the amphitheater stood the Colossus of Nero, a 30-meter-tall statue of gilt bronze, the work of the Greek sculptor Zenodoros. The statue originally represented the emperor but was modified to represent Apollo—god of the sun—after Nero's death. The last monument added to the square was the Arch of Constantine (Roman emperor 309–337 CE). It was erected in 312 CE by the Senate and people of Rome in honor of Constantine, who had liberated the city and the state from the "tyrant" Maxentius winning the Battle of the Milvian Bridge.

For nearly four centuries the Coliseum was the center of public entertainment and a symbol of power of the Roman empire. Its function as a venue for entertainment ended soon after the fall of the Roman empire in 476 CE. The Coliseum was abandoned for hundreds of years until medieval times, when warlords used it as a fortress. During the two millennia of its existence the Coliseum has suffered extensive damage from earthquakes, fires, neglect, and vandalism. Nevertheless, since the fifteenth century people have expressed a desire to restore the ancient architectural marvel. Today the remains of the Coliseum are one of the most visited tourist sites in the world.

Ying Wushanley

Further Reading

Balsdon, J. P. V. D. (1969). *Life and leisure in ancient Rome.* New York: Phoenix Press.

Cary, M. (1967). *A history of Rome, down to the reign of Constantine.* New York: St. Martin's Press.

Gelzer, M. (1968). *Caesar: Politician and statesman.* Cambridge, MA: Harvard University Press.

Harris, H. A. (1972). *Sport in Greece and Rome.* Ithaca, NY: Cornell University Press.

Lintott, A. (1993). *Imperium Romanum: Politics and administration.* New York: Routledge.

Matz, D. (2002). *Daily life of the ancient Romans.* Westport, CT: Greenwood Press.

Nicolet, C. (1988). *The world of the citizen in republican Rome* (P. S. Falla, Trans.). Berkeley and Los Angeles: University of California Press.

Salmon, E. T. (1982). *The making of Roman Italy.* Ithaca, NY: Cornell University Press.

Staccioli, R. A. (2001). *Rome: Past and present.* Rome: Vision S.R.L.

Starr, C. G. (1971). *The ancient Romans.* New York: Oxford University Press.

Zoch, P. A. (1998). *Ancient Rome: An introductory history.* Norman: University of Oklahoma Press.

Collective Bargaining

Collective bargaining is the process through which management of an enterprise and the workers (in the case of sport, the players) bargain over components of the working relationship. In a typical sport the league owners are the management, and the players collectively pool their voices to maximize their bargaining position vis-à-vis the owners. In sports collective bargaining issues typically involve financial remuneration (salaries, salary caps, pension contributions, per diem allowances), working conditions (modes of travel, scheduling, hotel accommodations), and code of conduct (punishments, drug-testing policies, public relations commitments and expectations). The ability of players to unionize in bargaining with management is established under the United States legal system.

U. S. Legislation Affecting Management and Labor

In 1890 Congress passed the Sherman Act, which was designed to shatter monopolies and establish an economic landscape that allowed businesses to freely enter and exit the marketplace and compete on equal terms with competitors. Though designed to limit the power of companies, numerous business entities utilized the Sherman Act to restrict the ability of workers to better their conditions. Many corporations successfully argued in court that employees who unionized and implemented strikes to force management to provide employment concessions restricted trade and were thus in violation of antitrust laws. In response the United States Congress passed the Clayton Act of 1914, which established that the labor of human beings was not subject to the Sherman Act. In addition Congress later passed the Norris-LaGuardia Act (1932) and the Wagner Act (1935), which established the right of labor to collectively act in its best interest when negotiating with management. The Wagner Act (known as the National Labor Relations Act) established the National Labor Relations Board (NLRB) to enforce labor laws and assist in governing labor disputes.

United States law enables workers to collectively pool their efforts in labor unions, to choose representatives to bargain their position, and to implement pressure tactics (strikes, picketing, etc.) to enhance their interest. In exchange for the power to bargain collectively, all members of a labor union agree to submit to the terms of their collective bargaining agreement with management and potentially to agree to terms that may diminish their individual rights.

Players Attempt to Unionize

Professional baseball began in the United States shortly after the Civil War. Most of the early years of professional baseball were disorganized and often underfinanced, but as uniform rules and a major league were established, leagues attempted to exert as much control as possible over players. In 1882 the National League and the numerous minor leagues that had been estab-

lished signed the National Baseball Agreement. The National Baseball Agreement established the reserve clause, which gave control of player services to the club. Effectively, the reserve clause allowed teams to retain the services of the players forever. The reserve clause would remain in effect until 1976.

The reserve clause and other antiplayer baseball decisions would occasionally incite the players to attempt to organize in one coherent collective effort. Prominent attempts at organizing labor in baseball included the Brotherhood of Professional Baseball Players in the 1880s, the Professional Players Fraternity of the 1910s, and the American Baseball Guild in the 1940s. Each attempt to organize the players eventually stalled and was destroyed by player dissension, ownership maneuvers, or the American court system.

Marvin Miller and the Major League Baseball Players Association

Undaunted by years of unsuccessful attempts to establish a cohesive and effective union, players continued to work to organize their voices to instigate change in Major League Baseball (MLB). During the 1953 season, All-Stars Ralph Kiner and Allie Reynolds attempted to negotiate with the owners for additional money for the players' pension fund. After meeting with continued resistance, the players hired lawyer Jonas Norman Lewis to represent their interests. The refusal of the owners to meet directly with Lewis frustrated and emboldened the players. In 1954 the Major League Players Association (MLBPA) was established, with aging star pitcher Bob Feller elected the first president of the new association.

Baseball's owners continued to increase their revenues through franchise relocation, broadened television exposure, and expansion. In addition, in 1965 the owners implemented an amateur draft, which severely limited an incoming player's ability to negotiate signing bonuses. Despite the efforts of the players and the MLBPA's attorneys, baseball's owners dramatically increased their profits while offering players only minimal increases in their compensation. The players decided

that they needed to hire an established labor leader who would work for them full-time. In 1966 the MLBPA hired former United Steelworkers of America representative Marvin Miller and changed the course of labor relations in American professional sport forever.

Marvin Miller approached his job as executive director of the MLBPA fervently, immediately attempting to change the mentality of the players. For years players in all American professional sports had been unable to approach management on equal footing; Miller enabled MLB players to realize that they could bargain from a position of strength if they remained united. After collectively bargaining with the owners, an agreement regarding pension plans and insurance was signed in late 1966. From there Miller led the players union in numerous battles with the owners, almost always helping the players to advance their cause. When Miller assumed his position as MLBPA executive director in 1966, the minimum MLB salary was $6,000 a year, and there were no opportunities for free agency (the opportunity to negotiate with any team in the league). Although the United States Supreme Court ruled in 1972 against outfielder Curt Flood in his bid for free agency, Marvin Miller and the Players Association continued to work tirelessly for the rights of players. In 1976, after reviewing the merits of a player-owner dispute regarding the application of the reserve clause, arbitrator Peter Seitz awarded pitchers Andy Messersmith and Dave McNally free agency, and the reserve rule established in 1882 was finally overturned. The initial efforts of Miller and the continued efforts of the MLBPA created a financial landscape in baseball that resulted in average salaries exceeding $2.4 million by 2004.

Modern Sport Unions

Players from the National Football League (NFL), National Basketball Association (NBA), and National Hockey League (NHL) have also established player associations in their sports. Utilizing collective bargaining, the unions have successfully increased their share of league revenues and have worked to achieve free agency and other working conditions more favorable to play-

ers. Unfortunately, each of the four major professional sport leagues has experienced labor difficulties over the past thirty years—often with fans being the real losers during the negotiations.

Strikes

Under the collective bargaining process, players not satisfied with management proposals may elect to withhold their services through strikes, attempting to force owners to satisfy player demands by stopping "production." In addition to postponing or canceling games, strikes increase media and fan attention on the disputed issues, which players hope will lead to concessions by owners. Additional stakeholders besides the union and management are affected by a strike. For every postponed or canceled game, media outlets lose revenue; facility employees working in concessions, security, hospitality, and the like potentially lose a portion of their yearly income; and hotels, restaurants, and bars near the stadiums lose their sport clientele.

Although there have been numerous strikes in the four major North American professional sport leagues, the most notable strikes have involved issues concerning salaries and free agency. The Major League Baseball strike of 1981 was a response by players to the insistence of the owners that teams losing free agents would be compensated with players from the team signing the free agent. The players correctly determined that if owners knew they would lose a player after signing a free agent, the potential salaries of players would be lowered. The strike resulted in a fifty-day shutdown, and 713 games were canceled.

During a strike players may elect to enhance their message of resolve to management, media, and fans by picketing. Often picket lines result in arguments or, occasionally, physical altercations between players and management. In some cases management may elect to employ nonunion workers or "scabs" to cross the picket lines. This occurred most prominently during the 1987 NFL strike as owners utilized replacement players in an attempt to fulfill media obligations while attempting to break the resolve of the striking players. Although the

Understand one thing. Nothing happens without the Game. We can talk about labor relations and relationships with owners and between the teams, and marketing and globalization. But we've also got the best game. Everything we do emanates from that. ∎ DAVID STERN

attendance and ratings for games played by replacement players was down considerably from usual levels, the games showed many striking players that the owners were committed to their position. The owners were successful in their tactics as scores of NFL players began to cross the picket lines to return to work. Eventually, the NFL Players Association was forced to end the strike and compromise with owners' demands.

Perhaps the most devastating strike in American professional sport history occurred in Major League Baseball in 1994–1995. The owners insisted on a salary cap and a detailed revenue-sharing system. The players, adamant in their stance against any form of a salary cap, announced a strike on 12 August 1994. The strike resulted in the shutdown of the remainder of the season, including the cancellation of the 1994 World Series. For the first time in ninety years, the October Classic was not played. The 1994 strike continued into the 1995 season, with the owners threatening to utilize replacement players. The parties were able to finally compromise on 25 April 1995. The usual schedule was shortened from 162 to 144 games and unfortunately, despite the posturing and strong negotiations on both sides, few changes to the basic agreement were made.

Lockouts

Owners unable to finalize collective bargaining agreements favorable to their position may elect to lock out the players from the workplace. During a lockout most owners attempt to portray the players as unreasonable in their demands. Although lockouts result in decreased revenue for management and players, sport owners hope the lockout will force players to return to the bargaining table, as they may be unable to financially survive without their regular paychecks.

Although the NHL had experienced relative labor peace from 1950 to 1990, in 1992 players had nearly shut down the postseason before some of their demands were met. In 1995 the NHL owners hoped to regain some concessions lost to the players in 1992, so they closed their doors. The 1995 NHL lockout lasted 103 days and resulted in the loss of 468 total games.

Although the owners were able to advance their cause, hockey lost significant momentum in its marketing efforts as a result of the lockout. The NHL continued to waiver on a financial tightrope as owners and players had not completely settled their disputes and failed to establish a financial system that insured future prosperity for owners and players as well as stability for fans. This labor unrest eventually caused the owners to lock out the players during the start of the 2004 season. Players rebuffed any attempts by management to implement a salary cap or significant luxury tax, while owners insisted that such measures were necessary to contain costs and ensure financial viability for every team in the league. The entire 2004–2005 NHL season was eventually cancelled.

Prior to the 2004–2005 NHL labor disagreement the most devastating lockout in American professional sports occurred in the NBA in 1998–1999. Historically, the NBA had attempted to maintain labor peace despite difficult financial situations. The NBA and its players had established the first salary cap in major professional sports in 1983 and had never lost any games to work stoppages prior to 1998. The owners and players debated the merits of the salary cap, free agency, minimum salaries, rookie compensation, and aberrant behavior during the 202 days of the lockout. Although the finalized collective bargaining agreement created an individual salary cap, greater sharing of resources among players, and a comprehensive drug-testing policy, the loss of thirty-two games for each team significantly tarnished the image of the NBA.

Current Issues

Although unions in professional sports act much like any other union to further the interests of their members, there are some subtle differences across industries. In sports, unions typically do not bargain for exact compensation for members. The union and management craft a basic agreement regarding minimum salaries, working conditions, and the like, but the individual player is free to negotiate yearly salary, bonuses, and incentives with his individual employer. Although most of the major professional sport leagues have established seniority systems (rookie wage scales, veteran minimum salaries), compared with most nonsport unions, professional athletes have far greater freedom to negotiate as individuals. As salaries for many professional athletes have increased dramatically into the millions of dollars, many have questioned the need for sport unions in MLB, NBA, NFL, and NHL. In fact attempts have been made by individual players to decertify their union in order for individual players to maximize their compensation. During the 1998 NBA lockout, Michael Jordan and other prominent players attempted to decertify the union after the union and management appeared close to agreeing to maximum individual salaries. Jordan and the other players hoping to decertify the union to garner salaries above the proposed maximums failed in their attempt as the vast majority of players realized the collective bargaining agreement between NBA owners and players would enhance the salaries of the majority of players, even if it artificially lowered the salaries for the ultra-superstars.

In recent years Major League Baseball and other professional sport leagues have discussed the possibility of implementing rules (salary caps, revenue sharing, payroll taxes) to enhance competitive balance (the opportunity for every team to have adequate resources to compete for player services). These rules are subject to collective bargaining since they potentially alter financial compensation for players. In some leagues owners have not been able to implement policies that might enhance competitive balance (and therefore potentially improve the overall long-term financial position of the entire league) because they have not been successful in convincing the players association that changes should be implemented.

The Future

As performance-enhancing drugs have become commonplace in sport, unions negotiating collective bargaining agreements with management have been placed in an awkward position. Union leaders are employed to negotiate the best possible deal for the players, and if performance-enhancing drugs cause irreparable harm to the players, the union will likely not wish to see its members use these drugs. However, the union must also be concerned for the public relations implications if players are caught cheating by using drugs. This dilemma has often delayed the adoption of meaningful drug-testing and punishment policies as union members are not eager to allow management to implement full-scale testing, even if the union hopes to protect its members from the detriments of drug use.

The rapid increase in revenues in intercollegiate athletics has caused many people to consider the possibility of forming a union to protect the interests of athletes competing for men's basketball and football teams in the National Collegiate Athletic Association (NCAA). For many NCAA Division I universities, revenues from media contracts, ticket and luxury suite sales, licensed merchandise, and other sources often exceed tens of millions of dollars a year. Numerous critics have noted that although players often receive scholarships to attend college, their value to the university is considerably more than what the school is providing them. Future discussions in this area are likely to lead to heated debates as players may elect to collectively bargain for a greater share of the revenue generated from their endeavors.

Mark Nagel, Daniel A. Rascher,
Matt Brown, and Chad D. McEvoy

See also Unionism

Further Reading

Helyar, J. (1994). *Lords of the realm.* New York: Villard Books.

Kuhn, B. (1988). *Hardball: The education of a baseball commissioner.* New York: McGraw Hill.

Lowenfish, L. (1980). *The imperfect diamond: A history of baseball's labor wars.* New York: Da Capo Press.

Miller, M. (1991). *A whole different ball game.* New York: Carroll Publishing.

Quirk, J., & Fort, R. (1999). *Hard ball.* Princeton, NJ: Princeton University Press.

Staudohar, P. D. (1996). *Playing for dollars: Labor relations and the sport business.* Ithaca, NY: Cornell University Press.

Zimbalist, A. (2003). *May the best team win: Baseball economics and public policy.* Washington, DC: Brookings Institute.

College Athletes

*F*ormer intercollegiate athlete students such as Kareem Abdul-Jabbar, Jerry West, Larry Bird, "Magic" Johnson, Cheryl Miller, Nancy Lieberman-Cline, Dominique Dawes, Wilma Rudolph, Jackie Joyner Kersey, Walter Payton, Jackie Robinson, and Jim Brown have become household legends. The terms *March Madness* and *football bowl games* have become synonymous with college sport. Yet, an historical critique of college sport represents a study of contradictions (i.e., student-athlete), player and coach scandals, crises management, perpetration of sport myths, academic dishonesty, and cartel-like behavior. College sports today represent an arena in which gender, race, hegemony, and social class are manifested.

Early College Contests

Sport records show the first college sports event was a crew race between Harvard and Yale Universities in 1852. The first recognized college baseball game was played in 1859 between Princeton and Rutgers Universities. Baseball became the most widely played sport on college campuses during the nineteenth century. Initial college athletic events and conferences were organized and governed by college students who scheduled games, wrote the rules, selected team captains, and organized clubs. "Colleges increasingly turned to the formation of athletic conferences as a means of regulating sports. Students had formed the first intercollegiate association in 1858 when Harvard, Yale, Brown and Trinity organized the College Rowing Association" (Rader 1999, 178).

The desire by college presidents to enhance college visibility and increase student enrollment and the lack of professional sports led to the growth in college sports. By the late 1800s, college sport programs, led by football, began to mature into "for profit" enterprises. What was once a student-organized activity came under the control of college administrators and athletic department officials. Colleges began to hire professional

coaches and build stadiums to support their sports programs. During this time, college faculty members were also cognizant of the rising influence of college sports. In 1881, Princeton University established the first faculty athletic committee. As early as the late nineteenth century, college sport began its transformation to meet the perceived needs of alumni, coaches, and college administrators. College sport was now seen as a vehicle to:

- Promote state-funded financial support
- Increase student body populations
- Enhance educational opportunities for students
- Mobilize alumni support

"Intercollegiate sports were instrumental in defining college identities, in giving them greater emotional depth, and thereby in bonding students, faculty, administrators, alumni, and social climbers into a single college community" (Rader 1999, 96).

By 1900, college sport became embedded in the structure of higher education. College sport began its transformation from an educational and student-centered activity to a corporate enterprise. The establishment and popularity of college football was instrumental in this transformation. Walter Camp, the father of American football, recognized the connection between football and business, stating, "American business has found in American college football the epitomization of present day business methods" (Gorn and Goldstein 1993, 158).

Football

Between 1890 and 1900, college football gained prominence on campus as a major revenue producer, second only to student tuition and fees. College football was played by Ivy League colleges, historically black colleges and universities, and regional and national colleges and universities. Early college football grew to be a brutal, yet popular activity. Formations such as the "flying wedge" resulted in the deaths of eighteen football players in 1905. As a result, President Theodore Roosevelt invited selected college presidents to his office to discuss the future of college football and, to some

*Going to college offered me the chance to play football
for four more years.* ■ RONALD REAGAN

extent, the future of college sports. The meeting led to significant rule changes and the establishment of the Intercollegiate Athletic Association. In 1910, the organization adopted its present name, National Collegiate Athletic Association (NCAA).

Early Reform

Between 1910 and the 1930s, college sports expanded and grew in popularity. The highly acclaimed and controversial 1929 Carnegie Foundation report labeled football as an organized commercial enterprise providing a level of professionalism on campus. The report focused on the status and future direction for college sports and asked three important questions: (1) How should financial aid be distributed? (2) Who should control college sport? (3) How does alumni support affect the college program? Unfortunately, these questions and others were never answered, and college sport continued to expand its influence on college campuses. As a result, the financial and human cost associated with intercollegiate sports continued to escalate into the 1950s.

Sanity Code

During the 1930s and into the 1940s, several noteworthy social and intercollegiate conditions (widespread professional gambling, college recruiting irregularities, and the establishment of preseason bowl games in football) led NCAA leaders to provide more oversight and better enforcement of its rules and regulations. On 22 and 23 July 1946, conference representatives met in Chicago to draft a document titled, "Principles of Conduct of Intercollegiate Athletes," which defined amateurism, stipulated academic standards, and determined qualifications for athletic ability. The NCAA membership endorsed these principles, better known as the "Sanity Code."

The Sanity Code was a very important piece of NCAA history because it tried to define amateurism and the role of the student within a collegiate sport environment. In a fundamental break with the long-held principle of the college amateur athlete, NCAA member institutions adopted the Sanity Code and the Constitutional Compliance Committee (to provide enforcement power) in 1948. This code permitted the extension of scholarships and jobs to athletes. Scholarships or jobs had to be awarded solely based on demonstrated financial need. Unfortunately, some college officials believed this code pushed recruiting parity too far, affecting financial aid for their college programs. Criticism of the code resulted in its repeal in 1951. A former athletic director at Bradley University said, "The restrictions in the Sanity Code were such that the majority of institutions felt they couldn't live by it" (Brown 1999, A4).

In an effort to provide athletic regulation and enforcement, the NCAA passed the twelve-point code on 29 August 1951. Specific guidelines focused on the following:

■ Limiting practice sessions and number of games in each sport
■ Supporting normal academic progress guidelines
■ Limiting the number and amount of financial aid to athletes
■ Providing guidance for student recruiting

The twelve-point code ultimately led to the establishment of the NCAA Committee on Infractions. During the next thirty years, this committee's power and authority expanded to include investigative and enforcement procedures.

The term *student-athlete* first appeared in NCAA publications following a highly publicized 1953 college football court case. A University of Denver football player was injured in practice. The courts determined the athlete was eligible to receive Workman's Compensation because he was viewed as an employee of the institution. The term *student-athlete* was instituted to prevent any additional litigation in this area. The NCAA continues to take the position that student-athletes should not be paid a stipend in addition to tuition, room, and books.

Corporate Sport

The concept *corporate athletics* is defined as a set of institutional "big sport" values associated with modern

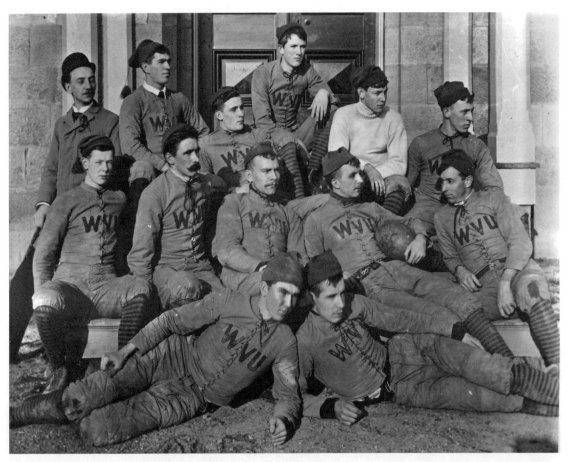

A rare image of the first football team at West Virginia State University in 1891.

Source: West Virgina School of Physical Education.

corporations. Literature supports two conflicting college sports models:

1. Amateur-education with its focus on the perceived educational value of sport. Under this model, college officials were able to view college sports as part of the larger university culture.
2. Commercial-education with its focus on corporate "big-business" aspect of sport.

The public began to recognize the contradiction between economics, college sport success, and student-athletes as amateurs.

The two models and the associated rising costs of athletic programs, concerns for student-athletes' rights, and other college sport deviant behaviors encouraged the public, college faculty, and administrators to advocate reforming college sports. In 1989, the Knight Commission (consisting of college presidents, business leaders, members of Congress, and NCAA representa-

tives) recognized that college sports with its corporate values negatively affects colleges' educational mission. The 1991 Knight Commission report offered strategies for change, including the one-plus-three model:

- Presidential control
- Academic integrity
- Financial integrity

Specifically, the report recommended the following:

- College presidents should exercise the same degree of control over athletes that they have over the institution.
- Student eligibility should be based on continuous academic progress.
- There should be greater institutional oversight and control of all athletic department business matters.
- Each NCAA institution should undergo an independent self-evaluation.

Prompted by the Knight Commission, the NCAA approved sweeping reforms in January 1991 aimed at controlling cost, reduced the length of playing seasons, established an annual coaches recruiting certification program, and phased out athletic dormitories. The rules prohibiting athletic dormitories at Division I colleges took effect in 1996. In 1995, 24 of the 302 NCAA Division I institutions had residence halls composed of more than 50 percent athletes. Not all of the 1991 commission recommendations were realized. Ten years later, the Knight Commission further deliberated strategies to address graduation rates and the athletic departments' "financial arms race."

Academic Admission Standards

Colleges and universities determine college entrance requirements and admission policies. Yet, in the case of NCAA college sports, colleges and universities have abdicated this responsibility to the NCAA. During the 1980s and 1990s, college faculty and the public voiced concerns about the perceived lack of student athletes graduating from college. In 1983, the NCAA tried to remedy the poor academic performance and low graduation rates of college athletes by passing Proposition 48, which was enforced in 1986 and required all freshmen athletes to be declared eligible by scoring at least 15 on the ACT or 700 on the SAT and a minimum GPA of 2.0 in at least core courses. Athletes could receive financial aid if they met one of these requirements.

In 1989, new NCAA guidelines led to the passage of Proposition 42, which prohibited colleges from providing athletic-related financial aid to athletes who did not meet their GPA and test-score requirements. The controversial legislation was passed in an effort to enhance academic performance and integrity in collegiate athletics. Unfortunately, the SAT/ACT cut-off scores disproportionately eliminated African-Americans from participation. African-American coaches presented the following arguments against the two propositions: (1) The minimum SAT score was arbitrary; and (2) the SAT and ACT tests were racially biased against minorities and students from low socioeconomic back-

grounds. Early reports found that 85 percent of African-American athletes lost eligibility status.

These propositions negatively affected the participation rates of African-American student-athletes attending historically black colleges and universities. As a compromise to Propositions 48 and 42, Proposition 16 was passed in 1996. This proposition raised the standards for the combined GPA and exam score necessary to qualify through use of a sliding scale. In 1999, the federal district court in Philadelphia struck down the NCAA Proposition 16. The court concluded it had a disparate impact against African-American student-athletes. One legal scholar argues, "Achieving racial equality in sports will require a shift in attitude: those in power positions . . . must commit to racial equality" (Davis 2000, 263).

Women's College Sports

Women's historical participation in college sports represents a struggle for equality, social justice, recognition, and respect. The early development of women's sports did not parallel that of their male counterparts. Women's programs were initially organized by women physical educators. Physical education philosophy stressed participation and educational value derived from playing sports. Fearing that participation would cause injury, educators discouraged women's participation in early competitive sports programs.

During the 1880s, women's sports gained a level of popularity in women's colleges. "In the 1880s, for example, women at Vassar and Smith, Mount Holyoke, and Wellesley played not softball or rounders or some gentler version of the game, but baseball" (Gorn and Goldstein 1993, 198). Similarly, in 1890, several colleges (i.e., the University of California, University of Wisconsin, and Goucher College) promoted women's participation in sport clubs (tennis, archery, bowling). In 1891, Dr. James Naismith invented the game of basketball. In 1893, Smith College was the first women's program to play basketball. Women's basketball soon became very popular on college campuses. In the 1890s, physical education programs began to introduce the

Football, fraternities, and fun have no place in the university. They were introduced only to entertain those who shouldn't be in the university. ■ ROBERT M. HUTCHINS

volleyball, field hockey, and basketball for women. These sports represented a departure from bowling, horseback riding, swimming, and gymnastics.

Between 1923 and 1936, intercollegiate athletic competition for women was limited. In 1930, the introduction of "play days" and "sports days" provided some measure of sport participation. These activities, stressing participation and enjoyment of sports, continued until the 1960s, by which time, competitive sports for women were viewed favorably by society. Various women's sports organizations have provided guidelines for women's sports participation. In 1957, the Division of Girls' and Women's Sports (DGWS) of American Alliance for Health, Physical Education, Recreation and Dance (AAHPERD) became one of the major advocates for girls' and women's sports. In a dramatic change in philosophy, DGWS members advocated female participation on highly competitive athletic teams.

Title IX: The Gender Issue

Two important milestones in the history of women's sports were the establishment of the Association for Intercollegiate Athletics for Women (AIAW) in 1971 and the passage of Title IX of the Federal Educational Amendment in 1972. "During the early stages of women's athletics, a concept, unique to women's athletics, was established: Student involvement in the establishment of policies and guidelines which would determine the path of women's athletes" (Acosta and Carpenter 1985, 315).

Physical educators and students provided leadership in establishing the AIAW, which replaced the Commission on Intercollegiate Athletics for Women (CIAW). By 1982, the AIAW offered forty national championships in eighteen sports across various geographical regions. Under the AIAW structure, women gained access to coaching and other leadership positions associated with college sports.

Title IX prohibits sex discrimination in federally assisted education programs: "No person in the United States shall, on the basis of sex, be excluded from participation in, be denied the benefits of, or be subjected to discrimination under any education program or activity receiving federal financial assistance" (*More Hurdles to Clear: Women and Girls in Competitive Athletics* 1980, 7). Title IX regulations took effect in 1976 and required physical education program and competitive athletic program compliance. This legislation had a positive dramatic impact on high school and college sports for women. Data indicated the number of sports offered to women and the number of female athletes participating increased significantly. "In 1976–77, 170,384 men (72.6 percent of all athletes) and 64,375 women (27.4 percent) participated in intercollegiate sports. The number of female athletes has increased 102.1 percent since 1971–72" (*More Hurdles to Clear: Women and Girls in Competitive Athletics* 1980, 21).

Interest in women's sports gained momentum and, in 1998, basketball, cross country, soccer, tennis, track, and volleyball were the most frequently offered women's sports programs across NCAA Division I, II, and III. As of 2004, according to Carpenter and Acosta (2004), there were 8,402 varsity women's NCAA teams. The passage of Title IX resulted in conflict between the NCAA and the AIAW. "The women's organization sought equal opportunity and equal treatment for women, charging that 'the men' wanted to take over the women's programs as a means of stopping them from getting a fair share of the money" (Byers 1995, 240). The 1980 NCAA Convention dramatically affected the future of the AIAW: The NCAA established ten women's championships and provided funding for women to attend these events. As a result, AIAW members joined the NCAA.

In February 1983, the AIAW lost its anti-trust lawsuit against the NCAA. The AIAW could no longer offer national championships or compete for financial support for its programs, which led to its demise. Today, Title IX remains one of the most controversial topics in college sports. Debate between male and female coaches, players, and alumni about the reduction of men's varsity

College Athletes

A Lesson Learned at the Summitt

The whistle emits a piercing shrill. All movement comes to a stop. I peel myself off the hardwood floor and come face to face with a pair of steely blue eyes staring daggers right through me. "Becky!" she barks as the rest of my teammates freeze in their spots on the court. I brace myself for a good tongue lashing from the most competitive, fiercest coach I have ever known in my nineteen years on earth. This young coach, just eight years my senior, was an Olympic silver medallist (1976 Olympics) as a basketball player for the USA, and already had five years of collegiate coaching under her belt. The previous season, her squad nearly upset the reigning champions of collegiate women's basketball—Delta State, to finish as runner-up in the AIAW (Association of Intercollegiate Athletics for Women) national championship game.

"Becky! What happened there? Tell me! You've got to get around that pick! You've got to see it coming!" She said impatiently. Coach Pat Head Summitt, took two steps toward me as I held my breath. None of us liked to be singled out. We were THE Lady Vols of the University of Tennessee. We were expected to excel at the highest echelons and Pat was going to make sure we succeeded. "Becky, tell me what just happened," Pat demanded. "Um, Coach, I didn't hear my teammates holler "pick" and slammed right into the offensive player." It wasn't surprising that I didn't hear the warning as I could not wear my hearing aids while playing because sweat destroys them. As a freshman in college, I was learning how to deal with my own progressive hearing loss, that I had no clue how the deafness was affecting my basketball skills. This excuse did not fly with Pat. "Becky, you know you will not be able to hear your teammates holler

"pick" or "screen." You must see the pick coming," Pat demanded as she moved me out of position and proceeded to model what I must do as a defensive player. She quickly switched to visual coaching, never letting up in her quest to achieve what seemed to me the impossible task of "seeing" what everyone else was hearing. As she assumed a defensive stance in denying the ball to her offensive player and stepping around the pick set by another player, she continued to teach and coach with such passion. "Becky, let yourself see the whole court. Use your peripheral vision, be aware of movement around and behind you as well as what you see in front of you. The key, Becky, is to ANTICIPATE. You've got to anticipate that pick and get around it. You are the only one on this team that is not allowed to 'switch' on defense because you cannot hear your teammates warn you. You've got to see it! Again, Becky, ANTICIPATE. ANTICIPATE the action, ANTICIPATE the movement and be ready! Ok, now let's try it again."

Coach Summitt taught me a valuable lesson during that practice session twenty-six years ago. I learned to anticipate, to sharpen my mind, and increase my awareness. I've developed a deeply analytical mind, which has served me well in all phases of my life. Although I am now deaf, I still hear Coach Summitt's voice urging me on to greater heights with one simple word, "ANTICIPATE".

Becky Clark, Guard 1979–1980
Lady Vols Basketball Team

Eds. note: In March 2005, Pat Summitt became the "winningest coach" in NCAA history when the Lady Vols' victory brought Coach Summitt's record to 880 NCAA wins.

level programs, the definition and interpretation of "gender equity," "proportionality," the reduction in the number of female college coaches and administrators, and the cost associated with the addition of women's programs continue at NCAA conferences and appear in popular press.

Controversies

NCAA Division I-A intercollegiate athletic programs have become a multimillion-dollar, market-driven allocation of power: revenue versus nonrevenue. The desire to win at all costs permeates all levels of college athletic endeavors. Discrepancies in funding available to revenue and nonrevenue sports, male and female coaches, and access to high pay-off college football bowl and NCAA basketball tournament games still exists. Thus, a system of inequity exists in college sports.

The NCAA marked its seventy-fifth anniversary in 1981. A review of the organization's history finds most of the rule changes and recommendations were aimed at restricting student-athletes' rights and providing parity across NCAA member institutions. Today, issues such as the following threaten to undermine the fabric and existence of college sports:

- Mis-education of college athletes
- Sport gambling
- The use of performance enhancement drugs
- Realignment of conference teams
- Increased participation rates by female student athletes and Title IX
- Apparent discrimination in hiring practices
- Low graduation rates of African-American student-athletes in certain sports
- Rising costs to fund the athletic programs

Once again, there is public demand for college sport reform and better oversight. A national public-opinion poll taken in May 2003 of the perceived status of higher education in America showed that Americans were concerned about affirmative action, tenure, and "big-time" athletics. Sixty-seven percent said colleges place too much emphasis on athletics.

Collegiate "athletes in overly commercialized, professionalized college sports programs have trouble reconciling the roles associated with their dual status of athlete and student" (Eitzen and Sage 2003, 122), and college faculty continue to voice concerns about the student-athlete's experience, college sports and its affect on the institution's educational mission. Mark B. Ellis, a professor at Ohio State's Mansfield Campus, said, "A successful program can be a source of pride for lots of folk, but the sheer magnitude of this athletic enterprise, and maybe any big-time athletic enterprise, always will present concerns for faculty" (Suggs 2002, A33). If intercollegiate sports hold promise and hope in the future, they must forthrightly focus on student-athletes' rights and positive educational experiences.

Dana D. Brooks and Ronald C. Althouse

See also Intercollegiate Athletics; World University Games

Further Reading

Acosta, V. R., & Carpenter, L. J. (1985). Women in sport and higher education. In D. Chu, J. Seagrave, & B. Becker (Eds.), *Sport and higher education* (pp. 313–334). Champaign, IL: Human Kinetics.

Acosta, V. R., & Carpenter, L. J. (2004). *Women in intercollegiate sport: a longitudinal, national study twenty-seven year update 1977–2004.* Smith College's Project, Brooklyn College of the City of New York.

AIAW Handbook. (1981–1982). Washington, DC: Association for Intercollegiate Athletics for Women.

Brooks, D., & Althouse, R., Eds. (2000). *Racism in college athletics: The African American athlete's experience.* Morgantown, WV: Fitness Information Technology.

Brown, G. T. (1999, November 22). The "Sanity Code" leads association down path to enforcement program. *The NCAA News,* A1, A4.

Byers, W. (1995). *Unsportsmanlike conduct: Exploiting college athletes.* Ann Arbor: University of Michigan Press.

Chu, D. (1982). The American conception of higher education and the formal incorporation of intercollegiate sport. *Quest, 34*(1), 53–71.

Davis, T. (2000). Race, law, and college athletics. In D. Brooks & R. Althouse (Eds.), *Racism in college athletics: The African American athlete's experience* (pp. 245–265). Morgantown, WV: Fitness Information Technology.

Davis, T. (1995). *A model of institutional governance for intercollegiate athletics.* Wisconsin Law Review, 1995), 559–645.

Davis, T. (1994). *Intercollegiate athletics: competing models and conflicting policies.* Rutgers Law Review, *25*(2), 270–327.

Durso, J. (1975). *Sports factory: An investigation into college sports.* New York: *New York Times Sports Department.*

Eitzen, D. S., & Sage, G. H. (2003). *Sociology of North American sport* (7th ed.). New York: McGraw-Hill.

Falla, J. (1981). *NCAA: The voice of college sports: A diamond anniversary history 1906-1981*. Mission, KA: National Collegiate Athletic Association.

Gerber, E. (1975). The controlled development of collegiate sport for women, 1923–1936. *Journal of Sports History, 2*(1), 1–28.

Gorn, E., & Goldstein, W. (1993). *A brief history of American sports*. New York: Hill and Wang.

Hart-Nibbrig, N. (1979). Corporate athletics: an inquiry into the political economy of college sports. In A. Yiannakis, T. McIntyre, M. Melnick, & D. Hart (Eds.), *Sport sociology: Contemporary themes* (3rd ed., pp. 156–161). Dubuque, IA: Kendall/Hunt.

Hart-Nibbrig, N. & Cottingham, C. (1986). *The political economy of college sports*. Lexington, MA: Lexington Books.

Keeping faith with the student-athlete: A new model for intercollegiate athletics. Report of the Knight Foundation Commission on Intercollegiate Athletics, (1991, March), Charlotte, NC.

More hurdles to clear: Women and girls in competitive athletics. (1980, July). Washington, DC: United States Commission on Civil Rights.

NCAA history: A chronology. (1981, March 31). *National Collegiate Athletic Association News*, 9–16. Retrieved January 7, 2005, from http://web1.ncaa.org/web_video/NCAANewsArchive/1981/1981 0331.pdf

Rader, B. G. (1999). *American sports from the age of folk games to the age of televised sports*. Upper Saddle River, NJ: Prentice Hall.

Sack, A. L. (1991). The underground economy of college football. *Sociology of Sport Journal, 8*, 1–15.

Selingo, J. (2003, May 2). What Americans think about higher education. *Chronicle of Higher Education, 49*(34), A10.

Shulman, J. L., & Bowen, W. G. (2001). *College sports and educational values: The game of life*. Princeton, NJ: Princeton University Press.

Sperber, M. (1990). *College Sports, Inc.: The athletic department vs. the University*. New York: Henry Holt.

Sperber, M. (1998). *Onward to victory: The crisis that shaped college sports*. New York: Henry Holt.

Suggs, W. (2000, June 16). A decade later, sports-reform panel plans another look at by-time athletics. *Chronicle of Higher Education*, A45–A46.

Suggs, W. (2002, November 29). How gears turn at a sports factory. *Chronicle of Higher Education*, A32–A37.

Witham, D. (1995, October 13). Many lament the NCAA ban on athletic dorms. *Chronicle of Higher Education*.

Commercialization of College Sports

Many people might say that commercialization has ruined sports. U.S. sports fans are, for the most part, nostalgic about the institution of sports as a way to enjoy leisure with one's family, to relax, to teach skills (most frequently people cite the development of leadership and team-building skills) that will allow athletes to find success after they leave the field of play, whether their career ends with Little League, high school, college, or even professional sports.

Sports sociology research often finds a sporting tradition at a high school that produces tennis champions or star quarterbacks or pitchers on an annual basis. For example, during the late 1970s the baseball program of Los Angeles' Crenshaw High School placed virtually every member of the roster in the minor or major leagues, including the former Mets and Dodgers superstar Darryl Strawberry. We rarely see an analysis wherein sports are used as the organizing principle to obtain goals that have little to do with running, throwing, jumping, and/or "social capital" obtained from parents. Frank Parkin, a sociologist, had this to say about this issue:

> What is especially remarkable about [sports] . . . is how relatively few of the children of successful footballers, boxers, baseball and tennis stars, or the celebrities of stage and screen have succeeded in reproducing their parents' elevated status. One reason for this would seem to be that the skills called for in these pursuits are of a kind that must be acquired and cultivated by the individual in the actual course of performance, and which are thus not easily transferred from parent to child. (1998, 130–131)

Sports force people to learn "sports skills" and how to sell those skills to the highest bidder—or, as economists like to say, whatever the market will bear. This situation brings about commercialization.

Deeply implicated in the commercialization of sports is what we can call the "athletic arms race." We see the athletic arms race in intercollegiate sports and, with free agency, in professional sports. Because of it, athletes and the sports they play come in second to ill attention to academic studies, contract disputes, unruly behavior, and movement from one team to another.

All of the aforementioned problems began in 1984 when the Supreme Court of the United States ruled that playing the sport of college football is an ordinary

Can't anything be done about calling these guys student athletes? That's like referring to Atilla the Hun's cavalry as weekend warriors. ■ RUSSELL BAKER

part of college business and that hence the National Collegiate Athletic Association (NCAA) has no right to force its members to abide by a central plan to broadcast football games.

Sports are an institution in U.S. society—and becoming one of the most important institutions—mirroring all that is important in our society, especially the importance of money. Although money is not the only measure of importance, it says a lot about what a society considers important.

"Show Me the Money," Professional Style

In July 2004 the most recent National Basketball Association draft took place. The outcome was astonishing. During the first round high school players were chosen over the more accomplished college and international players. Dwight Howard of Southwest Atlanta Christian Academy was chosen over everyone else, including the University of Connecticut's Emeka Okafor, perhaps the most dominant college player in the United States in 2003. Howard sported his Orlando Magic cap, his braces glistening in the spotlight, as he shook hands with NBA Commissioner David Stern.

Howard, and many others drafted, will earn $1.8 million for the first three or so years as a pro. Howard became the third high school player taken first overall in the National Basketball Association draft, touching off a record haul of eight prep players in the first nineteen selections for 2004.

Portland, with the thirteenth draft choice, selected Brooklyn prep star Sebastian Telfair, a cousin of NBA standout Stephon Marbury. Telfair, an eighteen-year-old, already has a lucrative shoe endorsement contract (he was on the cover of *Sports Illustrated* while still in high school) reportedly worth $12 million over six years. This sum of money is particularly potent when one realizes that Sebastian Telfair's high school coach, for whom Telfair played for only a month or two before the draft, makes a fraction of what Telfair will make going into his first NBA season.

"Show Me the Money," College Style

Just as salaries for professional athletes have skyrocketed (during the 1950s professional athletes earned *less than the median income* for men), money has become central to the administration of intercollegiate athletics as well. Athletic directors make salaries on par with university presidents, and coaches in the high-profile sports of football and men's basketball make five, ten, even twenty times more than the average college professor on the same campus. College athletic budgets are exorbitant and stretch into all aspects of sports: coaching salaries, stadiums, and recruiting.

Consistent with the search for student-athletes globally is the need for athletic programs to adopt a corporate model to upgrade facilities such as locker rooms and stadiums. This need is essential for two reasons: (1) to competitively recruit sophisticated student-athletes who are well aware of their needs for special amenities to which the college must respond and (2) to expand and retain a fan base that has become accustomed to luxury accommodations. These dual needs fuel the increasingly competitive athletic arms race.

Locker Rooms and Stadiums

Every male who has played sports, from Little League baseball to high school sports to intercollegiate sports, knows that locker rooms traditionally have been dirty and funky. However, those days are past, at least for high-profile athletic programs. A central part of the athletic arms race during the new millennium and especially at the Division 1A level is upgraded locker rooms and megastadiums.

In the autumn of 2003 the University of Oregon, at the expense of $26,667 per locker ($3.2 million total), acquired the best locker-room facility in the United States, better than those of most professional football and basketball teams. Inside this mammoth structure the doors open and shut at a rate of 1 meter per second and can accommodate eight players entering at once. The Ducks have 152-centimeter plasma TVs (at a cost of $15,000 each) that are outfitted for Xbox game systems. The locker room is a two-story structure, and each locker is equipped with its own ventilation system to "personalize" perspiration. Each locker has outlets for both video games and the Internet as well as a security system that is activated by a code that includes a player's uniform number and a scan of his thumbprint. Other schools in the PAC 10 and nationally have followed suit. Several, including Oregon, have also built new indoor practice facilities.

The athletic arms race also includes the expansion or construction of stadiums. Many Division 1A colleges have built new stadiums. For example, Folsom Field Stadium at the University of Colorado at Boulder has twenty-eight private boxes and nineteen hundred club seats and was built at a cost of $42 million. While the University of Colorado is investing in the new stadium, faculty in the Colorado system are fighting to keep the legislature from closing several institutions in the system. The University of Colorado also has spent the last year engaged in a series of lawsuits that charges Buffalo football players and coaches with a variety of uncivil behaviors.

Coaches' Salaries and Perks

Also part of the athletic arms race are the buying, selling, and trading of coaches. Before Steve Spurrier left Florida, the United States had two $1 million coaches. Coaches are expensive. They must have not only million-dollar salaries, but also full access to facilities during the summer to host their camps and contracts that have "appendages," such as a certain number of game tickets, airline tickets for travel, and product endorsements that monetarily are not tied to annual salaries. Before Matt Doherty was fired from the University of North Carolina at Chapel Hill he had a base salary of $150,000 but had a "shoe deal" with Nike worth $500,000.

Today approximately twenty-three U.S. coaches are paid more than a million dollars a year, many of them at programs that will never make the bowl championship series or break into the top twenty-five ranking.

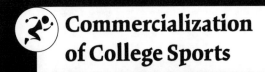

Commercialization of College Sports

Hunter S. Thompson on Commercialization in Sports

There is a progression of understanding vis-à-vis pro football that varies drastically with the factor of distance—physical, emotional, intellectual and every other way. Which is exactly the way it should be, in the eyes of the amazingly small number of people who own and control the game, because it is this finely managed distance factor that accounts for the high-profit mystique that blew the sacred institution of baseball off its "national pastime" pedestal in less than fifteen years.

Source: Hunter S. Thompson (1939–2005), American journalist.

Student-Athlete Perks

Another example of the athletic arms race was the promotion of University of Oregon quarterback Joey Harrington. The University of Oregon in Eugene, a public institution, under the direction of athletic director Bill Moos made headlines a few years back when it advertised, on the Times Square billboard in New York City, its Heisman Trophy quarterback candidate, Joey Harrington, at a cost of $250,000 for three months.

As frivolous as the Joey Harrington promotion was, perks for student-athletes are serious business. Such perks are institutionalized in the academic support services that are burgeoning on college campuses. Academic support services are a part of an athletic department's infrastructure designed to address the growing problem of the academic weakness—what Professor Cantor (1996) calls "underperformance"—of many incoming student-athletes. For example, at the University of Missouri in 1998 the Shelden Resource Center opened in a 900-square-meter facility with a budget of $130,000 for tutors and $500,000 for operating costs. It has seven full-time employees and thirty-six computers. At the University of Illinois seventy tutors, sixty computers, and ten full-time employees are housed in the 743-square-meter Irwin Academic Center. The athletic arms race is about expanding capitalism. The enterprise is used to attract student-athletes and fans to both athletic contests and the academic institution itself.

Faculty members at a number of major sports colleges have begun to question two elements of the athletic arms race. One element is the slip of paper that is brought to professors informing them that certain students are excused a certain number of classes, thus leaving the professors without control of their classrooms but knowing that every student in the classroom does not have this privilege. The second element is the number of athletic events that takes place during the school day. Not only has the number of such events increased, but also for a sport such as basketball, a team may play every day or night of the week. When combined with travel, this schedule results in even more missed classes. Many of these problems occur in high-profile sports, but they are not confined to Division 1A and exist even in the so-called lower-profile sports programs at liberal arts colleges. Student-athletes play sports such as golf and tennis nearly year around in schedules that include tournaments that may take student-athletes away from campus for a week at a time.

Athletic contests "on the road" also cost colleges financially. The costs of airline tickets, hotel rooms, and food for coaches and student-athletes can be a major portion of any athletic department budget. Moreover, many college football programs have adopted the practice of housing teams off campus in hotels on the night before home games. The cost of housing football teams off campus for home games can range from $6,000 per night to $50,000 for the home game season.

Finally, the athletic arms race can be viewed from another angle. Two colleges, Wisconsin and Michigan State, which are a few hours apart by bus, in 1992 traveled to Tokyo to play a regular season football game, forcing the colleges to delay final examinations. The NCAA, in connection with its TV deals (such as the $6 billion March Madness deal with CBS), is interested in increasing its fan base and TV market.

This globalization of sports follows the model of corporate expansion, thus taking control of intercollegiate athletics away from the colleges and placing that control in the hands of marketing and advertising executives who do not have a penchant for higher education but rather are interested only in profits.

Recruiting Practices

Perks for student-athletes begin long before they sign a letter of commitment and accept an athletic scholarship. Recruiting is also a central part of the athletic arms race and involves a large package of inducements.

Here is a description of seventeen-year-old high school recruit Willie Williams:

> Willie Williams tells us that after flying to Tallahassee in a private jet, he was taken to the best restaurant in the city by a Florida State University coach. After ordering a lobster tail at $49.95 and a steak at market value, he then saw that there was no restraint by others at the table. He called the waiter back and made his order four lobster-tails, two steaks, and a shrimp scampi. There were a dozen other recruits at the table.
>
> In Miami at the Mayfair House Hotel Willie's room, the Paradise Suite, featured a Jacuzzi on the balcony. He said he felt that he was living like King Tut and concluded that he would major in business so this lifestyle would continue. (Navarro 2004)

A central tool in the recruitment process is sex—everything from titillation to intercourse. Many colleges have begun to follow a practice—started by the legendary Alabama coach Paul "Bear" Bryant—of using co-eds to lure male student-athletes to their campuses. "Hostess squads" have nice names such as "Garnet & Gold Girls," "Lady Bells," and "Tiger Paws." Recently *Sports Illustrated* published an article on the widespread use of "hostess girls" to recruit male student-athletes that captured the essence of many hostess squads: "honeys for the boys."

The essence of the athletic arms race is that colleges must expand to remain competitive. That is, they must seek better ways of recruiting blue chip athletes, they must develop better relationships with fans and boosters, many of whom must be financially able, and they must provide facilities that lure both student-athletes and fans. The expenditures are not voluntary; they are a must to compete in big-time sports.

Although people most often think of the impact of athletic programs on the functioning of Division 1A colleges, as Bowen and Levin point out, because of the small student bodies at Ivy League schools and liberal arts colleges, which often field more intercollegiate teams than do Division 1A schools, the ratio of student-athletes is disproportionately greater, thus increasing the impact of their presence with each incoming class.

Athletics and athletic programs have a far greater impact on the composition of the incoming class (and perhaps the campus ethos) at an Ivy League university or a small liberal arts college than at most Division 1A colleges.

The Future

We often read news stories about law-breaking behavior at every level of intercollegiate sports. Coaches are fired for having sex with co-eds and strippers, student-athletes are arrested for everything from driving under the influence to rape, domestic violence, and murder, and even athletic directors and college presidents have begun to be arrested for such behavior: They, too, are now being scrutinized. The instances mentioned here are not random but rather are a result, either directly or indirectly, of the commercialization in all sports, professional and commercial.

Earl Smith and Angela J. Hattery

See also Amateur vs. Professional Debate

Further Reading

Finder, C. The big picture: Commercialism is here to stay in sports world. (2004, May 13). *Pittsburgh Post-Gazette.*
Navarro, M. (2004). Willie Williams' recruiting journey: On trip, FSU has Williams' number. *The Miami Herald.* Retrieved January 13, 2004 from http://www.miami.com/mld/miamiherald/sports/7857 927.htm.
Parkin, F. (1998). Marxism and class theory: A bourgeois critique. In R. Levine (Ed.), *Social class and stratification: Classis statements theoretical debates* (pp. 119–140). New York: Rowman and Littlefield.
Smith, E. (2005). *Race, sport and the American dream.* Boulder, CO: Lynne Rienner Publishers

Commodification and Commercialization

*S*ports are a prime example of an activity that has, at its higher levels, become a highly commercialized commodity. Commodification is the process by which a product or activity that once existed for utility or pleasure becomes something used to make money, to buy or sell, through promotion or utilization. Commercialization is the application of business practices where they were not formerly applied.

Sports have served as a form of public entertainment in many societies throughout history, but the commercialization of sports is more pervasive today than ever before. The prospect of making money has become both a motivation for sport organizers and a promise for athletes. The high monetary stakes associated with sports tend to drive interest and assist in building an audience. Today, money from television broadcast partners often dictates everything from team schedules to the scheduling of time-outs during a competition. Accomplished athletes have become millionaires through their sport earnings and endorsements. In essence, sport, as we know it today, has become corporate sport. It has been said that high-profile sport events could not exist without the support of corporate sponsorship.

Unquestionably, commodification and commercialization have changed sport in recent decades. Athletes can become a part of this phenomenon in two different ways. As professionals, paid to compete, they in essence become commodities. Their likenesses or images are sold to promote products. As amateur sports participants and spectators, they increase the market for sport-related products and advertising. The commercial success

An athlete cannot run with money in his pockets. He must run with hope in his heart and dreams in his head. ■ EMIL ZATOPEK

of sports has relied on the ability to generate revenue. Common sources of revenue include gate receipts, sale of broadcast rights, sale of licensed merchandise, and corporate sponsorship support. Successful commercialization occurs most often in or near large cities with many potential spectators who will spend money attending events and buying related products. People in urban areas must have the time, discretionary income, and means to travel to competitions. Commercialization of sport is the product of both urbanization and increasing marketing sophistication.

Commercial Success Factors

Commercial sport requires strong spectator interest. Communities often dictate the success of sport products and events. Spectator interest has appeared to be highest in places where the people value achievement, where a widespread system of youth sports programs exist, and where there is general access to newspapers, radio, and television. Spectator interest has increased worldwide, a phenomenon that has included women as well as men in many industrialized countries. One trend worth noting is that as more women have entered occupations with a strong emphasis on advancement and upward mobility, they have become more interested in following sports and attending games. Often spectators see sport as a model of the way they would like the world to operate. As they watch a sport event, they can see that hard work and the pursuit of excellence still lead to success and prosperity.

In addition to strong spectator interest, five key components have been found to exist where sports have received the most large-scale commercial success.

1. Commercialization of sport succeeds most often in market economies where material rewards are highly valued.
2. Societies with large, densely populated cities provide the needed concentration of potential spectators that translate to ticket buyers.
3. Consumers with access to means such as transportation, discretionary time and income, and media

outlets are those typically living in societies with higher standards of living and are a key component.
4. Large amounts of capital must be available to invest in the building and maintaining of sports arenas and stadiums.
5. Societies with high rates of consumption that emphasize material status symbols, such as clothing with specific team names and colors or brands that contribute to the person's identity, commonly are found where highly commercialized sport is successful.

This explains the success of multiple sports leagues and high-profile events in the United States. No other country has hosted separate winter and summer Olympic games within a six-year span of time. Few countries could finance the building of the needed facilities, provide the transportation and media, and guarantee the requisite spectator support.

Commodification of World Sport

Two primary factors have contributed to the globalization of commercialized sport:

■ Those who control sports work with those who promote and sponsor sports to find new ways of expanding markets. The return on investment dictates that new means for maximizing revenue are driving the latest initiatives.

■ Many corporations today are transnational in reach. With production and distribution in multiple countries, means are needed to introduce new products or expand services around the world. Sport becomes the vehicle for achieving this goal because of its ability to go beyond language and cultural barriers that may be more difficult to overcome with traditional marketing approaches.

Take the example of the Olympic games. The 1984 Los Angeles Olympic Organizing Committee (LAOOC) understood the potential that reaching a global audience would have to corporate sponsors. Instead of allowing 628 sponsors to attach themselves to the games, as was done in the 1976 Olympics, the 1984 games had only 32 sponsors that each paid between $4 million and $13 million in cash, goods, and services to be affiliated with this one-of-a-kind global sporting event. The result for the LAOOC was a net profit of $222 million, which had never been done before. The success of the 1984 games spurred corporate interest and increased both the cost as well as the potential for success. Companies such as Coca Cola, IBM, Visa, and Xerox have expanded into new markets, improved revenue, and maximized their transnational reach via the Olympic platform.

Sport organizations with a global interest logically would align sponsors with similar aspirations. Fédération Internationale de Football Association (FIFA), the organization responsible for both men's and women's World Cup soccer events, has benefited directly as a sports organization because of the commercial value associated with its global events and subsequent reach. FIFA events are held throughout world, as teams qualify for the World Cup. Cities throughout the world interested in hosting the World Cup of soccer compete for the privilege. Affiliated with hosting are numerous opportunities to gain investment from corporate interests, both locally and globally. Yet, sport properties that are more national have increasingly found ways to invest in expanding their reach; for example, the National Football League (NFL) has expanded beyond North American borders to manage teams and a league in Europe. The NFL Europe has had mixed results, yet, if the product of American football can be developed in European countries, the potential for corporate and media interests can similarly be developed.

Trends in Commercial Sport Development

The global sponsorship market has grown from $17.6 billion in 1997 to $37.8 billion during the summer Olympic year of 2004. By 2005, projections for the global sponsorship market amounted to $42 billion, in a non-Olympic, non-World Cup year. In addition, sport has been attributed to significant amounts of economic

impact for cities that host major events. In the United States, the 2002 Indianapolis 500 topped the chart with a reported impact of $336 million. The next highest figure was the $305 million reported for the Super Bowl in New Orleans. Even amateur sporting events can provide economic impact to host cities. The 2001 ESPN Summer X Games reportedly provided between $45 million and $50 million for the city of Philadelphia. Action sports are new to the landscape of commercialized sport, yet ESPN has illustrated the power in commodification with yet another genre. Women's sport also contributes to host cities. The 2002 National Collegiate Athletic Association (NCAA) Women's Final Four basketball championship was reported to have generated between $26 million and $32 million for host city San Antonio. The single best economic impact from an amateur event remains the NCAA men's Final Four basketball championship. In 2002, Atlanta benefited from a $75 million impact, and New Orleans reported a similar figure for 2003. Each of these examples illustrates the five components of commercialization, as well as the economic benefit sought by all parties involved. Sport is big business in the United States and around world.

Television Coverage of Sports

In 1980, NBC paid $87 million in television rights fees for the Olympic games in Moscow that were then boycotted by the United States. In 1984, however, the LAOOC was able to secure $225 million from ABC for domestic TV rights. The Los Angeles organizing committee was the last host-city organizing committee to retain the rights to sell all the sponsorship categories and negotiate the domestic television deal. The deal included a $75 million rebate in case the athlete pool was weakened by political boycott and if the telecasts failed to achieve agreed-upon ratings. The result was a prime-time rating of 23.2 (about 17.4 million households in 1984), which surpassed expectations. This unprecedented success paved the way for future television rights deals that now are represented by staggering figures.

In 2004, the NFL led all sports leagues in television rights deals. With a total rights fee of $17.6 billion paid for the contract period of 1998 to 2005, the average annual value for the league was reported to be $2.2 billion. ABC, Fox, CBS, and ESPN all contribute to these astonishing figures. The NFL also delivers some of the highest ratings in sports, which translates to value for the rights-fee holders. NBC has secured television rights for world-class events such as the Olympics and Wimbledon. The four-year deal to secure Wimbledon through 2006 amounted to $52 million. Television networks will, however, only purchase such rights if they have strong indications that they can receive a significant return on their investment. Thus, commercialization of sport has created a new field broadly accepted as sport marketing.

Commercializing Athletes

The opportunity to earn money as an athlete has transcended the sport for many of today's top celebrity athletes. The most marketable female athletes, such as Serena Williams, Annika Sorenstam, and Mia Hamm have potential to earn more from endorsements than from their sports performances. Michael Jordan, Tiger Woods, and Kobe Bryant were the top three men in 2002. Each of these athletes has earned a following that extends around the globe, which contributes to their high earnings for endorsements. Similarly, the female athletes represent sports that have a strong following beyond U.S. borders and commensurate appeal desired by companies when marketing on a global scale.

The ability that athletes have to cut through television clutter and deliver messages effectively for corporate partners has established them as some of the most effective commodities. For example, Lance Armstrong and his string of Tour de France wins have placed him at the center of a cable channel working to create an audience. The Outdoor Life Network (OLN) orients its programming around the three weeks during which the Tour de France is taking place. With six titles in a row, Armstrong has built a following that is valuable to OLN, as well as to the sponsors of riders, teams, and Armstrong. This world-class event extends company names to countries that may have little other exposure

to such brands. This proven strategy was initiated in 1984 in Los Angeles and continues in ever-evolving, innovative platforms.

Armstrong and the Tour de France also provide perfect examples of the future of sport commercialization. New categories of interest will continuously arise as exemplified by OLN's Tour de France success, while more companies will discover the power of brand building around athletes and sport properties. The past two decades have demonstrated that commodification of sport is limitless as long as creativity and innovation continue to evolve.

Nancy L. Lough

See also Brand Management; Marketing; Ownership; Sponsorship

Further Reading

By the numbers 2003: The authoritative annual research guide and fact book. *Sports Business Journal, 5*(36), 87.
By the numbers 2004: The authoritative annual research guide and fact book. *Sports Business Journal, 6*(36), 36–37, 77.
Coakley, J. (2004). *Sports in society: Issues and controversies.* New York: McGraw-Hill.
Howard, D., & Crompton, J. (2004). *Financing sport.* Morgantown, WV: Fitness Information Technology.
Lough, N. (2000). Financial management of sport. In H. Appenzeller & G. Lewis (Eds.), *Successful sport management* (pp. 71–84). Durham, NC: Carolina Academic Press.
Mullin, B., Hardy, S., & Sutton, W. (2000). *Sport marketing.* Champaign, IL: Human Kinetics.

Commonwealth Games

The Commonwealth Games concept dates back to 1891 when Reverend J. Astley Cooper proposed a gathering of sports and other cultural events for nations with ties to the Commonwealth. No event came from this proposal but twenty years later, in 1911, a celebration call the "Festival of the Empire" was held to commemorate the coronation of King George V. Athletes from Britain, Canada, South Africa, and Austral-

The price of success is hard work, dedication to the job at hand,
and the determination that whether we win or lose, we have applied
the best of ourselves to the task at hand. ■ VINCE LOMBARDI

asia (Australia and New Zealand) competed in a limited schedule of athletics, boxing, swimming, and wrestling in the midst of many other scheduled events.

British Empire Games

The bid for permanent games began in Canada, in 1924, when Canada's Amateur Athletic Union proposed a competition to be called the "British Empire Games." At the 1928 Olympic Games, Melville Marks Robinson, a reporter for a Hamilton newspaper who served at the Games as a manager for the Canadian track and field team, worked to promote the idea.

In 1928 and 1929 the Canadians moved forward with the idea, creating a British Empire Games Committee as part of the Amateur Athletic Union of Canada. Robinson led the Hamilton Games organizing committee, and a separate British Empire Games Association of Hamilton was created to provide opportunities for the public to assist the Games organizing committee with hospitality and with funding the Games.

The Canadians were able to convince eleven other nations to join in the first Games in Hamilton in 1930. Robinson is generally credited as the founder of the British Empire Games, and a high school in the neighboring city of Burlington is named after him.

From Empire to Commonwealth

The name of the Games and other symbols changed over time as the relationships of the nations involved changed from an Empire to a Commonwealth. From 1930 to 1950 the Games were called the British Empire Games, from 1954 to 1966 they were called the British Empire and Commonwealth Games, and from 1970 to 1986, they were called the British Commonwealth Games. Since 1990, the Games have been known as the Commonwealth Games.

The original governing body of the Games, the British Empire Games Federation, was formed during meetings at the 1932 Olympic Games in Los Angeles. That body is now known as the Commonwealth Games Federation.

The Games flag has also changed to reflect modern

sentiments. The Games emblem since 1954 had consisted of a chain surrounding a crown, which to some symbolized the strong links between Commonwealth nations. Others came to see the links as symbolizing colonial bonds that needed to be tossed off. The emblem was changed to a torch symbol in 2001.

History of Commonwealth Games

Since the games began in 1930, they have often been surrounded by controversy due to protests over the apartheid policy of South Africa. The issue of South African participation persisted in the Commonwealth Games (and in international sports) for much of the twentieth century.

1930 TO 1946: POLITICAL PROBLEMS

After the successful 1930 Games in Hamilton, the 1934 Games were scheduled to be held in Johannesburg, South Africa. However, the government policy of apartheid spurred protests and the Games were switched to London.

Sydney, Australia, hosted the 1938 British Empire Games. The February dates were convenient for the hosts, but out of season for the northern hemisphere guests. Australia used this advantage to top the medals table for the first time. Montreal, Canada, was chosen as the 1942 Games host, but the 1942 and 1946 Games were halted because of World War II.

1950 AND 1954: BREAKING RECORDS

When the Games resumed in 1950, Auckland, New Zealand, served as the host. Auckland chose the option of a grass track, conventional in New Zealand, but rare in other parts of the world. Skeptics were silenced when nine Empire Games records were broken, though it had been nearly twelve years since the last Games. England's Jack Holden ran the last seven miles of the marathon in his bare feet, after rain had ruined his shoes, and still won by more than four minutes.

The 1954 Games in Vancouver, Canada, became famous for the duel between Roger Bannister of England and John Landy of Australia over the mile distance.

Both men had broken the four-minute-mile barrier earlier that year—Bannister first, and the first ever to do so, and then Landy took the world record from him six weeks later. In Vancouver, Bannister bested Landy in the first race, with the two men running under four minutes in the mile.

1958: CARDIFF, WALES

The 1958 Games in Cardiff saw the introduction of the Queen's baton and relay, in which a baton was carried from Buckingham Palace, around the perimeter of Wales, to Cardiff. The Queen began the relay by inserting her message inside the baton at Buckingham Palace, and then the message was removed and read as part of the Commonwealth Games opening ceremonies. Since then, the relay has grown even more lengthy and complex.

Demonstrations against the South African team, which had no black members, took place in both Cardiff and London. South Africa withdrew from the Commonwealth in 1961, preempting its probable expulsion, and it did not return to the Commonwealth Games until 1994.

1962: PERTH, AUSTRALIA

The Games were again hosted by Australia in 1962, with Perth as host. In Perth a proposal was made to hold future Commonwealth Games during the Olympic year, a few weeks before the Olympics, in a Commonwealth city close to where the Olympics were to be held. The goal was to reduce travel costs, but the proposal was not approved. For the Games village, the government of Western Australia held a competition and built 150 homes from the winning design. The homes were sold at public auction after the Games.

1966: KINGSTON, JAMAICA

The first Games to be held outside of Canada, Great Britain, Australia, and New Zealand were the 1966 Games in Kingston. Jamaica, newly independent from Great Britain in 1962, proved doubters wrong who said that it was too small to host the Games. Jamaica could not provide television broadcasting facilities so the visiting broadcasters brought their own equipment and technicians. But Jamaica's new swimming pool was state of the art and one of the fastest in the world, and it saw fifteen new world records.

At the Edinburgh, Scotland, Games four years later, metric measurements were used for the first time, bringing the Games in line with international standards.

1974: CHRISTCHURCH, NEW ZEALAND

At the 1974 Games in Christchurch, New Zealand, security was strict in direct response to the terrorist attacks which occurred at the 1972 Munich Olympic Games. Christchurch made up for the added tension with its hospitality, even providing equipment and bicycles for Uganda's cycling team, who showed up empty-handed at the Games. Tanzania's Filbert Bayi bested New Zealand's John Walker in the 1,500-meter event, but both broke the 1,500-meter world record. Bayi won in 3:32.2, with Walker second in 3:32.5. Kenya's Ben Jipcho finished third in 3:33.2, adding a bronze to his gold medals in the steeplechase and 5,000-meter event.

1978: EDMONTON, CANADA

Edmonton, Canada, hosted the 1978 Games. It built a Commonwealth stadium for 20 million dollars, which it considered a bargain after the financial debacle of the Montreal Olympic Games. Stung by the African boycott of the 1976 Olympic Games, Canada worked extremely hard to prevent another full-scale boycott. In June of 1977, Commonwealth representatives met in Gleneagles, Scotland, and devised an agreement formally known as the Commonwealth Statement on Apartheid in Sport. The primary function of the agreement was to stop all sporting contacts with South Africa by other Commonwealth nations.

The Organization for African Unity (OAU) quickly gave its approval, but the Supreme Council of Sport in Africa (SCSA), led by Nigerian Abraham Ordia, was much harder to convince. In November 1977, the SCSA adopted a resolution endorsing African participation, but a few days before the Games, Nigeria announced that it would boycott them and tried to convince other nations to join the boycott. But Canadian diplomacy

Table 1.

Locations of the Commonwealth Games

Year	City	Country	Dates
1930	Hamilton	Canada	August 16–23
1934	London	England	August 4–11
1938	Sydney	Australia	February 5–12
1950	Auckland	New Zealand	February 4–11
1954	Vancouver	Canada	July 30–August 7
1958	Cardiff	Wales	July 18–26
1962	Perth	Australia	November 21–December 1
1966	Kingston	Jamaica	August 4–13
1970	Edinburgh	Scotland	July 16–25
1974	Christchurch	New Zealand	January 24–February 2
1978	Edmonton	Canada	August 3–12
1982	Brisbane	Australia	September 30–October 9
1986	Edinburgh	Scotland	July 24–August 2
1990	Auckland	New Zealand	January 24–February 3
1994	Victoria	Canada	August 18–28
1998	Kuala Lumpur	Malaysia	September 1–21
2002	Manchester	England	July 25–August 4

won the day and the African athletes participated in Edmonton.

Canada was rewarded by topping the medals table for the first and only time to date in Commonwealth Games history. Kenya's Henry Rono, denied the opportunity to compete in both the Montreal and Moscow Olympic Games due to boycotts, won both the 5,000-meters and the 3,000-meter steeplechase in Edmonton.

1982: BRISBANE, AUSTRALIA

In 1982 Australia hosted the Games and succeeded in avoiding a large-scale African boycott by strongly condemning the 1981 tour of New Zealand by a South African rugby team and reaffirming the Gleneagles agreement. Several protests for aboriginal rights occurred during these Games, and about two hundred people were arrested trying to gain access to the main stadium.

1986: EDINBURGH, SCOTLAND

When the Games returned to Edinburgh in 1986, the question of apartheid in South Africa had still not been resolved. When a New Zealand rugby team embarked on a tour of South Africa, a violation of the Gleneagles agreement, African and Caribbean nations both moved to boycott the Edinburgh Games.

In an effort to try and placate the boycotting nations, distance runner Zola Budd and swimmer Annette Crowley, both South Africans intending to compete for Britain, were excluded from the Games. But the attempt failed, and thirty-two nations stayed home while twenty-six took part.

1990: AUCKLAND, NEW ZEALAND

In 1990 at the Auckland games, the African nations threatened to boycott yet again in protest of another British rugby and cricket tour to South Africa. Anver Versi, of the news magazine *New African* had made strong arguments against a boycott, noting that African victories in the world sport arena was far more important to advancing the status of Africans than "all the speechifying and politicking that goes on every day." In the end, African nations went to Auckland and were successful. These Games saw the first drug scandals, when one Indian and two Welsh weight lifters tested positive.

1994: VICTORIA, CANADA

South Africa returned to the Commonwealth Games in 1994 in Victoria, Canada, after the apartheid government had been removed and the South Africans were able to send multiracial international sports teams.

Hezekiah Sepeng became the first black South African to win a medal in the Commonwealth Games by taking the 800-meter silver. (In the Atlanta Olympic Games in the United States, Sepeng would win another silver medal and become the first black South African to win an Olympic medal.) Horace Dove-Edwin from the small African nation of Sierra Leone also ran extremely well, finishing just behind Linford Christie of England in the final. However, Dove-Edwin then failed his post-race drug test for the same drug Ben Johnson had been found using in Seoul, South Korea.

Disabled athletes were included in the Victoria Games with events in swimming, athletics, and lawn bowls. Separate Commonwealth Paraplegic Games had been held from 1962 until 1974.

1998: Kuala Lumpur, Malaysia

In 1998 the Commonwealth Games were held for the first time outside an English-speaking country. However, in Kuala Lumpur a weak economy created budget difficulties, there was a water shortage, and smoke from forest fires that raged out of control in neighboring Indonesia. This led several countries to threaten to move or cancel their participation, but Malaysia held firm, and the Queen's baton was carried to the stadium on an elephant. It was presented to Prince Edward by Malaysia's first-ever Commonwealth-medal winner, Koh Eng Tong, who had won a bronze medal in weight lifting in the 1954 Games. The Malaysian spectators gave the delegation from Singapore a cool welcome because of political difficulties, and Nigeria did not compete because the nation had been suspended from the Commonwealth council.

The Commonwealth Games Federation took a new direction by adding team sports to the Games: Cricket, rugby, netball, and men's and women's field hockey were added to the upcoming schedule. Team sports had previously been excluded from the Games to emphasize the idea that the Games were between individuals and not nations. A proposal to award prize money at the Games was discussed by the Commonwealth Games Federation, but rejected.

Forty-year-old Judy Oakes of England won the shot put gold medal, becoming the oldest woman to win a gold medal at the Games. This continued her amazing streak of medal-winning: In six straight Games, Oakes won the bronze medal in 1978, the gold medal in 1982, silver medals in 1986 and 1990, and the gold medal in 1994. Kenyan runners dominated the distance events to no one's surprise, taking gold, silver, and bronze medals in both the steeplechase and the 5,000-meter event, and winning the 800-, 1,500- and 10,000-meter runs.

2002: Manchester, England

Manchester, England, hosted well-run Games in 2002, but not without controversy. Several medals changed hands during and after the Games due to drug suspensions, and there were disputes over officiating in boxing, field hockey, swimming, and table tennis. Athletes from Pakistan, Bangladesh, Nigeria, Kenya, and Sierra Leone could not be found at the conclusion of the Games and were thought to have defected. Two female swimmers from Pakistan became the first Pakistani Muslim females to compete outside a Muslim country. They participated in swimming events wearing new high-tech bodysuits, which were less revealing and more in line with Muslim cultural norms. In the end, Manchester was praised for its organization. Organizers hoped that the Games would raise the profile of the London bid for the 2012 Olympic Games.

The Future

Melbourne, Australia, was named host of the 2006 Commonwealth Games after all other bidders dropped out. New Delhi, India, beat Hamilton, Canada, for the right to host the 2010 Commonwealth Games.

Daniel Bell

Further Reading

Bell, D. (2003). Commonwealth Games. *Encyclopedia of International Games* (pp 108–126). Jefferson, NC: McFarland Publishing.
Black, D., Greenhorn, D., & Macintosh, D. (1992). Canadian diplo-

Tennis was given to me not to become a great player and a world champion. Tennis was given to me to keep me off the street corners of East St. Louis. ■ JIMMY CONNORS

macy and the 1978 Edmonton Commonwealth Games. *Journal of Sport History, 19*(1), 26–55.

British Empire Games Association of Hamilton. (1930). *Program and general regulations of the British Empire Games,* Hamilton, Canada.

Dheensaw, C. (1994). *The Commonwealth Games: The first 60 years, 1930–1990.* Victoria, BC: Orca Book Publishers.

Gallagher, D. (2002). Australia at the Commonwealth Games 1911–2002. Double Bay, Australia: Australian Commonwealth Games Association.

Newham, C., Richards, E., & Williams, J. (1958). *VIth British Empire and Commonwealth Games.* Cardiff, Wales: Organizing Committee of the VIth British Empire and Commonwealth Games.

New Zealand Olympic and British Empire Games Association. (1950). The story of the British Empire Games, Auckland, New Zealand.

Phillips, B. (2002). *The Commonwealth Games: The history of all the sports.* Manchester, UK: Parrs Wood Press.

Community

"Community" is one of the most common and multivalent concepts in the social sciences. At one end of the spectrum, community can refer to small, close-knit groups in which individuals have much in common, know each other intimately, and interact regularly. This is the definition made famous by Ferdinand Tonnies in his classic nineteenth-century characterization of *Gemeinschaft* as community under siege by the organization and force of modern societies (*Gesellschaft*). At the other extreme, community can denote extremely large and diverse collectivities of people who share little more than an idea or place of residence as in Benedict Anderson's influential reconceptualization of nationalism as an "imagined community." And conceptions of community vary not only in terms of size and type of interaction but also in terms of what communities are organized around and how organized they are. The community label can be applied, for example, to a neighborhood or a block club, a religious congregation or a social movement, to people who share a lifestyle or ethnic background.

In the popular vernacular—where the language of community also has remarkable currency—these various meanings are often indiscriminately employed and can thus obscure as much as they reveal. But what really stands out about everyday usage is how much moral weight and political baggage the term carries. No matter how defined or applied, "community" is invariably a good thing, a value in and of itself. This idealism actually reflects and reproduces tensions in liberal democratic social theory, where community is not just an abstract analytic category but often serves—as it did for the famous French sociologist Emile Durkheim a century ago and does for communitarian social theorists still today—as moral imperative or some larger, public good.

Community is, in short, a warm and fuzzy concept—"warm" in the sense that the term invokes good feelings and (in)tangible rewards, "fuzzy" in that the concrete empirical object of its affections is often vague and amorphous—and as such one of the more problematic terms in the social sciences to utilize properly much less summarize briefly.

In the field of sport studies, the term community appears in three fairly well-defined contexts. One is as an adjective describing a certain type of sport: namely, community sport or community-based sport. The other primary uses of the term come in the context of more analytical questions about the relationships between sport and various forms of social interaction and collective identification. They can be usefully divided into two main bodies of work—one that focuses on the impact sport has on social life, the other that attends to the ways in which community context and background affect peoples' experiences in sport and the social outcomes of those experiences. Each of these variations on the community concept in sport studies has its own issues, assumptions, and challenges; cutting across all of them, however, are cultural conceptions of sport that can be just as idealized and amorphous as the concept of community itself.

Community-Based Sport

The idea of community sport or community-based sport is the most concrete usage of the term "community" in the field of sport studies. It refers to active, participatory forms of sport organized (more or less) and practiced at

Community

Swimming Builds Character

Learning to swim should be a part of every boy's education. It adds so much to his health, happiness, and safety that it cannot well be neglected. With the building of large numbers of municipal, Y.M.C.A., school, club, and college swimming pools, it is a rare boy who has not opportunity to learn to swim. During the past year or two the Y. M. C. A.'s through many new swimming pools have been teaching thousands of boys to swim. In Boston, seven thousand boys were taught the crawl in only a few weeks' time. By the use of "water-wings" boys who had never swum a stroke learned the crawl in three or four lessons. This stroke is so similar to the "dog paddle" in the ease with which it can be mastered, and so striking in its results that boys pick it up in an amazingly short time. With swimming so easily learned and opening such vistas of sport and recreation, to say nothing of the protection of life, can any boy afford not to know how to swim?

Source: Kiphuth, R. J. H. (1914). Are you a swimmer? In P. Withington (Ed.), *The Book of Athletics* (p. 405). Boston: Lothrop, Lee & Shepard Co.

the local, grassroots level. Just how "local" and formally organized community-based sport is understood to be varies from person to person, from scholar to scholar, and across different social settings and cultural contexts. For some, it may involve simple recreational athletics—pickup basketball games at a local park, exercise classes, or swimming lessons at a recreational center. For others, it connotes more organized youth leagues or club sports sponsored by small businesses, civic organizations, or public parks and recreation programs. What these various forms of community sport all have in common may be best captured by contrasting them with what they are not, what they can be distinguished from: namely, high-performance, elite-entertainment sport.

The distinction between community-based sport and high-performance sport is not just a matter of how serious and skilled the players are, how structured their play is, or how many people pay attention to it. It is also and perhaps more importantly a matter of the purported values and rewards of the two sets of athletic practice. With its emphasis on intensive training, formal coaching, and high-level competition and accomplishment (not to mention spectatorship, marketing, and mass-media coverage), high-performance sport is understood as an end unto itself, with values and rewards intrinsic and self-evident for participants and spectators alike. In contrast, community-based sport typically puts the emphasis on the more intimate and immediate personal pleasures and long-term social rewards of physical activity: health and fitness, recreation and leisure, socializing with family and friends. In view of these commitments, community sport advocates typically stress mass participation and healthy practices, preferring to cultivate and support the participation of as many people in as many activities as possible regardless of athletic skill or ability.

In actual practice there is a good deal of overlap between community sport and high-performance sport. In part this is because community-based athletics often serve as training grounds and feeder systems for more competitive, performance-based sport, arenas for promising young athletes to be discovered, hone their skills, and thus move up the highly competitive, elite-sport ladder. The blurry boundaries between community and elite sport also have to do with the way in which the priorities of high-performance sport creep into community-based forms. Winning becomes more important than participating; formal structure and routinized practice push out the more pleasurable, playful aspects of physical activity; spectatorship and consumption are chosen over active participation. Advocates are so sensitive to these incursions that they often say community-based sport is not just different from high-performance sport but inherently in competition with high-performance sport and deeply threatened by it.

Ice fishing houses on a frozen lake. *Source: istockphoto.com/timeless.*

Low and decreasing rates of participation in healthful physical activity have been documented in recent years and have accentuated fears about the vitality and viability of community-based sport. Of particular concern for scholars and advocates are those social groups typically marginalized or excluded by sport's historic masculine, middle-class biases—women, minorities, the poor, and the disabled. And what critics call "bad practices" are not the only barriers these groups encounter. Equally problematic are the deteriorating facilities and declining levels of fiscal support that have resulted from the ascendance of neoliberal public policies. These cutbacks have been offset in more affluent communities by market-based, pay-to-play leagues, private health clubs, personal trainers, and the like. Elsewhere, community sports have become more dependent upon funding targeted at risk reduction, crime prevention, and public safety—objectives that skirt the traditional ideals of community-based sport and are in addition deeply racialized. Clearly, the future of healthful and equitable community sport depends not only on a recognition of the personal and social value(s) of mass participation, it also requires the infrastructure and funding to turn these ideals into institutional realities.

Sport and Community Building

A second sport-oriented context in which the community concept is present is in discussions about the impact that sport has upon groups and other social collectivities. This use of the term most often appears under the label of "sport and community building" and, more importantly, usually comes with the strong assumption (or even outright assertion) that sport builds, nurtures, and sustains communities. The belief that sport builds community is, at least in Western contexts, extremely broad and pervasive. It applies to virtually all types of sport, levels of sport, and forms of participation, and to the broadest and most elastic possible conceptions of

Basketball can serve as a metaphor for ultimate cooperation. It is a sport where success . . . requires that the dictates of community prevail over selfish impulses. ■ BILL BRADLEY

community. The communities believed to be built by sport can be as small as block clubs or office groups, as large as the whole of humanity itself, and anywhere in between—as exemplified by the language of civic pride, school spirit, and national identity that often appears in accounts of the communal value of sport.

Community building in and through sport can occur in many different ways. Recreational athletic activities can provide an environment and activity that bring individuals from disparate backgrounds and otherwise disconnected contexts into contact with one another. Recreational forms of sport can also provide a venue for people who already know each other from some specific context or social sphere—such as school, church, or work—to get to know each other better and think of themselves in more collective terms. The theory is that in moving people out of the narrow, one-dimensional roles they are accustomed to and into a collective activity stripped of tangible meaning and consequence, individuals will come to trust and understand each other and develop a stronger sense of themselves as a whole group, thus enabling them to work better together toward common ideals and objectives.

These community-building functions can be served through watching and following sports—and cheering for individual teams and players, and even in buying sports-related merchandise and apparel—as well as by playing them. Sometimes the more spectator-oriented interactions are concrete and face-to-face, as when workers in an office or members of a fraternity attend a sporting event together. But much of the community building that occurs in the context of elite-entertainment sport is of a different quality and type, usually more applicable to social entities that are larger and more diffuse. Interscholastic athletics, for example, provide a unique venue for student bodies to come together, and can generate unparalleled positive public attention. In many cities and towns, school sports teams take on even larger meaning and significance. Indeed, American public universities claim that over half of the interactions they have with ordinary citizens come via intercollegiate athletics. That these connections are typically

mediated through mass communications and market-based consumption makes them no less real; quite the contrary, such interactions can be the basis of community itself. It is no accident that sports and nationalism are so closely linked: sports teams or star players or even entire sports (think: hockey in Canada) provide an embodied form and rallying point for the otherwise intangible boundaries and sentiments of the nation. Anthropologist John MacAloon has argued that the popularity of the modern Olympic Games involves their success (in contrast to other global organizations and movements) in creating symbols and rituals that draw the various nations and peoples of the world together.

In each of these cases, the community-building powers of sport derive not only from the way in which sport draws diverse people together but also from its ability to cultivate among these people deep and abiding feelings of solidarity and belonging, unity, collective identity, and common purpose. Here, all of sport's unique cultural qualities—its inherent drama, its immediate physicality and emotion, its ultimate absolute clarity—are almost miraculously transferred to or even merged with the social groups teams or players are said to represent. No better evidence of this mysterious phenomenon may exist than the fact that sports fans the world over speak not of "my team" or "our team" but of "us" and "we." They feel the successes (and failures) of their favorite teams and players as their own.

There is a temptation to ignore the more problematic aspects of its relation to social collectivities. This is dangerous and inaccurate on several counts. In a very basic sense, sport can (and often does) break down community; it can, in D. Stanley Eitzen's terms, "divide as well as unite." This is frequently witnessed when a team has a disappointing performance or suffers an unexpected loss. Finger-pointing can take hold among players and coaches, fans begin to lose interest and disengage from the team and the larger collective entity it is said to represent. It can also happen when friends and acquaintances play against each other or root for opposing teams. And if athletic competition can bring out differences and animosities among people who already know

Community

Stilt Walking Indonesia

Stilt walking as performed by the Toradja people of Indonesia has several community functions as indicated in the following text.

Walking on stilts is also a favorite game among the east Toradja. The stilt (loko) is a bamboo or a strong pole on which a little block of wood, on which the foot rests, is tied with rattan. Or a hole is chopped in the stilt, in which a little piece of wood for the foot is stuck. Sometimes one uses as a stilt a bamboo stalk on which a piece of a branch has been left as a step. The foot is often placed crosswise on the step, such as children are wont to do among us. Most of the time, however, the foot is placed lengthwise on the step, whereby the stilt is clamped between the big and second toe, so that the foot cannot slip off. The stilts are not held down low behind the shoulder, but up on top in front of the shoulder.

All sorts of games are played on stilts: people hold races on stilts; they go to stand beside one another in a circle, in order then to jump around on one stilt and with the other alternately to stamp on the ground and strike the other stilt. During this the hollow bamboo makes a dull sound. In doing this, the montanggoli . . . is sometimes imitated. Or two persons on stilts approach each other and remain standing in front of each other; at the same moment they lift one stilt and balance themselves on the other; whoever can remain standing this way longer is the winner. Boys also try with their stilt to knock that of a companion out from under him, in order to make him fall.

A practical use of stilts is made when people chase birds from the fields with them; when they pick sirih fruits and pinang nuts with them, or when young men come to chat with girls who are sitting on the front veranda of their dwelling, plaiting mats or sewing.

No time is prescribed for walking on stilts, but one sees it done most in the period when the rice is ripening. It is possible that originally people wanted to exert influence on the growth of the crop by walking on stilts. Boys as well as girls walk on stilts, but boys do it much more than girls. For this the latter make use of coconut shells that are also called moloko. The half of the coconut in which the seed hole is found is used for this. Through this hole is pulled a rope, the end of which the girl holds in her hand. She puts each of her feet on the rounded side of a shell, with the rope between her big and second toe. By pulling the rope, the shell is wedged against the foot, and thus she strides along on it.

Source: Adriani, N. & Kruyt, A. C. (1951). *The Bare'e-speaking Toradja of Central Celebes (the East Toradja): Vol 3.* (pp. 606–607). Amsterdam: Noord-Hollandsche Uitgevers Maatschappij.

each other, it isn't difficult to realize that sport's purported community-building properties may fall short of the mark for people who have little in common to begin with. Sport's agonistic, winner-take-all structure doesn't just reproduce the social dynamics of group conflict and competition, it requires them and seems designed to bring out them out.

Given that the competitive qualities of sport are so pervasive and pronounced, the real question may be why the community-building possibilities of sport are so idealized in the first place. The explanation has as much to do with utopian liberal democratic ideals about community as with sport itself. For one, the making of a community is not as simple and straightforward as it first might appear. Bringing people together in a common space or collective enterprise does not automatically or inevitably generate social harmony. Indeed, it can accentuate the differences that distinguish one group of people from another—especially when the activity is competitive and there are tangible rewards to be won and lost.

On a deeper level, almost all communities are posited on social distinctions that marginalize or exclude others. That is, any sense of communal "we-ness"—who we

Athletes pose at the 1998 Amsterdam Gay Games. Gay athletes form a distinct community within the larger sports community. *Source: Agnes Elling.*

ment is a case in point: mostly white, middle-class reformers used sports ranging from Major League Baseball to neighborhood recreation to turn new European immigrants into "good Americans," thus creating one community (the nation) even as they were controlling, containing, and erasing various ethnic and immigrant minority cultures. In fact, a great deal of sport scholarship has been devoted to showing how hierarchies and stereotypes relating to race, class, gender, and sexuality have been perpetuated in and through sport, and how mass sport has been used as a tool for legitimating political power and the social status quo.

It can be difficult to square these scholarly critiques with the popular conception of sport as a positive, community-building social force. But instead of choosing one approach over the other, it may be better to think of sport as a sociocultural practice where people are constantly put together and pulled apart, where communities—in the plural—are made and often simultaneously unmade, where community construction occurs at multiple levels and often includes cross-cutting ties and allegiances that can have social implications far beyond the formal boundaries of sport itself. And what gives sport its unique power as a site for community building is not just its inherent agnostic structure; it has also to do with the paradoxical way in which sport is experienced and understood by so many of its participants and practitioners: as deeply significant, on the one hand, and yet ultimately trivial, playful, and unimportant. This peculiar attitude dictates that the consequential drama of community formation unfolds without the full knowledge and awareness of the players and audiences themselves.

Community as Mediating Social Force

A third and final line of work is focused on the role of communities—however defined and operationalized—in shaping and determining the experience of sport participation and its broader social impacts. In this context, the causal relationships between sport and community are reversed from the sport-as-community-building context. Here, "community" becomes the fac-

are—also implies and requires a sense of otherness—who we are not. And this otherness not only differentiates one group from another but often turns into a struggle for dominance (which of us is better?). Furthermore, most communities are far more multifaceted and internally differentiated than Western thinking usually allows. While these differences can be the source of divisive infighting, the bigger point here is that they can be used by one group to exercise power and authority over others, all in the name of a larger, communal good. One person's sacred "community," to put it succinctly, can be another's source of marginalization, subordination, or oppression.

All too often sport has been directly involved in privileging one set of community interests and claims over others. Some of this is built into the inflexible, one-dimensional structure of agnostic competition. Olympic athletes, for instance, must compete for their countries and cannot represent collective identities based upon race, religion, or gender. But it also results from sport's own exclusionary history and troubled complicity with the forces of power. The 1920s American play move-

tor or force (or independent variable) that impacts the form, quality, intensity, and social consequence of athletic participation.

Although not all of it uses the language of community explicitly, a great deal of research on this topic has been conducted. One of the first findings of sport sociology was that access to sport participation was clearly and predictably influenced by social factors such as class and education, race, and gender. Sport scholars have also found that the best determinants of whether young people will have fun in sports and continue to participate in them are social factors such as peers, parents, and coaches. More recently researchers interested in how sport participation is related to personal quality-of-life indicators such as mental health, self-esteem, educational aspirations and attainment, and social mobility have discovered that the relationship can be positive or negative and that the variation is shaped and determined by the way sports participation matches up (or interacts) with the communal context in which individuals are situated.

Important in its own right, this research serves as a counterpoint to Western tendencies to romanticize sport as an autonomous, pure-play realm, an arena uncorrupted—even unaffected—by the forces of the external world and whose own social impacts are always positive and progressive. The social force of sport is not one-dimensional or unidirectional but in fact variable and, moreover, largely dependent upon how sport interacts with other forces in the social environment. Thus, the relationships between sport and community are complex and multifaceted not only because of the many different (and often idealized) ways in which both community and sport can be conceived and experienced but also because of the reciprocal ways in which they interact. One cannot be studied or understood without the other—which is why the more we really learn about the deep structure and significance of sport in communities, the more we know about those communities and about modern, global society itself.

Douglas Hartmann

See also Fan Loyalty; Social Identity; Sport and National Identity

Further Reading

Andrews, D. L. (1999). Contextualizing suburban soccer: Consumer culture, lifestyle differentiation, and suburban America. *Culture, Sport, Society, 1*, 31–53.

Birrell, S., & Cole, C. L. (Eds.). (1994). *Women, sport, and culture.* Champaign, IL: Human Kinetics.

Bourdieu, P. (1978). Sport and social class. *Social Science Information, 17*(6), 819–840.

Calhoun, C. J. (1980). Community: Toward a variable conceptualization for comparative research. *Social History, 5*(1), 105–129.

Dyreson, M. (2001). Maybe it's better to bowl alone: Sport, community, and democracy in American thought. *Culture, Sport, Society, 4*(1), 19–30.

Geertz, C. (1973). Deep play: Notes on the Balinese cockfight. In *Interpretation of cultures* (pp. 412–454). New York: Basic.

Guest, A., & Schneider, B. (2003, April). Adolescents' extracurricular participation in context: The mediating effects of schools, communities, and identity. *Sociology of Education, 76*, 89–109.

James, C. L. R. (1993). *Beyond a boundary.* Durham, NC: Duke University Press.

Kidd, B. (1995). *The struggle for Canadian sport.* Toronto, ON: University of Toronto Press.

MacAloon, J. J. (1984). Olympic Games and the theory of spectacle in modern societies. In J. J. MacAloon (Ed.), *Rite, drama, festival, spectacle: Rehearsals toward a theory of cultural performance* (pp. 241–280). Philadelphia: Institute for the Study of Human Issues Press.

Pope, S. W. (1993, Winter). Negotiating the "folk highways" of the nation: Sport, public culture, and American identity, 1870–1940. *Journal of Social History*, 327–340.

Competition

Competition occurs in social relationships in which comparisons of performances are made according to shared standards, such that performances can be objectively evaluated and ranked.

Competition and the importance of striving for success are an inherent part of the ideology of many social institutions, in particular, the economy, military, and politics. However, competition in sport is not considered in the same way as it is manifested in many forms of social life. The structural aim of sport competition is to measure and rank competitors according to the results of athletic performance. The ranking is based on the principle of equality among sport competitors. This principle seems to be a unique feature of competition in sport.

Competitive Relationships

The Canadian sport sociologist John W. Loy has defined competition "as a struggle for supremacy between two or more opposing sides," in which opposing sides can "encompass the competitive relationships between man and other objects of nature both animate and inanimate" (Loy et al. 1981, 25). Thus, he has built a typology of competitive relationships to include competition between one individual and another, competition between one team and another, competition between an individual or team and an animate object of nature, competition between an individual or team and an inanimate object of nature, and competition between an individual or team and an ideal standard.

In general competition in sport can take the form of direct competition in which two opponents confront each other, as in ball games; or parallel competition in which contestants compete with one another indirectly, as in swimming; or competition against a standard, as in gymnastics.

Sport Competition from a Historical Perspective

In order to determine the outcome of a contest and the real winner in sports, it is essential to ensure equality and fair play in the competition. But have sport competitions as we know them always existed?

The concept of ranking athletes according to their performance required a certain equality of opportunity that seems similar to what today we would call "fairness." However, the principle of fairness in sports is a rather new phenomenon. In ancient Greece the ethical code of sportlike activities was subordinated to the requirements of bravery. In the Middle Ages, it was expressed by honor. In the period around the founding of the modern Olympics in the 1890s, *fair play* became a fundamental moral principle that incorporated ethical codes within the sports arsenal of detailed rules.

The development of sport and the emphasis on the concept of fair play as a standard reference for morally right and good behavior in sport competitions can be seen in light of an increasing social control of violence and aggression since the Middle Ages. As the British-German sociologist Norbert Elias (1897–1990) has noted, the passage of the term *fair play* into everyday language is linked to the growth of sport in the nineteenth century.

Elias found in his analysis of the genesis of sport that the need for competitions to be impartial and fair grew considerably with the increased popularity of gambling. For example, interest in putting money on a horse in horse racing depended on whether gamblers could rely on an impartial and just result.

The conception of sport, as manifested in the modern Olympic system developed at the end of the nineteenth century, was based on principles of equality and distinction. Sport constitutes a distinct social order in its regulation of the systematic endeavor to break records of competitive achievement. Moreover, the mode by which the pronouncement of losers and winners and the symbolic display of results is organized represents a new and modern order. These tasks are accomplished without causing the deaths of parties in the event, which was not always the case during sporting events of earlier times.

According to the Polish sociologist Zbigniew Krawczyk, the modern Olympic Games were built on the principles that sport should be practiced due to its immanent values and not for material gain; sportsmen and sportswomen should compete as people living in friendship and peace without nationalist emotions and wars; and victory means less than participation in sporting events. Unlike a society in which people are differentiated according to race and class, for example, in Olympic sport the goal is that egalitarianism should prevail. Thus, although the system of sport itself is structurally hierarchical in nature, participants experience egalitarianism and friendship.

Though it is possible to identify the modern order in contemporary sport, activities we today refer to as sport

Competition

Extract from *Tom Brown's Schooldays* by Thomas Hughes (1857)

The ball has just fallen again where the two sides are thickest, and they close rapidly around it in a scrummage: it must be driven through now by force or skill, till it flies out on one side or the other. Look how differently the boys face it. Here come two of the bull-dogs, bursting through the outsiders; in they go, straight to the heart of the scrummage, bent on driving that ball out on the opposite side. That is what they mean to do. My sons, my sons! you are too hot; you have gone past the ball, and must struggle now right through the scrummage, and get round and back again to your own side, before you can be of any further use. Here comes young Brooke; he goes in as straight as you, but keeps his head, and backs and bends, holding himself still behind the ball, and driving it furiously when he gets the chance. Take a leaf out of his book, you young chargers. Here comes Speedicut, and Flashman the School-house bully, with shouts and great action. Won't you two come up to young Brooke, after locking-up, by the School-house fire, with "Old fellow, wasn't that just a splendid scrummage by the three trees!" But he knows you, and so do we. You don't really want to drive that ball through that scrummage, chancing all hurt for the glory of the School-house—but to make us think that's what you want—a vastly different thing; and fellows of your kidney will never go through more than the skirts of a scrummage, where it's all push and no kicking. We respect boys who keep out of it, and don't sham going in; but you—we had rather not say what we think of you.

Then the boys who are bending and watching on the outside, mark them—they are most useful players, the dodgers; who seize on the ball the moment it rolls out from amongst the chargers, and away with it across to the opposite goal; they seldom go into the scrummage, but must have more coolness than the chargers; as endless as are boys' characters, so are their ways of facing or not facing a scrummage at football.

have developed and changed in relation to social and cultural change. As the Norwegian sport philosopher Sigmund Loland maintains: "Today's Olympians may have ideas of serving their country, their race, their ideology, or even their God. Still, secular goals of performing well, of winning, and of attaining fame and fortune are probably more common. During China's Cultural Revolution, the slogan was 'friendship first, competition second.'... This is in clear contrast with the Western high-performance sport mentality expressed in telling slogans such as that attributed to the Green Bay Packer football coach Vince Lombardi: 'Winning isn't the most important thing, it's the only thing!'" (Loland 2002, 10–11).

The competitive individualism of the market that dominates professional sports today is far away from ideas of the founders of the modern Olympic Games, who regarded sports competitions as existing outside the mainstream structures of society, separated from politics and commercializing tendencies. As is the case with commercial entertainment, modern sport would have had no meaning to them, and the social acceptance of women's participation in sports competitions in the late twentieth century would likely also have been unthinkable, as it was to most sport leaders in the beginning of the twentieth century.

Competition as a Defining Feature of Sport

The competitive character of sport regards rules of bodily movement in space and time that are linked with the achievement of a measurable result. The rules are directed at the aim of being able to pronounce a winner and, in contradistinction to premodern times, these rules are no longer local but have been systematized on a global level.

For the Finnish sociologist Juha Heikkalä, the core elements of the logic of competing are as follows (1993,

403): (1) setting individuals/teams against each other to produce a momentarily set hierarchy of performances; (2) maintaining a permanent state of scarcity, meaning that only one individual/team can, at a given time, occupy the position at the top of the hierarchy (i.e., win); (3) ensuring recurring possibilities of transcending one's own and/or opponents' performances and of occupying the top position of the hierarchy; and (4) instilling a will to win.

The Finnish sport sociologist Kalevi Heinilä has noted that in competitive sport these elements are combined in a process of an ascending spiral. This spiral of competition shows not only who is best, but also how good it is possible for an athlete to become, which seems to be infinite.

The logic of competing serves to demarcate sport from nonsport. Competition, according to this view, is identified as a constitutive feature of sport conceived as an action system, in contradistinction to its role in the fields of physical education, play, or game, in which it can have a function that is merely regulative. But what does it mean to compete as defined by the constitutive rules?

An individual's motivations for engaging in sport competition can be varied. They can reflect a desire for pleasure or health, for example. But a shared interpretation of "winning" is a necessity for meaningful competitions to be possible at all. As Loland has noted: "[C]ompetitions between groups of competitors each of whose ethos has radically different content become very hard if not impossible. There would be few shared norms and the sport in question may degenerate or even die" (2002, 8).

Different sports have sport-specific goals, and the constitutive rules of a sport provide a conceptual framework within which sport can occur. In sport, winning is logically dependent on using only the means defined in the individual sport's constitutive rules. Regulative rules, on the other hand, place regulations on activities that are logically independent of the process of competing, whether they be technical demands, norms about how to perform, or rules that define the size of the ball.

The sign shows that a winner steps up, a loser steps aside. *Source: istockphoto/calvinng.*

The process of competition, according to this view, is a defining feature of sport. Competition is not something that is optional within sport; it is part of sport itself. Athletic activity that is not competitive falls, by this definition, into the domain of play, physical exercise, or training.

Cultural Variances

In real life competitions are characterized according to various degrees of fairness and acting in accordance with the rules. For example, studies of football (soccer) players have shown that the interpretation of the rules of football (soccer) varies between professionals and amateur players and between different clubs. Yet, most sports are also seen to be relatively stable social practices.

Philosophical and social scientific approaches have analyzed and also valued sport competitions in various ways. A traditional interpretation is to distinguish between "formal fair play," which refers to rule conformity, and "informal fair play," referring to attitudes toward the game, toward other competitors, and toward officials. The historical and cultural change of sport

There's nobody you'd rather beat than your good friend. ■ CHARLES BARKLEY, about playing against MICHAEL JORDAN

competitions as right or not and good or not, respectively, can be seen in the perspective of how formal and informal fair play change in different settings.

When people interpret the meaning of sport for themselves, there will be a variety of the sports forms that they practice. However, it seems that the importance of competition is dependent on age and gender much more so than on nationality. Thus, competition has been indicated to be a more important component of sport for males than for females and for adolescents than for older people. In many cultures competitive behaviors are not considered appropriate for girls or women, although it has become much more acceptable in the late twentieth and early twenty-first centuries.

Several studies have indicated that sport undergoes cultural adaptation. For example, a comparative study has investigated the degree to which "achievement" criteria characterize the sporting behavior and sporting perceptions of adolescents in Berlin and suburban New York. In this study Berlin adolescents emphasized a more vague concept of sport, in that physical activity that was not competitive or "win-oriented" could still be sport, and was generally perceived to be enjoyable. "Achievement criteria such as the importance of practice, competition, and victory may be less central to the sports concepts of Berlin adolescents when compared with those of suburban New Yorkers" (Rees et al. 1998, 227).

Indeed, the role of sport in the system of education may be what determined the different views on sport concept, since interscholastic sport is largely nonexistent in Germany, whereas school sports and athletic scholarships have a pervasive influence in America. In addition to sport industries, educational institutions have been used socially to promote the virtues of competition in U.S. culture.

The Danish-German sport sociologist Gertrud Pfister has further noted that, in general, women participate in sports less for competition than for health and enjoyment. Yet, still more women enter the sports arenas, although their participation in competitive sport has been limited by ideology, economy, and family responsibilities. For example, about one-third of the participants in

the 2004 Olympics were women, and they are now allowed to compete in almost every Olympic event.

Competitive sport is rapidly becoming a worldwide phenomenon. Economic factors and the media have played a major part in its spread. Thus, what is meant by sport is becoming more uniform as international competitions such as the Olympic Games and the World Cup are televised worldwide. Though there are indeed an increasing number of sports forms that are practiced at the national or local level, at the present time competitive sport is the predominant form of sport from a global perspective.

Critical Perspectives on Competition

Is competition good or bad? Is competition an entirely destructive basis for interaction or a source of exhilaration, motivation, and self-knowledge? The American philosopher Michael L. Schwalbe asks these questions in his essay about a humanist conception of competition in sport. Proponents of competition stress that it spurs the participants toward excellence; that it fosters self-development, discipline, and respect for others; and that it is a legitimate source of pleasure. Critics emphasize that competition is a source of unnecessary stress, that it is less productive than cooperation, and that it celebrates domination.

To suggest that sport competitions are potentially meaningful and valuable social practices, the emphasis is on sport not as forced labor, but as an activity that includes a strong voluntary and playful dimension. The playful character of competition is seen in relation to the principle of equality. From this view it is argued that the symbolic meaning of competition is rendered meaningless unless the contestants in the competition, match, or tournament are also fairly matched. Social practices such as doping, for example, can corrupt the endeavors that ensure such conditions.

Competition in sport, critics have emphasized, ties physical activities to an ideology that stresses individual achievement and dominance over opponents in ways that do not emphasize partnership, sharing, open participation, nurturance, mutual support, and drug-free

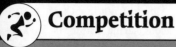

Competition

"Ex-Champions"
by Grantland Rice

"It's better to have won and lost
Than never to have won at all"—
This may be true enough, and yet
The far heights yield a greater fall;
And when one tumbles from the crest
Where he once held a golden sway
He carries something in his breast
That burns the living heart away.

I've watched them when the fickle crowd
Arose to give the victor cheers,
The haunted look within their eyes
That turned back through the vanished years;
The flame that leaped to sudden glow
To fade within their sullen stare,
As if they, too, had come to know
How soon the laurel withers there.

I've watched them as their burning eyes
Saw ghosts again from yesterday,
Where some new winner reaped the prize
Which they had known along the way;
"It's better to have won and lost
Than never to have won at all"—
But when one comes to pay the cost
The far heights yield the greater fall.

Source: Rice, G. (1924). Ex-champions. (1924). *Badminton*, pp. 128–129.

sports. Winning serves as proof of individual ability, worth, and character. Achievement is measured in terms of a never-ending quest to improve the "bottom line," according to the American sport sociologist Jay Coakley (2003, 329–330).

Moreover, the way in which the ideology of elitist competition can function to oppress women and children in sport has been discussed. According to feminist thinkers, the emphasis upon strategic relations and non-emotionality between competitors reflects a peculiarly male ethic of competition.

The humanist critique of elitist competition is first and foremost that "it encourages purely instrumental social relations rather than encouraging relationships in which people are valued as ends in themselves" (Schwalbe 1989, 47). Another criticism is that competition is morally objectionable if inequality is a desirable goal in itself.

However, since competition is intrinsic to sport as we know it, does sport as a competitive activity not seem worth preserving? Schwalbe suggests that competition in sport can be legitimatized, if we see sport as "a unique domain of social activity, competitors as critically self-conscious social actors, and competition as dialectically related to cooperation" (1989, 49).

In principle competitive sport can be seen as a unique domain that celebrates equality of opportunity even while it typically insists on inequality of outcome. The way in which striving to excel in relation to others is based on a dialectical relationship between competition and cooperation is explained by the following double premise:

■ Symbolically, we are enemies: We can only play together if you are also trying to win.
■ Symbolically, we are friends: We can only play together if there is fair play among peers.

This characterization of sport regards the conceptual level of clarifying points of similarity and difference among cultural phenomena.

Media and Large Corporations Highlight Competitive Success

Critical views of competitive sports have mostly concerned professionalization and commercialization of sport. According to Coakley (2003, 368), these processes have been realized because large corporations "use the bodies of elite athletes to represent their public relations and marketing images," and some high-profile athletes can "reaffirm a success ideology, which reproduces privilege among powerful people around the globe." Media-hyped rivalries are emphasized as more important than the way athletes enjoy friendships with other competitors. And Coakley continues by sug-

Competing in sports has taught me that if I'm not willing to give 120 percent, somebody else will. ■ RON BLOMBERG

gesting that the media tell about sports participation not from the perspective of the athlete but "in a way that supports the interests of those who benefit from cultural commitments to competition, productivity, and material success" (2003, 428).

As a media celebrity, the athlete is involved in a new form of competition within conceptions of sport as a commodity. In this context, play is paid labor, and professional sporting performers are paid well for doing their work well. And media celebrities seem to be a part of the traditional gender order. Women's sports have been televised more since the early 1990s. However, Coakley stresses that much of this coverage has been given to those sports that emphasise grace, balance, and aesthetics rather than to sports that are more competitive in nature.

Implications

Sport competitions are complex activities, and it seems reasonable to make a distinction, as Loland and Sandberg suggest, between sport competition as a system of ideas—a possible form of conduct defined by a rule system—and as a system of action, the realization of the rule-defined practice of certain persons at a certain time and place. Mostly, it is not competition per se that engenders the cultural forms of sport or the diverged answers to the question of whether competition is good or bad. In spite of a variety of individual, cultural, and social differences, in the Olympic Games, for example, athletes from all over the world, representing approximately 200 nations, are able to interact in an intelligible way in the contest arena.

Yet, the goals of sport competition differ and are objects for controversy. If the only purpose for engaging in sports is to win, then the only role that is required is strategic. The case of professional sports has illustrated this most starkly. Professional athletes are competitive athletes, but they are also workers. However, as Schwalbe emphasizes, "it is not competition per se that engenders this alienated labor," it is "an economy exploiting athletic ability to make profits" (1989, 56). "External goals, like fame and fortune, can only be re-

alized outside of the competition. Internal goals are linked to experiential values such as excitement, challenge, and fun, and can only be realized within the very activity of competing," according to Loland and Sandberg (1995, 231).

The invention of new games, for example, alternative and extreme sports in which the usual cultural values of competition are subordinated to values of cooperation, parallel the process of professionalization. However, competitive sport embodies mainstream values of individualism and competition as a means of gaining fame and reward, and new conceptions of competition and changing ethics of competition to a celebration of cooperation can hardly become universal in the very near future.

Inge Kryger Pedersen

See also Cooperation

Further Reading

Allison, M. T. (1980). Competition and cooperation: A sociocultural perspective. *International Review for the Sociology of Sport, 15*(3–4), 93–104.

Birrell, S., & Cole, C. L. (Eds.). (1994). *Women, sport, and culture.* Champaign, IL: Human Kinetics.

Coakley, J. (2003). *Sports in society: Issues & controversies.* Singapore/New York: McGraw Hill.

Elias, N., & Dunning, E. (Eds.). (1986). *Quest for excitement: Sport and leisure in the civilizing process.* Oxford, UK: Basil Blackwell.

Guttmann, A. (1978). *From ritual to record: The nature of modern sport.* New York: Columbia University Press.

Heikkala, J. (1993). Discipline and excel: Techniques of the self and body and the logic of competing. *Sociology of Sport Journal, 10*(4), 397–412.

Heinilä, K. (1982). The totalization process in international sport. *Sportswissenschaft, 12*(3), 235–254.

Krawczyk, Z. (1996). Sport as symbol. *International Review for the Sociology of Sport, 31*(4), 429–438.

Lenk, H. (1993). Fairness und fair play. In V. Gerhardt & M. Lämmer,(Eds.), *Fairness und fair play.* Sankt Augustin, Germany: Academia Verlag.

Loland, S. (2002). *Fair play in sport: A moral norm system.* London/New York: Routledge.

Loland, S., & Sandberg, P. (1995). Realizing ludic rationality in sport competitions. *International Review for the Sociology of Sport, 30*(2), 225–242.

Loy, J. W., Kenyon, G. S.,& McPherson, B. D. (Eds.). (1981). *Sport, culture and society: A reader on the sociology of sport.* Philadelphia, PA: Lea & Febiger.

McIntosh, P. (1979). *Fair play: Ethics in sport and competition.* London: Heinemann.

Pfister, G. (1998). Development of relationship to sport: Sport biographies of German women. *Women in Sport and Physical Activity Journal, 7*(19), 151–170.

Rees, C. R., Brettschneider, W.-D., & Brandl-Bredenbeck, H. P. (1998). Globalization of sports activities and sport perceptions among adolescents from Berlin and suburban New York. *Sociology of Sport Journal, 15*(3), 216–230.

Schwalbe, M. L. (1989). A humanist conception of competition in sport. *Humanity & Society, 13*(1), 43–60.

Seppänen, P. (1989). Competitive sport and sport success in the Olympic Games: A cross-cultural analysis of value systems. *International Review for the Sociology of Sport, 24*(4), 275–282.

Competitive Balance

Competitive balance describes the degree of uncertainty about the outcome of sporting events. Economists posit that uncertainty about the outcome of sporting events plays an important role in determining fans' interest in these events. In order to test this theory, some measure of the degree of uncertainty inherent in sporting events must be developed.

The interest of sports fans in sporting events depends on a number of factors. Fans enjoy watching athletes perform as well as the drama inherent in athletic competition at any level. Additional fan interest stems from watching gifted athletes perform at the highest level possible. But beyond these factors, a part of overall fan interest also depends on the perceived uncertainty of the outcome of the event. Sporting events with a predetermined outcome have no uncertainty and generate relatively little fan interest; closely contested sporting events have a high degree of uncertainty about the outcome and generate a relatively large amount of fan interest. Sporting events with a high degree of uncertainty of outcome are said to be "competitively balanced," and sporting events with a low degree of uncertainty of outcome are said to be "competitively imbalanced." Economists call the theory that fan interest varies with competitive balance the *uncertainty of outcome hypothesis*.

In general competitive-balance measures could be applied to any sporting event, from individual events like foot races, horse races, or figure skating to team competitions like the World Cup or America's Cup yacht race to hybrid events that combine elements of both individual and team events like the Tour de France. In practice competitive-balance measures are most frequently applied to sports leagues like the National Basketball Association or the English Premiership League (football/soccer). In the context of a sports league, uncertainty exists about both the outcome of individual games or matches and the final standings in the league. Competitive-balance measures are commonly applied to end-of-season outcomes in sports leagues.

Competitive Balance in Sports Leagues

The owners of teams in professional sports leagues and the organizations that oversee amateur sports leagues have an interest in competitive balance, although the perspective of these individuals and organizations differs from that of sports fans. The long-term success of sports leagues depends on the interest of fans, and owners and regulators have a vested interest in organizing sports leagues in a way that actively promotes the staging of events with highly uncertain outcomes.

Unlike leagues, individual teams have no natural interest in promoting competitive balance. Winning is the primary objective of any sports team. Sports leagues throughout the world contain examples of "dynasties"—teams that enjoy prolonged periods of success—suggesting that success in sports leagues may have a self-perpetuating component. In professional sports leagues, successful teams generate greater revenues, allowing these teams to hire better players and coaches. In amateur settings successful teams attract more talented players than unsuccessful teams. Although diminishing returns to talent tend to mitigate these advantages to some extent—a team will not find it's always advantageous to have the absolute best player at every position—some tension exists between the goals

*Competition is the spice of sports; but if you make spice
the whole meal you'll be sick.* ▪ GEORGE LEONARD

of individual teams and the goals of sports leagues. This tension often leads to a reduced competitive balance in sports leagues.

In addition professional leagues that grant individual teams exclusive geographic franchises—a common practice in North American sports leagues like the National Football League (NFL), the National Basketball Association (NBA), and Major League Baseball (MLB), as well as other professional sports leagues around the world—will have revenue disparities due to differences in market size that may also lead to competitive imbalances. These differences in market size may also be related to the existence of "dynasties" in professional sports leagues.

Research on Competitive Balance

Decision makers in professional and amateur sports leagues, sports management professionals, and economists have considerable interest in testing the validity of the uncertainty of outcome hypothesis and in understanding the effect of uncertainty of outcome on fan interest in sporting events. This interest spurs a large amount of research on competitive balance. The competitive-balance literature can be divided into two broad categories: measurement of competitive balance and tests of the uncertainty of outcome hypothesis.

Measuring Competitive Balance

Competitive balance depends on the perceived uncertainty about the outcome of sporting events. Uncertainty is a complex, multifaceted phenomenon that is difficult to reduce to a single quantifiable metric. Consequently, the literature contains no consensus regarding a single best measure of competitive balance. A large number of alternative measures of competitive balance exist, each with a different set of strengths and weaknesses.

The dispersion of winning percentages—the fraction of the total games played that are won by a given team within a sports league—is the most commonly used measure of competitive balance. At first glance average winning percentage may appear to be a good measure of competitive balance, but because each sporting event generates a win for one team and a loss for the other team (ignoring ties), the average winning percentage in a given league must always equal 0.500. The dispersion of winning percentages around this average reflects how much variation in winning percentage existed in the league, and it is also an indication of the extent of uncertainty of outcome in the contests played in the league.

Competitive Balance within a Single Season

From basic statistical analysis, *variance* is a common measure of the dispersion of a variable. The variance of winning percentages in a sports league is simply the average of the squared difference between each team's winning percentage and 0.500. Leagues with a greater degree of competitive balance have a larger variance of winning percentages. In practice researchers studying competitive balance use the *standard deviation* of winning percentage—the square root of the variance—because the standard deviation is expressed in the same units: percent of games won as winning percentage.

A number of other single-season measures of competitive balance have been developed. These methods include Gini coefficients for wins, Lorenz curves, and Markov chain methods. All of these measures share a common feature: They describe the distribution of wins across teams in a sports league in a single season.

Between-Season Competitive Balance

Because sports leagues exist for many seasons, sports fans may also care about the degree of uncertainty of outcomes for periods longer than a single season. Between-season measures of competitive balance focus on the amount of turnover in the relative success of sports teams from season to season. Unlike single-season measures of competitive balance, these measures of competitive balance focus on changes in the relative success of teams in a league, as measured by winning percentages or championships, over a number of seasons.

One approach to measuring between-season competitive balance examines the distribution of championships across teams in a sports league over some period of time. Sports leagues within which most championships are distributed among a small number of teams have a smaller degree of uncertainty of championship outcomes and have lower competitive balance; sports leagues within which championships are distributed relatively equally across teams have a larger degree of uncertainty of championship outcomes and have higher competitive balance.

A second approach to measuring between-season competitive balance calculates the dispersion of a single team's relative level of success over a number of seasons and compares this dispersion with the average level of dispersion in success across all teams in the league.

Level of Competitive Balance in Sports Leagues

Professional sports leagues generally exhibit a wide range of variation in degree of competitive balance. Even within a particular sport, different leagues will have different levels of competitive balance.

Table 1 shows the standard deviation of winning percentages in a number of professional sports leagues for the 2002 or 2002–2003 seasons in cases in which the season spans two calendar years (with the ALF exception noted). Recall that the greater the dispersion of winning percentages, the less competitive balance in that league in the 2002 season. The dispersion of winning percentages varies from a high of 0.22 to a low of 0.08 in this sample. The general pattern across sports indicates that baseball leagues had the most competitive balance, American football and basketball leagues had the least competitive balance, while football and ice hockey fell in the middle of these two extremes.

A careful reader will note that the pattern of standard deviations across sports leagues in Table 1 varies with the number of games played in each season by the teams in each league. Baseball seasons consist of between 140 and just over 160 games; basketball seasons consist of about 80 games; ice hockey seasons consist of between 50 to 80 games; football (soccer) seasons consist of between 30 to 45 games; and American football seasons consist of between 12 to 16 games. Seasons consisting of more games will generally have a lower standard deviation of winning percentage, no matter what level of competitive balance occurs in the leagues. To account for this, the actual standard deviation of winning percentages can be compared with an ideal standard deviation that would result from an evenly matched league of games playing a season of a given length. This ideal standard deviation can be calculated based on the case in which each team in a league has a 0.500 winning percentage—the maximum possible uncertainty of outcome in a single season—for a given number of games played by the teams in the league by dividing the square root of the number of games into 0.5.

Comparing the actual standard deviation with the idealized standard deviation for each league leads to a somewhat different picture of the relative degree of competitive balance in the leagues shown on the table. On average, football (soccer) leagues have standard deviations about 40 percent larger than the ideal standard deviation, American football leagues are about 45 percent larger, ice hockey leagues about 85 percent higher, and baseball and basketball leagues have standard deviations twice the size of the idealized standard deviation based on length of season.

Remedies for Competitive Imbalance

All of the standard deviations shown on Table 1 are larger than the ideal standard deviation for the league. Because the actual standard deviations exceed this ideal value in all leagues, some degree of competitive imbalance exists in all these leagues. It appears that competitive imbalance is a constant feature of most professional sports leagues. Also, recall that the owners of teams in professional sports leagues have an economic incentive to maintain competitive balance. This tension leads

Table 1.

Competitive Balance Indicators, 2002–2003 Seasons

Sport	League	Country	Standard Deviation
Football (soccer)	Premier League	England	0.14
Football (soccer)	La Liga	Spain	0.12
Football (soccer)	Serie A	Italy	0.15
Football (soccer)	Liegue 1	France	0.11
Football (soccer)	1st Bundesliga	Germany	0.11
Football (soccer)	Serie A	Brazil	0.10
Football (soccer)	Premier League	Argentina	0.12
Football (soccer)	MLS	USA	0.09
Ice Hockey	NHL	USA/Canada	0.10
Ice Hockey	Elitserien	Sweden	0.12
Ice Hockey	SM-Liiga	Finland	0.14
Ice Hockey	RHL	Russia	0.14
Australian Rules Football	ALF*	Australia	0.11
Baseball	Japanese League	Japan	0.09
Baseball	MLB	USA/Canada	0.08
American Football	NFL	USA	0.14
American Football	CFL	Canada	0.22
Basketball	NBA	USA	0.14
Basketball	Women's NBA	USA	0.15

Note: ALF standard deviation for all-time records, all others single season.

Source: Author's calculations.

sports leagues to impose rules in order to increase the level of competitive balance. However, most of these rules appear to have little effect.

One common rule aimed at enhancing competitive balance in sports leagues is the reverse-order entry draft. In these drafts the worst teams in terms of winning percentage in the previous season have the first choice of new players coming into the league. Presumably, bad teams will select the best new players and have the greatest chance to improve their performance.

Most evidence suggests that the institution of a reverse-order entry draft has no effect on the level of competitive balance in sports leagues. There are several reasons for this ineffectiveness. First, there can be a considerable amount of uncertainty about the quality of new players coming into a league. If coaches and managers have trouble determining the actual quality of incoming players, there is relatively little benefit to selecting earlier in the draft. Second, the success of the draft depends in part on the ability of the drafters. Bad teams are often run by bad managers and coaches, and less-able decision makers tend to make bad draft choices and bad trades involving draft choices.

Competitive imbalance often stems from imbalances in revenues. Revenue imbalances can come from differences in market size or differences in past success of teams. Some sports leagues attempt to reduce competitive imbalance by reducing the imbalance in revenues. Rules aimed at reducing revenue imbalance include sharing of revenues from ticket sales and revenues from television and radio broadcasts evenly among teams, rather than the team drawing the most fans or located in the largest market keeping these revenues. In some leagues, a "luxury tax" is imposed on teams with the largest payrolls. Finally, many sports leagues impose salary caps on teams in order to reduce competitive imbalance. A salary cap is a maximum payroll for players. Salary caps do not directly address revenue imbalances but instead equalize the amount of money that each team can spend hiring players. By limiting payroll, salary caps attempt to alter the distribution of talent across teams, thus changing competitive balance in the league.

Like the other rules aimed at reducing competitive imbalance, research suggests that salary caps do not reduce competitive imbalance, and in some cases they appear to increase it. One problem with salary caps is that it is very difficult to construct a salary cap system that cannot be manipulated by teams and players in some fashion. Players will often restructure the terms of contracts or agree to artificially low salaries in the early years of contracts and defer higher payments far into the future. In some instances teams have resorted to illegal side payments to players.

The Future

Competitive balance, and the related uncertainty of outcome hypothesis, have important implications for the behavior of sports fans, the owners of teams in professional sports leagues, and the organizers of amateur sports leagues. Fans, owners, and league organizers prefer a high degree of competitive balance in sports leagues. But competitive imbalance appears to be a feature of all sports leagues, and most rules aimed at reducing competitive imbalance appear to be ineffective. Future research on competitive balance will need to address this issue by (1) quantifying the relationship between the degree of competitive balance and fan interest in order to determine how much competitive imbalance should be tolerated, and (2) improving the understanding of why existing rules aimed at reducing competitive imbalance are ineffective and how to construct effective rules to improve competitive balance.

Brad R. Humphreys

Further Reading

Coase, R. (1960). The problem of social cost. *Journal of Law and Economics, 3*(1), 1–44.
Fort, R. (2003). *Sports economics.* Upper Saddle River, NJ: Prentice Hall.
Fort, R., & Quirk, J. (1995). Cross-subsidization, incentives, and outcomes in professional team sports leagues. *Journal of Economic Literature, 23*(3), 1265–1299.
Humphreys, B. (2002). Alternative measures of competitive balance in professional sports leagues. *Journal of Sports Economics, 3*(2), 133–148.
Kesenne, S. (2000). Revenue sharing and competitive balance in professional team sports. *Journal of Sports Economics, 1*(1), 65–65.
Leeds, M., & von Allmen, P. (2003). *The economics of sports.* Boston: Pearson Addison Wesley.
Quirk, J., & Fort, R. (1992). *Pay dirt: The business of pro team sports.* Princeton, NJ: Princeton University Press.
Rigotti, L., & Palomino, F. (2000). *The sport league's dilemma: Competitive balance versus incentives to win* (Working Paper Series: E00-292). Berkeley: University of California, Department of Economics.
Rottenberg, S. (1956). The baseball players' labor market. *Journal of Political Economy, 64*(3), 242–258.
Schmidt, M., & Berri, D. (2003). On the evolution of competitive balance: The impact of an increasing global search. *Economic Inquiry, 41*(4), 692–704.
Scully, G. (1989). *The business of Major League Baseball.* Chicago: University of Chicago Press.
Zimbalist, A. (1994). *Baseball and billions: A probing look inside the big business of our national pastime.* New York: Basic Books.
Zimbalist, A. (2002). Competitive balance in sports leagues: An introduction. *Journal of Sports Economics, 3*(2), 111–121.

Cooperation

Cooperation occurs when people work or play together to accomplish shared goals. Cooperation may seem an ironic entry in an encyclopedia of sport because most definitions of *sport* emphasize competition between opposing groups. However, sport provides many instances when the social processes of cooperation and competition occur separately and sometimes simultaneously.

Cooperative Games

People who oppose excessive competition in sport recently have stressed the importance of maximizing participation and cooperation. Critics both within and outside sport argue that sport should be open to all people—regardless of gender, physical abilities, or political philosophy. Jack Scott, first a professional athlete and then a critic of contemporary sport, has led a democratic movement to restructure sport to encourage the more humanistic values of cooperation, altruism, and interpersonal responsibility and to deemphasize the win-at-all-costs ethic of excessive competition and vio-

Cooperation is required not just for success but also for survival in the sport of mountain climbing.

lence. Other critics of competition in sport have stressed the importance of cooperation and have recommended a more radical examination of the value of competition in general, pointing to its dangers and destructive consequences. Their focus on cooperation is especially visible in discussions of the value of cooperative (or noncompetitive) games for both adults and children.

Cross-cultural studies have shown that not all cultures value competition as much as Western societies do. The sports and games of some cultures place far less emphasis on competition. For example, Galliher and Hessler note that the Chinese government's efforts to promote cooperation and interpersonal relations through sports ("friendship first, competition second") supposedly resulted in greater mass participation in sports.

Central to the theory of cooperative games is the notion of individual people or groups working together toward mutually beneficial ends. The main difference between competitive and cooperative games is that in cooperative games all participants cooperate and therefore, by definition, all win and none loses. An example of this approach is the scoring rules for infinity volleyball as described in the *New Games Book*:

> [T]his game is pure cooperation, and any number can play. The rules of standard volleyball still apply, including three hits per side before sending the ball over the net. The score, kept track of by both teams chanting in unison, is the number of times the ball is hit over the net to the other side without hitting the ground. Any score over 50 is good. Over 100 is phenomenal. And both teams always win. (Fluegelman 1976)

The goal of the cooperative games movement is to provide a radical alternative to traditional sports. Cooperative games (sometimes referred to as "new games") offer this alternative by stressing cooperating, participating, being spontaneous, and playing for fun, as opposed to competing, spectating, observing predetermined rules, and playing to win. Most importantly, cooperative games are subject to evolution—players are free to change the rules of the game and to improvise as they play.

Anticompetition Movement

The beginning of the cooperative games movement can be traced to the anticompetition movement in women's sports during the 1920s. During this period in the United States and in many other Western countries, women athletes increased their skill, and women became more competitive, vigorous, and organized. Women athletes began to participate in national and international competition. Pressure from Europe led to the inclusion of women's track and field events in the Olympic Games in 1928.

U.S. educators responded with more intense criticism of organized women's sports. Many educators disapproved of competitive sports for women altogether. However, their disapproval was not based on the earlier idea that women's sporting behaviors run counter to the Victorian ideals of womanhood of the late 1800s. Instead, critics argued that competitive sports for women would follow the example of men's sports and would focus on the elite athlete at the exclusion of the less skilled athlete. They feared that further commercialization of the woman athlete would discourage wider participation of women in sports and other physical

A team builds cooperation when the players and coaches put their hands together in a huddle. *Source: istockphoto/nano.*

activities. For example, a directive of the women's division of the National Amateur Athletic Federation (NAAF) stated: "The Women's Division believes in the spirit of play for its own sake and works for the promotion of physical activity for the largest possible proportion of persons in any given group." A half-century later research supports this belief: Physical activities that place greater emphasis on competition and winning are generally associated with lower rates of participation.

Orlick credits the origins of the cooperative games movement to the special role of women in many cultures. In his studies of North American cultures, he concludes that the humanistic strength of women holds most cultures together. Orlick credits women as being far more cooperative, caring, considerate, and depend-

able than men. As women's participation in sports increases, these qualities exert more influence on both which sports are played and how people think about sports in general

Cooperation and Gender

Social attitudes, in addition to cultural expectations, influence how people behave. Social scientists refer to the process of internalizing society's attitudes and expectations as "socialization." In every culture an important part of socialization involves people learning culturally acceptable gender roles and shaping themselves to fit them. Men and women have obvious biological differences as well as biological similarities. Cross-cultural research has shown, however, that many cultures exaggerate male-female differences, as in the notion that men and women are polar opposites.

The meaning that a culture gives to these biological differences is as important as the differences themselves. Gender differences, in sociological terms, are social constructions, and exactly what these differences are appear to be relative to each culture. People learn gender roles during childhood, and research shows how important games and play are to the development of a child's identity as either male or female, including the development of separate skills, attitudes, and interests between boys and girls. Games and play in essence are important ways of learning culturally appropriate conceptions of male and female.

Studies on this topic have focused on mainstream European and North American societies. These studies of boys and girls at play have consistently found that although the two genders sometimes play together, they more often play in groups of the same gender. Furthermore, studies have found that boys and girls often play using different types of play styles and games. For example, boys' games (like sports) tend to take place outdoors and in larger groups. Boys' games, too, have more elaborate systems of rules, and they place greater emphasis on competition. Boys' games also stress winners and losers, and status within the group is tied to winning.

The way a team plays as a whole determines its success. You may have the greatest bunch of individual stars in the world, but if they don't play together, the club won't be worth a dime. ■ BABE RUTH

Girls, in contrast, tend to play in smaller groups or even in pairs. Girls emphasize cooperation and intimacy much more than boys do. For example, in such traditional girls' games as jump rope and hopscotch, the focus is on taking turns with one another, and winning may not be all that important. In many girls' games skill, rather than winning, is the goal. Furthermore, many girls' games may not even have winners or losers, and girls more often settle conflicts while playing by stressing the importance of cooperation.

The gender segregation of younger children's play groups is reinforced later in school, and as Thorne indicates, evidence indicates that gender segregation among children is even more extensive in schools in formally organized sports.

In many Western societies cultural attitudes and gender socialization have limited women's athletic participation. Such societies have traditionally viewed sports as a more masculine activity, and different socialization practices have encouraged males to have a more competitive, serious, and professional orientation toward sports. Even when women do participate in sports, studies suggest, their orientations differ significantly from those of men. Studies have found, for example, that winning and competing matter more to men athletes than to women athletes. Time will tell, however, whether increasing participation by women at every level of sports may change this dynamic.

John R. Bowman

Further Reading

Bascow, S. (1992). *Gender: Stereotypes and roles.* Pacific Grove, CA: Brooks/Cole.

Edwards, H. (1973). *Sociology of sport.* Homewood, IL: Dorsey Press.

Fluegelman, A. (1976). *The new games book.* Garden City, NY: Doubleday.

Galliher, J., & Hessler, R. (1979, Spring/Summer). Sports competition and international capitalism. *Journal of Sport and Social Issues, 3,* 10–21.

Guttmann, A. (1978). *From ritual to record.* New York: Columbia University Press.

Leonard, W. (1993). *A sociological perspective of sport.* New York: Macmillan.

Orlick, T. (1978). *The cooperative sports and games book: Challenge without competition.* New York: Pantheon Books.

Orlick, T. (1982). *The second cooperative sports and games book.* New York: Pantheon Books.

Scott, J. (1969). *Athletics for athletes.* Berkeley, CA: Otherways.

Scott, J. (1971). *The athletic revolution.* New York: Free Press.

Singer, R,, Murphy, M., & Tennant, K. (1993). *Handbook of research on sport psychology.* New York: Macmillan.

Synder, E., & Spreitzer, E. (1979). Orientations toward sport: Intrinsic, normative, and extrinsic. *Journal of Sport Psychology, 1*(2), 170–175.

Tannen, D. (1990). *You just don't understand: Women and men in conversation.* New York: Ballantine Books.

Thorne, B. (1993). *Gender play: Girls and boys in school.* New Brunswick, NJ: Rutgers University Press.

Woolum, J. (1992). *Outstanding women athletes.* Phoenix, AZ: Oryx Press.

Country Club

Country clubs are leisure establishments that exist in most communities in North America and across the globe. They provide sports and community for their members. The term *country club* conjures images of privilege, separation, elitism, and difference. To people who are members of a country club, these images may be positive and welcomed. To many people who are not members or who are excluded from membership, these images smack of discrimination and a power imbalance based on wealth and social standing and, in many cases, race and gender.

History

During the early nineteenth century major cities in the eastern United States and Canada had an economic structure that clearly divided people into those who had wealth and social status and those who did not. The wealthy urban class had the means for considerable consumption of both material goods and leisure. Traditions of social stratification from Great Britain and France were reproduced in the young countries of the United States and Canada through clubs and other institutions that were formed to foster social discrimination. Wealthy, white men desired a collective identification of their socioeconomic prestige. This prestige was demonstrated not only by the men's homes and other possessions, but also by their leisure activities, which were qualitatively better than those in which the average person could hope to engage. The separation of people—men of privilege from everyone else—was the basis for the formation of "city clubs," the forerunner of today's country clubs.

City clubs were prominent institutions of privileged and private space for men of means in London. To replicate this exclusivity, people formed city clubs in the United States during the 1830s. One man or a group of powerful men would develop a city club with members from the social elite of the community. Restricted membership solidified the social status of the club members and the exclusivity of the club.

Following the format of their British forerunners, founders of clubs drafted constitutions for all aspects of club governance. Early concerns of clubs included admission standards and acquisition of an appropriate building to house activities.

Admission to a city club was based on social status. The socioeconomic standing of members provided a bond among these elites and set them not only apart, but also above the common person. Therefore, membership was selective. Members used the process of blackballing to deny membership to an applicant without the blackballers being identified. Each member of an admissions committee was given a white ball and a black ball, one of which he placed in a box. From one to three black balls in the box would deny membership to an applicant.

Women were always denied membership and in many cases even entrance to the club. City clubs were formed by powerful men of business. During the nineteenth century women were typically excluded from the public sphere of business. Only with great difficulty could women accrue the power status, if not the wealth, required for club membership. Some clubs allowed women to accompany their husbands; however, a "ladies entrance" was typically provided to ensure the sanctity of the men-only spaces in the clubs.

Cultural, racial, and religious groups were also discriminated against. Jews, Catholics, and African-Americans were generally excluded from membership in city clubs. In large cities wealthy Jews and Catholics formed their own clubs, and by the late 1880s African-Americans had amassed enough wealth to create exclusively black clubs. Social stratification in these clubs, however, paralleled that of the white clubs as the black elite separated themselves from the black masses.

Exclusive Spaces

Members selected the setting of a city club to present a visual indicator of the privileged nature of the space and the social elitism of those men allowed to enter the club's doors. City clubs were located in mansions or in facilities that were built with architectural styles that paralleled those of university, financial, or government buildings. The interior of a club was designed to meet the needs and desires of the membership. A club had a reception hall, library, dining room with a kitchen, and a bar. Most clubs also had lounging rooms for reading, playing cards, or smoking. Some clubs had a music room and separate meeting spaces for women. Some clubs had bedrooms for out-of-town guests or for the convenience of members.

Strict rules governed the dress and deportment of members. Clubs might require formal dress and top hats in the dining room, where smoking was usually prohibited, especially if women were allowed to be present. Men were often required to wear jackets of a club color in certain areas of the club—a tradition brought over from the clubs of Great Britain.

By the late 1800s members demanded more sporting facilities in their clubs. Although a number of cities had tennis and racquet clubs, clubs began to include courts, training rooms, and even swimming pools. During this time women's clubs were formed, many as athletic clubs. The availability of leisure time and discretionary money to spend on sporting and other leisure pursuits created a leisure elite among the social elite.

Activities

Many clubs offered sporting activities such as tennis, squash, croquet, billiards, and, in some clubs with the

Athlete: Th' athletic fool, to whom what Heaven denied of soul, is well compensated in limbs. ■ JOHN ARMSTRONG

space, baseball. However, the elite had the means to leave the cities and to engage in a variety of sporting and leisure activities. The elite desired more privacy than could be found in the increasingly industrialized, crowded, and less-than-sanitary urban centers of the nineteenth century. Sociospatial separation was an indicator of the status of the elite and their ability to discriminate against people whom they felt were below them as well as to escape from everyday life in the cities.

Participation in activities such as foxhunting, polo, horse racing, and yachting required not only large amounts of money, but also large amounts of leisure time, space, and equipment that were available only to the wealthy. "Though American elites were not homogeneous in their selection of sports, they nonetheless tended to select sports beyond the financial resources of non-elites" (Mayo 1998, 51). The types of leisure activities varied by the region of the country and the predominant weather. For example, foxhunting clubs were numerous in New England and Virginia; curling and ice skating prevailed in the North; yachting required access to the harbors of the East. In Canada cricket was the game of choice, although the first clubs outside of U.S. cities were primarily foxhunting clubs.

Control of the spaces in which such activities took place was an important aspect of the segregation and exclusivity that club members desired. Large tracts of land were required for equestrian sports, hunting, and eventually golf. Sometimes a city club developed a large parcel of land owned by a member, and access was by invitation only. At other times clubs leased or purchased land for the development of wilderness camps or resort-type developments that allowed families to vacation as a whole in protected and secluded locations. "Formed in 1877, the Adirondack Club was an early collective retreat. Renamed the Tahawas Club, the group leased 96,000 acres of land. In 1878, the first association to own land was the Bisby Club, which merged with the Adirondack League Club (formed in 1890) in 1983. One year later the club owned 116,000 acres and leased 75,000 acres in a joining parcel. In total the

Adirondack League Club privately controlled 275 square miles for exclusive fishing and hunting privileges to serve its membership" (Mayo 1998, 44). Only people who had access to such land could afford horses and carriages and employees to attend to them and could overcome the difficulties of reaching such secluded spaces.

Leisure activities away from the cities often entailed extended stays because of the distances that had to be traveled and the slow pace of horse-drawn transportation. Men of means who chose to segregate themselves even from their wives in their city clubs began to appreciate the opportunity that their country sporting venues afforded their families. The development of country clubs, sometimes as extensions of city clubs and sometimes as new clubs formed by wealthy men with similar leisure interests, became possible during the 1880s.

Necessary Factors

By the 1880s a number of factors precipitated the development of the country club. First, structures in place for the operation of city clubs could be easily transferred to country clubs, whose members were often members of city clubs. Second, members of the social elite increasingly participated in outdoor leisure activities. This increasing participation was necessary for a foundational membership base in country clubs to ensure sufficient finances to develop and operate them. Third, many major urban centers by this time had a public, affordable street car system, which was necessary to provide the easy access of employees and casual workers to and from a club.

The development of a successful country club had no single formula. Activities varied from club to club, and usually multiple activities were available, including foxhunting, polo, shooting, archery, boating, and croquet. Tennis courts were increasingly in demand at country clubs. Many tennis and racquet clubs already existed in the cities, and members demanded tennis of country clubs. Tennis was also an acceptable physical activity for upper-class women during this time; this acceptability was also a draw for country club membership. Although clubs still did not admit women as members, men whose wives played tennis, and later golf, were likely to see this acceptability as a membership advantage.

As in city clubs, in country clubs membership was strictly controlled by an admissions committee of the board. Not only did this admissions system ensure that new members had the financial means to pay the initiation and membership fees, but also it established the social status that might affect a club's continued existence. Obviously sufficient men of wealth existed in numerous cities because by 1900 more than one thousand country clubs were operating in the United States, mostly in the East.

Development

Regardless of the sporting activities at a club, the founders and board of directors had to attend to certain essentials in every club. The finances of the club had to be sufficient to maintain the facilities and services without undue financial commitment from the members and perspective members. Although the memberships of the first country clubs were some of the wealthiest men in North America, these members were also fiscally conservative people who did not want to risk their own wealth to ensure the solvency of the club. A club had to juggle carefully to have sufficient members to meet its financial needs and yet remain a fashionable and restricted enclave for its members.

Many early country clubs leased their land. Leasing kept costs down, but a club was at the mercy of the landowner, who could increase rent or sell the land, forcing the country club to counter with a higher purchase offer or move to another location. Limited liability corporations were set up among the members of some country clubs who chose to purchase land. Such a corporation reduced the financial liability of each member. The importance of the finance committee of early clubs paralleled that of the admissions committee.

A country club also needed a clubhouse. An existing farmhouse was frequently the first clubhouse for many country clubs. In some cases a barn was renovated. This renovation was less expensive than construction of a new facility and was less of a financial risk if the club failed. However, many of the wealthy clubs chose to build a clubhouse that would reflect the elite status of their members. The first clubhouse to be designed and built was for the Shinnecock Hills Country Club of Southampton, New York, in 1892. Clubhouse architecture would become a specialized genre of building design. Because members wanted the same grandeur that their city clubs had, architects used a variety of classical styles, including French colonial, Victorian shingle, classical revival, and French renaissance, to design a building with a unique functional form. Because family use was one of the attractions of country club membership the clubhouse needed to provide facilities for women and children as well as men. Women's and men's locker rooms, dining rooms, men's grill and card rooms, a kitchen, and a bar were included in the designs of clubhouses. Some clubhouses continued to provide bedrooms for members who could not return home because of poor road conditions. Shelters for horses and carriages were necessary facilities near the clubhouse before the automobile became the common mode of transportation during the early 1900s. The automobile, another symbol of elite status, was an important aspect of the development of country clubs outside of smaller cities that did not have public transportation systems to convey members to clubs. In small towns only the richest men had cars to easily take them beyond the city limits.

Impact of Golf

The first country clubs were formed around a variety of sporting activities. The more activities that a club offered, the more land that was required to adequately meet all of the wishes of members. This situation often caused conflict among the membership because the fox-hunting members did not want trees cut or land leveled to build tennis courts, swimming pools, or golf courses. Solutions to such conflicts ranged from the merger of clubs to consolidate activities to the development of new clubs for a specific sport or selected sports. Because of the popularity of tennis, many clubs were formed as tennis clubs. The growing popularity of golf, however,

Clubhouse at country club with golf carts parked waiting for players. *Source: istockphoto.com/Digiphoto.*

became the primary reason for the development of new country clubs. "The Royal Montreal GC, founded in 1873, was the first club in North America whose members played golf" (Barclay 1992, 11). In 1885 one golf club existed in the United States. By 1900 more than one thousand existed.

Golf courses had no standards during the 1880s. Country clubs developed the number of holes that their land could accommodate. Clearing and leveling land for fairways and greens required extensive human and animal labor. Finishing a course or adding holes to a course might take years. After the course was finished the maintenance was constant and costly. Some country clubs kept cows to graze the rough areas lining the fairways and sheep to keep the grass on the fairways short. Early mowers were contraptions pulled by horses whose hooves had to be covered to protect the greens. Securing adequate water for irrigation became an issue in country club site selection because clubs could not count on nature to provide adequate irrigation by rain. Clubs experimented with different types of grasses to find the most appropriate type for the climate. The in-

crease in the number of golf courses was so rapid that between 1910 and 1920 manufacturers were profitably producing motorized lawn mowers.

The nine-hole golf course became standardized during the 1890s. As country clubs acquired additional land many expanded to the eighteen-hole standard. Two loops of nine holes, both beginning and ending near the clubhouse, became the accepted design. Members could easily access the course from the clubhouse and could rest or eat between the ninth and tenth holes.

Golf course architects from Great Britain found almost unlimited work in North America as country clubs and golf courses were developed at a furious pace. By 1927 more than fifty-five hundred country clubs with golf courses existed in the United States. Golf course architects and clubhouse architects began to work closely together to create an integrated design that was functional as well as pleasing. Landscape architecture for country clubs lagged well behind, but eventually the incorporation of trees, flowers, ponds, and gardens became an integral aspect of the development of the country club.

Gender Wars and Blue Laws

Even though country clubs, unlike their city club ancestors, allowed women to participate, most clubs had special membership categories for women and did not provide membership for single women regardless of their wealth. Country clubs offered numerous social and arts activities. Women organized plays, dances, and holiday and costume parties. To further highlight the elite status of club members, debutante coming-out parties were often held at the clubhouse.

The greatest conflicts between men members and women members occurred around scheduling of tennis court times and tee times. Because people presumed that only men work through the week, the best tee times and court times on the weekends were reserved for men players. Playing time on the weekends was further restricted in some locations because of blue laws that prohibited a number of activities on Sundays. Some members played on Sundays in an attempt to get arrested so that blue laws could be challenged in court. Because politicians and judges were frequently members of country clubs, these protests were often successful.

To reduce such scheduling conflicts between men and women, some clubs encouraged mixed foursomes and doubles tennis on the weekends. Many clubs, however, made playing golf difficult for women. Some clubs required that women play a number of rounds under a particular score before they could schedule tee times or play a full round of eighteen holes. This requirement angered women, and some left to form their own clubs. Ada Mackenzie, arguably Canada's greatest woman golfer, in 1920 found that British women had much greater access to golf courses than women in Canada. Upon her return to Canada, she looked for an appropriate site for a women's club. "The answer was a rolling tract of land north of Toronto at Thornhill. Mackenzie signed an option on the property and then went to work. She organized a bond issue to raise the capital, issued shares, and in 1924, launched the Ladies Golf and Tennis Club of Toronto, the first (and possibly still the only) course in the world exclusively for women.

At least almost exclusively: there are restricted hours for men" (McDonald and Drewery 1981, 43). Most women's clubs did not fair as well, and the women either opened their membership to men or returned to their former clubs. Even today many clubs do not equitably schedule tee and court times for women and men.

Ups and Downs of the Twentieth Century

Nearly every decade of the twentieth century had an impact on the country club. In 1913 the United States passed the Sixteenth Amendment to the Constitution, which created a tax on personal income. This amendment reduced the amount of money that some people had to spend on leisure pursuits. Many people had to give up their club memberships.

The 1920s were a decade of prosperity, and country club development and membership flourished. Operating a club became a complex and time-consuming task that board members were often unable to undertake successfully. Board members hired managers, often from city clubs, to oversee the operations of all club facilities, activities, and services. In 1927 the Club Managers Association of America was formed. It sponsored annual conventions and developed a publication. A new occupation was created for the expanding industry of country clubs.

The stock market crash of 1929 had a devastating effect on many country clubs because their membership was made up of the socioeconomic elite, who were hurt by the financial downturn. Many clubs were financially unprepared for the upheaval.

Throughout the 1930s many country clubs attempted to "tread water" to remain open. To save money, they cut back on maintenance of the clubhouse and sporting facilities, laid off managers, and sold land that was not being used. Clubs searched for ways to increase revenue. They rented out clubhouses to "appropriate" groups for functions. They reduced membership fees and accepted members of lower social standing. In the United States, the end of prohibition, with passage of the Eighteenth Amendment, allowed clubs to reopen

their bars to entice members back to the clubhouse to spend what money they could.

Many clubs installed swimming pools, although a high initial expense, to entice families. Clubs hoped that members would spend more money on ice cream and drinks. Although clubs tried a number of strategies to remain afloat through the Depression, by 1939 more than 15 percent had closed.

For the clubs that weathered the Depression, World War II brought more chaos. Young members left to enlist in the armed forces, and many women took jobs in the defense industry or jobs vacated by the men. Clubs offered limited-term memberships at low rates to service personnel and defense industry workers in an attempt to keep up a cash flow.

Rationing of most goods made maintenance of the clubhouse and facilities difficult. Gasoline rationing limited driving to the club by members. Some clubs offered horse-and-buggy service to transport members from the cities. Club members donated vegetables from their victory gardens and fish and game from hunting to the club to keep the dining room operating.

An economic upturn followed World War II, but it was a slow upturn. Rationing of building supplies and other goods continued to hinder clubhouse and course maintenance and improvements, many of which had been on hold for nearly two decades. During the 1950s and 1960s urban expansion into suburban developments forced a number of country clubs to relocate. Roads and commercial developments in the new suburban areas also encroached on the seclusion of many clubs, causing them to reconfigure the golf course or parking lots and clubhouses.

To boost membership, clubs introduced powered golf carts, which promoted a faster round of golf and allowed more members to access the course on weekends and other busy days. Rebuilding and refurbishing clubhouses, especially the dining room and kitchen to accommodate the increased numbers at clubs, became priorities. Clubs turned their attention back to golf course maintenance and beautification.

The 1960s brought a variety of challenges to country clubs in the United States. The environmental movement focused public attention on the dangers of pesticides to plants, animals, and water supplies. Golf course managers were forced to find ways to keep the course green without polluting the environment or financially crippling the club. Improvements in this aspect of country club management remains a high priority.

The desire for exclusivity and elite privilege was carried forward into the newly formed country clubs. Not only was the membership drawn from the wealthy members of a community, but also racial, religious, and gender discrimination was still prevalent in most clubs. The civil rights movement and the women's movement of the 1960s did little to affect this aspect of country club membership. Private clubs were exempt from the 1964 Civil Rights Act, which prohibited discrimination. One might well question the motives of powerful lawmakers who remained members of the very clubs that were exempt. People protested the exemptions, arguing that country clubs are a site of business negotiation and transaction. The right of private discrimination interfered with the ability of women and racial minorities to conduct business in an open market. Because of such protests many states removed the exemptions granted to country clubs.

The Professional Golfers' Association (PGA) became the focus of protests when PGA tournaments were scheduled at clubs that had chosen to pay penalties to the government rather than change their membership standards. Because the PGA, the United States Golf Association (USGA), and the Ladies Professional Golf Association (LPGA) were experiencing an increase in the number of tour players from various racial groups, they decreed that their tournaments would not be held in country clubs with discriminatory membership policies, although this decree has not always been enforced.

Twenty-First Century

In the new millennium tens of thousands of country clubs exist around the world. Most have been formed as exclusively golf clubs, but many country clubs continue to offer tennis and swimming and other social activities to accommodate the needs of all family members.

The basic structure and functioning of country clubs have not significantly changed in 150 years, however. Country clubs remain sites where the economically elite engage in leisure pursuits in an environment that is controlled and private. Initiation fees can cost hundreds of thousands of dollars, and annual fees can be well beyond the means of most North Americans. Dress codes for the clubhouse and specific sporting venues reflect the heritage carried forward from the city clubs and are closely monitored. However, many clubs are more relaxed and accessible to a middle-class membership base, which helps to keep the clubs solvent.

Although membership restrictions on women and racial minorities have been loosened in many clubs, women still face challenges in obtaining prime tee times, and members of racial minorities find themselves an even smaller minority within the country club membership. Admissions committees may still have policies that allow virtual blackballing.

The Future

The future of country clubs in North America is secured. These private enclaves will continue to exist as long as social stratification exists. However, problems remain to be solved for country clubs as the social fabric shifts. Women are still second-class citizens in many clubs and are denied membership in others. People have filed lawsuits against clubs that admit gay and lesbian members but that deny membership benefits to their partners—even in states and provinces where same-sex marriages are legal. Environmental concerns still must be considered in golf course maintenance, especially concerns of water resources and pesticide use. Only with difficulty can we discern what other social changes will present challenges for the country club in the future.

The country club has been a part of the U.S. landscape since the Industrial Revolution. In many ways it is a reflection of the social and economic tapestry that

has made the North American culture what it is today. People of power and privilege will always seek to both demonstrate and protect their status. The country club will likely remain one institution that showcases that status.

Dayna B. Daniels

Further Reading

Barclay, J. A. (1992). *Golf in Canada: A history.* Toronto, Canada: McClelland& Stewart.

Cousins, G. (1975). *Golf in Britain: A social history from the beginnings to the present day.* London: Routledge & Kegan Paul.

Duncan, H. G. (1977). *Club Managers Association of America, 1927–1977: The first fifty years.* Washington, DC: Bassett Printing.

Mayo, J. M. (1998). *The American country club: It origins and development.* New Brunswick, NJ: Rutgers University Press.

McDonald, D., & Drewery, L. (1981). *For the record: Canada's greatest women athletes.* Toronto, Canada: John Wiley and Sons Canada.

Moss, R. J. (2001). *Golf and the American country club.* Champaign: University of Illinois Press.

Peper, G., McMillan, R., & Frank, J. (1988). *Golf in America: The first one hundred years.* New York: Abrams.

Veblen, T. (1953). *The theory of the leisure class.* New York: New American Library.

Cricket

Cricket, a bat-and-ball game, has long been regarded as the archetypal English game that became popular in British Commonwealth countries. The core rules of the game were formulated in the eighteenth century by wealthy landowners. By that time cricket had been established as a game between two sides of eleven that took turns batting. An inning was completed when ten of the eleven players had been dismissed—caught, bowled, stumped, run out, and leg before wicket being the chief means of dismissal. Play focuses on wickets in the center of an oval or field that consist of three stumps at each end of a 22-yard (20-meter) prepared grass pitch. An over (six balls) is bowled from one end to either one or the other batsmen, followed by an over at the other end. A batsman can hit the ball (on the full— or "fly"—or after it bounces) to any part of the field and

I have always imagined cricket as a game invented by roughnecks in a moment of idleness by casually throwing an unexploded bomb at one another. The game was observed by some officer with a twisted and ingenious mind who devoted his life to inventing impossible rules for it. ■ PETER USTINOV

a run or runs are scored when both batsmen safely reach the other end. If the ball reaches the boundary, four runs are scored; if the ball crosses the boundary on the full, six runs. Batsmen do not have to run when they hit the ball; they can continue to bat for hours and, in international cricket, for days on end.

Underarm bowling was the norm initially, but the laws were altered in the nineteenth century to allow round arm (1835) and eventually over-arm bowling (1864). The laws of cricket dictate that the ball should be bowled (with a straight arm) and not thrown. New traditions developed in the nineteenth century: The English three-day county game was instituted in 1864, and international contests known as test matches, which came to be played over five days, began in 1877. An abbreviated form of one-day cricket, limited overs, was introduced in 1963 and quickly became popular.

Cricket boasts a rich language with fielding positions such as "fine leg," "gully," "silly mid on," as well as bowling terms that include "bouncer," "yorker," "googly," and "wrong-un." Phrases such as "sticky wicket" and "it's not cricket" have assumed many broader meanings outside cricket. Cricket is one of the most literary of sports.

Origins of Cricket

The origins of cricket are obscure. The first authentic reference to cricket dates to 1598, and cricket was played in the south of England in the sixteenth century and increased in popularity in the next century. The involvement of wealthy landowners helped transform an informal intervillage pastime to a more organized sport in the eighteenth century. Aristocrats with abundant time and money helped codify the rules of the game to safeguard their substantial bets (up to £10,000) placed on matches. From 1711 articles of agreement, which set out the core rules, were drawn up for individual matches. These articles were later incorporated into the "laws" of the game of 1744, 1771, 1774, and 1788. By the end of the eighteenth century, rules covered the bat, ball, stumps, and bails; the size of the wicket; methods of batting and bowling; and ways of dismissal.

Development of the Game

Cricket appealed to English aristocrats because it was a complex and leisurely game amenable to class distinctions. The aristocrat could lead the side and bat, leaving the more physically taxing fast bowling to the estate laborer. Cricket paintings that adorn the walls of many a country house from this century suggest that at a time when England was undergoing rapid urban and industrial change, cricket conjured up an appealing vision of "Englishness": bucolic bliss and class cooperation on rustic swards during sunlit afternoons.

EIGHTEENTH CENTURY

With the number of cricket clubs expanding, matches were played between teams representing counties by the 1740s. Teams designated as "All England" also took the field. The Hambledon Cricket Club, which existed from 1756 to 1791 at Broadhalfpenny Down, Hampshire, was the most famous club of the eighteenth century.

From the 1730s to the 1770s, cricket found a London home at the Artillery Ground, Finsbury. The London Club was a forerunner of the powerful Marylebone Cricket Club (MCC), which was founded in 1787 and became cricket's governing authority. It was based at Lord's cricket ground, which took its name from a shrewd businessman, Thomas Lord. Lord's became the spiritual mecca of world cricket.

From the 1740s there were intervillage cricket games for women, particularly in the counties of Surrey and Sussex. Some of the games were robust and boisterous and involved gambling. There are many suggestions that women cricketers achieved greater acceptance in the eighteenth century than in later centuries. Their matches were advertised, gate-entry was charged, and large crowds attended.

NINETEENTH CENTURY

Cricket continued to grow in popularity in the nineteenth century. Matches between Eton and Harrow were first introduced to Lord's in 1805, contests between the Gentlemen and Players (that is, amateurs and professionals) in 1806, and Oxford and Cambridge universities in 1827. Star players, such as Alfred Mynn (1807–1861) and Fuller Pilch (1804–1870), who fired the public imagination, emerged.

The spread of the game throughout England and abroad and its growth into a highly profitable mass-spectator sport owed much to working-class professionals. William Clarke, a bricklayer from Nottingham, formed a lucrative All England XI in 1846. It became a successful professional troupe that traveled around England. The professionals helped take the game overseas to Canada and the United States in 1859, to Australia in 1862, and New Zealand in 1864. Their tours overseas proved immensely profitable and stimulated interest in overseas cricket. The professional John Wisden

(1826–1884) published his annual cricket almanac for first time in 1864; it soon became the bible of cricket collectors. The professionals also played an important role in establishing international cricket. The first test match was played in 1877 at Melbourne between an English professional team and an Australian eleven.

Class distinctions were incorporated into the game: The amateur was segregated from the professional in terms of accommodation and dining, and he even entered the field from a different gate. The amateur had his name and initials recorded in the scorebook, the professional was identified by surname only. It was also thought proper that England should be captained by an amateur; not until 1953, when the Yorkshireman Len Hutton became captain, was England captained by a professional.

Professional tours inspired colonial sides to tour England. The success of the Australians, who performed very creditably against the best English sides in 1878, helped install cricket as an international game. The Australian defeat of the cream of English cricketers at the 1882 test at the Oval gave rise to the "Ashes" mythology. An advertisement in the press a few days later declared that English cricket died on that day, that its body would be cremated, and that the ashes would be taken to Australia. Tests between England and Australia became known as the Ashes.

W. G. Grace (1848–1915), who dominated the cricket world for the last four decades of the nineteenth century, was a superstar who helped popularize cricket. Bearded and solidly built, he became one of the most recognizable Englishmen of his era. The era before World War I has been called the Golden Age of cricket, a period when the game itself was seen as a form of imperial cement that bound the British Empire together. An Indian prince, K. S. Ranjitsinhji, who played for England in the 1890s, became a potent symbol of empire.

By the nineteenth century, cricket was elevated to become a manly and character-building game. Women who took up the game in the late nineteenth century were viewed with suspicion as trespassers on male ter-

Cricket

The First Women's Cricket Match, 1745

Another proof that cricket was not confined to male players is furnished in the following paragraph transcribed from the issue of the "Derby Mercury" of 16 August 1745:

The greatest cricket match that was ever played in the south part of England was on Friday the 26th of last month, on Gosden Common, near Guildford, between eleven maids of Bramley and eleven maids of Hambledon, dressed all in white. The Bramley girls got 119 notches and the Hambledon girls 127. There was of both sexes the greatest number that ever was seen on such an occasion. The girls bowled, batted, ran, and caught as well as any men could do.

Sydney, W. C. (1891). *England and the English in the Eighteenth Century: Chapters in the social history of the times.* London: Ward and Downey.

The leg-break diagram shows the alignment of fieldsmen to be used with the leg-break bowl, which is bowled from round the wicket.

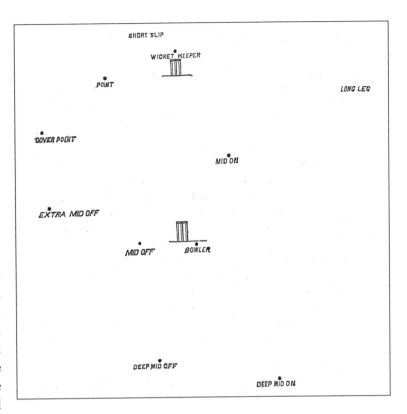

ritory. Women formed cricket clubs from the 1880s but battled to gain public acceptance—they were ignored or ridiculed.

TWENTIETH CENTURY

The twentieth century saw significant growth in international cricket competition and an ever-expanding program of international tours and contests. Many new competitors were accorded test status, including South Africa (1889), West Indies (1928), New Zealand (1930), India (1932), Pakistan (1952), Sri Lanka (1981), Zimbabwe (1992), and Bangladesh (2000). Many other nations have acquired associate status, including the Netherlands, Canada, Kenya, and the United Arab Emirates. The expansion of international competition led to the creation of a world cricket authority, the Imperial Cricket Conference (later the International Cricket Conference) in 1909.

International cricket for women dates from the 1930s, when England toured Australia in 1934–1935 and played three tests. Since then, a number of other women's teams have played test cricket, including New Zealand, India, and teams from the West Indies. For much of the twentieth century, women's cricket struggled to gain acceptance though the staging of a World Cup for women's cricket in 1973, two years before the men, was an inspired idea. Since cricket is still regarded as a man's game, there remains an onus on women who play cricket to prove their femininity. While women in some countries, such as Australia and England, play in a culotte (a divided skirt) to present a suitable feminine image, women in India and the West Indies compete in pants.

The infamous Bodyline series of 1932–1933 aroused great passion. To curb Don Bradman, the Australian run-machine, the English captain Douglas Jardine instructed his chief bowler, Harold Larwood, to bowl bodyline, a form of bowling which restricted scoring and provided greater opportunity for the batsmen to be hit. Australians regarded such tactics as intimidatory

and unsporting. The series strained relations between Australia and England and led to a change in the laws which sought to discourage bodyline bowling. The tour aroused great interest because it was the first to have ball-to-ball radio commentary in Australia.

With dwindling interest in three-day domestic cricket, limited overs cricket was introduced to English domestic cricket in 1963. The abbreviated format, with matches completed in a day, encouraged innovative play and proved an instant success. Limited overs internationals were played starting in 1971 and were featured in the 1975 World Cup in England. An epic final between the West Indies and Australia was watched by a substantial worldwide audience.

Television greatly extended the popularity of cricket in the 1970s. The game translated well on television and slow-motion replays helped unravel the intricacies of the game. This television-related boom in cricket made the game attractive to Australian media tycoon Kerry Packer, who virtually hijacked world cricket after he was denied exclusive Australian television rights. Packer signed up the majority of the world's best cricketers by offering players more generous payment. For two seasons establishment cricket and the World Series were locked in deadly combat before there was a truce

A cricket match at Cockington Court, Devon, England. *Source: istockphoto.com/BjornBP.*

in May 1979. Packer's great innovation in this period of crisis was to popularize day-night limited overs cricket, which proved commercially attractive.

The issue of South Africa and its apartheid regime dogged world cricket from the 1970s to the 1990s, and tours to the area were suspended during this period. The boycott of South Africa spawned a succession of "rebel" tours from various countries and resulted in suspensions for players who had accepted "blood money." Although many South Africans worked for multiracial cricket, progress was slow. South Africa reentered world cricket in the 1990s with the ending of apartheid.

The question of gambling and match fixing was widely debated in the 1990s when it was alleged that Pakistani, Indian, and Australian cricketers had accepted money from bookmakers from the subcontinent. South African captain Hanse Cronje received a life ban in 2000 after he admitted that he had accepted ap-

proximately $180,000 and offered some of his players money to underperform. Cronje was killed in a plane crash in 2002 before he had a chance to exonerate himself.

Spread of the Game

While the game became popular in England, it attracted less support in Scotland, Wales, and Ireland. Although cricket appealed to the working classes of Lancashire and Yorkshire, cricket was more of a middle-class game than soccer—the "people's game." English middle-class administrators of cricket considered the game to be the privileged preserve of the comfortable classes.

The British took cricket with them to all parts of their empire, though they made very limited attempts to encourage the indigenes of Asia and Africa to play the game. Indian teams were not formed until the mid-nineteenth century and did not play against European

The English are not very spiritual people, so they invented cricket to give them some idea of eternity ■ GEORGE BERNARD SHAW

teams until later in the century. In the twentieth century, however, cricket became the most popular sport on the four countries of the subcontinent, where it became far more popular than it ever was in England. The support of cricket by comprador communities, such as the Parsis of Bombay, and by many Indian princes endowed the game with glamor and status. Cricket on the subcontinent was able to reinvent itself to fit in with local culture and society and features passionate and noisy crowds and wickets that have encouraged slow bowling.

In the West Indies, too, cricket was initially a white man's game. C. L. R. James, in the cricket classic *Beyond a Boundary,* shows how West Indian cricket, although part of colonial oppression, was domesticated and transformed into a vehicle for the liberation struggle. Creolized West Indian cricket developed its own rich traditions, including "cricket as carnival," and produced outstanding teams that dominated world cricket from the mid-1970s to the 1990s.

Cricket clubs were established at an early stage in Australia and New Zealand, where playing cricket was a way to maintain their culture in remote and exotic locations. Cricket received a further boost in the late nineteenth century when test matches gave colonial teams a prized opportunity to thrash the motherland. Cricket comes close to being the national game of Australia, and it is also popular in New Zealand and South Africa, where it ranks second to rugby. Each of these countries transformed cricket to suit its particular climate, culture, and society. The hard and firm wickets of Australia, for instance, encouraged fast and leg spin bowling and confident shot making.

Although cricket was exported at an earlier period than soccer, it spread far less, remaining confined to the former British Empire. Allen Guttmann has claimed that this limited spread was probably due not to intrinsic factors, such as the greater complexity of the rules, but to the fact that by the time soccer was exported, in the later period of the empire, Manchester's economic influence was paramount and soccer was the favorite sport of Manchester. It is likely that cricket's failure to spread, for example, from local elites of Philadelphia and other social bastions to the broader population in North America was because these elites preferred to maintain cricket as an exclusive game.

The Future

Cricket as a sport has been a great survivor in that it has been able to reinvent itself many times over. It has evolved from the era of gentlemen who loved to gamble, to the time of the professional, to the amateur era, to the more commercial and professional era following World Series Cricket. In the 1980s and 1990s the balance of cricket has shifted away from England. It is ironic that the game is now more genuinely popular on the subcontinent and in Australia, than it is in England.

Cricket was played at the 1900 Paris Olympic Games, though it has not been recognized as an Olympic sport, and at the 1998 Kuala Lumpur Commonwealth Games. While it is unlikely to become a global sport in the foreseeable future, its global future seems secure because it is so dominant on the subcontinent, has a growing base in Africa (South Africa, Zimbabwe, and Kenya), and remains popular in Australia and New Zealand as well as England.

Richard Cashman

See also Ashes, The; Lords Cricket Ground

Further Reading

Birley, D. (1979). *The willow wand: Some cricket myths explored.* London: Queen Anne Press.

Brookes, C. (1978). *English cricket: The game and its players through the ages.* London: Weidenfeld and Nicolson.

Cashman, R., et al. (Eds.). (1996). *The Oxford companion to Australian cricket.* Melbourne, Australia: Oxford University Press.

Flint, R. H., & Rheinberg, N. (1976). *Fair play: The story of women's cricket.* London: Angus and Robertson.

Guha, R. (2002). *A corner of a foreign field: The Indian history of a British sport.* London: Picador.

Haigh, G. (1993). *The cricket war: The inside story of Kerry Packer and World Series Cricket.* Melbourne, Australia: Text Publishing.

James, C. L. R. (1963). *Beyond the boundary.* London: Hutchinson.

McPhee, H., & Stoddart, B. (1995). *Liberation cricket: West Indies cricket culture.* Manchester, UK: Manchester University Press.

Sandiford, K. (1994). *Cricket in the Victorian age.* Aldershot, UK: Scolar Press.

I can't really say I'm batting badly. I'm not batting long enough to be batting badly. ■ GREG CHAPPELL

Sissons, R. (1988). *The players: A social history of the professional cricketer.* Sydney, Australia: Pluto Press.

Stoddart, B., & Sandiford, K. A. P. (Eds.). (1998). *The imperial game: Cricket, culture and society.* Manchester,UK: Manchester University Press.

Cricket World Cup

The first attempt to create a world championship of cricket occurred in 1912 when Australia, England, and South Africa played a triangular tournament in England in the longer form of the game, Test cricket. The event, plagued by poor weather, was considered a limited success and not repeated. The first World Cup of cricket, known as the Prudential Cup, was played in England in 1975, and the championship has been held every four years since. Although the competition is primarily between the strongest Test-playing nations, some of the developing cricket nations, such as Canada, Namibia, and the Netherlands, have also participated.

Format and Venue Changes

The World Cup is the premier competition for an abbreviated form of cricket, known as limited overs or one-day cricket. (An *over* consists of six balls bowled in sequence by one player.) Whereas Test matches are scheduled for five days, and state, provincial, and county cricket matches occupy three to four days, the limited overs format—sixty six-ball overs per team in the first three World Cups and fifty overs since then—ensure that a match can be completed in one day, in approximately seven hours. The team that scores the highest number of runs in their allocated 300 balls—plus a few extra deliveries for wides (when a batsman cannot reach a ball to play a shot) and no-balls (primarily when the bowler oversteps the bowling crease) that have to be re-bowled—wins the contest.

The first three World Cups were played during daylight, and the traditional red leather ball was used. With the popularity of day-night cricket, some later World Cup matches involved play under lights—with one side batting in the afternoon and the other at night—necessitating the use of white rather than red balls because they were easier to see at night. Conditions frequently vary from day to night in light, heat, and even dew on the ground. Batsmen face an awkward period at twilight before the artificial lights take over.

The competition grew from eight nations and fifteen matches in 1975 to fourteen countries and fifty-four matches in 2003. In the first World Cup, the teams were divided into two groups, with the leading two teams in each pool advancing to the semi-finals. Since 1999, the best six countries advance to the Super Six playoffs. Under this system, performances in the preliminary matches count at the playoff stage.

Limited overs cricket emerged in England in 1962 when three-day county games were faced with dwindling crowds and declining revenue. The new format proved an instant success on television. The first limited overs international occurred almost by accident. After the first three days of a Test between Australia and England in January 1971 were abandoned because of rain, a hastily scheduled limited overs match on what would have been the fifth day of the Test attracted 46,006 spectators.

The first World Cup (for men) in 1975 was preceded by a World Cup for women, which was held at Edgbaston, England, in 1973, though this tournament was not the primary impetus for the men's World Cup. (The women's tournament is a smaller event because it has a smaller player base, and the game is popular only in a few countries, notably England, Australia, and New Zealand.) The 1975 World Cup final at Lord's in London was the first match broadcast live and in its entirety from England to Australia. The World Cup was an ideal format for television, and the BBC received £200,000 for the 1975 broadcast.

World Cup Events

The first three World Cups were played at Lord's in London and sponsored by the Prudential Insurance Company, but later World Cups have been played in a variety of Commonwealth countries including Australia,

Cricket World Cup

"I'm Here to See Cricket Played, Not Tiddlywinks"

In Dorothy Sayers's classic whodunit Murder Must Advertise *(1933), Lord Peter Wimsey unwittingly reveals himself at cricket. This passage presents a quintessentially English version of cricket, in which class and breeding show in every stroke. The Cricket World Cup is of a more global and democratic era, yet fans today share the same fascination with every nuance of the game.*

"The nincompoop! The fat-headed, thick-witted booby!" yelled Mr. Brotherhood. He danced with fury. "Might have thrown the match away! Thrown it away! That man's a fool. I say he's a fool. He's a fool, I tell you."

"Well, it's all right, Mr. Brotherhood, " said Mr. Hankin, soothingly. " At least, it's all wrong for your side, I'm afraid."

"Our side be damned," ejaculated Mr. Brotherhood. "I'm here to see cricket played, not tiddlywinks. I don't care who wins or loses, sir, provided they play the game. Now, then!"

With five minutes to go, Wimsey watched the first ball of the over come skimming down towards him. It was beauty. It was jam. He smote it as Paul smote the Philistines. It soared away in a splendid parabola, struck the pavilion roof with a noise like the crack of doom, rattled down the galvanized iron roofing, bounced into the enclosure where the scorers were sitting and broke a bottle of lemonade. The match was won.

Mr. Bredon, lolloping back to the pavilion at 6.30 with 83 runs to his credit, found himself caught and cornered by the ancient Mr. Brotherhood.

"Beautifully played, sir, beautifully played indeed," said the old gentleman. "Pardon me—the name has just come to my recollection. Aren't you Wimsey of Balliol?"

Wimsey saw Tallboy, who was just ahead of them, falter in his stride and look round, with a face like death. He shook his head.

"My name's Bredon, " he said.

"Bredon?" Mr. Brotherhood was plainly puzzled. "Bredon? I don't remember ever hearing the name. But didn't I see you play for Oxford in 1911? You have a late cut which is exceedingly characteristic, and I could have taken my oath that the last time I saw you play it was at Lords in 1911, when you made 112. But I thought the name was Wimsey—Peter Wimsey of Balliol—Lord Peter Wimsey—and, now I come to think of it...."

India, New Zealand, Pakistan, South Africa, Sri Lanka, and Zimbabwe. The establishment of the World Cup cricket is closely related to the rise and popularity of international cricket television coverage. The first six men's World Cups held some surprises and changes:

- The 1975 final between the West Indies and Australia was an exciting and fluctuating event with the West Indies winning by 17 runs after a fine 102 by captain Clive Lloyd and some outstanding West Indian fielding that produced 5 run-outs at crucial stages.

- The second World Cup in 1979 was disrupted by bad weather but a brilliant 138 by Viv Richards enabled to West Indians to win again, this time defeating England.

- India was the surprise winner of the third World Cup in 1983 when India dismissed the powerful West Indian side for a modest 140 and won by 43 runs.

- India and Pakistan hosted the fourth World Cup, known as the Reliance World Cup after a local sponsor, in 1987. Australia defeated England in Calcutta, India, by just 7 runs.

- Australia and New Zealand hosted the fifth World Cup the Benson & Hedges Cup, in 1992, Pakistan defeated England in the final by 22 runs at the Melbourne (Australia) Cricket Ground. This was England's second successive loss—and their third overall—in a World Cup final.

- The sixth World Cup in 1996, the Wills World Cup, was again played on the subcontinent with matches hosted by India, Pakistan, and Sri Lanka. Sri Lanka easily defeated Australia in the final at Lahore, Pakistan, by 7 wickets. Aravinda da Silva, who took 3 wickets and was 107 not out, was the man of the match.

In 1999, the competition was renamed the ICC Cricket World Cup, and a permanent trophy was created. This event was staged in England. Australia twice bettered South Africa in dramatic circumstances to reach the final. In a crucial qualifying match, Australia benefited when Steve Waugh was dropped at 56 before he proceeded to score a match-winning 120. In the semi-final, Australia secured a tie—which was all that was needed to qualify for the final—in the last over when South Africa appeared set to win. Australia comfortably defeated Pakistan in the final at Lord's in London by 8 wickets.

Australia won the 2003 World Cup, when it easily beat India in the final by 125 runs at the New Wanderers Stadium in Johannesburg, South Africa. Captain Ricky Ponting, 140 not out, and Damien Martyn, 88 not out, added 234 runs to register a World Cup record total of two wickets for 359 runs.

Of the first eight World Cups, Australia won the event three times, the West Indies twice, and India, Pakistan, and Sri Lanka, once each.

Controversies

Several events have affected World Cup Cricket:

- The 1979 World Cup was adversely affected by the World Series Cricket crisis. Caused by the issue of the television rights for cricket the crisis split the cricket world into two competing camps from 1977 to 1979. Australian media tycoon Kerry Packer signed up most of the world's leading players to stage World Series Cricket, challenging establishment cricket. A compromise was brokered in 1979 with Packer receiving the exclusive rights that he had sought. The crisis resulted in some under-strength national teams. Viewed in the longer term, however, World Series

Cricket popularized day-night matches and added to the status of the World Cup.
- Australia and West Indies forfeited their matches in Sri Lanka in the 1996 World Cup because of a bomb blast in Sri Lanka.
- The competition was skewed in 2003 when England refused to play in Zimbabwe and New Zealand chose not to play in Kenya; both England and New Zealand forfeited their points.

The Future

The Cricket World Cup continues to grow in popularity. The fifty-four matches in 2003 drew a record crowd of 825,000 and an estimated global television audience of more than one billion. Such has been the popularity of the World Cup that a "mini World Cup" based on a knockout format—the ICC Champions Trophy—was played in Bangladesh in 1998 to raise money for cricket development. The mini World Cup was played in Sri Lanka in 2002 and England in 2004. The 2007 World Cup will be held for the first time in the West Indies.

Richard Cashman

Further Reading

Baldwin, Mark. (2003). *The history of the Cricket World Cup*. London: Sanctuary.

Cricket Archive. (2004). Retrieved November 22, 2004, from http://www.cricketarchive.co.uk

Frindall, B., & Isaacs, V. H. (Eds.). (1985). *The Wisden book of One-Day International Cricket 1971–1985*. London: John Wisden.

Majumdar, B., & Mangan, J.A. (2004). *Cricketing cultures in conflict*. London: Frank Cass

Wright, G. (Ed.). (1976–). *Wisden Cricketers' Almanac*. London: John Wisden & Co.

Croquet

The modern sport of croquet—highly competitive but family oriented—originated in France during the early nineteenth century and was played with a unique mallet. This mallet, in its French peasant form,

Croquet being played on the lawn of Shadowbrook in Lenox, Massachusetts, in 1904.

Croquet might have grown in popularity to rival cricket as a major outdoor English sport if not for the arrival of another new sport that quickly became a public passion. Tennis was so popular that players took up all available grass space. Not surprisingly, by 1875 the All England Croquet Club had to add the words "and Lawn Tennis Club" to its name. Five years later the decline of croquet was spelled out when the club, based in Wimbledon, changed its name to the "All England Lawn Tennis Club." Croquet suffered from having neither the popular appeal of cricket nor the physical dash and style of tennis. One sports historian commented that "even the ladies grew bored and impatient with croquet's leisurely lack of vigor." By the turn of the century croquet was no longer played at Wimbledon, and croquet's international headquarters was moved to Roehampton and then to Hurlingham, both in England.

The American National Croquet League, founded in 1880, and the first Australian croquet club, founded in 1866, led croquet's international expansion. The Australian Croquet Council was founded in 1950. (Australia leads the world with more than six thousand registered players.) In 1896 the Croquet Association, an international body, was founded. The game's major impetus at the turn of the century was neither organizational nor regulatory: The emergence of star players from Ireland transformed the game into a sport.

During the nineteenth century croquet became an important vehicle by which women could move beyond the traditional boundaries of home, church, and school and attain a quasi-athletic pursuit. Writer Janet Woolum says that a milestone in women's sports was the 13 June 1877 founding of the Ladies Club for Outdoor Sports at New Brighton in Staten Island, New York. Club members took part in archery, lawn tennis, and croquet. Sport sociologist Jennifer Hargreaves, however, says that although croquet was "a highly sociable and fashionable

had a broomstick as a handle. The word croquet is derived from the French word *croc,* meaning "something shaped like a hook or a crook." Modern croquet probably evolved from an earlier game called palle mall in which players hit a ball (*palla*) with a mallet (*maglio*) through a series of iron rings. An account of a variation on that game appeared in a diary entry by the English essayist Samuel Pepys in 1663.

Origins

Croquet was transplanted from France to Ireland, where, records show, people played it regularly after 1852. After the game was introduced to England it flourished as Walter James Whitmore, the game's star player and tactician, promoted croquet and became the unofficial world champion in 1867 with his victory in the Moreton-on-Marsh, England, Croquet Open Championship. A year later he published a pioneering book entitled *Croquet Tactics.* The All England Croquet Club also was formed in 1868. Tennis historian E. Digby Baltzell, describing this period of the 1860s, was trying to be humorous but may have hit on the truth when he observed:

> There were more than half a million more women than men in England, most of them, with the help of their mothers . . . basically engaged in hunting husbands. On the smooth croquet lawns, as well as in the surrounding shrubbery looking for lost balls, proper, crinoline-clad Victorian ladies, more or less cunning, sought to capture the hearts of clean-cut English gentlemen (1995).

An English croquet lawn.

pastime," as women entered athletics they were stereotyped as the weaker sex capable of playing only gentle and respectable games. That is, women could acceptably perform only "the smallest and meanest of movements." Even with croquet, many people felt that women might more appropriately play croquet's indoor variations—parlor croquet, table croquet, and carpet croquet—instead of the outdoor version.

Hooping It Up

During the 1860s a croquet craze swept the United States as town clubs held competitions, and some scholars say that croquet was important in advancing women's rights. Nevertheless, during the 1860s, 1870s, and 1880s conservative groups in the United States and England feared the downfall of women who let

themselves be swept away by the excesses of such sports as bicycling and croquet. Despite such dire predictions, croquet flourished as a women's sport. In the United States, long before women took part in competitive tennis or basketball their first venture into competition sport was with croquet during the 1860s.

The croquet court consisted of nine hoops and two pegs at the first championship in England in 1867. The court's dimensions were 20 meters by 15 meters. The balls measured 9 centimeters in diameter, and the hoops had a maximum width of 20 centimeters. Three years later the court size was increased to 46 meters by 32 meters, and the hoops' width was reduced to 10 centimeters. The number of hoops was reduced to six in 1871. This configuration, called the "Hale setting," lasted from 1871 to 1922.

Straight and Narrow

Originally players struck the balls in a particular sequence (blue, red, black, and yellow), as in snooker. In 1914 this style of play was changed by the introduction of the either-ball game in which "the opponent could now play either of his balls. [This] meant that no easy break could be left for the next turn, for the opponent would remove the most useful ball to a safe position" (Arlott 1975). At the same time a 9.4-centimeter hoop was introduced. With a ball of 9.2 centimeters in diameter, the margin of error became minute, thus magnifying the importance of accurate ball striking. Perhaps only golf's putting carries the same premium on precision striking and ball placement.

Croquet is not a team sport. Almost without exception in croquet one player challenges another. Many descriptions of croquet make it seem as complex and cerebral as chess. However, the essence of the sport is its simplicity. The object is to score points by striking the ball through each hoop in the proper order and hitting the stake. Each player, in turn, tries to make a point or to *roquet*—to hit an opponent's ball with one's own. If an opponent scores a point he or she is entitled to another stroke. If not, the next player takes a turn.

Croquet continues to be an elitist sport. During its early days having croquet hoops on a lawn showed the house owner to be on the cutting edge of fashion. Today croquet club memberships still tend to be expensive and exclusive. Not surprisingly, the world's oldest "name" universities—Oxford and Cambridge—encourage the sport. In the United States croquet clubs exist in resort areas with an exclusive appeal, such as Greenbrier in West Virginia. The oldest U.S. university teams are at Harvard, Yale, and the University of Virginia. Only a few clubs exist in the Midwest, twenty-two in California, and more than that in the coastal resort townships of Florida. The largest concentration of croquet clubs is in the wealthy suburbs of larger northeastern cities such as Philadelphia, New York, and Boston. If croquet is to flourish, it must become more attractive to younger players.

Just as tennis has its Davis Cup, yachting its America's Cup, and golf its Ryder Cup, croquet has its Mac-Robertson International Shield. The Croquet Association, with headquarters at the Hurlingham Club in England, organizes all of the major championship events. In England these events consist of the open championship (singles and doubles), the men's, women's, and mixed-doubles championships, and four invitation events. The President's Cup is the most highly regarded of these latter events. Interclub croquet competition does not exist in the United Kingdom. In the United States croquet has been organized since 1976 by the United States Croquet Association.

A major, indeed, critical aspect of modern croquet is that it is a leader in terms of gender equality. Kay Flatten (2001, 281) notes: "Modern world rankings are combined for men and women, and the United States Croquet Association does not hold separate men's and women's championships."

Scott A. G. M. Crawford

Further Reading

Arlott, J. (Ed.). (1975). *Oxford companion to world sports and games.* London: Oxford University Press.

Baltzell, E. D. (1995). *Sporting gentlemen.* New York: Free Press.

Barnett, S. (1990). *Games and sets: The changing face of sport on television.* London: British Film Institute.

Blanchard, K., & Cheska, A. (1985). *The anthropology of sport.* South Hadley, MA: Bergin and Garvey.

Boga, S. (1995). *Croquet (backyard games).* Mechanicsburg, PA: Stackpole Books.

Brasch, R. (1971). *How did sport begin?* New York: David McKay.

Flatten, K. (2001). Croquet. In K. Christensen, A. Guttmann, & G. Pfister, (Eds.), *International Encyclopedia of women in sports.* New York: Macmillan.

Gaunt, D. (1993). *Croquet: Including games for the garden.* New York: McGraw-Hill.

Gorn, E. J., & Goldstein, W. (1993). *A brief history of American sports.* New York: Hill and Wang.

Holt, R. (1990). *Sport and the British.* Oxford, UK: Oxford University Press.

Lamb, W. E. (1997). *Croquet (know the sport).* Mechanicsburg, PA: Stackpole Books.

Lewis, R. M. (1991, Winter). American croquet in the 1860s: Playing the game and winning. *Journal of Sport History, 18*(3), 365–386.

Lucas, J. A., & Smith, R. A. (1978). *Saga of American sport.* Philadelphia: Lea and Febiger.

Michener, J. (1976). *Sports in America.* New York: Random House.

Reaske. C. (1988). *Croquet: The gentle but wicket game.* New York: Penguin.

Rooney, J. F., Jr., & Pillsbury, R. (1992). *Atlas of American sport.* New York: Macmillan.

Woolum, J. (1992). *Outstanding women athletes.* Phoenix, AZ: Oryx Press.

The act of taking the first step is what separates the winners from the losers. ■ BRIAN TRACY

Cross-Country Running

A form of competitive running, cross-country involves racing over outdoor courses of differential lengths and terrains, always "off-road." Courses are more than a mile long. An invention of nineteenth-century Britain, and primarily an Anglo-European event through the mid-twentieth century, cross-country running is a transnational sport today.

History

Cross-country developed as a competitive sport in early nineteenth- century England. Its origins were in a game called "hare and hounds" or "the paper chase," in which one runner or a group of runners created a trail for a second group of runners by dropping pieces of paper or other markers. The second group would try to follow the first group's trail, running through at a later time. The first formal competition, called "The Crick Run," was held at the Rugby School in 1837. Other public schools followed with competitions of their own, and when Oxford and Cambridge universities began to feature cross-country, this form of competition was consolidated as a sport. While hare and hounds continued to be a recreational and popular pastime, in serious competition this game was transformed into a cross-country race over a course that was clearly marked and established in advance over rough trails and open country. The English National championships were established in 1876. Two years later, William C. Vosburgh, a New York native, brought the sport to the United States. The first U.S. championship was established in 1880 and was run by the Amateur Athletic Union (AAU). The National Cross-Country Association was formed in

1887. Like many sports that developed at this time, it was primarily those who were well-to-do and well educated who participated.

Cross-country was introduced on the collegiate level at Harvard during this same period, but it was conceived as a form of fall training for distance runners who competed in track and field in the spring rather than as a specific sport in its own right. Other campuses followed Harvard's example. The first intercollegiate meet was held in 1890 between Cornell University, City College of New York, and the University of Pennsylvania. It was Cornell that developed the most pronounced interest in the sport and began to organize the first Intercollegiate Cross-Country Association in 1898. At the college level, the historical emergence of cross-country as a means to facilitate success in track rather than as a distinct sport continues to affect attitudes toward the event to this day. Cross-country is still somewhat seen as less exciting or viewer-friendly than track and is for the most part given less press and attention. It is rare that an athlete is recruited for cross-country alone, and it is always expected that if an athlete runs cross-country, that athlete will also run track (though not always the other way around). Because of the way scholarships are structured at major universities in the United States, wherein long-distance competitors in track are expected to compete in cross-country, it is also often considered a "service" or "feeder" sport. It is furthermore a point of consternation to aficionados of the sport that it is often confused with other forms of long-distance running like the marathon and road races. The sport of cross-country running, however, is distinct from all these forms in terms of terrain and distance.

International cross-country competition began in 1898 with a race between England and France. An annual championship meet, held at the Hamilton Park Racecourse in Glasgow, Scotland, was established in 1903, and included England, Ireland, Scotland, and Wales. The *International Amateur Athletic Foundation Magazine* notes that Alf Shrub, who led England to victory, "like most of his successors . . . was to transfer his talents to the track and during the next two years he set

14 world records" (lack of standardized distance for cross-country means no world records can be set in the sport). But although the idea of cross-country as a starting point for—or stepping stone to—track continued to follow the sport, it did grow, and other European countries began to take part in international meets the 1920s.

Women Compete

Though it is unclear who the first woman was to run a cross-country race, women as well as men were competing by the 1920s. F. A. M. Webster's *Athletics of Today for Women: History, Development, and Training* (1930) specifies that Rene Trente won the 1930 French Women's Cross-Country Championship for the seventh year in a row, and that in the English Women's Cross-Country Championship "Miss L. D. Styles retained her title" (97). The author was clearly an advocate of women's sports, for he reports that "it was to be proven even more conclusively in 1929 that women athletes have not as yet by any means reached the limits of their record breaking potentialities" (91). Contrary to any lingering stereotypes of delicate Victorian womanhood, Webster emphasizes that "despite adverse weather conditions and continuous showers of hailstones," on 13 and 14 May 1929 at the Women's Inter-University Championships in Birmingham, "the home university placed girls in every event, and carried off the Challenge Shield, which they had not held previously" (91).

In the United States, the annual NCAA Cross-Country Championship was established in 1938. The worldwide governing body for track and field, the International Amateur Athletic Federation (IAAF), assumed responsibility for cross-country in 1962 and established both men's and women's rules. The first international women's world championship was held in 1967, a year after the Amateur Athletic Union (AAU) held a national championship for women in the United States, so cross-country running for women emerged at roughly the same time as a national women's movement invested in securing equality of opportunity in all areas, including sports. Women's distance running in general

Cross-Country Running

Cross Country

For many decades, Cross Country coaches were somewhat isolated from a lot of the pressure basketball coaches faced. But lately those pressures have increased, in at least four areas I can think of.

1. Participation in high school Cross Country has always been a good stepping stone to college, but the competition for admission to a top-notch post-secondary institution has definitely increased.

2. With the advent of much more comfortable running shoes, coaches have had the opportunity to demand much more rigorous training, with the concurrent danger of stress fractures and other over-use injuries.

3. With the addition of girls Cross Country and the increased danger of eating disorders, a coach ignores that possibility at great risk.

4. Since it now is apparent that some illegal supplements can enhance a distance runner's performance, the temptation to use them is ever-present.

My hat's off to the Cross Country coaches who can cope with those pressures and keep their priorities straight. At the end of the season, it's a pleasure to see at the starting line a team's top seven runners: relaxed, healthy, confident and (hopefully) drug-free.

Source: Dougherty, K. (2004). My hat's off. *Cross Country Journal, XXII*(4), 2.

had a long and problematic history, and the emergence of a women's world cross-country championship at just this time was due to developments in this larger context. Although scientific data now show that women are actually more suited than men to endurance events, medical lore of the early twentieth century had stressed "moderate" exercise for women lest they compromise their reproductive capacities. This view was pervasive, for though women had been running in marathons since 1926 to no visible ill effect, the audience's distress at seeing women looking "exhausted" after their 800-meter runs in the 1928 Amsterdam Olympics led to an IOC (International Olympic Committee) ban that prohibited women from running a race any longer than the 200 meters until the 1960 Games in Rome. Marathon running in the United States was itself notorious for excluding women until that exclusion was publicized and challenged by Kathrine Switzer in 1967. Switzer entered the Boston marathon as K. Switzer, and despite the attempts of race officials to pull her entry number off her chest once they realized a woman was competing in the race, Switzer finished and called media attention to her cause, which was simply that women should be able to compete. Her quest had larger social and political implications, for the women's movement in the United States was gathering force at the time, and the push to include women in athletic events like the marathon paralleled the larger struggle for equal opportunity and revision of women's previously limiting gender roles. Switzer's struggle, along with that of other women pursuing equal rights in running elsewhere, cleared the way for their much larger participation.

Women's distance running developed against this history of gender relations, and that history had a profound effect on women's participation in cross-country. It has shifted from being primarily an intercollegiate men's sport early in the twentieth century to a sport that has far surpassed demands for equality of opportunity. Today, women's cross-country is more widespread and popular than men's, with the NCAA listing 890 schools that sponsored women's cross-country teams in 1998 as compared with 828 schools sponsoring men's teams (schools struggling to comply with Title IX requirements often add women's cross-country as a sport, because it has low overhead). At the high school level, 1995–1996 statistics compiled by the National Federation of State High School Associations show cross-country as the seventh-highest participant sport for girls with 140,187 athletes at 10,774 schools.

Nature of the Sport

The primary difference between a cross-country race and the 5,000 meters and 10,000 meters in track and field is that cross-country events are still run on courses that are technically "off-road." Such courses are not on any kind of synthetic surface such as a track or paved road; cross-country courses rather wind through parks, forests, and the dirt paths along golf courses. Unlike track, the marathon, or 10K or 15K road races, there is no standardized distance for cross-country. Courses vary between 10,000 and 12,000 meters for men, and 2,000 to 5,000 meters for women. It is also more a team sport than is track and field, the marathon, or road racing, with five to nine runners competing in a given race. The team's order of finish is determined by adding up the places in which team members finish— 1 point for first, 10 points for tenth, and so on. The team with the lowest score wins. Because it requires little equipment or special facilities beyond access to a park or other open space, it is an inexpensive sport that is accessible to many. Runners come from a wide variety of countries, traditions, and socioeconomic backgrounds. A latter-day derivative of cross-country running is trail running, for which special shoes were marketed in the mid- to late-1990s in the United States, but this is also a distinct sport of its own since competitions usually involve much longer distances than 12,000 meters.

As the generalist event of distance running, cross-country is a very competitive sport, because it draws runners from all distance specializations. Competitors from events as short as the 1,500 meters in track all the way through runners who compete in the marathon flock to cross-country racing in the fall, making the World Cross Country Championships notoriously difficult to win. A person who wins the world championship for the 5,000 meters in track (the most comparable distance) will not necessarily win in cross-country, where variable courses and terrains make every race a new challenge. In recent history, the dominance of African men and women in the sport, particularly those from Ethiopia and Kenya,

Men in turn-of-the-twentieth-century England competing in a cross-country race.

has caused controversy about whether or not there is some "long-distance gene" related to race, but such speculations largely have been discredited by the scientific community.

Competition at the Top

Although cross-country was an Olympic sport in 1912, 1920, and 1924, and then was dropped after 1924 because it was considered a bad fit with summer competition, it has continued to be a vital sport with its own national and international championships—the World Cross Country Championships for international competition, and the U.S. Men's and Women's Nationals at the national level. The superstars of cross-country tend to be successful across the distance-running spectrum. The best-known women's cross-country competitor of all time is Norway's Grete Waitz, who dominated women's distance running in the late 1970s and early 1980s. Though she is best known for her marathon victories, Waitz won five World Cross Country titles, four of them consecutively between 1978 and 1981. Waitz is typical of many runners in that she ran cross-country first, and her success there motivated her to try

other distances. Waitz was unbeaten in cross-country races for twelve years, until she was defeated in the 1982 Worlds by Romanians Maricica Puica and Fita Lovin. Her fifth World Cross Country title, however, came in 1983, when she won by over twelve seconds. Like Frank Shorter on the men's side, she remains best known, however, for her feats in the marathon, which included winning the New York marathon nine times, setting a world record four times, and getting a silver medal in the event in the 1984 Olympic Games.

American Lynn Jennings was also a formidable presence on the cross-country stage, beginning with her 1976 victory at the Junior National Cross-Country Championships. In 1985 she won the first of eight Athletics Congress National Cross-Country Championships. She competed in every single World Cross Country Championship between 1986 and 1993. She placed second in her first appearance, behind Zola Budd, and then had two fourth places and a sixth. In 1990–1992, however, she was undefeated in three consecutive Worlds, including the 1990 race, which she led from the start. She also won a bronze in the 10,000 meters in the 1992 Olympics, finishing behind Derartu Tulu of

Cross-Country Running

The Tarahumara of Northern Mexico

Training might almost be said to start at birth, because the Tarahumara runs from early childhood. Herding goats on the cliffs affords plenty of opportunity to develop endurance. Practice in running is hardly necessary; so the men practice kicking the ball. It is a common sight to see a man kicking a ball as he goes along a trail.

For three nights before a big race, the runners "cure" their legs. The first two nights they do this for themselves, using boiled cedar branches, and goat grease or olive oil. But all the runners spend the last night in the same house. Four old men, selected by the runners, watch over them. It is unlucky for these old men to sleep. (In some pueblos these guards are shamans.) All the paraphernalia of the race is gathered together and covered with a cross. All the runners are cured as follows: One runner takes the stick and the ball in his hands and gets bathed with a boiled cedar mixture—first one leg, then the other. (The bather is a special man, though not a shaman.) Then he makes three turns where he stands, and hands the stick and ball to the shaman again. He

takes a drink of laurel and goes back to his place to sleep. There are from three to four tcokéame (directors) who furnish coffee, tortillas, beans, esquiate, and other necessities for the runners. The food furnished by them is already prepared; and if a man is hungry, he eats and drinks. The water he drinks is warmed. He may smoke the strongest tobacco. Tesgüino or mescal is furnished for the shaman and the bather—not for the runners. Music and pascol dancing sometimes accompany the curing.

After a race the runner again cures his legs with a cedar wash. During the race the runners sometimes stop to get atole, pinole, coffee, mescal, or other sustenance. At other times they stop to get cured. The plant kotcínawa (Sp. sin vergüenza) is one reason for stopping. The leaves are ground and mixed half and half with tobacco and smoked by the spectators. This smoke, when blown toward an opponent, makes him very sleepy.

Source: Bennett, W. C. & Zingg, R. M. (1935). *The Tarahumara: an Indian tribe of northern Mexico* (pp. 337–338). Chicago: The University of Chicago Press.

Ethiopia and Elana Meyer of South Africa. Jennings recommends cross-country, especially for teens, telling *Runner's World* that it "provides the basis of excellence for track success . . . and most kids get their start as runners in high school cross-country. I'd like to think that my success with cross-country could serve as a kind of beacon to them." She was *Runner's World's* American Female Runner of the Year five times. Though she decided to concentrate her energies on track in 1994 (and most recently won 10,000 meters at the 1998 International Track and Field Championships), Jennings showed to a whole generation of cross-country runners that despite its usual backseat status, fame and fortune could be found in the sport.

On the men's side, the superstars include Oregon's Steve Prefontaine, who won the Individual NCAA men's title in 1970–1973, and has had two major mo-

tion pictures, *Prefontaine* (1997) and *Without Limits* (1998); a documentary, *One Day in September;* and another documentary that ran on CBS, *Fire on Track: The Steve Prefontaine Story,* made about his life. "Pre," as he is still known to fans, and who died in a car accident at the age of twenty-four, was the first athlete to sign a contract with Nike in 1974. His coach, Bill Bowerman, designed the first Nike running shoes along with Nike CEO Phil Knight. Other men's cross-country champions who had less notoriety but perhaps even more impressive records include Frank Shorter, who won the U.S. Men's National Cross-Country Championships from 1970 to 1973, and who became an Olympic marathon champion. Pat Porter won the Nationals in an unbroken streak from 1982 to 1989. In the World Men's Cross-Country Championships, John Ngugi of Kenya won the title from 1986 to 1989, and then he

Natural abilities are like natural plants;
they need pruning by study. ▪ RED AUERBACH

made a remarkable comeback to take the title again in 1992. Paul Tergat, also of Kenya, held the title from 1995 to 1999. Most recently, the title belongs to Kenenisa Bekele of Ethiopia, who won the championship in 2002, 2003, and 2004.

In the last seven years or so, African women have also been the dominant presence in women's cross-country, and Derartu Tulu, who won the gold in Jennings Olympics race (the first black African woman to win an Olympic gold), has been one of their leaders. She started her career in cross-country as well, beginning in 1989 on Ethiopia's women's junior cross-country team. She won the World Championships in 1995 and again in 1997, winning the latter with a strong kick at the end that surpassed Britain's Paula Radcliffe, who won the Junior Worlds in 1992. Tulu took the title again in 2000, while Radcliffe was the champion in 2001 and 2002. Ethiopia's Gete Wami also started on the Ethiopian junior team and won the World Cross-Country title in 1996. In the 1998 Worlds, though Irish runner Sonia O'Sullivan won the individual title, Kenya won the team title, followed by Ethiopia. The most recent individual champions have been Werknesh Kidane of Ethiopia in 2003 and Benita Johnson of Australia in 2004.

In recent NCAA cross-country competition, at the team level Stanford, Brigham Young University, and Villanova have continued to dominate. Individually, Kara Grgas-Wheeler of Colorado won the title in 2000, Tara Chaplin from Arizona in 2001, and Shalane Flanagan from the University of North Carolina in 2002 and 2003. One the men's side, Arkansas, Stanford, and Colorado have taken most recent team titles. On the individual level, Keith Kelly from Providence won in 2000, Boaz Cheboiywo from Eastern Michigan in 2001, Jorge Torres from Colorado in 2002, and Dathan Ritzenhein, also from Colorado, in 2003.

A More Positive Future

Though cross-country is still seen as a starting sport for runners who will later become the world's top marathoners and track and field competitors, the in-

creased rate of participation by girls and women shows that it is an important sport for meeting the mandates of Title IX, and that female competitors continue to demonstrate a facility for and interest in the sport. Two recent developments in the NCAA in the United States show a movement toward granting cross-country a more independent status: a move to require universities to offer scholarships to cross-country runners independently of track, and the 1997 subcommittee vote that extended the distance of the women's national championships from 5,000 to 6,000 meters (5,000 meters—3.1 miles—has been the distance since 1981). Coaches contend that the longer distance will also help make cross-country a sport with a firmer identity of its own. Furthermore, the 1997 realignment of Division I schools from eight districts into nine provides a better balance in terms of the number of schools sponsoring cross-country in each district. Better balance has made access to the championships fairer and increased the field sizes by 40 percent, up from 184 runners in 1997 to 255 in 1998. Increased access gives more teams and more athletes the chance to participate in a national championship, which raises the level of excitement in and commitment to the sport. Thanks to these improvements, in conjunction with the increased emphasis on separate scholarships for cross-country, it may not be long before cross-country outgrows its little sister status and emerges as a sport with a distinct identity and place.

Governing Bodies

Primary governing organizations include the International Association of Athletics Federation (www.iaaf.org), USA Track and Field (www.usatf.org), and the NCAA (National Collegiate Athletics Association, www.ncaa.org).

Leslie Heywood

Additional information was provided by Wayne Wilson (Amateur Athletic Foundation, Los Angeles), http://www. aafla.org.

Further Reading

Hickok, B. (2004). *Cross country running.* Retrieved April 23, 2004, from http://www.HickokSports.com.

IAFF Magazine. (2004). Retrieved April 23, 2004, from http://www.iaaf.org.

Johnson, A. J. (1996). *Great women in sports.* Detroit, MI: Visible Ink Press.

NCAA. (2004). *Women's cross-country.* Retrieved April 23, 2004, from http://www.ncaa.org

Webster, F. A. M. (1930). *Athletics for women: History, development, and training.* London and New York: Fredrick Warne.

Cuba

The largest island of the West Indies, Cuba is located 200 kilometers south of Florida and 100 kilometers west of Haiti. The capital city, Havana (with an estimated population of 2.3 million in 2003), is located on Cuba's northwest coast. Cuba's national population in 2004 was estimated at 11.3 million. Sport has been an important part of national life since the 1800s, but until mid-twentieth century, it involved mainly professional and amateur baseball, professional boxing, and amateur activities of the university and exclusive sport clubs. Cuba after the revolution of 1959 made sport a top national priority and established a developmental system that produced many great champions and coaches.

History

Indigenous people of Cuba and neighboring islands played *batos,* a bat-and-ball game. Colonial sports included cockfighting, bullfighting, and horseracing. Bullfighting and cockfighting are now prohibited by law, but horseracing continues. The game of *pelota vasca* also has continued since colonial times.

In the 1860s baseball came to Cuba by way of young men returning home from their studies in the United States. During the 1870s baseball teams already existed in Cuba, and a professional league began play. Largely through the efforts of Cubans, baseball spread to other Latin American countries. During the late nineteenth century and the first half of the twentieth century

Cubans played professional baseball in the United States (major leagues and Negro leagues) and in other Latin American countries. Adolfo Luque, Martín Di-Higo (a member of the U.S., Cuban, and Mexican Halls of Fame), Orestes "Minnie" Miñoso, and Luis Tiant Sr. were among the early great Cuban professionals. Before 1959 Cuba had supplied more U.S. major league players than any other country outside the United States. Beginning in 1949 interleague play for professional teams culminated in the Caribbean Series, a "world series" for Latin American teams, which Cuba dominated until after professional sport was banned by the new socialist government at the beginning of the 1960s. Cuba hosted the series championship three times and won it seven times during this period. During the late nineteenth and early twentieth centuries exclusive private clubs, such as the Vedado Tennis Club and the Club Atlético de Cuba, and the University of Havana had baseball teams and also played many other sports. Cuba has dominated international amateur baseball throughout its history.

Participant and Spectator Sports

As in the rest of the world during the late nineteenth and early twentieth centuries, sports in Cuba were largely limited to relatively wealthy and socially elite people, especially members of exclusive social clubs (such as the Vedado Tennis Club) and university students. Bullfighting, boxing, and baseball were professional sports before 1959. After the socialist revolution Cuba discontinued professional sports, encouraged sports participation for all Cubans, and initiated strong programs for the training of elite athletes. After a developmental period of ten to twelve years, socialist Cuba became a sporting power in the Americas.

Central American and Caribbean Games

Cuba had a large representation in the first Central American and Caribbean Games (called "Central American Games" until 1938) in Mexico City in 1926, where Cuba won baseball, all fencing events (Ramón Fonst won all), five of the eight field events, four of six swim-

Cuba

Key Events in Cuba Sports History	
1860s	Baseball is brought to Cuba from the United States.
1870s	A professional baseball league is formed in Cuba.
1900	Cuba participates in the Olympics for the first time.
1926	Cuba participates in the first Central American Games in Mexico City.
1926	The Cuban Olympic Committee is established.
1930	Cuba hosts the second Central American Games.
1949	The Caribbean Series is established as the "World Series" for Latin American baseball teams.
1951	Cuba participates in the first Pan American Games.
1959	The Castro government makes sports a national priority and bans professional sports.
1972	Cuban athletes win gold medals for the first time at the Olympics.
1984	Cuba boycotts the Summer Olympics in Los Angeles.
1988	Cuba boycotts the Summer Olympics in Seoul.
1991	Cuba hosts the eleventh Pan American Games.
1999	Cuba participates in the first Pan American Paralympics.
2002	Cuba boycotts the Central American and Caribbean Games.

ming events, and exhibition rifle shooting. Cuba hosted the second games in Havana in 1930 and subsequently participated in all years of the series except for 1959 (the year the revolution was completed) until boycotting the 2002 edition in El Salvador. Havana was host for the second time in 1982.

Before missing the 1959 games, Cuban men had won gold medals in 100 meters, 200 meters (Rafael Fortún won 100 meters and 200 meters in 1946 and 100 meters again in 1950 and 1954), 4×100 meters, and 400-meter hurdles, as well as several field events, baseball (1926–1938, 1950), boxing, soccer, fencing, gymnastics, swimming and diving, tennis, weightlifting, wrestling, and volleyball and silver medals in basketball. Cuban women had won gold in swimming and diving and a silver in basketball. Cuba won the most gold and total medals in 1930 and 1946 and most total again in 1935 and came in second in both categories behind Mexico in 1926, 1950, and 1954.

From the 1962 games through 1990 Cuban men won gold in 100 meters, 200 meters (Silvio Leonard

won 100 meters and 200 meters in 1974 and 1978), 400 meters (Alberto Juantorena in 1974 finished nearly four seconds faster than the next runner), 800 meters (Juantorena in 1978), 1,500 meters, 110-meter hurdles, 3,000-meter steeplechase, 4×100 meters, 4×400 meters, and the decathlon. Cuban men also won all field events (Javier Sotomayor set a high jump record of 2.34 meters in 1990), archery, baseball (1966–1978, 1986, 1990), basketball (1974, 1982), and boxing (eleven of twelve categories in 1986 and ten of twelve in 1990). Cuban men also won canoeing and kayaking, cycling, fencing (all events in 1978, 1982), field hockey (1982–1990), gymnastics (all medals in 1970, all golds in 1974, 1978, 1982, 1986), judo (all categories in 1978 and 1982 and eight of nine in 1986), rowing (seven of eight events in 1982), shooting, soccer (1970–1978, 1986), softball (1990), swimming, table tennis, tennis, volleyball (1966–1978, 1986, 1990), water polo (1966–1990), and weightlifting (all categories in 1978, 1982, nine of ten in 1986). Cuban men also won in wrestling (all Greco-Roman categories in 1982 and

The Cuban team is welcomed at the Pan American Games.

1986, all freestyle categories in 1986, and all but one category in 1982) and yachting, as well as silver medals in diving and tae kwon do.

Cuban women won gold medals in all women's track and field events, including pentathlon and heptathlon (Liliana Allen won 100 meters and 200 meters in 1990, María Caridad Colón set a javelin record in 1978 and bettered it in 1982, Ana Fidelia Quirot won 400 meters and 800 meters in 1986 and 1990), archery (all events in 1982), basketball (1970–1990), canoe and kayak, fencing (all events in 1978 and 1982), gymnastics (all medals in 1970, all golds in 1974–1986), diving, judo, rowing, shooting (all events in 1982), softball (1990), synchronized swimming, table tennis, tennis, tae kwon do, and volleyball (1966, 1974, 1978, 1986, 1990).

For most games of this period the Cuban athletic delegations were the most numerous, and Cuban athletes dominated track and field, boxing, baseball, basketball, fencing, gymnastics, volleyball, water polo, weightlifting, and wrestling. Among the weakest sports for Cuban athletes were equestrian , swimming, tennis, and yachting. Fearing for the safety of their delegation in San Salvador, Cuba did not participate in the 2002 games. As a substitute activity Cuba held the first "Olympics of Cuban Sports."

Through 1986 Cubans held fifteen of twenty-three Central American and Caribbean women's track and field records and eighteen of twenty-nine men's track and field records, one cycling record, all but one weightlifting record, all women's shooting records, and most men's shooting records, and had won 43 percent of gold and 28 percent of total medals.

Pan American Games

Cuba has participated in all editions of the Pan American Games from the initial games in Buenos Aires, Argentina, in 1951 through the most recent in the Dominican Republic in 2002. Havana hosted the eleventh games in 1991. In the first Pan Ams, Cuba won men's 100 meters and 200 meters (Rafael Fortún won both), baseball, three men's gymnastics events, and other medals in boxing, fencing, weightlifting, wrestling,

swimming, and shooting. From 1951 through 1959 Cuban men won Pan American gold medals in 100 meters and 200 meters, baseball (1951), boxing, weightlifting, other medals in 4×100 meters, 110-meter hurdles, triple jump, fencing, gymnastics, shooting, swimming, and wrestling. Cuban women won 60-meter and 80-meter hurdles and a bronze medal in discus. During this period of three Pan Ams Cubans won nine gold and forty-five total medals.

From 1963 through 1999 Cuban men won Pan American gold medals in 100 meters (Silvio Leonard in 1975 and both the 100 meters and 200 meters in 1979), 200 meters, 400 meters, 800 meters, marathon, 110-meter hurdles, 400-meter hurdles, 4×100 meters, 4×400 meters, high jump (Javier Sotomayor set records at 2.32 meters in 1987, 2.35 meters in 1991, and 2.4 meters in 1995), long jump, triple jump, shot, discus, javelin, and hammer throw. They also won baseball (1963, 1971, 1979, 1987, 1991, 1995, 1999, 2003), boxing (seven of eleven categories in 1975, eight of twelve in 1983, ten of twelve in 1987, eleven of twelve in 1991), canoeing and kayaking, cycling, fencing, gymnastics (all eight events in 1991), judo, karate, rowing, shooting, swimming and diving, tae kwon do, team handball (1991–1999), volleyball (1971–1979, 1991, 1999), and water polo. They also won in weightlifting (eighteen of twenty-seven categories in 1975, seventeen of nineteen in 1983, twenty-nine of thirty in 1991), Greco-Roman and freestyle wrestling (eight of ten Greco-Roman and five of ten freestyle categories in 1983).

Cuba Olympics Results
2004 Summer Olympics: 9 Gold, 7 Silver, 11 Bronze

Cuban women won gold medals in 100 meters, 200 meters (Liliana Allen in both), 400 meters, 800 meters (Ana Fidelia Quirot won both in 1987 and 1991, with a record in the 800 meters in 1987), 100-meter and 400-meter hurdles, 4×100 meters, and 4×400 meters. They also won high jump, long jump, triple jump, shot, discus, javelin (María Colón in 1979 and 1983), heptathlon, archery, basketball (1979, 1999, 2003), fencing, karate, gymnastics, rhythmic gymnastics, judo (eight of ten categories in 1991, all eight categories in 1995), kayaking, shooting, table tennis, tae kwon do, and volleyball (1971, 1975, 1979, 1983, 1987, 1991, 1995).

From 1951 through 2003 Cuba was in second place overall in total Pan Am medals won. Cuba's greatest Pan American successes have come in baseball, boxing, men's and women's basketball, fencing, volleyball, track and field, and men's gymnastics, weightlifting, and wrestling. Cuban athletes have been weakest in equestrian, roller skating, softball, swimming, and yachting. Through 1999 Cuba had won 654 gold, 464 silver, and 401 bronze medals for a total of 1,519. The comparable figures are 1,587, 1,154, 774, and 3,515 for first-place United States and 286, 451, 592, and 1,329 for third-place Canada. During the post-1959 period Cuba made its first great advance in 1971 (second overall in gold and total medals) and maintained this position in subsequent games through 2003, with the exception of first place in gold medals in 1991 and third place in total medals in 1999. Cuba also has had extensive participation in the Pan American Paralympics since the first were held in Mexico in 1999.

Olympic Games

Cuba's first Olympic appearance came in 1900 in Paris, where Ramón Fonst won a gold and a silver in fencing. Fonst won two more gold, and Cuba won a total of four gold, two silver, and three bronze medals in fencing in St. Louis in 1904. In 1948 Cuba won a silver in yachting.

After the revolution Cuban participation and success in Olympic Games began slowly but accelerated through the 1980 games in Moscow. In 1964 (Tokyo) a Cuban man won silver in the 100 meters; in 1968 (Mexico City) Cubans won two silver medals in boxing (Rolando Garbey won one of them) and silver in men's and women's 4×100 meters. The first gold medals came in 1972 (Munich, Germany): three boxing golds (including heavyweight Teófilo Stevenson). Other medals were one silver and one bronze in boxing, bronze in men's basketball, and bronze in the women's 100 meters and 4×100 meters. Gold medals in 1976 (Montreal, Canada) included three in boxing (including Stevenson), 400 meters and 800 meters (Alberto Juantorena won both), and one in men's judo; other medals were three silver and two bronze (including Rolando Garbey) in boxing, silver in men's 110-meter hurdles and bronze in men's volleyball. Cuba's best Olympic year at the time was 1980 (Moscow), when Cuba won six gold (Stevenson again), two silver, and two bronze medals in boxing, gold in javelin (María Caridad Colón), one gold and one bronze in weightlifting, silver in men's 100 meters (Silvio Leonard) and 110-meter hurdles, bronze in men's discus, two silver in men's judo, and one bronze in men's shooting. Cuba tied for third in gold medals (eight) and for fourth in total medals (twenty), however, ending well behind first- and second-place USSR and East Germany.

As a result of political conflicts and allegiances Cuba boycotted the 1984 (Los Angeles) and 1988 (Seoul, South Korea) Olympics. However, for the games in Barcelona, Spain, in 1992, Cuba won unprecedented numbers of medals for such a small country. Cubans won seven of twelve possible gold (including heavyweight Félix Savón) and two silver medals in boxing, gold in men's high jump (Javier Sotomayor) and women's discus, silver in men's 4×400 meters, bronze in men's 4×100 meters and men's discus, and bronze in women's 800 meters (Ana Quirot) and high jump. They also won gold in baseball and women's volleyball, one bronze in men's judo, one gold, one silver, and two bronze in women's judo, one silver in weightlifting, one silver and one bronze in men's fencing, one gold and one bronze in freestyle wrestling, and one gold and

Cuba

Cuban Baseball Players

The extract below from a 1924 sports publication bears out the fact that Cuban athletes have long been coveted players in the U.S. major leagues.

With the prestige of his Cuban predecessor in the big leagues to carve a place for him, Pedro Dibut, Cuban pitcher, comes up to join the Cincinnati team in the Florida training camp this spring. His is a protégé of Adolfo Luque, of the Reds, who last season was by long odds the best baseball pitcher in the world. Pedro has been coached during the winter in Havana by Luque, has a lot of speed and good curves, and, like all Cubans, is a high-class fielder and good hitter. One thing all Cuban pitchers can do, whether they can pitch much or not, is to field and hit like a regular player.

Source: *Sporting Life.* (1924, March), p.44.

two bronze in Greco-Roman wrestling. Cuba finished in fifth place in gold medals (fourteen) and fifth place in total medals (thirty-one). Comparable results for Cuba continued through 2004.

In 1996 in Atlanta, Georgia, Cuban medals included four gold (including Savón) and three silver medals in boxing, one gold in women's judo, gold in baseball and women's volleyball, one gold and one silver in Greco-Roman wrestling, one bronze in freestyle wrestling, one gold in weightlifting, silver in the women's 800 meters (Ana Quirot), one silver in men's fencing, one silver in women's judo, one silver in men's swimming, bronze in triple jump, one bronze in men's fencing, three bronze in women's and one bronze in men's judo, and one bronze in men's swimming.

In 2000 in Sydney, Australia, Cubans won four gold (including Savón) and two bronze medals in boxing, gold in men's 110-meter hurdles and long jump, silver in men's triple jump and high jump (Sotomayor), bronze in men's, bronze in women's javelin (Osleidys Menéndez), one bronze in men's fencing, two gold and two silver in women's judo, and one bronze in men's

judo. They also won gold in women's volleyball, one gold in Greco-Roman wrestling, one gold in men's tae kwon do, one silver in women's tae kwon do, silver in baseball, two silver in men's flatwater canoe, two silver in Greco-Roman wrestling, and one silver and one bronze in men's freestyle wrestling, tying for ninth place overall in gold (eleven) and in eighth place in total medals (twenty-nine).

Cuba's Olympic successes continued in 2004 in Athens, Greece, with gold medals in women's shot and javelin, silver and bronze in women's hammer throw, bronze in men's 110-meter hurdles, gold in baseball, five gold, three silver, and one bronze in boxing, one gold and one bronze in men's freestyle wrestling and one silver in Greco-Roman wrestling, one silver in flatwater canoeing, one silver and four bronze in women's judo, one bronze in men's judo, one silver in women's tae kwon do, one bronze in men's shooting (skeet), and bronze in women's volleyball, tying for ninth overall in gold (nine) and in eleventh place overall in total medals (twenty-seven).

Through 2004 Cubans had won sixty-five gold, fifty-four silver, and fifty-two bronze Olympic medals, with most outstanding performances in boxing, women's volleyball, and track and field.

Women and Cuban Sports

Postrevolution Cuba has given women many more opportunities than they had before to participate in sports and to develop into world-class athletes. Examples of the latter include Ana Fidelia Quirot (400 meters), María Colón (Olympic gold medalist in javelin), Osleidys Menéndez (present world record for javelin at 71.54 meters in 2001), Ioamnet Quintero (Pan Am high jump winner in 1991 and 1995), and Liliana Allen (100 meters and 200 meters).

Youth Sports

The Cuban model of sports proposes to expand mass participation in order to have the greatest chance of locating superior talent for international competition. Children who exhibit athletic ability are identified early in life and given opportunities to develop their ability. Sports schools (such as rural schools with sports emphasis, combining sports instruction with normal academic study) are available for all grade levels, and additional academies are specialized in particular sports or groups of related sports. Interscholastic sports competition is available from regional to national levels.

Higher-level training for the most accomplished athletes is available at other institutions and training centers, and the training of physical education teachers and coaches takes place at the university-level Instituto Superior de Cultura Física (Superior School of Physical Culture) in Havana and other teacher-training institutions in other parts of the country.

The Cuban Olympic Committee was established in 1926. The main sports organization in the country is the National Institute for Sports, Education, and Recreation.

Sports in Society

Prior to the revolution amateur sport had been largely the privilege of the socially and educationally elite class. Professional sports, in which anyone with enough talent could participate, included baseball and boxing. "Kid Chocolate" (Eligio Sardiñas) was Cuba's best-known professional boxer. After the revolution, the government's policy was to make sport available to all Cubans, to encourage talented children to develop their sport abilities, and to raise the level of Cuban elite sport to levels where international victories could bring prestige to the nation. Cubans had sports victories that surpassed expectations, remarkable performances including Alberto Juantorena's Olympic gold in 400 meters and 800 meters in 1976 and Javier Sotomayor's many medals and current world record in men's high jump (2.45 meters in 1993). In addition to programs that developed superior athletes, socialist Cuba promoted sporting and recreational activities for people in the military, workers, women, and the general population, both in cities and the countryside, with goals of attaining health and fitness.

Many principles used to develop Cuban sports were based on the Soviet model, and the Soviet Union supplied technical consultants for training athletes. Cuba also has provided many coaches to other nations—for example, in Central America—to help them develop elite athletes in many Olympic-type sports. In the absence of major governmental changes and/or negative economic conditions in the future, it is expected that Cuba will continue to stress sport for all and, especially, the preparation of superior competitive athletes.

Richard V. McGehee

Further Reading

Alfonso, J. (1988). *Puños dorados: apuntes para la historia del boxeo en Cuba* [Golden fists: Notes on the history of boxing in Cuba]. Santiago, Cuba: Editorial Oriente.

Bjarkman, P. C. (1994). *Baseball with a Latin beat.* Jefferson, NC: McFarland.

Capetillo, E. (1996). *Cuba: Sus aros de gloria* [Cuba: Her rings of glory]. Melbourne, Australia: Ocean Press.

González Echevarría, R. (1999). *The pride of Havana: A history of Cuban baseball.* New York: Oxford University Press.

Jamail, M. H. (2000). *Full count: Inside Cuban baseball.* Carbondale: Southern Illinois University Press.

Méndez Muñiz, A. (1990). *La pelota vasca en Cuba: su evolución hasta 1930* [Pelota vasca in Cuba: Its evolution until 1930]. Havana, Cuba: Editorial Científico-Tecnica.

Montesinos, E., & Barros, S. (1984). *Centroamericanos y del Caribe: Los Mas Más Antiguos Juegos Deportivos Regionales del Mundo* [Central American and Caribbean Games: The oldest regional games in the world]. Havana, Cuba: Editorial Científico-Técnica.

Ortega, V. J. (1991). *Cuba en los Panamericanos* [Cuba in the Pan American Games]. Havana, Cuba: Editorial Gente Nueva.

Pettavino, P., & Pye, G. (1994). *Sport in Cuba: The diamond in the rough.* Pittsburgh: University of Pittsburgh Press.

Senzel, H. (1977). *Baseball and the Cold War.* New York: Harcourt Brace Jovanovich.

Wulf, S. (1991). Running on empty. *Sports Illustrated, 75*(5), 60–70.

Cultural Studies Theory

Cultural studies is the general study of culture, the study of intercultural relations, and the anthropological study of culture. As theory and as practice, cultural studies is embodied in multiple histories and trajectories (e.g., institutional origins such as the Center

I think there are only three things America will be known for 2,000 years from now when they study this civilization: the Constitution, jazz music and baseball. ■ GERALD EARLY

for Contemporary Cultural Studies at Birmingham University, England; disciplinary affiliations such as sociology and education; and theoretical perspectives such as Marxism and feminism). Interdisciplinary projects within a cultural studies paradigm (framework) display a variety of theoretical and methodological approaches because the investigated issues are considered to be more important than the disciplinary constraints placed on what questions one can ask within an individual discipline.

British Cultural Studies

Cultural studies originated with the work of three founding fathers—Raymond Williams (1921–1988), Richard Hoggart (b. 1918), and E. P. Thompson (1924–1993)—and establishment of the Center for Contemporary Cultural Studies (CCCS) during the 1960s. British cultural studies emerged as an attempt to understand the changing sociopolitical and cultural environment of post–World War II Britain. This attempt to make meaning of contemporary culture meant undertaking such projects as critical analysis of Britain during the administration of Prime Minister Margaret Thatcher; retelling history from the perspectives of previously marginalized groups in society (e.g., "herstory" or history from women's perspective and undertaking "history from below" or history from the perspective of the working class); examining police brutality directed at black and working-class populations; taking seriously and studying such "unserious" movements and subcultures as the "hippies" and "skinheads"; and exploring popular culture forms such as pop music, talk shows, shopping malls, sports, and so forth and how the mass media operates in the production of meaning that society gives to these forms.

Numerous scholars affiliated with the CCCS displayed a range of divergent theoretical and methodological traditions that encompassed literary criticism, culturalism, structuralism, Gramscian Marxism (emphasizes class struggle and hegemony), feminism, and poststructuralism. Constantly evolving and seeking "unity-in-difference" (Grossberg 1989, 414), cultural studies has never been dominated by a single theoretical position and/or affiliation with a single academic discipline. British intellectuals, who were united by espousing leftist politics and generally working for progressive social change, used cultural studies as a means of undertaking progressive activism in an academic setting and of addressing pressing issues of social justice in and through culture in an interdisciplinary and also antidisciplinary manner.

Characterization

Stuart Hall, a contemporary leading figure of British cultural studies, is credited with asserting that cultural studies is not one thing. The various discourses of cultural studies are distinguishable by such factors as geographical location (e.g., British, Canadian, U.S., African, Nordic, Australian, Asian, etc.), by close disciplinary affiliation (e.g., closely related to communications and media studies, English and literary studies, sociology and anthropology, history, etc.), and by variations on theory/practice balance (although cultural studies is supposed to involve the blending of theory and practice in "praxis" (action), some versions are almost purely theoretical, whereas others maintain strong connections with grass-roots activism). Nevertheless, although different cultural studies theorists and activists would emphasize different characteristics or aspects, or even reject certain aspects, "openness" (in terms of theoretical and methodological approaches and in terms of content) is a pivotal characteristic of cultural studies. Thus, cultural studies is "always already" a contested terrain and is constantly mutating. As Lawrence Grossberg has warned, cultural studies should never be taken for granted:

Doing cultural studies takes work, including the kind of work of deciding what cultural studies is, of making cultural studies over again and again. Cultural studies constructs itself as it faces new questions and takes up new positions. In that sense, doing cultural studies is always risky and never totally comfortable. It is fraught with inescapable tensions (as well as real pleasures). In the U.S., the rapid institutional success of cultural studies has made it all a bit too easy. Cultural studies has to be wary of anything that makes its work too easy, that erases the real battles, both theoretical and political, that have to be waged, that defines the answers before it even begins. (Grossberg, Nelson, and Treichler 1992, 18–19)

Given the complexity and endless diversity of cultural studies discourses, some prominent cultural studies scholars, such as Grossberg, John Storey, and Handel Wright, contend that we would more usefully discuss the characteristics of a cultural studies project than attempt to define the field itself. The following shortened version of Wright's list of themes pinpoints broad characteristics that would delineate a cultural studies project:

- *Interdisciplinary, antidisciplinary, and postdisciplinary*—refuses to adhere to traditional disciplinary boundaries; draws upon a selection of traditional disciplines; transgresses and transcends disciplinary boundaries
- *Heavily informed by theory (especially cutting edge theorization)*—instead of dogmatically adhering to a certain theoretical position, borrows from and intersects with a number of theories and theorists; theoretical framework is determined by one's own politics and its relevance to one's work
- *Political*—concerned with issues of power, social difference, and justice; critically examines social and national identity/identification; draws on and forwards identity politics discourses; generally works toward progressive social change
- *Praxis driven*—intends to bring theory and practice together; not a purely academic endeavor but rather one that attempts to address real contemporary sociopolitical and cultural issues
- *Contextual*—positioned within a particular context; the method, theory, and politics of critical inquiry are connected to specificity of the geographical location and historical conjuncture
- *Self-reflective*—realizes the potential incongruity and transient nature of the knowledge it produces; resists creating and endorsing canons

Sports

Sports are an integral part of culture. They permeate various aspects of society and are inextricably connected with education, economics, politics, media, and even international diplomacy. Taking into account that cultural studies, as David Andrews indicated, can be conceptualized as a critical investigation into the politics of contemporary popular cultural practices and the magnitude of sports' constituency, we should not be surprised that sports have long been a persistent topic of interest in cultural studies.

The study of sports from a cultural studies perspective has enhanced our understanding of sports as a cultural practice that has definite social and political ramifications. For example, historically sports have been a public space where sex differentiation as a form of power is constructed and the hegemonic (relating to influence) power hierarchy and the male superiority rhetoric are reinforced. Cultural studies' analyses of the oppressive sporting culture have elucidated the ways in which this social institution is embedded in patriarchy and heterosexism as well as the role it plays in legitimizing popular values and social norms regarding women and homosexuals. These critical examinations have further unraveled sports' ability to perpetuate and worsen social discrimination against both marginalized groups. Moreover, cultural studies projects that examine the interrelationship between sports and the mass media have indicated that the patriarchal discourse of contemporary commodified sporting culture tends to trivialize women athletes, representing them not as active subjects but as passive sex objects. Thus, cultural studies as an approach to sports studies has played a crucial role in illuminating the process of meaning making in relation to cultural productions/commodities mediated through popular sporting practices.

Cultural Studies as Praxis Model

One of the emerging pedagogical (relating to education) models that articulates cultural studies characteristics (i.e., interdisciplinarity, exploration of social and cultural differences and social justice, the simultaneous focus on

A young woman showing her muscles. *Source: istockphoto/hidesy.*

both theory and practice, etc.) and has the potential to advance, if not radically alter the study of sports, is that of the cultural studies as praxis model, developed by Handel Wright at the University of Tennessee. This model blends the critical theory and literature of cultural studies (e.g., feminist, [neo]-Marxist, postcolonial theoretical perspectives, etc.), service learning as an activist/practice component, and empirical research (especially the critical forms of qualitative research such as critical ethnography, institutional ethnography, etc.) with progressive politics into everyday praxis.

A specific genre of service learning that Stephen Fisher coined as service learning for social justice is the principal practice and activist component of the model. This genre of service learning examines issues of social difference (i.e., race, social class, gender, sexual orientation, etc.) and addresses issues of discrimination based on social difference in or through institutions and organizations. Service learning for social justice articulated with cultural studies adds the element of pedagogy to the conceptualization and practice of service. It not only links the university with the larger community, forging town-gown relationships and collaborations, but also teaches students to approach local issues within the broader societal and global scope.

Cultural studies theory and qualitative examination of a particular organization and/or institution further students' understanding of how diversity and equity are constructed and operationalized in real-life situations, how power operates in everyday life, and how institutional culture shapes individual experiences. For example, within this frame, a researcher studying various factors that determine the college footballer's playing time on a team would look not only at his performance

skills and college status but also at his race and sexual orientation. The researcher would be interested in questions such as "Could it be that this talented receiver does not get a fair share of playing time because he is gay?" and "Is this just?" and "How do issues of power and privilege play a role in this situation?" and "What can be done to create a safe and just space for all athletes on the football team?" The cultural studies as praxis model thereby endorses empirical research as a factor that engenders cultural studies as praxis (i.e., theory-driven practice and theory informed by practice).

Thus, unlike passive forms of learning or internships that are divorced from theoretical references, the

cultural studies as praxis model pushes students to approach service (e.g., assisting an athletic trainer in the training room) from a research co-participant's point of view (i.e., observing daily interactions among staff members, between staff and athletes, etc.) and yet to theorize about the links between individual (i.e., athlete) and organization (i.e., athletic department) and between the organizational, the institutional (i.e., university), and the social. Because the model highlights four intertwined levels of social existence (i.e., individual, institutional, societal, and global) and puts emphasis on sociocultural difference, it creates a conducive framework for a reexamination of identity in general and of the identity of the athlete in particular. Instead of looking at the athlete in isolation as a whole, singular, unified individual, one looks at the athlete as a subject of multiple discourses of class, gender, race, sexual orientation, region, and so forth; a member of numerous social and cultural groups; and a part of the corporate culture of institutionalized sports immersed in a broader sociocultural and historical context.

Another implication of the cultural studies as praxis model for the study of sports is that interdisciplinarity inherent in the model opens up many more topics for inquiry. Traditionally, sports researchers adhering to the confines of a single discipline could not explore athletes' embodied experiences of being gendered, raced, sexualized, collegiate, or professional; the way athletes perform their identities/identifications and negotiate power in everyday life; or even athletic culture and sports subcultures in relation to cultural meanings. Cultural studies in general and the cultural studies as praxis model in particular provide powerful tools, both in terms of theory and methodology, for undertaking this type of work.

In sum the three principal components of the model (i.e., cultural studies theory, service learning for social justice, and empirical qualitative research), blended together as interrelated elements, transform the mundane everydayness of sports into an arena for social justice praxis work.

Posting the Future

Since the days of the CCCS cultural studies has approached the study of sports as an aspect of its project of challenging the binary opposition between "high" and "low" culture and taking popular culture seriously. Since those days cultural studies projects have attempted to make visible what is "not seen," reading actively against the grain of the common sense and taken-for-grantedness of sports as a neutral, apolitical activity. Cultural studies as an approach to sports studies has played a crucial role in elucidating the process of how the "common sense" is constructed and sustained through popular sporting practices (e.g., sports are a level field; men are better athletes than are women; blacks are natural basketball players; sports "lesbianize" women, etc.).

The relatively recent critical approaches to sports studies share cultural studies' conceptual framework because both display similar characteristics, such as interest in issues of power, human agency, and how individuals and social groups conform to, resist, and change existing power relations. Advocating the use of critical theories in sports studies, the sports sociologist George Sage has stated,

> A critical social perspective invites us to step back from thinking about sport merely as a place of personal achievement and entertainment and study sport as a cultural practice embedded in political, economic, and ideological formations. Relevant issues involve how sport is related to social class, race, gender, and the control, production, and distribution of economic and cultural power in the commodified sport industry. (Sage 1998, 11)

Thus, taken together, interdisciplinarity, considerations of social difference, power issues, culture and cultural theories, and especially cultural studies writings have meant that cultural studies has made inroads into sports studies such that we can now speak of a cultural studies of sports.

As stated, cultural studies is "always already" a contested terrain and is constantly mutating to reflect the swiftly changing conditions of the (post)modern world.

Influenced by the fact that cultural studies has been increasingly informed by poststructuralist and postmodern theorizing, cultural studies of sports initiated the poststructuralist project of sports. Drawing on the work of thinkers such as Jacques Derrida, Michel Foucault, and Pierre Bourdieu, a number of sports studies scholars have undertaken a critical analysis of the relationship between contemporary sporting structures, language, power, and subjectivity. In particular, these intellectual activists have exposed and demonstrated that sports language, televised sports, and athletes' representation are not neutral but rather are infused with national identity politics, power relations, and ideology; that the sporting body is disciplined and controlled through various technologies of power; that postmodern sports culture is dominated by the consumption of athletic commodities and celebrity spectacles; and that postmodern sports itself is both (re)producer and (re)produced by the postmodern culture. In sum, in the cultural studies of sports project, poststructuralist theories offer the most sophisticated and rigorous intellectual framework for examining the nature of (post)sports—at least for now.

Tatiana V. Ryba

Further Reading

Andrews, D. L. (Ed.). (2001). *Michael Jordan, Inc.: Corporate sport, media culture, and late modern America*. Albany: State University of New York Press.

Birrell, S., & Cole, C. (Eds.). (1994). *Women, sport, and culture*. Champaign, IL: Human Kinetics.

Blake, A. (1996). *The body language: The meaning of modern sport*. London: Lawrence & Wishart.

Davies, I. (1995). *Cultural studies and beyond: Fragments of empire*. New York: Routledge.

Grossberg, L. (1989). The circulation of cultural studies. *Critical Studies in Mass Communications, 6*(4), 413–420.

Grossberg, L., Nelson, C., & Treichler, P. (Eds.). (1992). *Cultural studies*. New York: Routledge.

Hall, S. (Ed.). (2000). *Representation: Cultural representations and signifying practices*. London: Sage.

Hargreaves, J. (1986). *Sport, power and culture*. New York: St. Martin's Press.

McDonald, M. G., & Birrell, S. (1999). Reading sport critically: A methodology for interrogating power. *Sociology of Sport Journal, 16*, 283–300.

Morgan, W. (1994). *Leftist theories of sport: A critique and reconstruction*. Urbana: University of Illinois Press.

Sage, G. H. (1998). *Power and ideology in American sport: A critical perspective* (2nd ed.). Champaign, IL: Human Kinetics.

Storey, J. (Ed.). (1996). *What is cultural studies?* London: Arnold.

Wright, H. K. (1998). Dare we de-centre Birmingham? Troubling the origins and trajectories of cultural studies. *European Journal of Cultural Studies, 1*(1), 33–56.

Wright, H. K. (2001–2002). Editorial: Cultural studies and service learning for social justice. *Tennessee Education, 31–32*(2, 1), 11–16.

Wright, H. K. (2004). *A prescience of African cultural studies: The future of literature in Africa is not what it was*. New York: Peter Lang.

Curling

Curling is a team sport played on a long, narrow sheet of ice. It incorporates the basic principles of lawn bowling or horseshoes. Each of four members of a team has a counterpart on an opposing team, and in alternating fashion the members of the teams throw (slide) objects toward a target. The target is a group of concentric circles called a "house" at the far end of the sheet; the largest of these circles is 12 feet (3 meters) in diameter. The objects that are thrown are round "stones" or "rocks," which must be less than 44 pounds (20 kilograms) in weight, less than 36 inches (1 meter) in circumference, and less than 4.5 inches (11 centimeters) in height.

After each player has made two throws—after a total of sixteen throws—an "end" (similar to an inning in baseball) has been completed, and at this time one point is awarded to a team for each of its stones that lies both in the house and closer to the center of the house (the tee or button) than any of the other team's stones. If neither team has a stone in the house, the end is "blank"; however, most ends result in one team counting between one and three points. A new end then begins, with players throwing toward the house at the other end of the sheet. A match is normally complete after ten ends. However, extra ends are played to break ties, and in recent years clocks have been introduced to speed up play, and occasionally a match is terminated because one team has used all the time allowed for its total of eighty throws.

The sheet of ice on which the game is played is called a "rink." The rink is 146 feet (44 meters) long, although only 132 feet (40 meters) are in play. As one moves down the sheet eight lines are encountered, each drawn straight across the ice, and many of the rules of the game preclude or allow particular activities within the specific sections of the ice created by these lines. The width of the ice varies from the 14 feet, 2 inches (4.2 meters) commonly found in Canadian curling clubs to the 15 feet, 7 inches (4.7 meters) used in other countries and in international play. The side boundaries are identified, often with wooden boards, and stones that touch or strike the boards are removed. The only important consequence of using the different widths is that in Canada one stone can fit in the space between the side boards and each house at the line drawn across the ice at the middle of the house (the tee line), but in other countries and in international events, two stones can fit there.

Teams

A team of curlers, often also called a "rink," is composed of a "lead," a "second," a "third" (sometimes called a "vice skip"), and a "skip." The four members throw their stones in order, and in the usual pattern the lead alternates with the other team's lead in throwing his or her two stones, then the second does the same, then the third, and finally the skip. Normally, though not necessarily, the skip throws last because usually he or she is the best shot maker on the team or at least the best shot maker under pressure. For this reason, and because the skip is given the responsibility for calling the shots that a team will attempt as an end unfolds, the skip is the most important member of the team. This explains why usually a team will be identified in the skip's name.

Shots

If one reduces curling shots to their essential purposes, only four types exist. The first is the draw into the

Curling
The Jolly Curlers

THE LAIRD'S DITTY

Tune: 'O for him back again'

Of a' the games that e'er I saw,
Man, callant, laddie, birkie, wean,
The dearest far aboon them a'
Was ay the witching *channel-stane.*

Chorus.—O for the channel-stane,
The fell-gude game, the channel-stane!
There's ne'er a game that e'er I saw
Can match auld Scotlands channel-stane.

I've been at bridals unco glad,
Wi' courtin' lasses wondrous fain:
But what is a' the fun I've had,
Compare it wi' the channel-stane?

O for the, & c.

Were I a sprite in yonder sky,
Never to come back again,
I'd *sweep* the moon and starlets by,
And play them at the channel-stane.

O for the, & c.

We'd boom across the *Milky-Way*;
One *tee* should be the Northern *Wain*;
Another, bright *Orion's* ray;
A comet for a channel-stane.

O for the, & c.

Source: Peek, H. (Ed.). (1901). *Poetry of sport* (p. 326). London: Longmans, Green, and Co.

house. The second is the hit, a faster-running shot designed to take out (remove) an opponent's stone(s). The third is the guard, a stone thrown with quiet weight that stops in front of the house (but it must be within 21 feet or 6.4 meters of the tee line to remain in play). The fourth is the tap-back, which might involve raising a guard into the house or simply moving stones to more advantageous positions.

In this skating and curling rink built in Carberry, Manitoba, in 1922, the skating surface is under the high part of the building, and two sheets of curling ice are under the lower, lean-to portion of the structure. *Source: Carberry Plains Archives.*

A curling stone is thrown from a "hack," which is now a rubber foothold but once was essentially a hole hacked into the ice. Two hacks are at each end, one for left-handed throwers and one for right-handed throwers, and each is 126 feet (38 meters) from the middle of the house at the far end. The curling stone is held by a handle, and as it is released the thrower imparts a spin or turn to the stone. If the thrower twists his or her elbow and hand out on release, then an "out turn" has been used, and if the thrower is right-handed the stone will rotate counterclockwise as it moves down the ice. If the thrower twists the elbow and hand in on release, then an "in turn" has been used, and it will rotate clockwise, again if the thrower is right-handed. As a stone moves along the ice toward the far house, and especially as it starts to lose speed, a stone thrown properly will move across the ice as well as down it. This fact means that a curler almost never throws directly at his or her target. A well-played curling shot is one that has been thrown with not only just the right amount of weight but also just the right allowance for sideways movement.

All of the players hold a curling broom or brush (the brush has become far more common since the 1970s), and this piece of equipment has different functions. The person throwing the stone holds the broom or brush in the nonthrowing hand and uses it to help maintain balance through the delivery. The skip uses his or her broom to provide a target for the thrower; when the skip is throwing, normally the third holds the broom. Almost always the broom is placed to the side of the true target to allow for the sideways movement. The other two members of the team use their brooms (brushes) to affect the speed and direction of the stone after it is on its way. Essentially, they sweep or brush in front of the stone and thereby cause it to slow down at a less rapid rate than it would if they were not sweeping. Just how sweeping affects speed is a matter of some controversy, but it seems to do so in several ways. It removes debris from the path of the stone, although in modern indoor rinks about the only debris that creates problems is the straw or hair left by other brooms or brushes. It affects speed also by temporarily heating the ice directly in front of the moving stone and thus

The greatest efforts in sports came when the mind is as still as a glass lake. ■ TIMOTHY GALLWEY

creating a slicker path, and perhaps by creating a bit of an air vacuum just in front of the stone.

Attractions

The attractions of curling are much like those of bowling and golf. Recreational players can be confident that serious injuries almost never occur to participants. They can be confident as well that even a novice can expect to make a few shots. For competitive players, the rewards can be the fame that comes with victory in prestigious club, regional, national, and even world championship events. The rewards also can be the valuable merchandise or, in recent years, substantial amounts of money awarded to victors. The most important reward, of course, is the knowledge that a player has achieved excellence in a sport that rewards coordination, skill, concentration, stamina, strength, strategy, and teamwork. Finally, for both recreational and competitive players, one of the attractions of curling is that it is a sport with many natural breaks in the action, and the time can be used for socializing with other players and even spectators.

Origins and Early Development

Games in which an object is thrown or rolled or slid toward a target are thousands of years old and have been played in many parts of the world. However, the game we would recognize as curling, featuring stones and brooms and houses, probably appeared during the sixteenth century, perhaps in northwestern continental Europe but more likely in Scotland. Certainly the Scots were responsible for the early development of the game, if not for its first appearance.

The early games of curling were played with stones that were simply held in the hand, although sometimes grooves or small holes might have been added to provide a better grip. The caliber of shot making must have improved dramatically during the seventeenth century when players began to use rocks with handles. The caliber of shot making improved still further during the latter half of the eighteenth century, especially as round stones became more common, and triangular or oblong ones became less. During the eighteenth century curling clubs began to proliferate. People established clubs for many reasons, but among the reasons were the desires to recognize meritorious play and to schedule regular competitions and social occasions for members.

Until early in the nineteenth century members of Scottish clubs curled with stones of differing weights, and perhaps even shapes. They used sheets of ice of assorted dimensions and a variety of rules to govern delivery, sweeping, and etiquette. Then, during the second quarter of the nineteenth century, improved transportation networks allowed curlers from different towns or districts to compete against each other, and standardized rules and regulations became desirable. The result was the formation of the Grand Caledonian Curling Club in 1838. This club was really an association, not a club. It became the Royal Caledonian Curling Club in 1843. It adopted and then promoted key rules that remain in effect today: Participants should not interfere in any way with an opponent's delivery; each team should have four players; each player should make two shots per end; only circular stones should be used; the sheet of ice should be 138 feet (42 meters) from "foot-score to foot-score"(the hack lines).

As the Scots were developing curling, they also were beginning to export it, often by emigrating, sometimes just by traveling. By the end of the nineteenth century the sport had been introduced into several countries, especially Canada, where in specific regions iron or wooden stones might be used. By the turn of the twentieth century curling in Canada was played mainly with "granites," and the sport was more popular in Canada than anywhere else in the world. This is still true today; Canada has about 1 million curlers, perhaps forty times as many as any other country.

Canadian Prairie

The region of Canada that especially took curling to heart was the Canadian Prairie, which was settled between the 1870s and the 1920s by peoples of European ethnic origins. Curling quickly became probably the most popular participant sport among them. Part of the reason for this popularity was that a significant number of newcomers were Scots, people already familiar with the sport moving in either from Scotland itself or from an eastern Canadian province. Another reason was that the basis of the Prairie economy was commercial agriculture, and winter was a slow time of the year. Finally, especially on the eastern part of the region, excellent natural ice could be maintained for three or four months each year, much longer than in Scotland or eastern Canada. The indoor, natural-ice curling rink was not invented on the Prairie, but it soon became far more prominent there than anywhere else. In small towns little two- or three-sheet sheds or "rinks," often joined to an indoor skating rink, were built almost as soon as schools or churches were, and in cities larger structures with perhaps eight or ten sheets were quickly constructed.

Canadians on the Prairie not only curled more often than people in other parts of the world, but also curled more seriously and more skillfully. Beginning in the 1880s the better curlers began to gather for bonspiels, which are curling tournaments of several days' duration at which prizes are offered to winners of events. The most skilled Prairie participants also introduced techniques and practices that made curling a better test of athletic excellence. In particular, they developed the shoulders-square-to-the-target delivery, a type of delivery that was facilitated by the permanent hacks that players could build in indoor rinks. On their temporary outdoor surfaces the Scots had used portable footholds (crampits), which encouraged a shoulders-sideways-to-the-target delivery that was not as efficient. With the squared-up delivery came improved accuracy and a style of play that featured hits rather than draws. Finally, during the 1920s the serious prairie curlers also worked hard to establish a Canadian (men's) championship event. It was first held in 1927, and prairie curlers dominated it until the mid-1970s. This championship was called the "Brier," after a product manufactured by the

sponsor, the Macdonald Tobacco Company. The Brier has been sponsored by other corporate entities since 1979, but it still goes by the same name, and it remains the most keenly followed national championship event in the sport.

Artificial Ice and Growth in Popularity

During the last half of the nineteenth century and the first half of the twentieth, Canadians and especially Prairie Canadians nurtured the old Scottish game of curling to new levels of popularity and athleticism. However, not until after World War II, with the availability of artificial ice, did the sport become truly international.

Artificial ice is created when a thin layer of water is sprayed onto a cold, hard floor, usually a surface of cement. The floor is cold because brine is pumped through pipes laid just below the floor surface. The sprayed water freezes, and the ice remains hard and true even if the air in the building is quite warm. Artificial ice was invented in England late in the nineteenth century, and it quickly began to have an impact on skating and ice hockey, but not until the prosperous 1950s and 1960s could large numbers of curlers in Canada and elsewhere afford to join clubs that installed an artificial surface. Then the technology began to have immense consequences.

One consequence, especially in Canada, was that more women began to participate. A few women had curled earlier, but the more comfortable, heated, artificial ice rinks drew women by the thousands, and by the 1970s and 1980s curling in Canada was truly a mixed sport. Another consequence was that curling could become much more popular and much more competently played in the moderate to warm weather regions of Canada. Finally, artificial ice led to internationalization. In the United States, in Scandinavian countries, in Switzerland, Germany, and other European nations in which the sport had been established earlier, curling now became much more popular. It also gained a small following in such unlikely nations (given their climates) as Australia, Bulgaria, Mexico, New Zealand, and Japan (in some of these nations the sport was not completely unknown prior to World War II). By the turn of the twenty-first century curlers competed in about forty countries around the world.

World Championships

Another reason for the rise in popularity of curling after the 1950s was the example of athletic beauty and excellence exhibited by elite players in world championship competitions. Almost always these competitions have featured a strong Canadian team, but competitors from other countries, notably Scotland, Norway, Sweden, Switzerland, and the United States, have won frequently. An unofficial annual men's world championship event began in 1959; it was sponsored by the Scotch Whisky Association. In 1966 the International Curling Federation was formed, partly in an attempt to have curling accepted as an Olympic sport. During the next few decades the federation (in 1991 it became the "World Curling Federation") helped to establish and then to oversee an annual world women's championship (first held in 1979), a world junior men's (1975), and (in 1988) a world junior women's championship (junior curlers can be no more than twenty-one years of age). In 2002 it established world senior (fifty years of age or older) championships for men and for women and a world wheelchair curlers' championship (wheelchair curlers use a stick to push the stone). These world championship events are, of course, preceded by national championship events in the individual countries.

Television

Since the 1980s many of the national and international championship events have become popular on television, as have other events in both North America and Europe that feature "professional" curlers (the money that curlers can win is not enough to live on year around, but it is substantial). Various curling organizations, including the World Curling Federation, have introduced or promoted initiatives to make curling a more attractive sport for live audiences as well as TV viewers. Among these initiatives are the use of clocks to encourage teams to quickly decide on a shot and then play it, the use of microphones on players so that the television audience has access to discussions about strategy, and especially the use of the "free guard zone" rule to increase the likelihood that the early stones thrown in an end will remain in play and that the last few shots will require great skill.

The Future

Curling likely will grow in popularity both as a participant sport and a spectator sport. Since 1998 it has been an "official" Winter Olympic sport; this designation assures exposure all over the world. In western Europe and in North America demographic trends suggest that recreational, easily learned, sociable sports such as curling will thrive. The sport is easily televised, and, as the Sports Network in Canada has discovered, a large demand for televised curling exists among retired people. Artificial ice has allowed the sport to be introduced in many warm weather countries, and the fact that curling has recently gained a few followers in Israel, Spain, and Greece suggests that this pattern will continue. Curling is enjoyed by men and women, by young and old, by highly competitive athletes as well as by people who want mainly a reason to laugh and talk with friends.

Morris Mott

Further Reading

Creelman, W. A. (1950). *Curling past and present: Including an analysis of the art of curling by H. E. Wyman.* Toronto, Canada: McClelland and Stewart.

Kerr, J. (1890). *History of curling, Scotland's ain' game and fifty years of the Royal Caledonian Curling Club.* Edinburgh, UK: David Douglas.

Kerr, J. (1904). *Curling in Canada and the United States, a record of the tour of the Scottish team, 1902–1903, and the game in the dominion and the republic.* Edinburgh, UK: George A. Morton.

Lukowich, E., Ramsfjell, E., & Sumerville, B. (1990). *The joy of curling: A celebration.* Toronto, Canada: McGraw-Hill Ryerson.

Maxwell, D. (1980). *The first fifty: A nostalgic look at the Brier.* Toronto, Canada: Maxcurl Publications.

Maxwell, D. (2002). *Canada curls: The illustrated history of curling in Canada.* North Vancouver, Canada: Whitecap.

Mitchell, W. O. (1993). *The black bonspiel of Willie MacCrimmon.* Toronto, Canada: McClelland and Stewart.

Mott, M., & Allardyce, J. (1989). *Curling capital: Winnipeg and the roarin' game, 1876 to 1988.* Winnipeg, Canada: University of Manitoba Press.

Murray, W. H. (1981). *The curling companion.* Glasgow, UK: Richard Drew Publishing.

Pezer, V. (2003). *The stone age: A social history of curling on the prairies.* Calgary, Canada: Fifth House.

Richardson, E., McKee, J., & Maxwell, D. (1962). *Curling, an authoritative handbook of the techniques and strategy of the ancient game of curling.* Toronto, Canada: Thomas Allen.

Russell, S. (2003). *Open house: Canada and the magic of curling.* Toronto, Canada: Doubleday Canada.

Sautter, E. A. (1993). *Curling—vademecum.* Zumikon, Switzerland: Erwin A. Sautter-Hewitt.

Smith, D. B. (1981). *Curling: An illustrated history.* Edinburgh, UK: John Donald Publishers.

Watson, K. (1950). *Ken Watson on curling.* Toronto, Canada: Copp Clark Publishing.

Weeks, B. (1995). *The Brier: The history of Canada's most celebrated curling championship.* Toronto, Canada: Macmillan Canada.

Welsh, R. (1969). *A beginner's guide to curling.* London: Pelham Books.

Welsh, R. (1985). *International guide to curling.* London: Pelham Books.

World Curling Federation. (2005). Retrieved March 4, 2005, from http://www.worldcurling.org/

Cycling

Cycling is an on-road and off-road sport with variations in terrain, slope, distance, and type of bicycle affecting its outcome. The sport began in France in 1868 and has spread throughout Europe, the Americas, Asia, Africa, and Australia.

History

The Industrial Revolution gave birth to the bicycle after nearly a half-century gestation period. The first crude two-wheeler of 1817 ceded the stage to the velocipede, the first bicycle with pedals, in 1863 when three French-

men, brothers Pierre and Ernest Michaux and their compatriot Pierre Lallement, claimed its invention. Yet the bicycle was not an immediate boon to sport in a century still in the shadow of Thomas Jefferson, Benjamin Franklin, and other philosophers of the Enlightenment. They had insisted that machines be useful and that they further the ideal of progress. No invention, lest of all a machine, was an end in itself, but instead it was to be a precursor of an even grander innovation. In this context sport gave way to utility. The bicycle was a new form of transportation as well as the herald of a new age of invention that would culminate in the automobile and airplane.

The ideology of the Industrial Revolution might have marred the future of cycling as a sport but for the rivalry between France and Great Britain. In 1868 business and civic leaders in Paris sponsored the first bicycle race, a 1,200-meter circuit of the Parc St. Cloud both to showcase the majesty of Paris and to celebrate the invention of the bicycle, the latest proof of French ingenuity. The event disappointed Parisians who watched Englishman James Moore rather than one of their own sprint to victory. The next year, Moore again deflated French pride, winning the 133-kilometer race between Paris and Rouen, a prelude to the stage races that would capture the French imagination, in 10 hours, 25 minutes. The event was the first to admit women, though once more the French could not claim victory. American Margaret Turner, who took the sobriquet "Miss America" to distinguish herself from her European rivals, captured the women's title to become the first American to win a bicycle race.

In 1878 cycling leapt across the Atlantic, with the first race in the New World in Boston, Massachusetts. The delay of nearly a decade between Turner's win and the first U.S. competition was cause by the tendency of Americans to brand European culture, including sports, as decadent. Yet Americans, even more than Europeans, were fascinated by machines and celebrated the bicycle for the freedom and mobility it gave riders. The bicycle helped democratize the United States, as it was available to men and women, both working class and middle class. The League of American Wheelmen, which could count only a handful of members in 1880, numbered 102,000 in 1889, triple the membership of the U.S. Cycling Federation in 1987.

But the league was no sanctuary from the racism of segregation that plagued the United States. The 1892 league convention erupted in dispute over the admission of African-Americans. White southerners opposed their admission, and the most militant racists stormed out of the convention. Others, repulsed by the thought of black men fraternizing with white women, were willing to admit blacks on condition that the league bar them from social events. A third group proposed segregated chapters within the league, modeled on the Jim Crow laws of the South. When the dust settled, league members voted to admit blacks so long as they were "gentlemen." The ambiguity of the word *gentlemen* gave white members the latitude to turn away blacks without cause, an injustice that lingered until the 1960s.

Cycles were built for transportation as well as sport. This carrier tricycle transports a worker, his ladder, and his toolbox.

By then France had reasserted supremacy with the Tour de France, whose origins are among the strangest in sport. In 1894 the French Army accused Alfred Dreyfus, a captain and a Jew, of spying for Germany, igniting a nationwide furor. Pierre Giffard, owner of cycling magazine *Le Velo,* thought Dreyfus the scapegoat of anti-Semitic military commanders and government ministers, whereas bicycle manufacturer and nobleman the Marquis de Dion declared Dreyfus a traitor. The feud grew so bitter that in 1900 Giffard refused to run an advrtisement from Dion, then *Le Velo*'s largest advertiser. Dion counted by founding his own magazine *L'Auto-Velo* in hopes of driving Giffard out of business. Desperate to attract readers, *L'Auto-Velo*'s editor Henri Desgrange organized a series of road races, among them the Tour de France, which he launched 1 July 1903.

Almost from its inception the Tour, which circuits France and portions of northwestern Italy, Switzerland, Belgium, and Luxemburg, claimed a mystique no other sporting event approaches. Although the course varies from year to year, it invariably sweeps across land once owned by the medieval Catholic Church and the Holy Roman Empire. It ascends into the Pyrenees and Alps traverses, passes through which the Carthaginian commander Hannibal marched his army in 218 BCE. The spectacle of cyclists streaming beneath the Arc de Triomphe recalls the grandeur of French Emperor Napoleon Bonaparte. In these and other ways, the Tour transcends sport in its evocation of religion, politics, and history. Pope Pius XI recognized as much when he elevated Gino Bartali to the status of Italian icon, blessing him "the Pious" on his winning the Tour in 1938.

The rise of the Tour as an elite event provoked a backlash during the 1960s in the United States among those who yearned for a mythic past when cycling was open to all. This impulse was strongest in California among white suburban teens who reveled in the excitement of motocross, a sport for motorcycle riders, and envisioned a new type of bicycle—and a new type of cycling. To be sure the road bike has virtues. The high

The bicycle is the noblest invention of mankind. ■ WILLIAM SAROYAN

frame permits full leg extension with each turn of the pedals. Slender, smooth tires reduce weight and roll resistance (the friction between tire and road), and aluminum or carbon alloys lighten the frame. High gear ratios maximize speed and the dropdown handlebars allow riders to crouch, minimizing air resistance. But the road bicycle lacks the ruggedness to withstand the shock of jumps and the maneuverability to negotiate the sharp turns of a motocross course. In 1963 the Schwinn Bicycle Company built the Sting-Ray, the prototype of the BMX (bicycle motocross) bicycle. Its short compact frame, small wheels, and thick studded tires absorbed the force from jumps and enabled riders to make abrupt turns. Despite its novelty the BMX bike is a throwback to the first chain-driven bicycles in having only one gear, for multiple gears offer no advantage in the frenetic sprint that is the motocross race. BMX began as an impromptu and informal affair with teens staging the first race in 1969 in Santa Monica, California. In 1975 some 130,000 cyclists competed in more than one hundred BMX races in California alone. BMX spread to more than thirty countries during the next two decades.

Around 1970 the off-road movement of which BMX was one manifestation spawned mountain biking, a phenomenon that combined sport, recreation, and communion with nature. Like BMX, mountain biking sunk roots in California, this time in Marin County, an upscale community that transferred the bohemian spirit and open terrain of cross-country running to cycling. Riders made do with the touring bicycle, the sturdier sibling of the road bike, or cobbled together their own contraptions until Specialized Bicycles owner Mike Sinyard built the Stumpjumper, the first mountain bike, in 1981. It was an eclectic model, borrowing the high frame and multiple gears of the touring and road bicycles and the thick studded tires, cantilever brakes, and flat handlebars of the BMX bike. But the Stumpjumper was not simply a touring-road-BMX hybrid. Its gears spanned a wider range than those of the touring and road bikes and shifted on the handlebar rather than

from levers on the frame. The result was a bicycle capable of covering a wide variation in terrain and slope and of igniting a sport. The National Off-Road Bicycle Association organized the first mountain bike championship in 1983, with the first world championship in 1987 and a debut in the 1996 Olympic Games in Atlanta, Georgia.

In all its permutations cycling has swelled in popularity. In 1992 bicycle production worldwide tripled that of the automobile, putting the number of bicycles at several billion according to one estimate. In 2003, 43 million Italians watched the Giro d'Italia, Italy's most prestigious road race. In 2004, 20 million Frenchmen and women thronged the stages of the Tour de France. So popular is cycling that it attracts sponsorship from Coca-Cola, Toyota, and other Fortune 500 companies. American millionaire Donald Trump has sponsored his own race, the Trump Tour, since 1989.

But popularity has not insulated cycling from controversy and scandal. In 1899 the state of New York banned cycling amid reports of riders hallucinating from exhaustion. In 1950 poor sportsmanship, a consequence of animosity between France and Italy, marred the Tour de France. Gino Bartali, in pursuit of his third triumph, surged into the lead in a stage in the Pyrenees. French spectators pelted him with bottles and stones and, when these actions failed, blocked the course and threw Bartali to the ground. Tour director Jacques Goddet broke up the mob with a stick and Bartali won the stage. That evening, he and the entire Italian team withdrew from the Tour. Goddet retaliated by changing the route so it would not traverse any Italian territory. No less pernicious has been the scandal of drug abuse. In 1908 Lucien Petit-Breton, two-time Tour winner, denied rumors that he used drugs to enhance his performance. Then as now, race promoters preferred to the look the other way rather than confront riders, but in 1924 Frenchmen and brothers Henri and Francis Pelissier rekindled the furor by admitting their use of cocaine, chloroform, and an assortment of pills. "In short, we ride on dynamite," confessed Francis. Drug abuse caused catastrophe, even death. In 1960 Frenchman Roger Riviere, high on amphetamines, was paralyzed when he crashed in the Pyrenees. In 1967 Englishman Tom Simpson died of cardiac arrest on Mont Ventoux. He too had been on amphetamines. In 1998 drugs threatened to unravel the Tour. Six days before its start, French customs officials seized a car laden with anabolic steroids and other drugs owned by the multinational team sponsored by the Swiss watch manufacturer Festina. The arrest of team masseur Willy Voet, director Bruno Roussel, and physician Eric Rijchaert forced Tour director Jean-Marie Leblanc to suspend Festina's cyclists from the race. In disgust over the scandal, 102 of the 198 riders quit the race, and Italian cyclist and eventual winner Marco Pantani refused to start the twelfth stage. The remaining riders joined him, provoking a confrontation between cyclists and Leblanc that threatened to end the Tour that year.

Nature of the Sport

The road race has been a staple of cycling since its inception. The surface of road varies among concrete, asphalt and stone, and the slope from flat to steep incline. A road race may traverse a single route in one day. Amateur races of this type often range between 100 and 120 miles and professional races between 150 and 190 miles. One type of road race is the criterium, which resembles a track race. Riders circuit a rectangle of streets as many as sixty times. Another type, the stage race, knits together a series of routes over several days or weeks. The Tour de France, the most famous stage race, averages about 2,000 miles over three weeks. Among its stages, which have varied between twenty and twenty-two since the end of World War II, is the time trial, unique in road cycling in requiring a rider to negotiate a course alone rather than as part of a group. One might expect the stage race in its diversity of surface,

---

Cycling

Cycling on Roads

Out of the road conditions of bicycling have at length evolved two postulates: (1) No roadway in a city, unless paved or macadamized, is fit for wheeling during wet weather if used by other vehicles; (2) in the country, safety and convenience demand that bicycles be separated from horse-drawn vehicles, because there is no immediate prospect of wagon roads reaching the needed condition of improvement in this generation of wheelmen.

The result has been the development of what, in the East, is called the "side path," and in the West, the "cycle-path," or "cycle-way." A cycle-path being narrower and cheaper to construct than a wagon road, a stated amount of money will make a correspondingly longer path. [. . .]

But the conviction is strengthening and rapidly spreading that bicycle-paths should be constructed by the public authorities with the use of public funds. The proposition that it is the duty of the highway authorities to improve the highways in such a manner as the public needs demand, would seem to require no argument to support it. This duty was recognized by the Supreme Court of Minnesota, recently, in a case in which the League of American Wheelmen employed special counsel to establish that principle and to sustain a law prohibiting the use of cycle-paths by any other vehicle.

Source: Choate, A. B. (1899, October). Bicycling. *Outing*, 1, 115.

slope, and type of stage to favor the well-rounded cyclist; yet the champion, American Lance Armstrong is an example, is usually the best climber.

This fact, counterintuitive as it may seem, stems from the aerodynamics and tactics of the stage race. At speed a cyclist dissipates 90 percent of his energy against the wind. By drafting behind one or more riders, he minimizes air resistance and thus energy expenditure. The stages on flat terrain bunch riders in a pack as they seek to draft behind their rivals. Riders seldom steal the race by surging ahead because the wind tires them and they fall back into the pack. Mountain stages, however, recast the dynamics of a race. The rigors of the ascent often fragment the pack, reducing the number of riders who can draft behind others and allowing a climber to surge, building a lead of several minutes. Once he breaks from his rivals, the leader looks to his teammates for aid. These teammates hinder what remains of the pack by staying in front of it but at a slow pace. When a rival tries to pursue the leader, teammates move to block the pursuit. Far from being unfair, these tactics reinforce the hierarchy of cycling: Each team has its star whose success the other members labor to ensure, even at the expense of their own ambitions. The cyclist who commands the mountains may amass a margin of nearly an hour, as Italian Fausto Coppi did in the 1952 Tour. Thereafter, the leader may finish the other stages in the pack without surrendering more than a few minutes of his lead.

Among the road races, the criterium has its parallel in the track race, a mainstay of the Olympic Games and popular in the United States until the 1930s. The 1,000-meter sprint, run over three laps, pits two cyclists against each other in a tour de force of speed and tactics. The two draw lots before the race to determine who must lead the first lap and thereby bear the brunt

An early cycling race. Note the three types of cycles used.

of wind resistance. At the end of the lap, the leader will try to force his rival ahead of him by coming to a virtual standstill, balancing precariously on his bicycle without falling or drifting backwards. His opponent, equally reluctant to lead, will respond in kind until 200 meters remain, when the clock starts and both cyclists bolt for the finish. The trailer has the advantage of draft and surprise but must time a surge correctly to win. If he moves too soon his opponent may recapture the lead in a countersprint, if too late, he will not overtake his rival. Sprint tactics are absent from the pursuit, a type of track race over 3,000 meters for women, 4,000 for male amateurs, and 5,000 for male professionals. Cyclists chase one another (hence the name pursuit) from opposite sides of the track. They compete as individuals or on a team. If part of a team, a cyclist may draft behind his mates, but the start on opposite ends prevents rivals from drafting or jockeying for position. In fact there is no passing in pursuit, for a cyclist who catches his rival wins the race. Otherwise, the cyclist with the fastest time wins.

The importance of drafting as a tactic diminishes in BMX because cyclists dissipate less energy against the wind than road and track cyclists and more on absorption of shock, roll resistance, and the effort to balance and maintain traction on loose terrain and sharp corners. With drafting less beneficial, advantage tilts toward the leader rather than pursuer. The danger of a wreck, compounded by loose terrain and tight turns, increases this advantage, for the leader will emerge unscathed with the opportunity to widen the lead. Consequently, riders sprint for the lead at the start. The leader into the first turn has the greatest probability of winning the race.

BMX favors technique rather than tactics. A cyclist who leaps a jump in an arc looks picturesque at the expense of time. While airborne a cyclist slows. Better to make a low jump, reestablish traction, and resume pedaling. This logic also applies to cornering. The shortest line through a turn, like the shortest jump, is fastest. As it does in BMX, rough terrain negates tactics in moun-

tain biking. The need to ford streams, climb steep banks, and wind down precipitous trails requires strength and stamina akin to that required to meet the demands of the mountain portions of a stage race.

Whatever the terrain and tactics, women have participated in cycling since it origin, though men have not always welcomed them. The form-fitting leggings women wore in competition struck nineteenth-century moralists as risqué. The scandal in the 1890s over male cyclists hallucinating from exhaustion bolstered the argument that the sport was too rigorous for many men let alone women. The argument countered the fact that in 1896 sixteen-year-old Englishwoman Monica Harwood rode 429 miles at the first women's six-day race in London, England, and American Frankie Nelson, "Queen of the Sixes," finished every six-day race she entered, losing only four times between 1896 and 1900. The conviction that women were too frail nonetheless persisted, leading the Tour de France and Giro d'Italia, Italy's most prestigious stage race, to bar women from competition in 1903 and 1904, respectively.

Women clawed their way back into cycling during the second half of the twentieth century, though the lingering belief in their inferior stamina and strength confined them to shorter distances than men raced. In 1984 Tour de France organizers created the Tour Feminin at 625 miles, less than one-third the men's distance and without ascents into the Pyrenees and Alps. The Hewlett-Packard Women's Challenge bills itself as the true equivalent of the men's Tour because it includes ascents into the Rocky Mountains, but at 688 miles in its inaugural year of 1984, it was little more than a third of the Tour. Since the inclusion of mountain biking in the 1996 Olympic Games, women have raced between 30 and 40 kilometers compared with between 40 and 50 kilometers for men. The women's road race spans between 100 and 140 kilometers compared with between 230 and 250 kilometers for men. On the track, women sprint 500 meters, half the men's distance. As noted earlier the women's pursuit covers 3,000 meters compared with 4,000 for men. The

The truth is, if you asked me to choose between winning the Tour de France and cancer, I would choose cancer. Odd as it sounds, I would rather have the title of cancer survivor than winner of the Tour, because of what it has done for me as a human being, a man, a husband, a son and a father. ■ LANCE ARMSTRONG.

3,000-mile Race Across America, however, does not distinguish between men and women. Both pedal the same course.

BMX has been the most successful among the types of cycling in recruiting youth, sponsoring races that admit participants as young as age three. Boys ages eleven and twelve, the largest cohort of BMX racers, have their own age division in state and national competitions. Small races group all youth under age sixteen, sometimes under eighteen, in their own division. Youth, particular in affluent communities in the United States, flock to BMX as they once did to Little League Baseball.

Competition at the Top

The Tour de France has been the jewel of cycling for a century. The world's best cyclists converge on France during the last three weeks of July. The winner conquers not merely a grueling course but the sport itself. Gino Bartali won the Tour in 1938, but during World War II, the Nazis conquered France and abolished the Tour. Undaunted, Bartali returned to the Tour in 1947 and won again in 1948 to become the only person to win two Tours a decade apart. The next year, and again in 1952, Fausto Coppi captured the Tour, establishing himself as the fiercest mountain climber of his generation. The *Campionissimo* (the Great Champion) climbed like "a homesick angel," gushed British journalist Phil Liggett. His revised twenty-nine-minute margin of victory in 1952 wounded French pride, causing Jacques Goddet to bar Coppi the next year. In addition to the Tour, Coppi won the Giro d'Italia five times, Italy's Milan to San Remo thrice, and France's Paris to Roubaix once. Barely past his zenith, he died in 1959 in Italy after returning from a criterium in Africa. The medical examiner declared malaria the cause, but the explanation never satisfied Italians who believed a rival poisoned Coppi. In 1999 Italian prosecutors reopened the case, but the evidence remains inconclusive. Frenchmen Jacques Anquetil and Bernard Hinault, Belgian Eddy "the Cannibal" Merckx, and Spaniard Miguel Indurain each won five Tours, but in

2004 Lance Armstrong eclipsed them to become the only six-time champion, a feat all the more remarkable because of his recovery from a near fatal case of testicular cancer.

Armstrong was not the first American cyclist to win international acclaim. Several may claim the honor, perhaps none more deserving than Marshall "Major" Walter Taylor, the grandson of slaves. In 1891 Taylor, then only thirteen years old, won his first competition, a 10-mile road race in Indianapolis, Indiana. His forte, however, was the track rather than the road. In 1898 he won the U.S. Sprint Championship and broke seven world records between one-quarter mile and 2 miles, twice lowering the time for the mile. He would shatter the record again in 1899 and 1900, setting the mark at 1:22.4 minutes. In 1899 Taylor won twenty-two races, including the World Sprint Championship. Between March and June 1901, he won 18 of 24 races in France, Belgium, Germany, Denmark and Italy. He won 42 races in 1901, 40 in 1902, 31 in 1903, and 159 overall despite the fact that rivals elbowed him and referees ruled against him in close races. In Paris in 1901, sprinter Edmund Tacquelin thumbed his nose at Taylor and *Le Velo* attributed his success to biology: Taylor was typical of blacks in having been born strong and fast at the expense of intellect. His American rivals Floyd MacFarland and Owen Kimble assailed him with racial epithets. Twice he retired from cycling, returning both times in search of financial security, only to die destitute in 1932.

Taylor's career coincided with the rise of cycling as an Olympic sport. The first Olympic Games since Greco-Roman antiquity, the 1896 Games in Athens, Greece, featured an 87-kilometer race, an out and back course between Athens and Marathon. Track cycling included the 1,000-meter sprint and 4,000-meter pursuit. In its emphasis on road and track events Olympic cycling mirrored track and field and the marathon, the staple of Olympic running events. Only in the last decade has Olympic cycling broadened its appeal with new events:

mountain biking in 1996, and keirin, a Japanese variant of the track sprint, in 2004.

Women Participate

Olympic and world cycling records dispel the myth of female inferiority. The sprint is the best comparison, being timed over the last 200 meters for both men and women. The men's Olympic and world records are 10.129 and 9.865 seconds, respectively, and the women's 11.212 and 10.831, a difference of only a second, or 10 percent, for both Olympic and world records. Two women, New Zealander Sarah Ulmer and Australian Anna Meares, hold both Olympic and world records for their events, the 3,000-meter pursuit in 3:24.537, minutes and the 500-meter time trial in 33.952 seconds, respectively. Ulmer and Meares signal the emergence of a new generation of women champions. French mountain-biker Anne-Caroline Chausson won twelve downhill and slalom world championships by age twenty-six. Former U.S. Olympic skier Juli Furtado turned to cycling in 1989, winning five U.S. mountain biking championships between 1990 and 1995 and the U.S. Road Championship in 1989. As with Coppi, disease truncated Furtado's career. In 1997 doctors diagnosed her with systemic lupus erythematosus, an autoimmune disease.

Other major competitions for women have included since 1984 the Tour Feminin, the Hewlett-Packard Women's Challenge, and the Race Across America. Ultramarathon cyclist John Marino founded the Race Across America in 1982, admitting women two years later, in hopes of generating enthusiasm for a long race unburdened by the rigidity and elitism of the stage race. Marino envisioned a less-commercial, more-spontaneous event. The 1984 women's race exceeded expectation, ending in a sprint between Shelby Hayden-Clifton and Pat Hines, both of whom finished in 12 days, 20 hours, and 57 minutes, the only tie in the race's history. Like the Tour de France and Tour Feminin, the Race Across America posts no records because of variations in distance and terrain.

The Future

Cycling may be entering a period of experimentation in which the traditions of the Tour de France and Giro d'Italia give way to a search for freedom and self-expression through sport. In 1984 writer, traveler, and cyclist Jacquie Phelan founded in Marin County, California, the Women's Mountain Bike and Tea Society, an organization that combines this new spirit of reverence for sport and impatience with the status quo. The society has organized mountain bike races for women in California, New Mexico, Alaska, and Massachusetts. Phelan wants to stoke competition not as an end in itself but as a mean of self-discovery. This is a vision of cycling as both sport and therapeutic escape from a high-tech world. In pursuit of this goal, cycling promises to attract a new generation of enthusiasts.

Governing Bodies

Governing organizations include the International Mountain Bicycling Association (www.imba.com), National Bicycle League (www.nbl.org), Union Cycliste Internationale (www.uci.ch), and USA Cycling (www.usacycling.org).

Christopher Cumo

See also Tour de France

Further Reading

Hickok, B. (2004). *Cycling.* Retrieved October 23, 2004, from http://www.hickoksports.com
Hughes, T. (1990). *The bike book.* London: Queen Anne Press.
Rendell, M., & Cheetham, N. (Eds.). (2003). *The official Tour de France centennial, 1903–2003.*
Wenzel, K., & Wenzel, R. (2003). *Bike racing 101.*
Wingate, B. (2003). *BMX bicycle racing: Techniques & tricks.*

Czech Republic

A small, strategically located country in Central Europe with a population of 10 million, the Czech Republic came into existence in 1993, the result of political changes that began with the disintegration of the Austrian-Hungarian Empire. Its mountains and plentiful streams and rivers, and the regular alternation of four seasons, permit a wide spectrum of summer and winter sports. The development of sports in Czech lands can be divided into four stages that reflect the dramatic political and social changes that have significantly affected all spheres of life since 1918.

The First Stage

The period leading to the establishment of an independent Czechoslovakia after World War I comprises the beginning of the Olympic movement, the fight for an independent state, and the development of sports societies in Czech lands. In the seventeenth and eighteenth centuries, when these lands were an integral part of Austria, sports such as horseback riding and fencing were performed mostly by the rich and socially influential to mark various celebrations.

An important milestone in the establishment of sports societies was the founding of the *Sokol* (Falcon) Society in 1862. As early as in 1871, a total of 131 *Sokol* clubs were active in Czech lands. The principal idea of its founder and chief representative, Miroslav Tyrs, lay in the belief that "in a healthy body dwells a healthy soul." The *Sokol* movement fueled an intense national feeling that furthered the establishment of an independent Czech state.

The enthusiasm for sports development in Czech lands facilitated efforts to establish and restore the Olympic movement. One of the first members of a new twelve-member International Olympic Committee (IOC) in 1894 was the Czech representative Jiri Guth-Jarkovsky, who in 1896 established the Czech Olympic Committee, whose objective was to strive for independent Czech participation in the Olympics. The first Czech team, represented by five athletes, participated in the second Olympic Games, held in Paris in 1900, and Frantisek Janda-Suk, a discus thrower, won a second place and introduced a new throwing technique—the turn.

From then on, despite the numerous hardships that followed the political integration of Czech lands with the Austrian-Hungarian Empire, the Czech Olympic Committee remained committed to its objectives and participated wholeheartedly in the international Olympic movement. From 1885 to 1913 a number of sports associations and societies grew up spontaneously (for example, the Czech Athletic Amateur Union, which encompassed not only cycling and rowing, but also the Football Association, the Ski Association of the Czech Kingdom, the Czech Ice Hockey Association, canoeing, and fencing). This period lay the foundation for organized sporting activities in the Czech lands.

The Second Stage

The second stage encompasses the period between the establishment of an independent Czechoslovakia in 1918 and the Communist coup of 1948, though between 1939 and 1945 it was interrupted by the German occupation of the Republic. The young democratic state created ideal conditions for the rapid and unhindered development of sports and the activities of sports societies. The physical education system in the then-free Czechoslovakia was marked by the proliferation of several independent sports organizations. Concurrently, the democratic Czechoslovakia saw the political polarization of these sports societies and associations—for example, the Association of Workers' Sport Clubs was left-wing, while *Sokol* was democratic. The activities of sports societies based on religious principles led to the founding of the *Orel* (Eagle) sports society.

The number of registered gymnasts and athletes in the 1930s totaled about 1.2 million. Sports and physical education activities developed rapidly and successfully, international contacts were renewed, and most importantly, the spread of the Olympic movement was accompanied by the increasing participation of Czechoslovak athletes in the Olympic Games. On the *Sokol* premises, a unique phenomenon developed—*Sokol* gatherings (*sokolské slety*) in which a huge number of gymnasts gathered to exercise together. As many as thirty thousand gymnasts might participate in one gymnastic set.

Fascism and the occupation of Czechoslovakia by Germany in 1939 suppressed sports development. Sports societies and associations were dissolved, and the many *Sokol* members who engaged in the resistance movement were ruthlessly pursued and killed. After the end of World War II, sports activities were restored, and the growing influence of the Communists after 1948 laid the groundwork for another wave of development of sports in Czechoslovakia.

The Third Stage

The third stage in the development of sports relates to the period from 1948 to 1989, when all activities in all spheres of social life were brought under central control by the Communists. In the sports domain, a new public authority was established, the National Board for Physical Education and Sports, whose objectives were to unify and control all sporting activities, beginning with national representation teams and including spontaneous individual sporting activities. *Sokol*, as the largest democratic organization, was gradually transformed into a body with an ideological direction dictated by the new regime. However, the difficulty of subordinating *Sokol* led to the setting up in 1957 of a volunteer organization, which was constantly under the system's control, the Czechoslovak Association of Physical Education (*CSTV—Ceskoslovensky svaz telesne*

Czech Republic

Key Events in Czech Republic and Czechoslovakia Sports History

1862	The *Sokol* Society is founded.
1896	The Czech Olympic Committee is established.
1900	The Czech team competes in the Olympics for the first time.
1885–1913	Many sports associations are founded.
1918	Czechoslovakia becomes an independent nation and sports become politicized.
1939	Sports is repressed by the Nazis.
1948	Sports comes under the central control of the Communist government.
1957	Czechoslovak Association of Physical Education is founded.
1980	Czechoslovakia wins the gold medal in soccer at the Olympics.
1989	Communist rule ends and independent sports organizations are revitalized.
1993	Czechoslovakia becomes the separate nations of the Czech Republic and Slovakia.
1998	The Czech team wins the gold medal in ice hockey at the Winter Olympics.

vychovy). Its emphasis was on the international representation of the country in sports.

Following the model of the Soviet Union, Centres for Sports Excellence (*strediska vrcholoveho sportu*) were established. The state provided financial guarantees for all spheres of sports activities, and athletes were prepared for achieving excellence. This emphasis on excellence bore fruit in the form of a series of international triumphs. For example, between 1945 and 1965 Czechoslovak athletes won eighty-eight titles in the World Championships, forty-four titles in the European Championships, and broke seventy-nine world records; additionally, Czechoslovakia organized thirty world and European meets. The *Sokol* gatherings, renowned for their mass performances, were replaced by *spartakiads,* which were intended to propagate the ideology of the current regime. This trend prevailed until 1989 when the Communist regime finally collapsed.

During this period, physical education and sports were regarded as healthy leisure-time activities for citizens, and millions of people were engaged in organized as well as occasional sports and recreational activities, including hiking, cycling, skiing (about 2 million skiers), jogging, volleyball, and football. On the international scene, Czechoslovak athletes continued to triumph in important meets—for example, from 1948 to 1988 they won seventy-six medals in the summer Olympic Games and twenty-one medals in the winter Olympic Games.

The Fourth Stage

The fourth stage, which began after the collapse of the Communist regime in 1989, has seen the gradual decapitation and restructuring of the centrally controlled sports system. Another milestone was the division of Czechoslovakia into two independent states in 1993: the Czech Republic (population 10 million) and Slovakia (population 5 million). Since then, a new way of organizing and managing physical education and sports has evolved and, apart from the central organization (*CSTV),* new sports associations have been established

and many private and group sporting activities have sprung up. On the state level, the sphere of sports is supervised by the Ministry of Education, Youth and Sports. Based on the former central organization, *CSTV* has assumed the form of a sports federation comprising seventy-three sports associations (the total number of registered athletes is about 1.3 million).

Parallel to this impressive growth are various independent sports organizations—for example, *Sokol* (170,000 members), *Orel,* the Czech Association of Sports Clubs (275,000 members), and the Czech Association of Sports for All (250,000 members). The Czech Olympic Committee and the Czech Paralympic Committee supervise and coordinate the preparation of athletes for the Olympic Games and together they form an integral part of the international Olympic movement. People have also been encouraged to play sports for pleasure and health. Currently, the estimated number of people who engage in a sport exceeds 2 million, which is about 20 percent of the total Czech population.

The spectrum of sports disciplines in the Czech Republic is very wide, and in many sports Czech athletes have achieved excellent results on the international level. The most popular disciplines are football (a silver medal in the 1962 World Championship, a gold medal in the European Championship in 1976, a bronze medal in the 2004 European Championship, and a gold medal in the 1980 Olympic Games) and ice hockey (multiple World Championship titles and winner of the 1998 Olympic Games in Nagano). The popularity of individual sports disciplines such as skiing, tennis, and water slalom depends on their success in important international meets. The number of disciplines in which Czechoslovak and current Czech athletes won gold medals at the Olympic Games illustrates the great variety of sports in this relatively small country: gymnastics, horseback riding, weight lifting, canoeing, athletics, boxing, rowing, cycling, diving, shooting, modern pentathlon, wrestling, tennis, water slalom, football, ice hockey, figure skating, and acrobatic skiing.

The most famous athletes are those who won more than one medal in the Olympic Games—these include Bedrich Supcík and Alois Hudec (gymnastics, two medals), Emil Zatopek (athletics, four medals), Dana Zatopkova (athletics, two medals), Vera Caslavska (gymnastics, seven medals), Jiri Raska (ski jump, two medals), and very recently, Martin Doktor (canoeing, two medals), Stepanka Hilgertova (water slalom, two medals), Jan Zelezny (athletics-javelin, three medals), Robert Sebrle (athletics-decathlon, three medals), and Katerina Neumannova (cross-country skiing, three medals).

In the free Czech Republic of today, sports opportunities for the handicapped are increasing, and the results achieved in the Paralympic Games reflect impressive talent. The international achievements of Czech athletes are also the subject of significant media attention, an important factor in motivating young people to play sports. An interest in sports activities organized on a noncompetitive basis for pleasure and for self-betterment is also increasing.

Frantisek Vaverka

Further Reading

Bosak, E., et al. (1969). *Stucny prehled vyvoje sportonich odvetvi v Ceskoslovensku I* [Short overview of the development of sport's branches in the Czechoslovakia I]. Prague: Olympia.

Cesky olympismus [Czech Olympics]. (2000). Prague: Olympia.

Klir, M., Kossl, J., Martinek, A., & Martinek, M. (1988). *Almanach Ceskoslovenskych olympioniku* [Almanac of the Czech Olympian]. Prague: Olympia.

Kossl, J., Kratky F., & Marek, J. (1986). *Dejiny telesne vychovy II (1848 do soucasnosti)* [History of the physical education II (1848 till present)]. Prague.

Kossl, J., Stumbauer, J., & Walc, M. (2002). *Vybrane kapitoly z dejin telesne kultury* [Selected chapters from the history of physical culture]. Prague: Charles University.

Stekr, V. (2000). *Olympijske hnuti–Olympijske hry* [Olympic movement–Olympic games]. Olomouc, Czech Republic: Palacky University.

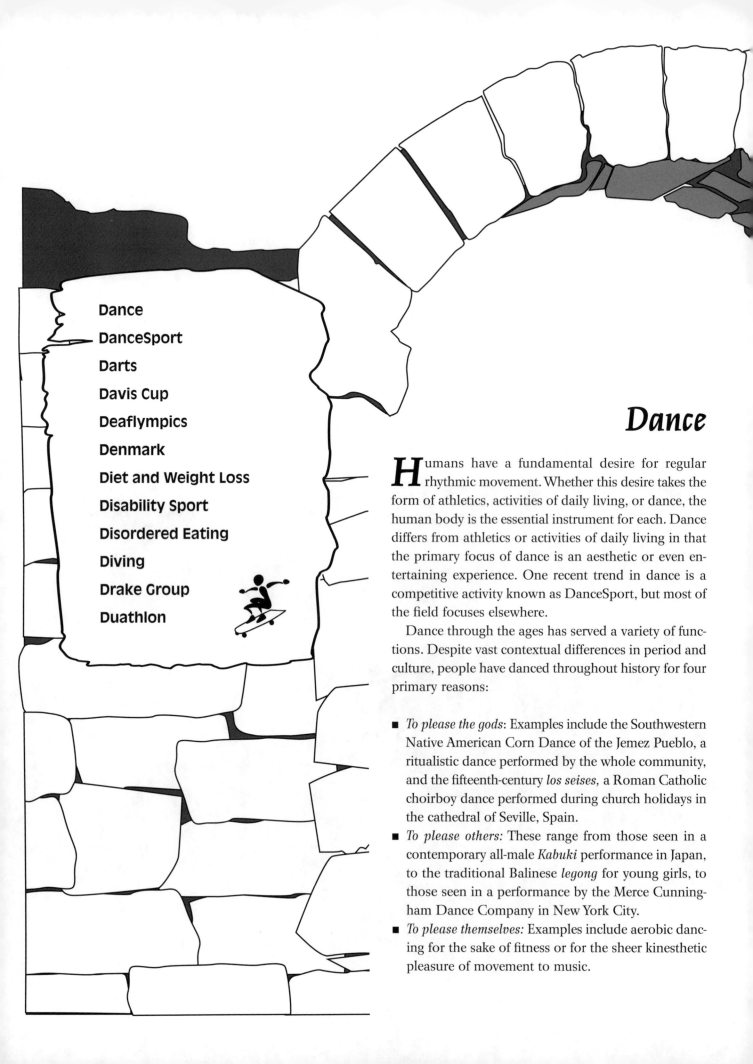

Dance

Humans have a fundamental desire for regular rhythmic movement. Whether this desire takes the form of athletics, activities of daily living, or dance, the human body is the essential instrument for each. Dance differs from athletics or activities of daily living in that the primary focus of dance is an aesthetic or even entertaining experience. One recent trend in dance is a competitive activity known as DanceSport, but most of the field focuses elsewhere.

Dance through the ages has served a variety of functions. Despite vast contextual differences in period and culture, people have danced throughout history for four primary reasons:

- *To please the gods*: Examples include the Southwestern Native American Corn Dance of the Jemez Pueblo, a ritualistic dance performed by the whole community, and the fifteenth-century *los seises,* a Roman Catholic choirboy dance performed during church holidays in the cathedral of Seville, Spain.
- *To please others:* These range from those seen in a contemporary all-male *Kabuki* performance in Japan, to the traditional Balinese *legong* for young girls, to those seen in a performance by the Merce Cunningham Dance Company in New York City.
- *To please themselves:* Examples include aerobic dancing for the sake of fitness or for the sheer kinesthetic pleasure of movement to music.

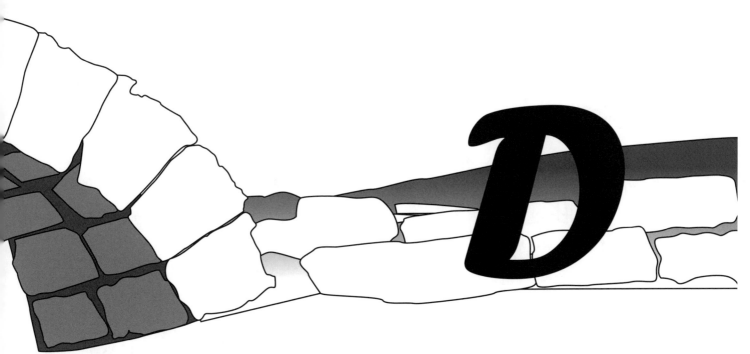

■ *To build community within an ethnic group:* Examples include *la marcha,* a group dance traditionally performed at Hispanic weddings; the *mayim,* an Israeli folk dance; and the *koko sawa,* a playful West African dance for boys and girls.

Global Dance Forms

Differences in dance forms and gender roles vary with culture and historical period. In traditional ritualistic dances, gender roles are a dominant factor. Women's dances often have themes of planting, harvest, relationships, or child rearing, whereas men's dances deal with war, hunting, or displays of physical prowess. Female ritualistic dancing often uses subtlety in its use of gestures and a compact use of space. Male dancers are usually more physically mobile with bold and energetic movements.

Dance forms also vary from culture to culture. Around the globe, identifiable characteristics may be associated with individual cultures.

ASIAN

Traditional Asian dance has remained closely linked with worship and generally has adhered to ancient forms and legends for its choreography, costumes, and musical accompaniment. Characteristics of Asian dance movement include a fluid body stance, with a flexible use of the spine. The hips, rib cage, head, and shoulders shift from side to side while the legs glide in a low level over the ground. The overall movement quality is multifocused, with a bound flow and a light use of weight.

The arms, fingers, hands, and eyes perform complicated yet expressive movements, and stylized facial expressions are used. In most Asian dance forms, one finds a distinction between more vigorous and athletic dancing for males, with more confined and subtle dancing for females. In certain traditional Asian dance forms, including Kabuki and Noh, male dancers perform all roles.

AFRICAN

African dance has evolved from a religious and community-building context into a means of personal fulfillment or theatrical performance. African dance has always been closely tied to the music with which it is performed. African dance, like African music, is frequently polyrhythmic, with contrasting rhythms and musical gestures occurring simultaneously. The movement style is strong and free flowing, with the body weight rooted in the earth. The head, shoulders, rib cage, and hips move in a flexible manner, often to independent rhythms, and the legs are often bent. In African dance forms, both males and females sometimes dance in a strong and grounded manner. However, some dances such as the *adowa* are gender specific, with the female version being more subtle and expressive, and the male version being more aggressive and exhibitionistic. African dance is often performed solo or in large unison groups that allow individual expression.

EUROPEAN

Most classical European dance is performed either with a partner or in choreographed group formations. It

These exercise illustrations from an 1829 German manual suggest the loose boundary between dance and exercise.

Broadway dance, lyrical jazz dance, and various street-dance forms (e.g., hip-hop dance).

■ Tap dance is derived from a mix of British Isles step dancing and dances of African slaves from the colonial United States.

■ Modern dance, which has European as well as American roots, incorporates a flexible use of the spine and a lower use of body weight than ballet technique uses. Although both men and women today dance leading roles in modern dance, many of the most significant early pioneers were women.

Origins of Western Dance

Since ancient times, dance has been associated with ritual and worship. In ancient Egypt, the goddess Isis was the center of a cult celebrating the rising and falling of the Nile River. Dance and music played a significant part in this agricultural ritual event. Egyptian priests, who were also astronomers, imitated the movements of the sun and cosmos during ritual functions. Egyptian courts and temples maintained specially trained dancers to participate in ceremonial functions.

The ancient Greeks have exerted a profound influence on dance in Western civilization. Dance flourished among the ancient Greeks during the classical period (540–300 BCE). The Greeks viewed the union of dance, music, and poetry as symbolic of the harmony of mind and body. Dance was seen as a metaphor for order and harmony in the heavens. Dance enriched theatrical presentations as well as religious festivals. Young men were taught to dance as part of their military training, professional dancers entertained guests at banquets, and at many religious festivals everyone danced—men and women, young and old, aristocrats and peasants.

According to Greek mythology, the cultivation and preservation of dance was entrusted to Terpsichore, the muse of dance. Two Greek gods also watched over dance and came to symbolize opposing types of art:

incorporates a stable and erect spine, with hips, shoulders, and arms held framing the torso. Classical European dancers often use bent legs only as a preparation to jump or to accentuate the extension of the legs. The body is generally held erect, with a light use of weight and an emphasis on intricate footwork. High jumps and leg extensions are frequently used in ballet technique and in some folk dance forms. Ballets often feature women in spectacular displays of exhibitionism, while the male dancers are often seen in supporting roles.

AMERICAN

American dance forms, with the exception of traditional Native American dances, are recent additions to world dance. Jazz dance, tap dance, and modern dance are uniquely American forms and vary widely in style.

■ Jazz dance has its roots in African dance and has developed into an eclectic mix of styles including

- *Apollo,* the sun god, symbolizes the ideals of intellect, formal balance, and an ordered perfection. Thus, a dance that emphasizes virtuoso technique and form may be considered "Apollonian" in Nature, for example, many traditional ballets such as *Agon* (1957), choreographed by George Balanchine (1904–1983).
- *Dionysus,* the god of wine and fertility, symbolizes artistic expression that is emotional and unrestrained. The Neo-Expressionist Japanese dance form called Butoh, with its sometimes grotesque movements, is a Dionysian response to the horrors of the atomic bombs dropped on Hiroshima and Nagasaki, as well as a reaction to the traditional etiquette of Japanese society.

Viewing dance according to its Apollonian or Dionysian elements can provide a framework for understanding contrasting artistic styles.

During the Roman Empire, dance became increasingly divorced from poetry and music. As a result, the art form that later became known as pantomime flourished. Over time, there grew to be a lewd, violent, and sensationalistic side to Roman entertainment. Scholars have cited instances in which captured slaves and condemned prisoners were forced to dance in an arena until the flammable clothing they wore was set on fire and they died in agony. In 426 CE, Saint Augustine denounced the cruelty of the arena games and the vulgarity of pantomime, blaming the debauched state of Roman society. The Christian church eventually adopted a policy discouraging all large public gatherings that included dance and theatrical performances and, by 744 CE, forbade all secular forms of dance.

As Christianity spread slowly throughout Europe during the Middle Ages, the use of dance in public festivals became limited. Unlike traditional Asian dance that has remained closely linked with worship, the idea of dance as worship struck many Europeans of the time as sacrilegious. The eighth-century English priest Alcuin characterized the situation in his admonition, "The man who brings actors and mimes and dancers to his house knows not what a bevy of unclean spirits follow them." Anyone engaging in public dancing was cast out of the church, ostracized from society, and denied Christian burial.

Although dance as public entertainment was severely limited because of restrictions imposed by the Christian church, everyday life during the Middle Ages was not devoid of dancing. Medieval guilds (representing workers in a particular profession) developed ritual activities, including dances that were specifically related to the occupations they represented. Musician guilds, founded by royal decree, provided music for social gatherings for the nobility and taught dance steps. Throughout Europe, licenses were granted for the teaching of dance after a person had demonstrated a thorough knowledge of music and the ability to execute dance steps, to create new dances, and to notate dances.

Renaissance Court Dance

During the Renaissance, members of the nobility organized an elaborate court life for themselves, their associates, and their servants. Intricate rituals of dressing, etiquette, and personal fashion evolved. Florence was the fifteenth-century cultural capital of Europe, with the Medici court a prominent cultural force. Dance masters were in great demand. Court entertainments became lavish spectacles, usually organized around Greek or Roman mythology. These spectacles served as powerful political propaganda for the ruling class—the nobility could display great wealth (and therefore authority), along with richly cloaked allegorical commentary on political and social matters.

In the mid-sixteenth century, Catherine de Medici married into the French court and brought with her the Italian ideals of lavish court entertainments, as well as proper culture and style. She hired Balthasar de Beaujoyeulx, an Italian dance master, to create entertainments for the court. His *Ballet Comique de la Reine* (1581) became what is considered by dance historians to be the first identifiable ballet because of its cohesive plot, poetry, music, dance, and décor. Although Renaissance court spectacles were often elaborate, the performers were all amateur dancers from the noble class. Dancing was one of the few acceptable ways for women of the nobility to engage in strenuous physical activity.

Many popular sixteenth- and seventeenth-century court dances survive today, preserved by the notations and descriptions made by dance masters during that time. Of these, one of the most famous dance manuals is *Orchésographie*, written in 1588 by Thoinot Arbeau. Skill in performing these dances was considered essential for a proper lady or gentleman of the nobility during this period:

- The slow and stately *pavane*
- The fast and athletic *galliard*
- The gracefully flowing *allemande*
- The playful and running *courante*
- The lively *gigue*
- The dainty and precise *minuet*.

Court dance reached its height during the reign of King Louis XIV of France (1638–1715), who used dance as a tool of power. He built the Palace of Versailles and invited French nobility to live together under one roof. The king staged elaborate dance productions in which members of the nobility were expected to participate. Men and women spent many hours each day learning dance steps to keep their status within the court. Missteps had grave consequences. Scholars have noted reports of persons being disgraced from court for poor dancing and having to climb through the social ranks slowly.

Louis XIV was himself a dancer; his teacher, Pierre Beauchamp (1636–1705), was the leading dance master of this era. Ballet fundamentals, including the five feet positions and standard arm movements, were classified under Beauchamp. As the dance steps became more complicated, the use of a ballet barre in training was developed. The barre is a railing attached to the floor or walls that ballet dancers gently grasp while practicing. Ballet turnout, an outward rotation of the hip sockets, was originally an adaptation of a fencer's stance. Dance masters found that turnout allowed a performer to open outward toward an audience and increased flexibility in the hips. By the middle of the seventeenth century, ballet had reached such a technical level that the first professional dancers arose in Europe.

Proscenium theaters began to be built during the seventeenth century, and dance moved out of the courts and onto the professional stage. Previously, audience members had sat on all sides of the performance, but proscenium theaters framed the stage as in a picture frame, with the audience seated on only one side. With the beginning of the Industrial Revolution and the rise of a new middle class, audiences flocked to these popular theaters for entertainment. The ascent of professional dancers gave rise to the first "balletomanes," or devotees of ballet, and to famous rivalries among dancers. This was one of the earliest examples of respectable middle-class women working outside the home in Europe.

Ballet and Beyond: Apollo versus Dionysus

As in other sports, there have always existed intense rivalries in dance. Apollo and Dionysus, the two Greek gods who symbolized contrasting types of art, were the prototypes for these dance rivalries. Apollo symbolizes the ideals of virtuoso technique, strength, and perfect form, ideals that also hold true for many sports. Dionysus symbolizes the ideals of artistic expression that is emotional, creative, and focused on content. This type of expression is present in certain sports including figure skating, ice dancing, and rhythmic gymnastics. Although these events have demanding technical requirements, the aesthetic component of the event is part of the criteria in judging. Dance is generally expected to include both Apollonian and Dionysian components—both form and content. Emphasis on dance technique alone ignores artistic expression, and emotional expression can rarely be effectively conveyed without a fully developed technique.

Two eighteenth-century dance rivals, exemplified the prototypical ballerina rivals:

Hungarian folk dancers in the early nineteenth century.

- *Marie-Anne de Cupis de Camargo* (1710–1770) was highly skilled in performing virtuoso jumps and leg beats that were usually the domain of male dancers. Although she caused a scandal by raising her skirts to ankle length to display her impressive technique and fast footwork, her athleticism and technical ability made her famous throughout Europe.

- *Marie Sallé* (1707–1756) was known for her formidable acting talent and expressive performance ability. Sallé also altered her costumes, not to display her technical abilities, but to heighten her emotional intensity in portraying dramatic characters as convincingly as possible.

For many, it is difficult to find a more sentimental image than that of an otherworldly Romantic ballerina floating across stage as an unattainable and tragic figure. During the golden age of Romantic ballet (1830–1850), female dancers rose to unprecedented prominence. Ballets such as *La Sylphide*, *Giselle*, and *Coppélia* feature women as the central figures, and male dancers were demoted from strong and muscular figures to assistants waiting to assist ballerinas in lifts. The most famous rival ballerinas during this time were Marie Taglioni and Fanny Elssler:

- *Marie Taglioni* (1804–1884), an Italian dancer, won fame through a combination of great technical skill and a demeanor of ease in performance. Her skill was the result of a demanding training regime directed by her father, Filippo Taglioni (1777–1871), who led his daughter through a rigorous daily physical routine until she was near fainting and had to have help dressing after rehearsal. Her strength, graceful ease, and ethereal lightness dancing *en pointe* in *La Sylphide* made her internationally famous.

- *Fanny Elssler* (1810–1884), the Austrian dancer, was a more Dionysian dancer. Elssler had impressive technique, yet audiences were drawn to her personal magnetism and theatrical ability. One of her most famous roles was a sensual solo dance called "La Cachucha," a Spanish-influenced dance in which she played castanets.

Taglioni came to be known as the ethereal "Christian dancer," and Elssler was loved as the sensuous "pagan dancer."

Dance

Dance in Africa

In the extract below, British missionary George Basden describes dance among the Ibos of Nigeria.

The twistings, turnings, contortions and springing movements, executed in perfect time, are wonderful to behold. Movement succeeds movement in rapid succession, speed and force increasing, until the grand finale is reached. . . . For these set dances . . . the physical strength required is tremendous. The body movements are extremely difficult and would probably kill a European. The whole anatomy of the performer appears to be in serious danger, and it is a marvel that his internal machinery is not completely thrown out of gear. The practice of such dancing leads to a wonderful development of the back and abdominal muscles. Moreover the movements are free, there is nothing rigid about them, and they produce no sign of "physical exerciser" stiffness. Every movement is clean, sure and decided, showing absolute control of the muscles."

Source: Basden, G. (1921). *Among the Ibos of Nigeria.* London: Seeley, Service and Co.

In the early twentieth century, a new company commanded attention throughout Europe—the Ballets Russes. The company manager, Sergei Diaghilev (1872–1929), managed to hire the most talented choreographers, composers, visual artists, and dancers of his time. Important artists who created work for this company included the following:

- Choreographers Balanchine, Nijinsky, Massine, Fokine, and Nijinska
- Composers Stravinsky, Prokofiev, Debussy, Satie, Poulenc, and Richard Strauss
- Painters Picasso, Matisse, Miró, Rouault, and Bakst

As before, two rival ballerinas embodying the Apollonian-Dionysian contrast arose:

- *Anna Pavlova* (1881–1931), who trained at the Maryinsky School in St. Petersburg, had a natural delicacy, lightness, and grace. After leaving the Ballets Russes in 1910, Pavlova formed her own company and toured the globe, often performing her celebrated piece *The Dying Swan,* choreographed for her by Michel Fokine (1880–1942). She was known for the Apollonian ideals of grace, beauty, and form.
- *Tamara Karsavina* (1885–1978), who danced as a soloist in the Imperial Ballet in St. Petersburg, was also a starring ballerina for the Ballet Russes. Although Karsavina had strong technical abilities, she impressed audiences with her dramatic and expressive qualities in ballets such as *Firebird* and *Petrouchka.*

Revolutions in Dance

Modern dance began in the early twentieth century, partly as a reaction to the strict confines of ballet technique but also as means for a new society to express its changing ideals following the world wars. Modern dance with its German and American roots, has flourished in an unbroken progression in the United States since its inception, while the devastating effects of World War II inhibited the growth of German modern dance for many years. Early German modern dancers such as Mary Wigman (1886–1973) believed that art is most powerful when form and content are joined. She was instrumental in developing the new dance form *Ausdruckstanz,* or "expressive dance." Wigman's dances were often about the struggles between conflicting powers, in which opposing forces were given corporeal shape. She studied with Émile Jaques-Dalcroze (1865–1950), who developed a system of expressing rhythm through bodily movements called *eurhythmics,* and with the important dance theorist Rudolph von Laban (1879–1958). Laban, who was also a dancer and choreographer, is perhaps best known for his work in the analysis of human motion and his development of a dance notation system. His Labanotation system is the most widely used dance notation system today.

By the end of World War II, German modern dance

Young Zulu women participating in a Zulu ritual dance in South Africa.

had been artistically weakened by the Nazi oppression and did not see an artistic phoenix until the rise of *Tanz-theater* in the early 1970s. Perhaps the best known of these *Tanz-theater* artists is Pina Bausch (b. 1940), whose productions are known for their dream-like imagery, dramatic intensity, and preoccupation with the struggles between women and men.

During the early part of the twentieth century, several American dancers made their fame in Europe. Among these are the following:

- *Loie Fuller* (1862–1928) was an early pioneer of modern dance who experimented with the effect of stage lighting on voluminous costumes of silk, which she manipulated through movement.
- *Josephine Baker* (1906–1975) devoted herself more to musical theater and cabaret. Her performances were considered suggestive for early twentieth century America, so Paris became the center of her activities while her international fame grew.
- *Isadora Duncan* (1877–1927) is considered one of the most important early pioneers of modern dance. She reduced costuming to silky tunics, performed barefoot, and used freely flowing movements inspired by nature, great classical music, and Grecian art. Duncan often performed solo dances to music by composers such as Beethoven, Wagner, Chopin, and Scriabin, and sometimes burst into impromptu speeches on the issues of the day.

All three women enjoyed international fame, albeit for differing approaches to artistic expression through dance.

Two of the most influential American founders of modern dance, may also be discussed in the context of form (Apollonian) versus content (Dionysian):

- *Doris Humphrey* (1895–1958) based her movement vocabulary on a reaction to gravity, yielding, and resisting gravity in a "fall and recovery." Her choreography centered around designs in space. Although she believed in a clear motivation for her dances, the manner in which her dancers interact in space suggests these motivations. Her works are seldom literal depictions, and her earlier works can be described as abstract "music visualizations."

- *Martha Graham* (1894–1991) based her movement vocabulary on the breath, or "contraction and release," believing that movement was a mirror into the expressive soul. Her choreography is angular, expressionistic, theatrical, and charged with tension and passion. She created an impressive body of choreographic work during a sixty-year period and was the first dancer to receive the Medal of Freedom, the highest U.S. civilian honor.

Later modern dancers had different aesthetic concerns. Choreographers such as Merce Cunningham (b. 1919) rejected the notion of dance as expressing emotions or stories. His work is abstract, and his experiments with chance choreography, the treatment of stage space as an open field for movement, and his regard for all components in a dance production (choreography, costuming, scenic design, lighting design) as independent entities, have made him an influential choreographer. He is also known for his collaborations with the foremost artists of the era, including the painters Andy Warhol, Jasper Johns, and Robert Rauschenberg, and his long-term collaboration with the experimental composer John Cage.

In the early 1960s, experimental choreographers from the Judson Dance Theatre explored the idea that everyday movements ordered in time and space can function as dance. Pedestrian movements, those that can be performed by nondancers in everyday situations, quickly came into vogue on the concert stage. Choreographers such as Yvonne Rainer, Steve Paxton, Deborah Hay, and David Gordon accepted the concept that almost any movement from the simplest, to the most complex, may legitimately function as dance.

Dance Training Today

Dance today has progressed dramatically from its origins. In the early part of the twentieth century, American choreographer Ted Shawn (1891–1972) characterized the relationship between dance and athletics by explaining, "Dancing is a manly sport, more strenuous than golf or tennis, more exciting than boxing or wrestling and more beneficial than gymnastics." First-class choreographers often began their careers as superb dancers, including the following:

- Martha Graham (1894–1991)
- Merce Cunningham (b. 1919)
- Paul Taylor (b. 1930)
- Alvin Ailey (1931–1989)
- Twyla Tharp (b. 1942)
- Mark Morris (b. 1956)

Dance training today shares much in common with athletics:

- Repetitive training that focuses on specific muscular patterns
- Practice sessions that emphasize strength, coordination, and balance
- Both individual and group training sessions

Most professional dancers attend daily dance technique classes, in addition to three to six hours of daily rehearsal for specific choreographic works. Many professional dance companies provide technique classes for company members, but others expect dancers to arrange their own personal training schedules. The need for rigorous training, as well as an aesthetic based on leanness, has caused some dancers to develop eating disorders and other addictive problems.

A famous dancer who suffered such problems is Gelsey Kirkland (b. 1953), who shocked balletomanes by leaving the New York City Ballet, where she worked with Balanchine, and joining the American Ballet Theatre to work with Mikhail Baryshnikov (b. 1948). After leaving the American Ballet Theatre, Kirkland revealed in her autobiography, *Dancing on My Grave,* that she was able to maintain such a svelte physique and perform with such speed and brilliance because of cocaine addiction and an accompanying eating disorder. Many critics cite Balanchine, founder of the New York City Ballet, for contributing to the problem of dancers' eating disorders. Balanchine, a seminal figure in American ballet, idolized the female form, albeit an extremely thin female form. This emphasis on an idealized female form is common to both dance and certain sports such as gymnastics and figure skating.

Athletics of Dance

Some choreographers who desire to find new sources for virtuosic steps turn away from standard dance techniques to sports, acrobatics, weightlifting, and gymnastics. The American company Pilobolus combines gymnastic movements with modern dance in witty, sculptural dances. Contemporary American choreographers such as Molissa Fenley (b. 1954), and Elizabeth Streb (b. 1950) are also interested in athletics. Fenley's grueling dances require great endurance, so much so that her training routine has included running and weightlifting, instead of the standard dance technique class. Streb's company, based in New York City, regularly performs on a series of trapezes and mats, presenting movements related to circus acrobatics and gymnastics.

However inclined choreographers may be to emphasize athletic movements, dancers are still refining their dance techniques in traditional ways. To gain strength

Chinese women participate in the highly ritualized "sport dancing" at the Temple of Heaven in Beijing in 2002.

and versatility, professional dancers often train in modern dance, ballet, and Pilates or other alternative training methods. Ballet technique develops speed, line, lightness, and articulate footwork, whereas modern dance emphasizes strength, weight, a flexible use of the spine, and asymmetrical and off-balance movements. Pilates develops strong core musculature of the abdominal and back muscles, whereas other alternative training techniques focus on different areas.

In contemporary dance, women and men are expected to have the strength and flexibility to lift other dancers, and to be lifted themselves. Although gender roles in dance have expanded in most Western concert dance forms, traditional forms such as classical ballet, flamenco, and some folk dances retain their historical gender role divisions.

Professional dance is a competitive field. Dancers usually audition for specific roles, or openings in professional companies through a highly competitive audition process. Dancers sometimes compete for prizes and titles in competitions such as the USA Interna-

tional Ballet Competition. Nonprofessional dance studios and dance teams commonly compete in regional and national competitions. Examples of these include Dancemakers, Inc., Dance Alliance, and the International Jazz Dance World Congress, among others. These competitions are a way for dance studios to compete with peer institutions and assess the quality of their training. The area of DanceSport, in which partners or teams of dancers compete in ballroom or Latin dance styles, has also become popular.

Athletes and their coaches are increasingly using dance training to improve coordination, flexibility, agility, alignment, and balance—for example, professional football teams in the United States regularly require their players to attend ballet class. Research clearly shows that dance technique has benefits for athletes in other sports as well, such as diving, track and field, and synchronized swimming. Nevertheless, although dance training can benefit athletes, its primary focus historically has been on aesthetics rather than on competition.

The Future

The dance of the future is multifaceted. Today, one can see dance on stage, on film, on video, and on computer screens all around the world. Technological advances have added to the complex nature of twenty-first century dance, from computer-generated dance images, to multimedia performances melding live dancers with projected images. Choreographic explorations now require dancers to improve not only their technical virtuosity but also their skills in music, acting, and a large variety of dance styles. The dancers of today generally are stronger, more flexible, and have more stamina than their historic counterparts, partly because of increased knowledge and application in kinesiology, diet, injury prevention, alternative therapies, and diverse training techniques.

Dance has also seen a recent return to content and expressionism as the focus for choreography. International artists working in this vein include the following:

- Anne Teresa de Keersmaeker (Belgium, b. 1960)
- Meredith Monk (U.S., b. 1943)
- Pina Bausch (Germany, b. 1940)
- Kazuo Ohno (Japan, b. 1906)

Other choreographers and dance companies—such as Bill T. Jones (U.S., b. 1952), Anna Halprin (U.S., b. 1920), and the Urban Bush Women—are more concerned with exploring social issues. Anna Halprin, for example, has become known for fusing dance with rehabilitation, particularly in working with AIDS patients.

National folk dance companies have also become common, as highly choreographed performances of these forms successfully tour to concert stages around the globe. Recreational dance enjoys increased interest with its cultivation of physical fitness and social enjoyment. Ballroom and other social dance forms are now popular as both recreational and competitive activities. Dance continues to grow and change as cross-fertilization of dance around the world increases.

Helen Myers

See also Capoeira

Further Reading

Acocella, J. (1995). *Mark Morris.* New York: Noonday Press.

Adshead-Lansdale, J., & Layson, J. (Eds.). (1994). *Dance history: An introduction* (2nd ed.). London: Routledge.

Anderson, J. (1997). *Art without boundaries: The world of modern dance.* Iowa City: University of Iowa Press.

Anderson, J. (1992). *Ballet and modern dance: A concise history* (2nd ed.). Pennington, NJ: Princeton Book Company.

Banes, S. (1994). *Writing dance in the age of postmodernism.* Middletown, CT: Wesleyan University Press.

Bond, C. T. (1990). An aesthetic framework for dance. In A. S. Akins, & J. LaPointe-Crump (Eds.), *Encores II: Travels through the spectrum of dance.* Reston, VA: American Alliance for Health, Physical Education, Recreation and Dance.

Cass, J. (1993). *Dancing through history.* Englewood Cliffs, NJ: Prentice-Hall.

Copeland, R., & Cohen, M. (1983). *What is dance?* New York: Oxford University Press.

Dance at Court. (1993). Prod. Rhoda Grauer, Thirteen/WNET in association with RM Arts and BBC-TV. Program four of eight-part series, 58 mins. Videocassette.

Dils, A., & Albright, A. C. (Eds.). (2001). *Moving history/dancing cultures: A dance history reader.* Middletown, CT: Wesleyan University Press.

Dyke, J. V. (1992). *Modern dance in a postmodern world.* Reston, VA: American Alliance for Health, Physical Education, Recreation and Dance.

Foster, S. L. (1986). *Reading dancing,* Berkeley: University of California Press.

Kraines, M. G., & Pryor, E. (2004). *Jump into jazz.* Mountain View, CA: Mayfield.

Lee, C. (1999). *Ballet in Western culture: A history of its origins and evolution.* Needham Heights, MA: Allyn & Bacon.

Mitoma, J., (Ed.). (2002). *Envisioning dance on film and video.* New York: Routledge.

Nadel, M. H., & Strauss, M. R. (Eds.). (2003). *The dance experience: Insights into history, culture and creativity.* Hightstown, NJ: Princeton Book Company.

Pruett, D. M. (1990). Ballet for divers. In A. S. Akins, & J. LaPointe-Crump (Eds.), *Encores II: Travels through the spectrum of dance.* Reston, VA: American Alliance for Health, Physical Education, Recreation and Dance.

Reynolds, N., & McCormick, M. (2003). *No fixed points: Dance in the twentieth century.* New Haven, CT: Yale University Press.

Stearns, M., & Stearns, J. (1994). *Jazz dance: The story of American vernacular dance.* New York: Da Capo Press.

Thomas, H. (1995). *Dance, modernity & culture: Explorations in the sociology of dance.* London: Routledge.